SCRUM WARS

SCRUM WARS

THE PRIME MINISTERS AND THE MEDIA

ALLAN LEVINE

DUNDURN PRESS
Toronto & Oxford

Editor: Judith Turnbull
Printed and bound in Canada by Gagné Printing Ltd., Louiseville, Quebec, Canada

Dundurn Press acknowledges the following for their permission to use extended quotations from copyrighted works:

One-Eyed Kings copyright © 1986 by Ron Graham. Published in Canada by Collins Publishers Ltd. Excerpts are used by permission of Ron Graham and HarperCollins Publishers.

Renegade in Power copyright © 1963 by Peter C. Newman, *The Distemper of Our Times* copyright © 1968 by Peter C. Newman, and *The Insiders: Government, Business and the Lobbyists* copyright © 1987 by John Sawatsky, A Douglas Gibson Book. Excerpts are used by permission of The Canadian Publishers, McClelland & Stewart Inc.

Mulroney: The Politics of Ambition copyright © 1991 by John Sawatsky. Excerpts are used by permission of Macfarlane, Walter & Ross.

Grits: An Intimate Portrait of the Liberal Party copyright © 1982 by Christina McCall-Newman. Excerpts are used by permission of Christina McCall.

The Decline of Politics: The Conservatives and the Party System, 1901–1920 by John English © 1977 by University of Toronto Press; *When Television Was Young: Prime Time Canada 1952–1967* © 1990 by Paul Rutherford; *Diefenbaker: Leadership Gained 1956–1962* © 1975 by Peter Stursberg; and *Diefenbaker: Leadership Lost 1962–1967* © 1976 by Peter Stursberg. Excerpts are used by permission of University of Toronto Press.

The publisher wishes to acknowledge the generous assistance and ongoing support of **The Canada Council, The Book Publishing Industry Development Program** of the **Department of Communications, The Ontario Arts Council, The Ontario Publishing Centre** of the **Ministry of Culture, Tourism and Recreation,** and **The Ontario Heritage Foundation.**
Care has been taken to trace the ownership of copyright material used in the text (including the illustrations). The author and publisher welcome any information enabling them to rectify any reference or credit in subsequent editions.

J. Kirk Howard, Publisher

Canadian Cataloguing in Publication Data

Levine, Allan Gerald, 1956–
      Scrum wars : the prime ministers and the media

Includes bibliographical references and index.
ISBN 1-55002-191-5 (cloth)   ISBN 1-55002-207-5 (paper)

l. Government and the press – Canada. 2. Mass media – Political aspects – Canada. 3. Prime ministers – Canada – Interviews. I. Title.

PN4914.P6L4 1993   070.4'08'83513   C93-094430-5

Dundurn Press Limited	Dundurn Distribution	Dundurn Press Limited
2181 Queen Street East	73 Lime Walk	1823 Maryland Avenue
Suite 301	Headington, Oxford	P.O. Box 1000
Toronto, Canada	England	Niagara Falls, N.Y.
M4E 1E5	0X3 7AD	U.S.A. 14302-1000

For

Angie

and for

Alexander & Mia

The press lives by disclosures; whatever passes into its keeping becomes part of the knowledge and the history of our times; it is daily and forever appealing to the enlightened force of public opinion — anticipating, if possible, the march of events. The statesman's duty is precisely the reverse. He cautiously guards from the public eye the information by which his actions and opinions are regulated; he reserves his judgement on passing events 'till the latest moment, and then he records it in obscure or conventional language.

John Thadeus Delane, editor, *The Times* (London), c. 1860

CONTENTS

PART THREE

The Unofficial Opposition, 1957–1992

Preface

The Battle of the Scrum

In the British game of rugby, a scrum or scrummage is when players from both teams gather tightly around the ball with their heads down and try to restart the play by breaking away or kicking the ball out of the massive human circle. It can be rough and brutal. In Canadian politics, a scrum is when reporters surround any available politician, thrusting microphones, cameras, hot lights, and notebooks in his or her face, and bark questions that demand quick and snappy answers. This too can be rough and brutal. Neither side particularly likes or enjoys this form of communication, but it has become one of the many enduring Ottawa traditions.

The modern scrum began when television took over political media coverage in the late fifties and early sixties. According to veteran journalist Charles Lynch, the term itself was first used to describe the chaos in the hallways of Parliament during the early Trudeau years. Since Trudeau often spoke in a hushed voice, journalists were forced to encircle him, resulting in some famous jostling matches.

But even in Sir John A. Macdonald's day a century earlier, reporters in the parliamentary press gallery waited outside the prime minister's office with pen in hand, hoping for a usable quote for the next edition. As a symbol, the scrum represents the test of wills, the contest of wits, and the battle for control that have characterized the relations between Canadian prime ministers and journalists for more than 125 years.

Indeed, if you were to ask either side in this "game," each would say that the scrum works to the other's advantage. Journalists would rightly argue that politicians can pick and choose when to hold a scrum, which questions to answer, and when to end it by simply walking away. The opportunities for manipulation appear endless. During one of the many first ministers' conferences on the constitution in 1981, John Gray of the *Globe and Mail* related how Bill Bennett, then premier of British Columbia, was scrummed: "He turned to walk through one door, changed his mind and walked back and was scrummed again, went outside and was scrummed again. All that effort, however, was a great success: he made the television news that evening, saying roughly nothing."[1]

Politicians would claim with equal justification that it is the members of the media who control and benefit from the scrum. Just ask former MP Erik Nielsen, no fan of the press during his many years in Parliament. "No one in the midst of ... a scrum, can think clearly, or enunciate policy on a complex matter, but, of course, that is not what the scrum is about," he wrote in his controversial memoirs. "The purpose of the scrum is to provide a fifteen- or thirty-second clip to be fed into the next news report. There are not many subjects in a complex world that can be dealt with intelligently in fifteen minutes, let alone fifteen seconds; the scrum provides the television editors with film over which the parliamentary correspondent can do a voice over – that is, substitute his own words for those of the politician, with one brief spasm of the victim's words to create the impression that what the viewer is seeing is news. It is commentary, but it looks like news, and it becomes news." If a politician refuses to go along with the scrum, he or she will be accused of "dodging the press" or of having "something to hide."[2]

Both sides have legitimate arguments. You need only have watched former prime minister Brian Mulroney work the press from his lofty position at the top of the House of Commons stairs, hearing what he wished to hear from the pack of journalists cowering below him, to figure out who had the upper hand. Still, it can go the other way. In January 1992 I was in Calgary, invited as an "ordinary Canadian" to participate in the constitutional conference on institutional reform. On the first day, Constitutional Affairs Minister Joe Clark got caught in a scrum. In response to reporters' queries about the likelihood of agreement on a Triple-E Senate – one that is elected, equal, and effective – Clark made the mistake of comparing such an eventuality to the "virgin birth." The message: a Triple-E Senate wasn't impossible, but it wasn't likely either. Reporters conveyed these remarks to Triple-E supporters, who not surprisingly reacted with concern. Clark had to backtrack and explain himself.

Nevertheless, Clark's virgin-birth analogy, a minor comment within the context of his more significant remarks, not to mention within the context of the delegates' wide-ranging discussions, was a lead item on CBC television's "The National" that evening and a headline story in the *Globe and Mail* and other major dailies the following day.[3]

While the press may believe in the fairness of this particular story, critics of the media would argue that this incident underlines many of the problems inherent in Canadian political news coverage and with journalism in general. The built-in antagonism, the media's dwelling on the trivial, and, more significantly, their power to select arbitrarily what is "news," are themes that run through this book, though to varying degrees.

At least until the 1930s Canadian journalists were much more respect-ful of the politicians they covered than they are today. Partisanship ran very deep in the parliamentary press gallery for decades, and even in 1958 Tory prime minister John Diefenbaker knew which loyal Conservative reporters and supportive Conservative newspapers he could trust. As late as 1963 Liberal prime minister Lester Pearson's office still classified the newspapers he received as "Conservative," "Liberal" or "Independent," and of the thirty-eight Canadian papers listed, only ten had no party affiliation. This did not mean that all journalists were party hacks. Long ago, John Willison, the influential editor of the Toronto *Globe* in the 1890s, observed that Canadian reporters "seem to feel that if the blow is not struck with a club, it will be taken for a caress."[4]

Television, with its emphasis on confrontation and dramatic moments, has only made matters worse. TV simplifies politics both by making it more personal and by turning the reporters who deliver the news into major Canadian stars with expert opinions on everything. The political analysis offered on television, media critic David Hayes has observed, tends to emphasize "presentation and superficial appearances, and favours conflict rather than extended exposition of ideas or complicated arguments."[5] As they watched their electronic colleagues take over the business in Ottawa and elsewhere – in 1964, 85 percent of the parliamentary press gallery's members were print reporters; in 1985 this figure had declined to 41 percent – news-paper journalists were forced to respond in kind in their columns and books.

Thus, around the time television was growing in popularity, newspaper and TV journalists took on the role of the "unofficial opposition," intent on exposing government corruption and protecting the public's interest as they defined it. In recent years this search for the truth has led to controversial, media-created news items, such as stories about former Liberal prime minis-ter John Turner's alleged drinking problem and Brian Mulroney's Gucci loafers.

Such adversarial journalism is said to benefit the public. To do their job properly, the journalists of today believe they must maintain a detachment from the subject they cover. No longer are prime ministers and reporters drinking buddies as in the days of old. As Arthur Siegel of York University has stated, "Politics has a seductive influence on the journalist, but the liai-son [between the reporter and the politician] must not become too close. Press and politics cannot live without each other, but they must also keep their distance if the public's interest is to be safeguarded."[6]

Fair enough. But in their quest to expose the truth, many journalists believe it their duty and right to harangue politicians as they see fit. Access to information legislation passed in 1983 now makes it virtually mandatory for reporters to question prime ministers about hotel bills and airfares, sometimes to the exclusion of questions of substance. By 1992 this trend had reached the absurd; even the *Globe and Mail*'s normally serious Jeffrey Simpson poked fun at the sheer ridiculousness of Ottawa journalists bothering Mulroney about his expensive Paris hotel room. Never mind the state of world trade, the environmental crisis, and the threat of nuclear proliferation, journalists were more interested in who ate what for dinner and who picked up the tab.[7]

In one of a 1989 series of advertisements promoting the CBC's "The National" and the celebrities who work for the corporation, correspondent David Halton was quoted as follows: "Politicians obviously try to manipulate the media, but it's our job to cut through those attempts and convey what's really happening."[8] The idea that journalists remain objective and above it all – neutral observers entirely divorced from the situation they are covering – is a myth. If this book shows anything, it is that since 1867 the personal biases of journalists have always entered into the political stories they have written and commented upon. In the partisan era of yesteryear, readers were not only aware of this fact, they readily accepted it. It was somehow comforting to know that the *Toronto Star* leaned to the Liberals and the *Globe and Mail* to the Conservatives. Only in the past few decades, when journalists have attempted to masquerade as independents, has their work lost some of its edge and honesty.

Throughout this book, there are many references to the terms "gallery," "journalists," and "media." Obviously the parliamentary press gallery, not even to mention the "media" as a whole, has never been, and is not now, monolithic. Print is different from television, English from French, *Alberta Report* from *Maclean's*, the *Sun* tabloids from the *Globe and Mail*, and the CBC from everyone. "The people who are lumped together as 'the gallery,'" journalist George Bain wrote in a 1985 *Saturday Night* article, "are rarely lumped together anywhere – except perhaps at prime ministerial press conferences in times of high excitement, and not all of them even then."[9]

Nevertheless, a strong case can be made that, as diverse as the components may be, there is such an institution as the "Canadian news media." Certainly politicians who see first-hand how they are covered by the journalists who patrol the corridors of Parliament – by the "pack," as they are irreverently called – would claim that the media have only one voice. In the reporting of information, or perhaps more accurately, in its retailing (George Bain's words), journalists pay heed to and follow each other's leads and thinking, and hence create the impression that they constitute a single entity.

In Ottawa, the *Globe and Mail* and CBC set the agenda for other papers and networks. Under enormous pressure to keep up with current news, journalists in the gallery habitually glance over at the competition in the office or desk next to them. And since no one wants to be caught ignorant of a particular story, everyone in the media ends up covering and following similar issues. This fact of journalistic life takes on even more significance during an election campaign, when reporters travel, live, and incestuously practise their craft together.

The story that follows chronicles the changing relationship between the prime ministers of Canada and the men and women of the Canadian media. As is common in so much of political history, the personalities of both politicians and journalists – as well as circumstances beyond human control – often shaped this liaison. For the chapters dealing with the prime ministers from John A. Macdonald to Lester Pearson, I used each prime minister's letters and papers as my primary guide; for the last chapters, from Pierre Trudeau to Brian Mulroney, I relied on the numerous books and articles dealing with this era as well as on the more than fifty interviews I conducted between 1989 and 1992. If I seem to have overemphasized the importance of the Montreal, Toronto, and Ottawa press, it is only because the prime ministers did. This book is by no means the final word on this subject. I make no claim to have examined every relevant newspaper report and column, but I have attempted to present a fair and objective account of many complex issues.

John Dafoe, the esteemed editor of the *Winnipeg Free Press* for more than forty years, after listing the many limitations of journalism argued that the journalist, nevertheless, "must go forward ... with a sort of reckless courage; and unless he is to fail, he must, out of his half knowledge and his intuitions, and his sense of values and his knowledge of life, tell a story which may not be accurate but is still true and which does not altogether lack suggestive power."[10] I hope readers, in judging this book, will keep these wise words in mind.

Acknowledgments

I conducted most of the major research and interviewing for this book between 1989 and 1990. Owing to the excellent leave program at St. John's–Ravenscourt School and generous grants from the Canada Council and the Manitoba Arts Council, I was able to relocate with my family to Ottawa for one year of intensive work. For this, I must thank John Messenger, the former headmaster of SJR, Robert Richard of the Canada Council, and James Hutchison of the Manitoba Arts Council. Travel funds were also provided by the J.S. Ewart Memorial Fund at the University of Manitoba.

Kirk Howard of Dundurn Press rescued the manuscript when it appeared it was going to spend the rest of eternity in my desk drawer. I am most grateful for his support as well as for that of his entire staff, particularly his assistant Nadine Stoikoff, marketing and promotions manager Jeanne MacDonald, and designer Andy Tong. Dundurn's senior editor Judith Turnbull was patient, enthusiastic, and great to work with. Her keen eye and fine editing skills have contributed much to the final product. The work of Christine Lumley and Matt Williams, as inputters and proofreaders, was also greatly appreciated. A special thanks also to my friend Heather Kluner for taking my picture.

I sincerely thank Maureen Hoogenraad at the National Archives of Canada, who acted as my guide through the papers of prime ministers and journalists. For more than a year, she answered my never-ending queries, and always with a smile. Also of assistance were Didier Cencig of Hull, who helped me with the Laurier Papers, Elizabeth Diamond, formerly an archivist with the Diefenbaker Centre at the University of Saskatchewan, and Erik Spicer, chief parliamentary librarian, who allowed me access to the valuable news-clipping files in the finest library in the country. Archivists and librarians at Queen's University, the Provincial Archives of Ontario, the Provincial Archives of Manitoba, the University of Manitoba, and the University of Calgary were helpful as well.

I have long been fascinated with both politicians and journalists. And to be completely honest, I admit it was exciting to meet and interview so many of Canada's major political and media stars. While a complete list of interviews may be found in the Bibliography, I would like to single out the following individuals for taking the time to speak with me: John Turner, Keith Davey, Richard O'Hagan, Arthur Irwin, and Charles Lynch (the latter for a memorable lunch at the National Press Club). J.W. Pickersgill, Robert Stanfield, and the late Bruce Hutchison not only shared their views and recollections with me, but also allowed me access to their private papers. I thank them, as I do Geoffrey Pearson for allowing me to research and quote from his father's prime ministerial papers.

For assisting me in arranging some of these interviews and for writing innumerable letters of reference, I thank Jack McClelland, Peter C. Newman (himself a candid interviewee), Shirlee Smith, and Winnipeg MP Dorothy Dobbie. Alas, my much-anticipated interview with Brian Mulroney did not take place, but it was not for lack of trying on Mrs. Dobbie's part. The unending constitutional saga unfortunately got in the way.

I benefited greatly from the keen insights and intelligent comments of Knowlton Nash, Jack Bumsted, and Mel Kliman (my uncle), all of whom read portions of the manuscript. I am especially grateful to Graham Fraser of the *Globe and Mail,* who befriended me when we first met in Ottawa, took time from his busy schedule to talk to me about his own experiences and those of his late father, journalist Blair Fraser, and wrote thoughtful commentaries on several chapters. Though I am certain he will not agree with all my conclusions, I look forward to future discussions with him.

I would be remiss if I did not acknowledge the contribution of historian and professor J.M.S. Careless, who for more than a decade has been a continuing source of support and encouragement for me. As always, his comments, reference letters, wisdom, and friendship are much appreciated.

It goes without saying that all omissions, misinterpretations, and errors of fact and judgment are solely my own.

There is no question that this book took its toll on my colleagues and family. At St. John's–Ravenscourt, Wendy Owen and Bruce Neal stood by me through the good and bad times, and I am sincerely grateful. At the bleakest moment, Wendy, in particular, remained optimistic when I had all but given up. I thank her for keeping the faith.

My parents, Bernice and Marvin Levine, were, as they always have been, helpful and excited about my work. Unfortunately, my father did not live to see this book in print, but I know he would have been proud.

As for my family, through every phase of this book's gestation – from packing up and moving to Ottawa for a year to awaiting publication – Angie and our two children, Alexander and Mia, have been more patient, understanding, and supportive than I had any right to expect. Though I have not always let Angie know it, this book would not have seen the light of day without her devotion and her confidence in me, not to mention her keeping the kids busy so that I could sneak away to my office. For all this and for much more, I dedicate this book to her and to them with all my love.

A.L.
Winnipeg
June 21, 1993

Prologue

The View from the Gallery

Here is my old accustomed place I sit with heart as true
And when your foes I used to face, and break a spear for you ...
I watch old friends, I note the new,
Half joyful, half in grief
To think my hand was naught to do,
Good Luck, God speed, my chief.

"The Gallery" by Martin Griffin,
dedicated to John A. Macdonald, 1876

Martin Griffin quickly finished eating his lunch. It was nearing three o'clock and he had to hurry back to the House to prepare for what would probably be a long sitting. Griffin was an editor with the Conservative Halifax *Herald*, and for this session he was working as the newspaper's Ottawa correspondent, a job he enjoyed and was good at. The Liberal government's March 1878 budget was the subject of debate, and the Conservatives, led by a reinvigorated John A. Macdonald, were on the offensive, gearing up for an anticipated fall election. This meant that he and the other journalists high above in the parliamentary press gallery would be extremely busy taking pages and pages of notes as the politicians below debated the young dominion's future, sometimes to the point of exhaustion for members and scribes alike. Griffin drank his ice water, finished his roast beef, and glanced around at the other lunch-time diners at the Russell House, Ottawa's finest hotel.

Over in one corner were two American visitors from Vermont, Colonel Fuller, who had distinguished himself during the Civil War, and William Noble, a leading lawyer from St. Albans. Both were in town to discuss the controversial fisheries question with Canadian officials. Sitting at a nearby table were the wives of two prominent members of Parliament, sipping on tea and chatting in hushed tones about poor Mrs. Newbanks who had recently dropped dead in a house on York Street. The coroner's findings released that day indicated that she had died from a congestion in her lungs caused by excessive use of alcohol. It was all very sad, the ladies murmured, but typical of the lower classes. In the rest of the large room sat a variety of

Ottawa's citizens – judges, politicians, civil servants and businessmen. It was just another typical day at the Russell Cafe.

Nearly everyone was talking about the Quebec constitutional crisis that had exploded five days earlier, on March 2. The province's Liberal-appointed lieutenant-governor, Luc Letellier de St. Just, had dismissed the Conservative administration of Charles de Boucherville over a dispute involving public money earmarked for the North Shore railway project. More to the point, Lettelier had then asked the Liberal leader in the Quebec assembly, Henri Joly de Lotbinière, to become premier.[1] This was all too much for Griffin, a dedicated and traditional Tory who deeply resented such slick Grit manoeuvres.

Griffin was born in St. John's, Newfoundland, in 1847 into a devout Roman Catholic family. His father was a captain in the Merchant Marine. The Griffins moved to Nova Scotia in 1854, and young Martin, a capable student who demonstrated at an early age a speed-reading ability and a love of literature, was educated at schools in Halifax. He later attended St. Mary's College, where he received a bachelor of arts, and then obtained a law degree from Dalhousie University. He was called to the Nova Scotia Bar in 1868.

For the ambitious Griffin this was not enough; he also had to make a decent living. In 1872 he married Harriet Starratt and they started their family very soon after. Like his good friend John Thompson, a lawyer and future prime minister of Canada, Griffin found that practising law in Halifax was difficult and not very lucrative. During the next decade he supplemented his meagre income in several different ways. He tried his hand at politics but was an unsuccessful candidate in the Nova Scotia election of 1874; he also worked for a brief time as a private secretary to James McDonald, a local Conservative politician. It was, however, in journalism that Griffin made his mark.

For five years, from 1869 to 1874, he edited the Halifax *Evening Express*, where his devotion to Catholicism was evident in his writings. When that paper folded, he became the editor of the new Conservative Party organ, the *Morning Herald*. On its board of directors was his close associate John Thompson. Not only did Griffin make the *Herald* a great success, but he established a reputation for himself as a highly partisan, harsh, and on occasion downright wicked writer.[2]

In all other respects Griffin was a mild, pleasant, and cultured man who revered British institutions and enjoyed reading fine literature and attending the theatre. He often used his favourite passages from Shakespeare to open his Ottawa reports. At the same time, in the editor's chair at the *Herald* and later with Toronto's Tory *Mail* in the early 1880s, he could rip the dreaded Grits to shreds. In 1878, after encountering Prime Minister Alexander

Mackenzie at a costume ball at Government House, he reported that "Mr. Mackenzie was present disguised as a gentleman." He was more cutting a few years later when covering a large Liberal gathering in Toronto, noting that the Grit group in attendance was "a motley collection of office seekers, looking around for free lunches and cheap whisky and sadly in need of a bath."

At about half past two, Griffin left the Russell House, turned up Elgin Street towards the Parliament Buildings, then crossed over to Sparks Street. He briefly stopped at Esmond's, a bookstore, to pick up a copy of Mark Twain's new book, *An Idle Excursion*, for fifty cents. If the session did not go on all night, he would read the book later in the evening. The weather was quite pleasant for early March, but the temperature of around 40 degrees Fahrenheit made things rather muddy. This was nothing new for Ottawa, still a small but growing lumber town with a population of roughly 25,000.

As he walked up Wellington Street, Griffin paused to admire the clock that Prime Minister Alexander Mackenzie had recently had placed in the Centre Block tower. Years later, on a cold night in February 1916, it, along with the rest of the Centre Block, except for the precious library where Griffin himself would soon work, would be destroyed by a terrible fire. That, however, was in the future. For the moment, Griffin entered the buildings by a side door, struggled up the narrow, dark, twisting staircase, and made his way to the mezzanine gallery, which in the old House "swoop[ed] dangerously low over the Speaker's chair."[3]

It was a different setting than the present-day House of Commons. Then the Speaker's chair was in the centre facing east and the members' seats (206 in 1878) were on either side but along the shorter walls of the rectangular room; in the rebuilt House, the Speaker's chair faces south and the seats are along the long sides.[4] From the perspective of the gallery, the Commons resembled a "deep pit," according to a young novice reporter, John Dafoe, who in 1884 at the age of eighteen had been sent to Ottawa by the *Montreal Star*. "At the bottom [of this pit] the members swarmed," recalled Dafoe years later when he was the editor of the *Winnipeg Free Press*. "It was enclosed by walls that rose sheer and unbroken, save for narrow entrances, for perhaps 20 feet, from the top of these walls the public galleries sloped upward and back to the outer walls. Gothic windows in these walls and skylights let in an uncertain measure of light."[5]

Martin Griffin took his seat in the gallery as the members took theirs below. Surrounding him were the other twenty-five or so correspondents who reported on events in Ottawa: Conservative friends from such newspapers as the Toronto *Mail, Hamilton Spectator, Montreal Gazette*, and *Ottawa Evening Citizen*; and Liberal rivals from the Montreal *Herald*,

Ottawa Free Press, Halifax Chronicle, and *Toronto Globe* – "the parent of all the journalistic scurrility" in Canada in Griffin's biased estimation. Indeed, just as the Commons was divided between Macdonald's Conservatives and Mackenzie's Liberals, so too was the gallery.

Paul Bilkey worked in the gallery in 1903 for the *Toronto Telegram,* but his recollections are even more appropriate to the 1870s and 1880s. "For a long time, the Gallery was divided into two bitter hostile camps," Bilkey wrote in his memoirs, "so that men who should have been friends hardly spoke to each other."[5] This animosity was a reflection of the partisan age to which Griffin and his fellow-correspondents belonged. Canada in 1878 and for many years to come was a world divided between two political parties; partisanship touched the fabric of day-to-day life in a way that is now hard to comprehend. Each side had its own hotels, lawyers, doctors, dentists, and businesses to frequent. Most important of all, both parties sponsored or supported their own newspapers. And these were read religiously by their respective followers.

It was considered as much a journalistic honour to work in the Ottawa gallery in 1878 as it is today. And, as now, the pay was not great. John Willison, the *Globe*'s correspondent, even by 1887 was earning only about $1,000 a year as compared with a successful Toronto or Montreal lawyer, who could make ten times that amount. In addition to covering the Commons proceedings, most correspondents were required to write editorials and columns. Some freelanced, wrote for more than one paper, or if they had the right connections, worked part time as a government clerk.[6]

Regardless of the long hours, the low wages, and the tedious chore of recording politicians' speeches, the job had prestige – at least the Ottawa journalists thought it did. It was, and is, the plague of the profession. "When I first came to mingle among newspaper men as a working associate," recalled Toronto writer and journalist Hector Charlesworth, "it secretly amused me to discern that they held a much higher opinion of their importance in the world than the business and social community with which they were surrounded actually accorded them."[7]

Prestige, however, had its price. In Ottawa this meant that the correspondent was supposed to heel to the beck and call of the party politician. It was a relationship of mutual manipulation. The politician, if he (no women in those days) was in the government or better still the cabinet, supplied the journalist with what he needed most: private information about appointments, election dates, and policy decisions. When John A. Macdonald liked a correspondent, such as Martin Griffin or the Toronto *Mail*'s Charles Belford, he could be very accommodating, granting access to himself and to the government's books. This did not make life pleasant for Liberal journalists during the Conservatives' long tenure in office from 1878 to 1896. "It was difficult, if not impossible, to secure information from the public departments," the *Globe*'s John Willison recalled with some frustration. "All appointments and statements of policy were reserved for party organs."[8] Pity the proud Willison, who, in order to discover the latest government strategy or action, had to hang around the telegraph office in the hope of sneaking a peek at the dispatches of Conservative correspondents.

There was also the question of money. During the 1870s it did not cost very much to establish a newspaper, anywhere from $5,000 to $10,000, readily available from businessmen seeking investment opportunities and politicians looking for a mouthpiece. It was surviving for more than a year that was the real problem. Newspapers came and went quickly in this era. In Winnipeg, a "journalistic cemetery," there were no less than six different Conservative newspapers between 1879 and 1887. It was said that if you were still in operation after two months you were doing well (one paper actually lasted for fifteen days before being absorbed by a competitor).

Explaining such commercial instability is easy. There were the initial expenses for presses and machinery, not to mention a building to operate in. But as historian Paul Rutherford notes in his study of the nineteenth-century daily newspaper, the costs of such things as paper, ink, type, and salaries proved to be the biggest financial burden. For example, in 1870 it cost George Brown, the legendary founder of the *Globe*, $60,000 a year for newsprint alone.[9] Add to this a few bad debts, clients who did not pay advertising and subscriptions, equipment that broke down and had to be replaced with the latest but more costly design, and it is not hard to understand why editors and publishers were constantly and desperately in need of cash.

Here was where the politicians and their party organizations came into play. In a world defined by whether one was a Grit or a Tory, it was usually good business for a newspaper to identify with one side or the other. This provided it with a loyal group of readers and gave some sense of purpose to its editorials.[10] The politicians, in turn, were grateful. They pushed their local party organs in speeches at Sunday picnics, helped raise capital if necessary, and if their particular paper had a correspondent in Ottawa, they channelled information his way.

Then there was the "pap," or government patronage, to be doled out in the form of advertising and printing contracts. An actual list was prepared to ensure that the right papers received the rewards of loyalty. This meant that except for the brief interlude of Alexander Mackenzie's administration in the mid-1870s, Liberal Party organs did not receive their fair share. But too much should not be made of the power of this patronage, since the money allocated to even the largest Conservative daily was never substantial. During 1888–89, for instance, the federal government's newspaper patronage totalled $77,359 for advertising and $115,335 for printing. The

Montreal Gazette, one of the premier Tory papers in the country, received the most: $1,689 for advertising and $5,606 for printing, not exorbitant amounts. The poor *Globe*'s share, on the other hand, was an advertising contract for $18.21.[11]

The fact was, as the *Hamilton Spectator* put it in January 1882, "no journal of standing of either party looks upon its government patronage as being of importance to it. Every journal has scores of private patrons whose account is vastly greater with it than that of the Government." Two years earlier, in an editorial of February 10, 1880, entitled "Organship," the London *Daily Advertiser*, a Liberal daily, was more succinct: "The alleged 'pap' in the shape of official advertisements is a very small item in the large returns which such a newspaper must have if it is to continue to exist at all. The profits from Government advertisements in any prominent newspaper for a whole year would not meet the publishing expenses of half-a-day out of the three hundred and sixty five."

If what the *Spectator* and *Advertiser* said was true, why then was John A. Macdonald's correspondence filled with letters from Conservative editors from every town and city across Canada who were not satisfied with their share of government contracts? The simple answer is that the money, no matter how small an amount, did make a difference to a struggling newspaper proprietor.[12] Realistic politicians like Sir John A. understood that in the newspaper business meagre government patronage was no substitute for a sound commercial foundation. This, however, did not stop him from trying to use patronage to ensure newspaper loyalty. Sometimes it worked, more often it did not.

From a politician's perspective, a good newspaper was one that spread his party's gospel daily to his loyal supporters so that on election day there would be no unhappy surprises. It was all very straightforward. For newspaper publishers, the realities of life were slightly different; they had other concerns, such as balancing the books and increasing circulation. More to the point, newspapermen did not like to be regarded as party slaves. With some subtle political cajoling they did usually toe the acceptable line, at least during the Macdonald era, but the relationship between the two partners was often strained by differences over policies and press independence. In his memoirs, John Willison recalls that Gordon Brown, George Brown's brother and editor of the *Globe* for many years, refused to be "only a speaking-tube for the political leaders." Willison himself left the *Globe* in 1902 to become the editor of the independent Toronto *News* because he couldn't tolerate Liberal Party interference.

Indeed, in some instances loyalty to a party cause was expensive. Conservative papers in the West in the 1880s were compelled to write editorials in support of the protective tariff on agricultural implements, not a popular measure among the farmers who were supposed to buy the newspapers. John Young, the editor of the Regina *Leader*, had been ordered by his boss, the indomitable Nicholas Flood Davin, the founder of the Conservative organ in 1883, "to support the Government on every occasion."[13] The same was true for Montreal's *La Minerve* and other French Tory dailies that suffered financially as the Conservative Party's fortunes declined in Quebec after the hanging of Louis Riel in 1885.

Such pressures eventually caused more and more papers to split from the party on some controversial or unpopular issues, and in some cases to declare their independence outright. Macdonald ran up against this more than once; his struggles to establish and maintain a loyal and viable organ in Toronto is only the most outstanding example. Macdonald valued journalists' work on behalf of his cause, and what he and other political leaders wanted, sometimes demanded, was loyalty and devotion.

All of which brings us back to Martin Griffin on Thursday, March 7, 1878, at 3 p.m. Sitting there in the gallery waiting for the session to begin, Griffin was no doubt aware of the role he played in John A. Macdonald's plans and understood as well the nature of his relationship with politicians. He didn't concern himself with gossip about John A.'s drinking binges – there was, as John Willison noted, consideration among gallery members "for men's private faults and foibles."[14] No, Griffin knew that his job was to present the Conservatives' perspective, to lambaste the Grits at every opportunity, and to portray his leader in the most favourable light possible. It was all so easy.

Events in the Commons unfolded as they should have that day. It was a month into the Fifth Session of Canada's Third Parliament, another three weeks were to follow. As noted, the House was in the midst of a serious debate on the economy. The Liberals were defending their proposed budget, which reflected the party's traditional stand on freer trade, while the Conservatives were finalizing their move towards a policy of protectionism that had begun five years earlier.

After some preliminary and routine business on transportation and railway matters, the debate began in earnest. John A. Macdonald, then in exile as the leader of the opposition but spry as ever at age sixty-three, rose to make a statement regarding some inappropriate comments made at an earlier date about Sir William Young, the seventy-nine-year-old chief justice of Nova Scotia. The offender in this case was the Liberal minister of militia, Alfred Jones from Halifax, whose feud with Young involved an incident that had occurred in 1869. This debate is fascinating, not so much for the issue itself, but as an example of Macdonald's uncanny ability to goad his opponents into a tizzy.

After about forty-five minutes of sniping across the Commons floor, the discussion on economic matters was about to resume. What followed first, however, was a bizarre and lengthy diatribe by Quebec Conservative Joseph Mousseau on the history of Canada, on whether or not a now-departed George-Étienne Cartier had been a coward during the Lower Canadian rebellion of 1837 (he hadn't been), and on why French Canadian Conservatives had refused to support bills establishing the Supreme Court in 1869 and 1875 (they were concerned about judicial decisions respecting Quebec civil law because only two of seven judges on the planned court were to be French). The dour Edward Blake, who had recently resigned from Mackenzie's cabinet for the second and last time, offered his partisan opinion about the French Conservatives' self-serving behaviour on the latter issue. This was too much for Macdonald, who challenged Blake's assertion about the Quebec members' loyalty and suggested that Blake examine his own record of deserting his party when it needed him most. He was as sharp and witty as ever.

Before the day's session ended at 12:55 a.m., Macdonald had explained his views on the future of the Dominion economy and moved a motion for the "adoption of a national policy" that involved a "judicious readjustment of the tariff."[15] It would be the platform that would bring him back to his rightful place on the other side of the House floor in late September.

From above, Martin Griffin watched Sir John A.'s performance with delight. Even surrounded by more than a hundred other men, he stood out. He was just as the satirical *Grip*'s J.W. Bengough's brilliant caricatures had captured him: tall, black curly hair clumped at the back and sides of his head, and "a long large nose ... that acquired ripeness, as it matured from years and whisky." Griffin and other correspondents heard his distinct "rich, soft voice" and witnessed his restlessness in his Commons seat. If Macdonald disapproved – or approved – of something, he let it be known. As Willison remembered from his days in the gallery in the late 1880s, "I could sometimes see shades of expression cross his face, the defiant jerk of the head when he was angry, the shrug of contempt for a mean gibe that was meant to wound, the quick, natural, human manifestation of pleasure over a generous word from an opponent or a tribute of affection and confidence from an associate."[16]

The men of the gallery, Willison and Griffin included, were much like the play-by-play commentators of present-day hockey games, although in this case Griffin's editorial correspondence for the March 7 session had more in common with a description of a one-sided boxing match. In the bout between the featured pugilists, Macdonald vs. Alfred Jones and Edward Blake, it was no contest. "It was a knock-down blow, delivered with a boxing glove, final, but not cruel," Griffin wrote. "Sir John never uses his sharpest weapons, except when he despises as well as opposes a man. With

Mr. Blake he contends with humanity. It is only when he deals with a person like Jones that he uses his force with the cruelty, necessary, and laudable, that one uses towards any kind of dangerous viper that gets out of its hole to sting." On Macdonald's questioning of Blake's solidarity with the Mackenzie government, Griffin reported that "never was there a better hit; it was perfect in tone and manner; it was complete in detail; it was stunning in effect. The House enjoyed it immensely."[17]

Far away in Nova Scotia, in a world without radio and television, this was the image of Macdonald that was conveyed to friend and foe alike. It was unlikely that many of the *Herald*'s readers would ever lay their eyes on the Conservative chieftain; in his later years Macdonald did most of his campaigning in Ontario and left the Maritimes to such colleagues as Charles Tupper. It was thus the writings of journalists like Griffin that made Sir John A. into a larger-than-life figure and ultimately had their effect counted on election day. As the political master of his time, Macdonald was quick to recognize the power of the pen. It was a reality that occupied a great deal of his time and effort, as it would those of his successors.

PART ONE

Partisan Partners,
1867–1913

CHAPTER ONE

A Controlling Interest

*I have been a good deal disappointed by the tone in which
political warfare is conducted by the press. The terms in
which you have been assailed quite exceed the license of
electioneering language.*

Lord Dufferin to John A. Macdonald, 1872

At the McGill University convocation in 1873, the governor general,
Lord Dufferin, delivered a lengthy speech entirely in Greek. In attendance were John A. Macdonald and his French Canadian colleague Hector
Langevin. On the train trip back to Ottawa, Langevin read a news report of
the event which noted that Dufferin had spoken "the purest ancient Greek
without mispronouncing a word."

"Good Heavens," said Langevin to Macdonald, "how did the reporter
know that?"

"I told him," replied Sir John.

"But you don't know Greek!" exclaimed Langevin.

"True," answered Macdonald, "but I know a little about politics."[1]

Indeed he did. We like to think of Macdonald as being something of a
charming and witty political genius. The truth was that he worked more diligently at the political game than any of his peers. While he had what is
referred to today as a charismatic personality, his great success was due
more to his ability "for managing other people," as Lord Dufferin put it. He
knew how to win over followers and keep them loyal. He treated back-
benchers with the same respect accorded his cabinet ministers, could recall
names of constituents he had not seen in five years, and "deemed no man
beneath his notice." "He never forgot," John Willison wrote, "that popularity was power."[2]

He could be devious, manipulative, even unscrupulous if it was necessary, although he was not corrupt. Apart from his exaggerated drinking
problem, Macdonald is best remembered for the Pacific Scandal of 1873. It
was alleged that he took money from Sir Hugh Allan in exchange for the
contract to build the Canadian Pacific Railway (CPR), but this was probably

more a case of foolishness and bad judgment than corruption. Those times dictated a different set of acceptable political rules than do current mores. It is often forgotten, for example, that there never would have been a Pacific Scandal had the Liberals not purchased stolen and incriminating documents for $5,000.

Such were the realities of political life in late nineteenth-century Canada. As a practical man, Macdonald accepted this; he also understood how to operate within the defined boundaries. Nothing illustrates this point more than his relationship with the press. Over more than a forty-year period, this was the arena in which Macdonald's best and worst qualities as a politician were utilized, refined, and tested.

In 1885 Macdonald's parliamentary office received thirty-seven daily and weekly newspapers from across the country. He read the major Montreal and Toronto papers each day, most often at bedtime, and later his secretaries prepared clippings for him to peruse. Even on his rare holidays he voraciously scanned the editorial pages. More importantly, he kept in close touch with most of the Conservative newspaper publishers in the Dominion, both large and small. He advised them what lines to take on policy, stroked their egos, and sometimes assured them that needed patronage was forthcoming.

No matter how trivial an issue, Macdonald refused to miss an opportunity to score a political point. The examples abound in his voluminous correspondence. As journalist Jeffrey Simpson has pointed out, Macdonald's letters "brim with attention to a thousand details of politics." In December 1868 he sent Daniel Morrison, the editor of the Conservative *Daily Telegraph* in Toronto, an article he had received from a Halifax Liberal paper that was critical of his rival George Brown. Nova Scotia Grits had never forgiven Brown for not consulting them before he joined the "Great Coalition" with Macdonald and Cartier in 1864 that led to Confederation. The article in question, Macdonald told Morrison, "pitches into Brown ... I leave [it] for your manipulation."[3]

Less than two years later he wrote to Morrison again, this time explaining at length why the aging Francis Hincks, who had returned after fifteen years from his retreat as governor of Barbados and British Guiana to join Macdonald's cabinet, had publicly attacked the *Telegraph*, a Conservative booster. Apparently Hincks had taken exception to comments made by one of the newspaper's reporters. Macdonald conceded that it was a misunderstanding and then proceeded to tell Morrison – in a way only he could get away with – how appreciative he was of the *Telegraph*'s contribution to the Tory cause. He acknowledged that the newspaper should not be regarded as merely "a mouthpiece of a government" and that its influence depended on it "being supposed to speak its real sentiments." Macdonald suggested that

Morrison send a correspondent to Ottawa whom he could confide in from time to time. "It might add to the interest of your paper," the prime minister noted. "However, you as a newspaper man know more about this kind of thing than I do."[4]

In fact, Macdonald knew a great deal more about newspapers than he was willing to admit. By 1871 he had been the Dominion's prime minister for four years and an active politician for twenty-eight. In the historic road he had travelled from his position as Kingston's member in the Legislative Assembly of the Province of Canada, through his participation in the debates over Confederation in the early 1860s, to his role as the new Dominion's first leader in 1867, Macdonald had received the best political education anyone would want. And from the day in April 1844 when the *Kingston Herald* published his first real political declaration, he was conscious of a newspaper's tremendous impact.[5] He also witnessed the rise of his opponent George Brown and the Liberals, assisted in no small way by the Toronto *Globe*, the most influential political organ of its time and for years to come. Using and manipulating the press to his own advantage became a part of Macdonald's political arsenal.

This was certainly the case during the 1871 negotiations with the United States over the Washington Treaty, one of the most serious issues Macdonald faced in his first term in office. Though the British still controlled Canada's foreign relations at this time, Prime Minister Macdonald was invited, in accordance with proper diplomatic etiquette, to join the British delegation in Washington during discussions about U.S.-Canada trade, fishing rights, and other issues still unsettled from the American Civil War years. (The Canadian government believed, for instance, that the U.S. government owed it compensation for the damage done during raids on Canada conducted by Irish Fenians from U.S. bases back in 1866.) Reluctantly, Macdonald left Ottawa for the American capital at the end of February 1871 and remained there for three long months. He was all too aware that he was regarded by the other members of the British negotiating team as a colonial inferior. He realized as well that the imperial government, desperate to establish friendly relations with the United States, would have no qualms about sacrificing Canadian interests to gain American favour. He was not disappointed.[6]

After months of dreary meetings and evenings spent socializing at Washington dinner parties, the Americans offered a cash payment for the use of Canadian fishing waters, a rather radical proposition, with no comprehensive reciprocal trade agreement as desired by Macdonald. By the time it was all over at the end of April, the British had bowed to the Americans' unfavourable terms. They had sold fishing rights in Canada without the Dominion's consent or approval.[7]

A frustrated Macdonald confided to Alexander Morris, one of his cabinet ministers: "Never in the whole course of my public life have I been in so disagreeable a position."[8] He was dejected, but not yet defeated. His strategy now revolved around whether to sign the treaty. He decided it would be best in the interests of the Empire to add his signature, but he did write formal letters to the British government noting his objections. These would be helpful later on.

His first general election as prime minister was about a year away. He knew that Brown and the *Globe* as well as other Liberal newspapers would attack him as a traitor. Controlling information about his position on the treaty therefore became essential. He instructed Morris "to make arrangements with the friendly newspapers ... to hold back, if possible, any expression of opinion on the Treaty when it is promulgated, until the *Globe* commits itself against the Treaty." The idea was that Brown and the Grits would think Macdonald supported the treaty and would criticize him accordingly, and then Macdonald could reveal that he too objected to it. He and Brown would be on the same side of the issue and the treaty would be forgotten by the time the election campaign began. If, however, he confirmed his opposition immediately, he feared that Brown would find some way to support it.[9] It was a shrewd manoeuvre by an experienced politician, and it worked.

As Macdonald anticipated, the *Globe* tore into the treaty and branded the prime minister a weak traitor. "Sir John Macdonald is but a poor parody of a statesman after all," declared a *Globe* editorial on May 31. "Neither in his personal or political character has he ever shown moral or intellectual strength. He is smart and cunning but has more than once before now proved himself to be 'too clever by half.' At Washington he found not subservient tools, but men of infinitely superior calibre to himself and the natural weakness of his character appeared." Such was the colourful language of 1871 editorials.

The loyal Conservative press was placed in a more difficult position because Macdonald had decided the best course to follow was silence. Amazingly, for twelve very long months he refused to comment; nor did he accept any invitations to speak at political gatherings, fearing that he would have to explain his treaty position.[10] But the Tory press adhered to its leader's wishes. Despite the *Globe*'s daily abuse, the Brantford *Courier* defended Macdonald's actions against the aggressive "Yankees," while future prime minister Mackenzie Bowell's *Belleville Intelligencer* argued that no opinion could be made about the treaty until Parliament debated it.

Eventually the British government came up with a guaranteed loan of £2.5 million for railways and canals in exchange for the Canadian Parliament's ratification. Macdonald finally spoke on the issue in a two and a half hour speech on May 3, 1872. He played up his role in assisting both

Anglo-American peace and the interests of the Empire.[11] Thanks in large part to his ability to manipulate and slant the news, he turned a potential disaster into a triumph and beat Brown and the *Globe* – in this round at least.

George Brown was a large man, over six feet tall and powerfully built. Even by age thirty-five, he was balding and wore long, bushy, mutton-chop sideburns, as was the style of the day. He was a hard, dogmatic, and passionate man with strong beliefs about the freedom of religion, free speech, civil liberties, and the separation of church and state.[12] Moreover, he was willing to fight for these ideas, no matter what the cost. He feared the power of the Catholic Church and resented how his French and English Conservative opponents, Macdonald and Cartier, had expanded the church's power in the schools of Canada West. From the day in 1844 when he founded the *Globe* in Toronto, Brown became a major player in the political life of the country by establishing what proved to be one of the foundations of a lasting Liberal Party. He also set the standards by which all other newspapers and journalists were judged.

As a pioneer of the Canadian newspaper industry, Brown ensured that the *Globe* always had the most innovative machinery. It allowed him and his brother Gordon (who was appointed managing editor in 1853) to refine and transform the paper from a "mammoth blanket sheet" folded once to make four pages of thirty-six columns to a smaller eight-page version resembling the newspapers of today. The Browns experimented with new and clearer type, sent correspondents all over the country to cover stories, reported foreign as well as local news, and attracted large audiences in Toronto as well as in nearby towns with serialized literature and stories about sensational murder trials. This plus the *Globe*'s "ferocious editorials," in which Brown and his writers "struck without mercy against the foes of Reform," made the newspaper a powerful weapon.[13]

No newspaper was referred to in House of Commons debates more than the *Globe;* nor was one more widely read. It was said that before many Liberal politicians would speak on an issue, they would ask, "What will the *Globe* say?" It was sold in every train station, hotel, and bookstore in Ontario. Its denunciations and strong opinions were a daily topic of conversation. As veteran Liberal politician Sir Richard Cartwright so aptly put it, "There were probably many thousand voters in Ontario ... who hardly read anything except their *Globe* and their Bible."[14]

For more than five decades, the *Globe*'s main target was John A. Macdonald, the Tory devil incarnate. No two men were as different in style and personality than Macdonald and Brown. Where Macdonald was easygoing, generally cheerful and good-natured, Brown was less accommodating, more strenuous and serious. That they clashed is not at all surprising.[15]

The root of their long feud stemmed from an incident in pre-Confederation days when they were both members from Canada West. In a violent outburst in 1856, Macdonald unfairly accused Brown of lying and falsifying evidence in his capacity as secretary of a major commission on conditions at Kingston Penitentiary that had reported in 1849.[16] Unlike Macdonald, who rarely held a grudge, Brown did, and in his opinion Macdonald never publicly apologized for his vicious remarks. Brown remained bitter about this for the rest of his life and it coloured his view of John A. and his political methods.

As for Macdonald, his personal feelings towards Brown were reflected in one of his most quoted remarks: that Canadians "would rather have John A. drunk than George Brown sober." Still, the *Globe* – the 'Grit Organ' as it was commonly referred to by Conservatives – could drive Macdonald to drink, and probably did on more than one occasion. He read it daily and had an army of newspaper publishers and supporters who kept him up to date on its most recent attacks.

For Macdonald, taking on the *Globe* was sometimes the best sport in town. When he was in Toronto, he stayed at the Queen's Hotel, where he would hold court in the Red Parlour. Usually camped outside the Queen's was the *Globe*'s Herbert Burrows, assigned to spy and report on Macdonald's activities. Burrows did anything for a scoop. In 1881 the Conservatives held a convention in Toronto at the Grand Opera House, and the *Globe* was not invited. This didn't stop Burrows. He paid off an Opera House employee and perched high above the stage, where he remained all day, taking notes. He was thus able to write an in-depth story, much to the anger of the local Tories. Macdonald admired Burrows so much that he later got him a job with the Toronto *Empire*, the Conservative Party organ in the late 1880s.[17]

More often, John A. received harsh and critical treatment by *Globe* writers, representative of the journalistic style of the era. He was condemned for his handling of Louis Riel and the Métis conflict in 1869 and for selling out Canada in the Washington Treaty of 1871. But in early April 1873, when Liberal Lucius Seth Huntington first raised the charges that Macdonald had awarded the Pacific Railway contract for a bribe, breaking the scandal that would ultimately cause the Conservatives' fall, the *Globe*'s vindictive and predatory character reached new heights.

From this point on, the newspaper hammered away at the government's corruption. Outraged, the *Globe* produced each new piece of the devastating puzzle, disclosing how Hugh Allan had been promised the presidency of the new railway and how desperately the Conservatives had needed Allan's "dirty" money during the election of 1872. "Immediate, private. I must have another ten thousand. Will be the last time of calling. Do not fail me.

Answer today," Macdonald had wired Allan's lawyer J.J. Abbott on August 26, 1872, near the end of the election. This plea for help, boldly published by the *Globe* and other Liberal papers on July 18, 1873, sealed Macdonald's fate.

Throughout the ordeal the *Globe* took the moral high ground. "Shall the highest servants of the nation, the chosen advisors of the Crown be suffered to maintain their position by selling the public interests and public lands for gold and pandering to the lowest and most sordid motives?" pondered an editorial on October 21. Macdonald finally resigned in early November but defended his position in a five-hour speech in Parliament. To the *Globe* this was "callous and repulsive." In words that today would be cause for a libel suit, the newspaper portrayed Macdonald as "the Hector of corruption" who "defied all the principles of right and justice, every dictate of morality, every sanction of conscience, every prescription of decency which belongs to the people of Canada."[18]

Brown's close associate, supporter, and friend, Alexander Mackenzie, became prime minister upon Macdonald's departure. Historians have not treated Mackenzie as a figure of much consequence. The truth is that John A. was a hard act to follow, although the diligent and honest Mackenzie, a former stonemason, would not have concerned himself with such matters. He accepted his party's call (no one else wanted the job) and with the help of Brown and the *Globe* faced the challenges of a depression and the indecisiveness of Edward Blake (who resigned twice from the cabinet).

Governor General Lord Dufferin referred to George Brown, appointed a senator in December 1873, as "the protector of my prime minister."[19] Every prime minister needs a confidant, someone trustworthy who will provide advice when needed. For Mackenzie this was Brown, his fellow-Scot and leader. It would be wrong to say Mackenzie worshipped Brown, but he did value his friendship and newspaper. On the other hand, he wasn't afraid to speak out when he thought the *Globe* was following the wrong course.[20] The *Globe* could not save Mackenzie from a resurging John A. Macdonald in 1878, but it was not for lack of trying.

April 12, 1878, was a Friday. In the House of Commons a debate was raging over the actions of Quebec Lieutenant-Governor Letellier de St. Just, who had dismissed his Conservative ministers. Macdonald, then leader of the opposition, wanted the debate to resume the following day; Prime Minister Mackenzie, impatient to be done with the issue, would not grant the requested adjournment; and thus the debate continued through the night, lasting until 6 p.m. on Saturday. In an act of defiance, the Conservatives used a variety of tactics to keep the discussion going. In fact, it was mayhem. Recalled journalist E.B. Biggar: "While the points of order were being argued members hammered at desks, blew on tin trumpets, imitated the crowing of cocks, sent up toy balloons, threw sand crackers or torpedoes and occasionally hurled blue books across the House."[21]

There were two different accounts of John A. Macdonald's conduct that night. According to his sympathetic biographer Donald Creighton, Macdonald, after leading the attack late into Friday night, retired from the House, had a few glasses of sherry with some oysters, and went to sleep on a couch in a committee room. The *Globe* and Alexander Mackenzie saw it differently. "John A. got very drunk," the prime minister informed George Brown, "and early this morning they had to get him stowed away somewhere ... About six this morning he drank a tumbler full of sherry and at eight [Liberal M.P. David] Mills saw him drink a tumbler full of whisky. The last dose laid him out and his friends hid him somewhere."[22]

The *Globe*'s correspondent in the gallery wrote a damaging story for Monday's edition, and an editorial entitled "The Disgraceful Scene in Ottawa" followed the next day: "To say that Sir John Macdonald was on Friday night somewhat under the influence of liquor would be a grossly inadequate representation of fact. He was simply drunk in the plain ordinary sense of the word." The *Globe*'s interpretation of the events spread across Ontario, Quebec, and the Maritimes and was retold and published by Grit editors eager to join the slanderous attack. From every little Liberal printing press, John A. was denounced as the devil, as dishonest, and as a drunk.[23]

Conservative papers, of course, rallied to their leader's side, while Macdonald himself ordered his lawyers to begin $10,000 libel suits against the *Guelph Mercury*, Brantford *Expositor*, and *Peterborough Examiner*. It is not clear whether a suit was also launched against the *Globe*, although Macdonald was encouraged to do so. The cases were to begin in October but were all dropped after the Conservatives were back in office.[24] Still, until the day he died in 1891 – a decade after his nemesis George Brown had suffered a similar fate (caused from a wound sustained from an assassination attempt) – there was no greater thorn in Macdonald's side than the *Globe*. The problem of combatting its influence and power took up more of his valuable time than he surely desired.

It wasn't that Macdonald was not concerned about the rest of Canada; Joseph Howe, Louis Riel, Honoré Mercier, and Thomas Greenway, among others, made sure of that. Yet during his career it was his home province of Ontario, where the roots of his legal, business and political profession were, that most concerned him. He spent the majority of his time in three Ontario cities, Ottawa, Toronto, and Kingston. It was not until he was seventy-one, in 1886, that he actually visited a Canadian region west of Ontario. He was a smart enough leader to realize that the inner political workings of Quebec and the Maritimes should be left with Cartier, Langevin, and Tupper, who understood the local dynamics of their communities. Ontario, with its eighty-two seats (ninety-two by 1891), was his territory. He was, as one writer observed, "an Ontario institution."

Macdonald did try to establish a network of viable Conservative newspapers across the Dominion. He appreciated, for instance, the support of the *Montreal Gazette* and the Quebec City *Chronicle*, his two main English papers in Quebec, and worried about the financial problems faced by the French Montreal daily *La Minerve*. He spent a decade assisting his Winnipeg supporters in their ultimately unsuccessful efforts to start a Conservative paper that would challenge the supremacy of the Liberal-leaning *Free Press*. Further west in Regina, he put out a call for capital to finance the founding of the *Leader* by Nicholas Flood Davin in 1883.[25] Nevertheless, because of Macdonald's own interests, political and personal, as well as the overwhelming influence of the *Globe*, it was the press situation in Ontario, more particularly Toronto, that mattered most.

Toronto at the time of Confederation was no longer "muddy little York"; it was not, however, the metropolis it is today. It was still a distant second behind Montreal as the dominating Canadian urban centre of business and culture, but it was growing. In 1871 its population was a little more than 56,000; within a decade it would rise to 86,000 and at the end of the Macdonald era in 1891 to 181,000. Toronto was in every respect a Protestant city: hard work, Christian values, and loyalty to Britain were its trademarks.[26] The wealthy played cricket and golf at the fashionable clubs, while labour leaders tried to reduce the average working day from ten hours to nine.

King Street was the social and business centre, although in 1869 Timothy Eaton had opened his store a few blocks north at the corner of Queen and Yonge. At Eaton's, it was cash only and the prices to be paid were as marked. There was no credit and no dickering, a radical departure from the way business was usually conducted. Torontonians soon learned to adapt to and even like the new ways. If you enjoyed sports, you could cheer on champion rower Ned Hanlan down by Lake Ontario or watch the Clipper baseball team practise in Queen's Park. There were outings to High Park (about the only place you could not drink), the highlight there being the fireworks display on Queen Victoria's birthday, and visits to the annual summer exhibition, where a dazzling display on electricity was staged in 1882. For the Liberals there was the *Globe* and the National Club. Conservative businessmen and lawyers preferred the confines of the Albany Club; what newspaper they read, however, varied from year to year.

The main reason Macdonald and the Conservatives had so much trouble establishing a legitimate contender to the *Globe* was that there was no Tory version of George Brown. The *Globe* publisher nurtured his sheet, giving it a vision and a personality. Ultimately the task of challenging the Grit paper became the responsibility of Macdonald and his most trusted advisers. Macdonald, as prime minister, had quite different priorities from Brown, who by 1867 was a newspaper proprietor first and a politician second, and herein lay the root of the problem. Besides a publisher, a successful party organ required a full-time competent team of dedicated editors, reporters, printers, and business managers. Brown had brought them all together; Macdonald was forever trying to find the right combination.

Until 1872 Macdonald was supported in Toronto first by the *Leader* and later by the *Daily Telegraph*. But both failed him. The *Leader* had been founded by James Beaty, a Toronto leather merchant, in 1852. Beaty was a supporter of Francis Hincks, and his paper, which was edited by Charles Lindsay (the son-in-law of rebel William Lyon Mackenzie), reflected Hincks's moderate tone, a fact that troubled Macdonald.

In those days, during the time of the union of the Canadas, the *British Colonist*, a Tory paper that dated back to the 1830s, also assisted Macdonald, although Macdonald's control was limited. In fact, in 1858 a disagreement between Macdonald and the *Colonist* over its fair treatment of George Brown's father, Peter (who had been unjustly charged by a Conservative member of the assembly with embezzling funds in Scotland years earlier), had led the prime minister to sponsor a paper called the *Toronto Daily Atlas*. It lasted only a short time before being taken over by the *Colonist*, which was eventually itself absorbed by Beaty and the *Leader*.[27]

Despite its acceptable service to the Conservative cause, the *Leader* could not keep up with the *Globe* in circulation or technological improvement. As David Macpherson, a prominent Toronto Conservative businessman, told Macdonald, who was in London watching the passage of the British North America (BNA) Act in February 1867, "The *Globe* is so much improved as a newspaper and the *Leader* so fallen off." The situation had not improved a year later. "How I wish your paper was in Toronto," Macdonald wrote in a letter to Thomas White, then publisher of the *Hamilton Spectator*. "I feel absolutely powerless there for want of an organ. The *Leader* is effete." Plans were arranged for White to relocate to Toronto, but the $10,000 needed for the move could not be raised. Macdonald and Macpherson then attempted to buy out Beaty, hoping to change the *Leader*'s tone and style by installing White as the new managing editor. This too did not work out. The eccentric Beaty, as Macdonald later admitted, had "an exaggerated value" of his paper and, besides, enjoyed having it as a "toy to play with."[28]

Next was the case of the *Daily Telegraph*. Established in 1866 by James Cook (formerly of the *Leader*) and John Ross Robertson (once the *Globe*'s city editor), the *Telegraph* started out as an independent Conservative paper.

Cook and Robertson favoured the British connection, Confederation, free trade, and John A. Macdonald. They also felt free to criticize any or all of these, a situation unacceptable to a politician like Macdonald, who needed daily partisan press coverage and editorials he could count on. Cook and Robertson were joined in the summer of 1868 by Daniel Morrison, an experienced journalist who had previously worked for the *Colonist*, the *Leader*, the *Morning Chronicle* (the Conservative paper in Quebec City), and most recently the *New York Times*. He returned to Canada at about the time the *Telegraph* was experiencing serious financial difficulties and within six months set out with Cook to raise the needed funds. Robertson, who did not want to owe anyone, especially politicians, favours, remained behind in Toronto, frustrated and angry.

During March 1869 Morrison and Cook presented Macdonald with their plans for a revised *Telegraph* that could compete more effectively with the *Globe*. They also met with Charles Brydges, the manager of the Grand Trunk Railroad and an associate of Macdonald's. Brydges did not hold either the *Telegraph* or Morrison (he had told Macdonald he was "certainly not sober when I saw him") in the highest regard. Nevertheless, in April Macdonald and Brydges arranged for $5,000 to be given to the *Telegraph* as a mortgage, and promised another $5,000 if the paper became as successful as Morrison and Cook claimed.[29]*

Even with Morrison as editor the *Telegraph* faltered. Then on April 12, 1870, Morrison died suddenly at the age of forty-three, and the *Telegraph* was returned to Robertson's hands. During the next year and half, much to Macdonald's displeasure, Robertson wrote critical editorials on the government's handling of the Riel crisis at Red River; further, his paper considered the Washington Treaty, as the *Globe* did, a betrayal of Canada. On 11 May 1871, the *Telegraph* accused the Macdonald administration of being "worn out political hacks of every shade of political views, without one common idea, save that of retaining power and place, by sacrificing every principle and every particle of honour." These were not the words of a party organ, nor it seemed of a financially viable newspaper. By attacking the government, Robertson was moving into the *Globe*'s territory, but there was not enough room for both in partisan Toronto. That May the *Telegraph*'s debt reached roughly $50,000.[30]

---

* In his unpublished history of the *Globe*, M.O. Hammond claimed that Macdonald and the Conservative Party had given the *Telegraph* $50,000. But the evidence in Macdonald's correspondence suggests that he had put in $2,000; John Sandfield Macdonald, then the premier of Ontario, $1,000; and Brydges, $2,000. Whether or not larger contributions were made by Toronto Conservatives is not known.

Robertson wasn't finished yet. He bought out his original partner, James Cook, for $3,000 and continued on his tenuous course. With an election fast approaching, Macdonald was getting desperate. The obvious thing to do was to appease Robertson and take control of the *Telegraph*. Starting a new paper was just not practical. While Conservative politician John Carling from Ontario believed Macdonald could "manage" Robertson, the prime minister was doubtful. He had been secretly kept informed of Robertson's activities by George Kingsmill of the *Telegraph* staff and was aware of the editor's principled position regarding his independence. No, the only route, Macdonald determined, was to buy out Robertson, his printing plant, and his valuable subscription list and quickly start a revised version of the *Telegraph* under an editor he could trust.[31]

Robertson was approached by David Macpherson, on Macdonald's behalf, and offered $20,000. This was declined by both Robertson and the paper's creditors. As the Conservatives planned their next move, an unknown financier named Ross bailed out Robertson with a $30,000 gift. This allowed Robertson to turn his venomous pen on Macdonald in a way that must have made his old boss George Brown proud. On March 11, 1872, the *Telegraph* editorial claimed that the paper "is not now and never has been the organ of Sir John A. Macdonald." This was followed by a harsh attack on May 6 labelling the prime minister and his Toronto friends a "perfidious ring" for trying to drive the *Telegraph* out of business. "Every vile perversion that the narrow intellects of the scurvy informers employed and directed by the chief trickster from his room at the Queen's could devise was blazoned wherever venom was calculated to penetrate."[32] Such were the words that made John Ross Robertson famous in the annals of Canadian journalism.*

Macdonald had realized as early as January that the *Telegraph* was a lost cause and clearly no Conservative answer to the *Globe*. He and his supporters now faced the challenge of establishing a new Toronto newspaper, one that would proudly carry the Tory banner.

---

*Robertson and the *Telegraph* were eventually forced out of business in October 1872 by the new Toronto *Mail* (see chapter 2). A bitter Robertson returned to the *Globe*, where he worked as a London, England, correspondent for two years. He later wrote for Goldwin Smith's *Nation*. In 1876 he started the *Toronto Evening Telegram*, a sensational one-cent paper that appealed to the common man. In so doing, he became a pioneer of so-called popular or people's journalism. (Rutherford, *A Victorian Authority*, 53–54)

Note: See Bibliography for full publication details of footnote sources, if not otherwise provided.

CHAPTER TWO

Party Organs

An impecunious paper and party organ is an impossibility.
A daily newspaper is a great tax on a man's constitution,
and the anxieties endless when politics are part of the
game, and the paper is owned by stockholders, all thinking
themselves privileged to grumble and all pulling in differ-
ent directions.

Thomas Patteson, c. 1902

I t was to be called the *Mail*. The Tory team that put it together in 1872 included David Macpherson, who was vying for the contract to build the CPR; John Sandfield Macdonald, the recently defeated premier of Ontario; John Carling, one of Sandfield's chief ministers; Frank Smith, a prominent Ontario Catholic; and Prime Minister John A. Macdonald, who was already busy in February soliciting supporters for funds.[1] The first order of business for this group was finding a capable manager and editor who could raise the required capital and get the paper off the ground before the campaigning for the summer elections began. Their candidate for the job was thirty-six-year-old Thomas Charles Patteson.

Patteson was a typical Ontario upper-middle-class immigrant. Born in England in 1836, he was educated at Eton and Oxford before coming to Canada in 1858. He brought with him a scholarly attitude, a devotion to the Empire, and a love for cricket and horses. In Toronto he studied law with John Hillyard Cameron, a leading Conservative politician, and was called to the bar in 1862. For a few years Patteson worked in the prominent Toronto firm of the Honourable John Ross, but at Confederation he joined the provincial government service as assistant secretary under Matthew Cameron, Premier Sandfield Macdonald's chief lieutenant.

In late January 1872 Patteson was working in his office at the old parliament buildings on Front Street when an excited Frank Cumberland, a local Tory, barged in, asking him to come to the Queen's Hotel at once. Patteson grabbed his top hat and walked the short distance to nearby Bay and King. Waiting for him in the hotel's "Red Parlour" were Prime Minister Macdonald, Macpherson, and the rest of the group. They offered him a

$2,800 salary for 1872 (later raised to $3,000), a managing position with the new *Mail,* and a federal government appointment once his task was completed. It was more than a generous offer, and he asked for twenty-four hours to think about it. Returning to his office, he applied for a raise, but was turned down by the recently elected government of Edward Blake (the premier apparently vetoed the increase himself). Patteson resigned his civil service position soon after and at a meeting on February 6 was officially appointed managing director of the *Mail.* His first act was to lease premises at the corner of Bay and King for $1,100 per year.[2]

In challenging the *Globe*'s position as the most widely read Toronto newspaper, Patteson had some daring ideas. He proposed that the Conservatives put their full efforts into an economic policy of protection to counter the Liberals' free trade cry. Macdonald immediately recognized the political advantage to be gained, but the switch made him uneasy nonetheless. "Now you are I know a hot Free Trader, and, in principle, so am I," he wrote to Macpherson. "But I quite agree with Patteson that our game is to coquette with the Protectionists. The word 'protection' itself must be tabooed, but we can ring the changes on a National Policy." Patteson took Macdonald's advice and hired "little red-headed" John Maclean, an excellent, although unpredictable, writer on economics who penned the articles that would bring Macdonald back to power in 1878.[3] Maclean was soon known around the *Mail* as "N.P. [National Policy] John"; he later founded the *Financial Post.**

By the end of March, the *Mail* was ready to roll off the presses. Patteson, with help from Macdonald and the other founders, had raised about $90,000, well short of the anticipated $250,000. There were fifty-one primary shareholders, among them Macdonald, who subscribed for ten shares worth $1,000. Charles Brydges of the Grand Trunk was the largest contributor with fifty shares for an investment of $5,000. The Mail Printing Company was incorporated on June 14 with a board of directors including Patteson, John Carling, William H. Howland, Angus Morrison, Donald McInnes, and James G. Worts.[4] It was John A. Macdonald's newspaper, nevertheless.

---

*Hector Charlesworth tells one interesting story about Maclean from this time. While slightly drunk Maclean had written a story on protectionism and his handwriting was harder to read than usual. The *Mail*'s chief proofreader, Edward Clarke, a good Orangeman, thought Maclean had written "protestantism." In the lead editorial of the next day's paper, Maclean's article came out as "Canadian interests demand more protestantism." Both Macdonald and Patteson were not amused. (Charlesworth, *Candid Chronicles,* 152)

The first edition of the *Mail* hit the streets of Toronto on the morning of March 30 with a declaration that hardly suggested it was the party organ it was designed to be. "With honest endeavor to do justice to the claims of new ideas and to the irresistible force of progress, the *Mail* will steer clear of partisanship," Patteson had written. "Not local purposes, not local prejudices ought to guide, but the general good." Soon, however, the paper's real intentions were clarified, "stabbing the Grits under the fifth rib every morning," as O.D. Skelton observed years later. George Brown was attacked as a threat to Confederation, and Alexander Mackenzie, soon to be the Liberal leader, was colourfully branded a "pharisaical brawler, rowdy rhetorician, and an incarnation of egotism."[5] Macdonald and his Ontario supporters could only cheer as the Grits and the *Globe* finally got back what they had dished out.

Still, there were problems. After six months of operation, the *Mail*'s advertising revenue was insufficient (only $2,200) and several reporters had difficulty working with Patteson, who himself was learning what it was like to answer to party chiefs for each and every editorial. "An impecunious paper and party organ is an impossibility," Patteson later wrote in his unpublished memoirs. "A daily newspaper is a great tax on a man's constitution, and the anxieties endless when politics are part of the game, and the paper is owned by stockholders, all thinking themselves privileged to grumble and all pulling in different directions."[6]

In Patteson's view, the prime minister was probably the worst offender, because for Macdonald there were no doubts or questions about the *Mail*'s chief purpose. During the weeks leading up to the July 1872 election and after, he wrote Patteson every other day with new leads to take and new attacks to pursue. His devious strategy was unparalleled. In September, when Edward Wood, a former member of Sandfield Macdonald's Ontario "patent combination" administration, joined the provincial Liberal government of Oliver Mowat, Macdonald advised Patteson to collect all the negative comments previously levelled at Wood by the *Globe*, then "sprinkle them singly over the *Mail* for a series of weeks until they are finished, keeping up the type of precious extracts and then publishing them ... It will be a pretty picture of the leading financial mind of the new Government."[7]

The election of 1872 and the Pacific Scandal that followed provided some of the dirtier moments in Canadian political history. It was a bitter, hard-fought, and expensive campaign. The Conservatives were forced to defend their record on the Washington Treaty, the Red River Rebellion, and the terms that brought British Columbia into Confederation the year before. The *Globe* and the *Mail* spent most of the campaign attacking each other rather than promoting the policies of their respective parties. In the end, such strategy, at least on the *Mail*'s part, did not pay off. Macdonald won thirty-eight seats in Ontario, down from forty-six in the last contest, while the Liberals made substantial gains.

Months later, in April 1873, Patteson was visiting Macdonald in Rivière du Loup. He told the prime minister that he had heard "something was going to be revealed which the Grits said would ruin him." Macdonald laughed and assured him the rumours were unfounded. On Patteson's return trip by train to Toronto the next day, he got hold of a *Globe* in Cobourg to learn about Huntington's charges, charges that eventually led to Macdonald's resignation. Patteson was upset that no one, and in particular not Macdonald, had warned him of the impending disaster. Alone at the *Mail,* he churned out editorials that dismissed Huntington's accusations as "base rumour." Privately he knew better.[8]

Throughout the rest of the year, Patteson had the unenviable role of having to defend the Conservatives' actions. Although he castigated the Liberals for using stolen documents and ridiculed the *Globe*'s treatment of the government, Patteson felt abandoned. "I have been left alone to fight the battle," he complained to Hector Langevin in July. "I have had to draw on my own wits, instead of on information supplied by the Government. One day I have ventured on one line of defense, to have it upset the next by the production of evidence not thought to be in existence."[9]

Financial difficulties caused by the poor economy of the 1870s, low circulation, and the fall of the Macdonald government all hurt the paper. It cost about $120,000 a year to operate the *Mail,* but revenues were only $110,000. In October 1874 the *Mail*'s debt had reached approximately $50,000, and in desperation Patteson made a deal with John Riordon, a wealthy paper manufacturer from St. Catharines who was owed $15,000 by the *Mail.* In lieu of payment, Riordon obtained a chattel mortgage for $12,000 and the *Mail* received its daily supply of newsprint.

Matters only got worse. By 1877 Riordon's mortgage had increased to $26,000, and under the terms of his contract he opted to take the *Mail* over. Patteson claims in his memoirs that when Macdonald was told that he and his friends had lost the newspaper, "he actually wept." Patteson resigned in November 1877 but had to wait until February 1879 to assume his government appointment as the Toronto postmaster. Riordon reorganized the *Mail,* putting in more capital and installing Christopher Bunting as managing director and editor, with assistant W.J. Douglas.[10]

Bunting was a distinguished-looking man, with a full beard and deep, penetrating eyes. He was well read in Shakespeare and was a supporter of the University of Toronto. Of Irish descent, he had come to Canada with his family in 1850 and had apprenticed as a printer with the *Globe.* Once he achieved success there, he entered the world of Toronto business, establishing a reputation as a merchant "of sound integrity, shrewd judgement and great enterprise." During a brief period, from 1878 to 1882, he also served as a member of Parliament. (In March 1884 Bunting was implicated in a bribery plot to unseat Ontario's Liberal government by buying off Liberal backbenchers. A provincial commission cleared him of any wrongdoing, but doubts lingered about his involvement.)

With the help of Riordon's money and Bunting's business sense, the *Mail* began to show promise. Superior presses were purchased, more-experienced writers were hired, and "the rights were acquired to the *New York Herald*'s cable dispatches." Within a year of the takeover, daily circulation had increased from about 8,500 to 15,000, reaching 22,000 by 1883. It was not long before the *Mail* was making serious inroads on the *Globe*'s influence in Ontario.[11]

From Macdonald's perspective, things had worked out nicely. It was true that he no longer had any direct control over the newspaper's day-to-day activities, but close ties with the editorial writers, most notably Martin Griffin (formerly of the Halifax *Herald*), who joined the *Mail* in 1881, ensured that his views were considered and followed. Indeed, during the election of 1878 and after Macdonald had regained power, the *Mail* staunchly supported both Macdonald and his National Policy. At the same time, the paper attacked the Liberals, its new leader Edward Blake, and the *Globe* at every turn.

Macdonald's correspondence with Martin Griffin during his five-year term as the *Mail*'s editor (1881–85) is especially fascinating. The letters reveal much about Macdonald's manipulative powers and the way he used the press to his own advantage. Griffin considered it the duty of a good party organ "to follow and not lead its chiefs." Macdonald agreed. Griffin received much advice from the prime minister on a host of issues, everything from the CPR monopoly clause to the place of Catholics in the government. Most of these dictates were transformed by Griffin into stinging editorials, as Macdonald wished. It was a convenient and favourable arrangement. John A. finally had the loyal and financially successful party paper he had always wanted in Toronto. Then "madness struck."[12]

The crisis at the *Mail* simmered slowly in 1882 and boiled to a thundering climax in 1887. At the crux of the problem lay age-old Protestant prejudice and fear of Roman Catholics. In 1881 Ontario had a predominantly Protestant population of 1.9 million. Catholics numbered 320,839, or 17 percent of the total. Still, as Peter Waite has written, in the view of the Protestant majority, "the Roman Catholic religion was a conspiratorial engine, designed to dominate, and ultimately destroy Protestantism." In some rural areas of the province where affiliations with the extreme Orange order were high and the number of Catholics very low, "it was possible to wonder what a Roman Catholic looked like."[13]

Since before Confederation, John A. Macdonald's political power had been based on the English-French partnership he had forged with George-Étienne Cartier in the early 1850s. A key ingredient in their successful platform was the protection of Catholic rights in Quebec and throughout the Dominion. In Ontario, support from the Irish-Catholic community was particularly cultivated. A few weeks prior to the general election of June 1882, Macdonald, always one step ahead of the opposition, strengthened his position when he asked his old friend Frank Smith, a leading Toronto Catholic businessman and a senator since 1871, to join the cabinet. At the same time, he appointed to the Senate Toronto lawyer John O'Donohoe, one of the founders of the Ontario Catholic League, a group formed in 1871 to fight for Catholic rights.

Meanwhile there were changes in the upper ranks of the *Mail*. At some point in 1882 John Riordon sustained a serious head injury after falling from a horse. He decided it would be best if he retired and transferred control of both his paper mill and the *Mail* to his brother Charles (although Charles did not officially become the president of the *Mail* until John Riordon died on September 21, 1884). An intelligent and industrious merchant, Charles Riordon enjoyed the finer things in life and frequently travelled to Europe to seek out the latest technology for his paper company. And while he was a staunch Conservative, his desire for higher profits was stronger than his party affiliation.[14] He believed, as Macdonald quickly found out, that the *Mail* would be more prosperous if it was more independent. He pushed Bunting, still the managing editor, in that direction, encouraging him to support popular causes that would sell newspapers. As an Irish Protestant, Bunting did not have to look very hard.

As is the case today, education could be an emotional issue, especially when religion was involved. First came a dispute in September 1882 over Sir Walter Scott's poem "Marmion," which was placed on university and collegiate reading lists but was later removed after a protest to Adam Crooks, the Ontario minister of education, by Archbishop John Joseph Lynch. An imposing figure, Lynch took exception to certain anti-Catholic passages about nuns breaking vows and friars committing adultery. What Bunting saw, however, was a Catholic prelate dictating orders to a politician who represented the majority. *Mail* editorials yelled about a conspiracy, with Crooks being the "donkey" and Archbishop Lynch the "donkey driver." From his exalted position on the pulpit, Lynch fought back with some critical remarks about the Conservative newspaper and party. This made a tense situation worse.[15]

During 1883 and into 1884, the conflict heated up over such issues as a proposed booklet of religious readings for Ontario schools that both Protestants and Catholics found objectionable. All the while, the *Mail* hammered away at Catholic and sometimes French arrogance. Even Conservative cabinet ministers were not immune. In February 1884 a group from the Quebec caucus, including Minister of Inland Revenue John Costigan, pressured Macdonald for more federal assistance for Quebec, threatening they would not support a CPR money bill then being discussed. As a protest, Costigan resigned from cabinet, although he was later persuaded by Macdonald to change his mind. In Bunting's eye, this was a clear case of French Catholic favouritism. In a vicious editorial on February 20, entitled "A Base but Unsuccessful Conspiracy," the *Mail* accused Costigan of accepting a bribe from the Liberals. Neither editor Martin Griffin nor Prime Minister Macdonald was pleased.[16]

Griffin, a devout Catholic, was in a difficult predicament. The archbishop was angry with him and his family was upset. "For months, I have been in an unfair and unpleasant position as regards Mr. Bunting and the *Mail*," he confided to Macdonald just prior to the attack on Costigan. "My present position is most painful for many reasons." Griffin believed Bunting was "foolish" to think he could win over Grit supporters by attacking "clerical influences."[17] Dejected, he started a campaign that would ultimately lead to his resignation from the newspaper and his appointment to the position of parliamentary librarian a year later.

In Ottawa, Macdonald was all too aware of what was happening with the *Mail*. Large numbers of Catholic supporters throughout Ontario began to write to him, expressing concern about "the course of the *Mail*." The letters would keep coming for three more years. When the suffering Griffin departed in 1885, the prime minister lost his last ally at the *Mail*.

The new editor was Edward Farrer. No one talks much any more about "Ned" Farrer, as he was called by fellow-newsmen, but he was the premier journalist of his day. A "short stocky, ruddy and bearded man with a twinkling eye and mind stored with state history" was how reporter Paul Bilkey remembered him. He was an expert in economics and a brilliant writer who could pen elegant, clever, and sarcastic prose. A man with a good sense of humour, he loved sports as much as politics and could tell equally delightful stories about both. Farrer, like other journalists, worked in black-bound notebooks in which he would scrawl, often in shorthand, random thoughts and quotations on economics, politics, and history. His wisdom and advice were sought by all.[18]

Born to an Irish Catholic family in 1850, Farrer was educated at Stoneyhurst, England, and the Jesuit College in Rome, where he was trained for the priesthood, but he changed his mind about this course. A trip to New York and Toronto in 1870 confirmed his destiny as a newspaper man, and his first assignment was with Beaty's Toronto *Leader*. He moved to the *Mail* under Patteson and was promoted to the editor's chair in

1878. A job offer from the *New York Herald* took him back to the United States in 1881, for a short time. In search of something more adventurous, he journeyed to Winnipeg in 1882 to edit the *Times*, the city's struggling Conservative Party organ, and later worked for the independent *Sun*. A call from Riordon and Bunting brought him back to the civilization of Toronto in October 1884.

The brewing Catholic issue was at the top of his agenda. Perhaps as a backlash against his Jesuit education, Farrer resented the moral dictates of the Catholic Church hierarchy, and it showed in his editorials – "masterpieces of invective," as one Conservative reader observed. The execution of Louis Riel in November 1885 and the ensuing outcry in Quebec provided Farrer with the excuse he needed to assail what he saw as French Catholic belligerence. His invective also proved to be a quite popular way to sell more newspapers.[19]

In an editorial on November 23, eight days after Riel's hanging, Farrer displayed his classic logic. He summarized the history of English-French relations since the union of the Canadas in 1841, adding, "Yet after all our efforts to establish amicable relations with them, even at the sacrifice of prosperity, the French-Canadians are now seeking to compel us to recognize their right to suspend the operation of the law whenever a representative of their race is in the toils." Two days later he questioned French Canadian allegiance to the Dominion and by February 1886 was attacking the educational privileges of Roman Catholics and the "despotism of ancient ecclesiastical laws." Soon the focus turned to Macdonald and Liberal leader Edward Blake for "buying the Catholic vote." "We maintain," a *Mail* editorial exclaimed on October 27, "that alike Sir John and Mr. Blake this trafficking in the Catholic vote gives the Church an exceptional and unparalleled station and authority in public affairs."*

At least Blake could denounce the *Mail* as Tory propaganda that should not be considered seriously. For Prime Minister Macdonald, it was another matter. He obviously did not countenance the *Mail*'s bigotry; nevertheless, Bunting, Farrer, and the *Mail* were becoming a serious political liability.

---

*Much of the outcry was caused by a speech made by Senator John O'Donohoe in May 1886 in which he recalled the establishment of the Catholic League in 1871 and noted how the association had promoted Catholic bloc voting in exchange for favours. As it turned out, O'Donohoe was actually upset because he was passed over by Macdonald for a much-coveted cabinet post. To the outraged *Mail*, however, Catholics were behaving like Swiss mercenaries selling their services to the highest bidder. Farrer considered the entire episode "immoral." (*Senate Debates*, May 14, 1886, 517–533; *Mail*, May 17, 21, 25, 1886)

Worse still, even the *Globe* was fairer to Ontario Catholics than was the *Mail*. Ironically, Macdonald no longer owned any shares in the newspaper, nor had much, if any, say in its policies. Unfortunately for him, no one payed any attention to that: the *Mail* was the Conservative Party organ, plain and simple. To anyone who would listen, Macdonald pleaded his case. "No one is more dissatisfied with the course of the *Mail* in Catholic matters than I am," he told T.H. McGuire of Kingston. "I have spared no pains to endeavor to induce Bunting to alter his course, but without success. He is quite independent of the Government or the Party and his conceit leads him to think that he knows more about politics and party expediency than anybody else in the world."[20]

To assist William Meredith, the leader of the Ontario Conservatives, who was facing a vote at the end of December 1886, and to boost his own fortunes for the coming federal election in February of the new year, Macdonald, now seventy-one years of age, toured southern and western Ontario for seven weeks. With Meredith and chief ministers John Thompson and Thomas White also on board, the prime minister's train departed Toronto on November 3. Huddled together in a special Grand Trunk rail car, the four men endured a horrid pace, travelling through blizzards and living in dirty clothes. "At every station there was a crowd, sometimes large, with a brass band, and always cries for 'John A.' Thompson would watch Macdonald go out, 'shake hands everywhere with everyone & kiss all the girls and ... come back to the car covered with snow."[21] Throughout the tiring trip, Macdonald faced hostile criticism of the *Mail*. Finally, at a stop in London, he repudiated the newspaper and with his schoolboy charm claimed that the Conservatives did not control any organ in the shameful way the Grits did the *Globe*. (But how he wished they did!) "I will not allow anyone to say," he declared to the cheering crowd, "that what is said in the [*Mail*] is the language of Sir John Macdonald." The next day's *Mail* argued that it was "an independent Conservative paper; a full declaration of its new position was to follow on January 8.

The results of the Ontario election on December 28 were telling. The Liberals under Oliver Mowat increased their seats from forty-eight to sixty-four, while Meredith's Conservatives dropped to a low of twenty-six. Certainly the *Mail*'s "No Popery Cry" played a part in delivering traditional Catholic Conservative votes to Mowat.[22] Stated one disgruntled Tory, "It is plain that the *Mail* and the *Mail* alone is responsible for alienating the Catholic vote while it brought nothing in return." An angry John A. wrote to Bunting on January 3, 1887: "There is no use crying over spilt milk – the mischief is done – I think you will admit now that the course taken by the *Mail* has not only resulted in Meredith's defeat, but prejudiced the Conservative party throughout the Dominion."[23]

It was too late for any reconciliations. Besides, for Bunting, business could not have been better. Daily circulation was hovering around 25,000, up at least 10,000 from Patteson's day, allowing the *Mail* to make gains against the *Globe* (which had an average circulation of 31,000 in 1887). With its aggressive anti-Catholic editorials, its independent political stand, and its championing of prohibition and municipal reform, the paper's popularity was never higher. This meant that the Conservatives and Macdonald had to survive the February general election without a powerful Toronto organ. Thought was given to purchasing the use of Billy Maclean's *World* for $10,000 but that did not work out (although the *World* was very supportive for the duration of the campaign).[24] Macdonald was lucky. Owing to Liberal leadership problems – Edward Blake was by then a tired old man – and a lack of policies that would seriously challenge Macdonald, the Conservatives were once more victorious.

There was a hint, however, of what was to come the next time around and the *Mail* was in the thick of it. Late in the campaign, *Mail* editorials began to support Blake's call for a reduction in the tariff, going so far as to label Macdonald's National Policy with its protective plank a "foolish experiment." During Farrer's earlier term with the *Mail* in 1878, he had aggressively supported protectionism. Now, nearly a decade later, he began to move in the opposite direction, seeing free trade as the answer to Canada's economic future and perhaps even imagining annexation with the United States.[25] Indeed, throughout 1887 and 1888, as the Liberals under their new leader, Wilfrid Laurier, formulated their policy of "unrestricted reciprocity," the *Mail* became the chief promoter of commercial union.*

For Macdonald, the *Mail*, as he proclaimed to a Quebec City audience a week before the 1887 election, was a "treacherous paper." He was not yet finished with it or Farrer. But for the moment the matter of establishing yet another faithful Toronto organ required his undivided attention.

David Creighton probably wished he had remained in the quiet confines of Owen Sound. The small northwestern Ontario town had been his home since 1855, when at the age of twelve he had immigrated to Canada with his parents from Scotland. He apprenticed there as a printer and later studied

---

*Historian Peter Waite offers the best definitions of these two terms. "Unrestricted reciprocity ... meant that everything Canada produced would be admitted free into the United States and vice versa"; commercial union went one step further: "Canada and the United States should have one tariff structure in common against the world, with all custom lines between themselves obliterated." (Waite, *Arduous Destiny,* 205–7)

law, but opted for a career in journalism. He joined the staff of the Owen Sound *Times,* the weekly Conservative paper, which he eventually took over in the mid-1870s. Politically ambitious as well, he won a seat as a Conservative in the Ontario legislature in 1875, holding it for the next fifteen years. Creighton was so popular that he claimed his election expenses never exceeded $75. He was a committed Anglican, a diligent worker with a remarkable memory for statistics, and a thoroughly likeable fellow.[26] In short, he possessed all the qualifications necessary to become the managing editor of Macdonald's new Toronto daily newspaper.

By the time John A. summoned Creighton in June 1887, the plans for the *Empire,* as the organ would be called, were gradually taking shape. With the able assistance of D'Alton McCarthy, a lawyer from Barrie and member of Parliament for Simcoe, Macdonald was already soliciting funds, as he had done for the *Mail* fifteen years before. The prospectus for the Empire Printing and Publishing Company, issued in July, offered 10,000 shares at $25 each; it stated that the firm would not be incorporated until $200,000 worth were subscribed, and promised investors a "handsome return" for their trouble.[27] The phrase had a nice ring, but in reality raising money proved to be difficult.

Macdonald himself initially subscribed for eighty shares totalling $2,000 and added another $2,000 by the end of the 1887. When Macdonald died in 1891, Creighton revealed that over the years he had contributed $1,000 every so often. He estimated John A.'s total share in the *Empire* to be $11,000, a fair amount considering the poor state of Macdonald's finances. Another investor of note was Alexander Campbell, a veteran Conservative politician and the newly appointed lieutenant-governor of Ontario. He did not want to be seen publicly discussing the *Empire* with Creighton, feeling it too risky to have "anything to do with a political paper," but he agreed to channel his contribution through someone else.[28]

By the end of the summer, only $100,000 had been pledged and little paid up. Raising capital in Montreal, for example, proved to be a disappointment. Richard White, the publisher of the *Montreal Gazette,* apparently spoke on behalf of his wealthy Tory friends when he commented to Creighton that it was "cheeky" for him to seek assistance for an "Ontario paper." Disillusioned, Macdonald even contemplated trying to win back the *Mail,* but McCarthy wouldn't hear of that. "No," he advised his chief, "we must start the *Empire* or prepare for defeat at the next general election – if not before that."[29]

Creighton's perseverance paid off. He gathered around him a competent team of journalists, including John Maclean ("N.P. John" from the *Mail*); John Livingston, the *Empire*'s first editor; and Louis Kribs, "a bulky blond figure who looked like a German comedian," formerly with the *Evening*

News. (Kribs had been responsible for a hoax a few years earlier when he ran the story that Macdonald had retired, a joke that gave John A. much pleasure.) Fred Cook, who defected from the *Mail,* was to be the paper's Ottawa correspondent.[30] With his rural, country-editor demeanour, as well as his habit of walking around the bare wooden floors of the newspaper office in his socks, Creighton put his staff to work. The *Empire*'s first edition came out on the morning of December 27, 1887. Its aim as a Conservative organ was clear: "to strengthen by all legitimate means the hand of the Party and the Government that have controlled the politics of the Dominion ever since the foundations of Confederation were laid." The paper's first editorials highlighted the internal strife of the Liberal trade policy and declared the *Empire*'s unquestioning support for the National Policy – a platform, in the newspaper's view, that had made Canada the greatest, happiest, and most prosperous country on earth.

Macdonald was generally pleased with his new "offspring." He respected Fred Cook, who as chief Ottawa correspondent was entitled to all state secrets (much to the chagrin of the *Mail*'s man in the gallery, John Ewan, who boldly asked Macdonald what purpose it would serve to discriminate against the *Mail*; he received no reply), and he also applauded the *Empire*'s strong rejection of "unrestricted reciprocity and commercial union with the United States."[31] Macdonald had a great deal of advice for Creighton and his staff over the next three years. Some of it was sound, some of it not. The trouble was that Creighton, as a party-appointed managing editor, was supposed to obey, no questions asked.

It was nearly impossible for the *Empire,* the quintessential party paper, to achieve financial success in a city of 175,000 already saturated with five newspapers (three in the morning, the *Globe, Mail*, and *World;* and two in the evening, the *News* and *Telegram*). Despite, Creighton's cheerful optimism, it is doubtful whether the *Empire*'s daily circulation ever rose above 14,000, more than 10,000 less than that of either the *Mail* or the *Globe*.

On top of this, Creighton's work was hampered by a board of directors composed of politicians and party hacks who knew little about the overhead costs and marketing strategies involved in operating a newspaper. At the *Empire*, politics, not commercial realities, came first. As a consequence, the journal earned a reputation, apparently well deserved, for being "dreary." "Our friends, almost without exception, say to me," Macdonald wrote to Creighton in mid-December 1890, "that while they subscribe to the paper they never read it" (future prime minister John Thompson among them).[32]

Creighton had a few complaints of his own. One was that the *Mail*, the paper that had turned against John A. in his hour of need, received more government advertising dollars than the *Empire*. In fact, everyone got more money than the *Empire*. During 1889–90 the *Mail* was awarded $2,590, the *World* (a Conservative supporter) $1,451, and the *Empire*, the chief party organ, a grand total of $731.26. Macdonald attempted to rectify the bureaucratic foul-up, but Creighton was seething mad.[33]

It did not help the situation, morally or financially, that he was also compelled to defend unpopular government policies. The Jesuits Estates Act was a case in point. In 1888 the Quebec government of Honoré Mercier decided to compensate the Jesuit order for property taken from it in 1773 (this had been done when the order was dissolved by the Pope, but it was reconstituted in the 1860s). The $400,000 allocated by Mercier was given to the Pope in Rome to divide. To some zealous Ontario Protestants fearful of Roman Catholic power, the Quebec government's act was an outrage. In their minds the legislation "endowed with public funds a religious organization and … it invited the arbitration of an authority unknown to the British Crown, the Pope."[34]

Leading the crusade for the federal disallowance of the Jesuit Act was the *Mail*'s Edward Farrer, who churned out dozens of "savage and unrepentant" editorials. In the House of Commons, the *Mail*'s cause was picked up by D'Alton McCarthy, a Conservative MP who had assisted Macdonald and Creighton establish the *Empire*. A vote on disallowance was taken in March 1889 but it was defeated 188 to 13. Not one to surrender, McCarthy and his friends created the Equal Rights Association, a rather strange name for an organization bent on promoting the supremacy of Anglo-Protestantism.[35]

Throughout the ordeal the Macdonald government (and a majority of the Liberal opposition) maintained that Quebec's legislation was that province's concern, and it expected its loyal party press to adopt and support the same position. The *Empire* faithfully did just this and then suffered the financial consequences. Protestant passions in Ontario were at the boiling point, and consumers turned to the one newspaper that made sense to them, the *Mail*. Its daily sales soared. All this posed a dilemma for the other journals. At first the *Globe* followed its party line and opposed disallowance. By March it had changed its editorial mind, after its circulation started to plunge. For the *Empire*, which had no alternative but to obey its political chiefs, valuable advertising contracts were lost and subscriptions cancelled.[36] The newspaper never regained its commercial footing; by May 1890 its deficit was $11,500 and rising monthly. But it had one more battle to fight on behalf of its leader.

During Macdonald's last years, questions were raised about the country's future and its economic relationship with the United States and Britain. Following the 1887 election, the Liberals under Wilfrid Laurier promoted a form of free trade known then as "unrestricted reciprocity." Macdonald's

Conservatives stuck with the protective tariff of the National Policy but were in fact open to Canada-U.S. free trade in natural products.[37]

The political situation in the fall of 1890 was dismal. The Manitoba government had abolished its dual Protestant-Catholic school system, established by the Manitoba Act of 1870, opting for a secular education system, and had also done away with French as one of the province's official languages. French Catholics cried out for federal help; the complex Manitoba Schools Question, as it is remembered, took six more years to settle. In Ottawa, renegade Conservative D'Alton McCarthy attempted to amend the North West Territories Act and abolish the use of French in the western courts. Then there were the scandals that hit the Conservatives. The most infamous indicted Quebec MP Thomas McGreevy, his brother Robert, and Hector Langevin, Macdonald's Quebec lieutenant. It was a complicated financial web involving kickbacks and campaign contributions.*

Economic and trade issues proved troublesome as well. In November the colony of Newfoundland had succeeded, without including Canada, in negotiating a trade and fisheries agreement with the United States. Macdonald considered this an attempt by James Blaine, the self-interested U.S. secretary of state, to keep British North America divided. He convinced Britain to stop the Newfoundland deal and hold out for a more comprehensive one that addressed Canada's concerns as well.

In December 1890 Macdonald and his ministers proposed to Washington and London that a joint commission be convened to discuss Canadian-American problems. Secretary Blaine, aware of Macdonald's plans for a moderate reciprocity agreement unacceptable to the new Republican administration of Benjamin Harrison, would not agree to formal talks, but said he would meet privately with British and Canadian representatives in early March. In correspondence between the three parties, nothing was said about not publicizing the Conservatives' proposals or the impending discussions.[38]

---

*In addition to being a member of Parliament, Thomas McGreevy was also his brother Robert's business partner in a variety of ventures, including Larkin, Connolly and Company. In exchange for campaign contributions to McGreevy and Hector Langevin (related to Thomas through marriage), this company was rewarded with lucrative public works contracts (Langevin was minister of public works). It was all very discreet until a greedy Thomas sued Robert over the profit distribution. After John A. Macdonald refused to listen, an angry Robert provided Israel Tarte, the editor of Le Canadien, a Liberal organ, with the incriminating correspondence. Among other things, it was revealed that McGreevy had supplied Langevin with election funds and money to establish the Montreal newspaper Le Monde in 1884. The scandal killed Langevin's chances of succeeding Macdonald; he resigned from cabinet in September 1891. (Waite, Arduous Destiny, 218–19, 230–37)

By January of the new year, there were rumours in the Canadian press about Macdonald's election plans and the potential for a new economic deal with the United States. The Conservatives wanted to make an official announcement about their forthcoming private talks, but Blaine and President Harrison would not permit it.

The Liberals, who were still formulating their platform for the next election, needed to know what was going on in Washington. Enter forty-year-old Edward Farrer. In 1890 the editor of the *Mail* had been wooed to the *Globe* by Liberal finance expert Richard Cartwright, who was impressed with Farrer's criticism of protection and his articles advocating commercial union. As the *Globe*'s chief editorial writer, Farrer decided to find out what the Conservatives were up to in Washington. He knew his way around that city. The year before he had made a similar visit when he was still with the *Mail,* possibly supplying information to Republican members of a Senate trade committee about the annexation of Canada (there are various versions of Farrer's activities in Washington).[39] The *Empire,* which had maintained a watchful eye on Farrer's activities, exposed the alleged plot, casting scorn on the whole *Mail* organization. For his daring journalism, Creighton was sued by Bunting for libel, although the action failed.

In any event, in late January 1891 Farrer was back in the U.S. capital. There he received a personal note from Blaine regarding the trade issue.[40] Blaine informed Farrer, as was reported in the *Globe,* that "there are no negotiations whatever on foot for a reciprocity treaty with Canada."

That was it. Macdonald had been double-crossed, and he was unable to explain what had transpired. The die was cast. On February 2, three days after Farrer's meeting, the general election was confirmed for March 5, 1891. Protectionism, the National Policy, and the British connection were to be the backbone of the Conservative platform. Trade negotiations with the United States were not ruled out, but they had to be on Macdonald's terms, not the Americans'. "As for myself, my course is clear," he declared in one of his most memorable speeches. "A British subject I was born – a British subject I will die. With my utmost effort, with my last breath, will I oppose the 'veiled treason' which attempts by sordid means and mercenary proffers to lure out people from their allegiance." No one made Macdonald look like a fool. Blaine was beyond his reach, but not Farrer.

Revenge came quickly and was sweet. Earlier, in November 1890, unbeknown to John Willison, the *Globe's* newly appointed editor, or to the Liberal Party hierarchy, Farrer had agreed, at the request of an American politician, to compose a pamphlet outlining policies the United States should adopt to ensure the annexation of Canada (this could have been for Senator George F. Hoar, head of a trade committee, although Farrer later claimed in the *Globe* that he wrote it for a non-political American friend).

As a personal favour and maybe for a bit of fun, Farrer wrote the piece and delivered it to the Hunter Rose & Company of Toronto for printing. In the pamphlet, Farrer suggested that the Americans not allow Canadians bonding privileges in the United States, cut the CPR link with American railways at Sault Ste. Marie, and increase tonnage duties on Canadian ships. "Political union with the United States," Farrer boldly proclaimed, "was the manifest destiny of Canada."[41] This was dangerous stuff.

In mid-January 1891 Macdonald got his hands on some of Farrer's proofs, most likely through the assistance of William MacDougall, who was given the documents by a loyal Conservative. The thief in question was Christopher St. George Clark, a compositor at Hunter Rose. He saw Farrer deliver the manuscript, and as a former *Mail* employee he was familiar with his former boss's handwriting. He claimed in an affidavit of January 30 that Farrer had insisted on secrecy when printing began.[42] (As a reward, Clark received a federal government appointment; he was later fired after he stole large batches of the private correspondence of his ministerial chief John Haggart!)

Although Governor General Lord Stanley expressed reservations about using Farrer's work, Macdonald, the consummate political strategist, had none. On February 17 the campaign was already two weeks old and the battle on the hustings was bitter. Richard Cartwright, whose recollections must be taken with a grain of salt, stated that the Liberals were impoverished, while the Conservatives spent lots of money – in his words, it "flowed like water." (In fact, it has been suggested that the Liberals received a large amount of American funds for election purposes.)[43]

The animosity was reflected in the official organs of both parties. The *Globe* and *Empire* fought each other editorial for editorial, both papers trying to define what it meant to be a loyal Canadian (just as in the election of 1988). For the *Empire*, John A. was the "old man" with the "old flag" and the "old policy" and the *Globe* and the Grits were in league with the Yankee devils. Until voting day, Creighton bombarded his readers with slanted statistics supporting protectionism; he published "The *Empire*'s Honour Role," which listed those Liberals who favoured annexation.[44]

The *Globe* was no better. For the Liberal organ, Sir John was not the "old man" but the "old dictator." Willison and Farrer countered the *Empire*'s protectionist propaganda and stressed the difference between unrestricted reciprocity and annexation. The *Globe* outdid itself and the *Empire*, however, when it published the Tory annexation manifesto of 1849 as an indication of Conservative hypocrisy.[45]

Without a doubt the highlight of the campaign was Macdonald's speech at the Conservative rally in Toronto on February 17. After a week of work and touring in Ottawa, Macdonald boarded the train for Toronto on Monday,

February 16. He arrived early the next morning and met with friends and supporters until late in the afternoon.[46] At 7:35 p.m a horse-drawn cab pulled up to the Academy of Music on King and Dorset. Out stepped Sir John with two local Toronto Conservatives, W.R. Brock, president of the *Empire*'s board, and Col. Fred Denison. They were met by a huge crowd that had been gathering for over two hours. The King Street streetcars could not move through the masses of people.

Inside the theatre, nearly 4,000 people waited, crammed together, with another 15,000 to 20,000 standing outside. Toronto police struggled to maintain order. The crowd was so dense in front of the theatre that Macdonald needed a police escort to reach the door. He entered the hall to the cheering and singing of "He's a Jolly Good Fellow." The screaming but friendly mob waved hats, flags, and handkerchiefs. Moments later Charles Tupper, the Canadian high commissioner in London, joined Macdonald and a large Tory group on the platform. Signs hung on the wall behind the stage and around it were emblazoned with such election slogans as "HAIL TO OUR CHIEFTAIN," "NO UNITED STATES SENATORS NEED APPLY," "THE OLD FLAG, THE OLD LEADER AND THE OLD POLICY," and "OTTAWA NOT WASHINGTON, OUR CAPITAL."

Emerson Coatsworth, the Conservative candidate in East Toronto, spoke first, followed by Tupper. Tupper could scarcely be heard over the yelling of the audience. He was interrupted when the police entered the hall to thin out the crowd and make a passageway down the centre aisle. Tupper then continued, praising Macdonald as the most eloquent and distinguished statesman in the world. The crowd was in a frenzy by the time it was John A.'s turn to speak.

He was now seventy-six years old. He began by speaking fondly of Toronto, noting how the National Policy had contributed to its growth. He gave his version of the events with Blaine, stating that Canadian traitors had gone to Washington to convince the Americans to "put the screws to Canada."

"Name, name," roared the audience.

"What is that I hear?" John A. asked. "You ask me to name him. In the first place, you know Mr. Farrer?"

"Hear, hear, cheers."

"People know who Mr. Farrer is. He was once editor of the *Mail*, when it was a Tory paper. He is now the editor, philosopher and friend of Sir Richard Cartwright and the controlling influence over that great, that glorious and consistent newspaper – the *Globe*. Mr. Farrer has been down to Washington, several times. Perhaps he is there yet."

From the back a voice yelled, "He is here tonight." And he was. Farrer was at the back of the hall with the other reporters. Macdonald waved the

proofs and read excerpts to the audience. He went through Farrer's arguments, point by point, about the best way for the United States to annex
Canada. "I think you will agree with me," he concluded, "that there is somewhere and among some people a conspiracy to drive Canada into the arms
of the United States." He struck out at Farrer, the *Globe*, and the Liberal
Party. He questioned Farrer's loyalty to Canada and told his supporters that
the Liberals' policy of unrestricted reciprocity was merely a cloak for something far more sinister.

As Macdonald took his seat, the crowd burst into song with "We will
hang Ed Farrer on a sour apple tree." The prime minister returned to the
Queen's Hotel with his secretary, Joseph Pope. Meanwhile the *Globe* management was so worried about retaliation that the police were summoned to
surround the *Globe* building. But there was no trouble. As the *Empire* put it,
"The call for help was quite unnecessary – the time has not yet come in
Canada when traitors are hanged to lamp posts – nobody went near the
place."

The next day Tory papers throughout the Dominion reiterated the
charges of a "traitorous conspiracy" and denounced the Liberal Party. It was
a case of guilt by association. At the *Globe,* Willison issued a curt statement
of denial. "Mr. Farrer is a newspaper writer; by unanimous consent, we
believe the ablest writer in the Canadian press. He was engaged by the
Globe to write for the *Globe* and his work has been most faithfully and efficiently performed," the editorial stated on February 19. "The *Globe* has
been thoroughly loyal. The *Globe* has not engaged in any movement for the
promotion of treason … It will not be held responsible for the opinions of
any of its writers nor for any opinions except those spoken in its editorial
columns."

Farrer accepted full responsibility for the consequences of his actions
and, according to Willison, "never seemed worried or distressed" by the
pamphlet's publication.[47] In a letter to his own paper, he claimed there was
no conspiracy by the Liberal Party and that the published pamphlet was not
connected with his work at the *Globe*. Declared Farrer, "I deny the assumption that the *Globe* or the Liberal party is bound or affected by anything
written, said or done by a mere writer for the *Globe* in his private hours or
private capacity … A newspaper is to be judged by its printed utterances
and is no more responsible for the acts or opinions of its staff outside of its
columns than what they choose to have for dinner."

He further admonished Macdonald for using his publication as he did.
"Intelligent men," Farrer wrote in the *Globe*, "will feel sorry that Sir John
should have been driven by the stress of the battle he has on his hands to
resort to so poor a subterfuge."[48] But Farrer should have realized that
Macdonald was merely playing politics as only he knew how.

The *Empire* called Farrer's version of events a "palpable falsehood," refusing to believe that Cartwright was not somehow involved. And there were yet more revelations. A week later, on February 24, Sir Charles Tupper, campaigning in Windsor, produced two letters sent in April 1889 to Erastus Wiman, a Canadian businessman living in New York and a supporter of commercial union and annexation. One letter was written by Farrer, the other by Congressman R.R. Hitt of Illinois. They revealed that Farrer and Wiman were involved in the promotion of commercial union – a fact long established and certainly not as astonishing as Tupper claimed.

This did not matter to the *Empire*. In its partisan opinion, the conspiracy was now "beyond all doubt." The newspaper sought unsuccessfully to link Cartwright and the rest of the Liberal Party to Farrer's sordid scheme. And Louis Kribs told Macdonald that he had evidence that the Grit leaders knew about the pamphlet in the first week of February, although no evidence of this ever surfaced.[49] Richard Cartwright publicly denied that he knew anything about Farrer's work and denounced Macdonald's tactics as "despicable."

The *Globe*'s Willison later argued in his 1905 biography of Laurier that "the significance of Mr. Farrer's pamphlet was greatly exaggerated and the deductions drawn from its discovery were wholly unwarranted. There was no plot. There was no conspiracy. There was no intrigue in Washington." Willison missed the point. Perception is everything in politics and the Farrer affair gave Macdonald the opportunity to turn the public's attention away from his government's problems towards the emotional issue of the U.S. threat to Canadian sovereignty. As Macdonald put it in a letter to George Stephen, "I have of course pointed out that U.[nrestricted] R.[eciprocity] meant annexation, and the movements of Cartwright, Farrer & Wiman enabled us to raise the loyalty cry, which had considerable effect."[50]

In fact, the results of the election on March 5 were surprisingly close: 123 for the Conservatives against 92 for the resurging Liberals under Laurier – a sign of things to come in the near future. Macdonald had his victory but he was dead within three months. As for Farrer, he resigned from the *Globe* (possibly forced out) a year later. He freelanced after that, worked in Washington, Toronto, and Montreal for several years, and returned to Ottawa in 1905. He was a frequent contributor to the *Economist*. Farrer died in April 1916 at the age of sixty-six, long remembered for the role he had unwillingly played in John A. Macdonald's last victory.

What of the loyal *Empire*? It had performed brilliantly during the 1891 campaign, but with Macdonald now gone, it lost a valuable supporter. Indeed, for Macdonald's four successors, the *Empire* became an unwanted burden. The newspaper was overly cautious when the schools question in Manitoba first developed and it was continually scooped on government news by the Toronto *World.* Soon no one but Creighton took it seriously. John Thompson, who became prime minister in November 1892, admitted to Archdeacon Kelly that he did not own any shares in the paper and rarely read it more than once a week.[51]

The *Empire*'s debts continued to mount. The economic depression of the early 1890s, the rising popularity of the Liberals in Ontario, and the fact that many Conservatives still looked at the *Mail* as the true Tory organ all contributed to the *Empire*'s problems. Meanwhile, behind Creighton's back a solution to rid the party of this liability was in the works. The idea that the *Mail* and *Empire* should merge had been suggested several times by Christopher Bunting and his business manager, W.J. Douglas. The *Mail* was also feeling the pinch of the depression and recognized the commercial absurdity of there being so many Toronto newspapers. In 1893 Bunting presented a plan to Thompson whereby the combined paper would continue to support the Conservative Party in exchange for a seat in the Senate for Charles Riordon. Given the *Mail*'s past record, the prime minister was rightly skeptical of Bunting's sincerity.[52]

The situation grew desperate. By October 1894 the *Empire*'s cumulative debt amounted to more than $100,000. "If the plant of the *Empire* were for sale tomorrow," Senator Frank Smith told Thompson, "it would not bring 25 cents on the dollar." He advised the prime minister to meet with Bunting again and send Creighton back to Owen Sound with a $2,000-a-year postmaster job.[53] Thompson planned to deal with the situation as soon as he returned from his trip to England. He died at Windsor Castle on December 12.

The details of what happened next are vague. The correspondence of Mackenzie Bowell, who reluctantly succeeded Thompson as prime minister, is not very useful in piecing the events together. Negotiations between the boards of the *Mail* and *Empire* (minus Creighton) took place in late December 1894 and throughout January 1895. At a meeting in a Montreal hotel room on January 30, the final deal was hammered out. As announced by the Toronto *World* on February 2, the merger was "a triumph for Bunting." The *Empire*'s loyal shareholders were given $125,000 of paid-up *Mail* stock and the promise that the new journal would support the party. A clause was added that gave the *Mail*'s owners the option to buy back the stock for $30,000 after eighteen months. This was done in November 1896.[54] Finally, the *Empire*'s staff, except for the competent Fred Cook in Ottawa, were all to be dismissed. The government made no provisions to assist the unemployed journalists, including, initially, Creighton, who was eventually appointed assistant receiver general of Canada for Ontario. To leave the rest without work in the middle of winter was a pathetic act.

The *Empire*'s last day was February 6, 1895. Over at the rival *World,* an indignant cartoon was splashed across the front page; entitled "The Wake," it depicted a coffin labelled *"Empire."* Yet Creighton was not bitter and he encouraged his staff to put out one final edition. Ironically, the main story that day was a Liberal rally at Massey Hall, with leader Wilfrid Laurier as the guest speaker.

The new *Mail and Empire* was not an immediate success. Both the new prime minister Charles Tupper, appointed in 1896, and his son J. Stewart lamented the newspaper's "weakness." Although it was making a profit of $30,000 by 1902, the *Mail and Empire* remained a "colourless ... paper without life."[55]

John A. Macdonald would not have been surprised by what had transpired with the *Empire*, but he would have been saddened. The paper's demise signalled the end of the absolute party organ. No more would publishers and editors merely obey. Political support would be offered, of course, but the dynamics of the relationship between prime minister and editor had clearly changed.

CHAPTER THREE

Laurier and the *Globe*

The Globe *is first of all a newspaper and an organ of public opinion. Its alliance with Liberalism and the Liberal party is a matter of history and of deliberate choice, not of convenience or of obligation.*

Globe editorial, January 1905

It was hard not to like Wilfrid Laurier. Almost everyone did. Conservative leader Sir Charles Tupper and his successor, Robert Borden, respected him; Henri Bourassa, his rival in Quebec, was in awe of him; John Willison, the editor of the *Globe*, worshipped him. Laurier possessed all the attributes of a successful political leader: a charming and magnetic personality, grace, wit and a good sense of humour. Physically he was not a strong man; he suffered from chronic bronchitis throughout his life and found the dry climate in Arthabaska in Quebec's Eastern Townships more suitable to his health.

Laurier was fluently bilingual and, according to legend, one of the finest orators to speak in Parliament. He first caught the public's attention with an impassioned speech on political liberalism in 1877. Nine years later, following a debate on the hanging of Louis Riel, he earned the well-deserved name "Silver-Tongued Laurier" for delivering one of the most eloquent speeches ever heard in the House. Lord Minto, one of the governors general during Laurier's term as prime minister, from 1896 to 1911, considered him "far the biggest man in Canada."[1]

He was well read, preferring biographies of great men like Abraham Lincoln and Napoleon, and a frequent patron of the Parliamentary Library. Both John Dafoe and John Willison, two of the most prominent Liberal journalists of their day but in the 1880s young gallery reporters, recalled that Laurier always got the best books first. Laurier did not have many close friends, but he had many admirers. "He had the gift of being loved," as Liberal politician Chubby Power put it many years later.

Among his numerous fans were the members of the parliamentary press gallery. "What news have you for me?" was Laurier's standard greeting for the Ottawa correspondents. As prime minister, he never held any formal press conferences and "refused to go between quotation marks." Parliament was the place for declarations of policy, not a newspaper column. Anything personal was also out of the question.

In March 1899 Godfrey Langlois, editor of *La Patrie*, a generally loyal Montreal paper controlled by Minister of Public Works Israel Tarte, requested information about Laurier's reading preferences for an article he was writing about the tastes of public men. The prime minister quickly refused. "I do not want my daily life to become public," he told Langlois. There were rumours and references in the society pages about Laurier's close friendship with Emilie Lavergne, the wife of his law partner, but none of this concerned the serious political reporters. What Laurier did in his private life was his own business.

Similarly nothing was revealed about the annual press gallery dinner. As M.O. Hammond, the *Globe*'s Ottawa correspondent in 1906, explained, tradition demanded that the music and the bright speeches would never "see the light of day, for on that night no newspaperman will labor." Apparently the merriment embraced everyone. Even Laurier let his guard down, loosened his tie, and smoked his annual cigarette. When a break in the House allowed it, there was much camaraderie between politicians and journalists, most notably before Speaker Tom Sproule, a devout Protestant churchgoer, closed down the parliamentary tavern in 1912, the scene of many a rowdy party. Senator Grattan O'Leary, who spent his long life covering the Hill, recalled a 1912 softball game, with Laurier and Borden as spectators. O'Leary, then a young writer with the *Ottawa Journal,* played third base. After only three innings the journalists were losing 33 to 7 and the "game was called for cocktails."[2]

Unlike John A. Macdonald and many other politicians, Laurier tried to treat Liberal and Conservative newspaper reporters equally. He gave off-the-record interviews to both, revealing enough state secrets to keep the newsmen happy. Interestingly, some members of the *Globe*, the chief Liberal organ, differed on this particular policy. The paper's Ottawa correspondent in 1896, Arnott Magurn, sent a memo to Laurier on November 9, five months after he took office, demanding that the practice of restricting official news to government papers continue. Magurn wanted his "enemies" of the Tory press to suffer as he had. But in Toronto, Magurn's boss, John Willison, a more forward-looking man, argued against this. Though he too had experienced partisan discrimination during his time in the gallery in the 1880s, he advised Laurier "against the perpetuation of this system which was essentially petty in spirit and vexatious in practice." Willison's position won out.[3] Although Laurier may not have been fully aware of it then, this change signalled a shift in some newspapermen's thinking about party organs and about the need for more independence. He would debate this issue with Willison many times in the near future.

Magurn and other traditionalists were satisfied that one aspect of political life remained as it always had been. As soon as the Liberals took over in 1896, new newspaper lists were drawn up to ensure that the printing and advertising contracts were awarded to loyal supporters first. Thus, the *Mail and Empire* lost a needed source of revenue, while the *Globe*'s efforts were finally rewarded.[4]

Laurier knew most of the gallery men personally: William Mackenzie, or "Mac," who wrote for the *Manitoba Free Press* as well as other Liberal papers; Fred Cook, the veteran writer for the Conservative *Mail and Empire* and the London *Times*' man in Canada; young John Garvin of the *Ottawa Journal;* and Paul Bilkey of the Tory *Toronto Telegram,* who had a "happy indifference to any and all political idols, and the freedom with which [to] smash them from day to day in his correspondence." As Bilkey recalled, he had little to do with Laurier personally and the prime minister did not care for his writing. "I have read some of his work," said Laurier, "and for my part I do not want to read any more."

Then there was the celebrated Ernest Cinqmars of *La Presse*. In an article of May 26, 1906, Cinqmars, under his pseudonym "Blaise," had written a slanderous attack on George Foster, a prominent Conservative member of Parliament. Arguing that Foster had maligned French Canadians, Cinqmars wrote: "He has but one principle, that of self-interest. He has only one desire, the desire to insult. He belongs to the school of lying, hypocrisy and cowardice. In his eyes the person to whom civic and political virtue are not vain words is an imbecile and a hot-head."[5]

Outraged, Foster demanded that Cinqmars be called to the bar of Parliament to answer for his libelous words, an ancient practice dating back to Stuart England during the early 1600s, when the English House of Commons was locked in a struggle with the Crown. Foster's political colleagues, including Laurier, agreed. On June 7, with the galleries full, Cinqmars, wearing a frock coat and a silk hat, stood at the bar to hear the charges. A week later the Quebec journalist read his statement of defence, suggesting that the article under protest was an editorial and therefore not a declaration of fact but only an opinion. In the lengthy debate that followed, Laurier explained his own particular philosophy about press freedom.

While the prime minister accepted without reservation the right of journalists to criticize and express their personal judgments, he believed there were limits to consider. "The press must understand," Laurier argued, "while it is possible, and not only possible but fair and within their rights, to criticize the act of any public man, they must do it in the language that is fair, and not in the language of mere vituperation." Cinqmars received an official vote of censure and became a gallery folk hero.[6]

Ottawa journalists considered Laurier a fair man, yet they also recognized that he had a darker side. "In the contemporary Liberal myth," wrote author Bruce Hutchison, "Laurier's arrival was the ultimate salvation of Canadian life." Indeed, Laurier has been portrayed as having been close to sainthood, high above the vulgar art of politics.[7] In fact, he was a pragmatic politician. "A man who had affinities with Macchiavelli as well as Sir Galahad" was how *Manitoba Free Press* editor John W. Dafoe accurately judged him in his 1922 book *Laurier: A Study in Canadian Politics.* No leader stays in power in Canada for fifteen years without blending compromise and charm with manipulation and deviousness. While Laurier's great challenge was to hold the country together, to "harmonize" English Canadians with French, he also understood and enjoyed power. He used patronage to consolidate his position and included in his cabinet such capable political managers as Clifford Sifton and Israel Tarte. "He told me once," Willison recalled about Laurier in 1919, "that he was in politics for one reason only – to beat the other man."

Born in 1841 in the tiny village of St. Lin, north of Montreal, Laurier had gained his political education as young Rouge. He was a follower of Louis-Joseph Papineau, the rebel leader of 1837 whose nationalism, anticlericalism, and radical ideas offended many Quebeckers. Like his leader, Antoine Aimé Dorion, Laurier opposed Confederation, but he later learned to work within the system. He was first elected as a Liberal to the Quebec assembly in 1871, moved to the House of Commons in the election of 1874 following the Pacific Scandal, and was in the cabinet of Alexander Mackenzie by 1877. During the next decade, he served as Edward Blake's Quebec lieutenant before his own election as Liberal leader in 1887.

For the next nine years, while the Conservatives under Macdonald and his four successors held power, Laurier attempted to strengthen his party's platform and standing. Unpopular Liberal trade policies were modified, and Laurier set about to convince English Canadians that he was not too French or Catholic (but Quebeckers that he was Catholic enough) to become prime minister. The support of moderate Quebec Conservatives or Bleu politicians led by J.A. Chapleau and Israel Tarte (followers of the "School of George E. Cartier"), who abandoned their party in favour of Laurier, was also a major factor in the Liberals' 1896 victory.

After spending so many years in opposition, Laurier valued loyalty above all else. Believing his goal of national unity could only be achieved if his party were united, he rarely tolerated dissent within the Liberal ranks. This was also the rule for the party's newspapers – loyalty and obedience came first. As a former newsman himself (in 1866 Laurier had edited

Le Défricheur, a Rouge anti-clerical, anti-Confederation paper that was published in L'Avenir), he understood the value of a devoted press. "It stands to reason," he explained to Edward Blake in 1882 in a letter about the poor state of Liberal newspapers in Quebec, "that as our adversaries have 21 papers to our 5, we must forever remain in the minority no matter what may take place in the political world."[8] Two years earlier, Laurier had joined with like-minded Liberal friends to establish the newspaper *L'Électeur* at Quebec City. Edited by his close companion Ernest Pacaud, it was to be his mouthpiece for the next several decades.

As prime minister, he immersed himself in the day-to-day troubles of numerous Liberal papers, especially those in Quebec, ensuring patronage support, worrying about circulation figures, and building up an impressive organization. For Laurier, as for Macdonald, a newspaper was a tool to deliver the party's message and to guarantee success at the polls. If he had one failing, it was that, as a man of the nineteenth century, he did not fully understand the transformation of journalism that was taking place as newsmen like Willison began to assert themselves. No more would the leader come first and the faithful organ second, as during the time of journalist Martin Griffin in the early 1880s. Confrontations were thus inevitable.

Nothing mattered more to loyal Ontario Liberals than the *Globe.* This was something twenty-seven-year-old John Willison did not fully appreciate in 1883, but he soon would. In his youth, Willison was a handsome man, with a full black beard and fire in his dark eyes. Born in 1856 in a small town north of London, Ontario, he had been raised in a Tory environment. The only newspapers allowed in his home were the Toronto *Leader* and the *Daily Telegraph,* two of John A. Macdonald's organs. After having been away at school for a number of years, Willison returned home an avid reader of the *Globe,* much to his father's displeasure. He developed an early affection for politics and was soon submitting short pieces to the local newspapers. Even in those years, Willison was bursting with confidence, his ego swelling by the day. It may not be fair to label him arrogant, but he did think highly of his own work and talents. Still in his mid-twenties, Willison had not yet developed the independent-mindedness that would make him famous in the annals of Canadian journalism, although something deep inside him found the master-servant relationship between politician and editor unacceptable.

Convinced he wanted to one day be the editor of the *Globe,* Willison set out to establish his career in journalism. In 1880 he tried to impress Gordon Brown, then managing editor of the *Globe,* with a collection of his writings but there were no job opportunities at the time. His first real break was courtesy of John Cameron, the editor and founder of the London *Advertiser,* a

Liberal Party organ. At three dollars a week, he started as a typesetter and proofreader, with promises of reporting duties to come. After a few successful local assignments, Willison had proved himself worthy of a raise of another three dollars a week (by the end of 1881, his weekly pay had increased to twelve dollars) and a job as a full-time newsman.[9] In December 1882 John Cameron left London to become the editor of the *Globe* and Willison followed him six months later. This move brought Willison in close contact with the Liberal Party hierarchy, marking the beginning of a highly charged relationship.

In fact, the *Globe* in 1883 was going through a difficult period. Three years earlier, on March 25, 1880, George Bennett, an alcoholic and former *Globe* employee, had walked into the office of publisher George Brown and shot him in the leg. The wound had seemed superficial, but within six weeks Brown was dead. At the time, Brown had been planning yet another costly expansion of the *Globe* and had recently purchased new presses that could produce a more compact newspaper of eight pages.[10] The financial state of the *Globe*, however, was precarious. George Brown was a great newspaperman, but he had lost a lot of money on his Bow Park farm.

Over the years, Brown had received financial help from his brothers-in-law in Scotland, William and Thomas Nelson. As collateral for various loans, Brown had transferred to the Nelsons a large bloc of *Globe* stock as security. By December 1882 Donald Smith, on behalf of the CPR syndicate, had been purchasing as many shares of the *Globe* as he could find and had approached the Nelsons. The plan was to take over the paper and silence its criticism of the railway, still under construction. Respecting the wishes of their sister, Mrs. Anne Brown, who would soon move back to Scotland and sell her own valuable *Globe* shares, the Nelsons tried to ensure that the *Globe* remain a Liberal paper. They thus informed Ontario premier Oliver Mowat of Smith's favourable offer to them. (When Smith died as Lord Strathcona in 1912, he possessed about $100,000 worth of *Globe* stock.)

Mowat gave the assignment of raising money to retain control of the *Globe* to Arthur Hardy, one of his key ministers. With the assistance of Liberal MP Richard Cartwright and W.T.R. Preston, the chief Ontario Liberal organizer, a group of Grit corporate sponsors was assembled. Leading the syndicate were Robert Jaffray, a businessman from Toronto who had made his money in railways and selling groceries, and George Cox, formerly from Peterborough but now a Toronto tycoon. Acquiring control of the *Globe* (actually Jaffray did not have total control until 1888) cost Jaffray, his sons, and Cox about $250,000.[11] As agreed, Jaffray and Cox and the other shareholders were allowed to name three directors to the Globe Printing Company's board, while the Liberal Party leaders named two. "The idea," recalled W.T.R. Preston, "was the *Globe* should be held in perpetual trust for the Liberal party, to act as its mouthpiece." No sooner was the new board in place than Gordon Brown was forced out of the editor's chair. Brown's business practices and independent attitude had never been popular with leader Edward Blake and other party chiefs. Blake much preferred his friend John Cameron from London.

On Cameron's *Globe*, John Willison first covered the Ontario legislature, and in 1886 he was promoted to the gallery in Ottawa. He became an ardent Liberal and an admirer of Wilfrid Laurier. While Laurier was Willison's senior by fifteen years, their careers caught fire at almost the same moment. In 1887 Laurier replaced Blake as party leader, the first French Canadian to hold such a position; three years later, Willison was made the *Globe*'s new editor following Cameron's return to London.

The *Globe* did not embrace Laurier with open arms. Nevertheless, Willison travelled with him during his first tour of Ontario in 1888 and visited him at his home in Arthabaskaville. The two men developed as close a friendship as Laurier probably had with any English Canadian. Willison's reverential feelings towards the Liberal leader were soon apparent in his writings. "The reputations of George Brown, Alexander Mackenzie and Edward Blake will be dear to the Canadian people for many a long year to come," Willison wrote in his column of April 6, 1888, "and on the same bed roll of fame the name of Wilfrid Laurier will have a bright and brilliant place ... His ability is as great as his popularity."[12] In later articles he placed Laurier on a pedestal high above the "trivialities of parish politics."

Once the search was on to replace Cameron as editor, Laurier quickly let it be known that he favoured young Willison, as did Robert Jaffray, now president of the Globe Printing Company. Richard Cartwright and Oliver Mowat were not as sure, but they agreed to give Willison an opportunity to prove himself during the Ontario election of June 1890. As Willison remembered later, "I knew that if *The Globe* made no capital blunder in the campaign and if the [Mowat Liberal] Government was sustained I would succeed Mr. Cameron, and that if the Government was defeated I would not."[13]

The Liberals and Mowat were returned to office on June 5, and everyone applauded the *Globe*'s performance. Two weeks later, on June 19, John Willison officially assumed his place "in the Chair of the Browns."[14] As the new editor set out to give the paper a fresh personality, the political advice began to arrive. Cartwright (who, it will be recalled, had Edward Farrer hired as a *Globe* editorial writer in 1890 to assist Willison) offered ideas on trade, while Laurier suggested the *Globe* remain silent about the separate school issue brewing in Manitoba.

The *Globe*'s daily circulation in 1890 hovered around 24,000, a bit of a drop from previous years. Part of the problem was the rising popularity of the now independent (formerly Conservative) Toronto *Mail* as well as the fact that under Cameron the *Globe* had not been consistent on a number of controversial issues, including the Jesuit Estates Act. Willison wanted to win back respect for the *Globe* and knew that straightforward and intelligently written editorials were required. The question was, could Grit politicians accept an independent-minded person as editor of their most influential organ?[15]

Willison was a devoted party man but would not countenance the suppression and misrepresentation of Conservative speeches and meetings, a policy that did not sit well with many Ontario Liberals. Following the 1896 election, Tory leader Sir Charles Tupper conceded to Willison that the *Globe* "had reported his speeches more fairly and fully than any other newspaper." Willison would later come to value the *Globe* above everything else, including Laurier. As Arthur Hardy noted in an 1897 letter to Charles Fitzpatrick, the Liberal minister of justice, "[Willison] is quite willing to serve the party, but it must be in his own way. In fact, he is drifting as steadily as a man can to a position of perfect independence."[16]

This transition did not occur quickly, although it wasn't long before Willison was in trouble with Liberal leaders. He was extremely critical of Quebec's Liberal premier, Honoré Mercier, after evidence of a political scandal surfaced in June 1890. Nor was he very tolerant of Mercier's nationalist pleadings or his campaign to extend provincial powers. Led by Cartwright and Preston, several Ontario Liberals urged the *Globe* board to fire Willison, but Jaffray and the other directors were pleased with his work. This was a clear indication of the party's declining influence over the internal operations of the newspaper.

Further problems arose because Willison believed the *Globe* did not need the party's permission to advocate reforms and policies. Laurier was understanding, but the two men eventually clashed when Willison committed his paper to positions not agreeable to his political friends in Ottawa. One such instance took place in the fall of 1892, when *Globe* editorials suggested allocating more federal subsidies and dealing away the money-losing, government-owned Intercolonial Railway to the CPR – long a Liberal villain – in exchange for a more efficient Atlantic steamship service. Laurier did not agree and told Willison so, but the overly sensitive *Globe* editor did not appreciate the mild rebuke. "The *Globe* is as anxious to serve the Liberal party as it ever was," he told Laurier, "but we must have some freedom of utterance."[17]

More serious was how Laurier and Willison dealt with the Manitoba Schools Question. In 1890 Manitoba abolished its dual Protestant–Roman Catholic school system guaranteed by the Manitoba Act of 1870, opting instead for one secular school system. Separate schools could continue to operate but without public money. Catholics in Manitoba and Quebec were justifiably outraged. Court rulings by the Supreme Court in Ottawa and the Judicial Privy Council in London eventually determined that the Manitoba legislation was constitutional but that Catholics, under provisions in the British North America Act, had the right to ask the federal government to pass remedial legislation. Federal disallowance was also a possible solution.

The significance in Canadian history of Manitoba's educational quandary probably has been exaggerated. Between 1890 and 1896, when Laurier was elected, numerous other issues also had an important impact: the death of Macdonald and the inability of the Conservatives to find a successor; the demise, as a result of the McGreevy scandal, of Conservative Hector Langevin's political career; the economic depression; and the defection of the moderate Bleu Chapleau Conservatives in Quebec to Laurier. Yet, for Laurier, the schools question was a thorny problem. As a Catholic, he would have preferred the restoration of Catholic rights, but he had the political sense to understand that supporting federal coercion of Manitoba was an unpopular position in Ontario, where the Liberals stood for provincial rights.

For four years, Laurier tried to avoid the schools question, or at least not commit himself on the issue. (In private, he argued that if Catholic children were forced to attend Protestant schools, he would "risk everything to prevent such a tyranny.") He finally revealed his policy to the voters in a speech in Morrisburg, Ontario, on October 8, 1895. He recalled the Aesop fable about the confrontation between the north wind and the sun: "[The government] have blown and raged, and threatened, but the more they have threatened and raged and blown the more that man [Manitoba Premier Thomas] Greenway has stuck to his coat. The Government are very windy. If it were in my power, and if I had the responsibility, I would try the sunny way."[18] Laurier's "sunny way" eventually carried the day, but the *Globe's* Willison never really appreciated the Liberal leader's predicament.

Willison staunchly believed that Canada was "an English-speaking country and that it will remain." National unity could only be achieved with "one language and a system of national schools." To Laurier's dismay, Willison had hammered away at these ideas in *Globe* editorials in 1891 and 1892. Bowing to the prime minister's demands, Willison toned down his Anglo-nationalistic and secular sentiments, but the pressure from the Conservative press to commit to a viewpoint on remedial legislation was too great.[19]

In a lengthy editorial on March 5, 1895, two weeks before the passage of a government order-in-council that threatened remedial legislation if Catholic rights were not restored, the *Globe* stood by its earlier policy against federal coercion. As Willison saw it, the newspaper had to take a position. "It is impossible for a newspaper to go on and on without an opinion," he wrote to Laurier the day the editorial appeared. "From the first, we have opposed interference in Manitoba. We cannot now turn heels over head, and it seemed to me that if we refrained from expressing an opinion before the conclusion of the argument at Ottawa ... we would be fairly open to the charge of waiting to see how the Government would jump. Then we would be of no use to either side." Laurier was not as certain. "To condemn interference absolutely and in all cases would simply revolutionize our constitution," he countered. "It is conceivable that occasions may arise so outrageous as to warrant interference."[20]

Years later, Willison told Manitoba editor John Dafoe that both Laurier and the *Globe*'s management had pressured him to come out in favour of remedial legislation. He was "ordered" to Ottawa, where he had a "most unhappy time" and where he was supplied with an article allowing the paper to make the editorial switch. But Willison convinced Robert Jaffray that such a change in editorial policy would be disastrous. The *Globe* stood fast and, in Willison's view, saved Laurier and the Liberals from political suicide.[21]

The *Globe* denounced the order-in-council once it was approved by the governor general on March 21. Laurier still refused to see the issue as purely one of provincial rights, as Willison did, and in a moment of anguish lashed out at the *Globe* editor. "You view it from the point of view of provincial rights. Let me ask you: Can there be here a question of provincial rights? How can this be pretended?" he wrote to Willison on March 30. "Does not the constitution expressly declare that in the matter of education the Provincial Legislature shall have exclusive jurisdiction ... There is an exception. What is it? You have it in Section 93 of the B.N.A. Act, and it is that in provinces where a system of separate schools exists, an appeal shall be given to the minority." Yet Willison could not be swayed.

The Manitoba government, not surprisingly, refused to comply with Ottawa's demands, so in early July the Conservatives, led by the inept Mackenzie Bowell ("a tiny figure with a jagged grey beard and hooded eyes set in a parchment face," as journalist Gordon Donaldson described him), announced plans to introduce remedial legislation at the next session of Parliament. The *Globe*'s response was an editorial on July 17 entitled "No Coercion," which reiterated its familiar arguments. But it was a comment about the reaction in Quebec that raised the hair on the back of Laurier's neck. "We believe that, left to himself, the French-Canadian citizen [in Quebec] cares very little about the question of Separate Schools in the Northwest," declared the *Globe*. "But it is quite possible that he may be worked in to a state of excitement by the appeals of politicians who will tell him that French-Canadians of Manitoba are being oppressed by the majority."

To say that Laurier was furious is an understatement. His feelings of anxiety that had been building over the past five years now exploded in angry admonishment. He felt Willison had betrayed their friendship. "The whole tenor of the article is as much an attack on the Liberal Party as on the Conservative Party," he told Willison in a letter written the day the piece was published. "The *Globe* seems to be of opinion that the whole of Canada is composed of one province ... I look upon your article as a very serious reflection on me personally and it has been a most painful surprise to me."[22]

Back in Toronto, Willison was upset. It was past midnight on July 20 when he sat down alone at the *Globe* office to pen "an emotional apology to the man he had worshipped for almost a decade." "Your letter pains me more than any letter I ever received," he wrote. "No one here thought we were attacking you ... Looking over the article I am bound to say that I think there are some rash sentences and that in this case there may be ground for complaint. It does seem to attack the Liberals."[23] By this time, Laurier had calmed down. He assured Willison a few days later that he had never doubted his friendship or devotion. But he did want Willison to be a little more sensitive to his politically sensitive situation.

The Conservative solution to the schools question now ran its course. On January 4, 1896, seven ministers resigned from the Tory cabinet because of Bowell's unwillingness to introduce the remedial legislation. Bowell himself resigned on January 13, enabling that aging political warhorse, Sir Charles Tupper, to return from his posting as Canadian high commissioner in London to take over the prime ministership. Within three weeks, the remedial bill was introduced in the House: separate schools were to be restored in Manitoba against the wishes of its citizens, who had re-elected the Greenway government on January 16 by a margin of 29 to 7.[24] Laurier wisely succeeded in blocking second reading of the bill for six months, so that it could be studied further, and the schools question debate was carried into the election campaign of May and June.

In another key move, Laurier displayed his political prowess and ability to manipulate the press to his advantage. He leaked a letter he had received on January 20 from Father Albert Lacombe, an outspoken and influential missionary who was acting as an intermediary between the Conservative government and Catholic officials. Lacombe, claiming he spoke on behalf of all Catholics, had repudiated Laurier's demands for a commission of enquiry and threatened to rise against him in the forthcoming election. Laurier had saved the letter for a month before handing it over to Ernest Pacaud at *L'Électeur,* his Quebec City organ. As planned, the letter caused a furor in Quebec and helped Laurier disarm the powerful Catholic forces arrayed against him.[25] That, together with the support of Israel Tarte and other Bleu politicians, enabled Laurier to win a majority in Quebec (49 of 65 seats) on June 23.

While Laurier was pleased with the *Globe*'s performance during the campaign, Willison was disappointed that he did not deliver to the Liberals more than 43 of Ontario's 92 seats (the Conservatives won 44; independents, the remaining 5). Nevertheless, throughout his life, the *Globe* editor believed he and his paper had played a significant role in the Liberal victory. This may have been an exaggeration considering the role of Tarte and the antagonism to the Conservative–Catholic Church connection in Quebec.[26] Moreover, as opposition leader, Laurier had the added advantage of being able to sit back and respond to the government's initiatives. In politics, it is always easier to attack than defend. Still, on June 23 the *Globe* regained its position atop the Toronto newspaper pack and John Willison became the most powerful editor in Canada.

In 1904, two years after Willison had quit the *Globe*, he confided to a friend that "party journalism meant for me simply a succession of quarrels." He had not found the paper's transition from an opposition to a government organ easy or desirable. He could not give unquestioning approval to everything the government did. Indeed, he put up with Liberal interference and the job for only six years. Willison refused to become a party patsy; even when appealed to by Prime Minister Laurier, he did not back down easily.

Laurier followed the *Globe* closely. Whenever he did not approve of an editorial (or even a political cartoon), he let Willison know. He did not like articles that reflected negatively on his Quebec colleagues and urged Willison to point out any inconsistencies in the Conservatives' policies.

The *Globe* editor grew defensive about any criticism of his work. In December 1897 Minister of Public Works Israel Tarte, also a high-strung personality, complained to Willison about a brief article mentioning the death of one of Tarte's political enemies. Willison tore into Tarte for his "absurd letters," believing a conspiracy was at work against the *Globe*. Willison saw further evidence of this the following April, when the government changed the postal rates, imposing postage on newspaper delivery within a ten-mile radius of the point of publication. Because the *Globe* was circulated throughout Ontario, Willison considered the legislation a plot to cripple his newspaper financially (it cost the *Globe* about $8,000 a year). He sent a nasty letter to William Mulock, the postmaster general, in complaint. A few days later he received a note from Laurier warning him to "beware of a quarrel with Mulock, because then you quarrel with us."[27]

The *Globe*'s correspondent in the parliamentary gallery was a point of contention as well. Willison expected his Ottawa reporter to be fully briefed by the government and realized it was important for federal ministers to trust and respect the journalist. Such was not the case with Roden Kingsmill, who worked for the *Globe* in the spring of 1899. Clifford Sifton, the minister of the interior and one of Willison's government friends, warned the editor that Kingsmill was too chummy with the Tory reporters in the gallery and was feeding them confidential information reserved for Liberal organs. Initially Willison gave Kingsmill the benefit of the doubt, but when it was clear that Kingsmill was being ignored by leading government members, he was replaced.[28]

Independently of both the prime minister and the party, Willison followed his own agenda. On January 9, 1900, in a *Globe* feature called "A Programme for Parliament," he set out a comprehensive nine-point platform dealing with everything from Canada's relations with the British Empire to the establishment of a non-partisan civil service. For Laurier, calls for reform were the concern of the opposition; he was not pleased with Willison's initiative. He considered some of the proposals too radical and wondered how the *Globe* could have published such an article without first advising the government. In his defence, Willison contended that the *Globe* had been pushing for many of the reforms for years and confirmed that he was a "devoted personal friend" and a "devoted friend of the government." He added, "Of course, I have never admitted that this should mean that the *Globe* should never seem to go a step in advance and should never offer criticism of any government measure. Such a paper I conceive would be useless to the government and a curse to the community."[29] The gulf between what Laurier needed in Toronto and what Willison offered with the *Globe* was widening.

Ontario Liberal politicians and supporters had already acted. In December 1899 a group of party stalwarts led by William Mulock, Timothy Eaton of department store fame, biscuit king William Christie, Peter Larkin of Salada Tea, and Senator George Cox of the *Globe* board (but who apparently represented Laurier) was organized to establish a loyal evening Liberal paper. The businessmen decided to spend $32,000 to purchase the *Evening Star,* a money-losing journal founded in 1892 by organized labour, and turn it into a profitable party organ. On Willison's approval, they offered the editorship of the *Star* to thirty-three-year-old Joseph Atkinson, a talented journalist formerly with the *Globe* and in 1899 the managing editor of the Montreal *Herald.* In Atkinson's opinion, the *Star* was to counter the independence of the *Globe*. "I understand the motive of Mr. Mulock is to have not only an evening Liberal paper but one that will be more 'ardent' and reliable than the *Globe* in the support it gives the party," Atkinson wrote to Laurier on December 1, 1899. "A newspaper is a good ally but soon useless as the subservient organ of a party."

Atkinson had no wish to create another Toronto *Empire*. He told the Liberals he wanted a yearly salary of $5,000, of which $2,000 would be in the form of *Star* stock, and demanded that he, not Ottawa politicians, have the final say on editorial policy. This is not exactly what Mulock and his friends had in mind, but believing that Atkinson would not become the same kind of problem as Willison, they reluctantly accepted his terms. Over the next few decades, the investors sold controlling interest of the paper to Atkinson, who in turn transformed the *Star* into the Liberals' most loyal Toronto organ.[30]

During the federal election of 1900, the *Star* joined the *Globe* in securing Laurier and the Liberals another term. But again Willison was not happy with the results (the Liberals lost fourteen seats to the Conservatives in Ontario), and Toronto Liberals grew increasingly dissatisfied with the *Globe*'s "common sense and justice" approach to politics. As the criticism of the *Globe* mounted, so did Willison's temper.

The best indication of his frame of mind at this time is found in a letter to Clifford Sifton on January 29, 1901, in which he released a decade of frustration and anger. Willison considered it an insult to his integrity as a journalist that some Liberals believed the *Globe* should restrict news and not report on Conservative events or declarations. He was a loyal party man, he told Sifton, and he expected a little more gratitude for his difficult endeavours. In fact, he argued, "The *Globe* owes the Liberal politicians nothing. The Liberal politicians do not contribute one dollar to its support. They hold little of its stock. They receive, however, absolutely, without fee or reward the service of one of the very best newspapers in Canada." Then he got to the crux of the issue: "I resent the assumption of every Liberal politician that I am his hired man, that he has the right to criticize and condemn me, and that he has the right to dictate or shape my course as a journalist."[31]

As Sifton replied a week later, it was not that the Liberals of Ontario did not appreciate the *Globe*, it was only that they wanted to fight fire with fire. And Tory papers like the *Mail and Empire* were not as fair or just to Liberals as the *Globe* was to the Conservatives. The truth was that partisan Canada was not yet ready to accept a journalist such as Willison, a newsman ahead of his time.

By the fall of 1902 he had had enough. Enough of the snide remarks from party hacks who did not know the first thing about journalism or the newspaper business. Enough of the questionable commercial dealings of *Globe* president Robert Jaffray and his sidekick George Cox, who, in Willison's opinion, had used him and the paper back in 1897 to lobby the federal government to support the CPR's bid to construct the Crow's Nest Pass Railway in British Columbia. Jaffray, however, had failed to inform his editor that he and Cox stood to make a sizable profit from selling to the CPR, as B.C. land in the area they owned contained lucrative coal deposits. This clear conflict of interest embarrassed Willison and he was reluctant to forgive his employers.

Willison's resignation was one of the biggest and most talked about political stories of the day. He was to go to work for Toronto capitalist Sir Joseph Flavelle, who purchased the *Evening News* for him at a cost of $150,000. The redesigned newspaper that first appeared on January 19, 1903, was to be totally independent and free from any political party influence. As its masthead declared, "An independent journal devoted to Politics, Education, Literature, the presentation of current news and the diffusion of useful information."[32]

Willison's friendship with Laurier remained intact for a few more years. He published an acclaimed but worshipful biography of the prime minister in 1905, and Laurier read the *News* as often as he could. Yet Willison's drift away from the Liberals came quickly. He disagreed with the government's transportation policies and gave only marginal support to Laurier during the 1904 general election. The following year when Laurier sought to restore separate (that is, Catholic) school rights in the autonomy bills creating Saskatchewan and Alberta, Willison sharply opposed the move. "The *News* savagely attacked the Autonomy Bills as a cleric-inspired attempt to fetter Western Canadians with the chains of sectarian education. For two months it carried a banner across its front page: A Free West, A Common School, Provincial Rights, and Religious Equality."[33] Even after the prime minister backed down (following Clifford Sifton's resignation from the cabinet), the damage to Laurier and Willison's relationship was done. The two proud men did not directly communicate with each other for three years.

By February 1908, when Willison finally wrote to Laurier ("a great relief" to the prime minister), the *News* was about to become a Conservative Party organ. An independent paper was still not financially viable in the saturated Toronto newspaper market; the *News* was losing more than $50,000 per year. Even for a wealthy entrepreneur like Joseph Flavelle, there was a limit to the losses that could be absorbed. In the spring of 1908, by which time the *News* had cost Flavelle approximately $375,000, he found a buyer. The paper was sold to a group of Ontario Tories led by Frank Cochrane, a provincial cabinet minister in the Whitney government. Laurier thought Willison would find it painful to write for the Tories, and tried to arrange his return to the *Globe* and the Liberal Party. Too much had happened; Willison refused even to visit Laurier in Ottawa to discuss the matter.[34]

John Dafoe rightly referred to Willison's *Globe* as "the laboratory" in which an experiment – a transformation in the relationship between a political party and its newspaper – was most thoroughly worked out. At times Willison wanted it both ways. He desired his independence but demanded special treatment from the government for the *Globe* and its staff. Nonetheless, despite Willison's later defection to the Tories, he should be credited with the achievement Dafoe noted. Laurier would have concurred.

Willison's effect on Canadian journalism can best be seen in what transpired at the *Globe* after he left. Succeeding him as editor was Reverend J.A. Macdonald, "the preacher journalist," a forty-year-old Presbyterian religious writer who had never edited a daily newspaper before. Still, he quickly made a name for himself and was not afraid to criticize the Liberals or Laurier. Macdonald was a tough, moral man. His idea of journalism "was to select each month some victim 'to drive out of public life' ... He knew no scruple in the matter of slanderous invective."[35]*

Laurier's relationship with Macdonald was amicable, though nothing like his relationship with Willison. Correspondence between the new editor and the Liberal leader was very businesslike, having none of the emotion that characterized the letters Laurier and Willison had exchanged. Laurier's relationship with Robert Jaffray and the *Globe* board had changed as well. This was made clear in an editorial of January 1905. "The notion that a newspaper whose political associations and affinities are with the Liberal party is under obligation to support or defend whatever may be done by Liberal leaders is unjust to those leaders and offensive to every self-respecting newspaperman," the *Globe* boldly declared. "The *Globe* recognizes no such obligations. Its loyalty is to those best ideals of its own past which put

---

*One of the *Globe*'s most celebrated cases during the Macdonald period involved George Foster, the veteran Conservative MP and at the time general manager of the Union Trust Company, a subsidiary set up by the Independent Order of Foresters (IOF) to handle its funds. In 1906 a royal commission on life insurance revealed that Foster had invested his trust company's funds (amounting to almost $3 million) in a land syndicate owned by some fellow Tories, including George Fowler and future prime minister R.B. Bennett. It was a favourable deal for the IOF, but allegations were made that Foster "pocketed considerable profits himself and [was] said to have accepted large commissions from the syndicate for turning ... IOF business to them." Led by the *Globe*, the Liberal press attacked Foster for two years. He was regularly referred to in *Globe* editorials as "the Rake," and during the 1908 election campaign editor J.A. Macdonald attacked Foster for accepting "a rake off." Eventually Foster sued the *Globe* and Macdonald for libel, for alleging in newspaper articles that he had robbed IOF dependents. When a judgment was rendered in February 1910, the jury found for Macdonald. They appreciated that Foster had acted in good faith, but his actions were open to question. (See Brown, *Borden*, vol. 1, 124; AO, M.O. Hammond Papers, Box 2, "Unpublished History of the Globe, 255–58)

the party above the politician, the country above the party, and the right and truth above all ... In the past, it has criticized, disapproved and sometimes condemned things said or done by Liberal leaders and Liberal governments. It stands ready to do so again."[36]

Within a few weeks these high-minded principles became a matter of practice. With the support of Jaffray and the other directors, Macdonald and the *Globe* opposed Laurier's version of the educational clause in the autonomy bills for the two new western provinces. Robert Borden and the Conservatives took up the provincial rights cry, proclaiming that the citizens in Alberta and Saskatchewan should decide for themselves the kind of school system they wanted. And most newspapers in Ontario and the rest of English-speaking Canada agreed. In April, once the final draft of the bill had been written and the controversial clauses amended, Laurier appealed to Macdonald to remain silent, noting how difficult it was to govern the country with Quebec demanding one thing and Ontario another. Yet the damage had already been done, and the Liberal leader blamed the entire mess on the *Globe*. "This trouble could have been entirely avoided," he bitterly wrote to Ontario Liberal organizer W.T.R. Preston a few weeks earlier, "if the *Globe* had frankly supported us, but as usual the *Globe* took to the fight and simply added fuel to the flames."[37]

After this, the more Laurier pushed, the more Macdonald and other *Globe* writers resisted. Ontario Liberals were particularly upset with how close to and supportive of Premier James Whitney and (to a lesser extent) federal leader Robert Borden the paper was. In 1909, when discussion in Ottawa focused on the development of a Canadian navy and assistance to Britain, the Liberal organ supported the Tory plan to make a direct contribution to the British Admiralty instead of Laurier's safer, more general proposal (acceptable to Quebec) to establish a Canadian navy at some future date. In demanding that Canada should "fling the smug axioms of commercial prudence to winds and do more than her share," the *Globe* was quite restrained compared with the Conservative press.[38] (Atkinson and the *Star*, on the other hand, supported Laurier's stand.)

Still, during the reciprocity debate and the election campaign that followed in September 1911, the *Globe* chose to stick by Laurier. Editorials praised Laurier, now age seventy, as one of the British Empire's "most distinguished" statesmen and reciprocity as a "great policy." Speaking to a crowd in Toronto during the campaign, Macdonald declared, "Sir Wilfrid Laurier more than any other man, has interpreted the sentiment and the purposes of the overseas Dominions of the King. It is owing to him and to his statesmanship ... that the five free self-governing Dominions of the Empire are to-day to the Motherland like the five fingers of a great hand." (A story circulating in Ottawa, concocted by Tory Sam Hughes, was that Macdonald had actually negotiated the reciprocity deal and was being paid off by a Boston publisher named Ginn.)[39]

Unlike the *Globe*'s editor, other Toronto Liberals, most notably such prominent businessmen as Sir Edmund Walker, J.C. Eaton, and R.J. Christie, rejected the trade pact. With former cabinet minister Clifford Sifton and John Willison at the *News* opposing reciprocity as well, Laurier suffered a humiliating defeat in Ontario (winning only thirteen of ninety-two seats) and lost the prime ministership to Robert Borden and the Conservatives.[40]

During Laurier's remaining years in Ottawa, this time as opposition leader, the *Globe* resumed its former policy. It was particularly hard on the aging Liberal leader for his preoccupation with Quebec. William Jaffray, who had assumed control of the *Globe* board following the death of his father, Robert, in December 1914, made it clear that the *Globe* was committed to Borden's administration at least for the duration of the war. In 1917 the newspaper supported conscription and Ontario Liberal leader Newton Rowell's entry into the Conservative-led Union government. So disgusted was Liberal Peter Larkin, the Toronto tea merchant, that he resigned his position as a *Globe* director. Under the younger Jaffray's tutelage, the once mighty and loyal Liberal organ pursued its own independent course to an even greater degree, making life miserable for Laurier's successor, William Lyon Mackenzie King.

From the day Laurier became Liberal leader in 1887, he found the *Globe* a difficult partner to control. It was a different story with the party's press in Quebec and other parts of the country.

CHAPTER FOUR

Under Liberal Management

It certainly is my firm belief that the publication of a news-
paper is of very great advantage always for the prosperity
and well-doing of a political party. In this modern age, the
press seems to be essential to the success of anything
which requires exertion.

Wilfrid Laurier, 1901

"Canada's Duty in the Transvaal" blared the headline in the *Montreal Star* of October 3, 1899. Britain was going to war in South Africa to protect British Uitlanders from harsh treatment at the hands of the Boers, descendants of Dutch colonists who governed the distant country. As a loyal member of the Empire, what would Canada do? In the opinion of the popular and zealous *Montreal Star,* the most widely read English newspaper in the Dominion, it was Canada's "manifest duty" to send troops to assist the mother country. Prime Minister Laurier was not as certain.

Questions about imperialism and Anglo-Saxon domination troubled Laurier. Like many French Canadians, he had no desire to participate in foreign wars and looked to the day when Canada would be an independent country. Still, he understood English Canadians' attachment to the Empire and their intense desire to remain linked to the British "Motherland." He was also aware that such a divisive issue could pit French against English and tear Canada apart. Thus, the Boer War presented him with a dilemma.[1]

Initially, Laurier downplayed the hostilities in South Africa, believing the trouble would be settled rather quickly. On October 3, the day the *Montreal Star*'s Boer War campaign began, Laurier gave a rare interview to the *Globe.* He stated that even if he wanted to send troops, Parliament's sanction of men and money was mandatory. With that out of the way, he boarded the Grand Trunk train to Chicago. The following day, the *Star* told Canadians that they should be "amazed and disgusted" by the prime minister's position.

In 1899 the *Montreal Star* was a unique newspaper. It had been founded thirty years earlier by Hugh Graham, a business "operator" of the first order, and George Lanigan, a brilliant writer. Copying the style of the one-cent popular press in New York, Graham (the partnership with Lanigan dissolved quite quickly) produced an exciting and innovative newspaper. Filled with stories about crime, foreign affairs, politics, and entertainment, the *Montreal Star* became an overnight sensation. Success allowed Graham to purchase more efficient presses, include more illustrations, and hire more reporters to flush out corruption in high places, a favourite *Star* preoccupation.[2]

It was Graham himself, however, who ensured the *Star* stood apart from all other Canadian newspapers. Graham was flamboyant, grandiose, and pretentious. He became a wealthy member of the Montreal elite and led the *Star* on numerous "righteous causes," including raising funds (more than $55,000) for the India famine in 1897. He was an ardent imperialist Tory and over the years contributed thousands of dollars to the Conservative Party coffers. Brenton McNab, the *Star*'s managing editor from 1892 to 1912, told Robert Borden in 1932: "During the period of fifteen years from 1897, my active political work, in attempting to forward the fortunes of the Conservative party, was inseparable from my executive journalistic activities."[3] Graham was always mixed up in some zany scheme, as Laurier would discover in 1904 in the famous plot to buy the Liberal paper *La Presse* and turn it into a Tory organ. As a reward for his defence of the Empire, Graham was knighted in 1909, the first Canadian journalist accorded such an honour. He later became Lord Atholstan, a title he proudly signed on his correspondence.

In 1899 Graham and the *Star* made the conflict in South Africa their own. While Laurier was away in Chicago, the Montreal paper hammered the government for its lack of "moral courage." On October 7 an entire page was devoted to what appeared to be messages from Canadian dignitaries, mayors, and soldiers affirming support for the *Star*'s position. (In fact, as historian Blair Neatby has noted, the messages were "really replies to leading questions submitted to them by the *Star*.")[4] With lurid stories about British women and children being blown up by the Boers, the *Star* challenged the "cowards" in Ottawa to do something. In one particularly wicked cartoon by the brilliant Henri Julien, Laurier was portrayed in one panel accepting his knighthood at Queen Victoria's 1897 Diamond Jubilee, and in another dressed in a military uniform cowering from view as Canadian volunteers "began their irresistible march" to join their British brethren.

Returning from Chicago, Laurier learned that war had broken out. Accompanying him and his wife, Zoë, on the train were Quebec journalist L.O. David, Raymond Prefontaine, a Liberal MP and mayor of Montreal, and *Globe* editor John Willison. "When we reached London on the homeward journey, we learned that the South African Republics had precipitated the conflict," Willison recalled years later. "Laurier had not believed that war was inevitable ... During the journey between London and Toronto he was very sober and silent. He recognized that the Canadian Government must reach an immediate decision, but he would not admit that the fact of war necessarily involved Canada in the conflict." Willison left the train in Toronto, urging Laurier to send a military contingent. But the prime minister "was still reluctant, unconvinced and rebellious."[5]

Laurier was back in Ottawa on October 11. Two days of "stormy" cabinet meetings followed. Israel Tarte, the minister of public works and the chief Quebec leader, was particularly adamant against sending troops or money. In the end, Laurier decided to heed the British plan and dispatched a group of 1,000 volunteers. The men were to be paid and sustained in South Africa by imperial authorities.[6] On October 30 the contingent, including *Globe* correspondent Charles Hamilton, who was there at Laurier's request, sailed from Montreal. Unknown to the men, publisher Hugh Graham had taken out policies, valued at more than one million dollars, insuring each of them against death and accident.

How influential a role Graham and the *Star* ultimately played in the government's decision is difficult to determine. Governor General Lord Minto later reported that "it is no exaggeration to say that it was a newspaper which saved the honor of Canada." And it was generally believed at the time that Laurier had caved in to the paper's demands. Certainly the *Star* reflected the majority view held by English Canadians about participation in the South African conflict, and the prime minister and the cabinet were under tremendous pressure to act.[7] In the larger context, the *Star*'s headline frenzy gave new meaning to the term "power of the press."

In Quebec Laurier faced a different problem: how to convince both his supporters and opponents that the decision to send troops was justified. National unity was on the line. The Liberal French press was dealt with first. On October 14, the day after the cabinet had rendered its verdict, Laurier wrote a long letter to his friend Ernest Pacaud, editor of Quebec City's *Le Soleil* (formerly *L'Électeur;* the name change occurred in 1896), enclosing an article to be published. "Here is the attitude you should take," the prime minister informed his editor. "The reason which led us to take this action is that we wish to be of service to England without launching into a military adventure."[8] Pacaud complied. In Montreal, *La Presse,* a Liberal daily with the largest circulation of any French newspaper, was supportive of Laurier as well. Owing to Laurier's powers of persuasion, Public Works Minister Israel Tarte and his organ *La Patrie,* which had strongly opposed participation of any kind, reluctantly followed.

The one casualty was Liberal Henri Bourassa, who resigned his seat in the House as a protest against the government's edict. A grandson of nationalist rebel Louis-Joseph Papineau, Bourassa believed that despite the government's claims to the contrary, sending troops to South Africa was only the beginning of future Empire entanglements for Canada. Although Bourassa, re-elected as an independent, continued to admire Laurier and support most of the government's policies, the seeds of future conflicts over imperialism were sown.[9] In 1910 Bourassa established the independent newspaper *Le Devoir* to protest the Liberals' naval policy. Laurier looked over his shoulder for Bourassa for the rest of his life.

Laurier's masterly control of the French press during the Boer crisis was a good indication of the extent to which he dominated Quebec during most of his political career. As prime minister he worked with his chief lieutenant, Israel Tarte, the Bleu defector who was in his cabinet from 1896 to 1902, overseeing newspaper patronage and ensuring his government had press support in Montreal and Quebec City.

The unpredictable Tarte was a fascinating man; "vibrating with intelligence, he had a style of writing that was nervous, mordant, and deadly."[10] A career journalist, Tarte's claim to fame was his exposé of the McGreevy scandal in the columns of his newspaper *Le Canadien,* an organ supportive of Bleu leader J.A. Chapleau. When Thomas McGreevy launched a $50,000 libel suit against Tarte in October 1890, Tarte chose Laurier to act as his lawyer, confirming his split from the Conservative Party.

In 1897 Liberal officials financially backed the acquisition by Tarte and his two sons of the Montreal newspaper *La Patrie,* which thereafter usually toed the government line. For his distribution of patronage and influence, Tarte earned the name "Master of the Administration" from the Conservative press, but there is no doubt Laurier pulled all the strings, as demonstrated by his control over Tarte in 1899. In 1902, while Laurier was out of the country, Tarte – never the true Liberal – got carried away in several speeches committing the government to a more protective trade policy. With the Liberal press up in arms, Laurier returned, demanded, and got Tarte's resignation.[11]

Not surprisingly, given Tarte's strong personality, he refused to relinquish control of *La Patrie* after he was out of the government. The paper became independent but suffered the dismal financial fate of similar journals. The loss of *La Patrie* forced the Liberals to establish yet another Montreal paper. In 1903 *Le Canada* was born on a shoestring budget of $40,000. Edited by Godfrey Langlois, a strong-willed individual who didn't always follow the party's orders and was plagued by a lack of funds, *Le Canada* struggled to stay alive.[12]

Of all the journalists Laurier dealt with, Ernest Pacaud was the one with whom he could be most himself. The two young Rouge advocates met in 1871 and a quick friendship developed. Pacaud's first foray into the newspaper business was a year later with the *Journal d'Arthabaska,* a weekly published in Laurier's hometown. Laurier contributed numerous articles and Pacaud made a reputation for himself as a hard-hitting journalist, though he was continually short of money.

In 1880 Laurier joined with a group of Liberals to establish the Quebec organ *L'Électeur* with Pacaud in the editor's chair. With the Conservatives under John A. Macdonald and Hector Langevin still strong in Quebec, *L'Électeur* scrambled to stay alive. In 1885 Laurier worked for three long weeks raising money to keep the newspaper in operation, and he personally assumed a large amount of the debt.

As a financial backer and a friend, Laurier was never without a piece of advice for Pacaud on how to conduct his journal. In the years after 1887, when Laurier was in Ottawa most of the time, directives were issued almost daily from Ottawa to Quebec City. His demands encompassed a wide range of items: a request in April 1889 to withhold criticism of two Liberal MPs who had voted against the party on an important issue; questions about *L'Électeur*'s correspondent in the gallery; ideas for articles on such Liberal policies as reciprocity during the 1891 election and the Manitoba Schools Question compromise of 1897; and, most notably, a plan of attack to expose the Tories' weaknesses.[13]

Laurier was quite ingenious. "Your article on Bowell did not strike the right note," he told Pacaud in a letter of December 1894 in the midst of the Manitoba schools debate. "All articles of a like nature are sure to have a counter effect in other Provinces, and will be used against us by reason of my French origin and religious beliefs ... The tactics I suggest would be to take extracts from all articles resembling the one last Saturday in [the Conservative] *La Minerve* ... and comment on each particular. I would draw the attention of the Catholic clergy to the extent to which such articles are a mockery. I would then take all the articles published by the *Empire, Mail* and other [English Tory] papers, wherein are to be found appeals more or less directly in favour of Bowell, by reason of his religion and draw attention of the public to these."[14]

Pacaud could not stay out of trouble. The most serious political crisis took place in 1890 when the editor, who had become close to Quebec premier Honoré Mercier, was implicated (along with Mercier) in the Baie de Chaleurs Railway scandal. As revealed at the hearings of the Senate railway inquiry, Pacaud had acted as Mercier's intermediary in transferring the charter for the Baie de Chaleurs Railway from one company to another. "The original company was reimbursed to the extent of $175,000. Of this sum $100,000 was promptly returned to Pacaud," who apparently used the money to pay off provincial Liberal Party debts accrued from the last Quebec election. Allegations that he kept part of the money for himself were heard but never confirmed.[15] This peculiar way of raising party funds tainted his reputation and upset Laurier, who attempted to alter the journalist's methods.

Like that of many newspapers of the day, *L'Électeur*'s language was hard and vengeful, a style not approved of by the more cultured Laurier. Pacaud faced a torrent of libel suits. He was lucky and escaped condemnation in dozens, until one legal action in 1894 cost the newspaper $130,000. This one had been in response to a reporter's attack on a Quebec Conservative. Thereafter Laurier implored Pacaud to make some changes, to keep "it above the vulgarities of the general press. No more personalities, no more poundings and violence." And presumably, no more libel suits.

Another crisis of sorts erupted in 1896 after Pacaud published excerpts from Quebec journalist L.O. David's pamphlet *Le Clerge Canadien,* which was "a mild criticism of the political activities of the Church."[16] The pamphlet and *L'Électeur* were declared forbidden reading by the sensitive Catholic hierarchy. Pacaud ceased publication of the newspaper on December 26, 1896, only to start up again two days later with an identical paper, *Le Soleil.* In this way, he and his subscribers would not be disobeying the church's edict. It was a shrewd move and the clergy let him get away with it.

Le Soleil remained Laurier's voice in Quebec throughout his term in government and after. Following Pacaud's death in 1904, the paper was taken over by a board of directors, including Simon-Napoleon Parent, P.A. Choquette, and Pacaud's son Lucien. Laurier sold his shares in 1907 to Liberal premier Jean-Lomer Gouin, but retained control of *Le Soleil*'s federal editorial policy until his death in 1919.[17]

Laurier could also count on the support of the popular paper *La Presse.* Founded by William Blumhart in Montreal in 1884 as an organ of the Chapleau wing of the Conservative Party, it did not become a commercial success until it was purchased by printer Trefflé Berthiaume in November 1889. A "stocky man with a thick mane of hair and beard," Berthiaume was a tough but sympathetic newsman. "Every night for the first two years of his presidency," according to journalist Mackenzie Porter, "[he] stood at the bottom of the stairs and as the staff departed for home shook each by the hand and thanked them."

Like his English counterpart Hugh Graham, Berthiaume was a clever publisher. Utilizing the most modern technology (he experimented with colour photographs as early as 1897, for example) and employing the best writers, he transformed *La Presse* into a popular paper that rivalled those owned by American publisher William Randolph Hearst.[18] Daily circulation, approximately 16,000 in 1889, reached an astounding 66,000 a decade later.

Chapleau's switch to the Liberal camp in 1896 brought along Berthiaume and *La Presse*. So aware was Laurier of *La Presse's* powerful influence that he went out of his way to ensure that everyone involved with the newspaper remained happy. In 1899 Berthiaume hired Arthur Dansereau as editor-in-chief. Dansereau, a close associate of J.A. Chapleau, had earned the nickname "Boss" for his patronage dealings during Chapleau's short stint as Quebec premier from 1879 to 1882.

Dansereau had known Laurier from school days at L'Assomption Collège in Quebec and had edited the Tory organ *La Minerve* during the 1870s. With the Liberals accession to power in 1896, he became the link between Chapleau, Tarte, and Laurier. As a reward, he was named postmaster of Montreal. Dansereau was not cut out to be a civil servant, and according to Postmaster General William Mulock, the Montreal office was in chaos. While Laurier was visiting Washington in early January 1899, Mulock decided to fire Dansereau. Aware that Dansereau had been offered the job at *La Presse,* Laurier, not wanting to make any trouble, countered his minister's decision and ordered Mulock to reinstate Dansereau in his postal duties. He even sent Mulock an outline for the apology letter that was to be forwarded to Dansereau.[19]

Although Laurier was skeptical of Dansereau's commitment, everything worked out nicely. Once rehired as postmaster, Dansereau promptly resigned to work at *La Presse* and went on to greatly assist the Liberals in the federal election of 1900. The newspaper's share of patronage increased and favourable postal rates were secured. In 1901 Laurier helped Berthiaume secure a much-needed $300,000 loan from Toronto financiers to consolidate some debts. In Quebec, *La Presse* became known as "l'organe principal et personnel de Sir Wilfrid Laurier."[20] The prime minister was not about to allow anything to disrupt this successful partnership, particularly some half-baked Tory plot to take over *La Presse* and turn it against the Liberal government.

The Conservatives had long coveted *La Presse*. In fact, by 1900 they were desperate for a decent French paper in Quebec. The days when John A. Macdonald commanded support in the press of both languages were long gone. *Le Monde,* a party organ until 1892, had died in 1897, and *La Minerve,* forever struggling financially, followed in 1899. Tory leader Charles Tupper was hopeful that Dansereau would return with *La Presse* to the Conservative fold after the way he had been treated by Mulock, but this was wishful thinking.[21]

With capital from Hugh Graham, Senator Louis Forget, and Louis Beaubien, yet another French Conservative organ was launched. *Le Journal* first appeared in December 1899, but it was a lost cause from the beginning. The Quebec Tories were hopelessly divided, and the new paper accumulated a deficit of more than $100,000 in less than five years. It ceased publication in 1905.[22] It was during this period that the infamous "*La Presse* Affair" was hatched, a classic Canadian political plot if there ever was one.

Starring in the lead role of the *La Presse* Affair was none other than Hugh Graham. "Cool-headed enough in his own business," once observed journalist Edward Farrer, "but in politics he is excitable, almost hysterical, and can be made to believe anything that promises to bring the Conservative party to power." This was the mood that characterized the entire episode.

Joining Graham was David Russell, a promoter who would have felt right at home at the present-day Vancouver Stock Exchange. He was born in Saint John, New Brunswick, but had established a career for himself in Montreal as a promoter with interests in shipping, mining, and land. He was also the owner of the Saint John *Telegraph,* a Liberal Party organ.

The supporting cast included J.N. Greenshields, a powerful Montreal lawyer and the solicitor representing William Mackenzie and Donald Mann, the two daring railway entrepreneurs who built the Canadian Northern; Robert Borden, who succeeded Tupper as leader of the Conservative Party in 1901; Andrew Blair of New Brunswick, Laurier's discontented minister of railways; and Trefflé Berthiaume and Arthur Dansereau of *La Presse.*

Piecing the story together is difficult. For one thing, every person implicated denied any involvement. Once Laurier heard rumours about Graham and his associates' activities, he hired the well-connected journalist Edward Farrer (himself familiar with political plots from the 1891 election) to investigate. Farrer's report, reproduced in O.D. Skelton's 1921 biography of Laurier, is an intriguing document but marked with gaps, as Farrer relied heavily on inside sources in his search for the truth. Correspondence in the papers of Robert Borden is the best guide. Borden, who regretted the day he became involved with Graham and Russell, seems to have been obsessed with the *La Presse* story and saved much of the evidence to help clear his name of any political wrongdoing.[23]

Essentially, the *La Presse* Affair involved a concerted attempt to defeat the Laurier government in the 1904 federal election. This was to be accomplished by a variety of means. Several influential newspapers – *La Presse* being the most important – were to be acquired and filled with articles containing damaging information about certain cabinet ministers, information that would bring the government to its knees. Liberal candidates in Quebec were to be bought off, and Andrew Blair, who resigned from the cabinet in July 1903 after a disagreement about railway policy, was to campaign against his former chief.[24] The end result would make Blair minister of railways in the new Borden government, halt the plans to build a new transcontinental railway as proposed by the Laurier administration, and mean the adoption of a railway scheme that would be more profitable to David Russell, who had investments in several money-losing Maritime railway ventures.

It was, in fact, the government's plan to build a second transcontinental railway that had initially given impetus to the plot. In 1903, after considerable discussion, the Liberals had entered into a controversial agreement with the Grand Trunk Railway (GTR), controlled by British and American interests. Under the terms of the contract, the government was to build the eastern section from Moncton to Winnipeg and, when this was completed, lease it to the GTR for fifty years. The construction of the more difficult western section was to be done by the Grand Trunk itself, but the government guaranteed the company's bonds and paid the interest on part of its building costs. Laurier maintained that the whole enterprise would not cost more than $13 million, a very questionable estimate. Plainly, the deal was risky and the public's money at stake.[25]

Andrew Blair had resigned in protest just before the government made the official announcement. As minister of railways, he did not approve of dealing with the GTR syndicate, supporting instead a publicly owned line. He was also close to Mackenzie and Mann, owners of the Canadian Northern in western Canada whose proposal to expand their holdings had been rejected by the government in favour of the GTR. (Laurier had unsuccessfully tried to form a partnership between the GTR and Mackenzie and Mann).[26] Hugh Graham had wanted Blair to switch political sides immediately, but the former minister was too cautious. He accepted Laurier's offer to become chairman of the Board of Railway Commissioners.

But Graham wasn't done yet. In October 1904, about a month before the November election, his associate David Russell purchased the Saint John *Gazette,* a paper that had supported Blair and the Liberals, and turned it into the *Evening-Times,* a Tory organ disguised as an independent journal. The *Evening-Times* and Russell's *Telegraph* were to be used to uncover "dirt" and ruin the careers of such key Liberal cabinet ministers as Clifford Sifton, Raymond Prefontaine, and Charles Fitzpatrick. Plans were also under way to bribe Quebec candidates – $10,000 apiece – to drop out of the campaign at the last moment, allowing the Conservatives to capture the seats with ease.[27] The deal for *La Presse* was next.

On October 11 Berthiaume and Dansereau visited the Montreal home of solicitor J.N. Greenshields. There they met Russell and several lawyers. As the men drank champagne late into the night, the lawyers drew up a contract for the sale of *La Presse.* Farrer later reported that Dansereau had been paid off to manipulate Berthiaume into signing *La Presse* away; Dansereau denied this and there is no real evidence to back the charge up. By remaining silent about these dealings, however, he did lose Laurier's friendship and trust.[28] For his part, Berthiaume claimed that he was so drunk he believed that Russell and Greenshields "were acting for Sir Wilfrid Laurier," a weak defence that Farrer rightly dismissed as "ridiculous and false." Whatever transpired, one thing was certain, Berthiaume left Greenshields's house at about 6 a.m. on October 12 with a $10,000 deposit on *La Presse,* the Liberal Party's prized newspaper.

Five days later, news of the deal was published in newspapers in Montreal and Toronto. A syndicate led by Hugh Graham and David Russell had purchased *La Presse* for $750,000.[29] The following day Andrew Blair resigned his position as railway commissioner. On October 20 David Russell's *Telegraph* announced that Blair would be campaigning against Laurier in the election fight.

What the papers did not know was that the total down payment required on *La Presse* was $400,000. The investors were in need of another $100,000 rather quickly. This was obtained with the assistance of Conservative leader Robert Borden, a personal friend of Graham's and presumably a recipient of the *Star* publisher's generous campaign contributions to the Tories. As a director of the Bank of Nova Scotia, Borden used his influence to have the bank advance Graham and Russell a short-term $100,000 loan. A bond issue of $1 million was to be offered to cover the rest of the financing of *La Presse,* and the CPR pledged to purchase $500,000.[30]

Even before the newspapers broke the *La Presse* story, Laurier knew about the plotting going on behind his back. Lawyer J.N. Greenshields, "playing the role of spy," had warned him about what was brewing in late September. Laurier was able to corroborate the facts on or about October 18 following a visit from William Pugsley, the New Brunswick attorney general, who was close to Blair and Russell and in the thick of the plot. Pugsley cleared his guilty conscience and revealed all the sordid details to Laurier. The prime minister acted quickly, neutralizing his opponents and showing to all that he truly was the "master of the administration."[31]

On Sunday, October 23, Laurier saw Blair in Ottawa. Whether he pressured him to remain loyal to the Liberal cause is unknown, but Blair returned to New Brunswick and remained silent for the rest of the campaign. In a public letter of December 3, Blair denied any involvement in a conspiracy. The CPR was next on Laurier's list, and the company's president, Thomas Shaughnessy, assured the prime minister that the CPR had no part in financing the scheme. Furthermore, no cabinet ministers resigned and no scandals were uncovered. With managing editor and Laurier loyalist Thomas Côté in charge of *La Presse* (Dansereau was in Europe), the newspaper supported the Liberals during the 1904 election, helping them sweep to victory.[32]

With the loss of the CPR's financial support, Russell and Graham could not meet their obligations to the Bank of Nova Scotia on January 17, 1905.

Russell decided to get out while he could and Graham was forced to follow. In a masterful stroke, Laurier arranged for railway promoters Mackenzie and Mann to buy *La Presse* on January 18, part of the deal being a signed agreement that the newspaper would continue to support the Liberals.[33] Thomas Côté was formally installed as editor, thereby ensuring *La Presse*'s loyalty.

There was still more to this bizarre tale. After all was said and done, Berthiaume, bored in his new life, pleaded with Laurier to help him get *La Presse* back. To exact an act of penance, Laurier made Berthiaume wait for a full year before he persuaded Mackenzie and Mann to sell *La Presse* back to its original owner (although Mackenzie and Mann retained shares in the paper). In the new deal signed November 1, 1906, Laurier's control of *La Presse*'s policy was consolidated to an even greater degree.[34]

And what of the conspirators? To the end, David Russell refused to apologize for anything he had done, claiming that he had simply been opposing Laurier's railway plans. Hugh Graham, in a public letter published in the press some three years later, also declared his innocence, insisting that the *La Presse* purchase had been merely a business deal.[35] Robert Borden, on the other hand, who was a minor though significant player, received the brunt of the public blame for the failed plot. A month after the election on December 6, Borden tried to clear the air by issuing a statement denying knowledge of Blair's resignation or the *La Presse* negotiations.

Craig Brown, Borden's biographer, gives him the benefit of the doubt with regard to his contacts with Blair, but concludes that Borden's correspondence with the Bank of Nova Scotia and the bank's own letters strongly suggest that Borden's denial was misleading. He had asked the bank to help Graham and Russell. How could he have not known what they were up to? As Brown writes, it was not in Borden's nature "to make a recommendation on a $100,000 transaction casually, or to exercise his responsibility and influence as a director of the bank lightly." " At the same time," argues Brown, "there was nothing illegal about the purchase of *La Presse*. And from the bank's point of view, it was a straightforward business deal."[36]

Aspects of the plot lingered for the next three years, haunting and humiliating Borden further. He did, of course, bounce back, but for the moment, *La Presse* and the election of 1904 belonged to Laurier and the Liberals.

Laurier did not control the press by himself. He was ably assisted by his intelligent minister of the interior, Clifford Sifton. If Quebec belonged to Laurier, then the West belonged to Sifton. "When one speaks or writes of the west at the turn of the century," Pierre Berton has observed, "one does not call it the Laurier period. It is the Sifton Era, the Sifton Decade." Laurier would have agreed. Sifton, according to Laurier, "was the master in

Parliament. He could discern the current political tendencies, put his finger on the popular pulse, better than any other man in my experience. His executive capacity was extraordinary."[37]

Sifton is best remembered for his open-door immigration policy, by which he employed business tactics to settle the vast West with "stalwart peasants in sheep-skin coats." But as Laurier's right-hand man from 1896 until he resigned from the cabinet in 1905 (over the prime minister's plans to restore separate schools in Alberta and Saskatchewan), Sifton was a skilful political manager. A "workaholic," he reshaped the civil service in his own image and used patronage to accomplish his political objectives. He had many enemies among the Tories, as well as within his own party, and was fittingly dubbed by the Toronto *Mail* the "Young Napoleon." And in 1896 at age thirty-six he was wealthy, good-looking, well dressed, and full of himself. (Sifton's wealth and lifestyle were a constant topic of discussion in the Tory press. The Conservative *Calgary Herald,* for example, usually spelled his name "$ifton." When he died in 1929, his estate was worth $3 million, about $20 million in current dollars.)[38]

Sifton had earned his reputation when he was attorney general in the Manitoba government of Thomas Greenway during the early 1890s, having used the *Brandon Sun*, a newspaper in which he held shares, to further his political career. He not only recognized the power of a loyal organ, but understood more than most politicians that a simple distorted piece of news was more valuable than a verbose editorial. An avid reader of at least seven newspapers every day, Sifton "constantly analyzed the news stories in the Liberal and opposition press for their political impact and systematically prepared carefully slanted news items for insertion into Liberal journals." He strongly disagreed with *Globe* editor John Willison's view that Liberal voters should read both sides of the political story, believing that suppression of Tory news was both smart and practical.[39]

What began as a series of newsletters to Liberal papers in 1898 became what one journalist labelled in 1900 the "Sifton Editorial Factory." Liberal newspapers across the West were encouraged to support all government policies, with no questions asked. Patronage dividends were awarded to those publishers and editors who complied. Within a few years of his coming to Ottawa, Sifton's machine had established "an efficient propaganda network" that published biased editorials and slanted news articles. These political pieces were churned out of his office in Ottawa, some written by him personally. Orders were issued, and the right news stories appeared exactly when Sifton determined they would have the desired effect. It was, by all accounts, a smooth operation.[40]

Sifton's methods were not always popular. Influential Liberal journalists like *Globe* editor Willison and his successor, J.A. Macdonald, for instance, rejected such party controls over their day-to-day operations. Macdonald made this admission in a 1911 speech following Sifton's break with Laurier on reciprocity: "During my nine years of editorship of the *Globe,* the Hon. Clifford Sifton, and what the Conservatives called Siftonism, was absolutely the heaviest and most irksome burden we had to carry."[41]

But it was hard to argue with the results. No one outdid Sifton at election time, when his machine was working at full tilt. During the 1904 contest he oversaw the Liberal "Press Bureau," which dispatched the party's literature and ensured that government organs adopted the correct line.[42] So impressed were the Conservatives by Sifton's press network that they decided to establish one of their own.

Sifton's prized jewel was the *Manitoba Free Press,* which, in typical fashion, he acquired in a shroud of secrecy. The *Free Press* had been established in 1872 by William Luxton, who had come west as correspondent with the *Globe,* and his partner, John Kenny, a farmer with some money. Luxton was a smart newspaperman with a domineering personality. His editorials, soon aimed at the Tory government of John A. Macdonald, were hard-hitting; he did not like protective tariffs or the CPR. Because of distance and communication problems, the *Free Press,* though favourable to the Liberals, followed its own western agenda. Luxton was not easy to control (CPR executive William Van Horne considered him "partially insane" and the "damndest fool" he ever knew).

Throughout the 1880s the Conservatives attempted, unsuccessfully as it turned out, to establish their own Winnipeg organ to compete with the *Free Press.* At the same time, Luxton, needing capital for new presses and building expansions, went public, offering shares in the Manitoba Free Press Company to the city's prominent businessmen. Among those tendering Luxton financial assistance was Donald Smith, long associated with the Hudson's Bay Company and a key member of the syndicate created to build the CPR. Smith and the CPR (which had also invested) gained control of the newspaper in 1893 and forced Luxton out of the editor's chair.[43]

For Van Horne and Smith, five years was long enough to be involved in the unpredictable and troublesome newspaper business. They wanted out. A secret deal was negotiated in January 1898 with Clifford Sifton, in which the minister of the interior purchased the *Free Press* for about $75,000. Sifton decided to buy the paper because he didn't trust the Winnipeg *Tribune,* the city's supposed Liberal organ, and its owner, R.L. Richardson. The fact was that Richardson, a member of Parliament who had started up the *Tribune* in 1890, saw himself as an "independent Liberal," true to his constituents but having no obligation to abide by party dictums. Richardson was a threat to Sifton's rule of the West. He was not a team player and clearly not the kind of politician Sifton could depend on. Before long, the two men resented each other, particularly after Richardson discovered who his new competitor was at the *Free Press*.[44]

The first editor Sifton hired for his new organ was Arnott Magurn, the *Globe*'s Ottawa correspondent, but after a few years it was clear that Magurn could not do the job. The next candidate, John W. Dafoe, worked out much better.

In 1901 John Dafoe was working for Hugh Graham in Montreal as editor of the *Weekly Star* (the *Montreal Star*'s weekly edition). This was his fifth position and already, at age thirty-five, he had made something of a name for himself as a respectable and capable journalist. He was a big man "with a shock of red hair, a shaggy moustache, and a long, flabby face with a nose to match."[45] His career as a newsman had begun in 1883 when Graham had hired him to work for the *Star*. At nineteen, Dafoe was in Ottawa as Graham's gallery correspondent. It was there that he first met Wilfrid Laurier among the stacks of the Parliamentary Library and heard Edward Blake eloquently speak in the Commons. The latter event, he later recalled, changed his political views forever. He entered the Parliament Buildings "not much interested in politics" and came out "a fighting Grit." (Asked once by journalist Grattan O'Leary why he was so dedicated to the Liberals, Dafoe replied, "I simply think of all the sons of bitches in the Tory party, then I think of all the sons of bitches in the Liberal party, and I can't help coming to the conclusion that there are more sons of bitches in the Tory party.") Later Dafoe worked for the *Ottawa Evening Journal,* spent a few years with the *Manitoba Free Press* in the late 1880s, but returned to Montreal in 1892 for an editorial position on the *Liberal Herald*. He resumed his relationship with Hugh Graham in 1895 and quickly doubled the *Weekly Star*'s circulation from 50,000 to 100,000.[46]

As a devoted Liberal and an admirer of both Sifton and Laurier, Dafoe jumped at the opportunity to join the newly organized *Free Press*. It was in Winnipeg that the Dafoe legend as Canada's premier journalist was established. In another era, *Free Press* editorials, or "leaders," were to become required reading in Ottawa, but that was not until Sifton left active politics in 1911. For at least his first decade at the *Free Press*, Dafoe was very much Sifton's employee. "He wrote what he was told," Pierre Berton has noted. "In those early years, he was as much a party hack as an editor."[47]

Sifton fed the *Free Press* editorials and news items from his Ottawa press bureau and Dafoe willingly complied. When publisher and editor differed over reciprocity in 1911, Sifton reluctantly permitted Dafoe to follow his own course and support Laurier in the pages of the *Free Press*. Sifton's decision was not based on anything other than the fact that it was good business for his newspaper to remain consistent. He himself opposed Laurier and helped defeat the Liberals in Ontario.[48]

With Sifton acting as an intermediary, Dafoe's personal relationship with Laurier was slow to develop. Until Sifton left the cabinet in 1905, any direct orders from the prime minister to the *Free Press* editor were first cleared through him. And even after Sifton's departure, Dafoe and Laurier never became particularly close – certainly not like Laurier and Willison had been.

Following the Liberals' defeat in 1911, Dafoe felt freed from the restraints placed upon government organs and looked forward to advocating reforms in future *Free Press* editorials. He did just that, giving the newspaper a "personality," and in the process made it the voice of the West and a newspaper of national importance. "In the past generation now it has been generally true," commented historian Frank Underhill in 1932, "that what the *Free Press* thinks today, western Canada will think tomorrow and the intelligent part of eastern Canada will think a few years hence."[49]

Dafoe remained loyal to Laurier until differences over Liberal participation in Borden's wartime Union government drove the two men apart. He believed that Laurier's obsession with Quebec and his fear of losing the province to the nationalists (and Henri Bourassa, the *Le Devoir* editor who opposed Borden and conscription) blinded him to the fact that partisanship and war were not compatible.[50] That was part of the problem. Laurier, twenty-five years older than Dafoe, belonged to an earlier era when Canada "was isolated from the world and, as far as possible, concerned only with its own pressing problems." Dafoe, on the other hand, viewed Canada "as part of a wider world in which it had international interests and responsibilities."[51] Consequently, the *Free Press* editor played a major part in bringing western Liberals to Borden's side. He campaigned against Laurier for the first time in the 1917 election.

Even in his old age, Laurier did not quit. Angered at losing Dafoe's support and concerned that the editor had grown too powerful for his own good, the Liberal leader, a year before his death in 1919, seriously contemplated starting his own morning paper in Winnipeg. No new organ was ever established. It would be left to the next leader of the Liberal Party to bring Dafoe and the *Free Press* back on side.

CHAPTER FIVE

Politics of Virtue

*I'm a Conservative, but also a free man. The party system's
all right, but I am not a machine.*

W.F. "Billy" Maclean of the Toronto *World,* 1908

M any years later, when he was preparing his memoirs, the entire affair
gave Robert Borden "much amusement." At the time the story broke
on Thursday, April 7, 1910, however, the Conservative leader was in a more
serious mood. All that week both Liberal and Conservative newspapers had
given ample space to the unsavoury rumours that Borden was in trouble.
According to Ottawa political gossip, the Tory caucus was so angry that it
was on the verge of ousting its temperamental leader.

Gerald Brown, a seasoned Ottawa correspondent who covered
Parliament for several Canadian and British newspapers, including the
Toronto Star, had reliable sources deep within both political parties. On or
about April 1, Brown had been approached by some disgruntled
Conservative MPs who believed that going public was the only way to halt
the inner turmoil that threatened their party. The *Star* published Brown's
lengthy dispatch on April 7, with the headline in bold print: "Borden's Want
of Tact Started the Discontent."[1] Brown speculated that there were seven
different factions within the Conservative caucus that were hostile to
Borden's continued leadership. He further suggested that among the eighty-
six Conservative opposition members, at least thirty-six were against
Borden.

One of the main troublemakers was William Northrup from Belleville,
Ontario. A Macdonald Conservative first elected in the 1890s, Northrup was
an ardent imperialist and hence extremely unhappy with Borden's performance during the 1909 naval debate as well as with his leader's reluctance
to approve an immediate contribution to the British navy. He was eager that
Borden's replacement be Richard McBride, the Conservative premier of
British Columbia and an outspoken supporter of an unconditional financial

gift to Britain. Adding fuel to Northrup's fire were lumber merchant William Price, who had fought in the war in South Africa, and Dr. John Reid, a politically astute Irishman from Prescott who had been elected to the House in 1891. There was also Thomas Crothers of St. Thomas, Ontario. A lawyer and teacher by training, Crothers had been elected only in 1908 but had his own leadership aspirations. According to the *Star*, Conservative organizer Major Thomas Beattie of London was Crothers's "chief man."

The most politically dangerous faction was the French Canadian wing of the party, led by Frederick Monk. Unlike Northrup, Price, and Reid, who demanded a more imperialistic policy, the Quebeckers proposed that a plebiscite be held before a final decision on the navy question was made. While Borden understood that support from Quebec was essential if he was ever to defeat Laurier, he and the majority of other English-speaking Conservatives were unwilling to disregard the party's long-standing British connection and devotion to the Empire. John Willison, a devoted defender of Borden and editor of the Toronto *News,* one of the most important and influential Conservative newspapers in the Dominion in 1910, considered Monk's demands "inconceivable." By the end of March, he had virtually "read him out of the party." Still, Quebec support was a large problem.

Challenging Borden as well were the usual group of party complainers, the uncontrollable Billy Maclean, founder of the Toronto *World,* being the most vocal. In his memoirs (published in 1938, a year after he died), Borden wrote rather matter-of-factly: "I am confident that W.F. Maclean had an ambition to succeed me, as on many occasions he took opportunity either to belittle or to attack me through his newspaper, the Toronto *World.*" Only a lawyer like Borden could have so understated the case.

Born in Ancaster, Ontario, near Hamilton in 1854, Maclean took his first job in journalism with the *Globe.* In 1880 he established the *World,* an independent Conservative newspaper. It was a "people's paper" with a popular Sunday edition. Guided by its owner's tenacious personality, the *World* fought for the underdog. Though a supporter of John A. on most issues, Maclean refused to be tied down by party strings and kept Conservative Party officials guessing as to his editorial intentions. From 1892 on, he became more active in politics, winning a seat in the Commons in a by-election held that year. He won by acclamation in the 1908 general election.

Maclean was far from enthusiastic when Borden became Conservative leader in 1901, no doubt believing he was a better choice for the position. With the *World* as his mouthpiece, he gave Borden a rough time about the *La Presse* Affair in 1904 and was morally outraged a year later when the Laurier government increased the opposition leader's parliamentary yearly stipend to $7,000, equal to that of a cabinet minister (regular MPs received a raise from $1,500 to $2,500).[2] Maclean even introduced a bill to have the indemnity legislation, including his own leader's salary, repealed, but it was defeated by a sizable majority. Maclean gave his $1,000 pay increase to charity.

The two other Toronto Tory papers, the *Mail and Empire* and the *News,* were extremely critical of Maclean's erratic actions. Many other political leaders would have expelled him from the caucus for disloyalty, but Borden liked to keep his enemies close at hand. In 1910 Maclean was furious when Borden, because of divisions between French and English Conservatives, postponed a party convention planned for June 15 in Ottawa. In a story that appeared in the *World* on April 6 and was reprinted in Liberal papers across the country, Maclean blamed the Tories' troubles on their weak leader. Maclean's assessment of the Conservative Party's problems was not entirely wrong.

Robert Borden was an intelligent, competent, and decent man. Born in Grand Pre, Nova Scotia, in 1854, he was trained as a lawyer and worked with his good friend Charles Hibbert Tupper, the son of "Nova Scotia's greatest politician." He married the elegant Laura Bond in 1899 and by the age of forty was one of Halifax's leading legal practitioners. His entrance into politics was a natural progression, but he chose to run for Charles Tupper's Conservatives in 1896 as the Laurier Liberal dynasty was about to commence. Five years later, through one of those quirks of fate, Robert Borden found himself leader of a party in disarray.

Nearly a decade of problems and heartache followed. A humiliating defeat in the 1904 election, coupled with allegations of impropriety in the *La Presse* incident, almost made him quit. In 1907 he unveiled his famous "Halifax platform," calling for reform of the civil service, the end of political corruption, the restoration of public lands to Saskatchewan and Alberta, free mail delivery in rural areas, and a public utilities commission to regulate railways, telephones, and telegraph companies[3] – quite an unusual menu for a Tory politician. Together with the assault on Liberal corruption during the 1908 campaign, Borden's new strategy almost worked. His skilful opponent, Wilfrid Laurier, however, co-opted several of the Conservative proposals, thereby neutralizing Borden's appeal as a reformer.

Though facing Laurier across the Commons floor was difficult enough for Borden, it was the comparisons in the style and personality of the two political leaders that did him in. In private, Borden swore, smoked cigars, drank whisky, and played bridge. He was an avid golfer, enjoyed riding his bicycle to work (in fact, he never learned to drive a car), and had a good sense of humour. In public, however, unlike the great Liberal chieftain, he was neither colourful nor charming. He lacked the magnetism that radiated from Laurier and won him the affection of every crowd he addressed. Borden was basically a shy, reserved man, uncomfortable on a public platform. His speeches in the House were thoughtful and powerful, but most had all the flair of a legal brief. Journalist Grattan O'Leary recalled that Borden was so "painstaking that his staff had to steal his fountain pen or he'd never stop correcting his speeches." To Borden, Parliament was work; to Laurier, it was an arena that allowed the display of his superior oratorical talents.

In 1910, as today, success in politics required a feel for people: egos had to be stroked and friends rewarded. While Borden understood this, part of him refused to accept it. A man full of contradictions, he took a lot of money from *Montreal Star* publisher Hugh Graham at election time, yet he disdained partisanship and the compromises and deal making that went with "brokerage politics." As prime minister, he hated dispensing patronage and generally left it to more "practical politicians" such as Robert Rogers and Dr. John Reid, though he did not hesitate to call on rewarded party journalists for favours. Most members of the Tory caucus neither understood him nor appreciated his dilemma. He lacked "political guts" was how Sam Hughes once put it. Others regarded his moody reserved style and the fact that he looked to provincial premiers, journalists, and businessmen for advice as a slap in the face.[4]

A *Toronto Star* story in April 1910 had it right. "While all [Borden's] men swear by his personal honour, his breadth of view, his intelligence and his culture," Gerald Brown wrote, "he lacks so much in tact and good fellowship in dealing with his men that he has lost their confidence." Whereas Laurier regularly visited the Liberal back benches once a session had ended to talk and laugh with his supporters, Borden quietly slipped back to his private office, which had "the air of a study rather than of a place where men come and talk things over." This behaviour made differences of opinion over Conservative policy and strategy all the more difficult to resolve.

As the *Star*'s story was going to press, Borden rather uncharacteristically made a bold move: on April 6, 1910 he submitted a letter of resignation to George Taylor, the chief party whip. When preparing his memoirs, he could not recall the events that led him to eventually withdraw this letter. His biographer Craig Brown suggests that he had no intention of leaving his office, rather he wanted to test the will of his party. Conservative premier Rodmond Roblin of Manitoba, a Borden supporter, told his friend to stand by his post with "the courage of a lion" and to exercise his rights "in as autocratic a manner as does the Czar of Russia."[5] The Tory leader did just that.

Borden met his caucus on the morning of April 12, and the issue of his leadership was hotly debated and put to a vote. Those identified by the *Star* accepted the group's decision, although Monk and the other French members remained a problem. Within eight months, Borden had appointed three trusted associates and friends – George Perley, Charles Magrath, and Herbert Ames – to important parliamentary posts and had regained control of the party.[6] As the new year began – a year that would forever change his life – he realized that maintaining his position of strength depended on daring and decisive action. His few friends in journalism could no doubt assist in attaining this objective.

Unlike his predecessors, Robert Borden in 1911 did not make the party's press a top priority. Indeed, there are few references to newspapers and journalists in Borden's two-volume, 1,044-page memoir. Though an avid newspaper reader, he questioned the press's influence and regarded it as another aspect of the unsavoury, partisan side of politics he so disliked.[7] It upset him when journalists misrepresented his opinions or printed stories about his private life. He was most displeased, for example, when John Willison, the editor of the Toronto *News* and a trusted adviser and friend, published a story about the Conservative leader's law practice in 1905. (On the other hand, in 1916 he was furious with the editor of the Halifax *Herald* because the Conservative paper failed to report the ceremonial presentation of colours at Camp Aldershot by his wife.)

Borden was admired and respected by members of the parliamentary gallery, but he was never as popular as Laurier. He handled the Ottawa reporters in much the same fashion as his caucus: he was friendly but he kept his distance. "There was no magnetism about him," conceded Paul Bilkey of the Tory *Toronto Telegram*.

While he was closest to such Conservative correspondents as Bilkey and Arthur Ford of the Toronto *News,* he insisted that access to him, as well as to government information, not be limited by a journalist's party loyalties. Ford recalls in his memoirs that during the war years Borden held weekly press conferences much like those convened by U.S. president Franklin Roosevelt during the Second World War. Comparisons with the brilliant and skilful Roosevelt stopped there. Borden never mastered, controlled, or catered to the press the way FDR did. He would meet reporters in his office after cabinet meetings with "notes of news." The problem was that Borden had his own strange ideas about what constituted good copy – he would not have lasted a day on the staff of the smallest newspaper in the country. Once, with the correspondents assembled with pencils at the ready, he informed them that a waterway pipe had been authorized for some town in Nova Scotia for $175. On another occasion, during the conscription crisis in 1917, Borden emerged from the cabinet room and offered this announcement to journalists who had been parked outside the door for three hours: "The cabinet met today. Military service was discussed. No decision was arrived at."[8]

At times Borden's style and fair-mindedness infuriated even an ardent supporter like Arthur Ford. In September 1915, after obtaining a rare exclusive interview with the prime minister, Ford reported back to his editor at the Toronto *News* that "despite all my pleading and arguments he insisted on handing out a copy of the interview I had dug out of him to all newspapermen who came along."[9] There were no scoops for Ford that day.

Still, Borden was politically astute enough to realize that a competent party press was necessary to his attaining power. He was particularly concerned, as John A. Macdonald had been, with the inadequate Conservative newspapers in Toronto, the city that was viewed as the pulse of the Dominion. "It is quite true," he told Willison in 1903, "that public opinion in Toronto reflects in an emphatic way the view entertained on public questions by the great majority of the English-speaking population of the country."[10] It was for this reason that in 1907 he worked with James Whitney, then the Conservative premier of Ontario, and Toronto MPs Edward Kemp and Edmund Osler to acquire the *Mail and Empire*.

Since its inception in 1895 the *Mail and Empire*, owned by the Riordon and Douglas families, had never been as dynamic or popular as the Liberal Toronto *Globe*. In April 1907 Tory politicians sought out Col. John B. Maclean, formerly a reporter on the old *Mail*, but by this time the successful publisher of the *Financial Post*. As the Conservatives' representative, Maclean offered the owners of the *Mail and Empire* first $300,000 and later half a million dollars for the paper; the deal, however, fell through.[11] Next came a plan to start a new Conservative organ, but the necessary capital could not be raised. In the end, John Willison and his paper, the Toronto *News,* emerged as Borden's chief Ontario allies.

As Willison, after 1905, transferred his allegiance from the Liberal to the Conservative camp, he quickly became one of Borden's key outside confidants and advisers. Considering both men's negative views on party politics, the friendship was not surprising. In 1907 Willison was one of the few people Borden consulted before publicizing his Halifax platform, and he stood by the Conservative leader during the 1909 naval debate. After the *News* was sold by Joseph Flavelle to the syndicate headed by Frank Cochrane in 1908, the once "independent" paper became the voice of the Tory party in Ontario. By 1915 it was, according to former prime minister Mackenzie Bowell, "the only consistent Conservative journal in Toronto."[12]

John Willison greatly admired Borden, although he was routinely frustrated by the politician's habit of waiting for problems to solve themselves. "In politics, the dramatic counts for everything," he once told Borden – advice the cautious Tory leader usually failed to follow. Near the end of Borden's political career, Willison joked with Clifford Sifton about "Robert the Unready's" indecisiveness: "You have no doubt heard why the ship that Borden was to christen at Halifax slipped into the water before the ceremony could be performed. It could not wait for Borden to make up his mind."[13]

Nevertheless, in 1911 Willison was instrumental in leading the crusade against reciprocity. During the election the Conservative Party's slogans were "NO TRUCK NOR TRADE WITH THE YANKEES" and "A VOTE FOR BORDEN IS A VOTE FOR KING, FLAG AND COUNTRY." Willison was more succinct: "VOTE AGAINST NATIONAL SUICIDE" was how he put it in the *News* a few days before the election. Borden repaid the favour twice; he recommended that Willison be knighted in 1913 and sanctioned the $50,000 grant made to the *News* by the Conservatives in 1915 to save the newspaper from bankruptcy.[14] The war and the idealism it generated relegated partisan politics to the back seat and drew the two men even closer together.

Borden's views on the usefulness of the press were equally shaped by his relations with Hugh Graham of the *Montreal Star* and his unhappy experiences in the attempt to steal *La Presse* from the Liberals in 1904. Given Borden's distaste for partisan politics, his long association with Graham, one of Canada's most famous "bag men," is an anomaly. In fact, he uncharacteristically spent years attempting to please the overly sensitive Montreal publisher.

It might have been Laurier who secured Graham's knighthood in 1909, but it was Borden who persuaded the reluctant British authorities to grant Graham a peerage in 1916. "I am under a debt of deep personal obligation [to Graham]," Borden admitted at the time. While the new Lord Atholstan was grateful, Borden was troubled and annoyed. A few months earlier he had described Graham in his diary as a "singular mixture of cunning and stupidity. His great weakness lies in his belief that he can hoodwink others ... Evidently he is consumed with immense desire for peerage. Speaks of it as a bauble hardly worthy of his acceptance."[15]

Why did Borden expend so much energy on Graham? Clearly, he could not ignore the *Star*'s tremendous influence; nor could he refuse Graham's generous contributions at election time. "I happen to be the owner of newspapers with vast interest in every province of the Dominion, more widely dispersed than those of any bank or industrial concern," Graham declared in a public letter of 1907. "So long as I have a dollar to spare, I will consider myself free to aid whichever party has, in my opinion, the policy best adapted to the needs of the country." The Tories nearly always fit the bill. During the 1904 election, Graham not only raised money for the Conservatives among his wealthy Montreal business friends, but donated at least $200,000 from his own bank account. Borden no doubt appreciated Graham's "enthusiasm and devotion" to the "Conservative cause."[16]

Nevertheless, Graham's fund-raising work became the focus of a serious dispute between the two men. In May 1905 Graham testified in the proceedings of a lawsuit that he had received a letter from Borden on or about

October 23, 1904, just prior to the November 3 federal election. According to Graham, Borden had ordered him to establish a Dominion-wide network of trustworthy Tories so that the party's money could be quietly distributed.[17]

Political gossip about these financial dealings appeared in the Liberal press over the next two years as Borden embarked on his "purity in politics" campaign aimed at exposing Liberal corruption. In August 1907 Borden revealed his Halifax platform with its promises of honest government, and on September 2 he arrived in Montreal to deliver his message. He was, however, still troubled by his devastating loss at the polls in 1904 and embarrassed by allegations that linked him to the *La Presse* conspirators and Hugh Graham's money. In the heat of the moment, he denied that he or any member of his caucus had ever written the letter alluded to by Graham in his legal testimony of 1905. In other words, the *Montreal Star* publisher was either mistaken or a liar. While the Liberal *Herald* reprinted Borden's speech, the *Star,* the chief Conservative paper in Quebec, did not. In a statement issued on October 25, 1907, Graham reaffirmed that Borden had sent him the letter in question. There the matter stood.

Borden's refusal to accept Graham's version of events apparently cost him the support of the *Montreal Star* during the 1908 election, and as a consequence the newspaper took an independent editorial position on charges of Liberal corruption. On September 19, five weeks before the vote, Borden attempted to win back the favour of the *Star* and its owner. In a key Montreal speech he described Graham as "patriotic and absolutely unselfish" and then dealt with the infamous letter: "In respect to some alleged or supposed discrepancies between Mr. Graham and myself with regard to a certain letter, the memories of men may be at fault from time to time with regard to the date or contents of a letter, but I would be the last to imagine ... that Mr. Graham would ever in the slightest degree deviate from the truth in any statement made by him under oath or otherwise."[18] His effort came a little too late, although even without the *Montreal Star's* backing the Conservatives gained a few seats on the Liberals in the 1908 contest.

Borden's retreat and apology were enough for Graham, who had every desire to see the Tories in power. As an ardent imperialist, Graham supported Borden's opposition to Laurier's naval bill the following year and threw all his resources behind Borden in the 1911 election and the fight over reciprocity. For Graham and the *Montreal Star*, reciprocity was "an altogether dangerous, seriously injurious, anti-Canadian, anti-British and anti-Empire policy." Consequently, the paper harassed Laurier for months, denounced the free trade bill as a threat to the British connection, and exposed the Liberals' efforts to suppress U.S. congressman Champ Clark's pro-reciprocity–annexation speech about "the day when the American flag will float over every square foot" of North America. In the *Canadian Annual Review*'s post-election analysis, Graham's *Star* played an unprecedented role in securing Borden's victory. "It is not very often in the history of a young, or indeed of any country," observed the *Review*'s editor, "that a single newspaper wields a powerful influence in the overturn of a Government and the defeat of political policy. Such, however, was the record of the *Montreal Star* in 1911."[19]

At the same time, Graham played his usual clandestine role behind the scenes. Reciprocity alone did not make the 1911 general election a historically fascinating event; the support Borden received from Quebec nationalists led by Henri Bourassa did the same. Borden had first met Bourassa when they shared the same Ottawa boarding house during their early careers as MPs in the late 1890s. Borden had gone on to become leader of a party with virtually no representation in Quebec; Bourassa, a confident man and an excellent bilingual debater, emerged as the chief spokesman for one brand of Quebec patriotism. In January 1910 Bourassa established the intellectual and independent newspaper *Le Devoir* in order to combat Laurier's threatening imperialistic naval policy.[20]

As Borden marched towards the prime ministership, he recognized that Bourassa might be the potential solution to his party's Quebec problems. Though the two men obviously disagreed on British imperial issues, they were united in their aversion to Laurier-style politics. Surprisingly enough, the first attempt to bring the two together was orchestrated by Hugh Graham. In 1907 he ordered *Star* editor Brenton McNab to act as an intermediary between Borden and Bourassa. The planned meeting did not take place, but the seeds for future cooperation had been sown.[21]

During the 1908 election Bourassa remained neutral. Yet by 1911, with *Le Devoir* as his public sounding board, he and the nationalists attacked Laurier and the Liberals over reciprocity and the naval question. Since most English-speaking Tories demanded a naval policy even more aggressive than the one proposed by the Liberals, Borden left Quebec and Bourassa in the hands of discontented French Conservative Frederick Monk. Money for the nationalists' anti-Laurier campaign was provided by none other than Hugh Graham.[22] The result of this so-called unholy alliance delivered twenty-seven Quebec seats to Borden, the most the party had won in the province since 1891.

A few days before the vote, Paul Bilkey of the *Toronto Telegram* ran into Sir George Foster, soon to be the new minister of trade and commerce, at the gates of the Parliament Buildings. "What are you going to do with these Nationalists after the election?" inquired the reporter. "Bilkey," said Foster solemnly, "one thing at a time." In fact, with Laurier out of power, the mismatched partnership quickly fell apart. Wrote historian John English,

"An unpopular naval policy, organizational decay, and Borden's lack of understanding of French Canada combined to undermine Quebec Conservativism between 1911 and 1914."[23]

In Ontario the Conservative victory was spurred on by John Willison's *News* and by the defection from the Liberals of former Liberal cabinet minister Clifford Sifton and eighteen other prominent Toronto businessmen and financiers who opposed the reciprocity pact.[24] Equally significant but less well known was the backroom work of the independent Conservative editorial committee chaired by Toronto lawyer C.A. Masten.

Similar to Sifton's Liberal "editorial machine" earlier in the decade, the Tory committee, organized in 1908, churned out propaganda for the party's press. During the 1911 campaign, about seventy newspapers across the country published hundreds of slanted articles prepared by committee members. The non-partisan Borden appreciated the work. "These articles were exceedingly helpful to our cause," he wrote to Masten following the election. Whether or not newspapers identified the authors of the editorials is not known; a random search through the Ontario press indicates they did not. More importantly, the committee was still in operation in 1930. It assisted Borden in 1917 during a wartime election that, in the prime minister's view at least, was supposed to be above partisan politics.[25]

On September 21, 1911, Robert Borden, fifty-seven years old, was elected Canada's eighth prime minister. He had overcome great odds to achieve this position of power: a fragmented caucus, almost no support in Quebec, and a charismatic and beloved Liberal opponent. Certainly his perseverance and hard work counted in the end, as did the Liberals' adoption of an unpopular and unacceptable economic policy. He was also aided by the advice of the country's premier journalist, the money of the most influential newspaper publisher in the Dominion, the writings of a French Canadian nationalist, and a backroom committee that distributed partisan editorials – all highly unorthodox for a man who did not hold newspapers in great esteem and spurned the seamier side of politics. Indeed, while Borden would have been reluctant to admit it, his press network and Conservative Party journalistic support had played a key role in his victory. Such assistance would be greatly valued as he and the country faced the most serious challenge in the Dominion's short history.

In September 1911 twenty-eight-year-old Arthur Ford was working as a news editor with the independent Winnipeg *Tribune.* He had come west from Toronto in 1905 after having spent a few years as a reporter with the *Stratford Herald,* the *Ottawa Journal,* and a financial daily in New York. His first news job in Winnipeg was with the *Telegram,* the partisan Tory paper that supported Premier Rodmond Roblin and his lieutenant, Robert

Rogers. Ford was assigned to cover the railways in the days when Winnipeg was the hub of the mass immigration. In time he met J.S. Woodsworth, who was then running the All People's Mission in the city's overcrowded North End. The two collaborated on a book, *Stranger within Our Gates,* published in 1909, in which immigrant groups were discussed and ranked according to their capacity to adopt "Canadian" ways.

After the *Telegram* moved him to the Manitoba legislature, Ford made a name for himself as a competent, loyal Conservative journalist. He was sent to Ottawa to cover the parliamentary session of 1907–1908. "I was so intrigued with Ottawa and so interested in politics and the Bohemian life of the Gallery," he recalled many years later when he was the editor of the *London Free Press,* "that I made up my mind, if the opportunity ever came, I would locate in the capital."[26] He had to wait three more years.

Soon after returning from his stint as a sessional, he switched to the Winnipeg *Tribune.* The day after Borden's victory, he called upon his former boss Mark Nichols at the *Telegram* and offered his services as a full-time gallery correspondent. A week later he boarded a train and arrived in Ottawa just as the new prime minister was naming the first Conservative cabinet since 1896. The Russell Hotel, still the best establishment in the city, was "abuzz with excitement."

For Ford and his colleagues who represented Conservative newspapers, it was as if the clock had been turned back to the days of John A. They again had access to government secrets and the confidence of influential ministers. Though Borden, like Laurier, believed that all journalists should be treated the same, regardless of which newspaper they worked for, the simple fact was that the new Tory ministers played favourites.

The *Winnipeg Telegram,* long a voice of Manitoba conservatism, had sent Ford east to report on Robert Rogers's jump to federal politics. "Hon. Bob," as he was known, brought with him a reputation for being tough and fiercely partisan. Rumour had it that there were numerous skeletons in his closet. After he was appointed minister of the interior, Rogers kept Ford up to date on government activities, but the two men never got along.

In 1914 Ford accepted a position with John Willison's Toronto *News* that brought him into closer contact with other key ministers, including Thomas White in Finance and Arthur Meighen, the solicitor general. The war had started by this time and both politicians supplied Ford with sensitive background material for stories that highlighted the government's accomplishments. White had a particular understanding of and appreciation for newspapermen, having worked as a reporter for the *Toronto Telegram* prior to becoming an important member of the Canadian business community. He was the first finance minister, for example, to allow gallery men to read portions of the budget before it was unveiled in the House.[27]

Access to Borden was more limited, but the prime minister liked Ford and Paul Bilkey of the *Toronto Telegram* and occasionally invited them to lunch. Though he steered the correspondents in the right direction and offered sound advice when necessary, Borden rarely revealed cabinet secrets to outsiders. Still, Ford was enough of a trusted friend to be able to admonish the prime minister for sticking "too close to his desk." In November 1914, when the war was but a few months old, he counselled Borden to "keep in touch with the people." This suggestion was followed, and public gatherings were arranged the next month in Winnipeg, Montreal, and Halifax.[28]

Robert Borden took over the prime ministership in 1911 with the intention of cleaning up the mess left by fifteen years of Liberal rule. The state, he believed, had a regulatory role to play in matters of economic development, transportation, agriculture, education, and bureaucratic administration. In a few short years, however, Borden and his colleagues discovered that "election planks were easier to formulate than fulfil." A promised overhaul of the inefficient federal civil service, for instance, did not take place, and many other proposed economic reforms were blocked or changed by the Liberal-dominated Senate.[29]

One issue that kept Ford and the other gallery members especially busy during 1912 and 1913 was the great naval debate. In the summer of 1912 Borden travelled to England to visit Winston Churchill, then first lord of the Admiralty, who impressed upon the Canadian prime minister the danger of a German naval build-up. Though Borden took this threat seriously, he began to speak about a "Canadian voice in imperial foreign policy." At home he faced another problem. Frederick Monk and the other French Canadian Conservatives opposed any commitments that would draw the country further into an imperialistic conflict. Borden did not want to lose Quebec support but rejected Monk's call for a referendum on the question of an emergency contribution to the British navy. Monk resigned from the cabinet on October 18, 1912. Soon after, when Borden invited Ford and a few other Conservative correspondents to chat with him, off the record, in his office, he asked the journalists to be "very tender in [their] treatment of Mr. Monk."[30]

On December 5, Borden outlined his naval policy: $35 million was to be allocated for the construction of three Dreadnoughts for the British navy. Laurier and the Liberals questioned the emergency and regarded such a measure as a threat to Canadian sovereignty. They called for the reinstatement of their own impotent plan for a Dominion navy, which had been discarded earlier. Discussion on "Borden's resolution and Laurier's amendment initiated the most acrimonious debate the House of Commons had ever witnessed." The debate began on January 31 and did not end until May 15. Though Laurier's motion was eventually defeated, the Liberals held up final passage of the bill for weeks. Following second reading assented to at the end of February, the House, in committee, sat continuously (except Sundays) from March 3 to 15.[31]

Throughout the ordeal, the men in the gallery watched the political duel from above. Paul Bilkey remembered that members "slept in their seats." His colleague, Grattan O'Leary of the *Ottawa Journal,* recalled that Quebec Liberal MP David Lafortune once spoke from midnight to 6 a.m. and was forced to stop because of "an imperative call of nature." Dr. J.P. Molloy, a Manitoba Liberal, declared that the book *The Great Illusion* by Norman Angell was relevant to the question under debate, and proceeded to read the entire volume into *Hansard.*[32]

The Grit tactics forced Borden to limit the debate by using closure, an action that caused another outcry. The naval aid bill finally passed third reading on May 15, but Borden anticipated trouble in the Liberal-dominated Senate. He curtly instructed C.A.C. Jennings, the editor of the *Mail and Empire*, to stress in editorials the irresponsibility of the opposition should the bill fail to make it through. In the prime minister's view, "the Liberal majority in the Senate are mere puppets who will dance whenever Laurier pulls the strings."[33] Despite the criticism of the *Mail and Empire* and the rest of the Tory press, the Senate sent the bill back to the Commons, killing it for good.

The naval bill suffered the fate of much of Borden's legislation during his first term – it failed. In this instance as with others, Borden rightly blamed the outrageous blockade set up by the partisan Liberal senators. In fact, he and Laurier were both guilty of vindictive and partisan behaviour. As Craig Brown and Ramsay Cook have argued, "Borden had unwisely cancelled Laurier's naval programme before he had any acceptable substitute to put before the nation. Laurier had replied by obstructing passage of the Naval Aid Bill. Borden had introduced closure; Laurier had forced an outright rejection of the bill in the Senate."[34]

Journalists like Arthur Ford experienced the same pettiness. At the height of the naval debate, when Laurier had declared his position, Ford was in the gallery taking notes. Conservative cabinet minister Douglas Hazen had spoken that day as well, but his speech was of no consequence. Ford was also writing for the Conservative Fredericton *Gleaner* and wired the editor in New Brunswick, James Crockett, a good friend of Hazen's: "'Sir Wilfrid Laurier has spoken on the naval question. How much do you want?' Then as an afterthought [he] added: 'Hazen spoke this afternoon. Do you want anything of his speech?' Back came the wire: 'Ignore Laurier entirely. Send Hazen verbatim.'"[35] Even Ford, a staunch Tory, was astonished.

The next four years, years of war and bloodshed, temporarily pushed some of these partisan attitudes to the background and off the front pages of Canadian dailies. Equally, the war revitalized Robert Borden's political career and showed him at his best.

PART TWO

No League of Gentlemen,
1914–1956

CHAPTER SIX

Wartime Headlines

That in Parliament and as far as possible in the public press, party warfare shall be suspended and the united efforts of both parties directed toward the best means of assisting to bring the war to a successful conclusion.

Robert Borden to Wilfrid Laurier,
November 3, 1915

The First World War changed the rules of politics. In the face of a crisis that threatened the freedom of the Western world, party politics, partisanship, and patronage were no longer acceptable – at least in public. Many politicians – Robert Rogers, Dr. John Reid, Sam Hughes, and even Laurier to a certain extent – could not or would not adapt. This was not the case with the prime minister. From the opening days of the conflict in August 1914, Borden relished his new role as a wartime leader. "The war had given Borden a cause to work for," Craig Brown writes, "a cause that was just and moral and on a higher plane than the parochial political affairs he had found so frustrating before."[1]

Changes were also evident in the press, yet it took actual fighting and a full declaration of war to convince the numerous skeptical editors of Liberal newspapers that a crisis existed. A confidential memo prepared for Borden on October 30 revealed that during the spring of 1914 opposition papers criticized the Conservative administration either for spending too much money on military preparations or for not doing enough.[2] The outspoken and indiscreet minister of militia and defence, Sam Hughes – "King Sam" to Liberal journalists – was singled out for his excessive spending habits. "What does it matter how many millions of dollars of the people's money King Sam is spending?" asked the *Ottawa Free Press* sarcastically. "Is it not worth the price just to have King Sam do the spending? King Sam says it is and that should be sufficient."

By the end of July, as the situation in Europe worsened, Liberal editorials offered a new message, calling for unwavering support and loyalty to the mother country. In the struggle between autocracy and liberty, it was essential that Canada champion freedom. "When Britain is at war, Canada is at war," the *Globe* declared on July 31. It was a sentiment widely accepted among English Canadians of all political stripes.

In Quebec the cry was more cautious, but there were exceptions. On August 5 Montreal's *La Patrie* stressed the dangers to both England and France; the flags of both countries were intertwined on its front page. "There are no longer French Canadians and English Canadians, only one race now exists united by the closest bonds in a common cause," the paper proclaimed. The majority of the French press, however, was more reserved. Henri Bourassa, the editor of *Le Devoir* and an opponent of imperial entanglements, was visiting Europe when war broke out, which tempered his initial reaction. Upon his return, he put things into perspective in a lengthy editorial of September 14 entitled "Le Devoir National" (The National Duty). He argued that while Canadian interests were not directly threatened, the country's "ethnic, intellectual and economic ties" with Britain and France justified an active Canadian role.[3] With this pronouncement, the Dominion's unity seemed assured for the duration of the conflict. But questions about bilingual schools, the number of French Canadians volunteering for military service, and age-old prejudices soon intervened. Within a few months, Bourassa had changed his mind and *Le Devoir* again was the government's most vocal and bitter critic.*

Quite different feelings were evident in the English press. One sign of its loyalty was its ready acceptance of wartime censorship. Under section 6 of the War Measures Act passed by the Borden government in August 1914, Ottawa officials were empowered to censor, control, and suppress any publications or writings deemed dangerous to Canadian or Allied security. Having no prior experience in this area, civil servants in the Department of the Militia formulated rules as needed on a day-to-day basis, and patriotic editors complied. It was a workable but admittedly inefficient system.

In July 1915 Col. Ernest Chambers was appointed press censor. Chambers had worked for the *Calgary Herald* in his younger days and had later become the editor of the *Canadian Military Gazette*. In 1904 he was

---

*Bourassa spoke at the Russell Theatre in Ottawa in December 1914. Hundreds of people forced their way in and the mob became unruly. The crowd, led by a group of vocal cavalry troopers, shouted Bourassa down and told him he was "rocking the boat." He was threatened with a whip and barely escaped in one piece. Mrs. A.G. Glennie, the wife of the meeting's organizer, for some reason blamed the *Ottawa Journal* for inciting the crowd that led to her husband breaking a rib. The following day, she stormed into the *Journal*'s office and used a dog-whip on one of the editors. (Kesterton, *A History of Journalism in Canada*, 188–89)

appointed the Senate's Gentleman Usher of the Black Rod. At age fifty-three, he was popular among the gallery correspondents, having earned their respect for trusting them to do their jobs. In the summer of 1915, he held meetings in Ottawa with most of the publishers and editors of Canadian dailies to explain the new rules and to clarify what sensitive military information was not to be publicized. In his report to Borden, Chambers noted that the "interviews thoroughly confirmed the view that there existed throughout the press of Canada a keen, patriotic desire to assist the naval and military authorities in every possible way."[4]

In general, Chambers's assessment of the journalists was accurate, but there were times when they felt that the public's right to know about military movements and activities took precedence over national security regulations. In July 1916 press reports in Ontario papers, fuelled by stinging editorials in Billy Maclean's Toronto *World,* stated (wrongly) that nickel from Canadian mines exported to the United States (which was still neutral) for refining ended up in the hands of the Germans for use in the construction of enemy submarines. In such cases, Chambers (and Borden) did little more than dispatch a stern reprimand. The prime minister was especially incensed by a *Mail and Empire* editorial on July 14 that commented on the Canadian-German nickel conspiracy; he curtly informed the paper's editor, C.A.C. Jennings, just how he felt.[5]

It was important that Chambers maintain a good working relationship with publishers and editors. To this end, he kept an elite group of prominent Conservative newspapermen up to date on sensitive information. In October 1915 reports circulated that a Canadian regiment had "misbehaved" in action. While an inquiry was under way, Chambers asked John Willison and a number of his "journalistic friends" to refrain from writing about the incident. "There is at stake," he told Willison, "an issue as to national pride." The editor of the Toronto *News* agreed to cooperate.

While Borden sanctioned the censorship of local foreign-language and socialist newspapers, he hesitated when it came to major publications like Henri Bourassa's *Le Devoir.* The nationalist editor was angered by the Ontario government's suppression of the French language under the infamous Regulation 17, which withheld public funds from schools that refused to comply with an English-only policy of classroom instruction. In a series of harshly worded editorials, he questioned why French Canadians should fight and die overseas for freedom when their rights were being trampled upon at home.

An anti-war article of May 30, 1915, particularly infuriated the governor general, the Duke of Connaught, who urged Borden to shut *Le Devoir* down. But the prime minister understood that such an action would only give the Quebec nationalists further ammunition. That day, contemplating the censorship of *Le Devoir*, Borden noted in his diary: "Bourassa would like nothing better. I would not be so foolish." He also knew that outside of Quebec *Le Devoir*'s influence was minimal; the English press routinely condemned the nationalist editor as "pro-German" and a "traitor."[6] (The major French dailies like *La Presse* and *Le Soleil* did not support Bourassa's radical anti-war position.)

Along with the English press's acceptance of censorship and the patriotic call-to-arms came demands that party politics be put aside. Many journalists found it intolerable that politicians should squabble while Canadian boys died in Europe. "Let there be co-operation between the political leaders to assist the mother country," Willison wrote in the Toronto *News* on August 1, 1914. "Let there be co-operation to steady markets and safeguard common interests." Laurier grasped the seriousness of the situation immediately, pledging soon after war was declared his party's support for government initiatives "as long as there is danger at the front." It was a brilliant manoeuvre by the wily veteran leader, catching the more partisan members of the government off guard. The Conservatives had been contemplating a wartime election, and the thrust of their campaign strategy would have been to stress the correctness and virtue of their naval bill while criticizing Laurier for obstructing it. This strategy was no longer suitable. "Laurier's speeches in August 1914, by their high-minded appeal to a greater interest beyond party and politics, had undercut the Tory hopes."[7]

Other Liberal supporters followed Laurier's lead. In Winnipeg, John Dafoe, the eloquent editor of the Liberal *Manitoba Free Press*, had harshly attacked the policies of the Borden administration for four years. Dafoe, an early advocate of Canadian autonomy within the British Empire, had denounced Borden's naval plans in 1912 as a "sell-out" of the country's interests. He equally rejected the protectionist slant of the Conservative budget and loathed Borden's selection of Robert Rogers, his long-time political enemy, as the Manitoba representative in the cabinet. Now, in 1914, Dafoe believed that Borden was "entitled to the co-operation, sympathy and support of the Liberal party in Parliament."[8] In other words, partisan attitudes had to be stifled for the general welfare of the country. A coalition government was the obvious solution and Dafoe's editorials were soon advocating this unique political experiment.

Getting partisanship out of politics and the party press was easier said than done. For Robert Borden there was no question that cooperation and a political truce were essential. As his government began its fifth and final year in October 1915, he held lengthy meetings with Laurier to discuss an extension for the duration of the war. He further proposed the suspension of "party warfare" in the House and in newspapers until the end of the war.[9]

Borden did not anticipate having problems convincing Laurier to follow his plan. Earlier, in a speech in Toronto in May 1915, the Liberal leader had expressed his aversion to a wartime election. But in November the old partisan Laurier returned. He offered to consider Borden's plan provided the prime minister reveal his future railway policy. These negotiations produced a deal for a one-year extension and set the stage for the wartime election of 1917. Significantly, Laurier agreed to use his influence to "minimize," not end, party conflict in the Commons and in the press.[10]

While it is certain Borden's intentions were good, the fact that for most of the war his cabinet included such party men as Robert Rogers, Sam Hughes, and Dr. John Reid makes his non-partisan stance appear somewhat suspect. For more than a year, he looked the other way as his minister of militia, the unpredictable Sam Hughes – "Sir Sam" to his friends (he was knighted in August 1915) – used the war to dispense Tory patronage as never before. This was directly contrary to Borden's assurances to Laurier in the fall of 1914 that war purchases and appointments would be free of such favouritism.[11] Equally damaging was Borden's continued support for Robert Rogers, who, like Hughes, used patronage to award his many friends. Once it had been confirmed that Canada was truly at war, the Liberal press returned to its former partisan ways. The actions of Hughes and Rogers gave credibility to its attacks.

Sam Hughes was a gallery favourite. A former newsman himself – he had been the publisher and editor of the Lindsay, Ontario, *Warder* from 1885 to 1897 – he had a soft spot in his heart for journalists; he also thrived on attention and publicity. According to one observer, he was "outspoken, aggressive and vain," all of which made him popular with the press. The entourage of reporters who daily gathered in his office could always count on Sir Sam for an outrageous comment for the next day's edition. He trusted newsmen like Arthur Ford with confidential war information and in return the Tory press was loyal to him.

When Hughes was appointed to Borden's cabinet in 1911 as minister of militia, he assured the prime minister he could be discreet and cautious, but as Borden later noted, "discretion did not thereafter prove to be a prominent characteristic." The war finally gave Hughes the national stage he so long had coveted; it also exposed his large ego ("insane egotism" was how Borden put it), erratic judgment, and extreme partisanship. Beginning in the fall of 1914, stories soon appeared in the press outlining the lurid details of Hughes's inefficient administration: the intolerable conditions at the military training facilities built at Valcartier, Quebec; the inadequacies of Hughes's favoured weapon, the Ross rifle; and charges of corruption and war profiteering levelled at Hughes's Shell Committee.[12]

Initially, while the Liberal press attacked Hughes, such Conservative newspapers as the Toronto *News* gave him the benefit of the doubt. Arthur Ford, the recipient of many private briefings by the minister of the militia, stood by his political friend. "The criticisms in regard to equipping troops, assembling them at Valcartier and getting them off is grossly unfair," Ford wrote to Willison in September 1914. "Col. Hughes has done wonders. He has made mistakes. His most serious one was trying to do everything down to the smallest detail and not putting sufficient responsibility upon his men. No man could have done what Hughes attempted to do."[13]

But as the war took its toll on the country's resources, even the Tory press questioned Hughes's ability to continue to function in a sensitive and key cabinet position. In short, inefficient war management and the abuse of patronage during such a national crisis were unacceptable. Among his colleagues in government, Hughes became a convenient scapegoat, and soon his loyal friends in journalism exposed his (and his department's) ineptitude. Eventually, Borden, though he had appreciated Hughes's loyalty over the years, had had enough. In the fall of 1916, against the prime minister's direct orders, Hughes reorganized the Canadian army command in Britain without first obtaining government approval. This led to a confrontation with Borden and a demand from the prime minister that Hughes resign from the cabinet.[14]

The extremely sensitive and paranoid Sir Sam was humiliated by his dismissal and became, as Arthur Ford remembered, "a rather pathetic sight." Publicly he blamed Borden, probably the only person in the cabinet who had defended him for the past two years. In reporting on Hughes's downfall for the *News*, Ford noted the minister's accomplishments but criticized him for attacking Borden. Sir Sam, who saw conspiracies behind every door, took exception to the *News*'s interpretation of the events. Recalled Ford, "Sir Sam came into the press gallery and I was the subject of a fine round of abuse for my article ... I was cut off from the list of Sir Sam's friends. Afterwards he never more than growled at me if he passed me in the corridors or on the streets."[15]

The Liberal and independent press was less tolerant of Hughes's antics. They were happy to see him go. Daily editorials in such papers as the *Globe*, the *Toronto Star*, the *Manitoba Free Press,* and the *Ottawa Citizen* found fault with the government's handling of the war effort. After Hughes's departure, the continued presence in the cabinet of Robert Rogers remained a sore point.

In Winnipeg, John Dafoe, whose *Free Press* "leaders" were usually confined to general criticism as opposed to political sniping, was disappointed and disgusted with both Borden and Rogers. "It is quite clear that Sir Robert Borden, his colleagues, associates and confidants do not want a readjustment of the cabinet on either a coalition or a national service basis," he wrote to his friend Professor George Wrong of the University of Toronto in December 1916. "They want the present government to stay in office in order that it may continue to be what it has been ever since August, 1914: a government devoted first to the interests of itself and its friends and then to the cause of the great war. The government, as at present made up is constitutionally unable to rise above the levels of selfish political considerations. The chief source of poison is Rogers."[16]

In 1914 Robert Rogers looked older than his fifty years and certainly not like the "immoral bad boy" of Canadian politics Dafoe and others wrote about. He was of medium height, slightly overweight, with a head full of white hair and an aging, haggard face hidden by a thick, white moustache. First as minister of the interior and then, in 1914, as an officer in Public Works, Rogers was the Borden government's master of patronage. Not a shy or reserved man, he spoke his mind and attacked the Liberals at every opportunity. The war did nothing to lessen his animosity or partisan attitude. On the contrary, as historian John English points out, "Rogers refused to accept a party truce and had used the abundant patronage which the war created to revivify the listless Conservative organization."[17] As with Hughes, past mistakes and his refusal to accept that the old ways of politics no longer worked led to his downfall. But Rogers did not give up without a fight. His long battle with the *Ottawa Citizen* was a case in point.

The *Citizen* was established as a Conservative organ in 1874, though it did not become a prominent paper until it was taken over in 1897 by William Southam, publisher of the Tory *Hamilton Spectator*. Southam's two sons, Wilson and Harry, took control of the *Citizen* and remained committed to Borden and the Conservatives through the election of 1911, despite their personal belief in reciprocity. Within two years, further differences over economic policy with both the federal and Ontario Conservative governments forced the *Citizen* to declare itself an independent newspaper. The Tories responded by severely reducing the *Citizen*'s federal patronage dividend.[18]

Like many other English-language newspapers, the *Citizen* initially rallied around the Borden government during the opening months of the war. While Southam papers in Hamilton, Edmonton (the *Journal*), and Calgary (the *Herald*) faithfully toed the Tory line, the independent *Citizen* analyzed each issue on its own merits. Its editor, Charles Bowman, had little patience for party hacks like Sam Hughes and Robert Rogers.

One evening in May 1916, a few months before Hughes's resignation, Bowman was invited to the office of Frank Carvell, a Liberal MP from New Brunswick. There he was handed a copy of a confidential letter, dated February 1916, from Gen. Edwin A.H. Alderson, then the commander of the Canadian troops in England. Carvell had cut off the name of the person the letter had been sent to (this had been Gen. Willoughby Gwatkin, chief of the General Staff in Canada). (It was Arthur Ford's opinion that Carvell had obtained the letter from Lord Richard Neville on the staff of the governor general.) Alderson, no fan of Hughes, listed for Gwatkin (at Gwatkin's request) the numerous deficiencies of the Ross rifle used by Canadian soldiers on the orders of the minister of militia. Hughes was predictably outraged when he learned of Alderson's attempt to undermine his rifle, suggesting to the general that some of the points raised "are so absolutely absurd and ridiculous that no one excepting a novice ... would be found seriously advancing them."[19]

In fact, the Ross rifle was superb in target practice and as a sniper weapon, but nearly useless in the heat of battle in the mud-filled trenches of France. Canadian soldiers literally threw their Rosses away and picked up the superior Lee-Enfields from the arms of their dead British comrades.[20] By July 1915 the Canadian First Division, over the objection of Sam Hughes, had quietly and happily switched from the Ross to the Lee-Enfield.

Rumours and negative comments about the Ross continued to circulate in Ottawa for the next year and half. On May 13, 1916, Borden cabled Field Marshall Sir Douglas Haig, British commander-in-chief, asking for a full report on the Canadian-made rifle. Three days later, Bowman ran the critical story of the Ross rifle on the *Citizen*'s front page, quoting from Alderson's damaging letter. Members of the government and military were understandably angry. As a result of the terrible fire a few months earlier that had destroyed the Centre Block and the House of Commons, Parliament had moved across the street to the Victoria Memorial Museum. It had been a difficult and tiring session and the exposé on the Ross caused a minor furor.

In the Commons debate that took place in the late afternoon of May 17, an aggravated Prime Minister Borden questioned the *Citizen*'s patriotism for publishing such a story in the midst of a war. Later, after consulting with Hughes, he denied that the government had ever received an "official letter of that character." (Since Hughes had not only read Alderson's February letter but had also replied to it, he was clearly misleading the prime minister.)

It was Robert Rogers's turn next. As one of Bowman's targets for the last three years, he did not hold the *Citizen* in high regard. "I am not surprised that that paper would be guilty of publishing this letter, or anything else by which they could hope to create excitement," he charged. Rogers further suggested that the culprit responsible for giving the letter to the *Citizen* should be thrown in the "tower of this building." The Liberals delighted in pointing out to the minister that the tower had burned down and that the museum did not have one. "I will promise ... to provide a suitable tower for the individual who wrote that letter," Rogers countered.[21]

Over the next week, newspapers across the Dominion reprinted the *Citizen*'s story. By early June, once Sir Douglas Haig had verified the problems and unpopularity of the Ross, the order was given for the replacement of the Ross by the Lee-Enfields for the Second and Third Canadian divisions. It is more than likely that the adverse fall-out from the *Citizen*'s article hastened this major decision.[22]

Robert Rogers continued to be the *Ottawa Citizen*'s favourite target. A year earlier, in the spring of 1915, his reputation had been tainted by his link to the scandal-ridden government of Sir Rodmond Roblin in Manitoba, which had resigned in disgrace. Once the provincial Liberals under T.C. Norris were in power, further investigations revealed in January 1917 that Rogers may have been tied to a kickback and fraud scheme in the construction of the Manitoba Agricultural College. (An independent federal inquiry appointed at Rogers's request reviewed the findings of the Manitoba Commission and in July 1917 cleared Rogers of any wrongdoing.)

The *Citizen* followed events in Manitoba closely. "Hon. Robert Rogers Found Guilty," declared an editorial on February 1. Its message was clear: Rogers must resign. More of the same followed throughout the week and the battle lines were drawn. In defending himself against "that petty little sheet," as he labelled the *Citizen*, Rogers implied that his department's refusal in 1914 to purchase a piece of property owned by the Southams in Montreal for a new post office was the real reason for the *Citizen*'s assault on his character. In fact, the evidence suggests that Rogers had told the Southams at the time the deal was being negotiated that "a more sympathetic attitude on the *Citizen*'s part" would result in the sale of the land, a title for William Southam, the family's patriarch, and senatorships for his sons.[23]

Not surprisingly, the *Citizen* denied Rogers's allegations and demanded an official investigation. In Hamilton, the *Spectator,* still loyal to the Tories, carried an objective report of the Ottawa paper's row with Rogers. Privately, William Southam was concerned enough to write Borden on February 9 reaffirming the *Spectator*'s devotion to the Conservative Party. "But it is a great strain upon our fidelity," he added, "to find one of your ministers, the Hon. Robert Rogers, without the slightest basis in fact, imputing unworthy motives to the *Ottawa Citizen* and the Southam family." Borden, in the interests of cabinet solidarity and loyalty, stood by his beleaguered colleague, noting that Rogers and the government "have been subjected to a great deal of attack and misrepresentation from the *Citizen* for more than three years." He hoped the *Spectator* would remain committed to the party, but guaranteed that the government would continue to defend itself against abusive and unfair press criticism.[24]

The Southams' two Alberta papers, the *Calgary Herald* and the *Edmonton Journal,* joined the *Citizen* in condemning Rogers but did not declare their independence. The *Spectator* in Hamilton stayed away from the controversy. In any event, Rogers resigned from the cabinet in August 1917 over Borden's plans for a coalition government.

His battles with the *Citizen* and other papers were a sign that things were changing in Canadian journalism. Certainly the war had made Rogers's partisan style unpalatable, but it was more than that. Lifelong Tories like William Southam, who placed political loyalty first and their businesses and families second, were a dying breed. A new generation of newspaper publishers was taking over. This new breed did not feel obliged to obey the parties' dictates as their fathers had. More and more, their support was not automatic but depended on issues, personalities, and business decisions.

Even more significant in the sphere of political news reporting was the creation of the Canadian Press in 1917. Regional wire services had been in operation since the 1890s, but Canadian papers had had to rely on larger American outfits for their foreign news. The rates were high and the stories deficient in Canadian content. In Winnipeg, for instance, local papers found it less expensive to obtain the details of a murder in Kentucky than the results of an election in Toronto.[25]

The first step towards a national service occurred in 1910 with the creation of Canadian Press Ltd., a newspaper cooperative that held the rights to the American Press wire, but there was as yet no link across the Dominion. The major obstacle was money. In 1917, the Borden government agreed to grant CP an annual $50,000 subsidy (this handout lasted until 1924, when it was refused on principle) to bridge the telegraph-wire gaps between Saint John and Montreal, Ottawa and Winnipeg, and Calgary and Vancouver. Eventually 6,000 miles of wire were in operation twenty-four hours a day.

For the first time, the proceedings of Parliament were covered in a non-partisan way. As Arthur Ford put it, the country "obtained a fair picture of what was going on at Ottawa." It was Ford's opinion "that the credit for the development of independent political thinking in Canada and the breaking down of party lines ... must largely go to the Canadian Press." Initially, however, some correspondents resented CP for stealing their jobs. Only later did they realize that CP freed them from the mundane chore of having to take Hansard down verbatim and allowed them to pursue other behind-the-scene stories. CP also paved the way for more political commentary and analysis.[26]

The new wire service had a great deal to cover in 1917, surely the most difficult year of Borden's prime ministership. To use the words of historian Ramsay Cook, 1917 was a year of "cultural tension and political upheaval." Borden's announcement in Parliament on May 18 that his government planned to introduce conscription – compulsory military service – and Laurier's subsequent refusal to support it in a coalition government eventually split the country apart, pitting French against English. On both sides, newspapers were employed as effective weapons in a war of propaganda leading up to the December 1917 federal election.

The two big English papers in Montreal, the *Gazette* and Hugh Graham's *Star*, supported conscription without reservations. The French press was initially divided. The government's two supporters, *L'Evenément* in Quebec City and *La Patrie* in Montreal, were hardly enthusiastic but understood the seriousness of the military situation and stood by Borden's decision for about a month. *La Patrie* in particular paid a price for its solidarity with the Tories. During the conscription riots in Montreal on May 24, its office windows were smashed (as were those at *L'Evenément*) and someone took a potshot at editor Louis-Joseph Tarte. *La Patrie*'s daily circulation dropped by at least 10,000, more than half its total. Later, in the fall, Tarte attempted to save his journal by favouring a conscription referendum. Albert Sévigny, one of the few French Canadian Conservatives who remained in Borden's cabinet, was so angry with Tarte for his change of heart that he wanted to throw him out of the party.[27]

Like Tarte, most Quebec editors wanted a referendum on conscription. Nationalist Henri Bourassa at *Le Devoir* remained silent on the issue for ten days. Then, in a series of brilliant articles during the week of May 28, he outlined his anti-conscriptionist philosophy, in which he also called for a referendum before the government could implement its policy. "Canada has furnished all the man-power she can for this war without grave danger to her own existence and that of her Allies," he wrote. He condemned both Borden and Laurier for going back on their promises of January 1916 that there would be no conscription, and warned that "everything in the application of compulsory service – however impartial it may appear to be – will tend to irritate the French Canadians, and generally all Canadians who are Canadians before all."[28] Such bold statements merely served to further alienate the English Canadian press, which generally accepted Borden's call for conscription. This included the major Liberal papers: the *Globe* and *Star* in Toronto and the *Manitoba Free Press* in Winnipeg.

In Ottawa, events moved quickly after Borden revealed his plans for conscription. Protracted negotiations with Laurier for a coalition government followed in the last week of May and first week of June. The crafty Liberal leader extracted a deal for a wartime election, but in view of his personal objection to conscription and the strength of opposition to it in Quebec, he ultimately rejected the prime minister's invitation.

But the coalition idea was not dead yet. English Canadian Liberals led by Newton Rowell, the leader of the party in Ontario, Frank Carvell, Clifford

Sifton, his *Free Press* editor John Dafoe, and *Toronto Star* owner Joe
Atkinson would not accept Laurier's decision. It took four months and rounds
of closed-door meetings but a Borden-led Union government was finally
announced on October 12, with a dozen Conservative ministers, nine Liberals,
and one labour. Rowell was the president of the Privy Council, but "most of
the senior portfolios, including finance, railways and canals, and trade and
commerce, continued to be held by Tories."[29]

That a coalition deal was made at all is amazing enough. There were
strong objections in both parties. Rogers and his small band of Tory parti-
sans, as well as large groups of English Liberals in Ontario and the West too
loyal to break with Laurier, were unwilling to accept such dramatic political
change.[30] The press was no different. With the exception of the *Manitoba
Free Press* and to a lesser extent the *Toronto Star,* which strongly supported
coalition, most editorials continued along partisan lines. In late June, for
example, as Borden and Rowell were coming together, the *Globe* and the
Star did not hesitate both to attack the prime minister and to praise Rowell
for his patriotic efforts. As well, through the summer of 1917 the *Globe* and
other Liberal papers repeatedly went after Robert Rogers for his supposed
role in a kickback scheme in the Manitoba Legislative Buildings scandal.*
The Liberals, conscriptionist or not, Rogers complained to Borden in
August just prior to his resignation from the cabinet, "have a strong press
through which they are promoting a most cowardly, malevolent campaign. I
am often made the target for many of their attacks."[31]

On July 26 editors of the major Liberal newspapers met in Toronto to
discuss Rowell's bid to form a Union government. After much discussion
the journalists passed a resolution supporting the war effort, the conscription
of men and money, and a coalition. They could not, however, resist taking a
cheap shot at the Tories: "Sir Robert Borden and his government have
proved themselves unequal to [the] tasks [of winning the war]. No other
purely party government at the present time could deal with them. A war
cabinet and government representing both parties and the strong forces of
the nation ... is therefore necessary." Such slurs on Borden's character
angered cabinet members who were already suspicious of the conscriptionist Liberals' real intentions, as well as Tory journalists like John Willison,
who used the columns of the *News* to trade insults with his Liberal rivals in
Toronto.[32]

---

*In May 1917 a provincial inquiry commission "declared that Rogers and Thomas Kelly, a
Manitoba contractor, had entered into 'a fraudulent conspiracy' to provide Conservative
campaign funds and to give Kelly a 'kickback' from the provincial treasury. Poor Kelly went
to jail; Rogers remained minister of public works." (English, *The Decline of Politics,* 147)

It was clear even to those who accepted the coalition that it was a temporary wartime measure. Clifford Sifton, a key backer of the arrangement, cautioned John Dafoe about pledging his enthusiastic allegiance to Borden: "The possibilities of the future hardly include the idea that the *Free Press* can support a party dominated by the Conservatives for any length of time and it might be awkward for you to feel that you had discussed matters too fully with the enemy."[33]

While Dafoe heeded the practical advice of his publisher, he became the voice of the Liberal Unionist forces in October 1917. (Sifton himself was one of Borden's key campaign advisers). During the bitter two-month election campaign that followed the formation of the Union government, the *Free Press* was unwavering in its commitment to Borden, conscription, and the war. In Dafoe's eyes, Laurier and the remaining Liberals by his side were the manipulated victims of Bourassa and the Quebec nationalists. "Shall Quebec, which will neither fight nor pay, rule?" the *Free Press* asked on December 11. For Dafoe the old rules of politics no longer applied; the choice, as he saw it, was between supporting a party determined to win the war and one that was not.[34]

Similar views were echoed in most other English newspapers, as journalists at the Liberal *Globe* and Conservative *News* in Toronto found themselves, probably for the first time, on the same side of a political battle. "English-speaking Liberals cannot afford to vote and work for a party in which they can be no more than a tail to the Quebec Nationalist kite," declared the *Globe* on December 4. Ten days later the *News* published a map of Canada with Quebec in black entitled "The Foul Blot on Canada." Worse still was the *Mail and Empire*'s depiction of Laurier and the German Kaiser as partners in crime.[35]

Partisanship had not disappeared – in fact, in many regions Liberal and Conservative Union candidates, workers, and reporters expressed contempt for one another – but it did take a break in the late fall of 1917, when journalists and politicians worked side by side, to guarantee a Union victory. John Willison was the Unionist publicity director, responsible for anti-Quebec and anti-Laurier propaganda as well as the coordination of a speakers' bureau. Meanwhile, to ensure that the soldiers overseas would vote correctly (as allowed for in the Military Voters' Act, a soldier could assign his vote to any constituency he wanted), a devoted group of prominent Liberal journalists led by Dafoe, Joe Atkinson, and the *Globe*'s Stewart Lyon dispatched cables to Europe in early December urging the soldiers to support the Union cause. They need not have worried, as the army and Union political workers made sure the military votes counted in the right constituencies.[36]

In Quebec, where conscription was not acceptable, the situation was serious. Political meetings were stormy to the point of violence. With the exception of *L'Evenément* (and *La Patrie* to a lesser degree), the French press, including Bourassa's *Le Devoir*, stood solidly behind Laurier and was severely critical of the few lonely Unionist French Canadians. In mid-November, a speech given by Albert Sévigny (who was dubbed "Judas" by francophone editorial writers) was interrupted by gunshots and smashing windows. He was burned in effigy in Montreal and, along with Joseph Barnard of *L'Evenément* and a Union candidate, threatened with lynching.[37] The Conservative press in Ontario published each episode in great detail as evidence of a Quebec conspiracy.

Borden took nothing for granted and believed, quite wrongly, that Bourassa was capable of hurting him outside of Quebec. He was extremely concerned about articles appearing in *Le Devoir* in early November that questioned England's integrity and stated that four million British men of military age were being kept in the factories to evade military service. Were these untrue reports being communicated in the English press, he asked his cabinet? It was important for Borden that they were, since in his view it was impossible for the government to have a "reasonable fair chance ... if the most inflammatory appeal can be made throughout Quebec without the English electorate knowing the nature of such appeals." In a memo of November 13 to George Foster, Charles Doherty, and John Reid, Borden offered this interpretation of political events: "Considering that Laurier and Bourassa have openly announced an alliance ... and considering that Bourassa is the real although not the ostensible leader in that alliance, it is absolutely criminal to permit these appeals to be made in Quebec without exposure thereof in every English-speaking paper from the Atlantic to the Pacific."[38] Less than a week later, Foster reported back to Borden that a survey of Bourassa's articles was under way presumably for dissemination to Union editors.

Such precautions and political manoeuvring were not necessary. The results on December 17 were as Union strategists had predicted: 153 Union and 82 Liberal, 62 of which were from Quebec. Disregarding the dangerous cultural split, the English press proclaimed a great victory for the country and the war effort; *Le Devoir* and other francophone papers hailed French Canadian nationalism.

At first, in the midst of a victory, the fact that the House was divided along linguistic and cultural lines did not disturb Borden. But later in the new year, after J.N. Francoeur in the Quebec National Assembly raised the possibility of Quebec seceding from Confederation (Francoeur's motion was discussed but eventually withdrawn), Borden better understood the seriousness of the issue. Rightly concerned that the Quebec debate on separation would be wrongly interpreted by the English journalists, he sent strong requests through MPs connected to newspapers asking editors not to make too much of Francoeur's motion.[39]

In the spring of 1918 further violence and rioting against conscription broke out in Quebec. A demonstration in Quebec City at the end of March resulted in four deaths and numerous wounded. The army had to be called in to restore order. Again Borden was concerned that these events not be blown out of proportion. A confidential memo was sent out to the English press on May 3. "There is the best reason for believing that a remarkable change of sentiment is developing in the province of Quebec in respect of the attitude of that province towards the war," Borden told the journalists. "The recent drastic change in the Military Service Act (the cancelling of exemptions) has been received in excellent spirit by the French-Canadian population." The response among the anglophone editors was very positive.[40]

Nevertheless, Union non-partisanship was but an illusion. On the long list of Ontario newspapers that received Borden's memo of May 3, for example, a "C" for Conservative or "L" for Liberal was noted beside the name of each paper from Aylmer to Woodstock. "Liberal Unionists held separate caucuses, maintained Liberal friendships, and thought themselves distinct."[41] Such distrust in the Union cabinet, coupled with Borden's lengthy absences in Europe and the general social and economic problems resulting from the war, slowly destroyed the government.

Newton Rowell, the Ontario Liberal leader and a member of the Union government, initially attempted to serve as a rallying point, but he was highly unpopular with Tories and Grits alike.[42] Rowell grasped that despite the non-partisan appeal that had given the Union administration its mandate, its survival depended, to a certain degree, on its behaving as a normal partisan government. But the war had changed the way things were done. Federal patronage, the backbone of the system, was not so readily dispensed; the reform (or rather sanitizing) of the civil service made sure of that. As well, for about a year after the election, the press of both parties toned down their partisan reporting.

Political control, however, was still possible. Rowell, like Clifford Sifton, understood the value of a good newspaper and firmly believed that the press could be utilized to shape public opinion.[43] Thus, it was Rowell who arranged for John Dafoe to join Borden in Europe in November 1918 so that he might write about the prime minister's accomplishments at the Peace Conference. This was not the assignment of an independent journalist covering a prime minister's overseas trip; on the contrary, Dafoe was an employee of and answerable to the Department of Public Information.

Borden was delighted. He had long considered Dafoe "a very able man" and a superior journalist. "As a writer [he] has no equal," Borden told Rowell. As his colleagues would testify to, Rowell was more difficult to please. He cabled Borden in February 1919 that Dafoe's stories, though good, were not "sensational" enough to compete with the many about President Woodrow Wilson and the American delegation's achievements carried in Canadian papers. Rowell urged Borden to tell Dafoe to send news features "which will put Canada more fully on the map." There is no evidence that the prime minister lectured the *Free Press* editor about his journalism; he did, however, seek Dafoe's advice on foreign affairs issues, as the two men were in agreement on the new autonomous role Canada would play in the Empire.[44]

Other members of the Liberal press were not as kind as Dafoe. As the Unionist bonds broke down in Ottawa, so did the bonds among editors at the *Globe* and *Star*. Never totally comfortable with the limitations placed on them by the wartime coalition, Grit journalists had, by the summer of 1919, resumed their attack on Borden and his Tory friends. Commenting on the weak Unionist leadership, the *Globe* noted rather caustically on July 24: "There is probably not a single member of Sir Robert Borden's government who will be among the political leaders of Canada fifteen years from now." The war was over, Laurier was dead, and a new Liberal leader was about to be chosen. Finance Minister Thomas White had recently retired, Thomas Crerar from the West had resigned from the cabinet because of a dispute over the high tariff, and millions had been spent nationalizing the Canadian Northern and Grand Trunk railways. Borden was a tired old man. The *Globe*'s support of the Union administration and conscription in 1917 was never intended to be permanent, and the paper had never advocated the destruction of the Liberal Party. In its view, the time had come for another election.[45]

The *Globe* would have to wait two years for its election. In the interim, William Lyon Mackenzie King became the new Liberal leader in August 1919, and a year later, following Borden's retirement, Arthur Meighen was chosen to be the new prime minister, head of a divided Tory party. He faced problems on all fronts. Labour, unhappy with the quashing of the Winnipeg General Strike in May 1919, was reorganizing. Canadian farmers, spurred on by the victory of E.C. Drury in the Ontario provincial election in October, were channelling economic discontent into concerted political action. Many members of the business community, traditional Tory supporters, were disheartened with the government's public ownership of railways. And it would take Quebec more than forty years to forgive the federal Tories for conscription.

In 1920 it was easier for Liberal newspapers, as it was for Mackenzie King, to respond to the changing political climate. The Tory press, on the other hand, whose loyalties remained with Borden, did not rush to defend the party's new leader. Indeed, Arthur Meighen soon discovered that he was alone in Ottawa, without a party press he could count on.

The style of political journalism had changed as well. This significant shift had started with John Willison in the Laurier era and grew stronger during the Borden years, as reflected in the career of John Dafoe. It was a question of who had the final word. Dafoe was highly partisan and supportive of the Liberals for the remainder of his long, distinguished career, yet on his own (and his employer's, Clifford Sifton's) terms. By the end of the First World War, publishing slanted news supplied by politicians was no longer acceptable journalistic practice. Those following Borden as prime minister would have to devise more subtle ways of controlling and manipulating the public.

CHAPTER SEVEN

The Undependable
Party Press

*It must be admitted that the press is the main vehicle of
prejudices. It is a trite saying that the press is today a great
power. It might be said that it is* the *great power, the
mightiest, most constant and efficient.*

Arthur Meighen,
"The Power of the Press," undated speech

B y the beginning of the 1920s, the newspaper business had changed, a
result of the technological revolution. Publishers could print more
newspapers in a shorter amount of time; photographs were transmitted over
a far-reaching wire service that linked the Dominion from sea to sea and the
Old World with the New; and as the educated population increased in
Canada, so too did the demand for newspapers. But just as in George
Brown's day at the outset of industrial change, technological improvement
had its price. Costs of paper, ink, postage, and labour doubled (newsprint
per ton, for example, rose from $76 in 1918 to $130 in 1920). Publishers,
who in the past had found most of the money they required from government patronage, political parties, and their followers, now depended more
than ever on advertising dollars from such enterprises as Eaton's and
Simpson's department stores. The emergence of professional advertising
agencies as "middlemen" between newspapers and businesses entrenched
this new system of dependency further. (In 1892, advertising represented 63
percent, or $18,703, of the *Ottawa Journal*'s total revenue of $29,688 compared to 84 percent, or $481,000, of a total revenue of $574,000 in 1920).[1]

There was no mystery to attracting profitable and steady advertising;
the greater a paper's circulation, the greater the revenue from advertising.
There was also no secret to increasing circulation: produce a newspaper that
appealed to a wide, diverse readership. "A newspaper today," noted the
Kingston *Standard* on November 20, 1924, "while still loyal to party is
essentially and first of all a business institution ... If a newspaper were to
depend merely on party loyalty and a party following it would starve to

death. Its chief dependence must be upon itself, backed by an ability to produce a good readable daily paper."

From the perspective of the Liberals and Conservatives, these facts of journalism proved disastrous. In small towns across the country and even in some cities, it no longer was possible to maintain two party papers. The result was amalgamations and the suspension of numerous operations. From 1914 to 1922, 28 daily newspapers died and 10 disappeared through amalgamations, leaving 125 dailies in existence. Of those that were gone, the most notable were the Liberal *Ottawa Free Press,* which merged with the *Ottawa Journal* in 1916; the *Winnipeg Telegram,* the organ of Tory Robert Rogers, which folded in 1920; Billy Maclean's Toronto *World;* and the Conservative Toronto *News.* Moreover, by 1926, from a total of twenty-five Ontario cities, only five had more than one daily newspaper, and out of twenty-one cities with populations under 50,000, only one city, Belleville, had more than one daily.[2]

Beyond this, the 1920s witnessed the birth of two long-term and significant developments in the history of the Canadian press: the "hyphenated" newspaper and the concentration of ownership. Adherence to the bottom line and an acceptance of commercial priorities created the *Quebec Chronicle-Telegraph,* the Saint John *Telegraph-Journal,* the Regina *Leader-Post* and the *Kingston Whig-Standard.* The realities of the newspaper business, in many cases, forced the merger of two extremely partisan organs, eventually leading to the disappearance of a particular political point of view. In Kingston, for example, the viewpoint of the Tories, preached by the *Standard* for decades, lost its voice.

It was inevitable, given the financial struggle, that control of the Dominion's newspapers would pass into the hands of corporate families like the Southams and the Siftons and to an elite group of press barons led by Lord Atholstan (Hugh Graham), the larger-than-life publisher of the *Montreal Star.* In this, Canada followed the pattern in Britain, where the press was dominated by three wealthy brothers, Lord Northcliffe, Lord Rothermere, and Sir Lester Harmsworth, and in the United States, where the Scripps and Hearst newspaper empires were consolidating and expanding their press holdings.[3]

By the summer of 1920 William Southam and Sons was capitalized at $5 million, five times its worth in 1904. Throughout the decade, William Southam, a kindly man who could not fire any employee, and his five enterprising sons, Wilson, Fred, Richard, Harry, and William Jr., were on the move, buying up papers and building a publishing empire that in 1929 recorded a net profit of $735,000, equivalent to at least $5 million in 1990s dollars. (Twenty years later the company made a profit of $1.2 million.) In 1920 the Southams already owned the *Hamilton Spectator* and the *Ottawa*

Citizen and had a controlling interest in the *Calgary Herald* and the *Edmonton Journal.* That year they added the *Winnipeg Tribune* to their stable, paying $50,000 cash and giving $190,000 in preferred stock to the paper's former owner, R.L. Richardson. Later that same year the company also acquired the remaining assets of the *Winnipeg Telegram* for $100,000, and the battle between the *Tribune* and John Dafoe's *Free Press* began in earnest. The Southams conquered the Vancouver market in 1923 with the purchase of the *Daily Province,* a profitable venture owned by Walter Nichol (later lieutenant-governor of B.C.) for about $2 million.[4]

One of the secrets of the Southams' success was that they gave their editors a great deal of independence. Except for the *Citizen,* which supported the agrarian Progressive Party during the twenties, the other papers more or less followed Arthur Meighen and the Tories. But as Meighen discovered, there were no guarantees. The Southam editors had their own interests and did not always agree with the Conservative agenda. *Manitoba Free Press* editor Dafoe studied the six Southam newspapers' editorials for six weeks in 1924 to determine if a common editorial policy existed. He found six quite different papers, each shaped by the strong personalty of its editor.[5] This "go as you please" attitude was evident as well in the Southam papers' election campaign coverage in 1925 and 1926.

Under the right management, the newspaper business could be quite lucrative. Here was an enterprise, free of government control, that produced a product with an ever-increasing demand and brought in a sizable return on investments. Is there any wonder that by the 1930s publishing was the business of choice for Canada's growing industrial elite?[6] It was not only the money that made owning a newspaper so attractive; it was (and still is) the power and influence that went with it. Lord Atholstan, Clifford Sifton, William Southam, William Jaffray, Izaak Walton Killam, and Joseph Atkinson in the 1920s and George McCullagh, J.W. McConnell, Max Bell, Lord Thomson, and Conrad Black in later years were all entrepreneurs whose tremendous impact on Canadian affairs stemmed, though to different degrees, from their control of the press. Some were more opinionated than others. By the 1920s Sifton generally bowed to the intelligence of his editor, John Dafoe (the two men held similar political views on most issues), and Izaak Killam, who purchased the Toronto *Mail and Empire* in 1927, remained in the background (he was just as conservative as the newspaper's editors), while Joseph Atkinson guided the editorial policies of the *Toronto Star* no less than Lord Atholstan in Montreal.

Newspaper publishers and editors in the 1920s wrestled with their dual responsibilities: what they owed to the public and what they owed to themselves and their coffers. "A newspaper must exist if it is to do any good of any kind," noted an editorial in the *Ottawa Journal* in June 1922. "A news-

Parliamentary Press Gallery, 1880. *Back row, left to right:* John T. Hawke (Toronto *Globe*), A. Horton (*Globe*), J.E.B. McCready (Saint John *Telegraph*), H. Pingle (Dominion Telegraph Co.), George Johnston (Halifax *Herald*), H. Higham (Montreal Telegraph Co.), and George Eyvel (Sarnia *Observer*). *Front row, left to right:* Arthur Wallis (Toronto *Mail*), A.C. Campbell (*Globe*), G.B. Bradley (*Mail*), W.T.R. Preston (London *Advertiser*), T.H. Preston (*Ottawa Free Press*), and E.J. Duggan (Montreal *Gazette*).

National Archives of Canada, C4515

Leading journalists of 1884: William Cameron (London *Advertiser*), Edward J.B.
Pense (*Daily British Whig*, Kingston), Hugh Graham (*Montreal Daily Star*),
E.E. Sheppard (*Toronto Morning News*), Thomas White (*Montreal Gazette*),
John Cameron (Toronto *Globe*), John Dougall (Montreal *Daily Witness*),
A.T. Freed (*Hamilton Spectator*), W.F. Luxton (*Manitoba Free Press*),
Goldwin Smith (*The Week,* Toronto), Honoré Beaugrand (*La Patrie*),
and John Ross Robertson (*Toronto Evening Telegram*).

Martin Griffin, journalist and
parliamentary librarian and friend
to John A. Macdonald.

National Archives of Canada, C70581

Sir John A. Macdonald, prime
minister of Canada 1867–73
and 1878–91.

Provincial Archives of Manitoba

George Brown, father of
Confederation, founder and editor
of the Toronto *Globe*.

Archives of Ontario, S16268

Edward Farrer, famed Toronto
journalist of the 1880s and 1890s.

National Archives of Canada, C4691

Ernest Pacaud, editor of *L'Électeur* in the 1880s and a close confidant of Wilfrid Laurier's.

National Archives of Canada, C15875

John Dafoe, the great editor of the *Winnipeg Free Press,* as a young newsman on Parliament Hill in the 1880s.

National Archives of Canada, PA 25579

Clifford Sifton, Laurier's minister of the interior, 1897–1905, and publisher of the *Winnipeg Free Press.*

Provincial Archives of Manitoba

Reverend J.A. Macdonald, successor to John Willison as editor of the Toronto *Globe,* 1903.

Archives of Ontario, Acc 6355 S9547A

Sir John Willison, editor of the
Toronto *Globe* in the 1890s and later
the editor of the Toronto *News*.

Archives of Ontario, S831

Sir Robert Borden, prime minister
of Canada from 1911 to 1920.

Archives of Ontario, 6355 S9044

Parliamentary press gallery at Montmorency Falls, Quebec, May 11, 1906.

Archives of Ontario, Acc 6355 S9041

The men of the *Winnipeg Free Press,* late 1930s. *Left to right:* Victor Sifton (publisher, seated), Grant Dexter (Ottawa correspondent), John Dafoe (editor, seated), and George Ferguson (managing editor).

Prime Minister R.B. Bennett, 1935. Note the radio microphone to the left.

Grant Dexter of the *Winnipeg Free Press,* c. 1940s.

Prime Minister William Lyon Mackenzie King in 1935.

Journalist and author Bruce Hutchison, in 1952, a friend to prime ministers King, St. Laurent, and Pearson.

Prime Minister Lester Pearson at the swearing in of three cabinet members,
Pierre Trudeau, John Turner, and Jean Chrétien.

National Archives of Canada, PA 117107

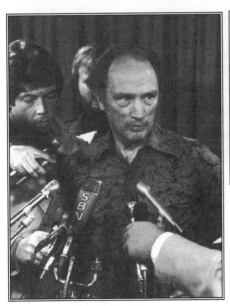

The May 13, 1979, television debate
between Ed Broadbent,
Pierre Trudeau, and Joe Clark.

National Archives of Canada, PA 142623

Prime Minister Pierre Trudeau
with reporters.

National Archives of Canada, PA 175947

Prime Minister John Diefenbaker and members of the press gallery in 1957, a relatively happy time. *Left to right:* Norman Campbell (*Ottawa Citizen*), James McCook (*Ottawa Journal*), Derek Bedson (clerk of the Privy Council), John Diefenbaker, Victor Mackie (*Winnipeg Free Press*), writer Peter Stursburg, Clark Davey (*Globe and Mail*), Tim Creery (*Montreal Gazette*), George Bain (columnist, *Globe and Mail*), Eugene Griffin (*Chicago Tribune*), and Maurice Jefferies (*Windsor Star*).

Prime Minister Brian Mulroney in a scrum on Parliament Hill, 1989.

paper business is a commercial attempt primarily, just as a butcher shop or a grocery ... store. It has to live as a business before it can do any good as an educator or an apostle. In short, newspaper publishers have to look out for number one, and they have a right to look out for number one in an honourable way ... before they look out for the public." Thus, high regard had to be given to space allocation and to the type of stories the paper printed.

At the same time, the *Journal* suggested that a publisher "should conduct his newspaper as he would conduct himself personally as a gentleman, using that word in its highest sense." The aim of the paper was to publish impartial and fair news: "to promote good causes and public advantage" and to see that "honest and decent" editorials were written. Its duty to the public also included exposing, "even at the risk of loss or libel," injustice and corruption. Above all, "the publisher should not use his newspaper for mean or small-minded purposes."[7]

Admirable as the *Journal*'s message was, the facts told a different story. Contrary to general opinion, it was a myth that the relationship which existed between newspapermen and politicians in the years following the First World War constituted some sort of intimate and cosy "League of Gentlemen." True, in some cases publishers were as "honourable, high-minded, public-spirited and patriotic" as the *Ottawa Journal* described, but as both Meighen and King learned, the wealthy czars of Canada's newspapers could be as petty, partisan, selfish, and egotistical as the next man.

Depending on the point of view, Arthur Meighen was either the greatest political failure in Canadian history or, next to Laurier, the finest and most skilled prime minister to hold office. Much of this difference of opinion was a result of Meighen's determined and often obstinate personality. As historian Roger Graham, his biographer, put it, "Meighen was incapable of neutrality on any important issue and it was impossible to be neutral about him. One had to be with him or against him, because on every question he took his stand and defined it with unhesitating conviction."[8] Even more than Borden, Meighen, also a lawyer, did not understand that politics was often emotional and irrational, that people sometimes voted with their hearts and gut feelings rather than with their brains. Meighen was honest and unwavering in his policies, while his hated opponent King was a master of vagueness. And it is always easier to vote against something specific than for an undefined alternative.

Consider how the two leaders dealt with the protective tariff, the backbone of Canadian economics since John A. Macdonald introduced the National Policy in 1878. For Meighen, a tariff was the only policy that made sense for Canada in the postwar years and after. This he preached across the Dominion, in Ontario and Quebec where it was favoured, as well as on the

Prairies where it was resented as a symbol of eastern domination. It made no difference to westerners that Meighen supported "moderate protection" or that the duties the Tories advocated in 1921 were lower than those adopted by the Liberals in 1911. "Meighen and his party were so completely the creatures of the 'big interests' whose vast power was inimical to the welfare of the West," writes Graham, "that nothing Meighen proposed could be looked at without suspicion." Mackenzie King, on the other hand, was typically non-committal – "tariff reduction if necessary, but not necessarily protection."[9] In the three general elections held between 1921 and 1926, the Prairies mainly opted for the farmer Progressive Party of Thomas Crerar, formed in 1920, and the Liberals.

Meighen believed that the protective tariff would win back support in Quebec for the Tories. He was dreadfully mistaken. Though Meighen was not anti-French or an imperialist, as historical legend has it, he was also not willing to place Quebec's demands and unique view of Canada above all else (while he took French lessons he was never bilingual). His proudest political achievements were four pieces of legislation he had put together as a minister in Borden's cabinet: closure, conscription, the Wartime Elections Act, and the nationalization of the Canadian Northern and Grand Trunk railways. However, these feats haunted him in Quebec throughout his career. Among French-speaking Quebeckers, he was vilified as "the champion of conscription," an indictment that King and the Liberals played up for all it was worth.

In July 1920, when Prime Minister Meighen was introduced to the Dominion, French editorials were vicious. "Mr. Meighen typifies in his person and temper ... whatever Anglo-Saxon jingoism contains that is most brutal, exclusive and anti-Canadian," declared *Le Devoir.* "His name is coupled to the most arbitrary and hateful measures passed by the Tory-Unionist government during the war."[10]

The one Quebec group that should have welcomed Meighen, the English-speaking Montreal business community, rejected him as well. In fact, because of their disgust with the public ownership of railways and their belief that Meighen would never win over French Canada, the so-called Montreal tycoons – Lord Atholstan of the *Star,* Edward Beatty of the CPR, Robert Smeaton White of the *Montreal Gazette,* and Sir Herbert Holt, president of the Royal Bank of Canada – abused, scorned and maligned Meighen like no Canadian political leader before or since. Liberal victories in Quebec in the federal elections of 1921, 1925, and 1926 were never in doubt. The final result: Mackenzie King was prime minister for nearly twenty-two years; Arthur Meighen for twenty months.

Meighen was born in 1874 in a small town in southwestern Ontario. His upbringing was quite traditional for the times. Showing an aptitude for school, Meighen attended the University of Toronto during the early 1890s, majoring in mathematics. He had already proven to be a brilliant debator. After graduation he tried teaching in Ontario before deciding on law out west. His move to politics in 1908 was, like that of so many of the country's leaders, a natural career change. By 1913 young, serious, and intelligent Arthur Meighen was the solicitor general in the cabinet of Robert Borden. Four years later he was promoted to a more senior portfolio, becoming minister of the interior, and at the age of forty-three was in the prime minister's inner circle of advisers. Upon Borden's retirement in the summer of 1920, Meighen got his job by a process of elimination.*

There is no doubting Meighen's skill as a parliamentarian. In a time when it mattered what went on in the Commons, Meighen had no equal. "He was incomparably the greatest parliamentarian of my time, probably the greatest Canada has ever had," recalled his lifelong friend and supporter Eugene Forsey, who watched him perform with delight. "Never a note; never a written word in front of him; never a hesitation; never a repetition; every name, every date, every quotation impeccable, never at a loss; invincible with interrupters and hecklers; never ruled out of order," he added. "The speeches were masterpieces alike in matter, structure, and manner; classical in their flawless English, memorable in their phrasing."[11]

For almost a decade the main target of Meighen's witty, clever, and vitriolic language was Liberal leader William Lyon Mackenzie King. Not since the days of George Brown and John A. Macdonald had Ottawa witnessed such a hostile political feud. Journalist Alex Hume of the *Ottawa Citizen* remembered that there "was never anything to match Meighen's hatred for King. It was unbelievable. Meighen had command of ... English and laced it to King to no end, and King was palsied with fear in the face of Meighen's withering attacks." Within time, the feelings were very mutual; King's contempt for Meighen was "too great for words."[12]

Meighen's "relentless pursuit" of King was symptomatic of the one irrational flaw in his character. He was not an easy man to get to know, but among his cadre of loyal and devoted friends he was admired and respected. This included several of the key Conservative Ottawa correspondents: Arthur Ford, who left his post in the gallery with the Toronto *News* in 1920

---

*Because of the unusual nature of the Union administration, members of the caucus – about 190 MPs and senators – submitted their individual choices to Borden, who ranked and selected the candidate. Thomas White was actually his first choice, but poor health prevented him from accepting. Borden convinced his chief ministers to accept Meighen. Mackenzie King, on the other hand, was elected at a Liberal convention in August 1919. He defeated W.S. Fielding in a secret vote. (Brown, *Borden,* vol. 2, 172, 181–84)

to become the editor of the *London Free Press;* Tom Blacklock, who worked for the *Toronto Telegram* and *Montreal Gazette,* among other papers; and the *Ottawa Journal*'s Grattan O'Leary. During his first term as prime minister between August 1920 and December 1921 and after, all three men, at Meighen's invitation, acted as discreet political advisers.

O'Leary was an especially close confidant. A legend in the gallery, O'Leary with his Irish background and jet-black hair resembled a leprechaun. He was the classic newspaperman, drinking scotch and playing the horses and poker (he was luckier at the latter than the former). He sat at his desk in the offices of the *Ottawa Journal* wearing a vest, a cigarette dangling from his mouth. Using two tobacco-stained fingers, he banged out on his old typewriter elegant but "explosive" editorials and columns.[13]

Born in the Gaspé, Quebec, in 1889, O'Leary first worked as a reporter in Saint John before joining the *Journal* in 1910 at age twenty-one. Its revered owner, P.D. Ross, paid his young reporter $17 dollars a week. Before long, O'Leary was in the gallery and writing the Conservative paper's political editorials. At the height of his career during the thirties, forties, and fifties, O'Leary was a news machine. His daily production included two or three *Journal* editorials, stories on Canada for the *Times* in London, a political column for *Maclean's*, and a short radio commentary that started in 1927.[14]

O'Leary belonged to an age when journalists made no attempt to hide their politics. "I am a party man. I am a partisan. I am a Conservative without prefix or qualification," he once said. Still, this did not mean he ignored his Grit colleagues in the gallery. (He was very close, for example, to Grant Dexter, his partner in his freelance radio work and the correspondent for the *Manitoba Free Press,* the great Liberal organ of western Canada. There is evidence that the two exchanged confidential information on more than one occasion, an indication that the partisan wall built in the days of Martin Griffin and Paul Bilkey was coming down.)[15] Nor did it mean he accepted everything the Tories did with open arms. Soon after Meighen became prime minister, O'Leary wrote a critical article in *Maclean's* arguing that the Conservative Party was "becoming divorced from its own supporters." Despite the anger of some Tories over the piece, Meighen accepted the comments and went out of his way to make O'Leary feel special.[16] It was kind treatment such as this that endeared Meighen to O'Leary and led to their lifelong friendship.* The Conservative leader cajoled O'Leary into running as a Tory candidate in the Gaspé in the 1925 election, but this foray into the political arena was unsuccessful.

---

*The friendship had its beginnings in 1912. That year, O'Leary wrote an article about Meighen in the *Canadian Magazine* entitled "The White Hope of the Conservative Party." O'Leary also wrote the introduction to Meighen's collection of speeches, *Unrevised and*

In June 1921 O'Leary accompanied Meighen to London for a major conference on imperial issues, most notably the question of renewing a treaty with Japan. Meighen, in consideration of American views and interests in the Pacific region, successfully argued against renewing the treaty in favour of convening disarmament meetings in Washington. It was a position that drew criticism from the imperialist wing of the Tory party and the wrath of Lord Atholstan and John Willison, then the Canadian correspondent for the *Times,* who believed that the prime minister had "sold out" the British Empire.[17]

O'Leary was by Meighen's side throughout the proceedings. He had been loaned to the Canadian Press by the *Journal* so that reports of the prime minister's exploits could be carried across the country. In fact, O'Leary regarded himself as Meighen's loyal "private secretary" and felt compelled to protect the Conservative leader's reputation. His dispatches, according to the Liberal press, bordered on "hero-worshipping," and by his own admission he did not report on one memorable evening when Meighen caroused with members of the Irish Party, a Westminster group who advocated home rule for Ireland, not a popular cause with imperialists back in Canada.[18]

The respect for Meighen shown by journalists like O'Leary and Ford was reciprocal. As a politician he understood the "power of the pen" and was impressed with their work. "Of all civil careers," he once wrote, "none [but journalism] require such qualities: a mind capable of assimilating all questions; a ready pen; the habit of work and a passion for it in spite of all obstacles; [and] the necessity of being prudent, prompt and thoughtful." Equally, he believed that journalists had a "great responsibility" to be honest and truthful.[19] Nothing bothered him more than misrepresentation by the press of his statements and positions.

Throughout his career, Meighen corresponded regularly with the key Conservative publishers across the country, explaining and interpreting his views. He even tried reasoning with *Manitoba Free Press* editor John Dafoe, but to no avail. From the day Meighen first entered the Commons, Dafoe had mistrusted him personally and detested his politics. The *Free Press* editor actually told Meighen in October 1920 that his paper was moving towards "independence"; a perusal of the editorials during the twenties tells a different story. Dafoe, a good friend of Thomas Crerar's, supported the Progressives on most issues and Mackenzie King and the Liberals when it counted at election time. Meighen was the defender of protectionism, the

---

(continued) *Unrepentant,* published in 1949. When Meighen resigned as leader of the Conservatives after he tried to make an unsuccessful comeback in 1942, O'Leary fondly told him, "God's blessing on you and your house! Not in my day will the Conservative party look upon your like." O'Leary's letters to Meighen dating from around the First World War until November 28, 1949, always began, "Dear Mr. Meighen." Thereafter, it was "Dear Arthur."

British imperialist opposing Dominion autonomy and consequently the enemy of the West and John Dafoe, its chief spokesman. "I can scarcely conceive of anything more dishonest than this conduct on the part of the *Free Press*," Meighen wrote Winnipeg journalist Mark Nichols in January 1924 after the publication of a particularly harsh editorial in the newspaper. "I would write Mr. Dafoe direct in answer to his editorial but I have found such a course in the past utterly useless." In Ottawa, Meighen regarded the dispatches of Dafoe's man in the gallery, the well-connected Grant Dexter, as being "violently Grit ... and very often glaringly dishonest" – an exaggeration to be sure, but years of abuse had coloured Meighen's opinions.[20]

He displayed the same anger with the treatment accorded him by the *Globe* in Toronto. While the *Globe,* under William Jaffray, pursued its own independent course during the twenties and was often at odds with Mackenzie King, it was no friend to Arthur Meighen. On August 3, 1920, within weeks of Meighen's becoming the new prime minister, he told his constituents in his home riding of Portage la Prairie that it was time to reunite Quebec with the rest of Canada. The following day the *Globe* praised Meighen's gesture as well as his controversial history with French Canada and recounted a story in which Laurier, responding to an anti-Quebec speech supposedly delivered by Meighen, angrily declared that Meighen hated Quebec and that he hated Meighen. As the new prime minister was trying to forge new links in the province, the *Globe's* article had a devastating effect on him.

Some months later, when speaking at Massey Hall, he alluded to the August editorial, challenging the *Globe* to name the date he had uttered the comments that had so offended Laurier. The *Globe* countered with another editorial ("Mr. Meighen and His Words"), asserting that it had no date for the incident but knew it to be true. It concluded by suggesting that Meighen would be better off working to translate "into deeds his recent praiseworthy professions of desire for national unity" than "endeavoring to escape the misfortune of accusing memories." It was a classic example of the press avoiding responsibility for its own words. Wrote Meighen to C.A.C. Jennings of the *Mail and Empire,* "This editorial ["Mr. Meighen and His Words"] is such a dishonest evasion and the *Globe* is in such an unescapable corner that I think it should be pounded hard." Jennings agreed: "We must keep prodding the organ until it breaks down and confesses, until it can be brought to the state of shame necessary for the acknowledgement of wrongdoing."[21] The *Globe* never recanted and the damage had been done.

The annual press gallery dinner was one of the rare occasions when Meighen relaxed and let his guard down. A witty man in private, Meighen usually kept humour out of his public remarks. But at the February 1924 dinner, he was in good form, making fun of himself and his attempt to learn to speak French. In his speech that night he drew a roar from the inebriated audience when he offered this view of the impartial Canadian Press news agency: "The function of the Press Gallery is to add to the importance of Members of Parliament. This is done by both laudation and by execration. With the Canadian Press it matters not whether the speech is good or bad, the report is the same in either case. The saddest hour in the life of a member of Parliament is to rise to speak and to see only the C.P. representative in the gallery. A man might as well speak in the Senate."[22]

A few months earlier, Meighen did not find the CP such a laughing matter. He long believed, without any hard evidence, that the wire service was "wholly Liberal" and out to get him. There were indeed cases when CP reporters had taken comments out of context or misinterpreted Meighen's speeches in the House of Commons, as in April 1923 over the complex issue of freight rates. In attempting to summarize in a 600-word dispatch a dialogue of approximately 7,000 words that took up ten pages of Hansard, the CP erroneously wrote that Meighen advocated removing Manitoba's low rates granted under the Crow's Nest Pass agreement; in fact, he argued that low rates be maintained across the Prairies and into British Columbia. While Arthur Ford at the *London Free Press* tried to convince Meighen that it was too dangerous for the Conservative Party to quarrel with such an influential organization as the Canadian Press, the Tory leader held on to his conspiracy theories for decades.[23]

If Meighen was slightly paranoid about the treatment given to him by the press, who could blame him? But nothing – not the *Free Press,* the *Globe,* or the CP – compared to the campaign waged against him by Lord Atholstan and the *Montreal Star*, beginning with the 1921 general election.

August 31, 1921, was a warm day in Ottawa. Grattan O'Leary was sitting in the den in Arthur Meighen's home on Cooper Street chatting with the prime minister. "I'm speaking tomorrow in London, Ontario, and announcing the date of the election," declared Meighen to his stunned journalist friend. O'Leary's eyes sparkled with thoughts of a big scoop, and he asked permission to use the information in the next day's *Journal*. At first Meighen hesitated, but a deal was worked out whereby the editorial revealing the election date would not be published until Meighen was on his way to London. "I made the proposal in absolute good faith and he accepted it the same way," O'Leary recalled. "We both forgot about Canadian Press, which had the right to use our material; somehow a copy of my editorial got over to the Canadian Press office and some enterprising fellow wrote a story and put it on the wire, attributing the announcement of the election to an editorial in the *Ottawa Journal*." The news quickly reached Toronto and made headlines in the *Globe*. Meighen did not change his mind and announced in his London speech, as planned, that there would be a general election on December 6.[24]

The political scene in the fall of 1921 was in a state of flux. The Liberals, following the death of Laurier in 1919, had regrouped under Mackenzie King, but he was as yet a largely untested leader and Laurier was not a man easily replaced. Out west, the Progressive Party, demanding lower tariffs and the re-establishment of a wheat board, was making gains. The party Meighen inherited from Borden was trying to find itself; it could not even agree on a name.

With the war over, "Union" no longer fit, since many of the key Liberals who had joined the coalition government in 1917 had now left. A few, such as James Calder of Saskatchewan (named a senator in September 1921), however, had remained in the caucus and pushed for the awkward-sounding "National Liberal and Conservative Party" (this unpopular label lasted until 1922, when the party's name was changed back to the "Liberal-Conservative Party," as it had officially been called in John A. Macdonald's day). Regardless, Meighen's group was divided and unhappy. The new leader's plan was to make the tariff the central issue in the election and in the process expose King's weaknesses. It was clear from the start that the West belonged to the Progressives and Quebec to the Liberals, but that some gains for the Conservatives were possible and Ontario's vote was anybody's guess.

While the organization of a campaign for a federal election was still primarily done at the local level, by 1921 there was more planning and money for public relations and press propaganda. In Ontario, for instance, Meighen had support from the independent Tory editorial committee that distributed favourable articles to newspapers throughout the province. Pre-election planning also included holding meetings with key Conservative editors and designing advertisements and cartoons for use by the "friendly press." A special effort was also made to target Jewish voters through their local newspapers. The entire PR package cost about $43,000.[25]

As Meighen suspected, Quebec proved to be a problem. French Canadians refused to forgive him for conscription, his greatest crime. "Escrasons Meighen, c'est le temps" (Crush Meighen, it's the time), demanded the Montreal Liberal paper *Le Canada*. A poster that circulated before Meighen spoke in the city was even more to the point: "Meighen is coming. Bring eggs."[26] Thanks largely to Lord Atholstan, the publisher of the *Montreal Star,* the reception he was accorded from English Quebeckers was no better.

Meighen, who was not impressed with wealth or intrigue, hated Atholstan and his newspaper. "I cannot think of any institution in Canada whose history is more putrid and whose conduct more uniformly despicable than ... the *Montreal Star*," he confided to a friend some years later. "Aside from the moral aspect of his course, the degree of sagacity and judgement used by its owner in public affairs has been a converging minimum which long ago passed the zero point. I know of nothing upon which his judgement is worth anything except how to run the character of newspaper which has been for so many years under his charge."[27]

The feelings were mutual. In 1921 Hugh Graham, aged seventy-two years, was a cranky but wealthy lord. He disdained Meighen's actions at the London conference as selling out British interests. Set in his ideas, he regarded the government takeover of the Canadian Northern and Grand Trunk rail lines – estimated to cost Canadian taxpayers in 1921 about $160 million – an economic disaster. A more logical plan, as put forward by Lord Shaughnessy, the CPR's past president, and approved by Atholstan, was for CPR management experts to assume control of the new system, with the government picking up the tab and guaranteeing the financing. This way, losses would be cut and the CPR would not face what was perceived to be unfair competition from a state-run operation. Graham's associates in Montreal (Senator Richard White, the publisher of the *Montreal Gazette,* and his cousin Robert Smeaton White, the paper's editor) and, not surprisingly, Edward Beatty, the dashing new president of the CPR, all agreed. But Meighen resisted. If that was not enough, the Tory leader was also, in the eyes of the Montreal tycoons, too close to various Toronto financiers, Sir Joseph Flavelle among them. In May 1921 Meighen appointed Flavelle chairman of the interim government board that was supervising the Grand Trunk's affairs prior to the organization of the Canadian National Railways.[28]

As the election campaign got under way, Meighen still believed he could bring Atholstan and the *Star* back on side. In fact, through November the *Star* was rather cool to both parties, urging voters to support candidates who "believed in protection and 'economy.'" But the baron, being a stubborn man, was unwilling to bend on the railway issue. When Meighen attacked Sir Lomer Gouin, the former Quebec premier and a federal Liberal candidate who favoured Lord Shaughnessy's plan, the *Star* went on the offensive, launching its infamous "roorback."* On November 30, the *Star*'s front-page headline declared, "Startling Rumour! Revolutionary Railway

---

*A "roorback" is political slander, especially an allegation that backfires. During the American presidential campaign of 1844, the Ithaca *Chronicle* in New York printed some alleged excerpts from an imaginary book called "Roorback's Tour through Western and Southern United States in 1836." It contained malicious and false charges against Democratic candidate James K. Polk. The charges were reprinted in other Whig newspapers, but Polk was nevertheless elected president.

Changes to Be Contemplated." According to the paper's Ottawa correspondent, Montreal was about to lose its place as the country's railway hub, as the government planned to relocate the GTR office to Toronto and consolidate it with the new CNR office in that city. The man behind this alleged plot was Meighen's friend and associate Sir Joseph Flavelle. Within days the Liberals made the best of this unsubstantiated rumour by taking full-page ads out in the *Gazette* and *Star:* "MONTREAL THREATENED. Destruction of One of its Greatest Assets. Removal of GTR Operation ... the Government is to blame ... Sir Joseph Flavelle is reported to have made millions during war ... WE MUST STAND IN OUR OWN DEFENSE." [29]

Both Flavelle and Meighen cabled curt denials to the *Star,* demanding to see the supposed evidence in the newspaper's possession. It was later discovered that the evidence was a letter sent by Flavelle to Howard Kelly, president of Grand Trunk in late November. Anticipating the integration of the GTR into the new CNR system, Flavelle had urged Kelly to "cut out the deadwood" by making some changes in his highly paid administrative staff. Four GTR vice-presidents were to be retired with sizable allowances. [30] Kelly, who disagreed with Flavelle's orders, not only refused to comply but sent copies of his correspondence with the chairman to the *Star*'s editors. (When Flavelle first questioned Kelly, he meekly answered that he had no knowledge of how the *Star* got hold of the letter). In the hands of Atholstan's news writers, the sensible decision to reduce staff was manipulated in the way that would best punish Meighen.

Across Canada, editors remained skeptical, but the damage was done. On December 6 the Conservatives were wiped out in Quebec; Tories blamed the *Star*'s roorback for the loss of three or four Montreal seats. Within less than a week of his disastrous defeat, Meighen got to the bottom of the *Star*'s actions. In Montreal on December 11 the Conservative leader, along with Flavelle and J.A. Stewart, the former minister of railways and canals, met with Lord Atholstan and his editor, A.R. Carman, at the Ritz-Carlton Hotel. "Where was the evidence?" Meighen demanded. The group immediately marched over to Howard Kelly's office, and according to Meighen, "the scene there was really absurd beyond words." An embarrassed Kelly pulled out the letters concerning the retirement of a few senior administrators and admitted that there was no evidence "to move anybody from Montreal." He and Carman, as Meighen recalled, "cut a sorry figure." But Lord Atholstan, who rarely apologized for anything, was "quite debonair" and even invited Meighen to lunch at the conclusion of the meeting. The invitation was refused. "I had the satisfaction of telling them," Meighen later wrote, "that the entire episode was the most despicable conduct I had ever known in my life. This they took without rebuke as well as other sentences of any equally flattering character." [31]

On December 14 the *Star* published its "evidence" together with a lame excuse defending its earlier story. Even the *Gazette,* no friend to Meighen, rebuked the *Star* for its atrocious conduct. Nevertheless, as in 1904 during the *La Presse* Affair, Atholstan remained adamant that he had done nothing wrong. He would not be satisfied until Meighen resigned the leadership of the party. The *Star's* anti-Meighen campaign simmered during 1922 but returned with a vengeance the following spring.

Humbled but not defeated, Arthur Meighen set out to reunite a very divided and dejected Conservative Party. There was no central organization to speak of, and this was the first order of business, a responsibility given to a group of MPs led by Dr. Simon Tolmie. Press support was another major problem, which Meighen tackled himself but with limited success. Money, or rather a lack of it, was the main issue. In fact, throughout the next few years, Meighen was inundated with requests from publishers for much-needed financial assistance. He did his best as a fund raiser and continued to send memos on Tory policy to friendly editors.

The truth was that the Liberals had more available cash than the Conservatives. "The Liberals have been making a policy of acquiring all the papers they can and their wealthy friends seem to be helping them," Meighen warned Mrs. I.E. Bowell, the daughter-in-law of Mackenzie Bowell and the owner of the *Belleville Intelligencer.* Mrs. Bowell wanted to sell, and a group of Liberals led by William Taylor of the Chatham *Daily News* and H.M. Houston and Allan Holmes of the Galt *Reporter* had approached her. Their objective was to turn the *Intelligencer,* a Tory organ since before Confederation, into a Grit newspaper. In order to uphold family tradition, Mrs. Bowell told Meighen that she would wait for an offer from the Tories. The asking price for the newspaper was $40,000 cash for 87 per-cent of the stock. It took more than a year and the help of Howard Ferguson, the Conservative premier of Ontario, for a deal to be put together to keep the *Intelligencer* in Tory hands. By December 1923, however, the new owner, S.B. Dawson, was in trouble and Mr. Bowell was called upon to help pay a $5,000 bill to the E.B. Eddy company for newsprint.[32]

Money problems also plagued the Toronto *Mail and Empire.* With the demise of the Toronto *News* in 1920, the *Mail and Empire* reclaimed its position as the chief Tory organ in Ontario. Though it had served Meighen faithfully during the 1921 election, its financial troubles continued. For one thing, the Mail Printing Company and its president, Charles Riordon, owed the federal government about $800,000 in taxes dating back to 1916. Promissory notes were forwarded to the federal finance department under an arrangement agreed to prior to the 1921 election, although the compa-ny's fortunes did not improve. In August 1925 Meighen personally wrote to a dozen leading Ontario Conservatives urging them to declare their support for the *Mail and Empire* as a way of increasing the paper's circulation. Eventually Riordon found a better solution. In October 1927 (after Meighen had resigned as Tory leader) he sold the newspaper to Montreal financier and millionaire Isaak Walton Killam. The new publisher, a quiet and publicity-shy man, was identified in the press as a "Conservative and a protectionist."[33] Killam ensured that the *Mail and Empire* supported the Tories, and for the next several years it remained the party's most important newspaper. Still, the *Mail and Empire* regarded itself as the "chief *independent* Conservative newspaper in Ontario" (italics mine). As Meighen (and King) discovered, a paper's loyalty to a political party was never written in stone.

Meighen had always had a good working relationship with the *Ottawa Journal* and its publisher P.D. Ross. A tall, lanky, and distinguished man, Ross had gained control of the struggling *Journal* in late 1891 when he was only thirty-three. For many years the paper took an independent line, but around 1904 Ross began to identify more and more with the Conservatives and the *Journal* emerged as the party's main Ottawa organ. Yet Ross never became the Tories' hired hand. He was, as his friend and colleague Grattan O'Leary recalled, a "newspaperman's newspaperman ... He was interested in news, the inalienable right of people to know; he believed in strong convictions strongly expressed." One of his strongest convictions was that an honest editorial page should not be the "mouthpiece" of a political party. "It may give allegiance to the policies and principles of a party [and] may support honestly and vigorously the platform of a party," Ross once explained. "But it cannot, if it is to put the truth first, or the public good first, support always and consistently the acts of a political organization."[34]

Ross had long admired Arthur Meighen as one of the "best speakers in the country." The *Journal* favoured Meighen's succession of Borden and backed the new leader during the 1921 election. Differences of opinion did, however, arise. In October 1922, during the last stages of the protracted railway consolidation and the organization of the CNR, the Liberals replaced the Conservative-appointed chairman of the board, D.B. Hanna, with Sir Henry Thornton, an experienced though outspoken British railway executive. Because of his past involvement, Meighen was extremely paternalistic when it came to railway policy, and he watched Thornton closely.

The new chairman had high hopes for the corporation, believing it could compete on an equal level with the CPR; Meighen thought otherwise. In the spring of 1923, Thornton purchased the Scribe Hotel in Paris for the CNR's European headquarters. While government authorization was required for the purchase, Thornton did a bit of financial manipulating to get around the rules and secure the required $2 million from the Bank of Toronto.[35] When news of the deal was made public, Meighen condemned

Thornton's "scandalous" actions. Few members of the government or the press shared his point of view. On the morning of June 9, the *Ottawa Journal* endorsed Sir Henry Thornton and published, much to Meighen's dismay, a stinging rebuke of the Conservative leader's speech. P.D. Ross found Meighen's criticism "largely technical" and his attitude to Thornton "deplorable." In the *Journal*'s view, Thornton, like Edward Beatty of the CPR, did not need the permission of his shareholders before he conducted business. (Years later O'Leary noted how wrong Ross had been: the CPR shareholders could sell their shares; CNR shareholders, the Canadian taxpayers, could not. Moreover, the Scribe Hotel, in O'Leary's opinion, was "second rate.")

Meighen was furious with Ross. That day, he composed a brilliantly detailed, legalistic, five-page response in which he discussed the responsibility of public companies to Parliament. Ross, like most newspapermen, refused to back down, suggesting that Thornton be given a fair chance to prove himself.[36]

Relations between Meighen and the *Journal* administration (other than O'Leary) remained cool. Yet Ross did stand behind Meighen when Lord Atholstan resumed his campaign to oust Meighen from the leadership of the Conservative Party. This time the attack had a particularly bizarre twist. On July 12, 1923, the *Montreal Star* published the first of a series of lengthy editorials entitled "The Whisper of Death." The main theme in these pieces of invective "was that Canada, staggering under an immense debt produced mainly by railway nationalization, stood teetering on the brink of disaster." According to the *Star,* there was one easy solution for the "impending peril" facing the country: "What is needed is new blood. Public life today does not seem to contain a man with courage, the foresight, the public confidence which would equip him to rescue the Dominion from the rapids ... It is our misfortune ... that our great men no longer seem to go into public life. They go into business, into finance, into transportation, into the learned professions. But in a time of national crisis we must 'dig them out.'"[37]

Certainly much of the *Star*'s criticism was aimed at Prime Minister Mackenzie King and the Liberals, but within a short time it was clear that the real target was Arthur Meighen. "He was a 'piffling' critic of the Government who had 'toyed' with socialism," the *Star* concluded, "a leader under whom the Conservative party had fallen prey to 'stagnation, astigmatism and amnesia.'"[38] Unlike Borden, Meighen refused to write any letter or do anything to appease Atholstan; nor would he resign the leadership. He suspected that Robert Rogers and possibly Howard Ferguson, the premier of Ontario, were in league with Atholstan to drive him from the party's leadership. Many of his supporters also reassured him that the *Star*'s influence was on the wane. Indeed, most Conservative and Liberal newspapers dismissed the "Whisper of Death" as "unspeakable nonsense," to use the *Globe*'s words. The *Ottawa Journal* rightly advised that "somebody should tie a wet towel around the *Star* editor's head, bathe his feet in hot water well-saturated with mustard, and after his temperature gets back to normal make him acquainted with the following facts: economic facts." (For instance, the *Star* claimed that the annual federal deficit was rising by the "hundred millions"; in fact, the deficit from June 1922 to June 1923 was $11.5 million.)

If anything, the "Whisper of Death" campaign backfired. Instead of getting rid of Meighen, it made him stronger and increased his popularity. Canadians sympathized with him, believing the treatment he was receiving at the hands of the *Star* to be unjust. But Lord Atholstan was not finished. In early November, the torrent of articles recommenced and the *Star*'s editors took every opportunity to lambaste Meighen. In a speech at Victoriaville in the Eastern Townships, the Conservative leader humorously denied he was "a hard loser and a poor sport" as the press portrayed him. On the contrary, he declared to the delight of the crowd, "I am a cheerful loser and have never spent two such happy years as since I left power." This was too much for the *Star*. On November 23, the Montreal newspaper's lead editorial – headlined "The Happy Warrior" – was a harsh critique of Meighen's leadership. "Most people have been under the illusion that he was trying to get into office," the *Star* sarcastically noted. "He appealed for votes to that end. He probably runs less risk than any other possible leader of the Opposition of having his happiness ruined by being conscripted into office." In concluding this diatribe, the paper observed that perhaps the reason for Meighen's happiness can be explained by the $14,000 paid to him as a parliamentary stipend.[39]

This editorial was viewed as going to far, even for Atholstan.[40] The Tory press rallied to Meighen's side, and from as far away as Saskatchewan the *Star* was charged with journalistic blasphemy. "The Montreal Judas," declared the editor of the *Moosejaw Times-Herald,* "violated every canon of British fair play, just as it did on the eve of the last election." Not surprisingly, Lord Atholstan was unphased and his attack on Meighen continued.

While there was no hope for the *Star*, the Conservative leader attempted, without success, to appease the Whites in order to win the support of the more respectable *Gazette*. In a Quebec by-election in 1924 (in St. Antoine, a Montreal riding), he went against the wishes of his caucus in backing an independent Liberal because that was the candidate the *Gazette* favoured. His actions troubled him. "If ever there was a case where a leader risked a great deal with his own party in order to hold the support of a newspaper," Meighen told Arthur Ford, "I did so in St. Antoine." In the end the *Gazette*'s candidate did not run and the Tories lost the by-election. Rather than blaming Conservative disunity, the real reason for the loss, both the *Star* and *Gazette* blamed Meighen.[41]

As the Conservatives prepared for the 1925 election, Meighen's press support in Quebec was no better than it had been in 1921. In fact, in many ways it was worse. Since the days of John A. Macdonald, Tory leaders had always counted on the loyalty of the Quebec City *Chronicle*. In 1925, however, economic realities altered this partisan relationship. There was a market for only one English daily in that city, and on July 1 the *Chronicle* merged with the Liberal-leaning *Telegraph*. Meighen lost a key supporter.

In Montreal "Meighen-baiting" remained a "very popular sport." The "editorials attacking Meighen," observed Roger Graham, "seemed to have a contagious effect and to stimulate a compulsive urge in the party of some people to join in the public elucidation of his inadequacies." This included such leading Conservatives as C.H. Cahan and Sir Herbert Holt, the president of the Royal Bank.[42] Joined by Atholstan and the Whites, these men believed that the only politician who could save the Tories in Quebec was E.L. Patenaude, a former member of Borden's cabinet who had resigned over conscription. A cultured and charming man, Patenaude had re-entered the Quebec legislature (his political career had started there in 1908) in 1923. He was extremely popular, or so Meighen thought. Negotiations to bring Patenaude back into the party began, but when the campaign was under way, Patenaude decided his best bet was to run as an independent.

Atholstan wanted Patenaude to renounce Meighen but he refused. Nevertheless, his presence in Quebec put the Tory leader in an awkward position. Not wanting to be seen as Patenaude's opponent, Meighen left the provincial campaign in Patenaude's hands. The *Gazette* and *Star* treated the returned politician as if he were the leader of the Conservatives, rarely mentioning Meighen's speeches.[43] It did not matter. The Liberals and their press, as in 1921, played up Meighen's past as the man who brought in conscription. And in Quebec the results were predictable: the Liberals won 60 seats, the Conservatives 4, and Patenaude was defeated.

Yet Meighen made a better impression in Ontario than Prime Minister King. There the Conservatives were vindicated with 68 seats to the Liberals' 11. King even lost his own seat in York North (he later won a by-election in Saskatchewan). Much to Meighen's delight, the Tories also swept the Maritimes, while the West was split. The final tally gave Meighen 116 seats, the Liberals 99, the Progressives 24, Labour 2, and independents 4. Clearly it was an impressive showing for Meighen, although he would have liked Quebec as well. As he assessed the situation, part of the blame was attributed to Patenaude's independent stand and part lay at the door of the bitter *Gazette* and *Star* for driving a wedge in the party. Still, it all came down to who controlled the French press, and in this area the Conservatives could not compete with the Liberals. Thanks to such papers as *La Canada* and *Le Soleil,* Meighen remained the hated symbol of Quebec's wartime experience. There was little he could do about it.

In November 1925 while Mackenzie King was pondering his future, Meighen waited patiently for the opportunity to lead the government. In Ontario the Conservative leader was more popular than ever, receiving countless invitations to attend meetings and dinners. Meighen, who was at his best in front of a supportive audience, attended one such banquet in Hamilton on November 16. He took the opportunity to make a speech declaring that, as a general rule, a decision by Parliament to go to war should be put before the people in a general election. "This would contribute to the unity of our country in the months to come," he said, "and would enable us best to do our duty."

Meighen had not suggested that a referendum be called before the country decided on war, as his detractors later claimed (and still do). He recognized that the government might have to make a quick decision in the case of a national emergency (he later made his position clear at the 1927 Conservative convention in Winnipeg, but to no avail), but his words were blown out of proportion and much of the Tory press was shocked. Such loyal friends as Arthur Ford in London were "dumbfounded" and remained silent, but others like Mark Nichols at the *Winnipeg Tribune* and P.D. Ross at the *Ottawa Journal* were highly critical. Nichols, in words he later regretted, went so far as to imply that the Hamilton statement was merely a play to win votes in a forthcoming Quebec by-election. This was also the view of veteran journalist Tom Blacklock, one of Meighen's oldest Ottawa friends, who was so angry that he actually stopped speaking to Meighen.[44]

The real trouble was that in 1922 when the British were about to go to war with Turkey over the Chanak crisis and had asked the dominions for military help, Meighen had had quite a different response. His famous answer had referred back to what Laurier had replied in August 1914 on the question of Canada's entrance into the First World War. "Let there be no dispute as to where I stand," Meighen told a Toronto group of Tory businessmen. "When Britain's message came ... Canada should have said: 'Ready, aye, Ready; we stand by you.'" That these highly charged comments were actually made in light of Canada's obligations under the Treaty of Sevres (which guaranteed a neutral demilitarized zone around the Dardanelles and Bosporus) and not as an all-encompassing military policy was overlooked. In 1922 the Canadian press portrayed Arthur Meighen as a great imperialist.[45]

Now, three years later, his jingoistic cry returned to haunt him. Grattan O'Leary, who found the Hamilton speech the "one strange inconsistency" in Meighen's career, best summed up the dilemma facing Tory supporters in

1925: "In 1922 ... Meighen said our answer should have been 'Ready, aye, Ready.' But now he was saying, 'Ready, aye, Ready ... *but after a general election.'*" Meighen tried hard to explain his position to Conservative editors, though with limited success. His arguments were logical and reasonable, but as Roger Graham pointed out, "logic does not govern politics or human affairs ... as much as ... [Meighen] thought it did. The fact was, whatever were the merits of his idea and however much it may have been misunderstood and misinterpreted, that in presenting it he had caused a disruption in the party at the very moment when it seemed to stand on the threshold of power, a disruption which someone more sensitive to the intricately varied currents of public opinion might have anticipated and avoided."[46] In outmanoeuvring King, Meighen needed all the help he could he muster, especially from his friends in the press. His so-called Heresy at Hamilton had achieved exactly the opposite.

The political drama that followed the 1925 election has been well documented. As was his right, King refused to relinquish the government to Meighen and attempted to hold power with the fickle support of the Progressives and independents. Had it not been for the discovery of corruption in the customs department, King's ploy might have succeeded.

During those eight months in 1926 as the Liberal government hung on by a thread, Meighen had his own problems. In April the *Montreal Star* launched yet another series of editorial attacks demanding Meighen resign the leadership because he could not win at the polls in Quebec. Although not as crass, the *Gazette* continued to be negative in its assessment of Meighen. Montreal businessman J.W. McConnell, who was to be the next owner of the *Star* when Atholstan died in 1938, arranged a meeting for Meighen with the "St. James Crowd" (as Grant Dexter of the *Manitoba Free Press* called them).

At a gathering in early May in Montreal attended by Herbert Holt, Senator White, and Edward Beatty, Meighen reaffirmed his intentions to stay on as leader. He also stated that in order to defeat the Grits he would need their financial help. Would they assist him, he asked? And could they call off the *Gazette* and the *Star*? The illustrious gentlemen demanded that in return for their money and press support, Meighen totally commit himself and the Tories to an economic policy of protection. With this he had no problem. No guarantees were given about changing the course of Atholstan and the *Star,* but it was agreed that money would be put up to purchase the former Liberal French newspaper *La Patrie* owned by L.J. Tarte. A group headed by Senator D.O. L'Espérance, named by Meighen to be Quebec's chief Tory organizer, took control of *La Patrie* on July 18, 1926. While this gave the Conservatives a francophone mouthpiece in Montreal for the first time in many years, it remained to be seen whether Meighen's Faustian pact with the St. James Crowd would pay off.[47]

By the end of June 1926 the Liberals were in serious trouble. The report of the parliamentary committee investigating the customs department had confirmed the worst: there was corruption at every level. Support from the Progressives and the independents led by J.S. Woodsworth appeared lost, and a vote of non-confidence was almost certain to pass. In a last-ditch effort to save his skin, King asked Governor General Lord Byng for a dissolution of Parliament so that another election could be held. In what was to be a critical moment in Canadian constitutional history, Byng properly refused and requested that Meighen attempt to form a government.[48] After much thought, Meighen agreed.

"No decision he ever made was so often and unreservedly criticized as this one – later on when things turned out badly," wrote Meighen's biographer. His acceptance of Lord Byng's invitation was interpreted by John Dafoe of the *Free Press* and others as a desperate grab for power. In fact, considering Byng's delicate position, Meighen had little choice but to accept; it was the right and honourable thing to do. In the end, little of this mattered. Meighen, unable to hold on to the Progressives' support on account of a parliamentary miscue, was defeated after being in office for three days. Byng then granted Meighen a dissolution and King got his election for September 14.

For Meighen the final results were extremely disappointing. He had run an aggressive campaign favouring the tariff and aimed at exposing Liberal corruption in the customs department and elsewhere. Moreover, he had solid partisan press support throughout the country. Even in Quebec, the *Star* was more or less positive about Meighen. King, on the other hand, made Lord Byng's refusal to grant him a dissolution the central theme of his platform. Backed by a much more powerful press in Quebec and aided by the potent pen of Dafoe in Winnipeg, King played up the "nationalist vs. British domination" conflict for all it was worth.

Dafoe's *Free Press* was by now the major voice in the West. The newspaper had favoured the Progressives for the past five years, but internal problems had divided the party and Manitoba Progressives were slowly moving back to the Liberals. Besides, as Dafoe argued, splitting the vote would only have allowed Meighen to reap the benefits. Thus, all the *Free Press*'s editorial efforts during the summer of 1926 were focused on exposing the imperialistic tendencies of Arthur Meighen and the unacceptable behaviour of Lord Byng. And no matter how many arguments were offered to show that Byng had acted properly, Dafoe in September 1926 and for the rest of his life saw the Liberal victory as "the triumph of Canadian nationalism over colonialism and sectionalism."[49]

Meighen, on the other hand, long blamed Dafoe and the *Free Press* for his total loss in western Canada. Out of 54 seats in the three Prairie provinces, the Liberals won 31 (including 7 Liberal-Progressive seats in Manitoba), the Conservatives held one seat in Alberta, and the remainder were divided up between Labour, independent, and farmer parties. Nearly a decade after Dafoe's death, Meighen admitted to O'Leary that he still did not hold the *Free Press* in high regard, "so long as it adheres to its abominable record over the Byng controversy." To another old friend he bitterly wrote twenty-five years after the fact: "The *Free Press* was the most pronouncedly and persistently antagonistic of any paper in all of Canada."[50]

In its post-election analysis, the Canadian press came up with dozens of explanations for the Conservatives' demise in 1926: resentment over the Hamilton speech, memories of conscription in Quebec, the party's rigid economic policies, and the constitutional issue. Meighen, who always believed he was more qualified to govern than King, wrestled with each of these factors for many years. The defeat in 1926 was indeed a bitter pill for him to swallow.[51]

He resigned as Conservative leader in the days following the election. Typically and with more than a slight degree of hypocrisy, journalists of every political stripe, many of whom had hounded him for close to ten years, extolled and applauded his accomplishments.

CHAPTER EIGHT

The Trials of Mackenzie King

My relations with King have never got to the point of warm friendship, but they have been close enough to give me an impression ... that there is more to this man than I have thought.

John W. Dafoe, January 13, 1943

A t half past five on a hot Ottawa afternoon in late July 1937, a dozen or so reporters congregated in the small anteroom in the north end of Parliament's East Block. They were prepared to wait for thirty minutes, perhaps a full hour, for the cabinet meeting in the large adjoining oak-walled chambers to end. Nearing 7 p.m. the door finally opened. James L. Ilsey, the minister of national revenue, not one to stop and chat, left briskly and headed back to his office in the Connaught Building. Next out was Ernest Lapointe, the tall, statesman-like minister of justice, and the prime minister's loyal Quebec lieutenant. The impeccably dressed Lapointe, age sixty-one, had been a member of Parliament since 1904. As was his custom, he greeted the journalists and exchanged a few quick pleasantries with the French reporters, but no hard news was forthcoming from him.

Behind Lapointe marched the rest of the distinguished Liberal cabinet: William Euler, whose booming voice could be heard down the corridor; the tall and slim Ian Mackenzie; Norman Rogers, the minister of labour, who looked as though he'd be more at home within the quiet confines of academe than in the political limelight; the veteran and genial Charles Dunning; C.D Howe, a no-nonsense engineer who had only recently entered the political arena; and former Progressive Party leader Thomas Crerar, the minister of mines and resources, who stopped to light his pipe. All followed Lapointe's lead, giving the reporters a casual "hello" but nothing that could be included in the next day's edition.

Finally, the "P.M." stood in the doorway, and the respectful journalists were on their feet. Carrying an armful of papers, William Lyon Mackenzie

King smiled when he saw the men of the gallery. "I don't think I can give you anything today," he said before any of them were able to blurt out a question. "We discussed many matters but they are not sufficiently advanced for me to say anything now." On hearing this, the group dispersed, wondering how they were going to explain to their respective editors the fact that the day's wait had not produced the anticipated scoop.[1] Such were "scrums" in 1937: courteous, sedate, and unproductive.

Life for the average gallery correspondent was not easy in Mackenzie King's Ottawa. For one thing, this complex, curious, and cautious man, who ruled Canada for nearly twenty-two years, was extremely secretive. Fearful to the point of paranoia of being misunderstood, undermined, or embarrassed, King rarely made impromptu public comments – especially not to the press. His keen and usually accurate political instincts had taught him to be prepared with answers, while his insecure and obsessive nature (some have said neurosis) made him defensive and circumspect.[2] All of this we know from King's unique benefaction to Canadian history: his diary, the rough, hand-written chronicle of his peculiar private and personal thoughts over more than five decades. Rarely happy with the way he looked – "short, squat, stocky [and] pudgy" have been the most common adjectives used to describe him – King tried to compensate for his apparent physical deficiencies by going to painstaking lengths to ensure that his public speeches and declarations in the House were flawless. Jack Pickersgill, a former Liberal cabinet minister and supreme political organizer who joined the prime minister's staff in 1937, recalls, "In private, King was amusing, gossipy and never at a loss for something entertaining to say. But in public, he had this 'Sunday-going-to-Church' style, and was concerned that he never appear informal."*

Unable to laugh at himself, King especially dreaded the annual parliamentary gallery dinner. He wrote in his diary about the "vulgarity of the affair ... [and the] course [sic] nature of the references to myself and others. The whole proceeding was wholly unworthy ... [of] thoughtful and serious minded men. As a matter of fact, it gives to the press an idea of their power to destroy reputations such as they should never be permitted to have."[3]

King thought he knew about the inner workings of the news business. To earn extra money as a student at the University of Toronto in 1895, King

---

*I interviewed many people in the course of gathering material for this book – Jack Pickersgill among them. Hereafter, where the source of a quote is not cited, the reader should assume the source is an interview. See Bibliography for a listing of those interviewed.

had taken a job as a reporter with the Toronto *News* for five dollars a week. A short time later he switched to the *Globe* and the paper's police beat. After he returned to Toronto following graduate work at the University of Chicago, he wrote a series of well-received articles for the *Mail and Empire* on Toronto's social problems. As a result of these early experiences, King had an affinity with the men in the gallery and understood their daily demands for information. But as a politician, he knew that to maintain his power he would have to control the flow of that information. Consequently, as Arthur Ford remembers, Mackenzie King "was never a good source of news" – or, as expressed by the Montreal *Gazette* in 1948, he was about as "informative as a gagged clam."

For most reporters, especially those representing Conservative-leaning papers, access to King was extremely restricted. Even for such correspondents as Thomas Wayling of the *Toronto Star,* a supportive newspaper which King held in high esteem, requests for on-the-record interviews were always refused. They just did not happen. Out of frustration, Wayling approached King in the hallowed halls of Parliament, to no avail. He was appropriately admonished. "I expressed my view," King wrote in his diary on September 21, 1926, "that press interviews with the leader of a party should be at proper times and places." Just precisely when the "proper time and place" was, he did not note.

Nothing had changed more than twenty years later when the jovial Charles Lynch arrived in Ottawa to embark on his long and distinguished career as a political journalist. After asking for an interview with the prime minister, Lynch was told to submit a list of questions, which he did. Weeks later, he received a letter with a table of King's speeches for the past six years, and was informed that the answers could be found in them.[4]

Anything resembling today's wide-open press conferences was out of the question. Large gatherings with the prime minister were "few and far between," as Arthur Ford recalls, "and as a rule not conducive to much news." When King visited Washington, the word at the National Press Club about the Canadian prime minister was "here comes Mr. King; he hasn't got a damn thing."[5]

During the 1930s relations between politicians and press in the U.S. capital were revolutionizing. The main catalyst for this was Franklin D. Roosevelt, widely recognized as "this century's prime manipulator" of the media, both newspapers and radio. FDR loved the gentlemen of the press and they loved him. He knew their first names and he shared their jokes; he was "one of the boys." All the while, he attempted, with great success, to have them write what he wanted.[6]

Before Roosevelt was elected president in 1933, Washington under his predecessor, the sedate Herbert Hoover, was a quieter and slower city –

more like Ottawa. The capital's press corps was required to submit its questions to the White House in writing and wait patiently for a written answer. Hoover's press conferences were few in number, about once a month. With Roosevelt, the doors were opened. He realized that if he wanted to shape what was written about his administration, White House reporters had to have access to him, though on his terms and in a setting he could control. Press conferences were thus held twice, sometimes three times a week (he held 337 press conferences during his first term, 374 in his second, and 279 in his third).[7]

King's respect for Roosevelt is well known. Their political friendship forged important links between Canada and the United States during the war years. The two were Harvard graduates, a fact which made King very proud. Roosevelt referred to his friend as "Mackenzie," the only person to use that moniker; in deference, King, the more formal and older of the two men, called FDR "Mr. President." Author and journalist Bruce Hutchison wrote: "King regarded Roosevelt with public adulation and privately with a mixture of admiration, amazement, skepticism, and some merriment. He thought many of Roosevelt's policies quite crazy, he looked on much of the New Deal as mere political hokum."[8] Apparently this included the American president's strategy for dealing with the media.

A Mackenzie King press conference in Ottawa was largely an exercise in futility. One day in mid-March 1937, the word reached the gallery that the prime minister wanted to meet with reporters at 6 p.m. in Room 16, then Parliament's common room, a place where MPs relaxed on the lavish splendour of green leather couches. Precisely at the appointed hour, King walked into the middle of the room, put on his reading glasses, which were attached to his vest by a black cord, and read his prepared statement to the journalists surrounding him. He was going to Washington to see President Roosevelt about matters "of mutual interest," he told them. "Any questions gentlemen?" "Sir, what is the purpose of your visit?" one Quebec correspondent asked. "To discuss the situation," he answered. Coming to the assistance of their French colleague, several more in the crowd asked if there were any other details regarding the trip. As if to tease them, King pulled a four-page, hand-written letter from the president out of his pocket and began to read it. But as soon as he got to the date of the letter, he stopped, deciding it would be inappropriate to reveal private correspondence. He shook hands with all the reporters and thanked them for coming. The journalists were bewildered and unsatisfied, feeling as if they had been just told by the girl of their dreams that she wanted to be a "friend."[9]

This scene was repeated on numerous occasions: Ottawa correspondents took many questions into a Mackenzie King press conference and left a half-hour later with the same questions unanswered. The gallery reporters, not a passive group by any means, grumbled from time to time about this intolerable situation. In December 1938 Alex Hume, a partisan Liberal journalist and one of Ottawa's first real press pundits, spoke with Walter Turnbull, the prime minister's assistant, for over an hour one day, listing the journalists' various grievances, among which were the following: ministers and their departments were releasing news items only to members of the Canadian Press wire service, thereby depriving other gallery members of their "bread and butter" stories; any news given out was so meagre as to nullify much of its value; too many important items were handed out on Saturday afternoons or late at night; interviews with the prime minister by individual members of the press were "granted so rarely ... as to amount to a boycott of newspaper men as individuals; and "the prime minister had not entertained the Press Gallery."[10] Turnbull suggested that his boss throw a party for the gallery members and their wives, but there is no indication that King followed his advice. He had his own methods for dealing with the press, perhaps not as flashy or as modern as Roosevelt's, but quite effective nonetheless.

Almost every day of his adult life, King carefully scrutinized the major Canadian papers, on the lookout for errors, favourable comments, and unjustified criticism. He was never without a pile of clippings prepared by his diligent staff, who by 1935 examined thirty-five English and eight French dailies, not to mention countless magazines. This left King with about 100–200 press clippings per day. In a 1946 *Maclean's* story, Blair Fraser estimated that from 1921, when he was first elected prime minister, to that time, more than 400,000 clippings had crossed King's desk.

Mackenzie King loved to be flattered. Nothing pleased him more than seeing positive words about himself in print. Though he told Fraser in 1946 that he did not let newspapers dictate government policy, there were occasions when he could be swayed or influenced. In late 1942 a cabinet debate was under way on the question of restricting liquor supplies for the duration of the war. Most of the ministers were against the idea, but King, who regarded himself a moral and religious person, believed something needed to be done. On December 12 Charles Bishop, a journalist at the *Ottawa Citizen* and an admirer of the prime minister's, wrote in his "Glimpses of Parliament" column that by standing up for his principles on the liquor issue King was showing real leadership. As his diary for that day records, King was very touched by Bishop's comments. In fact, Bishop's column, together with a telegram King received from a United Church minister, led the prime minister to push through an order banning liquor advertisements until the war ended.[11]

At the same time, the most minor mistake or misinterpretation upset and angered King out of all proportion. As events in Europe were nearing the breaking-point in April 1939, King stated in the House that Canada should support whatever may be "proposed" by the British authorities. The following day, the *Globe and Mail* correspondent noted that the prime minister had declared that Canada was prepared to support any action "decided" upon by the British. King was outraged. He labelled the story "willfully false" and "perverted" and suggested that the *Globe* reporter be "denied the privileges of the Press Gallery."[12]

The punishment demanded hardly fit the crime, but King long believed that the majority of the press was against him. And he took any criticism, constructive or otherwise, very personally. As Joy Esberey points out in her illuminating historical psychoanalysis of King, "Those who were not for him in everything were against him, and those who were for him were for him in everything; there was no room for half-measures."[13]

One journalist who particularly got under his skin was John Stevenson, for a time in the early 1920s the correspondent for the Liberal *Toronto Star* – a peculiar job for one of Arthur Meighen's closest friends in the press. But Stevenson was also a confidant of Thomas Crerar's and therefore indispensable to publisher Joe Atkinson during the Progressive Party's ascendancy. From the beginning of his long tenure as Liberal leader in 1919, Stevenson was unimpressed by Laurier's successor. "[King] is as full of noble sentiments as a new calved cow is full of milk," he wrote to John Dafoe, "but he is short on concrete plans for our regeneration." More than once Stevenson's growing disdain for King crept into his *Star* reports, forcing Atkinson, one of King's lifelong friends, to apologize to the prime minister for his employee's impertinence. Still, the *Star* publisher refused to fire Stevenson even after being asked to do so by King, a good example of just who was calling the shots in the relationship between the Liberals and one of its chief Ontario newspapers. Finally, in 1923, Stevenson was given notice after he had written anti-King pieces for another publication against Atkinson's direct orders.[14]

For a year, as his friend Arthur Meighen tried to secure him a job with the *Mail and Empire,* Stevenson worked as the parliamentary reporter of the *Farmers' Sun.* Eventually, much to King's dismay, Stevenson was appointed Ottawa correspondent for the *Times* of London, again becoming a thorn in the prime minister's side. (During this period John Willison was the London paper's "Canadian Correspondent," and when Willison died in 1927, Stevenson was promoted to that post.) While King claimed there was a "real danger to the Empire" in having the *Times*'s chief writer "a pronounced opponent of the government," the simple fact was that he did not know how to deal with people who did not like him.[15]

King regarded individuals such as Stevenson as part of the greater Tory conspiracy that (in his distorted view) he had been battling all his life. Moreover, he blamed much of the criticism he received in newspapers on the "commercialism" inherent in journalism, which constantly handicapped the Liberals because the link between the Conservatives and the businessmen who owned the papers was stronger than that between his own party and the owners. (It would have been difficult to convince Conservative Arthur Meighen of this.) But the Tory virus had also infiltrated the non-partisan Canadian Press, which by the 1930s, under the guidance of J.F.B. Livesay, had become quite fair in its political reporting. To King, however, CP dispatches were dismissed as disguised Tory propaganda.[16] (Again, it is fascinating that Meighen's view of the CP was exactly the reverse; he considered the organization to be pro-Liberal and anti-Meighen.)

In fact, the Liberals had more support in the gallery than King would admit. Partisanship aside – for there were among the small elite gallery club of the 1920s and 1930s such men as Grant Dexter, Bruce Hutchison, Alex Hume, and Charlie Bishop, Liberals one and all – success as a parliamentary reporter required a certain amount of deference to the government position. And except during Meighen's brief Conservative rule in the mid-1920s, or R.B. Bennett's from 1930 to 1935, this of course meant deference to the Liberal position. "There is no doubt at all," Mark Nichols of the *Vancouver Sun* explained to Meighen, "that the average Ottawa correspondent feels that he has to 'stand in' with the government in order to get the news. At times he will go out of his way to do something extra for a minister who gives him a special handout ... I think it possible that in some cases the reporter is reaching out to please the powers that be rather than to deprive a member of the opposition of the attention a particular performance calls for."[17]

Leaving the support of his policies to the discretion of journalists was nevertheless too risky for someone as obsessive as King. Nothing could be left to chance. He regarded the press in much the same way as had Laurier, his idol and mentor. Accordingly, to achieve his overall objective of national unity, King needed journalists at his disposal. His was a much more subtle approach than the one Roosevelt would follow in the 1930s. Though publicly King was not available for comment, he singled out several journalists he deemed trustworthy and loyal – two attributes very important to him – for special off-the-record discussions in his cluttered library on the third floor of Laurier House or at Kingsmere, his Gatineau estate. Most often, he liked first to flatter reporters and then to feed them ideas and opinions, allowing them to push a point of view as if on their own initiative.

Bruce Hutchison, a dignified and reserved man who could nevertheless grow passionate on occasion, arrived in Ottawa at the age of twenty-four in January 1925 to work as the correspondent for the *Victoria Daily Times*.

This marked the beginning of his long and impressive writing career.* As a wide-eyed journalist in 1925 he was an early victim of King's charm and manipulations.

Reminiscing many years later about his first private meeting with the prime minister, Hutchison recalled that King was not too busy to "take an hour to beguile an unknown young reporter, only because the remote *Victoria Daily Times* might come in useful some day. No stone of politics was too small for King to turn in an election year, no potential supporter too insignificant to be baited with favours and glued with birdlime." Hutchison was "easily ensnared." From their first encounter, he was a journalist King trusted and whose support he appreciated. Similarly, Hutchison, after he had left Ottawa to become the chief political writer for the *Vancouver Sun,* never hesitated to ask the prime minister for guidance or advice.[18]

King's closest contact in the gallery was probably Hutchison's friend Grant Dexter, the Ottawa correspondent for the *Winnipeg Free Press.* For at least twenty years no journalist knew more about what was going on in Ottawa than Dexter. No one had sources that reached as deep inside the cabinet or had as much access to the prime minister. He may not have been as elegant a writer as Hutchison or as electric as Grattan O'Leary, but he was the premier investigative reporter of his day and he wrote for the premier newspaper of his day, John Dafoe's *Free Press.* This last fact alone opened doors for him that were closed to most other gallery journalists. As soon as he arrived in Ottawa in 1923 at the age of twenty-seven, this tall, unassuming farm boy of Scottish stock became Dafoe's "eyes and ears." The correspondence between the two men was "a pile of papers three feet thick," as Bruce Hutchison ("Brucie" to Dexter) noted at the time of his friend's death in 1961.

And what correspondence! Besides submitting hundreds upon hundreds of news stories and commentaries to the "Chief" – as Dafoe was affectionately and reverentially called – Dexter also dispatched to Winnipeg neatly typed secret memoranda detailing the private thoughts of the country's political leaders. The breadth of his reports, as well as their origins, was remarkable: for example, he obtained a private interview with Mackenzie King

---

*Bruce Hutchison was a fascinating man. Until his death in September 1992 at age ninety-one, he was still writing columns for the *Vancouver Sun,* where he served as editor emeritus. I visited him in June 1990 at his cottage-like home on Rogers Street in Victoria, where he had resided for decades. It was the time of the last Meech Lake conference and he was quite despondent about Canada's future and the direction the Tories were taking the country. He told me that by the time my young children were adults, Canada as he had known it would no longer be. This was, he believed, a great tragedy.

about his troubles with Governor General Lord Byng in 1926; in the months leading up to the Second World War he was briefed on the latest cabinet strategy by Liberal ministers while playing a round of golf, a game Dexter never loved or was good at but endured as any dedicated newsman would; and he suffered through a heart-to-heart talk with R.B. Bennett in the men's washroom at the Rideau Club.

"The secret memos," as Dexter once explained to George Ferguson, the *Free Press*'s managing editor, "really developed as a means of communication between various people here and the Chief. These people were mostly ministers and they did not want to write directly but they wanted him to know certain things."[19] Had Dexter desired, he could have written the most sensational political bestseller of his day. But because he believed that much of what he was told in these off-the-record conversations was intended for Dafoe's ears only, he never gossiped and was extremely protective of his sources and memoranda (the only ones to read them, outside of his wife, Alice, who typed many of them, were Dafoe and Ferguson, and later, after Dafoe died, *Free Press* publisher Victor Sifton and Bruce Hutchison, who joined the paper in 1944 as an associate editor).

The fact that he could be trusted endeared Dexter to Liberals, Conservatives, and the growing civil service. During his two years as a *Free Press* correspondent in London, from 1936 to 1938, Dexter befriended a member of the staff at the Canadian High Commission office, Lester "Mike" Pearson, who proved to be a valuable source of confidential information then and for years to come. Within time, Dexter and his family became part of the Ottawa establishment. They lived in a nice house in exclusive Rockcliffe, belonged to the right clubs, and knew just about anybody of any importance. Like the politicians he covered, however, this journalist eventually came to inhabit a milieu somewhat remote from the real world. Author James Gray, in 1943 himself a young *Free Press* reporter on assignment in Ottawa, recalls how fascinated Dexter and his wife were with Gray's stories about his unemployment experiences during the early thirties. "It occurred to me," Gray observed, "that he had spent five years of his life in Ottawa during the Bennett administration [1930–35] writing thousands of words almost daily on the unemployment relief crisis, and yet had never become aware of what unemployment relief meant to the people on relief."[20]

Dexter considered himself a small-L liberal. He believed in a government responsible to the people, in free trade, and in the abolition of state privileges that enabled monopolies to exist. It would be unfair to label him a mere partisan (as Hutchison wrote, "Grant was much too big for that"), for it was only natural that his close contacts with King and members of his cabinet (especially Thomas Crerar, who revealed all government secrets to Dexter) drew him into the Liberal fold. King, the lonely bachelor, genuinely liked Dexter, and his feelings were reciprocated. While Dexter considered King "a queer sort of fish," he wrote about him in his memos with respect and admiration, on occasion referring to King as "the Great Man." At Laurier House, at his office in the Parliament Buildings, or at Kingsmere, Dexter was the perfect guest: he listened intently to what the prime minister had to say, offered supportive advice, and never publicly betrayed King's trust. After one such intensive discussion in January 1945, King wrote in his diary: "I told [Dexter] confidentially what was in my mind which he seemed to appreciate very much and with which he was in entire accord. It seemed to give him a great thrill. He was most friendly in every way."[21] All the while, of course, no less in King's mind was the thought that his private disclosures would be transmitted back to Winnipeg and used by Dafoe or Ferguson for the next day's editorial leader.

For King this was a convenient and beneficial arrangement. For Dexter, however, it meant that the line between being a good journalist and being a party hack was often blurred. More than once, his loyalty to the Liberal cause and to the belief that the Tories offered no superior alternative put him in a compromising position. He attended private Liberal "board of strategy" meetings where advice and recommendations on *Free Press* articles was freely given; in October 1941 he helped Jack Pickersgill revise a memo on price and wage control policy for the cabinet; and he was recruited by the National Liberal Federation (NLF) to write election propaganda, a task he privately resented. "I wrote the piece practically in the middle of Wellington Street," he wrote George Ferguson in a letter about work on a Liberal election pamphlet in February 1940. "I had to submit the job I did for Willie [King] to [Norman] Lambert [head of the NLF] and I camped in his office, using a typewriter there, with all the Grits in creation milling around. I am finished being a ghost, even for Mackenzie King."[22] This last sentence had more meaning than Dexter could have realized.

In a *Saturday Night* article published in September 1935 entitled "This Man Mackenzie King," Dexter had astutely observed that "his name rarely appears in the social columns. He dislikes publicity and lives as privately as the average private man." Mackenzie King, as we now know, was hardly the "average private man" Dexter described. The fact that King was a superstitious man obsessed with the hands of the clock, that he was a committed spiritualist who gazed into crystal balls and attended seances to seek advice from his dead mother and the departed Wilfrid Laurier, or that he and his friend Joan Patteson sat at a "little table" waiting for the spirits to rap their messages is not at issue here. Such bizarre beliefs and practices were probably more common than King's biographers have admitted.* What is far more fascinating was that Ottawa's probing journalists had no idea about King's "other life."

Newspapermen's attitudes about politicians' private affairs had changed little since the days of John A. Macdonald, and any ideas to the contrary brought a quick rebuke. Speaking at a Montreal dinner in late 1930, Robert Elson, the head of the Washington Bureau for *Time* and *Life* magazines, commented to his audience that a "public man has no right to privacy at all ... The fate of the nation can well turn on the accidental stumble of a great man." Canadian editors profoundly disagreed with this assessment. "We think a public man has a right to a decent degree of privacy in his private life," one Ontario newspaper argued in reply to Elson's comments, "that even in his official life he should not be constantly badgered by reportorial surveillance ... We do not want to know and indeed have no right to know who has tea with the Prime Minister, or goes to his dinner parties, or if Mr. King has a new Fall coat."

Mr. King agreed. He considered his private life sacred and of no concern to the press. Any intrusions were a betrayal. Even someone like Grant Dexter was severely reprimanded for writing in a *Free Press* feature story that King had taken a bath after his government delivered its budget in 1930.[23] But such incidents were rare. No one in the gallery, for example, speculated (in public in any event) about King's relationship with the married Joan Patteson. She was his hostess at many dinner parties at Laurier House and a constant companion, one of his only true lifelong friends. (In her book *More Than a Rose: Prime Ministers' Wives and Other Women*, Heather Robertson asserts that King had had an affair with Mrs. Patteson, but this is pure speculation, based on a reading between the lines of his diary.) Yet, as historian Charles Stacey has observed, King "took no particular precautions to keep the connection secret, but he would certainly have resented any publicity."[24] In those days, explained journalist Alex Hume, "you never covered a prime minister's private life." Had the newsmen

---

*Mackenzie King belonged to the late Victorian-Edwardian age before the First World War, a time when spiritualist activities were quite common among Britain's and America's upper-middle classes. As George Bernard Shaw remembered in *Heartbreak House* (1917), English society in the decades prior to 1914 was "addicted to table-rapping, materialization seances, clairvoyance, palmistry, crystal-gazing and the like to such an extent that it may be doubted whether ever before in the history of the world did soothsayers, astrologers, and unregistered therapeutic specialists of all sorts flourish as they did during this half century of the drift to the abyss." (See Janet Oppenheim, *The Other World* [London, 1985]; Ruth Brandon, *The Spiritualists* [New York, 1983]; and Ronald Steel, *Walter Lippmann and the American Century* [Boston, 1980])

known about King's crystal-ball gazing, they would not have written about it.

Consider the following episode as a good example of the journalistic practices of the time, an age without the omnipresent eye of television. On October 20, 1925, nine days before the general election of that year, the prime minister was in Kingston. The campaign troubled him. The mood in the country was grim and the Liberals were stumbling along. King needed some reassurance. At 3:30 p.m. the prime minister of Canada went to see a fortune-teller named Mrs. L. Bleaney. Not one journalist was there to witness this amazing spectacle. King attributed to Mrs. Bleaney, as he recorded in his diary, "one of the most remarkable – if not the most remarkable interview I have ever had." She had promised him a victory.[25]

Though King was somewhat disillusioned with spiritualism when Mrs. Bleaney's prediction did not come true on October 29 (see chapter 7), he resumed his otherworldly pursuits a short time later. The following year, during the election of 1926, Mrs. Bleaney was invited to Laurier House to perform her magic. Again, nothing about this fascinating visitor was noted by the press. The country's most visible politician indulged in further such adventures over the next twenty years – seances in Detroit and Brockville, consultations with mediums in England – and only his closest circle of confidants had any inkling.

Not long after King's death in July 1950, stories about his private activities began circulating. In 1937 King had attended a party in London hosted by his friend and fellow-spiritualist, the Duchess of Hamilton. Another guest at this party at the headquarters of the London Spiritualist Alliance in Queensbury Place, South Kensington, was a Scotsman named J.J. MacIndoe. After King died, MacIndoe wrote a letter to the *Psychic News,* a weekly journal for British spiritualists, stating that the recently departed Canadian prime minister had been a believer. The *News* sent a reporter to interview the Duchess of Hamilton, who confirmed MacIndoe's tale. On October 10, 1950, the *Ottawa Citizen* reprinted the *Psychic News's* story on King, setting off a journalistic investigation.[26]

A little over a year later *Maclean's* resourceful Ottawa editor, Blair Fraser, after travelling to England to interview the various mediums King had consulted, wrote his now famous piece "The Secret Life of Mackenzie King, Spiritualist," published in the magazine's December 1951 issue. The country's political pundits were stunned.

"I was astounded," said Bruce Hutchison. The resourceful Alex Hume, who thought he knew everything about King, later admitted after reading accounts of the prime minister's private life and thoughts that the information in "such excerpts ... comes as an intense shock to many of King's admirers." Grattan O'Leary, a man who had as many contacts as Grant

Dexter, suggested in his memoirs that there had been gossip about King's escapades, but it was "shoved under the rug during his lifetime. You don't quarrel with success. As far as his fellow Liberals were concerned ... it wouldn't do at all to let it get about that the Prime Minister of the country, the leader of the party for nearly thirty years, was a frequenter of mediums and a gazer into crystal balls when he wasn't busy communicating with the shades of departed friends."[27]

Through a combination of journalistic respect for privacy, faithful companions like Mrs. Patteson, and sheer luck, Mackenzie King's private affairs remained secret during his lifetime. As far as the press was concerned, King's public politics provided enough of a story.

By the time he was forty-six years old, in 1921, King was a competent political player. In 1900, after completing his formal education at universities in Toronto, Chicago, and Cambridge (Massachusetts), King had joined the new Department of Labour set up by his family friend, William Mulock, the postmaster general in the Laurier cabinet. Ambitious and determined, he was deputy minister within months, at twenty-four probably the youngest person to hold such a position in Canada.

For the next eight years, King worked diligently, establishing a reputation for himself as something of a labour relations expert, a pioneer in the field. Far from satisfied with the civil servant's role, he jumped into politics in the 1908 election. By June 1909 he was in the cabinet as minister of labour. Caught in the protest against reciprocity in the election two years later, King was defeated. He eventually accepted an offer from the prestigious Rockefeller Foundation to head its new Department of Industrial Relations.[28] Laurier brought him back to Ottawa for the contentious wartime election of 1917. Although he was again defeated, he proudly stood by the old leader, a show of support that would endear King to Quebec for the next thirty years. Following Laurier's death in 1919, he was chosen the new leader of the Liberal Party. Within two years, he was prime minister.

The party King inherited in 1919 was in a mess. Quebec Liberals demanded a policy of economic protection, while westerners, many of whom had deserted Laurier in 1917 over conscription, favoured low or no tariffs. The party's organization was nothing to speak of, and real press support was limited, particularly in English Canada.[29] Organizational details were left to Ottawa lawyer Andrew Haydon, the appointed executive secretary of the National Liberal Council (who, as Reginald Whitaker points out, effectively ran "a one-man national organization throughout the 1920s"), while King tried to bring newspaper editors back on side.

The idea was to establish a viable newspaper network right across the country. This objective required money and business acumen, neither ever in great supply. Pleas for financial help, for instance, from two prominent Alberta organs, the *Edmonton Bulletin* and the Calgary *Albertan,* went unheeded. Direct ownership by the party was also frowned upon, and in fact only on one memorable occasion was it attempted, a bungled job from beginning to end. Here is a brief account of that tale: In 1923 Haydon, with King's full support and knowledge, put in motion a plan to start up an English Liberal evening newspaper in Ottawa. At the time, the city's small population of 130,000 (including Hull) was served by four English newspapers (the *Journal* and *Citizen* each had a morning and evening edition; *Le Droit* was the French paper). Clearly the market was saturated, but Haydon persevered. He submitted an application for membership in the Canadian Press cooperative, mandatory for any newspaper, and consulted with W.F. Herman of the *Border Cities Star* in Windsor, who was also interested in an Ottawa paper. Here Haydon's plans ran into trouble. First, Herman was astute enough to recognize a losing venture; second, he did not have any interest in fronting a party organ. According to CP rules, both profitability and competition in the field were major considerations in admitting a new member. On both counts, Haydon's application failed, as William Southam of the *Ottawa Citizen* was quick to point out.[30] It was duly and rightly rejected by a CP committee, and with it the plans for a new Liberal daily.

King and Haydon were more successful when they worked behind the scenes to secure the necessary capital from wealthy party men. In February 1922 the Regina *Leader,* a loyal Liberal paper since Laurier's day, was in financial difficulty. Haydon brought together a syndicate of Liberal senators from Ontario and Quebec to guarantee a Royal Bank loan of $250,000 so that the Leader Company could survive. A year later, Haydon was also instrumental in keeping the Saint John Publishing Company, owners of two dailies, under the management and financial control of a Liberal board of directors.[31]

King himself was more actively involved in saving the London *Advertiser.* This newspaper had consistently supported the party since the 1880s and had gone against the tide during the First World War by backing Laurier and his opposition to conscription. This last action did not sit well with many of the *Advertiser*'s loyal readers, and by 1922 its owner, lawyer Thomas Purdom (who had lost money on other bad investments), wanted to get out of the newspaper business. King liked the *Advertiser.* More to the point, its editors routinely checked with him (or the local Liberal MP) about the performance of the paper's Ottawa correspondent and whether front-page stories "secured the proper political slant." In an era when newspapers were turning their backs on their former political masters, no prime minister could have asked for a more faithful servant than the *Advertiser.*[32]

In early September 1922 word reached King in Ottawa that Purdom was about to sell the *Advertiser* to W.F. Herman, the publisher of the *Border Cities Star,* for $175,000 (Purdom's initial asking price was $500,000). Herman was an ingenious and successful newspaper man, but in King's view he was too independent and headstrong to be controlled. A flurry of letters between Ottawa and London eventually killed the deal. By early December King had convinced his friend Joe Atkinson, the publisher of the *Toronto Star,* to purchase the *Advertiser* for $180,000.[33]

This was one of Atkinson's few errors in judgment. Even with public endorsements from King and other Liberals, the *Advertiser* could not compete in a limited market with the Toronto *Globe* (then perceived to be the party's main paper) and the more popular Tory-leaning *London Free Press.* Within three years, the *Advertiser*'s circulation had dropped from about 26,500 to 23,000, with financial losses reaching close to half a million dollars.[34] In February 1926 Atkinson sold the paper for the bargain basement price of $112,500 to the only buyer to make him an offer, Arthur Blackburn, the owner of the rival *Free Press.* Although over the next decade Blackburn ran the *Advertiser* as a Liberal paper – thereby ensuring that a Blackburn publication was in the home of virtually every London resident – King never gave up hope that a real party supporter would reclaim it. It was not to be; the London *Advertiser* died a peaceful death in 1936.

In his struggle to maintain a loyal press, as with many things in his life, Mackenzie King viewed himself as the beleaguered underdog. "The [Conservative] Government ... has exercised a very considerable control over the Press Gallery, both in direct and indirect ways," he wrote to one friendly publisher in Vancouver in June 1920. "Indeed, the one hope the Government has of being able to retain any kind of support at the next election is what they expect will come to them through the extensive and expensive press and publicity propaganda they have been able to establish."

What King did not understand then and throughout his career was that editorial endorsements by this time could not be won by flattery or meagre government patronage. As his hated rival, Tory leader Arthur Meighen, also discovered, the twenties were a period in which Canadian newspapers, in the hands of powerful and unpredictable owners, increasingly pursued their own agendas.

Robert Cromie, the handsome, eccentric, and high-strung publisher of the *Vancouver Sun,* proved this point. Originally from Quebec, Cromie had moved to Vancouver in 1906 at the age of eighteen. After attending business school, he went to work for railway entrepreneur Colonel Jack Stewart. With Stewart's financial backing, Cromie acquired control of the *Morning Sun* in 1917, the Liberal Party's struggling organ in Vancouver. Within a few months the Sun had absorbed one its chief competitors, the *News-Advertiser,* and was on its way to becoming a successful operation.[35]

These developments should have been good news for the Liberals, but Cromie did things his own way. He was a Vancouver booster and a friend of Gerry McGeer, the city's popular maverick mayor in 1935. Cromie had definite ideas on just about everything. Now he dangled his paper's support in front of Mackenzie King's nose like a bone before a hungry dog. He demanded lower freight rates and more grain elevators; he argued that the tariff was too high, that the Liberals' trade policy was wrong, and that the government was not marketing itself properly. By 1930 King was thoroughly frustrated. "Mr. Cromie … is a very difficult person to satisfy on anything," he observed. "We are anxious to retain his friendship, and also to meet his wishes wherever that can be done with due regard to the public interest."[36]

The "friendship" quickly dissipated after the notorious Beauharnois scandal broke in 1931. Investigations by a parliamentary committee revealed that the Beauharnois Power Company, which the King government authorized "to divert St. Lawrence River water for hydro purposes," had contributed more than half a million dollars to the Liberal Party's 1930 election campaign.[37] To make matters worse, it was discovered that King's expenses for a holiday in Bermuda had been paid by the Beauharnois corporation. The humiliated Liberal leader was eventually cleared of any wrongdoing and forgiven by the public and most of the press. Bob Cromie, however, wanted King to resign the party leadership.

Subtle suggestions began to appear in *Vancouver Sun* editorials, and Cromie encouraged Harry Anderson at the Toronto *Globe* to join his crusade. The *Globe* did not need much prodding. When King vowed to work to reclaim the prime ministership from Bennett, Cromie became more vocal. "He is set. He is stodgy. He has got himself into a rut," a *Sun* editorial declared of King in early October 1932. "Withdrawn within himself and living the intellectual life of a recluse, he is out of touch with the trends and with people. He is living in a groove as deep and as narrow as a political grave." King was furious. After more than twenty years in political life, he was not about to let a West Coast newspaper publisher push him out of his cherished position. From this point onward, Cromie was regarded as an enemy and part of the Tory conspiracy.[38]* Indeed, the

---

*In 1936 Robert Cromie dropped dead of a heart attack at age forty-eight. The management of the *Sun* was taken over first by his son Robert Jr. and then by his son Don. The paper returned to the Liberal fold in 1938 when Roy Brown was hired from the rival Vancouver *Province* to be editor. He brought the talented Bruce Hutchison with him to write about politics. In a letter to King of December 22, 1938, Hutchison assured the prime minister that "the Sun … will be the most important Liberal influence west of the Rockies." Mackenzie King, not surprisingly, was delighted. (NA, King Papers, J1, vol. 252, Hutchison to King, December 22, 1938)

Conservatives made the most of the situation by using critical *Sun* editorials in their 1935 election campaign literature – supposed examples of how the "Liberal" press really felt about its leader.

John Dafoe at the *Manitoba Free Press* presented King with an even greater challenge. In order to reunite the Liberals and bring western party members who had defected to the Progressives back where they belonged, King needed Dafoe. Dafoe, age fifty-four in 1921, had, over the following years, firmly established his reputation as the country's most powerful editor and the *Free Press* as the only newspaper in Canada that, as argued by historian Frank Underhill, exercised anything approaching a "national influence." In Underhill's opinion, only George Brown's *Globe* at the time of Confederation compared to Dafoe's *Free Press* of the 1930s.[39]*

Very much a Liberal-Progressive in 1921, Dafoe had not had much faith in King's leadership abilities, nor did he trust him. A few years later Dafoe and Grattan O'Leary were on a ship together travelling to Australia to attend the Imperial Press Conference of 1925. As O'Leary subsequently told Meighen, Dafoe had confessed that he could not find a single young man in Canada, Liberal or Conservative, who liked or trusted Mackenzie King. "The truth is," Dafoe had said, "I don't trust him myself." Yet because he anticipated that the Progressives' life as a third party would be short, Dafoe had decided to give the new Liberal prime minister the benefit of the doubt.

The two men were drawn closer together in the fall of 1923, when Dafoe, at King's request, accompanied him to the Imperial Conference in London. It was intended that Dafoe – as he had done in 1919 for Robert Borden – would dispatch back to Canada favourable news and opinion pieces about King's performance. In fact, as soon as they boarded the ship, Dafoe, who had rigid opinions on most issues but especially on Canada's status within the British Empire, became an "unofficial member" of King's board of strategy. Thus, Dafoe's diary reveals that he was kept up to date throughout the ensuing conference by the prime minister and his chief adviser, Oscar Skelton, a professor at Queen's University who was later appointed under-secretary for external affairs. When he wasn't writing, Dafoe spent much of his time urging the cautious King to push for a policy

---

*After Sir Clifford Sifton, the *Free Press*'s owner, died in 1929, Dafoe had virtually total control of the newspaper's editorial policies; Sir Clifford's sons would never have dared to argue with the great editor. By this time, too, the Sifton family company had purchased two newspapers in Saskatchewan – the *Saskatoon Star-Phoenix* and the Regina *Leader-Post* – and had expanded into radio. Net profits from the Siftons' three papers were close to $1 million, yet this was only the beginning of their communications empire. (See Hall, *Clifford Sifton*, vol. 2, 323–26)

that would give an autonomous and clear voice to Canada in imperial affairs.[40]

In the end, King's refusal to be bowled over by Lord Curzon, the British foreign secretary, who strongly favoured a central imperial foreign policy, earned him Dafoe's respect. "I don't think much of King as a party leader in Canada," Dafoe wrote to journalist John Stevenson upon his return, "but I am bound to say he handled himself pretty well in London." Thereafter, the *Free Press* more or less gave King its support, though never automatically. The fact was that, as much as Dafoe doubted King, he still detested Meighen and the Tories (and equally, Meighen's successor, R.B. Bennett.)[41] These feelings were further reinforced by the events of 1925–26 and the controversy surrounding Governor General Byng's decision to refuse King a dissolution of Parliament.

Dafoe, always much on King's mind, was offered a House of Commons seat in the 1926 election, but he told King he would "sooner be the editor of the *Free Press* than the Prime Minister of Canada." In 1935 it was a cabinet position and then a diplomatic job in Washington; again both were graciously refused. Finally, in 1937, Dafoe accepted King's invitation to be a member of the important Royal Commission on Dominion Provincial Relations, headed by N.W. Rowell and Joseph Sirois, which examined the country's constitutional problems.

At the same time, Dafoe no less resisted anything that jeopardized what he perceived as the *Free Press*'s independence. In February 1935, for instance, Norman Lambert, the head of the National Liberal Federation, sought Dafoe's permission to use *Free Press* editorials in a campaign booklet. Dafoe quickly rejected the idea. "It has taken us a good many years to escape from the position which we once occupied as a recognized organ of the Liberal party," he explained to Lambert, "and we have no desire to put ourselves in a position which might lead to the impression being gathered by the public that we had resumed that relationship."[42]

Through the 1920s and early 1930s, moreover, Dafoe's autonomous approach in backing Liberal policies forced King to be on his guard, and was part of the reason King had so much time for *Free Press* correspondent Grant Dexter. Bruce Hutchison (who joined the paper only months before Dafoe's death in 1944) astutely summed up the King-Dafoe relationship in this way: "From the Liberal Party the *Free Press* sought and received no rewards. Nor could the government punish it, and it had its own zone of power, jealously guarded from the politicians of all parties. If the paper had detached itself from the Liberal Party altogether, life might have been easier for Mackenzie King ... Dafoe had believed, however, and his successors agreed ... that an uneasy marriage of convenience or loose liaison, a continuing wrangle between members of the same ideological family, would give the paper an influence for good denied to outsiders." The great editor was right.

As an Ontarian, and a pragmatic as well as vain politician, King was always very conscious of the coverage given to him in Toronto by the two main Liberal newspapers there. The *Star*, the most widely read paper in the country in 1921, was rarely a problem. Publisher Joe Atkinson had known King since the 1890s and had once offered him the job as a news editor after his electoral defeat in 1911. King considered Atkinson one of his "truest friends," though Atkinson's biographer doubts whether the publisher felt the same way.[43] In any event, no one, not even a Liberal prime minister, controlled Joe Atkinson – a fact King learned when the *Star* tycoon refused to fire his Ottawa correspondent, John Stevenson, as King had requested. The *Toronto Star*, in short, was not a party organ. Rather, it independently supported Liberal policies. On occasion, it advanced ideas and issues even before the party had taken action, as it did in the 1940s with respect to social reform issues.[44]

The Toronto *Globe* was another matter.

Mackenzie King had long understood the mythical power of the *Globe*. As early as 1907, when he was planning his entrance into politics, one of the first things King did was to ensure that the paper reported a speech he had given at a banquet in Berlin (later Kitchener). Following King's inaugural election victory the next year, the *Globe* proclaimed him to be the Liberal's "man of the future." King saved these yellowed clippings for the rest of his days.

A newspaper, however, has the habit of reflecting the personality of its owner. In 1921 the *Globe* was as sombre as its publisher, William Gladstone Jaffray, a man at least as strange as King himself. He had inherited the newspaper in December 1914 at the age of forty-four after his father, Robert, had died. His education had been typical of that for any son of a member of Toronto's WASP business establishment: Upper Canada College, training as a stockbroker, and a job at his father's newspaper by the time he was thirty-one. Those who worked for Jaffray found him a narrow-minded, stubborn, and miserly employer. At the same time, his astuteness as a businessman allowed him to pay off a $175,000 mortgage on the *Globe*'s property within a decade of his father's passing.

But what most people remembered about Jaffray was his passionate religious zeal, a trait imprinted on every page of his *Globe*. Arthur Irwin, who worked at the paper before he became editor of *Maclean's,* recalls one occasion when Jaffray was caught in a terrible dilemma. "Jaffray was informed in the middle of the night that Jesus's second coming was to happen at 5:00 a.m. the next morning," Irwin says with a smile. "He wrestled all night whether or not he would tip the *Mail and Empire* off or keep the scoop for himself."

In fact, Jaffray was a moral crusader opposed to divorce, gambling, and all other forms of enjoyable vice. As Pierre Berton noted, Jaffray refused thousands of dollars in advertising for "cigarettes, girdles, whiskey, sanitary pads and cheap clothing. [The *Globe*] panned sexy movies and covered every religious revivalist who came to town. It refused to praise Sinclair Lewis' novels because the author was an atheist."[45] Indeed, because of Jaffray the *Globe* was one of the first large secular newspapers in the world to publish a regular religious editorial.

Religion also played a significant role in Mackenzie King's life, but in a simpler, less complicated way. King never outgrew the black and white Christian tenets he had been taught as a young boy at Sunday School. "His religious faith," wrote Blair Neatby, "was not so much a belief that with God's help he could be a Christian as a faith that he was a Christian. He did not flaunt his religious observance. He read the Bible and had private prayers every morning and attended church regularly but he avoided publicity and was indignant when his church attendance was referred to in the press."[46]

Unlike Jaffray, King was not a fundamentalist; nor did he try to impose his version of morality on the rest of the world. He recorded his sins in his diary like a good Puritan and promised to work harder to overcome his inner weaknesses. Basically, King believed he was "truly good." His critics, Jaffray included, were skeptical of that happy evaluation. "They watched his tactics, saw through his political scheming, and knew he was intensely ambitious," Neatby observed. "When he talked of his selfless dedication to Canada or humanity, they talked of hypocrisy. King's naive faith in his own virtue incited cynicism."[47] Even if this flaw in his character had been pointed out to him, King would never have grasped its meaning. While he eventually acknowledged that Jaffray did not like him, he never accepted this fact on a certain level because he could not admit his own failings. With great frustration, he tried for more than a decade to win over both Jaffray and the *Globe*.

Jaffray's personal animosity towards King was only part of the problem, though it was a significant factor. Journalist Melville Rossie, who wrote for the *Globe* in the early twenties, told King in 1935 that Jaffray was "always trying to poison my mind against you." Arthur Irwin had similar memories: "Anytime I said anything critical of King, he just beamed." Apart from Jaffray's unwavering opinion that King was an opportunist bent on staying in power at any cost, it was, remarkably, the publication of horse-racing results that was at the root of much of the friction between the *Globe* and the Liberals.

In 1920, in an attempt to combat the "evil influences of the handbook" (that is, the betting that took place in nearly every hotel and barbershop in Toronto), Jaffray ordered that the *Globe* no longer publish horse-racing odds or news. This righteous move cost the newspaper at least 10,000 sub-scribers, since its competitors had no such qualms (during the early twenties the *Globe*'s daily circulation hovered around 95,000; the *Star,* the *Mail and Empire,* and the *Telegram* were each over 100,000).

But Jaffray's morality knew no bounds. In exchange for the *Globe*'s support, he wanted King to pass an amendment to the Criminal Code ban-ning the publication of all racing news. Given the popularity of the races and the country-wide circulation of American and British newspapers, busi-nesses beyond the control of the federal government, Jaffray's demand was unrealistic. Nonetheless, on three separate occasions, King made an effort to appease the *Globe* proprietor, clearly an indication of how much he valued the paper's editorial page. Yet, each time – in 1923, 1925, and 1930 – the Liberals pushed the amendment through the House only to have it rejected by the Senate. And after each failure, it was the King administration that was blamed. "It was obvious for some time past," a *Globe* editorial declared following the last defeat, in May 1930, "that the King government lacked the energy or the earnestness necessary to overcome the sinister interests in opposition to the proposal."[48]

In many ways Mackenzie King was Jaffray's hostage, much more than Laurier had been John Willison's when Willison was editor of the *Globe.* As Jaffray grew increasingly unhappy with King, the newspaper distanced itself more and more from the Liberal Party. The average Canadian Grit was con-fused. As one astute Ontario lawyer explained to King in 1929, "At the pre-sent time there are thousands of Liberals in Canada who read the *Globe* as their morning Bible fully believing that it is a Liberal organ and when they see Liberal policies or principles attacked by the *Globe* they naturally lose faith in their party leaders." It was a predicament the prime minister had been well aware of since 1924.[49]

For about four years the *Globe* gave King moderate support. Still, it was clear even by 1923 that Jaffray no longer felt obliged to adhere to the arrangement agreed to by his father and George Cox back in the 1880s: that the *Globe* was to be held "in perpetual trust for the Liberal party to act as its mouthpiece." In Jaffray's view, put forward in a *Globe* editorial in early 1923, "politicians can no longer command the support of the press, [they] have to win it." This newly defined relationship offended King and his key advisers. Behind the scenes his close associate and benefactor, the tea mer-chant Peter Larkin, then Canadian high commissioner in London, started putting together a group of Liberal businessmen to buy back the *Globe,* but Jaffray was not interested in selling his prized possession.

As the 1925 federal election drew closer, King's political prospects did not look bright. Not wishing to upset the Progressives (who held sixty-five seats from 1921 to 1925), King had implemented a cautious and unimpressive legislative program during his first term. In Ontario, Arthur Meighen's prospects appeared brighter. Consequently, King was desperate for an influential newspaper in Toronto. "If we could only get back the *Globe* as a first-class Liberal organ," he confided to Larkin in September 1924, "we would be able to keep the party in power for many years to come."[50]

Not one to surrender without a good fight, King had spies everywhere. Inside the *Globe*, editors John Lewis and Hector Mackinnon kept the prime minister informed of Jaffray's strategy and actions.[51] In August 1924 Lewis, a gracious, tolerant, and talented writer of Welsh extraction, was made the paper's managing editor upon Stewart Lyon's retirement. Initially it looked as if Lewis would be able to keep the *Globe* in the Liberals' corner, despite Jaffray. The new editor wrote to King in September indicating that he wanted them to work together to secure a Liberal victory. On receiving the letter, the prime minister was overcome, and in responding was at his poetic best: "Your letter has come like the breaking of a fresh dawn upon the political horizon." Shortly after, Lewis was hired by the Liberal Party to write a favourable biography of King for use as election propaganda.

The fragile partnership collapsed four months before the vote, in June 1925, following the defeat of the government's second attempt to outlaw horse-racing statistics. Jaffray, furious with King for not being able to control the Senate, began to meddle with Lewis's pro-King editorials. Within weeks, Lewis had had enough. He resigned from the paper on August 14 along with Ross Munro and Melville Rossie, two other loyal Liberal editors. Stewart Lyon, who was recuperating from a serious illness in North Carolina, was forced by Jaffray to return to the editor's chair (Lyon had shares in the *Globe* worth about $20,000). Eventually, when Lyon was too sick to continue, Harry Anderson, who also hated Jaffray but coveted the editor's position more, took over the paper. He remained the *Globe*'s editor until 1936.

Mackenzie King was surprised and upset by Lewis's departure. He offered Lewis (who, he noted in his diary, "helps to restore my faith in journalists and in real Liberalism") a vacant seat in the Senate, and Lewis graciously accepted. As well, the party paid the salaries of Rossie and Munro for the remainder of the year. Losing the *Globe* this late in the campaign was bound to have serious repercussions. One plan, suggested at a private dinner at Laurier House on August 17, 1925, with King, Lapointe, Haydon, and Larkin, among others, in attendance, was to try again to buy Jaffray out. Senator W.L. McDougald (later forced to resign his seat as a result of the Beauharnois scandal), also present, offered $50,000 towards the purchase.

Yet King believed, probably correctly, that such attempts by the party would only have antagonized Jaffray further.

It was difficult for King, a man with a sizable ego, to accept that Jaffray could not be charmed into supporting him. With the help of Reverend John Inkster, a long-time family friend, a meeting with Jaffray at the *Globe* office in Toronto was arranged for the first week of September. Going into the meeting, the Liberal leader recognized he had only a slim chance for success. Inkster had told King that Jaffray seriously questioned the sincerity of King's Christian beliefs. The fateful meeting took place on the morning of September 5. "It was the horse racing business most on his mind," King observed later. When he left Jaffray, he believed the *Globe* might still be helpful, a complete misreading of the situation.

The prime minister should have paid more attention to a lengthy *Globe* editorial entitled "The *Globe* and Partyism" published September 1, five days before his meeting with the paper's owner. There in black and white was Jaffray's reply to the Grits, contained in an encapsulated history of the *Globe*'s long and often tortuous relationship with the Liberal Party. "The *Globe* is an exponent of Liberal principles. It is not and has not been since Confederation the organ of a party," declared the paper. "We have criticized and shall continue to criticize the Government of Mr. King when that Government fails, as we believe it has failed ... The *Globe* will remain neutral in the coming election ... It proposes ... to advocate the principles of political Liberalism as it has advocated them for the past eighty years. That assuredly does not mean subservient support of a policy of political drifting which involves the evasion of issues that should be faced courageously."

William Jaffray had spoken. But the neutrality of the *Globe* was interpreted by Liberals and Conservatives as nothing less than a total repudiation of Mackenzie King. Jaffray's pronouncement, coupled with the fact that support from John Dafoe and his *Winnipeg Free Press* was also less than favourable, caused devastating political damage. "No party was ever so handicapped in its press," conceded King in his diary a few weeks before the vote. "Both the *Free Press* and the *Globe* ... are betraying the cause hourly."[52]

At the *Globe,* Hector Mackinnon, the city editor who had served as a sessional in the parliamentary gallery, secretly kept King up to date on Jaffray's election editorials. Working with Arthur Irwin (who did not know about Mackinnon's correspondence with the prime minister), Mackinnon had prepared editorials in defence of King's "tariff for revenue." When Jaffray refused to run them, the two men resigned. As he had done before, King promised that the party would pay their salaries for the remainder of the year. That, however, turned out to be unnecessary, for both were hired by *Maclean's* within a short time. Arthur Irwin became the magazine's editor in 1945, a position he filled with distinction for five years.

As noted, on October 29, 1925, Mackenzie King suffered a bitter defeat, particularly in his home province of Ontario. He won only eleven of eight-one seats and lost his own seat in York North. The *Globe,* which was partially responsible, interpreted the results as a "severe want of confidence passed upon the Administration." Rank-and-file Liberals were upset with the newspaper's conduct and wondered why the Tory *Mail and Empire* had been fairer to King than the *Globe* had been.

Mackenzie King himself was both furious and wounded. About a month later he wrote an emotional nine-page letter to Peter Larkin in London spelling out the various reasons for the loss. He blamed Meighen's dishonesty; he blamed the "millions of dollars" of Montreal Tory money that had been used to discredit the Liberals throughout the country; and he blamed the appeal of the Progressive Party that captured twenty-four seats. In Ontario, however, there was only one guilty culprit: the "treachery" of the *Globe.* "There is hardly a doubt," King bitterly wrote, "that the ... loss of Ontario ... was due to the attitude of the '*Globe,*' which bewildered many of our own party who felt that there must be something radically wrong or we would not have been stabbed front and back by that journal as we were."[53]*

Jaffray had no regrets. On the contrary, he believed the *Globe* had acted in the country's best interests. "We feel that country comes before party and we could not conscientiously support the Liberal party in the last election," he informed one irate Liberal subscriber in November 1925. "What claim has the official Liberal party upon the support of the *Globe,* may we ask? The *Globe* has given a very great deal of support, during all the years of its history, to the Liberal party and debt, it seems to me, is all on the other side. The Liberals should not expect the *Globe* to be subservient."[54]

Through the next stormy months, as King and then Meighen tried to retain power, Jaffray and the *Globe* became disillusioned with both parties. King's resignation over scandal in the customs department was no better than Meighen's failed bid to govern by playing tricks with the rules of Parliament. When another election was called for September 14, 1926, the paper was not optimistic. "Let us be frank and honest with ourselves," the

---

*According to King, the *Globe'*s influence knew no bounds. As he told Larkin, there was a report from one of the teachers in the Toronto Institute for the Blind, "who, being herself a good Liberal, read aloud the 'Globe' to the inmates of the institution all through the campaign with the result that when the day of polling came these poor physically blind young women each and every one voted against the Liberal party because the 'Globe' had told them it was the only right thing so to do." (NA, King Papers, J1, vol. 117, King to Larken, November 26, 1925)

Globe stated on September 4. "The recent record of our political parties – both of them – has shattered public confidence. The people of Canada are weary of watching the unseemly struggle to 'get in' and 'keep in' – the long selfish, wearisome strife for office for partisan aggrandizement."

Again, as in 1925, the *Globe* refused to endorse King (or Meighen). But this time the Liberals, to quote the paper, were "lucky." King's victory in his constitutional fight with Governor General Byng returned more than a dozen Ontario seats, and he made slight gains in the West and the Maritimes. It was just enough to put him back in his "rightful" place as prime minister.

King, however, was still troubled by the *Globe* and by Jaffray's attitude to him personally. As much as he tried, he could not understand why the Toronto publisher, who admittedly did not know him very well, opposed him so emphatically. For King, the complexities of politics were reduced to a schoolboy's fight with the class bully. Why was Jaffray picking on him? At the prime minister's urging, Reverend Inkster set up a meeting for February 1927. As Grattan O'Leary later told Meighen, the story that made its way around the gallery went as follows: "The three men, preacher, premier and publicist, met in the latter's sanctum, and while King stood with bowed head the Rev. John Inkster, with hand uplifted, prayed that these two great and noble souls might become reconciled to work for the good of their common country. What a moving, immortal scene that must have been!"[55]

Apparently, King's call for divine intervention paid off. During 1927 and 1928 the *Globe* slowly came around. It supported the government's tariff policy and its development of trade within the British Empire, though Jaffray continued to press King about banning horse-racing results and stopping illegal liquor smuggling from Canada to the United States. The now workable partnership made King very happy. "A new beginning" had been made, he believed, and a great burden had been lifted from his shoulders. "It has been often a source of pain to me that the relationship between ourselves ... was not as close as I should have liked it to be," he wrote to Jaffray in August 1929. "I have never yet really understood just what it was that kept us apart."[56]

And now that he had Jaffray on side, King made every effort to keep him there. Against the advice of many members of his cabinet, legislation aimed at curtailing the illegal traffic in liquor was introduced in March 1930. In May of the same year, Finance Minister Charles Dunning's budget, which lowered duties on British imports, reflected Jaffray's thinking on the economic problems that had arisen since the stock market crash of October 1929. While King, like most Liberal politicians, believed the economy would rebound, Jaffray was deeply convinced from his reading of the Bible that the world was entering a period of hard times.[57] Furthermore, King insisted that Ernest Lapointe, his minister of justice, drop in at the *Globe* office to explain to Jaffray why the amendment to the Criminal Code on horse-racing statistics had been rejected by the Senate at the end of May 1930. No newspaper publisher had ever been courted so royally.

In mid-July the appeasing of Jaffray seemed to have paid off. Another election campaign was in full swing, and the *Globe* under the direction of Harry Anderson remained very supportive of the Liberals. But not even the *Globe* could save Mackenzie King as the Great Depression spread. Haunted by his infamous partisan declaration in April that he would not give any Tory provincial government "a five-cent piece" to combat soaring unemployment, and crippled by Canadians' loss of faith in his cautious management style as a cure for the gravely troubled times, King suffered a sweeping defeat on July 28. The election results gave R.B. Bennett and the Tories a commanding 138 seats, while the Liberals were reduced to 87 seats, a decline of 29 from 1926.[58]

The *Globe* reluctantly accepted the people's decision. "The arbiters of the national fate and of political fortunes have exercised their sovereign right by rejecting a Government with a good record," the paper observed the day following the election. Liberals everywhere must have been pleased with the *Globe*'s lead editorial on July 30: "Mr. King has been defeated, but in departing from office he can look back on nine difficult years of service in which his government piloted the country through a period of rejuvination from the turbulent and uncertain war aftermath to unparalleled national prosperity." The *Globe* failed to point out that it had made these "nine difficult years" even more difficult.

If Mackenzie King believed that he had won over the Toronto newspaper for all time, he was mistaken. Jaffray was outraged by the sordid details of the Beauharnois scandal that emerged in 1931. He went so far as to write a harsh anti-Liberal editorial entitled "A Discredited Party," but Harry Anderson persuaded him not to run it.[59]

Over the next few years, as the Liberals attempted to rebuild their organization and put Beauharnois behind them, King tried to please Jaffray's every whim amid rumours in Ottawa and Toronto that the *Globe* was to be merged with Isaak Killam's *Mail and Empire*. Despite some serious health problems, however, Jaffray was not ready to give up the paper he envisioned as Canada's London *Times*, a journal that espoused causes rather than parties.[60]

Relations with King remained cordial, but the publisher was clever enough to keep the Liberal leader off guard, never really sure if he could count on the *Globe*. Cabinet ministers visiting Toronto were instructed to pay their respects, while Jaffray was invited by King himself to lunches and visits to Kingsmere. Luckily for the Liberals, by the summer of 1935 Jaffray had given up any hope that R.B. Bennett could save the country. Beginning in August and for the remainder of the election campaign, *Globe* editorials fully endorsed King and the party. "The *Globe* is urging support of the Liberal party in this election," the newspaper explained on October 12, two days before the vote, "because it believes the principles it stands for will serve the welfare of the country most favourably at this time."

Canadians felt the same way, and Mackenzie King was returned to the prime ministership once more. The victory of October 1935 marked the start of two decades of uninterrupted Liberal rule. But it would also be the last election for many years in which the *Globe* stood as a Liberal friend.

Like many of his personal and business relationships throughout his long political life, Mackenzie King's association with William Jaffray had been characterized by a lengthy struggle to avoid confrontation. Whether the *Globe* was as influential a newspaper as King believed or whether it was worth all the aggravation it caused him remains open to debate. Even with today's modern polling techniques, measuring a paper's real power is still difficult. The point, however, is that King stubbornly insisted that the *Globe*'s support was mandatory if he was to fulfil his destiny as prime minister. That insistence ensured that Jaffray, a man with his own rigid agenda, largely dictated the terms of his newspaper's relations with the Liberal Party hierarchy. The *Globe* would discover that Conservative leader R.B. Bennett was not as accommodating in his own dealings with the press as King had been.

CHAPTER NINE

R.B. in Charge

*Mr. Bennett likes the radio better than the newspapers
because the radio cannot talk back to him.*

John Bassett Sr., June 1, 1934

Richard Bedford Bennett, "R.B." to his friends and foes, Conservative prime minister of Canada for five of the harshest years in this century, didn't much care for the press. And the feelings were very mutual. "The reason that Mr. Bennett finds fault with reporters and editors is that our Prime Minister is an orator rather than a thinker. Meaningless words flow from his agile tongue like water over a millrace while his brain is as arid of thoughts as an African river in the dry season," explained the *Vancouver Sun* in a February 12, 1934, editorial entitled "Why Bennett Hates Newspapers."

No prime minister had ever bullied reporters like Bennett did. None had ever threatened to throw editors in jail for publishing the truth. By the time Bennett was finished, he had alienated even the most ardent Tory journalists and, in so doing, had accomplished what no Canadian political leader had achieved before: he united the partisan parliamentary gallery. They now had a common enemy.

From the perspective of the press and most everyone else, R.B. Bennett was an easy target to condemn. Only his small circle of friends knew of his good nature and charm. In public his personality and demeanour were more suited to the private confines of a boardroom. He dressed like a turn-of-the-century banker, sporting a top hat, striped pants, and a morning coat. A bulging waistline rounded out his appearance. Often lacking a sense of humour, he could be rude, arrogant, and spiteful. If this were not enough to turn off journalists, his loathing (learned through his Methodist upbringing in New Brunswick) of tobacco, liquor, and gambling – favourite gallery vices – surely was.[1] In short, R.B. Bennett rarely had much fun. As a sixty-year-old prime minister, he worked until he dropped and enjoyed few of life's pleasures, although he could have afforded anything he desired.

To be fair, perhaps Bennett did allow himself a few indulgences. Stories about his escapades with the ladies – particularly older more matronly women – made the rounds in the press gallery, but, of course, not much of this got into the papers. Nevertheless, it was well known "that Bennett was no virgin." In May 1931 there was public speculation that he would marry Mrs. Elfie Rowley, the widow of the Eddy Match Company's managing director. But nothing came of that. As Bennett once told his friend Lord Beaverbrook, a wife "must while being domestic in her tastes have such large sympathies and mental qualities as to be able to enter into the ambitions and hopes of her husband, whatever they may be."[2] Even in the 1930s, this was a tall order.*

Needless to say, Bennett remained a lonely but very rich bachelor his entire life. Indeed, in a time when many Canadians could not put food on the table, Bennett, the millionaire, lived comfortably in a suite of rooms at the Chateau Laurier Hotel. While he had earned much of his money as a successful corporate lawyer in Calgary before he became Conservative Party leader in 1927, his enormous wealth was mainly due to his friendship with Jennie Shirreff Eddy and her brother Joseph, the major shareholders of the E.B. Eddy Company. Jennie, E.B. Eddy's widow, had died in 1921 and Joseph followed in 1926. Bequests from both gave Bennett a controlling interest in the largest match company in the country and a sizable fortune. During his term as prime minister, from 1930 to 1935, his annual income from investments and salary was never less than $150,000 – at least half a million in 1990 dollars. Journalists like Bruce Hutchison earned about $2,500 per year, while a seamstress at Eaton's was paid approximately $600 or less annually, if she was lucky.[3]

Beyond questions about his personality and wealth, Bennett was criticized then and since for being a poor administrator, a terrible political strategist, and a failure as a prime minister. He trusted few members of his cabinet and unlike Mackenzie King did not delegate responsibility. As the now famous story goes, a visitor to Ottawa in late 1930 was walking with his friend, a resident of the city. As they rounded a corner, they saw a man coming towards them talking to himself.

---

*In fact, Bennet would have married Hazel Kemp Colville, a young, wealthy, and attractive widow whom he courted in 1932–33. But she refused his offer. The few love letters and poems Bennett wrote Hazel reveal a much more passionate man than historians have portrayed: "I shall think tonight as I journey west of a week ago & the sunlight ... And I will be sad & pity myself & be thankful that I know you & grateful for all you have meant to me ... It would so please me to see your handwriting & have a few words from you ... I miss you beyond all words & I am lonesome beyond cure without your presence & so I go on with all my love." (Cited in Waite, The Loner, 74–75)

"Who is that man and why is he talking to himself?" the visitor asked his friend.

"That's Mr. R.B. Bennett, the new prime minister," replied the friend, "and he's holding a cabinet meeting."[4]

Since his days as a businessman and lawyer in Calgary, total control had been part of Bennett's style. As a political leader he made the mistake of taking on too much and worrying about too many details. At the beginning of his term, not only was he prime minister, but he also took on responsibility for Finance and External Affairs (the Finance portfolio was eventually given to Edgar Rhodes in the spring of 1931). In an effort to keep tabs on the growing civil service, Bennett encouraged "the practice of tattle-telling," *Winnipeg Free Press* correspondent Grant Dexter told John Dafoe in 1935. "There are literally hundreds of people in and out of the civil service who either run to him with gossip (very often untrue) or write him private letters."[5]

Driving Bennett was the fact that during the 1930 campaign he had promised, as Canadian journalists would remind him, that he would save the country from imminent economic disaster. He intended to end unemployment and use high protective tariffs to blast his way into the world's markets for the betterment of all Canadians. Single-handedly, R.B. Bennett was going to halt the Depression.

As with most Depression-time leaders of industrialized nations, including Mackenzie King, Bennett did not comprehend the extent of the economic disaster that gripped the world in 1930. Critics who argue that he should have opted for the untested theories of John Maynard Keynes forget that the British economist's ideas were not widely known upon Bennett's election; nor did Canada then have a central bank or any "experience in operating a large-scale social insurance scheme." Still, the Conservative government's record in its first four years – before Bennett attempted to turn the country upside down with his New Deal reforms of 1935 – indicates a sincere attempt to tackle the severe economic problems of the day. As historian Larry Glassford has recently noted, during the 1930–34 period "the Bennett government provided unprecedented sums for emergency relief, propped up the prairie wheat pools, increased coal subsidies, provided a temporary bonus on wheat exports, increased the federal share of old age pensions, nationalized radio broadcasting, negotiated a treaty with the United States to construct a St. Lawrence deep waterway, hosted an imperial economic conference, negotiated new trade treaties, set up relief camps, forced the two great railways into cooperation, helped to create international silver and wheat cartels, drafted legislation for unemployment insurance, established a central bank, set up natural product marketing boards, eased credit problems for farmers, and launched a major public works program."[6] That the Tories' solutions did not have the desired result was hardly Bennett's fault. It is highly doubtful that King and the Liberals would have done any better.

In taking on the elimination of unemployment from the face of Canada, Bennett showed that his political skills were not perfect. Too often his hard-nosed stubbornness and rigid business approach got in the way of a success-ful strategy. Yet it is too simplistic to dismiss him as a failed politician. He understood the political value of a good newspaper and put up his own money to prove it. And long before King did, he grasped the immense power of the radio as a supreme political tool. "Though his ideology was wrong," reflected Bruce Hutchison, "he has been underestimated. Bennett was an extremely able man."

In 1927 Bennett inherited a divided and discontented party. His predecessor, Arthur Meighen, had faced a similar situation seven years earlier. Meighen had been unable to unite the Conservatives; Bennett promised in his stirring acceptance speech at the Winnipeg national convention to "dedicate his tal-ents and his fortune to the interests of his party and his country." Tory dele-gates as well as the Conservative press were convinced that their party now had the "aggressive and virile" leadership required to unseat the Liberals. Preparations for the next election campaign began immediately.[7]

The view prevalent among the majority of Canadian editors and publish-ers in the late 1920s was that they were masters of their own destinies and editorial pages. This posed a problem for Bennett. In order to ensure proper press support, he would have to become more personally and directly involved. At first, Bennett was inundated with requests for money from groups across the country that were keen to establish friendly newspapers with his capital. In Ontario, on the recommendation of Tory Edmund Ryckman, he decided to back a weekly Conservative newspaper, the *Canada News,* that was launched by a publishing company from Port Hope. After negotiations, Bennett guaranteed a $2,500 loan at the Bank of Montreal and supplied Peter Brown, publisher and editor of the weekly paper, with a list of 20,000 names of potential Tory subscribers. The first issue of the *News* came out on July 1, 1928, but it had financial troubles and ceased publication about a year later.[8]

Politically, the situation in the West was far worse. Bennett, in fact, had been the only Conservative elected on the Prairies in 1926, and there was nothing in the way of a Conservative organ in the entire region. Years earlier as a member of the Alberta provincial assembly, Bennett had, together with his mentor and law partner, Senator James Lougheed, endeavoured to take over the Calgary *Albertan,* a Liberal organ. They were able to obtain only 46 percent of the shares, and control of the newspaper and its editorials, much to Bennett's dissatisfaction, remained in the Liberal hands of editor and publisher William Davidson. This failed attempt did not dissuade the ambitious Bennett from trying again.

In late October 1927, only a few months after Bennett had assumed the leadership of the party, a proposal was put forward for the establishment of a strong Tory newspaper in Saskatchewan, then the Prairie province with the most seats in the Commons. Start-up costs were estimated to be about $250,000.[9] Matters became urgent after the Liberal-leaning Sifton interests acquired the province's leading dailies in 1928, the *Leader* and *Post* in Regina and the *Star* and *Phoenix* in Saskatoon. Without a paper of their own, some Tories feared they might never win another seat in Saskatchewan.

Recognizing that the age of the out-and-out political organ was over, the Tories decided to launch a seemingly independent paper, the *Regina Daily Star,* which by its own choice would support the Conservative cause in the coming election. Curiously, Bennett entrusted the operation to Vancouver businessman Charles Campbell, a self-proclaimed Liberal who, with his partner, Alberta entrepreneur George Bell, had recently acquired control of the *Edmonton Bulletin.*

Bennett's part in the *Star*'s evolution was mostly financial. He initially arranged for a $40,000 loan from his Calgary bank, and another $150,000 was loaned to the *Star* by his Calgary law firm. He also helped Campbell secure Tom Blacklock as the paper's Ottawa correspondent and had his private secretary, A.W. Merriam, dispatch hundreds of letters urging Tory businessmen to advertise in the new independent, but friendly, journal.[10] The first edition of the evening *Regina Daily Star* was published on Monday, July 16, 1928, with a declared circulation of 10,000 and a pledge to be honest and non-partisan. It was only trouble after that.

Nothing went right at the *Star.* Despite the fact that the Conservatives won eight new Saskatchewan seats in the 1930 election, the *Star* was no match editorially for the more polished Sifton dailies; nor could it compete for advertising. The business side was terribly mismanaged by Campbell, who was more concerned with his investments in Edmonton and was absent from Regina for long periods. Moreover, provincial Conservatives, distrusting him because of his Liberal affiliations, refused to have anything to do with the paper. All of this meant that the *Star* quickly became a bottomless pit for Bennett's money. It lost $60,000 during its first year and usually ran at a monthly deficit of between $3,000 and $10,000.[11]

At Bennett's insistence, Campbell was finally forced out in 1933 after the *Star*'s accumulated debt had reached about $120,000. Bennett wanted to be rid of the entire operation, but in the midst of the Depression finding a buyer for a losing proposition was close to impossible. Things got so bad that the prime minister himself had to cover the staff's payroll on more than one occasion.

Had Bennett been able to devote more of his own business expertise to the newspaper, the *Star* might have become a great Canadian success story. But that was not possible. As it turned out, the paper was a financial disaster and of limited political use. Bennett was not able to dispose of the *Star* until 1939, by which time he estimated this foray into the publishing business had cost him more than $100,000.[12] (The *Star* ceased publication in 1940 after its assets were acquired by the *Leader-Post.*)

This experience probably made Bennett leery of putting up money to save the Montreal French newspaper *La Patrie* in 1931. The Conservatives had won twenty-four seats in Quebec in the 1930 election, the most since 1911. Memories of Riel, conscription, and Arthur Meighen seemed to have finally vanished, and many Quebec Tories felt the time was right to re-establish a strong French organ.

La Patrie, it will be recalled, had been purchased for Meighen by a Conservative syndicate in 1926, but with limited results. The paper, which billed itself as "independent Conservative," had a daily circulation of only about 30,000 in 1930, not even close to the Liberal *La Presse*'s 160,000. Around the time of Bennett's victory, *La Patrie* had been sold again to another group of Tories, led by Senator Lorne Webster, and it was now managed by Joseph Bender, a former manager with the Royal Bank. The purchase was not the most astute business decision ever made. Faced with mounting debts and a dwindling number of cash-strapped advertisers, Webster and Bender offered Bennett complete editorial control for $200,000 (the money was desperately needed to help guarantee a $400,000 bank loan).[13]

They planned to make the newspaper the party's official Quebec organ and to sell it to French readers throughout the province and country. The boost in subscribers would naturally lead to a boost in advertising dollars. There was only one hitch: while Bennett favoured the scheme in theory, he was unwilling to pay the price. Consequently, within two years, *La Patrie* was taken over by *La Presse* for $500,000 – a good deal considering the paper and property were worth close to $900,000 – and the Tories were without a francophone organ for the next election.[14]

A far more serious error in political judgment was Bennett's decision to shut down Maj.-Gen. Alexander McRae's propaganda and publicity operation, which accounted for more of the Tories' success in the 1930 election than the new prime minister would have liked to admit. It was the money of Bennett ($60,000) and of *Montreal Star* publisher Hugh Graham ($100,000) that financed the campaign, but it was McRae's organizational genius that put the funds to good use.

An imposing man, tall and square-jawed, McRae had been born in a small town in rural Ontario in 1874. His years on the farm had made him one of the best judges of horse flesh in the country. After spending nearly seven years in northwestern United States, he returned to Canada and accumulated an impressive fortune in real estate, lumber, and colonization work in western Canada. When the Great War began, Sir Sam Hughes placed McRae in charge of the remount section, which supplied horses to all branches of the service. McRae was so competent at this job that he was promoted to director of supply and transport for the entire Canadian Expeditionary Force. Near the end of the war, he was loaned to British authorities, working as an assistant to the minister of information. It was in this capacity that he learned the value of good propaganda.[15]

McRae returned to Vancouver and became active in the Conservative Party, winning a seat in the Commons during the 1926 election. The following year his reputation as a major political player was further enhanced when he brilliantly organized the party's convention in Winnipeg. When an undecided delegate asked him which candidate he should support, McRae directed him to vote for Bennett. "He's got the money and he can get the money," he said.[16]

And McRae knew what to do with Bennett's money. For two years, he travelled from one end of the country to the other, gathering names, meeting with local Conservatives, and establishing a grass-roots network of faithful followers. By the time the election was called for the summer of 1930, McRae's central office in Ottawa, complete with the latest printing technology – multigraph plates and addressograph machine – could churn out 250,000 Tory pamphlets and distribute them across Canada in about three days. More importantly, the office was able to deal very quickly with Liberal campaign literature, sometimes putting responses in the hands of Conservative editors before the Grit material had been sent from its headquarters.[17]

If not for McRae, Bennett would not have boarded his private railway car in early June 1930 for a 14,000-mile journey that took him to cities and towns throughout the country. With his future brother-in-law and confidant Bill Herridge as travelling companion, Bennett delivered close to seventy speeches in which he promised to save Canada from Mackenzie King and the Depression.[18] McRae also arranged for Bennett's opening speech in Winnipeg to be broadcast on the radio, a bold experiment in 1930. It was in this speech that Bennett made his famous declaration about using tariffs "to blast a way into the markets" of the world.*

---

*According to Grant Dexter of the *Winnipeg Free Press* (who heard it from Grattan O'Leary), Bill Herridge, who knew how to spice up a dull speech, had thought up the "blast" line. Bennett had struck it out when he first saw it on paper, but Herridge, without Bennett's knowledge, had put it back in when the final draft was typed. When Bennet was delivering the speech, he came upon the phrase "and was unable to get by it." (NA, Dafoe Papers, vol. 8, Dexter to Dafoe, January 4, 1935)

Assisting McRae in Ottawa was Robert Lipsett, a bright and competent journalist who had worked for the *Winnipeg Telegram* and more recently for the *Montreal Star.* Bennett liked Lipsett and was one of the few people who called him "Dick."[19] As director of publicity for the campaign, Lipsett supplied 99 Conservative weeklies with partisan articles and editorials and another 165 with more objective political letters. McRae and Lipsett's invention, the Standard News Service, exemplified their true shrewdness.

Starting in 1929, 645 weekly newspapers with a total circulation of 750,000 (of mostly rural readers) from British Columbia to Prince Edward Island received national news stories free of charge and with just enough of a Conservative slant to make a difference. What made this network so politically ingenious was that the unsuspecting and grateful editors had no idea the Standard News Service was in reality a Tory propaganda operation. The deception would have even made Clifford Sifton proud. "We have thus far been successful to such an extent," Lipsett reported to Bennett in August 1930, "that we have an imposing file of testimonials from publishers declaring that it is the first useful and *non-political* service ever offered to weekly newspapers." In Lipsett's view, the news service together with the editorials and articles provided, at a cost of approximately $700 a month, the kind of political advertising that the party could not have bought for less than $20,000. He urged the newly elected prime minister to keep the office functioning, primarily to educate the public about the realities of the economic crisis. "What I have been endeavoring to do is to stress the fact that your government faces actual conditions much more serious than was anticipated and that with the legacy left by Mr. King you have truly a Herculean task upon your shoulders," Lipsett wrote.[20]

It was advice Bennett foolishly ignored. In 1931, as economic conditions worsened and Bennett increasingly believed he could save the country by himself, McRae's office was closed, the staff dismissed, and – quite stupidly – the valuable multigraph plates destroyed. (Four years later, MP Earl Lawson, in charge of the 1935 campaign, had to start from scratch, while the Liberals were much better prepared.) After turning down a cabinet position, McRae accepted his appointment to the Senate in September 1931, soon after Bennett had made Bill Herridge (who married his younger sister Mildred the same year) Canada's ambassador to the United States. According to journalist Arthur Ford, it was Herridge's appointment that caused a serious rift between McRae and Bennett, and left the Conservative leader without the services of the general – one of the country's best political architects.[21]

As for Robert Lipsett, he got his revenge by becoming an Ottawa correspondent for the Liberal *Toronto Star,* one of several papers that went to war with R.B. Bennett in 1931.

At first, only those reporters who worked for Liberal newspapers suffered Bennett's wrath. Joe Atkinson of the influential *Toronto Star* was never a man to hide his feelings. He had long questioned Bennett's prime ministerial qualifications, regarding him as a "platform politician" and a "political lawyer." The *Star* had strongly backed King in the 1930 election and was disappointed with the results. Its coverage of Bennett was harsh and critical ("studied contempt," as Ross Harkness put it). When Parliament was reconvened in August with Bennett as prime minister, the *Star*'s headline on the first day of the session read, "Pooh Bah Is on Job at Capital."[22]

The *Star*'s men in the gallery in 1930, Wilfrid Eggleston and Thomas Wayling, paid the price. Soon after Bennett assumed power, both correspondents were literally thrown out of the prime minister's office and warned never "to approach the new government for news or assistance." Bennett had nothing personal against either reporter, but business was business.[23]

Such heavy-handed actions did not make Bennett popular with the close-knit gallery. The ever-powerful Grant Dexter of the *Free Press,* who found that his contacts in the civil service were still willing to talk, found the prime minister "incredibly arrogant and domineering." Fortunately for Dexter, his Conservative journalist friends (Grattan O'Leary, Tom Blacklock, Norman McLeod, and John Stevenson) kept him up to date on the government's closely guarded secrets. But the list of newspapers critical of Bennett grew at a steady pace, and within a matter of months political connections made no difference. Soon the *Ottawa Journal* and *Montreal Gazette* were viewed by Bennett with almost the disdain he reserved for the *Toronto Star,* the *Winnipeg Free Press,* and the *Financial Post.*

Unwilling to accept advice from anyone, let alone a newspaper, Bennett continued to stir the pot. In a speech in the House in early September 1930, he observed how newspapers regularly misinterpreted politicians and stated how glad he was to have the option of speaking on the radio so that he could tell the Canadian people the "right" news. Editors around the country were infuriated. Writing in *Saturday Night,* E.C. Buchanan, the gallery's vice-president at the time, suggested that Bennett ought to be grateful to the newspapermen for making him so well known.[24]

The *Ottawa Journal,* a Bennett supporter during the 1930 campaign, was especially upset. The "*Journal* Men" – P.D. Ross, Norman Smith, and Grattan O'Leary – still regarded Bennett as "a politician of intellectual integrity," but they were insulted by his attack on their integrity. Contrary to what Bennett now said (he claimed to have been quoted out of context), their own analysis of the *Journal*'s coverage of his speeches showed that there had been no misrepresentation of the prime minister's words over the past few months. A proud and overly sensitive man, Bennett did not like to be challenged, and he let Norman Smith know that he considered the *Journal*'s editorial "disgraceful." Smith was perplexed. "For one who seriously criticized his own party some years ago, he has an extraordinary objection to independence in the press," the *Journal* executive told John Dafoe.[25]

That Bennett lashed out at the Liberal press is understandable, but that he alienated his allies at Conservative newspapers is more difficult to fathom. He had, he believed, a mission and a duty to lead the country back to the land of prosperity. During that first session in August and September 1930, he had earmarked $20 million for provincial governments for relief purposes and had raised tariffs to levels not seen since Sir John A.'s day. Nothing happened. He attended an economic conference in London and convened another impressive gathering in Ottawa in the summer of 1932, where he pushed for a system of preferential tariffs within the Empire. The economy failed to respond as he had promised it would; instead poverty and despair became more widespread.

Bennett grew increasingly bitter and frustrated, perceiving any criticism or editorial comment as nothing short of treasonous. If the Tory press dared write anything positive about King, he accused it of printing "Grit editorials." "When the *Ottawa Journal* ran an editorial criticizing the government, Bennett failed to recognize me," Grattan O'Leary remembered. "The next day he flung his arms around me." As the papers continued to throw his 1930 election promises back in his face, he became thoughtless and downright mean. "It must be galling for a man who dramatized himself as the Saviour of his country to find that all his plans are going badly and he became the target for continual and well-founded criticism," John Stevenson, Ottawa correspondent for the *Times* of London, observed. "Of course, [Bennett] is afflicted with Mussolinian megalomania and wants in his blind rage to trample upon everybody who criticizes or thwarts him."[26]

Initially, reporters in Ottawa tried explaining to Bennett that they had no desire to embarrass the government "in its effort to promote the national interest." On a few occasions early in his term, Bennett invited several gallery members back to his office for "frank" off-the-record discussions. Yet such friendly gatherings were few in number. Either Bennett ignored reporters altogether, as he did in January 1931, when he failed to tell them that the Earl of Bessborough was replacing Lord Willingdon as governor general, or he resorted to intimidation, threatening to throw editors and reporters in jail for a year under section 136 of the Criminal Code, which concerned the illegality of spreading false news. It was a rarely used law but Bennett had done his homework, as Floyd Chalmers, editor of the *Financial Post,* discovered in the fall of 1931.

The influential Toronto business paper, like its highly eccentric and legendary owner Col. John Bayne Maclean, was, and had been since its inception in 1907, more Conservative than Liberal in its politics. At first, the

Colonel was willing to give the new Tory administration his support. "I think the work that Bennett is doing, and doing it thoroughly and conscientiously in the public interest – working under excessive pressure – might be commented on favourably and sympathetically," he told his senior editors in late 1930.[27] As the economic situation worsened, however, the *Post*'s editorials became negative. By July 1931, the paper had lost faith in Bennett's judgment. "He is making many mistakes and apparently has some bad advisers," declared one editorial. "Some of his policies are very unjust to established Canadian interests. He is finding many conditions are not what he thought they were."[28]

That October, in desperate need of money to carry out his plans, Bennett pleaded his case before New York financiers, asking them to support an issue of Canadian government bonds. Grant Dexter, a frequent contributor to the *Post,* wrote an innocuous article summarizing the predicament, noting that "the bond issue would be unwelcome in the U.S. 'until Canada came to grips with its costly railway problem.'"[29] (At the time, Canadian National Railways' staggering deficit was approximately $1 million or more a week.) Had Dexter's story appeared only in the *Post,* it probably would have been overlooked in Ottawa, but versions of it were picked up and published in the *Wall Street Journal* and the *Times* of London. Bennett, sick in bed with a temperature, was outraged.

Acting on the prime minister's direct orders, Minister of Justice Hugh Guthrie attempted to reach Colonel Maclean, but he was out of town. Editor Floyd Chalmers was next on the list. As he recalled the incident many years later, he was sitting at home on a Sunday afternoon when his phone rang.

"The law officers of the Crown have taken note of this article and require your presence in Ottawa tomorrow at ten o'clock in the morning," Guthrie stated firmly.

"This is such short notice, couldn't the meeting be delayed until Tuesday?" asked Chalmers.

"No, I'm sorry. Unless you give me your word right now that you will be here tomorrow morning I shall instruct the law officers of the Crown to have you brought," countered the minister.[30]

Chalmers was on the next train to Ottawa. He arrived at Guthrie's office at the appointed hour to find Bennett's henchman slightly embarrassed with the role he had been asked to play. Explaining that the prime minister had been running a high temperature all week, he read a stern and formal legal letter directed to Colonel Maclean, ordering the *Post* to publish a retraction. In the brief, Bennett referred to section 136 of the Criminal Code. He "cited cases from English law based on the statute *De Scandalis Magnatum* passed in the reign of Edward I, which compelled British subjects to keep a civil tongue in their heads ... The statute had not been enforced for 221 years and was repealed in 1888, but Bennett summoned it out of legal antiquity to strengthen his case."[31]

Like any proud newspaperman, Chalmers refused to retract anything, despite the threat of jail. Not knowing what to do next, Guthrie telephoned his chief, who told him – amazingly – to lock Chalmers up in the "Tower." As far as Guthrie knew, there were no cells in the tower of Parliament and he assumed that Bennett's high fever had conjured up hallucinations of "merry old England." Wanting no further problems, Chalmers reluctantly agreed to draft an article that presented Ottawa's official view, namely that the Dominion's financial position was sound. The solution received Bennett's approval, and the matter was resolved.[32]

This episode was only the beginning of Bennett's battles with the *Financial Post* – or "The Fanciful Post," a Bennett sarcasm. It was not as if Chalmers and his writers disagreed with everything the Conservatives tried. They supported his initiatives on imperial preferential tariffs in 1932, but together with other major newspapers, they attacked the London Wheat Agreement of 1933 for restricting the size of Canada's wheat crop. Nevertheless, in Bennett's eyes the *Post* was not only never right, it was also somehow responsible for Canada's problems. "His reasoning seemed to be," observed Chalmers, "that if we stopped saying his economic policies were dreadful, his economic policies would stop *being* dreadful." What further fuelled Bennett's anger was the fact that occasionally the *Post*'s criticisms were based on inaccurate reports found in the Tory *Mail and Empire*. Editor F.D.L. Smith, who generally agreed with Bennett's assessment of the *Post* (himself calling it "one of the most sensational, erratic and unreliable publications in the country") could only sheepishly apologize for his reporters' errors.[33]

There was more trouble in November 1933. On a national radio broadcast Bennett attacked the *Financial Post,* claiming it had run a story which stated that Ontario apple exporters were facing economic ruin under the Empire trade agreements negotiated a year earlier. The prime minister fingered Grant Dexter (whom he called the *Post*'s "Ottawa Correspondent") as the author of the article and insinuated that he was under instructions from either the *Post* or his other employer, the *Winnipeg Free Press,* or both, "to send news against the Government – and particularly against [cabinet minister] Bob Manion and the Prime Minister."

This time it was Chalmers who was outraged. In a two-column, front-page editorial, he listed and dismissed Bennett's comments, falsehood by falsehood: there had been no story on the destruction of the apple industry in the paper during the past year; Grant Dexter was not, and had never been, the *Post*'s "Ottawa Correspondent"; the paper's reporters had never been instructed to attack Manion or Bennett; the *Post* had not tried to "delude" the people through "fanciful statements"; and lastly, despite what the prime minister charged, the *Financial Post* had always supported the 1932 Empire trade agreements.[34]

Grant Dexter and his superiors in Winnipeg, John Dafoe and George Ferguson, were equally angered by Bennett's attack. A stinging rebuttal appeared in the *Free Press* on November 13. This had not been the first time the Winnipeg newspapermen had clashed with the prime minister. Indeed, Bennett and Dafoe's five-year feud was one of the bloodiest fights between a politician and a journalist ever waged in Canada.

John Dafoe had never liked Bennett personally or politically.* In 1928 he considered the Conservative leader's views on international trade to be "mercantilist theories of the eighteenth century," and he argued that on imperial questions Bennett had not "moved forward a step in forty years." The *Free Press* editor, a staunch advocate of free trade and the tenets of Manchester liberalism, was appalled by Bennett's 1930 campaign promise to raise the tariff to new heights. He was even more appalled when Bennett won the election, and publicly said so. As George Ferguson remembered, "Day after day, edition after edition, Dafoe explained to his readership, much of which had voted for Mr. Bennett, because it was sick and tired of Mr. King, that it had made a terrible mistake."[35]

Dafoe, in fact, had prepared his staff to do battle. The plan was to "fight the [Bennett] government on ... every aspect of its policy." In Ottawa, Grant Dexter was ordered in early August 1930 to write an editorial listing (and ridiculing) Bennett's countless campaign promises. "The record should include such things as [the prime minister's] reference at Regina that if Italy doesn't want our wheat he would see that they were not allowed to sell Italian goods in Canada," Dafoe instructed Dexter.[36] The correspondent's piece appeared in the paper on September 6 with a challenge to Bennett to fulfil his numerous pledges.

Significantly, Dafoe viewed the *Free Press* not as a Liberal organ, but as an "opposition paper" free to make its own choices. "We shall carry on our own brand of warfare against Bennett without much regard as to

---

*The feelings were mutual. During the 1927 Conservative convention in Winnipeg, Bennett was interviewed by a young reporter.

"Mr. Bennett, I represent the *Free Press*."

"Yes, of course, the *London Free Press*."

"Mr. Bennett, have you ever heard of the *Winnipeg Free Press*?"

"Well, now, let me see."

"Surely, Mr. Bennett, you have heard of Mr. Dafoe?"

"Dafoe? Oh yes, of course! He is the man who wrote *Robinson Crusoe*." (Cited in Waite, *The Loner*, 61)

whether or not it fits in with the plans of the Liberal board of strategy," he announced to Dexter, "and I should not be surprised if we do more execution than they."[37] Here was one of the earliest statements to elevate the press's role to that of the "unofficial opposition" – a fact of life in Canada that would not become commonplace for two more decades, but Dafoe was always a journalistic trend-setter.

After Dexter informed his editor and mentor of Bennett's arrogance, Dafoe replied that "if the prime minister of Canada is a rude and arrogant boor, it will be news to let the public know about it."[38] That he did. With the devilish cartoons of Arch Dale – one of the most polished practitioners of the art – portraying Bennett as a fat cat capitalist, the *Free Press* pilloried him for the next five years.

Not everyone in Manitoba supported this brutal attack. The Conservatives had captured eleven of the province's seventeen seats in 1930 with close to 50 percent of the popular vote. Even if Dafoe was not willing to give the Tories a chance, many Winnipeggers were, and the *Free Press*'s circulation actually dropped by more than 2,000 in the first sixteen months after Bennett assumed office. Readers were unhappy with the newspaper's uncompromising approach, and so was John ("Jack") Sifton, one of Sir Clifford's five sons, who had inherited the publisher's job at the *Free Press* following his father's death in 1929. After Dafoe left for his winter vacation in Bermuda in January 1931, Sifton wrote Dexter a confidential letter declaring that despite the great editor's orders, it was not the *Free Press*'s duty "to move Heaven and Earth to attack Bennett and the Conservative Party and organization on every possible occasion." He added that, like many in Winnipeg, he would rather "read the editorial page of the *Tribune* than that of the *Free Press*."[39]

Dexter obligingly wrote that he would follow these suggestions. Still, he only had one master at the *Free Press* and it wasn't Jack Sifton. Critical editorials, particularly on the futility of protective tariffs, continued to be a major focus of "the page." According to Dexter's sources inside the Tory cabinet, Dafoe was routinely characterized by the prime minister as "unfair, partisan, mean and unscrupulous." In view of all this, it seems remarkable that Bennett wrote to Dafoe in June 1932 asking for advice about the Imperial Economic Conference. The fact remains, however, that while Bennett regarded Dafoe as his "most malignant opponent," he was astute enough to see that the editor was "one of the ablest men" in Canada.[40]

The exchange of correspondence sent Ottawa buzzing. Of course, Dafoe did not tell Bennett what he wanted to hear – that his plan for an imperial trading bloc was feasible – rather he pointed out that "no matter how valuable the British market was to Canada, it alone was insufficient to meet Canadian export needs."[41] This was one of many negative points harped on by the *Free Press* during the conference that Bennett felt impeded his efforts to negotiate a better deal with the British delegation,* as was later made clear to Grant Dexter in an encounter with the prime minister in the washroom of the Rideau Club.

The story goes something like this, as Dexter later reported to Dafoe: Noon, Friday October 14, 1932. Dexter, as was his usual custom, was lunching at the Rideau Club, home to Ottawa's establishment. He was chatting in the washroom with lawyer Ken Green about the tariff issue when the toilet flushed in one of the lavatory compartments and out stepped the prime minister of Canada.

"Well, Dexter, what falsehoods have you been disseminating today?" asked Bennett while washing his hands.

"None that I am aware of, Mr. Bennett," an embarrassed Dexter replied.

"Doubtless you have written only your usual quota of misstatements," he continued.

Dexter moved towards the door, trying to escape, but Bennett refused to stop the strained conversation.

"Why Dexter did you write so many falsehoods during the conference?" the prime minister asked, shaking his finger as if he were scolding a child.

"I am not aware that I wrote any."

"Oh yes you are. You can't tell me that you were not actuated by malice."

"On the contrary, Mr. Bennett, I had the very best of reasons for believing that everything that I wrote on the conference was true."

"You had not."

At about this moment, in walked former prime minister Arthur Meighen, who, seeing the uncomfortable predicament Dexter was in, "smiled broadly behind R.B.'s back and went along." With the interrogation over, Dexter flew out of the washroom and sought refuge in a secluded corner of the club's dining room to eat his lunch. As Dexter began to read the

---

*Led by Neville Chamberlain, the British delegation, in fact, considered Bennett to be a bully "who alternately blustered, sobbed … prevaricated, delayed and obstructed to the very last moment." While much was made of the conference's accomplishments, from an economic viewpoint little actually changed. Wrote historian Blair Neatby: "The harsh fact was that Imperial solidarity was a myth. It was obvious, for example, that trade agreements and preferential tariffs would mean little if any Dominion could subsequently alter the value of its currency unilaterally. A stable exchange rate was required. The delegates understood the importance of the monetary question but the interests of the different parts of the Empire were so divergent that nothing could be done." In the end, Canadian wheat, apples, and lumber were accorded some preferential treatment in the British market. "The total impact on Canadian exports [was] not great," concluded Neatby, "but it … help[ed]." (Neatby, *King, 1932–39*, 19–22)

menu, Bennett appeared in front of his table; Dexter invited the prime minister to sit down.

The *Free Press* correspondent ordered soup; the prime minister, oysters. Again, Bennett started in on Dexter's coverage of the Imperial Conference. Again, Dexter declared his innocence, pointing out that he relied on his own sources because Bennett was not available for him. After attempting to pry the name of these sources from Dexter, an exercise in futility, Bennett pointed out how the *Free Press* and the *Toronto Star* had nearly "wrecked" the conference. "One of the saddest consequences of this conference for me," Bennett added, "is that throughout the entire proceedings some Canadian journalists – Dafoe at Winnipeg was one of them – and you, young man [Dexter was thirty-six years old], were another, did everything in their power, stopped at nothing, to discredit your country's representatives, and your own prime minister. Is that fair journalism, is it common decency?"

Dumbfounded by Bennett's lack of understanding of journalistic work, Dexter reiterated that he was not guilty of "malignant distortion." Bennett concluded that he was therefore "abysmally ignorant of what took place." As Dexter's face reddened, Bennett outlined his version of the conference's events. At the end of this self-serving diatribe, which described in great detail Bennett's Herculean efforts to save the Empire, it was agreed that Bennett would become, to use post-Watergate terminology, Dexter's "Deep Throat," supplying the correspondent with background information and confirmation of confidential details.[42]

Back in Winnipeg, Dafoe expressed astonishment on hearing of the interview. He encouraged Dexter to maintain close contact with Bennett on the condition that it was understood that it was both the *Free Press*'s "right and duty to oppose him to the extent of our ability and this we propose to do until he and his policies are eliminated from our politics."[43] This hard-line position, along with Bennett's huge ego and a deteriorating economy in 1933, meant that Dexter did not become the prime minister's close confidant. Instead, the *Free Press* continued to demand a change of government. This led to numerous confrontations, including one in November 1933, when Bennett publicly declared that the Winnipeg paper, the *Financial Post,* and Grant Dexter were conspiring against him.

Earlier, while in Washington for a conference on disarmament, Bennett held a briefing for the press at the Canadian Legation. Dexter, who was covering the meeting, arrived with fellow-journalist Grattan O'Leary. "In one of the large reception rooms R.B. was surrounded by a crowd of American and Canadian reporters," remembered O'Leary. "As soon as R.B. spotted Dexter he drew himself up as though confronted by a striking adder. 'Ladies and gentlemen,' he pontificated, 'there will be no press conference. I refuse to say anything in the presence of Mr. Dexter, the emissary of John W. Dafoe of the *Winnipeg Free Press,* whose only purpose here is to distort and misrepresent Canada's position.'" The stunned newsmen filed out of the room in disbelief.[44]

The *Free Press,* as well as other major Canadian dailies, was a convenient scapegoat for far greater problems. If he could have done so, Bennett would certainly have censored the press altogether, an idea he actually hinted at in May 1934 after the *Montreal Gazette* had mistakenly reported that the government was eliminating the excise tax on sugar.[45] In an editorial on May 22, 1934, the *Toronto Star* was forced to remind him that Canada was "not a Fascist country." "A free press is the bulwark of democracy," declared the *Star,* "and the Prime Minister will find little support for any proposal to make Canada's press other than free."

By December of that year, Bennett was in trouble. There was severe discontent in General McNaughton's military-style relief camps, where Canada's unemployed were treated like prison inmates; a Communist threat hovered over the country, or so Bennett believed; and Tory Trade and Commerce Minister Harry Stevens's year-long campaign to expose "sweatshop conditions" and excessive profits in department stores, meat-packing plants, and other businesses had led to his resignation from Bennett's government after a well-publicized feud with the prime minister.[46]*

Desperate, Bennett needed to do something. And he did – he went on the radio.

Large American advertisers were the first to comprehend radio's real power. When "Amos 'n' Andy" was on the air, everyone stopped to listen; when Pepsodent sponsored the show, sales of its toothpaste tripled within weeks. By 1931 one major U.S. tobacco company was spending more than $19 million annually to advertise its cigarettes on the radio.[47] It was not long before

---

*Dafoe and the *Free Press* were in the middle of Harry Stevens's crusade as well. Stevens's investigation had begun as a select parliamentary committee in February 1934 and had evolved into a full-scale royal commission on price spreads by July. In the meantime, without Bennett's knowledge, Stevens had put together an interim report that was published and distributed on his orders. Included in the pamphlet were some harsh words about Simpson's department store and Sir Joseph Flavelle, one of the store's major shareholders and a leading contributor to the Conservative Party. The *Toronto Star* and *Ottawa Citizen* were the first to quote from the report and then Dafoe got his hands on it. He published the entire incriminating document in the *Free Press* on August 7. The whole issue exploded in Bennett's face, causing Stevens to resign from the cabinet and eventually from the party. He formed his own Reconstructionist Party, which split the Conservative vote in the 1935 election. (Richard Wilbur, *H.H. Stevens, 1878–1973* [Toronto, 1977], 132–43; Watkins, *Bennett,* 205–13)

politicians made the same connection: radio could also sell politicians and policies.

In an attempt to control their potential rivals, newspapers were the first to get into the radio business. On July 27, 1922, the *Manitoba Free Press* opened one of the most powerful radio transmitting stations in North America; it could be heard up to 1,900 kilometres away. But it was the CNR's popular train-radio cars that tapped into a national market. Travellers would not board a train unless it was radio equipped – much to the chagrin of rival CPR ticket agents whose company was slower to respond to the demand. And in Calgary in 1925, a relatively unknown Bible instructor named William Aberhart went on the air with a weekly Sunday-afternoon sermon that became one of the most popular shows on the Prairies. The decade's most polished political artist on radio went from this flamboyant beginning to become, in 1935, Alberta's Social Credit premier.[48]

In 1925 approximately 100,000 Canadians owned their own radio; by 1930 the figure had risen to 500,000, even with the dollar-a-year licence fee (which many avoided). The new activity of "listening in" had killed Sunday-evening church services and had made the radio "the central piece of furniture in the living room."[49] Most Canadians tuned into popular American shows like "Amos 'n' Andy," "Moran and Mack" (the Two Black Crows), and "The Happiness Boys," prompting the federal government to appoint the royal commission chaired by Sir John Aird in 1928, the first of forty such inquiries to study broadcasting problems. To counter the effect of this overpowering American influence, which according to the commission "has a tendency to mold the minds of young people in the home to ideals and opinions that are not Canadian," it was recommended that a publicly owned and operated broadcasting system be established. This led to the creation of the Canadian Radio Broadcasting Commission (CRBC, now the CBC) by the Bennett government in 1932.

News reporting and political commentary developed simultaneously. Since the early 1920s, Canadian newspapers had fought to protect their supremacy in reporting the nation's news, restricting their stations to short bulletins that had already been published. Finally, in 1933, a deal was worked out between the Canadian Press and CRBC "to supply stations nightly with a 1200-word newscast compiled from material supplied by CP."[50]

Political commentary was first heard over the CNR's network in January 1932. Grattan O'Leary (with help from Grant Dexter of the *Free Press*) broadcast the fifteen-minute "Canada Today" show, which discussed current issues covered by O'Leary's paper, the *Ottawa Journal*. His intention was not "to take sides" in any political controversy, but to give listeners "an intelligible picture of the week's events ... [and] a clearer grasp of the nation's business." In deference to the prime minister, O'Leary had sought Bennett's permission before the program was first aired. Like a schoolteacher, Bennett had replied to the Ottawa editor's request by admonishing him to "take great care to be absolutely certain of accuracy in the use of figures." Before long, however, O'Leary had become embroiled in a dispute with American authorities over remarks he had made concerning U.S. policy on German war reparations. Bennett was caught in the middle of it.[51]

Like their counterparts in advertising, American politicians were quick off the mark in using radio as a propaganda tool. No one took to the radio or dominated it as did Franklin Roosevelt. He was, in the words of journalist David Halberstam, the "first professional of the art." "For most Americans of this generation, their first memory of politics would be sitting by a radio and hearing *that* voice, strong, confident, totally at ease." Roosevelt's predecessor, Herbert Hoover, had received about 40 letters a day; after FDR went on the air, the president's daily mail reached 4,000 letters. Not by chance, Halberstam concluded, was FDR president of the United States for an unprecedented twelve consecutive years.[52]

In Canada things moved at a slower, less exciting pace. As early as 1927, during the country's Diamond Jubilee celebrations, Mackenzie King had been impressed with the cross-Canada broadcast of the gathering (and his speech) from Parliament Hill. But he was also concerned about how he sounded on the radio. Today it is almost painful to listen to King's high-pitched, whiny voice in speeches that droned on for hours. Back then the reviews were mixed. In June 1930 the *Globe* maintained that there was no public speaker anywhere "equal on the air" to King. After his speech in Kingston in August 1935, which was broadcast over CRBC, the *Ottawa Journal* praised the Liberal leader for his "soothing, pleasant voice." On the other hand, in 1929 a prominent Ontario Liberal wondered why King sounded "so sick," and a decade later the Victoria *Colonist* called his New Year's message "boring and verbose."[53]

The secret to Roosevelt's radio success was that he was relaxed, intimate, and personally charming. Listeners felt as though he was in their living room, talking directly to them. A 1936 memo in King's papers on "how to talk on the radio" suggested just that approach – that "[you] speak to the listener as you would in the privacy of your own home." But King was never relaxed or comfortable in public and certainly was not while speaking into a microphone. Jack Pickersgill, who joined King's staff in 1937 (and was by all accounts the country's first backroom media expert), tried to tell King that it was sound rather than content that really mattered in a radio broadcast. The Liberal leader did not have to put everything he knew into every sentence. As Pickersgill recalls, "Mr. King paid no attention to this advice." Still, by the time he became prime minister again in 1935,

Mackenzie King finally understood that radio could be used to compensate for his loss of direct control over the press.[54]

R.B. Bennett had learned this political lesson earlier. The radio was tailor-made for Bennett's ostentatious oratory. In the House he was a powerful speaker, with a "speed of delivery ... so rapid that he was known as Richard 'Bonfire' Bennett." His speeches broadcast during the 1930 election left the listener with the image of a confident and strong political leader. Not everyone, though, was impressed with Bennett's speaking style. His opponent Mackenzie King, for one, was appalled. After hearing the broadcast of Bennett's memorable Winnipeg speech in early June, King noted in his diary: "I really blushed as I listened to him – such demagoguery, declamation & ranting, there was nothing constructive, nothing really destructive in any concrete fashion of the government's record or policy ... I really believe Bennett is one of our greatest assets. I cannot see how he can hope to win to his side men of any real intelligence. It was a terrible chaos, hectic utterances throughout ... I pray God I may escape coming into that class of oratory."[55] King need not have worried; his own broadcasted speeches did not come close to reaching the same feverish pitch.

That Bennett chose to use the radio to unveil his latest scheme for economic recovery five years later was thus not surprising. He had received sound advice from Major General McRae during the 1930 campaign; now he looked to Bill Herridge, his brother-in-law. As Canada's representative in Washington, Herridge had watched FDR conquer the country with his "fireside chats" and his New Deal, a government interventionist reform plan designed to save capitalism. That the American New Deal was not entirely successful was beside the point. It was the political ramifications of the experiment that impressed Herridge. For him the New Deal was the "Pandora's box" from which Roosevelt pulled a lot of "mysterious things most of the people never understood ... any more than they understood the signs of the zodiac." Bennett, Herridge suggested, needed his own Pandora's box, "by which the people can be persuaded that they also have a New Deal." The results would be self-evident: soaring political popularity and a boost to the staggering economy.[56]

On Wednesday afternoon, January 2, 1935, Grattan O'Leary was invited to the prime minister's office, where he found Bennett with his executive assistant Rod Finlayson and Bill Herridge. He was handed the text of Bennett's first two broadcasts on the economy. (It was more than a little ironic that it was an Ottawa journalist who was sent for; no one in the Tory cabinet was told, let alone asked for an opinion, about the radio talks.) After reading them quickly, O'Leary told the trio that the speeches were too vague. He suggested to the prime minister that he should state his proposals more clearly. "Bennett was inclined to agree with this view but pointed out that his main purpose was [to] arouse public interest in the later broadcasts and speaking tours. Herridge disagreed very strongly with the criticism; Finlayson said nothing," O'Leary later told Grant Dexter.[57]*

That evening Bennett delivered the first of five sensational New Deal broadcasts as prepared by Herridge and Finlayson. The speech was carried on thirty-eight stations, and Bennett was reported to have paid $10,000 for the air time himself.[58] As Dexter reported to Dafoe, everyone in Ottawa was "tremendously excited" with Bennett's apparent about-face.

It was a personal appeal to all Canadians in the best humble style of FDR. "If you are satisfied with conditions as they now are," Bennett declared, "if ... you feel that the Government is not required to do anything more – then I am not willing to continue in this office. For if you believe that things should be left as they are, you and I hold contrary and irreconcilable views. I am for reform. And in my mind, reform means Government intervention. It means Government control and regulation. It means the end of *laissez faire*." By the time the last broadcast was aired on January 11, the entire country (those without radios gathered around their neighbours' sets for "Bennett parties") had heard the Tory leader's bold plans for minimum-wage laws, regulations governing the maximum hours of work a week, unemployment insurance, and agricultural marketing boards.[59]

Reaction to the broadcasts was unsettling. Right-wing members of the Tory cabinet, led by C.H. Cahan, were skeptical and hostile, and Cahan later privately admitted his disbelief that Bennett could "espouse the economic fallacies of Karl Marx."[60] Cahan was a staunch defender of Montreal business interests and close to the publisher and editors of the *Gazette*. In an editorial the day of the second broadcast the traditionally Conservative newspaper declared it was not prepared "to fly the flag of Socialism side by side with the historic banner under which Conservatism heretofore has always made its appeal to responsible, sober-minded Canadians."

In Liberal quarters, Mackenzie King, who believed that most of Bennett's ideas were probably unconstitutional (for intruding into provincial jurisdiction – which some did), was "sickened and disgusted" by "the absolute rot and gush" delivered by the Tory leader. John Dafoe in Winnipeg was extremely cynical of the Canadian version of the New Deal; in his mind

---

*According to Grant Dexter, a few days later Bennett's secretary, A.W Merriam, telephoned O'Leary for his reaction to the first broadcast. O'Leary indicated that he was not impressed with Bennett's delivery, which was shaky in spots. Bennett was later told that O'Leary thought he was "rotten," and as a result, it was the last contact O'Leary had with the prime minister and his office for the duration of the speeches. (NA, Dafoe Papers, vol. 8, Dexter to Dafoe, January 12, 1935)

it was nothing more than a desperate ploy concocted by the Conservative leader to remain in office. "Canada is not the United States. Bennett is certainly not Roosevelt and 1935 is not the year 1933," Dafoe sarcastically observed.[61] *Free Press* editorials lambasted the prime minister as they had done for the previous four years.

Eight months later both Bennett and King were back on the air. The intervening months had been a trying time for the Conservative prime minister. In Parliament, the New Deal had not panned out as planned. Bennett had suffered a mild heart attack in February, which kept him holed up in the Chateau Laurier Hotel for about two months, and then he had had to deal with a large contingent of unemployed men "trekking" their way to Ottawa. After a violent confrontation in Regina between the relief workers and the Royal Canadian Mounted Police, Bennett declared that he had saved the country from a Communist takeover; the press, however, "condemned his actions as 'those of a dictator rather than the head of a great and free people.'"[62] More troubling for Bennett was the defection of Harry Stevens and his formation of a new reform party – the Reconstructionist Party – "to reestablish Canada's industrial, economic and social life to the benefit of the great majority."[63] Not a quitter, R.B. Bennett still had one last fight in him.

The 1935 campaign was more polished. There were catchy slogans: "King or Chaos" for the Liberals and the less exciting "Stand by Canada" and "Vote Bennett" for the Tories. The Liberals were the better organized party – through the office of the National Liberal Federation – and had raised close to $1.2 million in Montreal and Toronto alone. The radio played an integral part in both campaigns. In Ontario, for example, out of a total publicity budget of $116,323, local Liberals spent nearly $47,000 on radio publicity (compared to $18,000 for press advertising).[64] King considered his opening broadcasts so important that he sequestered himself for the month of July to prepare his speeches.

While King's three radio talks "contained no surprises," many editors were impressed with his style. "The Liberal leader commands a stately diction, is blessed with an excellent voice, has that historical background which, in the case of any speaker, makes for distinction," observed the *Ottawa Journal* on August 1. "It would be difficult to imagine him, no matter what the circumstances, making what is called a bad speech." *Journal* editors were less satisfied, however, with the content of the broadcasts, which they found vague.

Bennett too took to the air to defend the last five years and received similar praise for his "unshakable confidence ... conveyed through a microphone." But it was six dramatized Conservative broadcasts (the first was fifteen minutes, the other five thirty minutes each) near the end of the campaign that were most unique to the 1935 election.* When Canadians turned on their radios late in the evening on September 14 for the second installment, they were invited into "a typical home, in a typical Canadian town" and greeted by "our friend and neighbour, Mr. Sage – the old political observer" – and his family. Mr. Sage knew a great deal about Canadian politics, and what he knew about the Liberals and Mackenzie King, he didn't like.

"We've only got to take what that Mr. King said about Mr. Bennett," Mr. Sage told his wife. "What's that, Ma? He said a lot of things, didn't he, but mostly harm. Oh! You mean about blaming Mr. Bennett for the World Depression. Well, he's got to say something. He doesn't care whether it helps or hinders the people of the country so long as it helps him to be Prime Minister. That's the pity of it ... [Mr. King] is frightened of losing the leadership ... It seems to me he's just like the movie star who is losing her appeal to her public and she's afraid that one of her smarter and better looking rivals will put her nose out of joint. Mr. King's so fearful that he does anything at all that he thinks will please his crowd."[65]

The Sage series was the brainchild of R.L. Wright of the research department of the J.J. Gibbons Advertising Agency, the Toronto firm responsible for the Tories' publicity, and was produced by Don Henshaw, "a capable and versatile radio writer and executive who had come to Canada from the United States." Three of the shows were made in the CRBC's Toronto studio and the others in that of CKCL. Sparing no money, some of the best radio performers in the city were hired, including Rupert Lucas, who played Mr. Sage in the first two broadcasts, and Grace Webster, in the role of Mrs. Sage (Webster later played "Martha" in the long-running CBC farm show "The Craigs," from 1939 to 1964).[66]

Apart from the dialogue, which an outraged King later described as "scurrilous," "libelous," and "insidious," what really angered the Liberals was the fact that the first broadcast, on September 7, was not identified as a Conservative Party production. Norman Lambert of the National Liberal Federation immediately telephoned Hector Charlesworth, head of CRBC, to express his outrage and suggest that the show violated the commission's

---

*The Conservatives were not the first to employ this type of presentation. Starting in October 1934 in Alberta, the Social Credit inaugurated its "Man from Mars" radio series, in which an actor, playing a Martian, questioned a group of actors in the role of typical Albertans about the disastrous state of the province's economy. At the end of the show, "the Man from Mars would ask pointedly why earthmen weren't intelligent enough to accept Social Credit teachings as the solution to their problems." The series ran until February 1935, and in historian John Irving's view, was " the most dramatic of all the ingenious devices developed by Aberhart for arousing and maintaining public interest in Social Credit." (Irving, *Social Credit,* 110–11)

regulations by broadcasting defamatory statements about King. Charles-worth then advised R.A. Stapells of the Gibbons Agency that the next broadcast had to be clearly identified as a Tory election production. The problem, said Staples, was that Earl Lawson and his Conservative campaign organization had not read the first script and had not actually been involved. For the second broadcast, the sponsor and writer was declared to be "R.L. Wright." But this still did not satisfy Charlesworth or the Liberals. After further protests it was agreed that the sponsor would be listed as "R.L. Wright and a Group of Conservatives."[67]

So incensed were the Liberals over Mr. Sage that upon their return to power a full-scale investigation into the matter was launched. The result was that under the new restructured CRBC (now CBC), dramatized political broadcasts were outlawed, sponsorship of anything remotely political had to be clearly identified as such, and political broadcasts were taken out of the hands of private stations and placed under the full control of the CBC. The outgoing chairman of the CRBC, Hector Charlesworth, rightly regarded the Sage controversy as a "piffling affair."[68] Indeed, Mr. Sage had not had the desired effect. R.B. Bennett was resoundingly defeated on October 14. Within three years he had left Canada for good, a lonely and bitter man (the Conservatives won only 40 seats to the Liberals 173, with third parties accounting for 32 seats).

How much of an impact did radio actually have on the outcome? Journalist B.K. Sandwell, the brilliant editor of *Saturday Night,* didn't think much at all. Writing in the magazine's October 19, 1935, issue (under his pseudonym Lucy Van Gogh), he argued that radio as "a force in politics" was overestimated. It alone could not win or lose an election that was dependent on campaign volunteers and hard work. "Even an ideal broadcaster like [William] Aberhart would never have been able to rally a party to the polls merely by rushing to the microphone three weeks before the elections," Sandwell observed. So Bennett's superiority to King as a radio performer mattered little when the voters cast their ballots.

There was much in what Sandwell said. Bennett was a victim of the times and of his own churlish personality, and the radio could not change that. Still, the importance of radio in permitting prime ministers to bypass the newspapers and deliver their messages directly to the people, free of the filter of editorial analysis and bias, cannot be overestimated. As John Bassett noted, R.B. Bennett had known this since 1934 and probably earlier; Mackenzie King now knew it too.

CHAPTER TEN

Managing the War

*I may say to you that [King] is much concerned about the
demand which he feels may arise for conscription. This
rises, not from an inherent opposition to the principles of
conscription, but from a profound fear which he has of the
divisions it would create in the country.*

T.A. Crerar to John Dafoe, May 10, 1941

Soon after Mackenzie King returned to office one of his great wishes
finally came true. William Jaffray sold the Toronto *Globe* to the flamboyant C. George McCullagh. Backed financially by miner millionaire
William Wright, McCullagh paid $1.3 million for the newspaper. It was
more than ironic that Jaffray had sold his prized possession to two horse-
racing fanatics. Within days, the *Globe* had a new look, including cigarette
ads and results of the races at Pimlico. But this was only the beginning.
Within a month McCullagh's promise to drive the rival *Mail and Empire*
out of business had convinced its publisher, Isaak Killam, to offer
McCullagh the *Mail and Empire* as well. (Killam had first tried to sell the
paper to a group of prominent Tories, but the proper financing could not
be arranged.) Wright coughed up another $2.25 million and the *Globe and
Mail* was born. At thirty-one George McCullagh was, to the surprise of
everyone but himself, the king of the Toronto newspaper world.[1]

Every generation of Canadian business has its "wonder boy." In the
1980s it was Conrad Black; in the 1930s it was Clement George
McCullagh. He looked, said R.E. Knowles in a 1936 *Saturday Night* article, like the "Arrow-collar advertisement man in the flesh: dark, crisp hair,
of medium size but broad-shouldered with an athletic build. Readily, he
smiles or jokes, glibly he damns or consigns to hell what does not meet
with his approval. But underneath this congenital exterior is an alert analytical mind – one that misses nothing, one that sizes up constantly and
one that acts without hesitation."[2]

Born in 1905 into a working-class family in London, Ontario,
McCullagh was a go-getter at an early age. In an era when it was still possible to start at the bottom and work your way up the economic ladder, he did

just that, and more brilliantly than anyone else of his day. He started as a newsboy selling the early-morning *Globe* on street corners in London. In 1921, at sixteen, he worked in the *Globe*'s circulation department, regularly outselling every other employee. For a short period he was employed as a financial reporter, which enabled him to make important connections with the Toronto business community. Legend has it that after being forced to leave the *Globe* in 1928 for violating Jaffray's no-smoking policy, he promised to return some day as the paper's owner.[3]

He moved on to a job as a broker on Bay Street, where he not only made a lot of money in oil and mining investments, but was befriended by William Wright. As Pierre Berton put it in a 1949 profile: "In the Canadian scene there are two sure-fire ways of becoming a success. One way is to find a gold mine. The other way is to find a man who has found a gold mine. Bill Wright found the gold mine. George McCullagh found Bill Wright."[4]

Around 1911 Wright, a struggling British immigrant who had served in the cavalry during the Boer War, struck it rich prospecting for gold in the Kirkland Lake area. Another stake a short time later led to the formation of the extremely lucrative Lakeshore Mines. Wright had become a very wealthy man. A better prospector than businessman, Wright's affairs were in a mess by the time a young hustler named George McCullagh came calling with a stock offering. Though Wright turned him down, he was impressed with the sales pitch and later hired McCullagh as his assistant. McCullagh quickly sorted out his ledgers and accounts.[5]

Wright was genuinely fond of McCullagh. The two men shared a passion for horse racing and a belief that hard work paid off. The millionaire miner needed little convincing to finance his young partner's newspaper venture. He was also content to remain in the background.

Mackenzie King was visiting England and the United States when the Toronto newspaper business was turned upside down. King was ecstatic. "In the seventeen or more years of the leadership of the Liberal party," he wrote to McCullagh soon after his return, "I have hoped and prayed that some day 'The Toronto *Globe*' might again become the exponent of Liberal principles and policies." (In private he was a little more circumspect, noting in his diary a few days later that the new paper "may become in time a big interest, Fascist organ.") King wanted not an organ, but a partner. McCullagh, who regarded himself as a liberal in every sense of the word, replied favourably. "I knew that you would be pleased that the *Globe* had been purchased by a person who is a firm believer in democratic principles," he told the prime minister, assuring him that his *Globe* would be "a constructive and helpful voice" for running the country.[6]

The first issue of the *Globe and Mail* appeared on November 23, 1936.

Most of the staff from the old *Mail and Empire* were released, with little hope of finding work in the midst of a depression, and the new paper now reflected a Liberal bias. King liked what he saw, but it did not take long for the vulnerable partnership to fizzle. One major obstacle was McCullagh's friendship with Ontario Liberal premier Mitchell Hepburn, an erratic and unpredictable man who despised King.

From the day Hepburn was elected in 1934, he had taken exception to any attempt by the federal party to dictate policy or ideology to him. In his own mind, he was the master of Ontario. King's decision, following his return to the prime ministership in 1935, to implement more-centralized control from Ottawa was therefore greatly resented. By 1937 Hepburn had publicly declared that while he was a Liberal, he was not "a Mackenzie King Liberal any longer."[7] From King's perspective, Hepburn was a serious threat, not only to the unity of the Liberal Party, but to the unity of the entire country.

McCullagh had first met Hepburn in 1934 through his connections on Bay Street, and he had worked on his campaign. There is also evidence (a private letter dated January 29, 1937) that McCullagh had helped the Ontario premier amass a small fortune in gold mine investments, though Hepburn had lost it all by the time he died in 1953.[8] The two high-powered men complemented each other. Hepburn used his influence to have McCullagh appointed a governor of the University of Toronto, the youngest to hold such an esteemed position; McCullagh used the pages of the *Globe and Mail* to support Hepburn's rabid anti-union stand in the Oshawa General Motors plant strike in 1937.*

Fearful that the "Bolshevik" Committee for Industrial Organization (CIO) was leading the campaign to unionize at GM and would soon turn its sights on the mining industry, McCullagh encouraged Hepburn to be as ruthless as possible. King thought it ludicrous when the premier asked the federal government to send in the RCMP to crush the strikers; he blamed McCullagh – as did the *Toronto Star* – for stirring up much of the trouble.[9]

McCullagh was uncontrollable. Rather unrealistic when it came to politics, he believed it was his destiny to save the country.[10] Terribly unhappy with Hepburn's close association with Quebec premier Maurice Duplessis and disillusioned with politicians altogether, he decided in December 1938 to go on the radio himself to express his personal views on a wide range of

---

*"So vicious were the *Globe and Mail*'s editorials and so slanted the news coverage of the strike that the workers were prevented from beating [*Globe* writer] Ralph Hyman to a pulp only when a union organizer jumped on the hood of a car and explained to the mob that it was the publisher, and not the reporter, who was responsible." (Siggins, *Bassett*, 37–38)

important subjects. When he was rightly denied air time on CBC (only recognized political parties could buy air time), he claimed there was a government conspiracy at work.

In fact, the initial decision to block McCullagh was not taken by King or his staff, but by Leonard Brockington, the corporation's chairman. This marked the beginning of the long debate over the federal government's relationship to the CBC that lasted into the 1960s. On occasion King's partisan needs compelled him (and C.D. Howe, the minister responsible for the CBC under the Broadcasting Act of 1936) to try to dictate what went on the air. But generally, because of his sense of freedom, national unity, and fairness, he did not interfere with the CBC's programming.[11]

Not one to surrender, McCullagh recorded a series of Sunday-night sermons that were later broadcast over about thirty private stations. Little escaped his wrath: he attacked patronage, political corruption, high taxes, Communists, and fascists. King was described as a "poor" and "bumbling" leader. These broadcasts spawned McCullagh's short-lived Leadership League, a group designed "to enlarge public interest in public affairs." Many ordinary Canadians wrote McCullagh words of support, but offered little money for his cause. By the time the league dissolved in June 1939, the whole exercise had cost the *Globe* more than $100,000.[12]

Despite some critical comments about the prime minister in his radio speeches, McCullagh's break with King and the Liberals did not take place until the Second World War was well under way. Even in September 1939 the two men had kind words for each other. But McCullagh was too much of an imperialist for King's liking. "He was a fierce Anglophile," according to journalist Maggie Siggins, "as loyal a defender of the King and the Union Jack as any British lion standing guard in Trafalgar Square." McCullagh fancied himself a member of the British upper class who happened to reside in Canada. His friends included Anthony Eden, the Duke of Kent, and Lord Beaverbrook, "Max" to the publisher. Would it be possible for King and the Liberals to meet the newspaper publisher's demands for a total war commitment in Europe and still keep Quebec happy? This remained to be seen. As early as September 1938, one year before the conflict began, King already had grave concerns about the *Globe and Mail*'s overly enthusiastic views on Canadian participation in a European war.[13]

The war was only a few months old when the campaign of the "Mackenzie King Haters," as they were labelled by the *Winnipeg Free Press*, began in earnest. Starting in the spring of 1940 the *Globe and Mail*, the *Toronto Telegram,* and the *Montreal Gazette* went after King with a vengeance.

The first shots against the prime minister were fired even before the war had begun. In the fall of 1938 the *Financial Post* and *Maclean's* magazine, both owned by the Maclean's Publishing Company, began a relentless attack on the Department of National Defence (DND). What had started as an investigation of the DND's Bren gun contract in 1938 turned into a full-scale assault on the Liberal government's bureaucracy, and particularly Defence Minister Ian Mackenzie.[14] The articles in *Maclean's* in September 1938 and a more extensive series in the *Financial Post* the following year – researched and written by Arthur Irwin – broke new ground in press coverage. Together they exposed a pattern of wasteful spending, patronage, costly land flips, and sheer ineptitude.

Irwin discovered, for example, that over a three-year period Mackenzie, though he had been accorded a budget of more than $26 million for the air force, had assembled a fleet of only 14 "modern service type planes"; the minister's publicly declared minimum target in this category had been 312. Many politicians, including Prime Minister King, believed the Maclean's Company had crossed the line of acceptable journalism. Still, the articles had the desired effect: soon after the war began, Ian Mackenzie was replaced as minister of defence by Norman Rogers, who had been minister of labour.[15]

Swept away by a momentary pang of patriotism following Canada's declaration of war on Nazi Germany on September 10, 1939, the *Financial Post* reviewed its editorial stance against the government, but by early October it had renewed its attack. The paper now focused not only on the inefficiency of the defence department, but also on the "government's ability to lead the country in war."[16] Other major newspapers followed its lead.

In September 1939 such Tory papers as the *Montreal Gazette* and the *Toronto Telegram* were generally supportive of the King administration. Robert Manion, who had succeeded Bennett as Conservative leader a year earlier, had failed to impress the party's press. In the wartime election of March 1940, the *Gazette* did not push for Manion and was quite satisfied with a Liberal victory. The *Globe and Mail* had also expressed its faith in the government's ability to win the conflict, but "it was not happy with the vagueness of what the prime minister intended to do to finish the job." By the spring of 1940 George McCullagh was calling for a coalition government. As yet he was not willing to support the position of his one-time friend Premier Mitchell Hepburn, who had sponsored a resolution at Queen's Park in January critical of the federal government's war effort. At the *Telegram*'s office on Melinda Street, editor C.O. Knowles shared McCullagh's feelings about the need for a Union government. No fan of King's, he had even less faith in the Liberals' ability to do what was needed to protect England and ensure an Allied victory.[17]

King's wartime leadership and integrity were questioned on two counts. First, his decision to delay the institution of conscription as long as possible was interpreted, not unjustifiably, as pandering to anti-war sentiments in Quebec. And second, because of military and economic agreements negotiated with President Roosevelt in 1940 and 1941, King was accused of moving Canada closer to the United States and away from the British Empire.[18]

Behind every decision and act taken by King during the five-and-a-half-year war lay a sincere desire to keep the country united. Having witnessed the terrible consequences of conscription in 1917, he was not about to be trapped or pushed by Tory imperialist editors into adopting a measure that was sure to cost him his undisputed claim to Quebec. "Conscription," as historian J.L. Granatstein so succinctly put it, "was an issue King correctly feared."[19]

His busy schedule during the war years allowed him even less time for journalists. Those around him – Arnold Heeney, Walter Turnbull, Jack Pickersgill, and Brooke Claxton – scanned editorials in Quebec and the rest of the country, trying to gauge public opinion. A memo from Heeney to Ernest Lapointe in October 1939 indicated that while *Le Devoir* opposed an aggressive Canadian war effort overseas, the major Liberal papers (*Le Soleil, Le Canada,* and *La Presse*) were more supportive. King was pleased but realized he would have to walk a fine line to keep Quebec on side.[20]

Even more than his leader, Brooke Claxton understood the significance of controlling information during a crisis. A lawyer from Montreal, he was first elected to Parliament in the general election of 1940 at the age of forty-two and later served as King's parliamentary secretary. For shepherding the family allowance bill through the House, he was made the first minister of national health and welfare in October 1944. Described by Bruce Hutchison as "a young man with a look of owlish wisdom, a tough mind, and an almost unbelievable energy," the tall Claxton was an intelligent political tactician and a competent campaign organizer.[21] (He also was one of the first Canadian politicians to recognize the usefulness of polling.) He had observed how the Nazis had used propaganda to promote their unique brand of evil. The same methods, employed in a different way, Claxton believed, could help win the favour of both the public and the press.

"This is war for survival," he told King in a May 1941 memo about the role of the Wartime Information Board. "It is a war of ideas as well as between nations. Victory depends on sea power, air power and morale. The Department of Information is concerned with morale." In Claxton's view it was the agency's job to defeat fear and anxiety, Hitler's only allies in Canada, and "arouse in every Canadian a burning conviction that *his* effort will bring not only victory but a better life." As a means of achieving this goal, he recommended managing the news as opposed to censoring it. He further advised King to use radio extensively and make the newspapers write the stories he wanted to see in print.[22] This was the clever thinking behind the government's order less than a year later that prevented a Quebec nationalist group, La Ligue pour la defence du Canada, from broadcasting over CBC radio its anti-conscriptionist "Non" position in the plebiscite campaign.*

Actually, censorship of the press or radio was never a long-term option for King or his wartime cabinet. It was not necessary. As in the First World War, Canada's loyal press, including *Le Devoir,* for the most part unconditionally cooperated with government censors. As Wilfrid Eggleston, a veteran gallery man appointed press censor in November 1939, reported at the war's end, "newspapermen were in general as anxious as anyone else to win the war."[23] Mackenzie King's liberal and political instincts told him to look the other way even when in September 1940 Leopold Richer, *Le Devoir*'s Ottawa correspondent, wrote a scathing article comparing him to a dictator, or when his other nemesis, the *Globe and Mail*, ignored the censor's ruling and in early 1945 wrote about the NRMA (National Resources Mobilization Act – soldiers for home defence) deserters fleeing before they could be conscripted for overseas duties.[24] In fact, when the conflict was over, only one of the country's one hundred or so dailies had been suspended (the *Clarion,* a Communist paper published in Toronto) and only four had been prosecuted (three were found guilty and paid a small fine).

Claxton's advice on press management was also followed. King never hesitated to communicate his feelings to the press. In response to Hitler's successful march across Europe in 1940 he telephoned and wrote various editors requesting that they help him maintain "a calm attitude amongst the people of Canada." The *Toronto Telegram*'s C.O. Knowles for one was "disgusted" by this blatant attempt at manipulation. "The logic of events has forced King's hand out but how reluctantly he moves," confided Knowles to Arthur Meighen. "He summons the fire brigade only when his own roof is blazing."[25]

He was broadcasting on the radio more than ever as well. The election of March 1940 marked the first occasion that political parties were allocated free air time by the CBC. King spent days obsessively preparing his radio

---

*On April 27, 1942, Canadians were asked to answer the following question: "Are you in favour of releasing the Government from any obligations arising out of any past commitments restricting the methods of raising men for military service?" At the government's urging, the CBC ruled that "only recognized political parties would have free access to the airwaves ... This tactic meant that only the parties in Parliament, all calling for a 'Yes' vote, would be heard." Still La Ligue's position won out when 72 percent of Quebecers voted "Non" compared to 82.3 percent in Ontario, who said "Yes" to the Liberals. (Granatstein, *Canada's War,* 224–27)

speeches, revising and checking every word.[26] It wasn't long before some of the country's leading newspapermen felt King was ignoring them. His assistant, Walter Turnbull, urged him to meet regularly with major editors to appease them. He was, however, reluctant to do so, choosing instead to give off-the-record information to trusted writers like Grant Dexter.

One positive step in improving relations with Ottawa journalists was taken by the Department of External Affairs in October 1941, when more-regular informal press conferences were held to give the gallery a clearer picture of Canada's overseas operations. In charge of the briefings were Norman Robertson, External's competent under-secretary (Oscar Skelton had died in January), and his two able assistants, Hume Wrong and Lester "Mike" Pearson, who was particularly adept at handling the boys of the press.

In general, however, the war – and the fears and fiery emotions it generated – encouraged an incorrigible partisanship in the press. Editorials in Liberal papers like the *Winnipeg Free Press* and *Toronto Star* went after Arthur Meighen when he attempted to regain the Conservative Party leadership in 1942 with the same zealousness shown by the *Globe and Mail*, *Montreal Gazette,* and *Toronto Telegram* in their assault on the Liberals' war effort. But the newspapers saved their harshest words for each other, hurling charges of "gutter journalism" across the country.

In early March 1941 a *Toronto Star* editorial entitled "Mr. King and the Rumour Factory" showed that the accusations made against King by the *Globe* and the *Montreal Gazette* were false. The next day the *Globe*, in a piece harking back to the days of George Brown, responded with "From the Journalistic Gutter": "The *Toronto Daily Star,* of all papers in Canada, has undertaken to lecture the *Globe & Mail* and the *Montreal Gazette* on newspaper morals. This slavish party organ, with a reputation for violating every known code of newspaper ethics and all other ethics to gain its ends, which colors its news to suit its aims, is a strange creature to pretend to principles of honest journalism." A furious Joe Atkinson launched a $100,000 libel suit against the *Globe,* but when the case went to trial, the jury ruled there had been no libel in the *Globe*'s editorial.[27]

Beginning in about the spring of 1941, the Tory press demanded the creation of a national government as well as full-scale conscription. As Mackenzie King persevered along his tortuous course to avoid such action, which he regarded dangerous to Canadian unity (not to mention his power base in Quebec), he was denounced at every turn. King could tolerate the attacks from the *Gazette* and *Telegram*, widely recognized as partisan Conservative newspapers. He was more bothered by the *Globe and Mail* and McCullagh's alliance with Ontario political leaders Mitchell Hepburn and George Drew. Though he regarded McCullagh as an "amateur" who was in over his head, he thought that the great Liberal tradition of the

"*Globe*" part of the paper made the newspaper more capable of shaping public opinion against the government. Nevertheless, with the future of the country at stake, King was not about to let himself be manipulated by Tory journalists into instituting conscription or a Union government.

One of King's most ardent defenders was *Winnipeg Free Press* editor John Dafoe. Until his untimely death in January 1944, the great newspaperman championed the Liberals' cause. During the late thirties, Dafoe had profoundly disagreed with what he perceived as King's uncommitted approach to the League of Nations, specifically his reluctance to sanction the principle of collective security. (In private, however, Dafoe conceded as early as 1936 that the league was "doomed and that King could not have saved the institution.")[28] The *Free Press*'s criticism annoyed King, a fact that seemed to please Dafoe. The paper's independence was more important than ever to Dafoe at this point in his career. In a 1936 article in the *Canadian Historical Review*, he argued: "The newspaper whose support of a party is bought and paid for directly or indirectly, out of party funds, is a propagandist sheet and not a public journal."[29]

Yet when the war finally broke out in 1939, as Dafoe feared and predicted, he rallied to the Liberal leader's corner, accepting the government's rejection of conscription and a coalition. These were the two causes he had endorsed in 1917 and the two policies that had led him to split with Laurier. Now, more than twenty years later, he had mellowed. He recognized the tremendous difficulties in forming another union administration and, more especially, had come to appreciate Quebec's opposition to conscription and the threat it posed to national unity.[30]

To ensure he could count on the *Free Press,* King paid a quiet visit to Winnipeg in the early summer of 1941. There, in the newspaper offices on Carlton Street, the prime minister met with Dafoe and his managing editor, George Ferguson. According to Ferguson's account of the meeting, Dafoe reaffirmed his belief that conscription might be necessary and that the *Free Press* could not support the government if it was "opposed to conscription on principle." King assured Dafoe that if conscription was required he would "tackle it," but he spoke at length about the dangers. Before leaving, King raised the possibility of holding a plebiscite on the Liberals' "no conscription" pledge, a plan Dafoe did not object to.[31]

Later, when the plebiscite was announced, Dafoe described it as "an unheroic expedient to protect this country against the dangers and consequences of ill-considered courses urged by reckless men." Privately, he admitted that his respect for King had soared. "I think that in this moment in which we have arrived," he wrote to a friend in February 1942, "King is about as indispensable for Canada as Roosevelt is for the United States or Churchill for Great Britain."[32] Though results of the plebiscite revealed the

English-French division on conscription, Dafoe was prepared to give King the benefit of the doubt for the sake of the country. At the same time, he was pleased the government had opted to amend the NRMA, which meant that conscription could be a reality if necessary.*

From the beginning of the conflict, Dafoe never wavered in his public support for Mackenzie King; nor did he hesitate in putting the Tory eastern Canadian papers in their place. In a harshly worded editorial of May 1941 entitled "The Hymn of Hate Once More," Dafoe wrote: "No occasion passes on which the Canadian prime minister achieves some outstanding success ... that the little group of mean-minded and bigoted men whose chief spiritual solace is to be found in the columns of the *Toronto Telegram* and the *Montreal Gazette* begin to cry 'King must go!' This is a false statement and the writer[s] must have known it to be false." In Dafoe's view, the Tory party and press were guilty of perpetuating the myth that King was not providing strong leadership. This he compared to the Nazi propagandists who advocated the "big lie": "You say it long and loud enough and the public will buy it."[33]

Despite the best efforts of the Conservative press, King somehow manoeuvred around implementing full-scale conscription. Indeed, after all was said and done – the harsh firing of Defence Minister J.L. Ralston in favour of Gen. Andy McNaughton in November 1944; the eventual decision to dispatch a few thousand NRMA "zombies" (those conscripted for army service on the home front) to Europe – King, as he usually did, survived brilliantly with most of his cabinet and party intact.

Dafoe, who did not live to see the end of the war, would not have been surprised by the political outcome. In February 1942 he had told journalist John Stevenson, a long-time critic of the prime minister, that King was doing a good job. "No doubt he has made many mistakes," the Winnipeg editor conceded. "His methods of doing business may exasperate people, and he may at times have confused national and party interests. In short, he is a miserable sinner. But aren't we all?"[34]

---

*During second reading of Bill 80 on June 10, 1942, King made his famous declaration that his policy was "not necessarily conscription, but conscription if necessary." In fact, as Jack Pickersgill recalls, he had brought a file of clippings with him to Laurier House on June 9, including a *Toronto Star* editorial of April 28 interpreting the plebiscite vote. In preparing his speech, King had incorporated the catchy phrase into his notes. As the *Star* had put it, "Not necessarily conscription, but conscription if necessary – that is the significance of Canada's overwhelming 'Yes' vote on the plebiscite." (Granatstein, *Canada's War*, 234; Nolan, *King's War*, 87–88)

CHAPTER ELEVEN

Uncle Louis

I will be more interested in seeing people than in talking to cameras.
Louis St. Laurent to a television reporter, 1957

It was like a breath of fresh air. Ottawa journalists could not believe what they heard with their own ears. Two days later they were still not sure it had happened. A Canadian prime minister had called a press conference and had actually answered the correspondents' questions, openly and honestly.

After nearly fourteen consecutive years of dealing with Mackenzie King, the reporters had become accustomed to secrecy, ambiguity, and double talk. They expected more of the same on a Friday in late October 1948, when Louis St. Laurent invited them to his office in the East Block.

The sixty-six-year-old corporation lawyer who had joined the Liberal cabinet in 1941 (to replace Ernest Lapointe as chief Quebec lieutenant) had now reluctantly agreed to take over the reigns of power from King, who was retiring after an unprecedented twenty-nine years as Liberal leader. As minister of justice and external affairs, St. Laurent, though pleasant and charming, had abided by his leader's rules in dealing with the press: say as little as possible. So it was with a feeling of cynicism that the journalists trudged over to the new prime minister's office. The meeting turned out to be the most exciting event in Ottawa that week.

With the newsmen gathered around, St. Laurent made a few announcements and then asked for questions. Will the government oppose George Drew, the newly elected leader of the Conservative Party, in an upcoming by-election? When will the next session of Parliament be held? Does the government plan to airlift supplies to Berlin? What is Canada's position with regard to India? To the delight and amazement of every journalist assembled, St. Laurent answered each question frankly and without hesitation. Most of the reporters could not remember the last time such a thing had occurred. "Hail to the new era," they declared as they thanked him and left to write their stories.[1]

The press gallery's glee with St. Laurent lasted about four years. By September 1952 there were rumblings about the fact that he had not called a press conference in eight months. By 1956 he was portrayed as a cranky old chairman of a corporation who needed to be replaced. The press's discontent with St. Laurent was a reflection of Canadians' dissatisfaction with more than two decades of uninterrupted Liberal government. During the period of St. Laurent's prime ministership, from 1948 to 1957, popular sentiment changed dramatically, from a reverence for "Uncle Louis" to a disdain not seen in Ottawa since the days of R.B. Bennett.

While much of the disillusionment was the result of the infamous "Pipeline Debate" of May 1956, regarded at the time as the greatest instance of arrogance and parliamentary abuse in Canadian history, a more general transformation in the game of politics was a factor as well. Behind the scenes, advertising executives had developed campaigns to sell politicians like used cars or jello; the polling phenomenon (or plague) had begun in earnest; and most important, television's grainy, black-and-white screen now emphasized just how old St. Laurent was compared to his vibrant new Tory opponent, John Diefenbaker. The people watched, the press wrote, and the Quebec lawyer, who hadn't wanted to be prime minister in the first place, went down to defeat – not as a sore loser, but as the debonair gentleman he always had been.

The nature of Canadian politics had changed gradually. There was nothing to suggest to journalists in 1948 that, by the end of St. Laurent's tenure, so much would be different. The gallery itself, still a private club for newspapermen (and a few token women, such as the "acid-tongued" Judith Robinson, Ottawa columnist for the *Toronto Telegram*), was much as it been for the past sixty years. It had, of course, increased in numbers. From twenty-five men in 1930, it had grown to sixty-five (with seven associate members) by 1950. Yet the same room in the Parliament Buildings was still reserved for the gallery's use. It was so crowded that the members' desks were, in the words of one reporter, "packed as close as herrings in a barrel." Many journalists were forced to work in the hallway, and the "hot room," as it was called, became a major fire hazard.

The proceedings of the House of Commons were the focus of reporting, especially for the wire services, though a few enterprising journalists (like Ken Wilson of the *Financial Post* and Blair Fraser of *Maclean's*) developed close personal relations with the growing civil service, which led to greater specialization. Wilson, for instance, according to his boss Floyd Chalmers, "was the best informed business writer in the capital. He was trusted – and indeed beloved – by cabinet ministers and Opposition critics alike, by deputy ministers, back-benchers, and low-placed civil servants." More than once, C.D. Howe had used Wilson's column to test his economic policies.[2] His untimely death in a plane crash in 1952 was widely mourned.

Fraser was more interested in people, politics, and social policy. Because his stories were due every two weeks, his "Back Stage at Ottawa" column and feature articles were always meticulously researched and well written. Fraser stood apart. He had a university education in an era when most Ottawa reporters had started to climb the newsroom ladder fresh out of high school. By all accounts, he was the closest thing Canada had to the legendary U.S. pundit Walter Lippman, and like the American, the first columnist to analyze issues in a way that allowed the average person to understand the inner workings of government.[3]

A tall, thin, but strong man, Fraser worked the bureaucracy the way Grant Dexter worked the politicians. He had come to Ottawa in 1943 at the age of thirty-four, when Jack Pickersgill, Mitchell Sharp, and Lester Pearson were making their mark as mandarins under Mackenzie King's watchful eye. They became his professional and personal friends, leading to the often repeated accusation that he was a partisan Liberal – a charge that troubled him, and one that is vehemently refuted by his son Graham Fraser of the *Globe and Mail*. "I thought it was unfair and blurred a lot of distinctions," he says. "My father believed in a strong central government. He believed that Quebec had an important place in Canada and he believed in the creation of social programs – beliefs and values held by the senior civil servants. Consequently it was much more natural for him to be seen to be a Liberal than a Tory." Later, partisan criticism of Fraser was further reinforced by the fact "that he and John Diefenbaker hated one another."

On a day-to-day basis, there was now less partisanship among gallery members than during Laurier's day. As Peter Dempson, who became the Ottawa correspondent for the Conservative *Toronto Telegram* in 1949, remembered, the practice of exchanging "blacks," or carbons, of stories was quite common among reporters of every political stripe.[4]

Nevertheless, St. Laurent and his cabinet ministers were more likely to play favourites. In their minds, the *Toronto Star* and *Winnipeg Free Press* were the government's supporters, while the *Globe and Mail* and *Toronto Telegram* were the enemy. And it was true that criticism of the Liberals appeared more often in the latter than the former, most notably at election time. When Clark Davey arrived in 1955 to cover Ottawa for the *Globe and Mail*, he was summoned to the office of C.D. Howe, the minister of trade and commerce (plus everything else) and St. Laurent's second in command. Assigned to write a story on the wheat economy, one of Howe's responsibilities, Davey asked the powerful minister about a particular policy. Howe answered the question as best he could and then gave Davey the name of the department official who could supply the rest of the information. "Once the interview had ended," Davey recalls, "he warned me about double-crossing him. 'If you want to kick me, don't do it from behind,' he told me, 'come in front and kick.'"

Access to St. Laurent was generally restricted to such loyal supporters as Bob Taylor of the *Toronto Star* and Alex Hume of the *Ottawa Citizen*. Neither journalist hid his partisan feelings. Former *Globe and Mail* writer George Bain recollects that during the Liberals' huge election rally at Maple Leaf Gardens in 1953, Taylor stood on the stage applauding St. Laurent and his cabinet as they entered the arena. "There was no doubt," Bain says, "that he was a Liberal." Hume not only idolized St. Laurent, but also wrote propaganda for the National Liberal Federation and advised the prime minister on everything from how to attack the Tory leader, George Drew, to how to get along with the members of the press gallery. He remained in St. Laurent's corner to the end, going so far as to defend the government's heavy-handed use of closure in the 1956 Pipeline Debate in Parliament.[5]

As Hume recalled in a 1973 interview, St. Laurent "respected the press and media as having as important a job to do as Parliamentarians." But this did not mean that St. Laurent was willing to be "scrummed." Reporters would stand patiently in an East Block corridor waiting for cabinet meetings to end. When they approached the prime minister with a question about what had been discussed, he would usually cut them off curtly. "You have no right whatsoever to examine my mind," he'd tell them. "If there will be some action, I will let you know." On one occasion, Kenneth Brown of the CBC "jumped" on St. Laurent while he was walking across the Hill. (In 1953 a prime minister could still walk the streets of Ottawa without an entourage of bodyguards). He pushed a microphone in the prime minister's face and asked a question. Ever the gentleman, St. Laurent answered Brown's query, but once the tape stopped, he said, "Young man, don't you dare do that to me again." And Brown didn't.[6]

St. Laurent was much more reserved than his genial Uncle Louis image suggested. His daily schedule was regimented: he was at his desk by 9:35 a.m. in his East Block office; he lunched at the Rideau Club or at his apartment at the Roxborough (the St. Laurents moved into the prime minister's official residence on Sussex Drive in 1951); then he was back at work until 6:30 p.m. (Even at cocktail parties, St. Laurent followed a strict regimen. As noted in a 1955 *Maclean's* profile by Ian Sclanders [January 1, 1955 issue], "He arrives punctually, drinks a single drink, smokes one of the fifteen straight Virginia cigarettes he allows himself a day – using a black holder – and leaves in exactly half an hour.") Only on the hottest days did St. Laurent remove his jacket, and it was an unwritten rule that the forty-four members of his staff could work in their shirtsleeves only if he did. "He was so natural and wonderful with a large crowd," says Jack Pickersgill, who served as St. Laurent's chief assistant before becoming clerk of the Privy Council and

then a member of the cabinet in 1953. "But in private he was not particularly good company. There was no small talk." Pickersgill recalls, too, that St.
Laurent did not have an exalted opinion of himself. "Working for Mr. St.
Laurent," he says, "you never thought you were working for him but working with him." He was a humble man, devoted to his wife and family and
proud of his French Canadian heritage.

Every morning at breakfast St. Laurent read the *Gazette*. His focus was
more on Montreal than on Toronto, unlike Mackenzie King, who had paid
more attention to Toronto. Yet like his illustrious predecessor, St. Laurent
became upset with newspaper errors and inaccuracies, even occasionally
going so far as to write letters to the editor for publication – unprecedented
then and now. So long as the journalists who wrote about him and travelled
with him on the election campaign trains maintained a proper distance, they
had no trouble with St. Laurent. Going beyond what he regarded as acceptable drew a quick rebuke, as Eugene Griffin discovered.

In August 1950 Griffin, the *Chicago Tribune*'s Ottawa correspondent,
wrote a straightforward article on the St. Laurent family's vacation at their
summer home in St. Patrice, a resort 190 kilometres east of Quebec City.
The prime minister was infuriated and later stopped a press conference in
mid-sentence to lecture Griffin publicly on proper journalistic etiquette.
"People here know what to publish and what not to publish," he told him.
Stunned, not one member of the gallery came to Griffin's defence.[7]

In large part, St. Laurent's attitude towards the press and its coverage of
his activities was shaped by two factors. First, he had lived most of his life
as a private citizen in the confines of his law office, unaccustomed to the
scrutiny of probing journalists. Second, he was not a young man. He served
as prime minister from the age of sixty-six to the age of seventy-five, and
this eventually caught up with him. By the 1953 election, Uncle Louis had
become "Grandfather St. Laurent": "His face was still ruddy and [he] held
himself as erect as ever, but his hair and stubbly moustache were completely
white."[8]

He could be blunt and testy. On a visit to Manitoba during the flood of
1950, he was asked by a *Winnipeg Tribune* reporter what the federal government planned to do for the "little man." "Directly, nothing!" he exclaimed,
which the press regarded as a "strange outburst" and "hardly in good taste."
Newsmen repeatedly questioned him about his plans to retire, a topic that
drew his ire.[9]

There was no doubting St. Laurent's intellectual abilities. His mind,
observed Bruce Hutchison, was "superior to King's, and quicker." He dominated his cabinet, "not by imposing his authority," writes Jack Pickersgill, "but
by his sheer intellect, his wide knowledge, and his unequalled persuasiveness."
In Parliament, too, he was a convincing speaker in both English and French,

especially after he toned down his corporation lawyer demeanour and put some passion into his speeches. Asked by the *Ottawa Journal* about the difference between appearing before the Supreme Court and in the House of Commons, he said, "In the Supreme Court it is fatal to lose your temper. In Parliament, it is fatal not to pretend to lose your temper."[10]

Yet St. Laurent was never the political animal Macdonald or King had been. He was a man of "broad liberal views," said Chubby Power in 1951, but he was not a "team player."[11] Having joined the Liberal government at the height of its power in 1941, he did not know what it was like to be in opposition. Consequently, he was more interested in providing the country with good government than in working for the greater glory of the Liberal Party.

In some respects, he was fortunate that in Quebec the rule of thumb was to vote "bleu à Québec, rouge à Ottawa." The federal Liberals won huge majorities in the three general elections during his prime ministership. And though he was a committed federalist, St. Laurent was astute enough to maintain a working relationship with the all-mighty Union Nationale premier, Maurice Duplessis. Such cooperation included giving in to the Quebec government's demand for its own income tax system. Except for *Le Devoir,* which was generally critical of Duplessis and St. Laurent, the Quebec press (including the three major Montreal papers, the *Gazette, Star,* and *La Presse*) supported the federal Liberals.

More partisan matters were left to the ministers C.D Howe, Brooke Claxton, and Jack Pickersgill. In their deft hands, the Liberals' destiny as "the Government Party" was guaranteed. As the prime minister's partisan alter ego, Pickersgill was, according to Peter C. Newman, "the most powerful backstage influence in Ottawa" during the period from 1937 to 1957. As head of the Prime Minister's Office from 1945 to 1952, first under King and then under St. Laurent, "'I've fixed it with Jack' became tantamount to prime ministerial approval among members of the Liberal cabinet." Newman wrote that Pickersgill "looks more like a prankster than a politician and is handicapped by the awkward limb movements of a sleepy penguin."[12]

In June 1952 Pickersgill was promoted to secretary to the cabinet and clerk of the Privy Council, a non partisan civil servant job. Consequently, as noted by St. Laurent's biographer Dale Thomson, the prime minister "lost one of his most trusted advisers for ... Pickersgill disqualified himself from playing the role of political adviser in which he was so valuable." In his own memoirs Pickersgill asserts that he attempted to remove himself from political and partisan concerns. It was a difficult transition. Though he had cut his ties with the National Liberal Federation, he still advised St. Laurent on the federation's executive structure.[13]

More significantly, he called Bruce Hutchison in November 1952 with an urgent request that a recent speech by St. Laurent, which he felt had been "grossly neglected by all the newspapers," receive some attention. In the same telephone call, he lambasted Hutchison's associate Grant Dexter for *Free Press* editorials critical of the government's management of the economy. Since the Winnipeg newspaper was supposed to be the administration's friend, its criticism, picked up by the Conservative papers, made the Liberals look particularly bad. "Jack added specifically," Hutchison later reported to Dexter, "that if the government were defeated next year ... the *Free Press* would be largely to blame."[14] Too political to be wasted in the bureaucracy, Pickersgill, with the able assistance of Premier Joey Smallwood, won a Commons seat representing a Newfoundland riding in the 1953 election. He joined the cabinet and remained at St. Laurent's side for the next four years.

Another figure behind the scenes was forty-seven-year-old H.W.E. "Bob" Kidd of the Cockfield, Brown advertising agency. Kidd became secretary of the NLF in 1949 – a sure sign that politics, public relations, and mass selling were coming together. In fact, the advertising agency continued to pay Kidd's salary while he was seconded to the NLF.[15]

A dedicated backroom operator who abhorred public attention, Kidd, with guidance, of course, from Pickersgill, supervised all aspects of the Liberals' public relations, including "monitoring the press, planting stories, admonishing hostile reporters and generally watching for opportunities to put the best Liberal face forward." This propaganda work would have included lobbying for a story in *Maclean's* about the successful management of the Canadian economy, arranging meetings for St. Laurent with the publishers and editors of the leading newspapers, and preparing the prime minister for a radio broadcast.[16]

The Liberal PR team was extremely sensitive to anything resembling negative commentary. In the months prior to the 1949 election they went after the Canadian Press for what they regarded as its unfair coverage. In their view, CP was guilty of building up Tory leader George Drew and carrying out a vendetta against the St. Laurent administration. But a close examination of the allegedly biased seventeen articles does not bear out this conspiracy theory.[17]

What seems to have really bothered the Liberals was the CP staff's efforts to spice up their otherwise mundane prose, a fact not lost on Claxton. "Brooke is wild about Canadian Press slanting against the government and has a file to prove it," *Free Press* Washington correspondent Chester Bloom told Dexter, then serving as editor in Winnipeg (a job he had from 1946 to 1954 before he returned to Ottawa). "He doesn't suspect corruption but believes the CP boys are incompetent and prejudiced, and in their new style of attempting to jazz everything by fastening on some 'angle' instead of writing straight reports, invariably distort everything."[18]

By far the most politically successful ad campaign, however, was one that began during the 1949 election – the selling of Louis St. Laurent, the dour Montreal lawyer, as every Canadian's loving, paternal Uncle Louis. Despite his naturally formal mien, it was St. Laurent's genuine humility, gentleness, and affable public personality that made this possible. Before he left for his first cross-country election campaign by rail in 1949, there was concern about how the new Liberal leader would mix with ordinary Canadians. Quite quickly reporters noticed how at ease he was. One morning, very early, his train pulled into Field, B.C. Alex Hume and Norman Campbell of the Tory *Toronto Telegram* awoke to find the sixty-seven-year-old St. Laurent working the group of women and children already gathered on the platform. "I'm afraid Uncle Louis will be a hard one to beat," Campbell remarked. That day he used the term in his dispatch and other journalists soon picked it up. Much to the dismay of Drew and the Conservatives, Uncle Louis became the country's most popular celebrity.[19]

The NLF and Cockfield, Brown made the most of this welcome opportunity, then and in 1953, promoting St. Laurent's new image whenever and wherever possible. There were photographs of St. Laurent kissing schoolchildren. Newspaper advertisements focused on his kindly personality, portraying him as the head of the team bringing prosperity and a national health care scheme to Canada. Never before had a general election been so "dominated by a consciously manipulated media image of the party leader."[20]

Thinking back, Tory strategist Dalton Camp, whose background is in advertising, doesn't understand how the Conservatives could have been caught so off guard. "While the [Tory] advisors ... pored over every published word uttered by the Prime Minister and his cabinet, no one looked up to see that the Liberal leader had changed his clothes. I recall no one saying, for example, how devilishly clever it was to take this man, a wealthy corporation lawyer, and convert him into some Gladstonian version of 'The People's William' so as to magnify the contrast with Mr. Drew, who had unwillingly acquired the image of a harsh, malevolent partisan – and stuffed shirt to boot." Ironically, it was Drew much more than St. Laurent, says Camp, who "sensed the value of media [and] the latent power of advertising." But he received bad advice from men who believed elections could be won like a court case – through "great debates, logic, persuasion and forensic skills."[21]

Only later, after the ballots had been counted, did someone of the stature of Grattan O'Leary, the editor of the *Ottawa Journal* and a committed Conservative, question the fact that the Liberals had hundreds of "press agents in Ottawa to glorify ministers and put out political propaganda." One day in 1953 O'Leary bumped into Bob Kidd. "You know, you people do an exceedingly fine job for your clients. I wish you were doing our work," he told Kidd. "You seem to have acquired a certain political flair for what you are doing, and something which we can't seem to find with our people."[22]

Journalists had created Uncle Louis in 1949, and many people were then (and for the next eight years) caught up with the sentiment surrounding the man. "Talking to the PM is like warming your hands near a stove on a cold winter day," said Richard Jackson of the *Ottawa Journal*. "He's the most charmingly courteous person I've met. Children are magnetized by him." Yet those reporters travelling with him noted that this sixty-seven-year-old man was not enthusiastic about campaigning. "He found it an ordeal," Peter Dempson recalled. "He was testy with newsmen most of the time. His speeches were stilted and colourless, usually far too long. As soon as a meeting was over, we didn't see him again that night."[23]

Dempson's view of St. Laurent may have been tainted by his employer and the sensational newspaper war the *Telegram* waged against the *Toronto Star* during the campaign. Indeed, other than Uncle Louis, the best thing the Liberals had going for them was the *Star*'s determination to defeat federal Conservative leader George Drew at any cost. Publisher Harry Hindmarsh – the tough and relentless son-in-law of Joe Atkinson, who had died in 1948 – actually spent more than $5,000 establishing a bureau in Quebec, complete with French-speaking reporters. The plan was to keep track of the Tories' campaign and any connections they might have with Duplessis or Camilien Houde, the outspoken former mayor of Montreal who was interned during the Second World War. Because Duplessis's brand of nationalism offended many English Canadians, it was felt that exposing any friendly ties between the Union Nationale and the federal Conservatives would embarrass Drew in British Ontario.[24]

The fight between the Conservative leader and the Toronto paper had been going on for at least a decade and escalated during the war after Drew teamed up with George McCullagh of the *Globe and Mail* and Ontario premier Mitchell Hepburn to oppose Mackenzie King. After Drew was elected premier of Ontario in 1943, he told a *Star* journalist that "no reporter from the *Star* will ever have access to my office, or even be welcome at the Parliament Buildings."[25] He was true to his word.

The situation worsened two years later when the *Star* (which had moved further to the left, supporting such social programs as family allowances) gave prominence to allegations made by the Ontario CCF (Co-operative Commonwealth Federation) that Drew had established a secret Gestapo-like police force to spy on his labour opponents. In an editorial of May 25, 1945, Drew was compared to Nazi Heinrich Himmler, head of Hitler's SS.

Drew's friend George McCullagh became more involved in the battle in November 1948 after he purchased the *Toronto Evening Telegram* from the estate of founder John Ross Robertson for $3.6 million. He declared that he intended to build up the lagging *Tely*'s circulation and to attack the *Star*, which he regarded as a Communist organ. "I'm going to knock that fucking rag right off its pedestal," he told his staff. (McCullagh did not have mild words for publisher Harry Hindmarsh either. In a *Time* magazine interview, he said that "that fellow Hindmarsh is so ugly that if he ever bit himself, he'd get hydrophobia.") With respect to politics, the flamboyant media baron claimed publicly that his *Telegram* would be "independent in politics [and] seek to give fair treatment to all parties."[26] Few who had read his *Globe and Mail* believed him.

During the 1949 federal campaign, the Toronto papers went after each other's favoured candidate (and each other) with the same bitterness and hostility. It wasn't only the editorials that were slanted – that was acceptable journalism – it was the news coverage as well.* Not since the 1860s had facts been so distorted. Peter Dempson discovered that the stories he filed received prominent play on the *Telegram*'s front page only if he made St. Laurent look bad. One night the Liberal leader was addressing a crowd of about 2,000 people in Ottawa. Dempson estimated that there were probably about fifty empty seats. "I had the photographer accompanying me take two or three pictures of the yawning seats," he remembered. "I also made a note of the two or three interruptions when St. Laurent was speaking. The *Telegram* splashed the picture of the empty seats across four columns the next day. My story, which also played up the empty seats and the interruptions, was given line treatment."[27] *Star* reporters were just as guilty.

And so it went for the rest of the campaign. The *Telegram* matched the *Star* headline for headline: "Ready to Aid Any Plan to Build Decent Homes St. Laurent Declares," noted the *Star* about the prime minister's speech at Stratford, Ontario, on housing; the *Telegram*'s version of the same story was "St. Laurent Fatigued Cuts Handshake Hurries from Meet."

The final, and by any standards of decent journalism, lowest blow was delivered by the *Star* two days before the election. Desperate to prove that

---

*In a *Maclean's* article entitled "How Toronto's Evening Papers Slanted the News," journalist Sidney Katz concluded that during the period from May 10 to June 27, election day, the Liberals received 1,734 inches in the *Star* and only 290 inches in the *Telegram*, while Drew and the Conservatives received 355 inches in the *Star* and 1,402 inches in the *Telegram*. Of the *Star*'s 85 campaign photographs, 73 were of St. Laurent, his family, or other Liberal candidates; there were only 2 pictures of Drew throughout the campaign. The *Telegram* countered with 40 of 43 campaign photographs of Drew and other Tory candidates. (*Maclean's*, August 15, 1949)

Drew had formed a "sinister alliance" with Duplessis and Houde, the *Star* had sent editor Alex Givens to Quebec to collect evidence. *Star* photographers tracked Houde's every move and took pictures that played up the former mayor's large paunch.[28] On Saturday, June 25, the *Star* ran its now infamous headline in huge 110-point letters across the front page:

KEEP CANADA BRITISH
DESTROY DREW'S HOUDE
GOD SAVE THE KING

The story below, which was accompanied by "the most revolting picture of Houde" in the paper's collection, stated: "This man will be one of the rulers of Canada if voters Monday elect George Drew as head of a Conservative government. He is Camilien Houde, isolationist, ex-internee, foe of Britain." Even the *Star*'s executives were appalled, and in later editions the last line was changed to "VOTE ST. LAURENT."[29]*

Not wishing to be outdone, the *Telegram* blew out of all proportion the fact that the *Star Weekly* did not pay the 8 percent sales tax on newsprint. In a radio broadcast prior to the publication of the story, McCullagh had noted how it was a "cute trick" that the *Weekly* was classified as a magazine – which it was – and therefore exempt from the tax. None of this mattered. "Liberals Paying Off Star," screamed the *Telegram*.[30]

This, as well as other biased newspaper coverage (for instance, Grant Dexter's editorials in the *Winnipeg Free Press* were vehemently anti-Drew), had a limited effect on the final outcome, which gave St. Laurent a large majority. Life was good for Canadians under the Liberals. Why should they cast them aside?[31] But it was the last time such partisan mud-slinging took place. Embarrassed editors at both the *Star* and the *Telegram* agreed that such one-sided writing, if it had to exist, belonged on the editorial page and not in the news columns.

As a sign of things to come, the *Montreal Star* in its post-election analysis used a poll to examine the results. It found that when its "representative" group was asked what each of the parties stood for, 62 percent could not

---

*The *Star* actually wanted it both ways. Two days earlier, an editorial had equated Drew's opposition to family allowances in 1944 with being anti-Quebec – "because he did not want Quebec to profit from her large families ... If Mr. Drew had had his way, 1,250,000 children in Quebec who are happier today because of family allowances would not be receiving them." The paper concluded that Drew "too often has indicated a strange antagonism towards the French race that unfits him for national leadership." (*Toronto Star,* June 23, 1949)

define the objectives of the Conservatives, 54 percent those of the Liberals, and 49 percent those of the CCF.

For a time it seemed as if St. Laurent and the Liberals could do nothing wrong. During its first term, the administration's list of achievements was impressive. Even before the election of 1949 Newfoundland had become part of Canada and the country a member of the North Atlantic Treaty Organization (NATO). Federal financial assistance to the provinces for a trans-Canada highway was implemented; St. Laurent weathered the storm in 1950 created by the Korean War; the government established the Massey Royal Commission on National Development in the Arts, Letters and Sciences; old-age pension legislation was passed; and Quebec premier Maurice Duplessis was kept at bay.

The Liberal victory in the election of August 10, 1953, was predictable. From the perspective of Tory Dalton Camp, the campaign of 1953 "was an experience in futility. The result was never in doubt." Travelling with the prime minister on the campaign train – nicknamed the "Uncle Louie Limited" by the reporters – Richard Jackson of the Conservative-leaning *Ottawa Journal* noted that it was impossible not to be "charmed and warmed by his personality. He can turn the indifferent or the doubtful into a starry-eyed partisan."[32]

Responsible for much of the Liberals' success was C.D. Howe – minister of trade and commerce and defence production, "the Boss of all political affairs," the "Minister of All the Talents," "the Great Pooh-Bah." In a 1961 CBC television interview, St. Laurent said that he regarded Howe as "the most effective general director" of the Canadian economy since Confederation.

An American-born civil engineer who moved to Halifax in 1908, Howe became a successful businessman, building huge grain elevators from his base in Port Arthur, Ontario. Through contacts with Norman Lambert, he entered politics as a Liberal in the 1935 election; he was appointed to King's cabinet; and he brilliantly guided the Canadian economy through the Second World War. He was, in Grant Dexter's opinion, "good-natured, affable, with a ready sense of humour, but a mind that is razor-edged." By 1948 Howe, according to Grattan O'Leary, "was above criticism, an untouchable of the government, a man who got things done, a man who could do no wrong."[33]

Even so, while Howe was a shrewd judge of people, he had little patience for such political realities as Parliament. He was not the best debater and sometimes got caught in the opposition's barbs. His corporate dictatorial style made him an easy target for the Tories, and he later became their chief symbol of Liberal arrogance. What's more, Howe, a true "North American," did not distinguish between Canadian and U.S. dollars. "C.D. did all he could to entice, cajole, prod, even bully Canadian businessmen into the big projects he loved and rightly saw as necessary," said Tom Kent, a former editor of the *Winnipeg Free Press* and an adviser to Lester Pearson. "But when the response was inadequate, as in many sectors of the economy it inevitably was, C.D. was not going to let that stop him."[34] For Howe, American capital was as good as Canadian. His sense of urgency and strong desire to get the job done at any cost set the stage for the pipeline fiasco of 1956.

By 1954 St. Laurent had come to resemble the distant chairman of a massive corporation, letting his ministers, or managing directors, do as they wished. Moreover, his increasing years had begun to affect his work. "St. Laurent's condition is indicated by a lack of power to concentrate," Grant Dexter noted after a long talk with Jack Pickersgill in May of that year. "His capacity to master a question has left him. He is aware of this inability to concentrate. He is irritable ... and finds discussion in the cabinet or in the House excessively trying. Jack says they hope that a long summer holiday will restore him. Otherwise we might have a new leader sooner than we expect."[35]

The Liberal hierarchy was quite protective of its leader. CBC Radio, for example, had tried to get St. Laurent to chat on the air with journalists about his six-week trip to Europe and Asia, but his loyal secretary Pierre Asselin vetoed that idea. Though radio broadcasts were a fine way for a prime minister to reach the public directly, the time had not arrived for a leader to be publicly interrogated. That was better left for a private press conference.[36]

Howe, too, at sixty-eight, was starting to show his age. "He [now] looked," his biographers have written, "like a wounded bear, destined to be baited by the opposition, and doomed to rise to the bait every time ... [His] temper was perceptibly shorter." When the new CBC television service announced its plans to run a documentary on unemployment, drawing attention to the government's failings in this area, Howe "blew up." In a telephone call to the corporation's president, Davidson Dunton, he threatened to fire Dunton and his staff. A talk with colleagues cooled him down; he called Dunton back to apologize and calmly explained his position.[37]

The press – Liberal, Conservative, and independent – had begun to treat the government more critically by the spring of 1955. St. Laurent had not held a press conference since the summer of the previous year, and the *Winnipeg Tribune* editorial of April 20 suggested that "he could loosen up a little." He was to wait a full fourteen months more before calling one.

The first sign of serious trouble for the Liberal regime was Howe's attempt to make permanent his extraordinary – some said draconian – powers under the Defence Production Act, which had been passed during the Korean War but would expire at the end of July 1956. (Under the act, Canadian businesses, for instance, "could be required to make what the gov-

ernment wanted at prices fixed by the government.") A renewal of the measure might have been in order, but with no new national emergency looming
there was no good reason for making the powers permanent, other than that
in doing so, Howe would be freed from "having to make his case in
Parliament" every four years.[38]

Once the debate on the bill started, St. Laurent, tired and depressed,
remained silent, letting Howe carry the show. The Tories attacked "Dictator
Howe" and prolonged the discussion into the hot days of July. Editors
across the country wondered why the Liberal minister needed these special
powers if, as he said, he did not plan to use them.[39] At the *Free Press* in
Winnipeg, Tom Kent (who had succeeded Dexter as editor in 1954) was sufficiently perturbed that he personally wrote to the prime minister urging him
to withdraw the bill. Without consulting Howe, St. Laurent struck a deal
with George Drew to end the debate, allowing the extended powers to
remain in force for only a few more years.

Nevertheless, the damage had been done. Not since the days of R.B.
Bennett had newspapers been so united in their opposition to the government. Such supportive papers as the *Free Press*, the *Vancouver Sun,* and the
Montreal Star harped on the Liberals' arrogance. The *Ottawa Journal* went
further, noting how the power of the press had played a crucial role in the
outcome. "It was Mr. Drew who organized, inspired and kept his small band
of House followers in determined action against the Government's proposals," Grattan O'Leary wrote in an August editorial. "But it was the press,
almost unanimous across the country against the Government's position,
which gave the knockout blow. The public at first was indifferent; uninformed. The press, sensing the rightness of Mr. Drew's position provided
the necessary information, revealed to the country the basic principle at
stake, created and stirred up a public opinion for Parliament's rights such as
Canada had not experienced in years."[40] The battle was only beginning.

Every so often political events take place that are recognized at the time and
later as major turning-points in history. Such was the case with the Pipeline
Debate of 1956. At first there seemed to be nothing terribly startling about
C.D. Howe's plan to construct a pipeline to channel Alberta gas to Ontario
consumers (through an all-Canadian route) or the government's decision to
loan the U.S. controlled TransCanada PipeLines Ltd. $80 million. The gas
was desperately required in the East and the terms of the short-term loan
were favourable. What ultimately caused the furor was the fact that the bill
had to be passed quickly in order to meet budget demands. As a result, in the
same breath that Howe introduced his loan bill he also instituted closure to
limit parliamentary discussion. Thus, it was not the pipeline that became the
focus for debate in the Commons in May and June of 1956, but the St.

Laurent government's questionable tactics, further complicated by the arbitrary rulings of Speaker René Beaudoin. Anticipating the imminent end of the Liberal regime, Blair Fraser, soon after the bill had finally passed, wrote that "political historians may well conclude that the Liberals fell, not because of any one policy, and certainly not a pipeline policy of which the average voter knew little and cared less, but because they failed to observe the proper limits of power."[41]

The Pipeline Debate's legacy in the folklore of the gallery was that it marked a significant change in the way journalists treated politicians. As June Callwood put it, "The press gallery [in 1956] found itself caught up in a spirit of flaming outrage and abandoned all pretensions of writing impartially … 'Don't quote me,' [one civil servant had told Callwood], 'but since pipeline the real party in opposition is always the parliamentary gallery.'"[42]

Callwood and her bureaucrat friend were overstating the case. Journalists did not suddenly band together, disregard their partisan allegiances for all time, and form a common front. Indeed, during the federal election held a year after the Pipeline Debate, the Liberals maintained the support of many of the newspapers that could not accept new Conservative leader John Diefenbaker as head of the country. The editorials of the *Toronto Star*, *Kingston Whig-Standard*, and Regina *Leader-Post*, to list only a few, prompted Grattan O'Leary of the *Ottawa Journal* to make this observation a few days before voting day: "Over the past few weeks Government spokesmen from the Prime Minister down, with assists from propagandist and journalistic chore-boys, have tried desperately to obscure, distort and misrepresent what happened last June."

A significant consequence of Howe's attempt to ram the pipeline bill through Parliament was a disillusionment with the Liberals on the part of such long-time friends as Bruce Hutchison, George Ferguson, and Grant Dexter, who privately believed the government had gone "nuts." *Winnipeg Free Press* editor Tom Kent assailed Howe and the cabinet for its "appalling" strategy and extreme measures, referring to the use of closure as "an abomination to the heart of every man of every party who cares for free discussion and democratic institutions."[43]

The debate's effect on younger gallery members was more important. Much less partisan, they disapproved of the government's heavy-handed tactics. The Pipeline Debate left this new generation of Ottawa journalists a more questioning group, which made life more difficult for St. Laurent's successors. "It was the start of adversarial journalism," says media critic George Bain, then a thirty-six-year-old writer for the *Globe and Mail*. Bain's associate, Clark Davey, who arrived in Ottawa in 1955 at the age of twenty-seven, recalls that it was a very exciting time in the gallery's "hot room." Not only were most of his colleagues shocked by the government's behaviour, but they also wrote about it. This distressed veteran Alex Hume of the *Ottawa Citizen*, who, together with a few Liberal loyalists from the *Toronto Star*, stuck by the government. "There has been much purblind reporting," lamented Hume in a June 10, 1956, column, "some of it by younger writers with brief experience of Ottawa parliamentary work, giving a lop-sided picture of what actually has been taking place." In Hume's judg-ment, it was the "power-hungry Conservative opposition," with its "obstruc-tionist" filibustering, that was guilty of political sin.

The members of the public who were paying attention thought other-wise. The immediate result of the Pipeline Debate was a 10 percent drop in the Liberals' opinion poll rating. Traditional government foes like the *Globe and Mail* stepped up their campaign, denouncing Liberal arrogance and challenging St. Laurent to call an election. That perception did not improve in the wake of the Suez crisis during the fall of 1956, when the Tories and their supporters criticized the government for siding with the Soviet Union and the United States in their stand against "Israeli 'aggression' and the Anglo-French 'intervention.'"[44]

An analysis of Suez press coverage compiled by Bob Farquharson at the Canadian embassy in Washington convinced External Affairs Minister Lester Pearson that there was a concerted effort by Canadian editors to dis-tort their U.S-based correspondents' reports. Ambassador Arnold Heeney told Pearson that Farquharson's survey "reveals both a shocking bias against the United States and, even worse, an unwillingness to hear and print the truth when it is unpalatable." Briefing St. Laurent on the survey, Pearson called it "a very depressing picture of the influence exercised by Canadian newspapers on their correspondents."[45]

In an attempt to get the gallery back in his corner, St. Laurent convened a press conference in late September, the first one since July 28, 1955. With forty-five journalists crammed into his East Block office, the prime minister was in good humour. He talked and answered questions for more than an hour. But as queries about the pipeline and the next election were put for-ward, his responses became sharper. "There is a limit to what you can pry from my mind," he informed the group of reporters. Over the next two months, as gallery members pressed him about the crisis in the Suez, his mood soured. A background briefing for gallery members might have cleared the air, but the government chose the opposite course. "It was the worst PR failure the government has ever had," George Bain later said. "The immediate reaction here was that [Pearson] was selling out Britain. It could have been avoided if the gallery had been kept abreast of what Canada was trying to do and why."[46]

Asked about Canada's attitude to the British entry into Egypt in early November, St. Laurent "almost bit the nose off a reporter." "It's too bad you can't come into the cabinet meetings and tell us how to do it," he lectured the correspondents. A few weeks later, when the government allowed only one CP reporter to travel on the plane carrying Canadian troops overseas, journalists were up in arms. St. Laurent informed them that he was "under no obligation to provide facilities for newspapermen." In the eyes of the gallery, Uncle Louis had become "Louis the Terrible."[47]

There was another reason why the prime minister was testier than usual. Every time he stepped from his office, he was caught in a scrum. Not only did he have to face fifty print reporters with their pens at the ready, but glaring at him were the lights and camera of CBC television. And Louis St. Laurent was no TV star.

About six months after CBC television first went on the air (in September 1952), Tom Earle, an enthusiastic twenty-six-year-old former press agent for the CPR, signed on with the corporation's Montreal station. Within two years he was in Ottawa with a one-man show. By today's technological standards, it was a Stone Age operation. "I would record an interview one day with a huge tape machine, which would be used on the radio, and get the pictures the next day for TV," Earle says. "You couldn't do both at the same time. That would be too daring." For reports and commentaries, he hired newspapermen like Blair Fraser and Arthur Blakely of the *Montreal Gazette*. Fraser took to the new medium immediately. "Fraser could write a script, give it to you and then read it back to you on camera word for word," recalls Earle. "He was incredible."

The St. Laurent government had passed the necessary legislation creating the television network, found the money for it (about $9 million in 1953, rising to $42 million by 1957), and generally did not interfere in its day-to-day affairs. By 1956, however, the CBC's objectivity was not always appreciated. The Liberals, noted Blair Fraser in March of that year, "have the worst persecution complex of all political parties in their relations with the CBC. They think the CBC is in a dark chronic conspiracy to malign the government and they recite examples with the fluency of a hypochondriac describing his symptoms."[48] C.D. Howe, as noted, had threatened to fire the entire staff over the televising of a documentary on unemployment in 1954. The government procrastinated for more than a year before approving the CBC's plans for free-time political broadcasts; it made a big fuss over a proposed TV panel discussion on Harry Ferns and Bernard Ostry's unflattering 1955 biography of Mackenzie King (the show was never aired); and the Liberals felt that the reporting on the Pipeline Debate was biased against them. Regarding the latter, the bias in the reports flowed from the fact that most of the journalists doing the commentary were opposed to the government's actions in Parliament (though when the matter was raised in the

House, Conservative George Hees argued that the CBC's coverage was as fair as that of the wire services).[49]

From the Liberals' perspective, television entailed two key considerations: money and political value. In October 1956 St. Laurent, as a "private citizen" (or so he later claimed), wrote CBC chairman Davidson Dunton to complain about comments aired on the network regarding his administration's foreign policy. Dunton wrote back with an apology, but pointed out that it was his impression the CBC was "responsible for its own programming." St. Laurent's rejoinder was very telling. "I find it difficult to admit," he replied, "that it is the proper function of the Canadian government to recommend appropriations to the CBC to be used to subsidize the propagation of ideas which it believes, and I think has the support of the large majority of the Canadian public in believing, are unsound."[50] (No matter what Dunton did, he could not please everyone. In the spring of 1957, Leslie Frost, the Conservative premier of Ontario, complained that CBC newscasts favoured the Liberals!) Decades later, the CBC's relationship with the government would still be a matter of public discussion.

As early as 1950 the National Liberal Federation was examining the political aspects of television. A report prepared by Cockfield, Brown's research department in March of that year concluded that in the United States, when it comes to TV news, entertainment, or political coverage, "people want it." But while further investigations looked into how make-up or clothing could enhance a person's TV image, and referred to television's intangible "intimacy," the so-called experts didn't really know what they were dealing with. "None of us clearly saw what was coming," says former Tory ad man Dalton Camp, "which was a medium that would profoundly change politics, campaigning, reporting, and politicians themselves. Perhaps, had any of us realized its potential and its implications, we might have been frightened by it. Instead, we considered television a kind of extension of radio."[51]

The initial hint of TV's awesome power naturally came from the United States. The political party conventions and presidential election campaign of 1952 were extensively covered by the new medium. Television allowed an estimated fifty-eight million viewers to be part of a national party convention, until then "a private closed affair." Republican organizers for General Dwight Eisenhower, the ultimate victor, budgeted close to $2 million for television and radio and wisely purchased the more expensive prime-time hours for their candidate. The strategy paid off.* The British were the next to catch on. In the election of 1955, Conservative Anthony Eden, who looked as handsome and natural on television as he did in person, hired a special media adviser to prepare him for his broadcasts. It was ironic that a year later TV coverage of trouble in the Suez would be the British prime minister's undoing.[52]

On the question of television, St. Laurent reacted more like Eden's elderly predecessor, Winston Churchill; he hated it.† St. Laurent was good on the radio and enjoyed it. Listeners across Canada responded warmly to his voice. But television was something else. He resented having to wear make-up, refused to play to the camera, and did not tailor his speeches. The result during the 1957 election campaign was a disaster.

"I will be more interested in seeing people than in talking to cameras," St. Laurent had told a reporter at the outset of the campaign. It was a good plan. Television, observed journalist David Halberstam, "encouraged youth ... liked vigor ... and made old men look even older." St. Laurent was seventy-five years old in 1957, and though he was healthy, he tired easily. The camera highlighted his wrinkles, making him look wearier than he actually was. In an early broadcast, he sat at his desk reading a script, barely looking up. "If you cannot loosen up and be like ordinary people," recommended a *Winnipeg Free Press* editorial, "it would be decidedly to the advantage of the Liberal party to give up the television time that has been allotted to you." It was advice that was soon followed.[53]

Much to the dissatisfaction of Bob Kidd at the NLF, the Liberals – except cabinet minister Ralph Campney – ignored lessons on how to handle TV appearances given by CBC broadcasters (René Lévesque taught francophones) at a "dummy studio set up in the garage of its Ottawa headquarters." The attitude to television, Kidd said, was "one of caution and fear." About a month before the fateful ballots were cast, he reluctantly cancelled the rest of the planned Liberal TV broadcasts.[54]

---

*American scholar Stanley Kelley, Jr., in his 1956 book *Public Relations and Political Power*, one of the first books to analyze the relationship between politics and the media, pointed out that "the Republican message reached larger audiences than the Democratic one." Newspaper coverage of the Republicans was much stronger, and according to the Nielsen ratings, Eisenhower was seen and heard on TV and radio by a considerably larger number of Americans than was his Democratic opponent, Adlai Stevenson. Interestingly, Kelley also notes that on the subject of TV no candidate was more astute than Eisenhower's running mate, Richard Nixon. (Stanley Kelley, Jr., *Professional Public Relations and Political Power* [Baltimore, 1956], 177–200)

†British journalist Michael Cockerell wrote: "Churchill remained convinced that television had no real part to play in politics; in any case at the age of seventy-eight, the Prime Minister felt he was far too old to start to learn the techniques of the new medium." In 1954 Churchill relented and arranged a secret BBC screen test. He was not pleased with how his bulldog face filled the TV screen. (Michael Cockerell, *Live from Number 10: The Inside Story of Prime Ministers and Television* [London, 1988], 14–24)

The Tories and their new leader, John Diefenbaker, were another matter. In "McLuhanese," Diefenbaker by 1957 standards was a "hot" image on the screen – electric, vibrant, energetic. He was a natural ham, and his party quickly used the new medium to focus the campaign on their most potent weapon. "Television is the most pervasive and influential medium of them all," Dalton Camp wrote in a perceptive February 1957 pre-election memo. "It is likely that the Liberals will use television in the 'commercial sense,' since it is apparent I believe even to them that the Prime Minister does not like the medium. This affords us the opportunity for a certain advantage."[55]

Camp had been impressed with Diefenbaker's performance at the Tories' December 1956 convention. The CBC had broadcast the gathering, the first political event to receive such coverage in the country, and Diefenbaker rose to the occasion, as he did in the election that followed. In these early years, TV took the perspective of an outsider looking in. (This is in sharp contrast to the approach taken by "The Journal" in its controversial documentary of the 1989 NDP convention. CBC producers pinned a microphone on candidate Simon de Jong, which he inadvertently left on during a candid conversation he had with Dave Barrett, another contender.)

The 1957 campaign saw the first Canadian television battle between political leaders. Nothing in those days, however, could compare with today's public debates on TV. Besides TV time that was paid for, the CBC had allotted each party a certain number of free broadcasts (the Liberals received eight, the Conservatives seven). Forced to defend two decades of Liberal rule, including the Pipeline Debate, in three televised talks (or rather lectures), St. Laurent made the usual promise that the Liberals would continue "to do our best." In contrast, a relaxed Diefenbaker (prepared by Tory public relations expert Allister Grosart) first thanked viewers for "allowing me this short visit with you in your own home" and then delivered a stinging rebuke of the Liberals – as only he could. "His folksy manner, his look of sincerity, and his extravagant rhetoric worked well to fashion the image of a Lincolnesque figure," observes media historian Paul Rutherford. "Diefenbaker was the country's first master of the art of politics in the dawning age of television."[56]

On the evening of June 10, 1957, close to ten million Canadians (about 60 percent of the population) tuned in to the premier election-night broadcast. With Morely Safer as producer, Charles Lynch as anchor, and Blair Fraser as chief commentator, plus a team of commentators around the country (including a young intellectual lawyer named Pierre Trudeau in Quebec), the CBC's show was a polished, though sombre, broadcast.[57] "We were seized with it," recalls Lynch, who, in the days when it was permitted, smoked a pipe the whole night. "We were the only channel in town and had the country 'by the balls.'" The *Montreal Gazette* considered the show "a fine job of reporting the best drama of the year."

Careful to avoid charges of partisanship or favouritism, the CBC bent over backwards to appear impartial. Consequently, the show was far from a lively affair. Still, as returns rolled in, the journalists, so used to Liberal governments (the Liberals had won the last five elections), were astonished by the trend that resulted in a minority government for Diefenbaker. Near the end of the show Lynch lit up a huge cigar given to him by the crew. "I got shit from the control room for editorializing," he says. "But I was not being partisan, merely rejoicing in the story." But Fraser, according to Lynch, was "shattered" because he "hated Diefenbaker so much."

Because television is such a "dramatic medium," it is easy to exaggerate its effect on political contests. The 1957 campaign still belonged to the newspapers, and many in Quebec and elsewhere stuck by the Liberals. But the appeal of Diefenbaker the underdog was difficult to resist, even for a loyal Grit paper like the *Toronto Star*.* Like everyone else, most journalists assumed the Liberals would win. *Maclean's* even went so far as to predict a Liberal victory in their June 22 edition, which was written before the votes were counted: "For better or for worse, we Canadians have once more elected one of the most powerful governments ever created by the free will of a free electorate."[58]

With hindsight, it is easy to see that by 1957 the Liberals were in serious trouble. The Pipeline Debate was still on the public's mind, and Finance Minister Walter Harris's pre-election budget was less than satisfactory. Simply put, the party's leaders were too old, too out of touch with the concerns of the electorate.

Consider C.D. Howe's unfortunate campaign foray into Manitoba. At a rally in Morris, a town south of Winnipeg in an area that had been a safe Liberal seat for years, the Minister of All the Talents was unable to answer basic questions about grain policy to the satisfaction of those in attendance. Finally, when one man's query turned into a commentary, Howe shouted at him, "When your party organizes a meeting, you'll have the platform and we'll ask the questions." The man turned out to be Bruce Mackenzie, head of the local Liberal association.[59] Not surprisingly, this and similar episodes

---

*Supporting the Liberals were all the francophone papers in Quebec (except *Le Devoir*), the *Montreal Star,* Montreal *Herald, Toronto Star, Ottawa Citizen, Kingston Whig-Standard,* and the Sifton papers – the Regina *Leader-Post, Saskatoon Star-Phoenix,* and *Winnipeg Free Press,* which grew more critical as the campaign progressed. In the Conservatives' corner were the *Montreal Gazette* (with some qualification), *Globe and Mail, Toronto Telegram, Ottawa Journal, London Free Press,* and all the Southam papers (except the *Citizen*).

were widely reported in the *Free Press*, whose editors by then had lost faith in the Liberals.

Howe, like St. Laurent, could not adapt to television and went down to defeat at the hands of Douglas Fisher of the CCF, then a Port Arthur teacher who made exceptionally good use of the new medium. Later, in assessing what had happened to him, Howe noted that "my opponent was a polished television artist, and his gains all took place within the area covered by television. I may tell you that television is no good for us 'old boys.'"[60]

He may have been right. Though it is impossible to know its real impact on the outcome of the 1957 election, television might have played a contributing role. In Ontario, for example, a province with the most TV-equipped households in the country, the Tory popular vote increased from 770,000 in 1953 to 1.1 million in 1957. Of course, there is a strong possibility that Diefenbaker would have received these votes in any event. Television created "impression," as Dalton Camp noted. "The question that begs at every occasion of a political television broadcast in the viewer's mind is, 'Do I like and do I trust him?'" he observed.[61] In June 1957 there were a lot of Canadians, including most of the reporters in the Ottawa press gallery, who answered that question about John Diefenbaker in the affirmative. Television had done its job; it remained to be seen whether the new prime minister could do his.

PART THREE

The Unofficial Opposition,
1957–1992

CHAPTER TWELVE

Dief vs. the Gallery

To read the press for the period of my government ... is often to read the opposite of what actually took place.

The Memoirs of the Right Honourable John G. Diefenbaker, 1976

B y the end of the 1957 campaign there were only three of them left on Diefenbaker's whistle-stop tour. Clark Davey, the young *Globe and Mail* correspondent had been ordered by his boss Oakley Dalgleish to "stick with Dief"; veteran Peter Dempson of the *Telegram* was covering his third general election; and Mark Harrison of the Liberal *Toronto Star* was keeping a skeptical eye on the Prairie lawyer who was threatening to dethrone the "Government Party." Alan Donnelly of the Canadian Press had been with them at the beginning but was forced to depart the last week because of his health; his nerves were shot from an excessive workload. Diefenbaker was speaking seven and eight times a day, stopping the train at every small town across the country. "At the end of the day he was wiped out," remembers Davey. "We did not know how he did it. Near the end, he was in Edmonton and he made a speech that was absolutely incomprehensible. It was gibberish, but the people didn't give a shit. They cheered him anyways."

Two days after his surprising victory on June 10, Diefenbaker invited the three reporters to join him for a short fishing trip at Lac la Ronge, about 200 kilometres north of Prince Albert, his home riding. They travelled there by float plane and spent a relaxing day fishing – Diefenbaker's favourite pastime – and listened to the new prime minister talk about his choices for a cabinet. With Diefenbaker, however, such conversations were always monologues. As Davey recalls, "It was the happiest time in his life. He was full of stories and anecdotes and boasted that Donald Fleming and Alvin Hamilton could have any portfolios they wanted" (Fleming chose Finance; Hamilton, Northern Affairs and Natural Resources). The party returned to Prince Albert in time to catch the Trans-Canada Airlines red-eye back to Ottawa.[1]

In the confusion, one of Diefenbaker's suitcases was misplaced. "He had a temper tantrum and jumped up and down like a little kid," Davey says. "'Don't they know who I am,' he shouted, 'I'm the new prime minister.' I was on the phone talking to the rewrite man at the *Globe* and I repeated what Dief had said. The lead for the story was changed to 'An angry John Diefenbaker flew out of his hometown tonight.' When we arrived in Toronto, someone handed Diefenbaker a copy of the morning *Globe*. And Christ, Dief went berserk at me."

For the seven turbulent years Diefenbaker was prime minister, he went "berserk" at many people, but especially at journalists who he felt had betrayed his trust and friendship. The sixty-one-year-old lawyer, while brilliant on a platform and engaging before an audience, was equally insecure, often emotionally immature, and unskilled at managing other people. He was overly sensitive about the pronunciation of his German-sounding name and could rarely laugh at himself. He also possessed a huge ego, unmatched in Ottawa.

He allowed his pride and emotions to govern his stormy relationship with U.S. president John F. Kennedy, a fateful error for any prime minister. Unable to compete with JFK's charismatic style and youth, and bothered by the American president's view that Canada should blindly follow U.S. foreign policy, Diefenbaker grew hostile. When he accidentally found one of the president's confidential briefing memos prepared by adviser Walt Rostow for Kennedy's meeting with Diefenbaker in Ottawa in May 1961 ("What We Want from Ottawa Trip"), he not only failed to return it to the Americans, but threatened to blackmail Kennedy with it. In late 1962, when Diefenbaker learned that Kennedy was meeting privately with British prime minister Harold Macmillan in Nassau to discuss the troubled state of East-West relations, he pouted because he had not been invited. "He was just like a little boy being left out of a game of tag," said his secretary Bunny Pound. "He was practically in tears."[2]

The acquisition of power changes most people. Some are able to rise above the trivialities that go along with their new status, but not Diefenbaker. He tasted power and enjoyed it. No one, not even his closest friends, dared call him "John" after June 10, 1957; he was "Mr. Prime Minister."[3] "I may be wrong," he would say pompously to reporters, "but I have never been on the side of wrong." In his mind, he was in the same league as his heroes – John A. Macdonald, Abraham Lincoln, Winston Churchill, and Franklin Roosevelt – and faced the same tough decisions and challenges they had. Diefenbaker saw himself as a nation builder like John A., the "unsworn enemy of injustice," and the protector of the common man against "the powerful establishments" that ran the country. Confronting him in this quest to attain national salvation, he believed, was a grand conspiracy – led by the Liberals, supported by the money of Toronto's Bay Street, encouraged by the media, and planned by the Americans. "He was paranoid, neurotic and had a 'Nixonian' complex even before Richard Nixon," says Clark Davey. "'They're out to get me,' he would say, but you couldn't find out who the 'they' was." No matter, by 1963, following the revolt in his cabinet over the acquisition of nuclear weapons, "there was no question," Diefenbaker later wrote, "that everyone was against me but the people."[4]

A good deal of Diefenbaker's insecurity was a consequence of the fact that it had taken him so long to achieve political success. He was born in 1895 in Ontario, but moved west to Saskatchewan when still a young child. He was educated at the University of Saskatchewan, where he obtained a master's in political economy and a law degree. He later exaggerated his legal achievements, but as a small-town lawyer first in Wakaw, Saskatchewan, and later in Prince Albert, he was competent and worked very hard. It was in the courtroom that he developed the oratorical skills that were to make him one of Canada's greatest political campaigners. In those early years he was a loner with few close friends, except for his first wife, Edna, who died in 1951.

His real passion was politics, but his rise to power was not easy. Defeat followed defeat as he tried to build a career as a Conservative politician from the West. He was constantly campaigning, usually as the underdog, in federal and provincial elections. He even ran for mayor in Prince Albert in 1933, but lost by forty-eight votes. It was difficult being a Tory in Saskatchewan in the late twenties and early thirties. When Diefenbaker finally became the lonely leader of the provincial Conservatives in 1936, he inherited a party with "no office, no staff, no riding organizations, no candidates – only the fiction of a provincial organization, and no money." Moreover, he was no match for the "alluring remedies of socialism and monetary reform" offered to the voters by the CCF and the Social Credit.[5]

His elusive quest for a real political opportunity was finally fulfilled with his election to the House of Commons in 1940. During his many years in opposition, he gained a national reputation as the champion of so-called ordinary Canadians.[6] Twice prior to 1956 Diefenbaker attempted to win the Conservative leadership. In 1942 he lost to John Bracken, the former premier of Manitoba, who transformed the party into the "Progressive-Conservatives," and six years later he was defeated by Ontario premier George Drew. This latter loss, more than anything else, embittered him against the Toronto party establishment, which had engineered Drew's victory. Notorious for holding grudges, he would not soon forgive those who voted against him in 1948, including Grattan O'Leary, a party stalwart and the editor of the *Ottawa Journal*.

O'Leary was blamed for rigging the 1948 convention against Diefenbaker, a charge he found "absurd." Nevertheless, after Diefenbaker became prime minister, O'Leary was initially shunned by the new party hierarchy. Eventually, Diefenbaker, who was smart enough not to allow a resource like O'Leary go to waste, had the editor write his speeches as well as the preamble to the Bill of Rights. Interestingly, Diefenbaker was probably justified in not fully trusting O'Leary, since he was passing on secrets to Val Sears of the *Toronto Star.* "O'Leary did not admire Dief," says Sears, "but supported him as a good Tory. He told me one day the 'son of a bitch' Diefenbaker could not get it right. He delivered his northern Ireland speech in the south, and his southern Ireland speech in the north." At age seventy-three, O'Leary was finally rewarded for his long years of service with an appointment to the Senate in 1962, though Diefenbaker still remembered 1948. "O'Leary had never been one of my supporters," he wrote in his memoirs, "but he had served the party over a long period and I hoped that this recognition would contribute to the unity of the party."[7]

At first members of the parliamentary gallery, like the rest of the country, were captivated with John Diefenbaker. Reporters of both Conservative and Liberal newspapers were impressed with his magical oratory, the emotional outburst he generated everywhere he visited, and his vision of Canadian prosperity. In 1957 Diefenbaker's mangled French and his distortion of facts and statistics were overlooked.

On a purely theoretical level, Diefenbaker was an ardent defender of freedom of the press, although he differed with journalists over where the line was to be drawn between their right to report and a politician's right to govern. In a 1966 speech he declared that "no politician can expect favours or soft treatment from the news media as a matter of right. No politician can expect blunders, mistakes or indiscretions to be covered by a friendly press. But everyone in public life is entitled to expect fair, full and factual reporting and let the editorial arrows fly where they may."[8] Yet he also believed that, given the right circumstances – as in the turbulent months following the 1962 election – the press could grow too powerful.

In essence, Diefenbaker accepted freedom of the press only as long as the press played by his rules. This meant, as Peter Newman observed, that "the various communications media ought to act as a direct transmission lines between himself and the public – passing on nothing but his version of the valiant efforts he was making on behalf of 'the average Canadian.'"[9] In the high-stakes game Diefenbaker waged with journalists, he was only happy when he felt he had the upper hand.

Diefenbaker hardly needed lessons in self-promotion, but he did take the advice of Allister Grosart. Grosart had managed George Drew's 1948 leadership campaign, and Diefenbaker was not too proud to ask for his help in 1956. During the election the following year, it was Grosart who came up with the slogan "IT'S TIME FOR A DIEFENBAKER GOVERNMENT," which focused on the man rather than the party. With a penchant for detail, Grosart, as the national director of the Conservative Party from 1957 to 1963, utilized the most current polling techniques and prepared Diefenbaker for the television age.[10]

Grosart convinced the new prime minister to hire James Nelson as his press secretary, the first person to hold such a title in the Prime Minister's Office. In the summer of 1957 Nelson was the president of the gallery and the bureau chief of United Press, the British wire service. He wrote to Grosart requesting more work space for his colleagues and guaranteed access to Diefenbaker through regular press conferences, and suggesting that a full-time press secretary be appointed. Diefenbaker never agreed to the idea of weekly meetings with the gallery, but he did offer Nelson the job of press secretary.[11] In mid-August Nelson was designated "senior information officer" on an annual salary of about $6,000.

It was a difficult, if not impossible, job, a real pressure cooker, as Nelson remembers it. The hours were long, and as one of the few bachelors on the prime minister's staff, he travelled a great deal with Diefenbaker and his second wife, Olive. He tried to be non-partisan and did not attend any political meetings. To be successful, a good press secretary must have some control over communications between the gallery and the prime minister. Diefenbaker, however, did what he wanted when he wanted. "Diefenbaker did not need advice on press relations, and I don't think I tried to give him any," Nelson says with a grin.

The prime minister loved being the centre of attention. He knew what the press wanted in terms of "quotable quotes" and was conscious of deadlines. During a campaign he carried around a huge file with everything in it from coal to wheat. If he had promised reporters a statement on, say, coal and he was speaking about grain transportation, he would somehow fit it in. This led, as Clark Davey recalls, to some famous non-sequiturs. "In the middle of his speech, he would look at the press table and remember. 'You ask me about freight rates,' he would say, 'I'll tell you about coal,' or 'You ask me about lobster fishing in Atlantic Canada, I'll tell you about the Crow's Nest Pass rates.'"

Most of all, Diefenbaker loved the challenge of sparring with reporters in the hallways of Parliament. This led to the famous impromptu corridor conferences that Nelson was unable to control. The corridor outside the cabinet meeting room in the East Block was always crowded, just as it had been during the King and St. Laurent years, except that now the prime minister acknowledged the journalists' presence – at least he did early on in his administration. "Mr. Diefenbaker would come out of the Privy Council chamber after a cabinet meeting, and if you stopped him ... he would stop and talk to you, because he liked the press, and he liked to verbally fence with the press," Victor Mackie of the *Winnipeg Free Press* related in an interview with Peter Stursberg. "If an important issue had developed, you could question him about it and he would either answer the question directly or he'd say, 'I can't give you a comment on that; you know better than to ask me what we decide in cabinet,' and grin and make a couple of off-hand comments and disappear into his office. Eventually the crowd grew until there were maybe two dozen people standing in the corridor. Diefenbaker would make his usual comments and quips, and they would be blown up into big stories. This began to get him into trouble."

Nelson was able to restrain him to a certain extent, although often Diefenbaker would stick his head out of the cabinet door waving a newspaper. "Where is so and so," he would yell, "boy did he ever put himself out on a limb," and then slam the door. Diefenbaker became more cautious after radio and TV reporters were officially admitted into the gallery in 1959.* He liked to be in control, and a microphone thrust in his face made him nervous. "He didn't mind talking to us privately," remembered Mackie, "because he knew that when we wrote our stories we'd say 'the prime minister said this' or 'the prime minister did that.' But he suddenly realized this was being recorded."[12]

Indicative of this attitude was a minor incident in 1958 involving Tom Earle of CBC-TV. At this time, radio and TV reporters could attend press conferences, but no recording was permitted. They were therefore forced to repeat their questions in the corridor or in an adjacent room afterwards. British prime minister Harold Macmillan was visiting Ottawa, and newspapermen had asked him whether the offer of free trade with Canada that Britain had made months before was still open. When Macmillan and Diefenbaker left the conference, they found Earle waiting for them. "Just to be polite," Earle says, "I told Macmillan that I was going to ask him the same question on free trade." Diefenbaker, who did not favour the proposal, suddenly intervened. Overhearing Earle's conversation with the British leader, he yelled, "No, no, you cannot ask that question." While Earle had

---

*There was a great reluctance by press reporters, who earned their money freelancing for the CBC, to admit radio and TV journalists into their private club. In May 1958 CBC reporters were required to sit in the visitors' gallery and were not allowed to take notes. Finally, the Speaker of the House, Roland Michener, reserved four seats for them so that they did not have to compete with tourists. After repeated requests, Michener urged the gallery executive to open its doors to their colleagues in the electronic media and they eventually complied. But news reporters hated the cables and equipment that came with them, and as Tom Earle remembers, they often made life miserable for CBC interviewers by using clickers to ruin sound bites or swearing as the camera was rolling – "Jesus Christ, Sir" or "For fuck sakes, senator!"

no option but to adhere to Diefenbaker's order, other journalists, he recalls, stood with their "mouths gaping."[13] Diefenbaker's flagrant interference – which he vehemently denied – blew up into a major controversy on the front pages and later in the House of Commons, where he was attacked by Pearson for his blatant attempt to censor the media.

Though Diefenbaker was uncomfortable with television's probing power, he recognized its political potential – it enabled him to appeal directly to his true supporters, the Canadian people. It is not surprising that in the midst of most of the major crises that crippled his administration, his appearance on TV was mandatory. In the beginning, he did have a strong TV presence, and then, as the weight of the job took its toll, so did the impact of the hot TV lights. Interviews conducted after 1961, "where his faced looked old and his hand might shake, increasingly suggested a man who was in an advanced state of decay."[14]

For Diefenbaker, as for other politicians, the real change in how Ottawa was covered began in 1959 when Norman DePoe was appointed to the CBC-TV parliamentary bureau. A daring reporter with a "weathered Mississippi river boat gambler's face," according to *Toronto Sun* reporter Robert MacDonald, DePoe was the first of a long line of CBC media celebrities. "When DePoe comes on in his rumpled seersucker suit and five o'clock shadow, hoarse voice, short of wind, he has the smell of news on him," wrote the *Globe and Mail's* TV columnist, Dennis Braithwaite.[15] More importantly, DePoe was the first television journalist who could compete on an intellectual level with the other stars of the gallery – Blair Fraser, Arthur Blakely, Grant Dexter, and Peter C. Newman. "No one at CBC had the power that DePoe had," asserts Tom Earle. "He actually knew Canadian history and read books. He was the star."

Norman DePoe was born in Portland, Oregon, in 1917, and his family moved up to Vancouver when he was only six. He attended the University of British Columbia in the late thirties and served in the Canadian Army during the war. He resumed his education at the University of Toronto in 1946, where he was managing editor of the *Varsity*. He also began freelancing for the *Globe and Mail* and CBC Radio. He started full time with CBC in 1948 as a rewrite man on the news desk. By 1951 he was editor of "News Roundup" and moved onto the air permanently a year later, after he impressed CBC executives with his coverage of the Republican convention in Chicago. Thereafter, he travelled the world for the CBC until he landed in Ottawa in 1959. It was not long before Diefenbaker recognized "that the most important reporter he spoke to was the CBC's Norman DePoe." Only once did Diefenbaker publicly complain about DePoe. One day in 1968, long after he was out of power, he met DePoe outside the Commons. In reply to a question, Diefenbaker responded, "You Mr. DePoe, have consistently defended the Liberal Party." DePoe, who took pride in being non-partisan and objective, took offence. "I categorically deny that," he declared. Diefenbaker just scowled at him and he scowled right back.[16]

Next to the CBC, Diefenbaker had high regard for Toronto's two Conservative newspapers, the *Telegram* and the *Globe and Mail*. Though he always voiced his disdain for the power of Bay Street and the way in which Ontario moguls dominated the Conservative Party, he actually craved their approval. Both John Bassett, the debonair publisher of the *Telegram*, and Oakley Dalgleish, the one-eyed editor and publisher of the *Globe and Mail*, were strong Diefenbaker supporters during the elections of 1957 and 1958.

Bassett often flew to Ottawa to visit the prime minister and his wife at 24 Sussex Drive. In 1960 Diefenbaker offered to appoint him Canadian ambassador in Washington, seeing him as a match for John Kennedy, but he refused. That same year Bassett and his business partners were granted the first private television licence (from which Baton Broadcasting and the CTV network were born), but there is no evidence that Diefenbaker personally intervened in the decision of the Board of Broadcast Governors.[17] Bassett split with Diefenbaker in 1963 over the nuclear weapons question.

It was the same story with Dalgleish, only he lost patience with Diefenbaker a lot sooner. He saw Diefenbaker as an obvious choice in the 1956 leadership race and offered him advice and support for the next two years. In December 1957 he wrote to Diefenbaker with an offer to hold back an article on the sugar trade written by Fraser Robertson so that the government would avoid embarrassment and could take the proper "corrective action." "Dalgleish did the prime minister a favour," says former *Globe* editor Richard Doyle, "that would have resulted in dismissal for any other *Globe* editor who tried it."[18] According to Clark Davey, the *Globe*'s publisher also often acted as an intermediary between Diefenbaker and Toronto cardinal James McGuigan, who was code-named "Red Hat." "We used to get calls from Dalgleish, to tell the old man [Diefenbaker] that Red Hat says this or that," Davey recalls. "Dief was sensitive to what the cardinal had to say." The fallout between Dalgleish and Diefenbaker began with the cancellation of the Avro Arrow jet interceptor contract in February 1959. Ontario premier Leslie Frost attempted to mediate a settlement between the two proud men, but he was not successful. Thereafter *Globe* editorials were critical of the Conservative administration.

Meanwhile, on the front lines in Ottawa, Diefenbaker also cultivated close relations with journalists, many of whom had known him during his opposition years as "John" or "Johnny." He regularly consulted with James Oastler, the Ottawa bureau chief of the *Montreal Star*. The two men usually spent an hour together each morning between six and seven in the East

Block. "Oastler knew what was going on," says Clark Davey. "He was the real pipeline to Dief. If I had a story I wasn't sure of, I would go to Oastler and ask him to check it out with the prime minister. He would usually come back and confirm my story for me." But given his paranoia, Diefenbaker was never quite sure who his real friends were in the gallery. "He was always wondering which newsmen he could trust and who would boast," says James Nelson. "So he planted seeds around and sat back to see which would sprout." His favourite trick was sending up trial balloons to test the reaction to a new policy or appointment. It made no difference to him if his intentional leaks embarrassed members of his own cabinet (as they did in early 1962 when he allowed the rumour to circulate that he was removing Donald Fleming as finance minister; instead of killing the gossip at once, he let it fester in the press, much to Fleming's dissatisfaction).[19] Fearful of making the wrong decision, Diefenbaker needed to court public approval, which was why he had so much time for Peter Dempson of the *Toronto Telegram* and Richard Jackson of the *Ottawa Journal*.

In an age when it was still possible to be buddies with the prime minister, Diefenbaker viewed Dempson and Jackson as a friendly audience he could rehearse with. "He knew they would never knife him," recalls Gowan Guest, who worked in the PMO from 1958 to 1960. In fact, Diefenbaker often toyed with the two journalists, treating them like schoolboys. After the sudden death, on March 16, 1959, of Sidney Smith, the newly appointed secretary of state for external affairs, Diefenbaker let Dempson and Jackson believe he was going to move Donald Fleming from Finance to External Affairs. The story was prominently carried on both newspapers' front pages, which led to loud criticism of the move. As it turned out, Fleming remained at Finance and Howard Green was named the new external affairs minister, a fateful appointment considering that Green's opposition to nuclear weapons later split the cabinet in 1962.* In his memoirs, Dempson wrote what must be one of the great understatements in the gallery's history: "[It] became apparent to Jackson and me that Diefenbaker had used us, and our papers, to test public reaction about Fleming. When our stories evoked a prompt and negative reaction, he dropped the idea."[20]

The truth was that the two reporters were at Diefenbaker's mercy. At

---

*Unknown to Diefenbaker, Green, a Vancouver MP, leaked confidential information to his good friend Bruce Hutchison, then editor of the *Victoria Daily Times*. "I often called on Green," Hutchison later recalled. "His door was always open to me. I could ring him on the telephone at any hour. I trusted him absolutely and he seemed to trust me well enough to speak with indiscretion that would have horrified Diefenbaker." (Hutchison, *Far Side*, 255. See also University of Calgary Special Collections, Hutchison Papers, 1.2.6, Hutchison to Dexter, March 5, 1960; 1.2.7, Hutchison to Dexter, January 29, 1961; November 8, 1961)

the height of the government's feud in 1961 with James Coyne, the governor of the Bank of Canada, Diefenbaker "punished" them by not revealing that the cabinet was about to demand Coyne's resignation. The reason – Jackson had written an insignificant story about a development in the civil service that had hit Diefenbaker the wrong way. "You should have known better," he scolded. On another occasion, he berated Dempson for a story in the *Telegram* written by one of the newspaper's other Ottawa correspondents.[21]

What ultimately soured Diefenbaker's relations with Dempson and Jackson, as well as with other Ottawa correspondents, was the prime minister's insecurity and extreme sensitivity to every article about him and his administration. Publicly he claimed that while politicians might disagree with what was said about them, the freedom to voice such criticism, whether justified or not, was for him the "essence of democracy." In practice and in private, however, it was quite a different matter. He refused, according to James Oastler, "to understand that good newspapermen – even those who were his cronies – can't let personal feelings interfere with their objectivity. Because he can't comprehend the motives of correspondents who write critically about his administration, he interprets their comments as personal insults."[22]

Diefenbaker read about ten newspapers each day and religiously scanned piles of clippings. Knowing his sensitivity, his staff attempted to keep the most critical stories out of his sight, yet he always found out about them from his network of confidants across the country. Consequently, he wasted considerable time and energy in anger over a minor story or broadcast. As journalist Patrick Nicholson put it, Diefenbaker was "extremely sensitive to even the most trivial criticism by the most immature commentator in the most insignificant newspaper."[23] When the attack came from someone of stature, like Charles King of the Southam press, he was livid.

In September 1958 the prime minister, Lester Pearson, and M.J. Coldwell, the leader of the CCF, were invited to the University of British Columbia to accept honorary degrees. Following the ceremony, Diefenbaker departed for a fishing trip in the Yukon. In reporting these events, King pointed out that Pearson and Coldwell received louder applause than the prime minister. To make matters worse, King sarcastically noted that due to the necessary security and the decision of the CBC and National Film Board (NFB) to film the trip, Diefenbaker's fishing excursion cost Canadian taxpayers about $10,000. When Diefenbaker read the article the next day in Edmonton, he chewed King out in front of the other reporters on the plane and never trusted him again. Four years later, during the 1962 election campaign, the fishing story resurfaced in a more famous clash between King and the prime minister.[24]

Diefenbaker was notorious, as well, for phoning journalists (or having his senior people do it for him) any time during the day or night to let them know his opinion on an article or editorial. Former newspaper correspondent Clark Davey remembers one such incident. In December 1957 a Conservative government was introducing a budget for the first time in twenty-two years, and Davey had written, as he says, "some good stuff" in advance. "Two days before the budget was to be brought down, the phone rang at 5:30 or 6:00 a.m. My wife answered the phone and looked at me. 'It's the prime minister,' she said, 'and he doesn't sound happy.' I took the phone and was chewed out for fifteen minutes. 'Young man,' he began, 'You are fiddling with the national accounts. You don't know what this will do to the Canadian dollar in New York.' He went on and on. He was very upset, but I just let him blow off steam."

Diefenbaker enjoyed a honeymoon period with the media for about a year and half. At one of his first meetings with gallery members in his East Block office in late June 1957, the newly elected prime minister shook hands with all the reporters, calling them by their first names, and told them some hilarious stories about his early days as a Prairie lawyer. Most publishers and editors across the country were elated with the turn of events, promising Diefenbaker their support. "I have no doubt that it lies within you to become one of Canada's truly great prime ministers," wrote Basil Dean, the publisher of the *Calgary Herald*. "For our part, we shall do whatever we can to support and sustain you. More specifically, [editor] Dick [Sanburn] and I propose to give you and your government unquestioning support for the first year that you are in office." As a sign of the new atmosphere of honesty and openness in Ottawa, Diefenbaker, following his return from the Commonwealth Prime Ministers' Conference in London in the first week of July, went right from the airport to the lounge of the gallery to speak with reporters. "He may not have made news with every answer," the *Ottawa Citizen*'s Frank Swanson observed, "but he at least was there to give the answers, and the pressmen are genuinely grateful." Grey Hamilton of the *Globe and Mail* was more skeptical, taking a wait-and-see approach, but Gerald Waring of the Canadian-American News Service expressed the view of many journalists in a letter to Diefenbaker on August 5: "There has been little warmth between the prime minister's office and the press gallery since November 15, 1948. Probably neither side was blameless, but it is a situation which I hope will never develop again."25

Behind the scenes, journalists like Patrick Nicholson, the Ottawa bureau chief of Thomson Newspapers, had a larger role to play. Nicholson, who had known Diefenbaker for more than a decade, referred to him in a 1955 commentary as "perhaps the greatest Canadian in Parliament today" – kind words that Diefenbaker never forgot. Once he became prime minister, he looked to Nicholson for sound advice and speech notes on a number of topics. Nicholson's biggest unreported scoop occurred in the fall of 1957, when he came across a March 1957 economic forecast signed by Mitchell Sharp, then associate deputy minister of trade and commerce, predicting, among other things, a rise in unemployment. In the House, the Liberal opposition was claiming that Conservative economic policies, in place for only a few months, had caused the jump in the unemployment rate reported in September 1957. "Tory times are hard times," they declared. But the fact was, as verified by Sharp's secret and confidential report, that the Liberals had known the country was headed for an economic slump before they had called an election for June 10. In an age when journalists still respected the government's right to confidentiality, Nicholson took the report directly to Diefenbaker, who put it away for safekeeping.[26]

Several months later, after the new leader of the Liberal Party, Lester Pearson, foolishly blamed the Conservatives for the continuing rise in unemployment and challenged them to resign so that he could put "the country back on the Liberal highway of progress," Diefenbaker produced the secret report. As the prime minister berated the Liberals for misleading the country, Pearson could only squirm in his chair. While much was made (and still is by Mitchell Sharp) of the fact that Diefenbaker probably tore the "secret and confidential" cover off the study, thereby placing the civil service in a compromising position, the Liberals had been indeed "guilty of ignoring ... Sharp's warnings in their super-roseate election propaganda, dedicated to the proposition that Canadians had never had it so good."[27] Within two weeks, Diefenbaker called an election for March 31, 1958. In that election Pearson and the Liberals would meet their bleak fate.

In less than a year, the Tory government had accomplished a great deal. Old age pensions were raised, more money was allocated to agriculture, and there was a slight reduction in income taxes. Diefenbaker had also approved, without much cabinet discussion, the Liberal plans to join the United States in NORAD – the North American Air Defence Command – as part of an integrated defence system to protect the continent from the Soviet Union. In his haste, Diefenbaker did not sufficiently consider the "degree of consultation between Ottawa and Washington that would take place before NORAD swung into action in an emergency."[28] His poor judgment on this matter would return to haunt him.

In the early spring of 1958, however, life for the prime minister could not have been much better. On the hustings Diefenbaker asked Canadians to "catch the vision" – a vision of northern development, new roads, and a new National Policy – and they opened their hearts to him. While the Liberal *Toronto Star* in an editorial of April 1 regarded such declarations as "humbug and flapdoodle served up with an evangelistic flourish," it was acknowledged that Pearson did not offer an alternative, nor could he compete with

Diefenbaker's electrifying style. The journalists travelling with the Tory "Chief" were in awe. "Not since the days of Sir Wilfrid Laurier has a politician had the magnetic appeal of this tall, lean 62-year-old Prince Albert lawyer," claimed Peter Dempson in a *Telegram* report of March 25. On election day (March 31), the results were astonishing. The Conservatives won 208 out of 265 seats, including 50 of 75 seats in Quebec (courtesy of the assistance of Premier Maurice Duplessis and his Union Nationale organization). It was the greatest electoral victory in Canadian history to that point.

This one-sided win did not turn out to be the best thing that could have happened to the Conservatives. After March 31 John Diefenbaker thought he was invincible. As Douglas Harkness, the minister of defence who resigned in February 1963, later reflected, "This very large majority, in my view, gave Mr. Diefenbaker a case of megalomania. It persuaded him that he was in an unassailable position. He was able to persuade himself that his views were always correct and that he could carry the Canadian people with him."[29] This imperious attitude in turn altered his relations with the press. Journalists now looked more critically at this powerful government, which incensed the prime minister and caused him to react negatively, thereby destroying the good will that had been established. It was a fact Diefenbaker acknowledged many years later. "One of the results of our huge majority," he observed, "was that, generally speaking, the press became the Opposition; no matter what we did, however beneficial, the powerful press condemned us." Nevertheless, Diefenbaker needlessly alienated reporters who would have carried the message of his administration to the people (this included inviting gallery members to a garden party at 24 Sussex Drive on the hottest day of the summer of 1958 and serving them only hot tea and lemonade). The Conservatives, instead, practised terrible public relations and were forced to pay the price four years later.[30]

Consider the manner in which Diefenbaker handled the cancellation of the Avro Arrow contract in February 1959, a decision that cost him the support of the *Globe and Mail*. Even before Diefenbaker had come to power, the Liberals had determined that the Arrow jet was too expensive. In 1958 the price of the CF-105 delta-winged jet soared from its initial estimated cost of about $2 million per plane to $12.5 million. In addition, after the Soviets' successfully launched an intercontinental missile in 1957, the U.S. Pentagon became reluctant to purchase a costly plane they regarded as ineffective. With no buyers in sight, the Canadian military and government decided to cancel the contract, opting instead to install less expensive U.S. Bomarc anti-bomber missiles at bases in Ontario and Quebec. That the missiles had to be armed with nuclear warheads seemed clear to everyone but many members of the Tory cabinet.[31]

On February 20, 1959, Diefenbaker announced his fateful decision, forcing A.V. Roe Canada Ltd. in Malton, Ontario, to give notices to 14,000 employees. Since Diefenbaker had already put the project on hold, in September 1958, the cancellation was surely no surprise to either the company's executive or the media. Moreover, it was the only decision the government could have made. But instead of focusing on the jet's technical problems and high cost, Diefenbaker tried to convince the public that the decision had to do with defence priorities. "The foolishness of this judgment," says historian Michael Bliss, "helped feed the monstrous Avromyth, which was also stoked by former Avro employees and starry-eyed aircraft buffs, creating the legend of an amazing aircraft destroyed by bumbling politicians, who were secretly manipulated by the evil Americans."[32] Diefenbaker was assailed in the press for single-handedly killing the town of Malton and for apparently weakening Canada's engineering and research potential.

Soon, too, stories began appearing about Diefenbaker's dictatorial style of government, a charge that in hindsight does not hold up. But the prime minister's quick temper and a few public contradictions of his ministers left the impression of a one-man administration.

This image was further reinforced during the "Preview Commentary" affair of June 1959. Though Diefenbaker and his cabinet had always maintained that they did not interfere in the day-to-day workings of the CBC, they did not appreciate it when negative assessments of their government were broadcast across the country. Discussion in cabinet in April 1959 focused on how the CBC chose its radio and TV commentators, many of whom, it was felt, "were being unjustifiably and unnecessarily critical."[33] Ernie Bushnell, a CBC veteran, was then the acting president of the corporation owing to the illness of Alphonse Ouimet. On June 11 Bushnell ordered Charles Jennings, the CBC comptroller, to send word to Toronto that "Preview Commentary" was to be cancelled within two weeks or unnamed "heads will roll." The program was a three-minute public affairs editorial usually given by an Ottawa-based reporter (now called simply "Commentary") following the 8 a.m. news. Among its regular listeners were Prime Minister Diefenbaker and George Nowlan, the minister responsible for the CBC. Both were unhappy with the daily barrage of criticism levelled at the Tory administration, and Diefenbaker let reporters know what he thought. Four days later, Frank Peers, supervisor of the CBC's public affairs department received a memo from Jennings ordering him to cease production of the commentary. In protest, Peers and his three associates resigned; they were followed by about thirty radio and television producers.[34] CBC officials had no choice but to reinstate the program.

In the subsequent review of the affair by a special parliamentary committee, Bushnell claimed that he had acted completely on his own without political interference, a fact attested to by George Nowlan. Bushnell had felt that the daily commentary did not permit "a considered approach" to the problems of governing the country. Hence, even after Jack Pickersgill and Douglas Fisher finished interrogating Bushnell and Nowlan, no evidence of political interference was uncovered. An examination of the testimony, however, reveals the likelihood that Nowlan was well aware of Diefenbaker's feelings that the CBC was biased against him and that this message was conveyed to Bushnell.[35] All in all, the "Preview Commentary" affair left a bad taste in the mouths of Ottawa journalists, making them ever more vigilant in their investigations of the Diefenbaker government.

The *Toronto Star,* no fan of the Conservatives, led the way. According to a November 1959 eight-page memo prepared by Diefenbaker's staff, the *Star* was waging a "hatchet campaign" against the prime minister. "Its consistency and persistence indicates," the memo observed, "that it is deliberate and firmly based on the principle 'everything goes' no matter how lacking in truth and basis the attack may be."[36] Indeed, the *Star* had been extremely critical of the cancellation of the Avro Arrow and had published speculative reports on other controversial decisions made by the government. "Diefenbaker had a war with me and the *Toronto Star* regularly," remembers the newspaper's correspondent Val Sears. In a feature article on September 24 staff writer Bruce MacDonald insinuated that the prime minister, a supposed champion of freedom of the press, had threatened to cancel *Time* magazine's 20 percent tax exemption (on the advertising revenue of its "Canadian" edition reinstated by the government in 1958) because of a story in the magazine's June 8 edition about the Tories' "Nehru-style" neutralist foreign policy. This charge was later denied in a letter to the *Star* by Time Canada's managing director, but the paper continued to be tough with (and sometimes wrong about) Diefenbaker.

When the government's feud with Bank of Canada governor James Coyne broke wide open in June 1961, the *Star* as well as other Liberal newspapers, the *Winnipeg Free Press* and *Ottawa Citizen* among them, whole-heartedly backed Coyne's claim that he was the victim of a conspiracy. There is no question that Coyne and Donald Fleming, the minister of finance, were at odds over economic policy for at least three years and that Coyne overstepped the bounds of his position by publicly speaking out against the government in 1959 and 1960. There is also no question that Coyne would have probably resigned without fanfare had he been treated with respect. But when the Diefenbaker government implied that Coyne had acted improperly by accepting a sizable increase in his pension (to $25,000 a year – a raise passed according to the bank's by-laws), the governor had no choice but to fight back.[37]

The media have always loved an underdog and the Coyne story was too good to pass up. Donald Fleming got the worst of it, as he remembered. "In the aftermath of the Coyne uproar," he wrote, "the Liberal press indulged to its heart content in vicious criticism of me. All of the false accusations and innuendoes emanating in unceasing profusion from Coyne and his Liberal allies were propagated as the truth. The *Toronto Daily Star* outdid itself, ending up demanding my resignation."[38] Conservative papers like the *Ottawa Journal* and *Winnipeg Tribune* were more understanding. "The charges and accusations in the latest Coyne communique are so extreme as to be almost ludicrous," the *Tribune* observed on June 27 after correspondence between Fleming and Coyne had been leaked. "The governor of the bank seems to have lost his sense of proportion in his eagerness to score off the minister of finance."

The fact was, however, that the cabinet appeared petty and partisan (it is not surprising that the events of this episode are remembered quite differently in the various memoirs and recollections of Tory ministers). Indeed, so inept were Diefenbaker and Fleming in handling this matter that, according to historian Jack Granatstein, "they had achieved the impossible": they had made "James Coyne, an aloof and sometimes arrogant man whose policies were not even supported by the Opposition, into a sympathetic figure."[39] That the Liberal-dominated Senate rejected the government's bill ordering Coyne's resignation was predictable (he resigned on his own as soon as the verdict was known).

The government's public image and relations with the media were forever tainted by the Coyne affair. Fleming, especially, was hounded by the press. Rumours flew that he was to be fired for his conduct. That autumn he and George Hees, minister of trade and commerce, attended the Commonwealth Economic Advisory Council meetings in Accra, Ghana. On the first day at a closed session, both ministers spoke out against Britain's planned entry into the European Common Market, a development that it was perceived would have a negative impact on Canadian and Commonwealth trade.

Journalists covering the conference, including Christopher Young of the *Ottawa Citizen* and the Southam papers, filed stories claiming – to use Young's words – that "the nations of the Commonwealth, led by Canada, have ganged up on Britain." Though they had not heard the speeches of Hees and Fleming first-hand, the reporters had been briefed by the ministers' assistants. Though Young's choice of verbs may have been questionable, his article did confirm what had taken place behind closed doors. Alan Donnelly, the correspondent for the impartial Canadian Press, for instance, that same day wrote that "Trade Minister George Hees of Canada led a concerted attack by a number of Commonwealth countries today on Britain's move toward the Common Market."[40]

Back in Canada the stories caused a minor sensation, angering

Diefenbaker as well as editors of Conservative newspapers, who accused the government of selling out the "mother country." Upon his return, Fleming, in his own defence, lashed out at the press and at Christopher Young in particular (Young happened to be Lester Pearson's nephew through marriage). In a one-hour speech in the House, Fleming accused the press of lying and later implied that Young, because of his relationship with Pearson, had purposely written a biased report. Twenty-four years later, Fleming's anger had not subsided. Writing of Young's article and similar stories on the Accra conference in his memoirs published in 1985, he observed that "in all my political career, I never encountered a more misleading distortion of the truth."[41] But nowhere does he point out that it was his own assistant, Grey Hamilton, a former *Globe and Mail* writer, who gave Young and the other journalists the information for their explosive stories. It is hardly likely that Hamilton was acting without his minister's orders. Here is a classic case of selective memory.

Young himself, who soon after Accra was named the *Citizen*'s editor, in a column in January 1962 dismissed Fleming's criticism that he had acted in a partisan manner as "false, dishonest and grossly unfair." He feels the same today. "Their own guys briefed us," says Young, "and then they got mad because their boss the prime minister got mad. It was absolute nonsense." Fleming later apologized to Young for his remarks about the Pearson connection (though he repeated the accusation in his memoirs).[42] More importantly, while it may have been the press that reported the stand the government had taken in opposition to Britain, it was the Liberals led by Pearson, Jack Pickersgill, Paul Martin, and Lionel Chevrier – the so-called Four Horseman – that stirred up the anti-British charges.

Heading into an election year, the Conservatives could hardly have had worse relations with the media. Much to Diefenbaker's dissatisfaction, his off-the-record comments in the scrums outside the Privy Council chamber were turning up on the front pages of the newspapers. In an attempt to improve the situation, the prime minister held a rare, free-wheeling press conference in his office in early November 1961. In the opinion of his friend Richard Jackson of the *Ottawa Journal,* he "fielded the queries easily with short, quick direct answers or with simply one of a dozen variations of the well-known 'nothing to say.'" His true feelings towards the press, however, were revealed less than three months later, in a speech he delivered on January 13, 1962, at the seventy-fifth birthday celebrations of the Progressive Conservative Association of Toronto held at the Park Plaza Hotel. In reviewing his government's economic accomplishments, Diefenbaker stated that their efforts to improve Canada's economic position had been questioned by a "servile press" that worked hand in hand with the opposition to "degrade" the country.[43]

Making the media a scapegoat for the economic and political difficulties faced by his administration was not a wise strategy. Like everyone else in Canada in the spring of 1962, journalists could point to Diefenbaker's failure to make good on his 1958 campaign promises. Unemployment remained high, as did the federal deficit; Canada had not diverted 15 percent of its trade away from the United States in favour of Britain and the Commonwealth; and northern development had not taken off.

From Avro to Accra, the cabinet had done little to counter the view, as expressed in an August 1960 *Globe* editorial, that "its members gave the impression of men baffled by the problems which confronted them, unsure of their course, anxious to put off action in the hope that something would turn up." And the prime minister was as suspicious, temperamental, and self-righteous as ever.[44] Thus, on the eve of the 1962 election, Peter Newman wrote: "The feelings between the country's political press and the Prime Minister had deteriorated to such a degree that some Ottawa correspondents were convinced Diefenbaker was trying deliberately to goad reporters into intemperate criticism so that he could appeal to the elector's sympathy as the victim of a spiteful press that deliberately distorted all the good he had tried to do."[45] If this was Diefenbaker's strategy, it did not work.

"To work, gentlemen. We have a government to overthrow," declared Val Sears to his fellow reporters as the 1962 election campaign got under way. Diefenbaker took the *Toronto Star* correspondent's exhortation literally and considered it irrefutable evidence that members of the media were a significant part of the grand conspiracy working against him. Sears's caustic remark earned him the prime minister's scorn and the nickname "Mr. Snears."[46]

In truth, though Diefenbaker was deluded about the existence of a plot, by 1962 most Ottawa journalists had lost faith in his leadership. To counter the prime minister's dwindling popularity, Allister Grosart, Conservative Party president and campaign chairman, set out to stress Diefenbaker's great achievements and contributions to "Canadian nationhood." The effects of negative journalism, he felt, could be neutralized through control of television images. According to his plan, a field crew would accompany the prime minister on his daily activities and would shoot one to three minutes of news footage. This footage would then be fed to an editorial pool in Toronto and released to the CTV network and private stations. "There has been and will be a hostile carping press," Grosart wrote in a confidential strategy memo, "and part of the antidote to that is the concerted, united effort of the national party to put before Canadians the remarkable image of this remarkable leader." In Grosart's partisan opinion, Diefenbaker truly was "the Man for ALL Canada."[47]

As remarkable as John Diefenbaker might have been, Grosart's plan fell short. The campaign of May and June 1962 was indeed about Diefenbaker's leadership – that is, about "his indecisiveness, his pettiness, his economic mismanagement, and his quarrels with [President John] Kennedy."[48] The devaluation crisis during the first week of May, which forced the government to peg the Canadian dollar at 92 ½ cents U.S., was terribly handled. Instead of admitting the seriousness of the problem (in all, Canada's foreign exchange fund lost about $1 billion during the first six months of 1962), Diefenbaker pretended that everything was marvellous and that a lower dollar would be a boost to Canadian tourism.

Neither the Liberals nor the media bought this line. In the long term, the devaluation aided Canadian exports, but in the public mind it was, as Diefenbaker himself later admitted, "associated with [the Conservatives'] gross mismanagement of the economy." Thus was born the 92 ½-cent "Diefendollar," first depicted in a brilliant cartoon by Peter Kuch in the *Winnipeg Free Press* on May 4. The cartoon, showing Finance Minister Donald Fleming nailing to a flag mast a 92 ½-cent dollar with Diefenbaker's face on it, was reproduced in the thousands. It was exploited by the Liberals for all the propaganda it was worth.[49]

In addition, the press caught Diefenbaker distorting the truth. In a speech at the Ukrainian Centre in Montreal, the prime minister tried to win over voters by declaring that while Pearson was "soft on Communism," he was not. He recalled for the crowd a tough speech he had made at the United Nations in 1960 and claimed that it was in response to his comments that Nikita Khrushchev had pounded a desk with his shoe. The next day Diefenbaker's speech was on the *Toronto Star*'s front page along with a story by Jack Brehl, who had reported on UN events in 1960, clarifying the famous shoe-banging incident. Apparently, it had occurred more than two weeks after Diefenbaker had spoken and in reaction to remarks by a Philippine delegate. Never one to admit he was wrong, Diefenbaker the next day publicly attacked the *Star* and its correspondent Val Sears for misrepresenting him. A tape recording of the comments the prime minister had made in Montreal proved that the newspaper had got the story right.[50]

Typically, Diefenbaker's most serious battle with the media developed over something petty: attendance figures at Conservative rallies. Throughout the 1962 campaign, the sixty-six-year-old prime minister was showing his age. He was often cranky and sullen, a mood made worse by the fact that he was not attracting the large crowds he had in 1958. It was a difference the journalists with him hardly could have ignored.

During the last week of May, Diefenbaker was in Edmonton. As reported by Charles King of Southam News, the prime minister drew a crowd of only about 1,400 people in the city where four years earlier he had been mobbed and cheered by twice as many. "In the same city where the Conservative campaign caught fire in 1958," King wrote, "the Diefenbubble burst Friday night." Two days later, the Tory entourage moved westward to Trail, B.C., where the prime minister was handed a copy of King's story. Diefenbaker was livid. That evening, when King attempted to interview Diefenbaker, he refused to speak with the reporter. He accused King of writing "diabolical concoctions" and reminded him of the 1958 Yukon $10,000 fishing story. "I have nothing to say to you at all," Diefenbaker told King. "Anybody else can ask me questions but not you."[51]

The following day the prime minister would not allow King on the campaign plane heading to Vancouver. Other reporters protested, as did Diefenbaker's assistants John Fisher and Roy Fabish. Finally, after Mrs. Diefenbaker calmed her husband down, King was permitted to board the aircraft. When the plane landed in Vancouver, a crowd at the airport greeted the Diefenbakers with signs reading, "Charles King for Prime Minister."

On the way back east, in a stopover at Red Deer, Alberta, someone in the assembled crowd yelled out during Diefenbaker's speech, "What does Charlie King say about that?" "My friend, we're not dealing with matters like that now, I'm dealing with facts," replied the prime minister to the delight of the partisan crowd.[52] Such witty and sarcastic remarks merely united the gallery further in its opposition to Diefenbaker.

On June 18, 1962, the Conservatives were reduced to a 116-seat minority government. Diefenbaker had lost 92 seats, including 36 in Quebec, where the first rumblings of the Quiet Revolution were evident. Though the Liberals, under Pearson, increased their seats from 49 to 100, the balance of power was held by the 19 NDP and 30 Social Credit members (of the latter, 26 were led by Quebec Creditiste leader Réal Caouette). More significantly, although Diefenbaker had held on to his support in rural areas, he had been devastated in the cities, where the devaluation of the dollar and his dealings with James Coyne haunted him. "The outcome," wrote political scientist J.M. Beck, "was a deeper rural-urban cleavage than the country had heretofore experienced."[53]

Never had there been as emotional and tumultuous a period in Canadian politics as in the ten months following the 1962 election. The economy was in a terrible state, the world was on the brink of nuclear war, Canada's relations with the United States were at an all-time low, and the Conservative cabinet was in disarray. Throughout this period not only did the media continue to slash away at Diefenbaker, but several of their most important members themselves became key participants in the political process.

As Tom Van Dusen, one of the prime minister's chief assistants, later remembered, "A number [of journalists] had felt [Diefenbaker's] wrath, privately and publicly and in many cases had added to the Liberal leanings of their newspapers. The result was that in his final period in office, press animosity became a powerful political factor contributing to his defeat. There was little justification for this situation." By early 1963 "the majority of those in positions of control in the media were against him. Liberal newspapers and television stations opposed him on partisan grounds; the Conservative press in great measure had written him off and wanted him out. He was thus subjected to fierce criticism from both sides as the Liberal and Conservative press attempted to outdo each other."[54]

Diefenbaker himself set the tone for his relations with the media soon after the election. He was so angry with his coverage in *Maclean's* that he cancelled his subscription and encouraged his associates to do the same. And the Tories' austerity program, most notably a $1-billion loan (from the United States and European money funds) to stabilize the Canadian dollar, drew the ire of Canadian editors. The Liberal *Winnipeg Free Press* declared that Diefenbaker had transformed Canada into "an under-developed Asian state in need of charity."[55]

But it was Diefenbaker's convoluted foreign policy, especially his relations with the United States and his indecision on whether to arm the Bomarc missiles and the five squadrons of Voodo interceptor jets with nuclear warheads, that journalists concentrated on. The acceptance of nuclear weapons appeared certain after Diefenbaker cancelled the Avro Arrow in 1959 and opted for the Bomarc-B anti-aircraft missiles. There was no point installing the missiles if the nuclear warheads were not installed as well. Yet nothing was ever that straightforward with John Diefenbaker, and to make matters worse in this case, his cabinet was divided on the issue. In one corner was Secretary of State for External Affairs Howard Green, who was "horrified at the prospect of nuclear war"; in the other was Douglas Harkness, the minister of defence who saw no other option but to accept the warheads. Complicating the matter further was the question of Canadian commitments in NORAD and NATO as well as pressure exerted by U.S. president John Kennedy, who more than Diefenbaker worried about a Soviet attack on North America.

For more than two years Diefenbaker did what he did best: he stalled. He was not going to be pushed around by a "young pup" like Kennedy; nor was he convinced that the Canadian public supported the nuclear acquisition. At a meeting in Ottawa in May 1961 Diefenbaker had given JFK assurances that a decision in favour of U.S. demands was imminent. The crisis in Berlin over Soviet demands that NATO forces withdraw from West Germany intensified, and Kennedy wrote the Canadian prime minister a confidential letter on August 3, reminding him of his commitment. Diefenbaker wrote back suggesting action was forthcoming. (On August 13 the East Germans cut Berlin in half by building a wall between the east and west sections of the city.) About a month later, these letters were leaked to *Newsweek* magazine and made headlines in Canada. "JFK Presses Canada on Nuclear Warheads" blared the *Montreal Star.* Because *Newsweek*'s publisher, Philip Graham, and its Washington editor, Ben Bradlee, were Kennedy confidants, Diefenbaker could not help but conclude that the leak originated in the White House Oval Office. This incident infuriated him.[56]

Meanwhile, in Ottawa the Canadian military propaganda team led by Wing Commander Bill Lee, later a premier lobbyist and political strategist for the Liberals, urged his many friends in the press gallery to write stories about "the lunacy of Diefenbaker's nuclear policy." The U.S. ambassador to Canada, Livingston Merchant, who found Diefenbaker impossible to deal with, was busy lobbying as well. In the home of his assistant, Chuck Kisslejack, he held a series of off-the-record chats with Ottawa journalists to offer the American perspective on Diefenbaker's indecisive foreign policy. Later, when the prime minister discovered this "scandalous school" (as he labelled the briefings), he became further convinced of a Kennedy-led conspiracy to destroy him. More than anything, though, his feelings were hurt because none of the reporters let him know about the meetings.[57] That Diefenbaker would have expected such loyalty from the group of men he had scorned for the past four years is a good indication of just how warped his political antenna had become by the spring of 1962.

In the fall of that year, the world watched as Kennedy and Khrushchev battled each other over the discovery of Soviet missiles in Cuba. Diefenbaker learned of the Americans' decision to impose a blockade around the island only two hours before the president appeared on television to announce the policy, and was rightly upset that he had not been consulted, merely "informed." By this time, apparently, Canada was an ally that could not be trusted.[58] In any event, Diefenbaker at first refused to order Canadian forces to full-alert status (known as "Defcon 3") as the Americans requested, suggesting an on-site inspection instead. The order finally came two days into the crisis (Harkness had actually ignored the prime minister and approved it earlier), but the press lambasted Diefenbaker for his cautious attitude. "For those who have had to watch the indecisive Diefenbaker Government in action," editorialized the *Toronto Star,* "this will seem like extraordinary haste." (The *Star* made much of the fact that at the height of the crisis on October 24 Prime Minister Diefenbaker had spent the day planting tulip bulbs with his wife in their Sussex Drive garden.) The real point, however, was that when the alerted Canadian military stood at the ready, its Bomarcs and Voodo jets were missing the necessary nuclear warheads, much like, in columnist Patrick Nicholson's words, "bows without arrows."

Once Khrushchev backed down and the threat of nuclear war subsided, at least for the moment, Douglas Harkness and other cabinet ministers determined to resolve this issue. Events moved quickly after this. On January 3, 1963, retiring American NATO commander Gen. Lauris Norstad held an impromptu press conference in Ottawa. When asked by Charles Lynch of Southam News if Canada had made a commitment to NATO to acquire nuclear weapons, he responded in the affirmative. Pierre Sévigny, the associate minister of defence, knew "that all hell would break loose" after Diefenbaker heard about this.[59] He was so right.

Then, to make matters worse for the government, Lester Pearson, who had publicly opposed nuclear weapons since 1945, heeded his political advisers (including Jack Pickersgill and Brig. Richard Sankey Malone, the publisher of the *Winnipeg Free Press*) and declared in a speech in Scarborough on January 12 that Canada did indeed have a responsibility to live up to its NATO commitments. The nuclear warheads had to be accepted, the Liberal leader boldly stated. Diefenbaker condemned both General Norstad's interfering comments and Pearson's about-face. He found an unlikely ally in Pierre Trudeau, then a constitutional law professor and writer in Montreal, who labelled his future boss "the unfrocked priest of peace." Still, editorial opinion was almost completely against Diefenbaker and in favour of Pearson (some exceptions were the *Winnipeg Tribune* and *Ottawa Journal,* which ridiculed the Liberal leader's sudden change of policy).

In Toronto John Bassett, the publisher of the *Telegram* and until this point a strong supporter of the prime minister, had lost faith in Diefenbaker's judgment, as the *Globe*'s Oakley Dalgleish had a few years earlier. The Liberal press, led by the *Toronto Star* and *Winnipeg Free Press,* was even more vehement in its criticism. In a January 3 editorial reviewing the Conservatives' foreign policy, the *Free Press* commented that Diefenbaker's actions had "reduced our defence policy to fiasco, poisoned our relations with the American people and humiliated the people of Canada. To such a record of pugnacity abroad and indecision at home, there is no parallel in Canadian experience. Canada has behaved for the last five years like a small boy with a chip on his shoulder who asserts his strength by snarling at grown men." This might have been an exaggeration, but the moment of decision for Douglas Harkness, at least, had arrived. He told the prime minister that he would resign if the nuclear weapons were not accepted.

On Friday, January 25, in the Commons, Diefenbaker delivered the most important speech of his career. But instead of clarifying his stand on nuclear weapons, he left his colleagues, the opposition, and journalists shaking their heads. "It was a masterpiece of confusion," wrote Maurice Western of the *Winnipeg Free Press.* "Far from clarifying the Government's defense policy," added the *Globe and Mail,* "Prime Minister John Diefenbaker ...

left the picture more confused than ever." Diefenbaker also offered his unique interpretation of his talks with the United States, describing how, at a recent meeting in Nassau, Kennedy and British prime minister Harold Macmillan had agreed to move away from nuclear weapons and towards the use of conventional arms.[60]

Howard Green, as well as most members of the media, viewed Diefenbaker's remarks as a rejection of nuclear warheads, but Douglas Harkness thought exactly the opposite. When he read the editorials the next day, Harkness decided, without first consulting Diefenbaker, to issue a press release clarifying the intent of the prime minister's speech. Diefenbaker was far from pleased with Harkness for this initiative and determined to proceed on the nuclear issue in his own way and on his own schedule.

The best was yet to come. Angered by the prime minister's attempts to twist what had transpired at Nassau, the U.S. State Department, acting without the authorization of the president, issued a harshly worded press release on January 30 that basically called Diefenbaker a liar. Journalists were shocked by the critical tone of the American document, but little sympathy was forthcoming for Diefenbaker. As the *Toronto Star* put it in an editorial the next day, "Canadians have every reason to resent the tone of this message from Washington ... Yet indignation over American high-handedness should not blind us to the fact that this quarrel is very largely the fault of the Diefenbaker government." The prime minister, curiously, was delighted with this turn of events, believing he could fight the next election on an anti-American platform, as John A. Macdonald had in 1891. This idea was greeted with little enthusiasm from other Tory ministers or most editors.

In Washington, President Kennedy was outraged with his adviser McGeorge Bundy and Acting Secretary of State George Ball, who had approved the State Department press release. He used his good friend Max Freedman, a brilliant Canadian journalist who wrote for the *Winnipeg Free Press* and *Manchester Guardian,* to spread the word that he had not authorized the department's communiqué. (Among other things, Freedman assisted Kennedy in preparing his inaugural address of January 1960 and acted as an intermediary between JFK and Lester Pearson.)[61]

On Saturday, February 2, 1963, two events of note occurred: Chief Justice Patrick Kerwin died and the annual parliamentary press gallery dinner was held. Out of respect for Kerwin, Diefenbaker decided that the attending politicians would not give their usual witty speeches at the dinner; the prime minister was obviously in no mood for revelry. The evening did not go well. The hit song of the reporters' musical review was a tune that insinuated Diefenbaker had "Harkness's disease." Rumours had been circulating in Ottawa for years that the prime minister's constant shaking was caused by Parkinson's disease. With his poor hearing, Diefenbaker believed the irreverent reporters were mocking him about this in their song. Following the performance, Walter Gray of the *Globe,* who was in charge of the evening, received one of Diefenbaker's famed tongue-lashings. "I couldn't believe it," Gray later told his editor, Richard Doyle, "he was certain the whole thing was a part of the plot against him. He had said that the *Globe and Mail* was at the bottom of his trouble. It was fantastic. He stood very close to me and shouted. I could feel his spittle on my face."[62]

That same evening a minor argument erupted between Charles Lynch and his guest, Douglas Harkness, over the fact that the minister had not yet resigned. If there was anything Harkness prided himself on, "it was his integrity," said Agriculture Minister Alvin Hamilton. Harkness had reached his breaking-point. The next day, at one of the stormiest cabinet meetings ever held at 24 Sussex Drive, "all hell broke loose" – again. By lunch time Harkness had declared his intention to resign. As reporters watched the comings and goings both at the prime minister's residence and in the corridors of Parliament that Sunday and Monday, a picture of a well-organized plot – or "coup d'état," as Peter Newman later called it in his book *Renegade in Power* – began to take shape in their minds.

Reading the memoirs and comments of the participants thirty years later, one can see that what journalists took for a conspiracy was nothing more than the actions of several unhappy and confused cabinet ministers who were desperate to save their government, their honour, and their power. At the same time, through their apparent clandestine and unexplained gatherings, these ministers were as much, or more, to blame for the formulation of the conspiracy theory as anyone. As Pierre Sévigny recalled, "The tragic nonsense that marked our actions during those four momentous days was the total lack of communication among the members of Diefenbaker's entourage. If only the ministers and other key members of the Party had been reasonable enough to get together in a full dress, co-ordinated discussion of our political problems, a solution would have been found, and all this cloak-and-dagger political juggling might have been put aside."[63]

A few meetings, as early as December 1962, were held at the home of columnist Patrick Nicholson, who acted as an intermediary between the Social Credit's novice leader, Robert Thompson, and some disgruntled members of the Diefenbaker cabinet. Thompson had no desire to bring down the government, but he felt that he and his French colleagues could no longer support the prime minister.[64] Later, in the panic over Harkness's resignation, George Hees, Davie Fulton, and Senator Wallace McCutcheon, a Toronto businessman who had joined the cabinet following the 1962 election, proposed to Diefenbaker that he resign in exchange for an appointment as the new chief justice. Diefenbaker, not surprisingly, refused.

On Tuesday morning, February 5, Hees convened a private meeting in his Commons office to discuss with some of his colleagues – the so-called anti-Diefenbaker faction – the Liberal motion of non-confidence made the day before and to brief them on talks George Nowlan had had with Robert Thompson. The Social Credit MPs were prepared to support a "caretaker government" headed by Nowlan. But just as the meeting got under way, it was learned that someone had leaked its whereabouts and agenda to the media. As Immigration Minister Richard Bell recalled: "While the meeting was in progress, and before anything had been discussed in anything than the most informal way, we heard a newscast in which it was reported that a group of ministers were in George Hees's office engaged in a conspiracy. At the time the newscast came on the ministers had said almost nothing ... By the time we left George Hees's office, the corridor was filled with Press Gallery people. We were running the gauntlet and the story was out that this had been the grand conspiracy ... I deny completely having been at the time involved in any discussion of the dislodgement of the prime minister in any-thing more than what was really an academic discussion. These were Bob Thompson's terms: Nowlan as caretaker prime minister."[65]

Throughout the day, as reporters tracked the conspiracy story, Robert Thompson was waiting for an answer from Nowlan and Michael Wardell, the publisher of the Fredericton *Gleaner* and a close friend of Diefenbaker's, who had been asked to act as a mediator. By 7:00 p.m., when no reply was forthcoming, the writing was on the wall. A little over an hour later, the Diefenbaker government was defeated on a motion of non-confidence, 142 to 111. An election was soon set for April 8.

Across the country the overwhelming consensus among editors and commentators was that Diefenbaker had to go. "The man who could not lead the government into action to cure Canada's economic difficulties is unfit to lead the Conservative party into action in this election," declared a front-page *Globe and Mail* editorial. "For the sake of the party and the country, he should give up the leadership." Even the *Hamilton Spectator*, loyal to the Tories since John A. Macdonald's day, concluded that "the Diefenbaker administration has broken its coherent links with the Conservative tradition, and jeopardized principles for which the party has stood for decades."[66]

This political melodrama was not over yet. Diefenbaker's supporters had moved up the time of the regular Wednesday-morning caucus to nine o'clock, before the scheduled cabinet meeting. It was rightly believed that the prime minister's popularity was still strong among the backbenchers. As predicted, the caucus backed Diefenbaker and reduced George Hees to tears when he argued for the prime minister's resignation. At exactly the right moment the doors of the meeting room flew open so that the waiting mob of reporters could hear the cheers of solidarity. "The prime minister is still the prime minister and will be after the next election," Senator McCutcheon declared as he left the room. "We've never been more united," added Hees. "We're going to kick the hell out of the Grits."[67] Poor Douglas Harkness was left to stand as the lone renegade. The dumbfounded journalists and their editors could not believe what they were hearing.

At the *Globe,* Oakley Dalgleish, for one, had had enough. Unwilling to believe that there had not been a cabinet revolt, he wrote in an editorial on February 8, entitled "A Matter of Morality," that Hees, McCutcheon, and others were not telling Canadians the truth. Moreover, he resented the blame directed at the media for conjuring the whole thing up. "It is simple to blame the press and the other media," he wrote. "It is easy to speak in confidence on one day ... and then the next day to deny it and accuse the media of falsification. This newspaper has had enough of it. We want no more of these treacherous confidences." Here was the most significant shift in journalistic thinking since the Pipeline Debate of 1956.

Following the caucus meeting, Hees spoke on the phone with Eddie Goodman, the Ontario Tory organizer, and John Bassett of the *Telegram.* They expressed shock at Hees's public support for the man he had wanted replaced and urged him to have the government meet its defence commitments. On Saturday, February 9, after two days of drinking and endless talking, Hees – along with the acting minister of defence, Pierre Sévigny – handed Diefenbaker their resignations. (Sévigny was upset that Diefenbaker had told a reporter there was no chance Sévigny would become the permanent minister of defence.) Tories later blamed Hees for the subsequent Conservative loss, while newspapers questioned his integrity and his actions over this critical week. John Diefenbaker, who as the *Globe and Mail* had observed on February 8, was "so busy seeking out conspiracies" that he had "little time for anything else," would come to regard the resignations of Hees and Sévigny as a last and desperate ploy to drive him from the prime ministership.[68]

In all, three key cabinet ministers resigned and three more – Fulton, Fleming, and Halpenny – chose not to run for re-election in 1963 for personal reasons. Back in his accustomed role as the besieged underdog, Diefenbaker put on a great show in the early spring of 1963, attacking the Liberals, the Americans, and the "sinister interests" that were plotting to dethrone him.[69]

The media, both Canadian and American, were in this last category of villains. The Tories in particular made good use of the February 18 issue of *Newsweek,* which had as its cover story "Canada's Diefenbaker: Decline and Fall." In Ottawa it was sold out hours after it hit the newstands. The cover photo itself was worth a thousand words – Diefenbaker, angry and deranged, his hair and eyes blazing.

Written by staffer Dwight Martin, presumably with instructions and editorial advice from his boss, Ben Bradlee, the feature article was as partisan an attack on Diefenbaker as had ever been published. "Britain's Prime Minister Harold Macmillan can hardly bear the sight of him, and President Kennedy dislikes him cordially. His Tory colleagues in Britain's House of Commons say: 'it would be too flattering to dismiss him just as a superficial fellow – he's really much dimmer than that." (When told by a Canadian reporter that his article had been condemned by the Conservatives, Martin replied, "Really, well I find that unusual because there was certainly no direct criticism of Mr. Diefenbaker.")[70]

If it was Bradlee's intention to embarrass Diefenbaker, then the article had exactly the opposite effect. Dalton Camp, the national chairman of the Conservative campaign, dispatched copies across the country, encouraging constituency presidents to "condemn it in the strongest terms." Diefenbaker made the most of the situation. "The *Newsweek* article was all part of a plan to destroy me," he told an audience in Charlottetown near the end of the campaign. "A man came from Washington and met with the Who's Who of the Liberal Party. They planned that. They awaited that. It was conceived in Liberal headquarters in Ottawa."[71]

Though Diefenbaker was more entertaining than ever on the campaign trail, he had lost his credibility with the major newspapers and urban voters. Not since 1917 had so many papers turned on one political leader. Other than the *Ottawa Journal, Winnipeg Tribune,* Vancouver *Province,* and Fredericton *Gleaner,* all other metropolitan dailies came out against Diefenbaker. "The Tories of 1963," opined the *Edmonton Journal* on March 15, "are disorganized, dispirited, disrupted and disgraced. And they should be dismissed."

It took John Bassett of the *Telegram* until March 30, eight days before the vote, to publish an editorial supporting the Liberals: "The *Telegram* has consistently supported the principles advocated in the past by the Progressive Conservative Party. In now advocating the election of Mr. Pearson and his Party, the *Telegram* has not deserted these principles. But the *Telegram* believes the Prime Minister has so compromised these principles that Canada's position at home and abroad will immeasurably deteriorate under his continued leadership. The election campaign has hardened and sharpened this view." That day Bassett sent Diefenbaker a telegram apologizing for the editorial. "Son of a bitch," was apparently Diefenbaker's response. Many Ontario Tories were dumbfounded by the switch. "It is [as] though devout Christians have had to face the fact that the Bible is a false spurious document," one of them told *Telegram* columnist Douglas Fisher. John Bassett, too, regretted his decision. "The '63 election was very difficult," he remembered. "But I thought that as a matter of policy [the Conservatives] had been wrong."[72]

Diefenbaker's loss of urban media support as well as his indecisiveness on the nuclear issue ultimately cost him dearly at the polls on April 8. Still, he was popular in the West, where his rantings against the "eastern interests" won favour. Pearson and the Liberals came within a few seats of a majority (129 out of 265), but lost too many constituencies to the Social Credit in Quebec (of the province's 75 seats, the Liberals won 47, the Social Credit 20, and the Conservatives 8).

Press and TV reporters would forever remember John Diefenbaker as "Canada's greatest political actor of the century," but at this point they had become cynical about the politicians they covered. Yet Lester Pearson deserved a chance. They, like the rest of the country, looked to him for the leadership that had been sorely lacking for the past year. He had the vast majority of journalists in his corner on April 8, 1963. The question was, could he keep them there?

CHAPTER THIRTEEN

One of the Boys

I don't think this is any way to report important events.

Lester Pearson in a scrum, April 1968

Long before he became the prime minister of Canada in 1963, Lester "Mike" Pearson had sought out journalists as friends and confidants. His relaxed style and self-effacing wit made him a gallery favourite. "You meet Mike Pearson two or three times and you begin to think of him as an old pal," wrote Blair Fraser in a complimentary April 15, 1951, *Maclean's* magazine profile.

Pearson's appreciation of the importance of maintaining good relations with the press stemmed in part from his own ambition. In 1952 Grattan O'Leary considered Pearson "an upstart careerist" and was sickened by how the newspapers "fawn on him."[1] Indeed, Pearson relished the attention and notoriety and was aware how useful it was to his future plans to have the press in his corner.

While working at the Canadian embassy in Washington during the early 1940s, Pearson had become close to James Reston, the influential *New York Times* columnist. Though he disapproved of the way American politicians catered to Reston and other U.S. media stars, he used his own press contacts to spread Canada's "message."[2] Like so many of Mike Pearson's perplexing actions, it is difficult to say whether he was guilty of outright manipulation or whether he was simply fulfilling his duties. Whatever, says Richard O'Hagan, his former press secretary, Pearson "understood what it meant to share information. He understood the brokering function and he understood how one could conceivably disarm critics by taking them into your confidence and explaining."

On a philosophical level, Pearson believed in open and honest government, which he recognized would entail a well-informed press. As a politician he was conscious of the "natural conflict of interest" between the government and the media; yet he accepted that in a democracy the public's right to know should rarely be impeded. In this regard both ministers and journalists had important responsibilities. "It is wrong and indefensible for government to withhold information to which the public has a right, by marking it 'secret' or 'confidential,'" Pearson argued in his memoirs. "It is as bad, or worse, when the media or the public accept the right of every private citizen to decide for his own purposes whether information so labelled can be made public without prejudice to the national interest." In walking this fine line between the state and its citizens, Pearson acknowledged that "on rare occasions calculated leaks ... can be condoned because of the increasing practice of government to label anything 'confidential' merely because its disclosure might be inconvenient or embarrassing politically where no question of national security ... is at issue."[3] Yet Pearson would have been the first to admit that defining these "rare occasions" was difficult. His collegial style of management allowed such powerful baronies to grow within his cabinet that by 1966 the Pearson government had few secrets.

As he methodically worked his way up the ladder at External Affairs, from a lowly secretary in 1928 to under-secretary by 1946 and finally to minister of the department in the St. Laurent administration in 1948, his political theories meshed with his personal goals and made Mike Pearson one of the best sources in town. It was not by accident that he was one of the most famous Canadians of his day. He encouraged reporters to cover his trips and diplomatic exploits, supplying them, particularly such favourites as Grant Dexter and Bruce Hutchison, with in-depth, off-the-record background information.[4]

His close contacts with Dexter nearly got him in trouble early in his career. Both men were in London in the dark days preceding the Second World War, Dexter writing for the *Winnipeg Free Press* and Pearson working under Vincent Massey at the Canadian High Commission. The two men and their wives had become fast friends, and Pearson briefed Dexter daily on events surrounding the Munich crisis of 1938. Dexter in turn relayed the information to George Ferguson in Winnipeg and James Bone, London editor of the *Manchester Guardian*.[5] Such indiscretion was risky. "Mike has felt a little nervous now and then, for fear Ottawa would notice the similarity between our cables and their information," Dexter wrote in September 1938. "But I think the facts were sufficiently changed and much has gone confidentially ... Mike is taking his life in his hands talking out of turn. You can imagine what [Mackenzie] King would do to him. And Mike is a bad devil when he wants to be."[6]

On his return to Ottawa in 1941, Pearson was appalled by how poorly informed the press gallery was about the war and pushed for weekly press conferences that would be almost entirely off the record. Veteran journalist Bill Wilson, then writing for British United Press, remembers that he and his colleagues, stifled by limited access to Mackenzie King, were astonished and pleased. "He got into detail with a degree of frankness none of us had ever encountered before," Wilson says. "And he did it quite deliberately." These revealing sessions continued to an even greater degree after Pearson became more powerful at External as well as when he jumped from the bureaucracy to politics in 1948.

Through Grant Dexter, Pearson had met Bruce Hutchison, who also came under the spell of his wit and charm. Reflected Hutchison: "I was devoted to Pearson; he was the only prime minister I was really friends with." Because of Pearson's prowess on skates – in his student days he had starred on the Oxford University Hockey team – he was cryptically referred to by Hutchison as "the hockey player" in reports to Dexter (Hutchison and Dexter worked together for the *Free Press* from 1944 to 1950). Pearson held back little. "Often on returning from London or Washington," Hutchison recalled, "he would tell Dexter and me the top secrets of the British and American governments, his conversations with a prime minister or a president, even military secrets which both of us promptly put out of our minds and wished we had not heard."[7]

Pearson's trust was never betrayed, and journalists like Hutchison considered themselves fortunate "to know Mike's mind."[8] For Pearson, such loyalty and friendship were critical. As partisan journalists, Dexter and Hutchison provided Pearson with sound advice, free publicity, and editorial assistance with his speeches. On occasion Mike demanded even more. Both men were with Pearson when he was proclaimed the new leader of the Liberal Party in early 1958, and Dexter tried to counsel him against doing anything rash when he faced Diefenbaker in the House for the first time as leader of the opposition. Things turned out very differently.

The day before Pearson's fateful non-confidence motion that played into Diefenbaker's hands, Dexter had been informed that something "momentous" was to take place. (Clark Davey recalls Dexter walking into the parliamentary gallery "rubbing his hands with glee at the thought of what the Liberals were going to do to Dief.") Pearson was to do a television interview following his appearance in the House "to celebrate his [predicted] triumph," and he wanted Hutchison to be the interviewer, following a pre-arranged script. Hutchison had initially refused because of an appointment in Washington with Dean Acheson, former U.S. secretary of state, but he relented when Dexter pressed him on the eve of the occasion.[9]

It was a political disaster. Hutchison arrived in time to witness Pearson's ill-planned strategy and watched with horror as Diefenbaker used the "secret" economic report to expose further Liberal arrogance. Hutchison found Pearson dejected and his wife Maryon, no lover of politics, "muttering to herself" as she paced the room.[10] But the show had to go on.

"You've got a script ready?" Hutchison asked. "Some questions I can put to you? We'd better go over them together. There's not much time."

Pearson showed him the "statistics" and "teeming memoranda" his advisers had prepared, all deemed "no good" by Hutchison. A new list of questions and answers was quickly put together, and the two men made their way to the studio. Somehow the painful interview was completed, and Hutchison escaped back to Washington, hardly knowing why he had come in the first place.[11]

Hutchison remained close to Pearson during what he called those "six wretched years of parliamentary opposition," even though he had serious reservations about Walter Gordon and his economic plans for the new Liberal administration. A wealthy, affable Toronto accountant, Gordon was the most important member of the "Pearson team." He had first met Mike on a trip to London in the early 1930s, and their paths continued to cross for the next two decades. Then, in 1958, Gordon managed Pearson's Liberal leadership campaign. Probably no one, with the exception of Maryon, was closer to Pearson than Gordon. "In fact," writes Peter Newman, "for most of the decade from 1958 to 1968, Walter Gordon was so inextricably linked with Lester Pearson that it was difficult to discuss one without the other. It was as though the two men absorbed from each other the kind of knowledge and strength they lacked separately."[12] Gordon infected Pearson with his own passionate economic nationalism and concern over excessive American capital and control in Canada.

It was one of the flaws in Pearson's character that he sometimes, in an attempt to appease a supporter, said one thing but later did exactly the opposite. In a candid conversation in the fall of 1959, Hutchison was told by Pearson that the only chance for a Liberal success "lay in both the image and the fact of responsibility." There would be no easy solutions or vast expenditures. But the problem with Mike, as Hutchison saw it, was that in economic affairs he was "entirely at sea and [didn't] know what he would do or how to do it." Consequently, he was too easily influenced by Walter Gordon and his inflationary policies. By July 1961 Hutchison was writing Grant Dexter privately that "instead of the image of responsibility, carefully nurtured by Mike, there appeared [in the aftermath of the Liberal rally of January 1961] the image of irresponsibility and reckless promise, including the ultimate insanity of tax reductions."[13] Besides on Gordon, blame for Pearson's apparent about-face was placed on Tom Kent, the *Free Press* editor who became his chief adviser and speech writer.

In the hope of restoring the Winnipeg newspaper to the glory of the Dafoe days, publisher Victor Sifton in 1953 had recruited the Oxford-educated Kent from his position as assistant editor of the *Economist*. He had previously held the same job with the prestigious *Manchester Guardian*. At the age of thirty-two, he was extremely bright, self-confident, and somewhat intolerant of those who did not catch on to new ideas as fast as he did.[14] "I had a job to do and I did it the best way I knew how," he now says about his style at the *Free Press* and later in Ottawa. He arrived in Winnipeg in 1954 with a mandate to modernize the paper. Grant Dexter, who had been unhappy in the editor's chair, returned to the press gallery in Ottawa, but there was little room for Hutchison's editorial contributions at Kent's *Free Press*. (He had already taken on new duties as the editor of the *Victoria Daily Times* two years earlier.)

As editor of the Winnipeg newspaper, Kent was slowly drawn into the circle of men advising Pearson. He helped the Liberal leader with his Nobel Peace Prize speech, which Pearson had been awarded for his diplomatic resolution of the Suez crisis, and played a key role in devising the Liberal platform for the 1958 election – a platform that included the tax reductions and expenditures so detested by Bruce Hutchison, a believer in balanced budgets and free trade.

Kent resigned from the *Free Press* in 1959 over a dispute with Victor Sifton, opting for a corporate job in Montreal. He ensured his place in the Liberal intelligentsia at the party's "thinkers" conference in Kingston in 1960, where he delivered a paper on social security. Though neither the conference nor his paper produced many ideas that had not already been accepted as party policy, the journalists present were impressed with Kent and the gathering. A year later arrangements were somewhat finalized when, on Walter Gordon's recommendation, Kent was appointed special consultant to the Liberal leader and the National Liberal Federation. No fan of Kent, Hutchison regarded this decision as a worse blunder than Mackenzie King's five-cent speech.[15]

No one was madder about Kent's appointment than John Connolly, the federation's president. Both Gordon and Pearson had failed to advise him of it. In October 1961 Connolly visited Hutchison in Victoria and told him, according to the journalist, "a remarkable story" about his discussion with Pearson regarding Kent. As Hutchison reported to Dexter and Dick Malone (who became publisher of the *Free Press* on Victor Sifton's death that year): "Mike said he was desperate for a speech writer because, at that time there was still talk of an autumn election, his two assistants were going to run and there was no one to do the work. But to save the feelings of these two, Mike had decided to announce that Kent would work for the Liberal Federation mainly, and partially for him. Connolly blew up and said that to appoint a high official of the Federation without consulting him, the President, was 'a shoddy business' ... Connolly believes Gordon foisted Kent on Mike. He thinks Mike appealed to Gordon for help and Gordon came up with the Indispensable Man."[16] With Pearson and the Liberals "in the hands of the head shrinkers," as Hutchison called them, he and Dexter (who died on

December 12, 1961), as well as other old party supporters, worried about where it would all lead. It wasn't that they were disloyal to Pearson, but they wondered what would happen if the party was victorious in the next election. "Who, in short," Hutchison asked, "will govern the country when Mike seems so easily swayed by his palace guard?"[17]

Along with Tom Kent, the men most responsible for Pearson's image and media relations were Keith Davey and Richard O'Hagan. Davey, who was appointed to the Senate in 1966, is probably Ottawa's most celebrated back-room boy and consummate election-campaign organizer. He was "The Rainmaker," an uncomplimentary and ironic nickname he was given when he failed to deliver a majority government to Pearson, but which later took on miracle-worker connotations. It was this latter reputation that he private-ly cultivated, though in public he has always been full of humility – in his words, "just an ordinary guy who had been lucky."[18] No matter, Pearson and the Liberals could not have found a better "cheerleader," to use Walter Gordon's term for him.

Davey was thirty-four when he moved from Toronto to Ottawa in 1961 to assume his duties as the Liberal Party's national campaign director. With a background as sales manager of Toronto radio station CKFH and experi-ence with the Ontario Liberals, he was the skilled and dedicated ad man the federal party needed. Like many of his generation, Davey was in awe of U.S. president John F. Kennedy and, more significantly, the imaginative political organization and manipulation – not least the Kennedy charm that worked so well on television that led to his 1960 victory. When journalist Theodore White wrote his bestseller *The Making of the President* in 1961, Davey devoured every page. "I was," he says today, "a creature of that book; it was my bible." One of the first things he did was bring Kennedy's pollster, Lou Harris, to Ottawa to run some polls in preparation for the 1962 campaign.[19] (Davey recalls that once Pearson was prime minister, he had an aversion to polls and to Harris. The pollster would arrive at 24 Sussex to be greeted by Pearson as follows: "Hi Lou, how bad am I this month?")

Some of Davey's ideas and gimmicks backfired. This was the case with the children's political colouring books that were never distributed and with his Truth Squad, whose purpose was to expose Diefenbaker's fibs but which only embarrassed Judy LaMarsh, one of the squad's reluctant members. The "Campaign Colleges" that he set up to train Liberal candidates were much more effective. He taught his "students" to be as forthcoming as possible in dealing with the press. "What do editors want?" one campaign handbook on publicity began. "They want to hear about amusing or heartwarming inci-dents during the campaign. They want to know about the candidate's family."[20]

Davey was adept at handling the Ottawa media. He knew how to culti-
vate contacts with journalists like Peter C. Newman and how to obtain the
best coverage possible. Early on he was pleased to get *Maclean's* to publish
a story on two rising female Liberal stars, Judy LaMarsh and Pauline
Jewett.[21] Otherwise, he says, he did his best work at the regular dinner parties held by Richard and Wanda O'Hagan, to which members of the gallery
were always invited. "I would get some guy in a corner and tell him what
was going on," he says sheepishly. Two days later Davey's insight would be
the basis of a newspaper column.

Richard O'Hagan had joined the Pearson team just prior to Davey's
arrival in Ottawa. Born in New Brunswick in 1928, he had studied journalism at Fordham University in New York before joining the *Toronto
Telegram* as a reporter in 1949. He left journalism seven years later to work
for MacLaren Advertising's public relations department. In 1959 the large
Toronto firm aggressively went after and won the business of the Ontario
Liberal Party; it was soon preparing studies for the federal Liberals as well.
With the federal election about a year away in 1961, Pearson required the
services of an efficient and innovative PR man. The agency loaned him
O'Hagan. He remained with the Liberal leader until his appointment, five
years later, as minister-counsellor for information at the Canadian embassy
in Washington. He returned to Ottawa a decade later to assist Pierre
Trudeau. In 1979 he joined the Bank of Montreal, where he is now senior
vice-president of public affairs.

In the early sixties, as now, O'Hagan was an enthusiastic and energetic
individual, a man who enjoyed the finer things in life. "He had his hair cut
in Toronto, his shirts with his initials sewn into the neck were made by an
Egyptian shirtmaker, and he loved to do all the things that were *in*," Peter
Newman observed. Like Keith Davey, he too was fascinated with the power
of the Kennedys.

For someone so young, O'Hagan was extremely competent at his job.
Nothing was left to chance. Whether it was preparing Pearson for a press
conference or television talk, arranging a cocktail party at the Park Plaza for
editors of ethnic newspapers, or convincing the prime minister to agree to
an interview, O'Hagan was the consummate press secretary – the first real
practitioner of the art in Ottawa. Because, as he says, he was not a "gallery
person," he had the advantage of starting fresh with the parliamentary correspondents, a relationship that involved a great deal of ego-stroking. At the
end of November 1963, for instance, O'Hagan and Tom Kent had a long
talk with *Montreal Star* columnist Bill Wilson in order to clarify "the
Liberal [Party's] view," which was later reflected in Wilson's "constructive
and helpful" articles on the federal-provincial conference held at the time.[22]
More often, as he recalled, he would write to friendly reporters with this

approach: "The prime minister would like to tell you how much he enjoyed your article."

Gallery members were generally receptive to O'Hagan's overtures and congenial personality, not to mention his Saturday-night parties. But on occasion they did grumble about background briefings, trial balloons, and the withholding of information. When Pearson had his famous encounter with President Lynden Johnson at Camp David in April 1965 – following the prime minister's speech in Philadelphia in which he argued against further U.S. bombing in Vietnam – O'Hagan told reporters that the talks between the two leaders "had been friendly, frank and informative. There was no serious disagreements [sic]." After the American press revealed that Johnson had in fact verbally assaulted Pearson, O'Hagan was forced to admit he had not been as "discreet" as he could have been. "I didn't deliberately try to mislead the Canadian reporters," he said. "I guess I just didn't tell them enough."[23]

While O'Hagan admitted in a 1963 TV show that he was "something of a propagandist," he denies he was engaged in a "disinformation campaign" or that he managed the news. His job, he says, was "to sell the message," and as an advertising man he employed the media as a tool to achieve this objective. As early as 1961 he suggested in a memo on Liberal publicity that "the media, used successfully, represent the 'heavy artillery.' They soften up the ground, create the proper atmosphere, put the electors in a receptive mood." He astutely observed, as Clifford Sifton had decades earlier, that "a legitimate news story is worth a dozen propaganda releases," and recommended that whenever Pearson and other party spokesmen delivered speeches, "every available newsman should be cultivated and provided with script copies, and every other aid necessary to ensure good coverage."[24]

Above all, he expounded in a report to Keith Davey in September 1961, was "the incalculable importance of television as a force in modern politics." This meant making use of the free time available by the CBC show "The Nation's Business" as well as improving the quality and sparkle of generally dull, stuffy broadcasts.[25] Davey, who agreed with O'Hagan's assessment, had already signed on Bob Crone, a thirty-year-old independent and multi-talented Toronto film producer, to work with Pearson on his TV presence and to oversee the party's television spots. Along with Walter Gordon and Tom Kent, O'Hagan, Davey, and Crone made up the NLF's TV subcommittee of the Communications Committee for the 1962 and 1963 election campaigns. Great technical debates raged over everything from the use of graphics and voice-overs to whether or not Pearson should wear a bow tie. (They recommended he should not, advice he didn't follow.)[26] Ultimately, however, all their public relations schemes and television plans boiled down to one factor: the image of Mike Pearson.

Both Davey and O'Hagan now say it was never their intention to recast Pearson's personality. "You simply cannot change a person from what he is," Davey asserts. "You can do small things and we could get Pearson to change a little. But Mike Pearson was the way he was." Surveys indicated that the public's perception of Pearson was of an academic "smart aleck." "We tried to stop him from smiling at the wrong time ... and we persuaded him to tuck his thumb in his fist when he was being emphatic," Davey related.[27]

At first, the Liberal leader was open to most of his advisers' suggestions. Crone worked "to make him look as warm on TV as he was with small groups of friends" and filmed him in a variety of settings – "intimate soirees, crowd scenes, living-room shots [and] interviews with academics."[28] While Davey and his subcommittee were full of encouragement, telling Pearson after the 1962 election that he had "arrived as a political TV performer," the truth, as Keith Davey wrote years later, was the opposite: "The best television Mike Pearson would ever do would be the programs in which he thought he was simply practising. We used these frequently."

It was probably for the best that John Diefenbaker spurned Pearson's 1962 campaign challenge to have a Kennedy-Nixon–style debate on television, for unlike his Tory opponent, Pearson was not an actor. "Pearson's personality is the same on the hustings, in his office and on TV," Peter Newman wrote. "Diefenbaker has the ability to make a role out of a TV appearance. On the platform his righteous rhetoric can shake the second balcony; on television his lofty diction can genuinely touch his listeners."[29]

With his noticeable lisp (in a TV appearance in 1962 at the time of the Coyne affair, Pearson repeatedly referred to "Mithster Coyne"), high-pitched voice, and trademark bow tie, he looked like either someone's professorial uncle or the neighbourhood Little League baseball coach circa 1950. "Unlike many public men," commented Dick O'Hagan, "[Pearson] found it difficult to elevate himself, to motivate himself to give a spirited statement or deliver a speech with vigour sitting isolated in front of a television camera."[30] Pearson was the first to admit he needed help, particularly for his TV style. "I always felt uncomfortable before a television camera," he noted in a CBC interview. "I could never feel at ease speaking at a television camera ... I learned something of the technique as I went along. But I assure you, I never felt like a natural performer and this is a great handicap in a politician these days."[31]

This was no more evident than in CBC's famed *Mr. Pearson* film of 1964. Influenced by the new film trend of the day, *cinema verité,* the plan of director Richard Ballentine was to probe the prime minister's inner soul. To do so required hours of film footage of Pearson going about his daily routine, meeting with officials, and talking with his aides. For some reason

Pearson, a very private person, agreed to CBC's request to be its star guinea pig. As part of the deal, he was permitted to view the film before it was shown and could suggest editing changes.[32]

It was a fiasco from start to finish. Tom Kent recalled, "I was horrified one morning to find [the TV crew] ... in his office and was told by Mr. Pearson to behave as if they weren't there." There were hazy close-ups, muffled conversations, shots of Pearson watching baseball, and even a few racy phrases – one "Lord," one "God," a "damn," and one "oh hell." The real star of the film turned out to be Jim Coutts, then the prime minister's young, baby-faced appointments secretary. "Where Mr. Pearson on film seemed gentle, unaggressive, tentative at best and at times waffling and uncertain, Coutts was bright, eager, confident." Kent added, "If Mr. Pearson or anyone else had hoped the film could correct the public image of him as a weak man, they could not have been more wrong."[33]

Pearson and his aides were not the only ones to dislike the final version of the film. CBC president Alphonse Ouimet was not impressed with its "amateurish" quality and decided on his own to leave *Mr. Pearson* on the shelf. It was not shown until April 1969. Nevertheless, the Tories and NDP members wrongly charged Pearson with censorship. To this day, Dick O'Hagan does not know exactly what happened. "I'm not sure why CBC backed off. I don't think they needed to or they should have," he says. "I don't think Pearson had anything to worry about, although he became worried by concern shown by the cabinet. The whole thing spun out of control. It was just a case of nervous 'nellyism.' The film was experimental and I suppose you should not experiment with the government and prime minister."

Until the 1958 election, Lester Pearson had experienced few defeats in his career, let alone the humiliation he endured after the Liberals were reduced to forty-nine seats. It was to his credit that the Liberal Party was able to regroup, reclaim power five years later, and with a minority government pass legislation that has had a lasting effect on the country. The path to this success, however, was rocky.

From the perspective of the journalists who covered the Pearson administration on a day-to-day basis, there was nothing but infighting, poor judgment, and inappropriate behaviour that in a few instances bordered on criminal. "It was a time of national distemper," wrote Peter Newman in his chronicle of the Pearson years, "a time when the political affairs of the country were in such a state of disorder that there was something faintly absurdist about their unfolding, a time when many Canadians were left with the feeling that much of what was happening had no meaning and that all they could do was ask themselves a series of unanswerable questions: Is the country being governed by fools? Or is it ungovernable?"[34]

Naturally, most of the negative analysis by journalists and academics then and later focused on the personal inadequacies of a sexagenarian prime minister who in time showed his years. There was no denying that most people who came into contact with Mike Pearson liked him immediately, but as a politician he had his weaknesses. While he enjoyed meeting large crowds on the hustings, he did not exude a charismatic presence or communicate a "political passion."[35] He was not a good organizer; nor did his charm and sincere nature, so evident in small groups, come across on television.

In cabinet he governed by his diplomatic instincts. He exercised, as he explained, "loose and flexible control" and relied "on consensus rather than compulsion." More significantly, he examined "every side of a question before coming to a decision," a management style not always suited to the heat of political battle.[36] His style also contributed to the popular notion (one he would not have argued with) that the prime minister was only as good as his cabinet. Mitchell Sharp, a loyal friend and a minister in both the Pearson and Trudeau administrations put it like this: "When I sat around the cabinet table when Pearson was prime minister, I said to myself, 'The prime minister would not be here if we were not here.' You would never have said that about Trudeau."

Still, descriptions of Pearson by such adversaries as his outspoken health minister, Judy LaMarsh, who thought him "gutless," or Tories like Grattan O'Leary, who considered him "feeble and indecisive," did not tell the whole story. Tom Kent, who worked more closely with Pearson than anyone else had during his first two troubled years in office, saw his soft and whiny side, his "weakness at the knees," but ultimately he judges him a success. Much of Pearson's trouble, says Kent, was his weak image in Parliament and the fact that he was continually whipped in front of the nation by Diefenbaker, his detested rival. "The impression of Mike as a weak Prime Minister derived chiefly from his performance in the House of Commons where, under pressure, he was often uncertain, even obviously confused," Kent observed. "But while those and other weaknesses imposed great strains on his colleagues and associates, and above all on L.B. Pearson himself, they had little bearing on his strategic ability and none at all on his determination."[37]

Even to his closest advisers, Pearson never revealed his true self. Some, like Bruce Hutchison, tried to psychoanalyze him and understand his idiosyncrasies, describing his mind as being "constructed layer by layer in a series of Chinese boxes [which] had never revealed its inner content to any colleague, perhaps not even to its owner." In a column he wrote after Pearson announced his intention to retire in mid-December 1967, Hutchison postulated that no one had ever touched Pearson's "inner core." "It was always hidden under the disguise of the boyish look, the quick grin, the bow tie, the feet on the desk – an apparatus of convincing camouflage worn so naturally that the wearer may sometimes even believe it." At a dinner in his honour in Toronto in February 1968, Pearson could only laugh when he noted that "in some quarters I'm supposed to be a subtle, mysterious, lonely person." Maryon Pearson, on the other hand, his wife of forty-three years, regarded Hutchison's assessment as "accurate enough, however incomplete."[38]

The side of his complex personality he revealed to journalists was usually the friendly, down-to-earth, easygoing demeanour. In short, Pearson wanted to have fun and be liked. In contrast to dealing with Diefenbaker, who in his last years had blamed the press for many of his problems, reporters found dealing with Pearson delightful. "It required constant lip biting to refrain from calling him 'Mike,'" recalled Stewart MacLeod. "In the light-hearted bantering that often occurred on his aircraft [during a campaign], 'Mr. Prime Minister' just didn't seem natural to him."[39]

He had known many members of the gallery for years, and at least initially his relations with the press were wonderful. "When you saw Pearson," Peter Newman remembers, "it was like going to see your uncle. He had this ability to make you feel sorry for him in the sense that he had all these problems on his shoulders running the country. But at the same time you'd sympathize on how he was trying to solve them. So he had you on side not by trying to convince you what was right or because you were his friend, but simply by pointing out in a real way what the problems were he had in running the country."

During the 1963 election campaign, not only had traditional Liberal newspapers such as the *Winnipeg Free Press* and *Toronto Star* backed Pearson, but so too did those guardians of Ontario Toryism, the *Globe and Mail* and the *Telegram,* which had lost both patience with and faith in Diefenbaker. Yet the honeymoon ended within a few months of the Liberals' accession to power. There was, as Pearson reflected during a CBC television interview on April 1, 1968, "an inevitable hostility between the head of a government and newspapermen." During the campaign the Liberal leader had promised to solve the nation's woes in his first sixty days, committing his new administration to an unrealistic timetable that begged for critical media commentary.

Matters began to unravel when Finance Minister Walter Gordon presented his first budget in June 1963. With some incentives to ease unemployment and raise revenues, Gordon's plan for the economy was not as horrific as commentators made it out to be at the time. But his speech was too partisan, and editorials in the major papers, including the *Globe and Mail* and *Winnipeg Free Press,* attacked a "Draconian ... 30 per cent sales tax on takeovers of Canadian companies by non-residents" that was equally resented by the business community.[40] Additionally, Gordon had gone outside the finance department bureaucracy and brought in his own men to assist him in the preparation of the budget. Although this was not entirely unprecedented, the fact that he only revealed the participation of these external experts after the NDP's Douglas Fisher raised the matter in the House did not look good.

The positive aspects of the budget were lost in the headlines and columns calling for Gordon's resignation. Word had it that Pearson asked his press secretary, Richard O'Hagan, to poll gallery members for their thoughts on whether his finance minister and friend should depart.[41] "This was Walter Gordon's version of events," says O'Hagan. "I was, in fact, doing my job as press liaison. Mr. Pearson had not ordered me to 'poll' the gallery. But the issue was under discussion and the topic came up in my frequent meetings with journalists."

Regardless, Gordon decided to stay in the government, but the takeover tax was withdrawn and the budget considerably revised. These events in the early summer of 1963 hurt the reputations of both Gordon and Pearson as well as the entire cabinet. Senator Thomas Crerar, the aging politician who had led the Progressives in the 1920s before serving in Mackenzie King's government, summed up the feelings of many Liberals: "So far Mike has not given evidence of a capacity for clear, original, forceful thinking. In some respect, he is too much 'one of the boys.'"[42] Some members of the parliamentary gallery had similar thoughts.

By 1964, due in large part to admittance of radio and TV journalists five years earlier, the gallery's numbers had swollen to about 130 members. They worked in a space in the Parliament Buildings – provided at a cost to Canadian taxpayers in excess of $100,000 annually – meant for no more than 30. (This of course, included a small closet that was transformed into a bar, the most popular spot on the third floor of the Centre Block.) Many reporters were forced to move out into the adjacent hallway, creating a fire hazard and a "cluttered journalistic slum."[43]

In a 1965 *Maclean's* article on the gallery, June Callwood offered this snapshot of the "hot room": "The decor is Early Squalor, with sprightly touches of dust, empty beer bottles and solitary galoshes ... The main newsroom [is] crammed with antique oak desks, stalagmites of yellowed *Hansards* and elk-horned coat racks ... [While the corridor outside] now contains thirty-two desks, fifty-eight filing cabinets, fifteen coat racks, twenty-four bookcases and a festoonery of wastepaper baskets, cigarette machines, electric fans, watercoolers, Teletype machines, telephone booths and whiskey cartons rakishly stuffed with old budget debates."[44] After a considerable amount of complaining and haggling, the government forcibly moved the newsmen's offices across the street to the Norlite Building in the summer of 1965.

In general, the journalists in Ottawa during the sixties were more impatient, aggressive, and demanding than ever before. Their battles with Diefenbaker had made them crankier and more suspicious, even less respectful, of politicians. Television put pressure on print reporters to be more critical of the government and more passionate; it also turned those politicians and journalists who appeared regularly into media celebrities. Press conferences and scrums in the corridors of Parliament were transformed into technological mine fields, with electronic equipment of every shape and size. Cigarette smoke was thick and discarded butts were strewn about the East Block as the media horde waited for members of the cabinet. Judy LaMarsh described the chaotic scene in front of the East Block cabinet meeting room in 1963: "We ... opened the swinging door to find pandemonium – a crush of reporters worse than any I have seen, with cameras, flash bulbs, T.V. lights, tape recorders at the ready – it was almost impossible to squeeze out of the room and through them."[45]

Whereas Diefenbaker relished the challenge of the corridor debates, Pearson found them impossible. "His voice did not carry well and only newsmen at the front crowding around could hear his comments as he spoke into microphones pressed close to his face," noted one reporter who had experienced first-hand the pushing and shoving match. "Others at the back pressed forward. He is of medium height and was often lost in the crowd of newsmen with the TV cameramen desperately trying to find him. It was a shambles. Something had to be done."[46]

At the suggestion of press secretary Dick O'Hagan, the journalists were moved into a special conference room. Pearson was to stop by to brief reporters following his daily cabinet meeting. But as his administration became bogged down in one scandal after another, he had good reason to avoid these daily confrontations. Some of the journalists were relentless, firing questions at him from every direction. "Do you really expect me to answer a question like that?" he said to one reporter who had shouted rudely from the back of the room. Two long and trying years went by before Pearson finally banned this media circus from Parliament's hallways for the duration of his term in office. The *Toronto Telegram* considered it an attack on freedom of the press.[47]

The gallery's new attitude was no better epitomized than in the style adopted and promoted by the controversial television show "This Hour Has Seven Days," CBC's hard-hitting investigative program. The "Seven Days" team – including interviewer Warner Troyer and Ottawa editor Roy Fabish – were legendary, even going so far as to trample over their CBC colleagues in the news bureau led by Norman DePoe. With warlike strategy planning, they arrived at scheduled press conferences early so that they could sit in the front rows and dominate the questioning. Politeness to politicians and fellow-journalists went out the window. "Someone on the ['Seven Days' staff] actually stole news film from the [CBC] news service, which infuriated newsmen so much that the local news union came out with a denunciation of the arrogant pilferers," Paul Rutherford related.[48]

It was not surprising that Pearson refused an invitation to participate in one of the show's famed "encounter" sessions and ordered his ministers to do the same. "I watch 'This Hour Has Seven Days' whenever I can, always with interest," he told Laurier LaPierre, the program's debonair co-host. "Naturally, that interest is not always favourable because the program is designedly – at times it seems even aggressively – controversial."[49]

Hardly a week went by in 1965 when Pearson did not receive a bag full of letters from Canadians upset with the show. A satirical skit involving the Pope and a segment in which the "Seven Days" producers pitted two Ku Klux Klansmen against a young American black civil rights leader are two examples of the kind of programming that outraged – or fascinated – TV viewers across the country. Questions about its ethics arose as well.[50] Pearson could not appease those who objected to the show by saying that the CBC was a separate public corporation responsible for its own day-to-day affairs.

There is no evidence that Pearson himself had any involvement with the infamous decision in the spring of 1966 not to renew the contracts of "Seven Days" hosts Patrick Watson and Laurier LaPierre, a decision that led to a hysterical melodrama. If the prime minister was guilty of anything, it was of trying too hard to once again be the Nobel Prize–winning mediator. First, he allowed the "Seven Days" dispute, which was an internal CBC matter, to be investigated by the Parliamentary Standing Committee on Broadcasting, a body usually concerned with broad policy issues. And second, over the objections of the minister responsible for the CBC, Judy LaMarsh, he appointed *Vancouver Sun* publisher Stuart Keate to review the case. Keate's report did not settle the dispute, and it dragged on for a few more months.[51]

Though the show was off the air, it had a left a lasting impression. With its mandate to reveal all, "Seven Days" determined what kind of stories it wanted, and then set out to get them in any way it could. The "Seven Days" team's determination was tested to the utmost in 1966 when Larry Zolf attempted to interview Pierre Sévigny about his romantic involvement with Gerda Munsinger, his East German girlfriend accused of being a spy. In a famous altercation in front of Sévigny's Montreal home, the former Tory minister beat Zolf with his cane. The segment was never broadcast. Whatever the opinion newsmen had of the show, they could not argue with its success. Gradually the "Seven Days" style came to be imitated by other media members. This initiated a more adversarial form of journalism, observed Ron Haggart of the *Toronto Star* in 1966, "in which the journalists themselves decide what are the issues of concern and importance, a journalism in which the issues are established not by politicians, but by those who watch them with pencil and film." Now began the battle between the two sides to establish the public agenda.[52]

As the self-proclaimed moral guardians of the people's rights, it was the duty of journalists everywhere to uncover corruption and expose ineptitude. Of course, "the underlying assumption was that the politicians were always motivated by personal or partisan self-interest, at odds with the public interest – the assumption proved an all too convenient way of explaining just about everything that happened in Ottawa."[53] Nevertheless, the view most political reporters had had of themselves since Diefenbaker's day – as the "unofficial" opposition – was further entrenched.

In print the star of the gallery during the Pearson years was unquestionably Peter C. Newman (columnist George Bain of the *Globe and Mail* was as influential and respected in Ottawa, but he did not reach nearly as many readers across the country). A Jewish Czech immigrant, Newman had escaped the Nazi ravaging of Europe, arriving with his parents in Canada in 1940. He was eleven years old. Following his education at Upper Canada College and the University of Toronto, where he earned a graduate degree in commerce, he embarked on his path to journalistic fame, joining the *Financial Post* in 1951 and becoming the newspaper's Montreal editor in 1953. He was wooed back to Toronto in 1956, however, by one of his mentors, Ralph Allen, the legendary editor of *Maclean's*.[54]

After less than two years as assistant editor at *Maclean's,* he was asked to join Blair Fraser in Ottawa. "I was very lucky," he says, "because Blair Fraser wanted to do more travelling around the world and *Maclean's* had to have someone to cover Ottawa when he was away." It was here that this tall, intense, hard-working scribe earned his renowned reputation. From the viewpoint of other gallery members, however, Newman was different and purposely so. "As a Jew and an immigrant, I was an outsider," he states. He did not frequent gallery parties or socialize very much (although Newman and his then wife Christina McCall did throw some marvellous parties for Ottawa's who's who). "The gallery was a small English club in the late fifties and early sixties. Everyone who left the gallery got a mug made out of pewter except me, because I did not play by the club rules. I had my own path," he says proudly.

The path Newman chose was constant work. "When others quit for the day, Newman was still tracking down facts; when those facing daily deadlines copied from each other's carbons, Newman prepared his material from scratch," Elspeth Cameron noted in a 1982 profile. He was one of the first print reporters to use a tape-recorder, a large bulky UHR machine; he courted ministers and their "talkative young aides." He was decidedly non-partisan, more than willing to praise and criticize all politicians equally. "Newman," says journalist and former MP Douglas Fisher, "was like a prowling bird dog." His march to the top continued. In 1959 at age thirty, he published his first book, *Flame of Power,* intimate profiles of eleven Canadian business giants. The book sold well, cementing his fascination with power and those who wielded it.[55] He would return to writing about businessmen more than a decade later with *The Canadian Establishment* and its sequels.

A year after the release of *Flame of Power,* he succeeded Fraser as *Maclean's* Ottawa editor and began to assemble the data for his next best-seller, which would document the rise and fall of John Diefenbaker. He conducted, he says, nearly one thousand interviews and arranged for cabinet ministers and other officials to keep diaries for him. The result was the publication of *Renegade in Power* in October 1963.

Until then, Canadian prime ministers had been written about primarily by official biographers and academics, all looking in from the outside. In 1952 Bruce Hutchison had written a flattering biography of Mackenzie King, who had died two years earlier, while Bernard Ostry and Harry Ferns responded with *The Age of Mackenzie King.* In its day the Ostry and Ferns book caused a minor furor, but compared to *Renegade in Power* it was a rather tame academic study, focusing on King's eccentricities and his ambitious quest for the prime ministership. Newman wanted to offer the insider's view so that he could tell the story of government the way it was: the personality conflicts, the backstabbing, the political jousting. "I quite openly modelled myself on [American writer] Theodore White [author of *The Making of the President* (1961)] who got inside the U.S. election campaigns," he explains. "And I saw no good reason why I couldn't get inside the term of a prime minister."

Renegade was a sensation. Newman's "account of Diefenbaker's uncontrollable paranoia, particularly during the last year of the government, was the best Ottawa gossip Canadians had ever been allowed to read: unlike every other political journalist of the day, Newman wrote in public the way everyone in Ottawa talked in private," noted *Saturday Night* editor Robert Fulford. "His frankness changed Canadian journalism, and helped change the way Canadians saw their government."[56]

Newman presented the human side of Diefenbaker, with all his foibles, but overall the book offered a tough assessment of the defeated prime minister. "John Diefenbaker had a large, abiding love for this country," Newman wrote in the book's prologue. "He gave prodigious energy to his office and tried hard to bring the federal administration into a more meaningful relationship with the average citizen. Yet he only rarely had the courage to follow his privately held convictions. The right instincts were in him, but throughout his stormy stewardship, they languished in the cupboard of his soul."

Tories such as Alvin Hamilton, Grattan O'Leary, Allister Grosart, and Burt Richardson (the former editor of the *Toronto Telegram* who became Diefenbaker's special assistant in February 1963) were understandably outraged. They criticized Newman for not getting all the facts right; they complained that the CBC was giving the book too much free publicity by scheduling programs around it; and mostly they yelled about the title of the book, arguing that Diefenbaker was not a "renegade" in the sense of being a traitor or a deserter. Never one to take criticism, Newman stood his ground. He defended his choice of title by pointing out that Diefenbaker was indeed a "renegade to his own cause [and] an apostate to the principles of Canadian Conservatism" – a modern-day Robin Hood fighting the Establishment.[57]

On this point, Newman was probably pushing his thesis too far. The Conservative Party of that era did not have an "entirely coherent ideology" Diefenbaker could have followed, as political scientist Denis Smith argued in the 1971 reprint of *Renegade*. In any event, according to Smith, "Diefenbaker was true in faith to the Macdonaldian myth of national development, to the liberal mystique of small business enterprise, and to the symbols of the British connection."[58]

There were other errors in interpretation of events and motives (Newman may have exaggerated the so-called coup d'état of 1962, for example), yet in a book of such magnitude, based on nearly one thousand (largely anonymous) interviews, most of the mistakes singled out were of no great significance. The real question, Douglas Fisher observed, was not so much one of accuracy – for what is truth in politics? – but one of "authenticity" (ask two cabinet ministers about a particular event and they will offer two quite different versions). Here Newman succeeded as no journalist had before. He was able to sort through the "kaleidoscope of anecdote and rumour" that swirled around any prime minister, but especially Diefenbaker, and capture his subject's "contradictory personality" perfectly. This, said Fisher, made Newman's book authentic.[59]

Diefenbaker, not surprisingly, thought otherwise. Within days of the book's publication, Newman presented Diefenbaker with a copy inscribed with the words "With deepest respect." Diefenbaker took one look at the inscription and remarked to his press assistant Tom Van Dusen, "That is the worst of all." Diefenbaker claimed never to have read the book (although his wife Olive did). But a story that made the rounds in the gallery was that soon after the book was published, an aide happened upon Diefenbaker in his office, devouring every page.[60]

Diefenbaker was so angry with the book that he never spoke to Newman again ("He only glared at me," Newman recalls). He regarded *Renegade in Power* as a Liberal conspiracy and Peter C. Newman as a Liberal "propagandist." A scribbled note in Diefenbaker's own handwriting (verified by archivists at the Diefenbaker Centre at the University of Saskatoon) that was discovered in his papers attests to the former prime minister's fury, volatile state of mind, and meanness.

The note is undated but was probably written in late 1963: "Then there is Newman. He is the literary scavenger of trash. Manufactured and concocted. He is in close contact with the Liberal hierarchy and gets his briefings from them as that what he should publish. False propaganda. Vicious. Health of my wife [presumably referring to Newman's reference in the book that Diefenbaker's first wife, Edna, died of leukemia]. Cruel Stories. Caricatures." (Diefenbaker actually had Burt Richardson type out this note as if it was to be used in a speech. Richardson took the liberty of adding that "[Newman] seldom attends Parliament and what he finds out about the Conservative Party he learns via corridor gossip and key-hole peeping.")[61]

In the fall of 1963 Diefenbaker's apologists initially believed that the public would not be fooled by Newman's work. A confidential, seventeen-page commentary in Diefenbaker's "Renegade in Power" file put it as follows: "Newman is not the issue in this matter; nor is Newman's book. The issue is simply whether the people in this country will be prepared to accept an interpretation which shows bias initially in its title; and secondly, in the refusal of the author to take responsibility. To accept Newman's book at face value, in view of the purpose as indicated by the title is an act of faith of which the majority of Canadians will not be capable ... This ... book will never be used as a source book by serious historians, or even by serious journalists."[62]

The commentary was wrong on all counts. Canadians loved Newman's hard-nosed, critical approach, and reviews were very positive. Within a short time the book sold more than 50,000 copies and was the subject of countless television news shows. More importantly, if being imitated is a sign of success, then Newman had succeeded resoundingly. Since 1963, dozens of journalists have tried to copy Newman's style by writing books about other Canadian politicians; few have matched his gusto or sales record. *Renegade in Power* became the most talked about book in Canadian politics. Soon regarded as the standard history of the Diefenbaker years, it was mandatory reading for doctoral students in Canadian history and was reissued as part of the Carleton University Library series.

The next phase in Newman's career started when he left *Maclean's* to become the Ottawa editor of the *Toronto Star* in 1964. As a syndicated columnist, he was the Canadian version of the *New York Times'* James Reston. By 1969 his columns appeared in thirty newspapers, including French translations for *La Presse,* reaching an unprecedented two million readers. Politicians could not ignore such journalistic power. His column, observed Pearson's assistant Hal Dornan in a confidential 1966 memo, "is in many ways more important than any combination of commentaries because it is the basis for a large number of editorials, interpretative pieces and even news stories."[63]

Newman had sources everywhere, including inside the Liberal cabinet, a fact that angered Pearson. On one occasion, Newman remembered, "I'd broken a story about one of the many splits within the Pearson cabinet, [and] the Prime Minister began a meeting with his ministers by inveighing against me and my kind. He ended his lecture by saying he was fed up with reading about his government's intimate deliberations before they were cold on his tongue and that he was imploring his ministers not to talk to Newman." With a straight face, Walter Gordon remarked that Pearson should give Newman a chair. "It must be pretty uncomfortable for Peter to have to crouch under the table while the Cabinet's in session," he said. Two minutes later, the prime minister and several ministers looked under the table to see if he was really there.[64]

The truth was that Peter Newman did have unprecedented access. One key friend was Keith Davey, the national director of the Liberal Party, whom Newman met in 1961. "I leaked a lot of stuff to Peter," Davey says, "but Peter published a lot of generous stuff about us." Apart from helpful executive assistants, Newman had close contact with such ministers as Walter Gordon and Mitchell Sharp. According to Hal Dornan, Sharp had accepted Newman "as a very influential fact in political life. He has made devastatingly positive use of Newman's influence by the simple method of keeping him (too much) in his office's confidence."[65] That a great debate raged in the Prime Minister's Office in November 1966 when Newman requested an interview was testimony to his authority as a journalist.

Like others in the gallery, Newman had grown more critical of Pearson by this time, but he desired that this "estrangement" between himself and the prime minister end. He proposed an interview and agreed to submit his twelve questions ahead of time as well as a transcribed version of the conversation prior to publication. At first Dornan was not too keen on the idea. Yet, given that Newman was preparing a sequel to *Renegade in Power,* about the Pearson years (*The Distemper of Our Times* [1968]) and that he was a "knowledgeable contemporary popular recorder of history in the making," to use Dornan's words, the interview was granted. It took place just before Christmas.[66]

While Newman was as tough on Pearson as he had been on Diefenbaker, he recalls that the prime minister "was a very forgiving man. I wrote some terrible stuff about him and he still talked to me." In hindsight, he says, he may have been a little too hard. "I don't take a word back I ever wrote about Dief, but I think Pearson achieved a lot we did not give him credit for. When you think that with a minority government, medicare and a pension plan, among other legislation, were passed. The trouble was it was so untidy. Pearson looked as if he was stumbling from one crisis to the next ... Still, the record was impressive and I think I for one did not give him enough credit in *Distemper of Our Times*."

Pearson complained about too much analysis and too little factual reporting, and urged journalists to be less sensational and more responsible. "Newspaper editors are always bleating about the refusal of politicians to produce mature and responsible discussion of the issues," he said. "The fact is, when we do discuss policies seriously, we are not reported at all or reported very inadequately. Reporters do not appear even to listen, until we say something controversial or personal, charged with what they regard as news value."[67]

For a while, Pearson stayed clear of journalists altogether, and reporters complained that the Liberal government was too secretive. As for controversial subject matter, the various Pearson scandals provided copy too good to be ignored. From the dark tale of narcotics gangster Lucien Rivard, who escaped extradition by bribing several prominent Liberals and whose case led, unfairly some have argued, to the resignation of Justice Minister Guy Favreau, to the "furniture deals" in which another Quebec minister, Maurice Lamontagne, entered into a questionable credit arrangement when he purchased expensive furniture from a store run by the bankrupt Sefkind brothers, "characters on the fringe of the Quebec underworld," the Pearson government was mired in muck. (In *The Distemper of Our Times,* Newman lists no less than seven scandals that entangled the Liberals. Apart from Rivard and Lamontagne, there were revelations about links between Liberals and Hal Banks, the "despotic head of the Seafarers' International Union"; the bungling of the deportation of criminal immigrant Onofrio Minaudo; the controversial land deals of Liberal MP Edmund Asselin; the corruption of cabinet minister Yvon Dupuis; and the citizenship claims of gangster Harry Stonehill. This does not account for the most famous scandal of them all, the Munsinger Affair, which ensnared both the Liberals and the Conservatives.)[68]

Both the Tories and the press had a field day. In the furniture case, for example, Minister of Citizenship and Immigration René Tremblay, who had legitimately bought furniture from another Sefkind store, was tried and convicted on the front pages along with Lamontagne despite his innocence. Pearson was accused of waffling in his handling of this affair, as with most of the others, but he believed the media had gone too far. "I thought some aspects of this were badly handled by the press," he later commented in a CBC interview. "[There were] some ... commentators ... who would take statements that were made in the opposition which we knew to be untrue and which later we managed to show were not true, and would use them as a basis of sometimes rather superior moralistic comment on the depths to which these Parliamentarians had descended." For Lester Pearson, a politician who favoured partisan friends and discreet off-the-record discussions, there was nothing appealing about this new aggressive style in the gallery.

Partisanship was a cloudy issue. Despite the fact that among the 38 Canadian daily newspapers received by Pearson's office in 1963, 27 were classified as either Conservative (15) or Liberal (12), partisanship among journalists themselves was on the wane. Writing in 1965, June Callwood reported that only a minority of correspondents were devoutly partisan; about twenty-five journalists were regarded as "hard-edged" Liberal Party supporters.[69] Younger gallery members tended to follow the lead of columnists Peter Newman, George Bain, and Charles Lynch; they valued journalistic independence and viewed all politicians critically.

Pearson wasn't entirely sure which reporters he could trust. He did, however, like to chat with them. Whenever he travelled across the country by train, a small media entourage accompanied him. "Every night he would invite seven or eight reporters to his private car for talks," recalls former *Globe and Mail* bureau chief Anthony Westell. "These discussions were off the record, but if you really wanted to use something you could ask him. He would say, 'Yes okay, but don't attribute it to me.'"

Yet such small gatherings and off-the-record briefings, so much a part of Pearson's style since the 1930s, were becoming less popular in some quarters. Pearson would learn this the hard way. In May 1964 Pearson was to give a speech in Winnipeg at the Royal Canadian Legion's annual meeting. There he planned to unveil his choice for the design for the new Canadian flag, three red maple leaves (later changed to one) on a white background. The prime minister felt very strongly about his historic decision to go forward with the flag change, a campaign promise he was going to keep. As a preliminary precaution, he decided to test journalists' reactions to his bold proposal, and in the process release what he would have called a "trial balloon," designed to prepare the legionnaires and the rest of the skeptical public.

A few days before Pearson's Winnipeg departure, Richard O'Hagan invited about eight gallery correspondents to an intimate gathering at 24 Sussex Drive. Among them was Walter Stewart, then a thirty-three-year-old writer with the *Toronto Star Weekly.* Stewart had known O'Hagan when they were both working for the *Toronto Telegram* in the mid-fifties. "This isn't going to be one of those bloody background briefings?" he asked when O'Hagan called. "Because I don't play by those rules." He was assured that it would not be. "In fact," Stewart recollects, "it was just that." (To be fair, O'Hagan states that Stewart did not make his position clear until *after* the meeting. "It is memory in dispute," O'Hagan says.)

When he arrived at Pearson's home, Stewart found a curious assortment of journalists – no francophone reporters, no one from Canadian Press or the CBC. After some friendly banter and tea, Pearson showed his captive audience his choice for the new flag. The party then ended. Stewart wondered what came next. Was he supposed to write an article praising Pearson's taste in flag design? Or about the hospitality at Sussex Drive? Anthony Westell of the *Globe and Mail,* who was also invited, told him that he was planning to write a story for the next day's paper reporting on the new flag but "attributing the information to a 'reliable source' and making no mention of the prime minister."[70]

Stewart had no intention of abiding by such restrictions. "If you are privy to a high-level decision like that, you can't help but be prejudiced," he commented later. "If you're there when the egg hatches, it becomes your chick. It's human nature. And that's no way for a government to behave."[71] The result was two articles in the *Toronto Star,* one by Stewart about the flag, citing the prime minister as the source, and the other by Val Sears, detailing the blatant political manipulation behind the tea party.

In the House on May 21, John Diefenbaker, who favoured retaining the red ensign on the flag, raised the issue of Pearson's press party. He asked about the accuracy of Sears's story, which noted that the prime minister "personally had chosen a flag design" and had informed the Queen of his choice before the matter came to a vote in Parliament. Pearson retorted that Sears had not been at the "social gathering in question," and suggested that his report was not correct. As for his meeting with the journalists, he remarked, "Mr. Speaker, I met with certain members of the press at a social occasion. I do not deny that. Indeed, the right hon. gentleman does that himself quite frequently. I hope that when he meets his friends from the press at his home they have a good time as I hope they would have at my home. Mr. Speaker, we had a cup of tea, and there was some discussion of the question of national emblems. The national flag issue certainly came up, and I expressed in a personal way to my friends my views on that subject."[72] It was vintage Pearson at his witty best.

Privately he and his officials were outraged, as were some members of the gallery, who treated Walter Stewart as if he were a pariah. He had broken one of the unwritten rules of their cosy network. "They knew I was the one who 'ratted' and they did not like it one bit," he says. Stewart rocked the boat further when a short time later he wrote an article drawing attention to the fact that press secretary Dick O'Hagan had remained on the payroll of his former employer, McLaren Advertising, while working in Pearson's office.

For a time, the flag incident had some important ramifications. June Callwood noted that Pearson "no longer leak[ed] important announcements with such '007' intrigue and ... Walter Stewart [was] treated with the caution one would accord a ticking mailbox." Stewart, who was never again invited to one of Pearson's garden parties, says he wants Callwood's characterization of him carved on his gravestone.

Pearson, in fact, did not stop the private briefings. He liked talking to journalists, even if his loquacity might (and did) lead to other misunderstandings. On April 2, 1967, Pearson flew to Santa Barbara to receive an honorary degree from the University of California. That day, U Thant, the secretary of the United Nations, appealed to the United States to take the lead towards peace by declaring a unilateral cease-fire in Vietnam. Reporters travelling with Pearson asked for his opinion, and in what the prime minister and his staff regarded as an off-the-record conversation, he said that U Thant's proposal was unrealistic. This was more in line with U.S. thinking at the time and less with Pearson's 1965 speech in Philadelphia, in which he urged the Americans to stop bombing North Vietnam.

Covering the trip for the *Globe and Mail* was reporter George MacFarlane from the newspaper's Vancouver bureau. In his view, Pearson's comments were on the record and as such wound up on the *Globe*'s front page on April 3. It was 3 a.m. in California when the *Globe* hit the streets in Toronto, and instantly, recalls Pearson's acting press secretary, Don Peacock, "my phone was ringing off the hook. The other newspapers were furious, because their reporters had respected the prime minister's confidence and then had been scooped." Pearson was enraged, and Peacock let both MacFarlane and the *Globe*'s editors know how the prime minister felt. In a letter to Pearson a week later, MacFarlane denied betraying the prime minister's trust. Peacock reported to Pearson that he believed MacFarlane had not taken notes and had relied on memory. "It was," said Peacock, "an unforgivable breach of journalistic ethics." In pencil, beside Peacock's statement, Pearson wrote, "Agreed."[73]

By the time he announced his retirement a few months later, this "we against them" attitude, so much a part of the gallery's character in 1967, had taken its toll on Pearson's patience. Dick O'Hagan remembers, "Pearson was the most reasonable of men, that was what he was renowned for; that's what his life's work was founded on, reason and fair-mindedness and listening to the other point of view. In the end, even he became exasperated with the media."

For the Liberals, everything was supposed to come together to produce a great victory in the federal election of November 8, 1965. At least that was what Pearson's top advisers – Walter Gordon, Tom Kent, and Keith Davey – had told him that summer. Desperate for the majority government that had eluded them in 1963, the Pearson team had no qualms about calling the fourth general election in less than eight years. "We have a right to ask for a vote of confidence," the prime minister noted in a memo in mid-August. "Indeed, we have a moral obligation to give the Canadian people *now* the opportunity to give us one – or reject us for some other party."[74]

Editors and commentators across the country saw it differently. One newspaper after another criticized the impending decision. The *Globe and Mail,* which had deserted Diefenbaker and the Tories in the previous con-test, was extremely skeptical of Liberal strategy, as were such loyalists as the *Toronto Star* and *Winnipeg Free Press.* With Pearson indecisive about whether to go ahead, Tom Kent, who had had reservations about an election (calling it the Liberals' "death wish") but had given way to Walter Gordon, who thought it necessary, assured the prime minister that the press's views were not the issue. "We aren't running against the *Globe and Mail,* the *Winnipeg Free Press,* etc.," he explained in a memorandum of August 10. "We're running against the opposition parties. Do they object to an election now?"[75]

It is hard to understand how a former newspaperman could have under-estimated the importance of press opinion in an election campaign. When Pearson finally set the election for November 8, newspapers that had sided with the Liberals in 1963 deserted the party in droves. Of the more than thir-ty Canadian dailies that had favoured Pearson two years earlier, sixteen switched to the Tories.[76]

The most notable was the one paper Pearson read religiously each day, the *Globe and Mail.* As the paper's editor at the time, Richard Doyle, recalls, the decision to abandon Pearson was not an easy one. For over a year Diefenbaker had been attacked from within his own party but had somehow withstood the assault. The *Globe* was impressed with his resilience early in the campaign. He was the Dief of old. Finally, with less than ten days to go, Doyle penned a long editorial, entitled "The Instruments of Power," critical of Pearson's secret dealings with Quebec and his govern-ment's scandals and deficiencies. "The philosophy of the Liberal is very simple," wrote Doyle, "say anything, think anything, or what is better, do not think at all but put us in power because it is us who govern you best." When Doyle had weighed all the positive and negative factors, he found that

Diefenbaker and the Conservatives did not look as bad as they had in 1963.[77]

The Liberal strategy was to ignore Diefenbaker and sell Pearson as the prime minister who would continue to lead the country down the path of prosperity. This was the last Canadian election that would not be totally dominated by television (as an example, on election night Dick O'Hagan vetoed CBC's request to have Pearson wear an ear plug so that he could be interviewed by Norman DePoe and Knowlton Nash at the Toronto anchor desk). Still, with TV sets in the living rooms of more than 91 percent of Canadian homes, a great deal of time and money was spent filming Pearson and preparing him for his major appearances (air time on private TV stations alone cost the Liberals $292,369 – $86,000 more than was spent by the Conservatives and $206,000 more than was spent by the NDP). For the prime minister's benefit, substantial efforts were made to have an "easy, relaxed atmosphere" in the studio, while Bob Crone introduced some "movement" into the prime minister's usually unexciting monologues.[78]

But once again all the pre-election arrangements could not compensate for Pearson's personal weaknesses as a politician – a sixty-eight-year-old one at that. The campaign was a long, difficult, and agonizing one for him. Diefenbaker was stronger and more outspoken than anticipated, attacking the Liberals' appeal for a majority mandate as representing nothing but a desperate desire for power. Reporters were not impressed with either leader, although their sympathies lay with the Tory underdog. They condemned Diefenbaker for distorting facts and snickered at "poor old pooper Pearson," a nickname they gave the prime minister for being unable to exude any enthusiasm in front of the numerous small crowds he attracted.[79]

By 1965 it was an accepted political dictum that during a campaign, "next to the leader himself, the most important people involved are the reporters covering it," as a Conservative strategy paper put it.[80] Keeping journalists happy (with scotch if need be), catering to their every whim, and making sure they had time to file stories, had access to the candidate, and had something to write about each day were considered critical to electoral success. Yet reporters travelling with Pearson, while well taken care of, viewed with increasing cynicism the Liberals' attempt to produce another American-style campaign. Pearson had never been a great performer on the hustings, nor could he exploit the media in the way that Kennedy or even Diefenbaker had. And like St. Laurent in 1957, his age had begun to show.

In Toronto Dave McIntosh of the Canadian Press had heard Pearson tell local Liberals that if the majority was not won this time, another election would be held the following year. McIntosh wrote the story, and a radio station broadcast Pearson's taped remarks. When NDP leader Tommy Douglas learned of Pearson's apparent plans, he denounced them. All the while,

Pearson was on a plane headed to Vancouver. By the time he arrived, Douglas's critical comments were the latest news and the plane was met by reporters who wanted to know if Pearson had indeed promised another election should he not receive a majority. For some reason, he denied the statement that had already been aired. Quite quickly, radio stations were broadcasting the prime minister's original remarks together with his denial that he had ever said them. Dick O'Hagan was embarrassed and Pearson incensed. "The tape-recorder episode was a minor flash of an event during a long election campaign," Peter Newman observed. "But it was highly significant, because it helped reinforce the public image of Lester Pearson as a weak, forgetful man who didn't seem to know his own mind."[81]

When the ballots were counted, the Liberals had only two more seats than they had held previously. "Pearson Wins but Loses" was the way the *Montreal Gazette* described the results. Only the outcome in Quebec, where the Liberals' "Three Wise Men" – Jean Marchand, Gérard Pelletier, and Pierre Trudeau – were elected, suggested any promise for the future.

Quite quickly, the Pearson team dispersed. Walter Gordon, who had pushed hard for the election and had never been popular with the business community, was the designated sacrificial lamb. He resigned from the cabinet with his lifelong friendship with Pearson nearly ruined. Tom Kent moved out of the Prime Minister's Office to become the deputy minister of manpower and immigration. Keith Davey resigned as the party's national organizer and was appointed to the Senate, where he would fight a few more campaigns. Dick O'Hagan took over public relations duties at the Canadian embassy in Washington. Pearson himself only had a few years left in him before he too called it quits.

There was no denying that these men as well as others in the Liberal administration had done a remarkable job under often difficult circumstances. And their legislative legacy, including the Canada Pension Plan and medicare, was impressive. Where they failed, curiously, was in public relations. Despite the tremendous increase in the number of government information and press officers, the Liberals' message did not get through to the media or the people. Pearson's image in the public imagination remained as it had been since he assumed power in 1963 – a "good man in a wicked time."[82]

Canadians needed a vibrant new leader and journalists needed a hero they could respect. In 1968 both got more than they bargained for.

CHAPTER FOURTEEN

The "Crummy" Press

*I've been told hundreds of times I should have four or five
press people at the end of the afternoon having a drink
around this office. Quite frankly, at the end of the afternoon
when I finish my work, I'd rather go home and see my kids.*
Pierre Trudeau, 1977

In Pierre Trudeau's well-ordered and rational world, there was little room
for emotion or human failing. For those who worked for him he was a
difficult taskmaster, expecting excellence and near perfection. He demanded, says his former press assistant Patrick Gossage, "a level of articulation
not many of us were capable of meeting. I remember more than one memo
which was returned with the large notation scrawled across it – 'Not English
I Won't Read It.'" Trudeau's biographer George Radwanski wrote that "he
assumes that other minds function like his – and, indeed, have comparable
intelligence – and shuns any other approach as a failure to meet the standard
of acceptable human behavior."[1]

As a realist, however, Trudeau accepted the limitations of the day-to-
day workings of the Canadian government and had "no qualms about making decisions as prime minister which [fell] short of, or even appear[ed] to
contradict, some of his stated beliefs."[2] He rarely, if ever, admitted in public
to making a mistake and could explain away any inconsistency in his
actions with a dose of that famous Trudeau logic or merely with a shrug.
Yet when it came to the members of the media, he maintained different
standards.

Growing up and working in the Catholic Quebec of Maurice Duplessis,
the all-powerful Union Nationale "Chef," had made Trudeau highly suspicious of the press. From 1944 until his death in 1959, Duplessis controlled
every aspect of the province in an authoritarian manner not witnessed in
Canada before or since. Through a blatant patronage system, the Union
Nationale rewarded those who were loyal to the party. Quebec's towns and
cities learned quickly that funding for their churches, universities, schools,
and even the paving of roads was dependent on support for the Duplessis
regime on election day.

Smaller newspapers in rural areas as well as the Montreal and Quebec City dailies were especially vulnerable. Like a throwback to Macdonald's day, Duplessis awarded much-needed and lucrative printing and advertising contracts to those papers that toed the party line. To guarantee favourable editorials, he presented some Quebec journalists with generous gifts. The result was that during the 1950s the Union Nationale had the support of the majority of the province's English and French newspapers. (Notable exceptions were *Le Soleil*, a Liberal organ, and the independent *Le Devoir*.)[3]

While Trudeau was never an avid reader of newspapers, he saw in Duplessis's control of the press a tremendous danger to individual freedom; newspapers, he later wrote, were potential "instrument[s] of oppression." "I do feel that the press can exercise a tyranny," he argued in a 1977 interview, "and they are a power which like every other power has to be analyzed, studied, controlled, and criticized if necessary."[4] When he arrived in Ottawa after the 1965 election, he regarded the press, rather unfairly, as part of the political establishment he had been fighting since the days of the Asbestos Strike sixteen years earlier.

Influenced by such classical liberal thinkers as John Locke and John Stuart Mill, Trudeau believed that freedom of the press was based on a "free exchange of ideas among well-informed individuals." This had been borne out by his experience as a young writer with the Quebec magazine *Cité Libre,* the intellectual journal founded by his close friend Gérard Pelletier in the early 1950s. Each article published by the "Citélibristes" – as the young group of idealists associated with the magazine came to be known – underwent a rigorous editing process in which its ideas were challenged and revised.[5]

After his election as prime minister in 1968, Trudeau expected a similar high level of intellectual aptitude and professionalism in the Ottawa press gallery. Instead, in his opinion, he found a group of inferior journalists with limited knowledge about the events they covered, men and women who were more interested in his marital difficulties than in the constitutional and economic issues of the day. "He was always surprised at how ill-prepared so many members of the media were," says Tom Axworthy, his last principal secretary. "They would instantly ask questions about personality without really getting into the substance of issues." Near the end of his term, Trudeau would actually thank reporters for asking insightful questions at his press conferences.

Trudeau did not really understand the journalistic process. He failed to appreciate the time constraints of the job: the hours of research and analysis required to understand complex economic issues were simply unavailable to a reporter – the instant expert – who had to file a story by the end of the day or do a ninety-second television piece on short notice.[6] Nor did he see that asking of a lot of black-and-white questions was a necessary part of the game. "He wanted a seminar situation," recalls Peter Newman, "where he could explain things in a long-winded way. The interviews with him were useless. He'd go on and on and you would be enthralled, but reading it after you didn't know what the hell he was talking about."

Trudeau lumped media people into one monolithic group of "raving jackals," to use Patrick Gossage's term. He made little distinction between the lightweights and those like Bill Wilson of the *Montreal Star*, George Bain of the *Globe and Mail,* or Bruce Philips of CTV who knew what they were talking about. While he probably felt more comfortable with the small number of francophone reporters in the gallery – they, unlike English journalists, were unconcerned with his personal life – he was disdainful of their nationalist feelings and separatist sympathies.

On a personal level, there was absolutely nothing to link Trudeau with the members of the gallery, many of whom were caught up in their own self-importance. Unlike every other prime minister, Trudeau would not stroke journalists' egos, grant them the access they required, or cater to their needs. In early 1978, cajoled by his press handlers into an interview with Michel Roy and Lise Bissonnette of *Le Devoir*, he only frustrated them with "laid-back restatements" of his federalist position on Quebec. He would not even comply with a CBC request to thank or say good night to Barbara Frum following an interview on "The Journal." "Why should I say that?" he asked. "The interview is over."[7]

Having determined that the popularity of a prime minister in the gallery would decline over time no matter what he did, Trudeau decided that he would never grovel for its support. "I don't have much time for the press, in the sense that I don't curry their favour or try to be palsy-walsy with them or butter them up," he told Radwanski. "I know that some politicians think it's part of their job to be nice with the press ... I just don't have time to do it."[8] And though he scanned the front pages of the major dailies on the way to work each morning and read the stacks of clippings prepared by his office at his desk in the Commons, he was truly indifferent to what newspapers or television, which he rarely watched, had to say about him.

Typical of Trudeau, however, he expected much more than he gave. On one level he understood that it was the job of journalists to investigate and criticize his government's actions, while it was his task to create and execute public policy. Yet he believed that the media had some sort of undefined responsibility and duty to promote for the greater good of the country such controversial policies as bilingualism and wage and price controls.

That Trudeau refused to give journalists the respect they felt they deserved made life difficult for his various press secretaries and fostered a tense, often hostile, relationship between the prime minister and the media –

with many memorable moments. He could not or would not remember names, not even that of his biographer political columnist George Radwanski (during a lunch he continually referred to him as "Peter").[9] There were shoving matches in the parliamentary hallway scrums and luncheon meetings with prominent media barons that turned sour or deathly silent.

Jim Coutts recalls that at one such uncomfortable dinner with Beland Honderich, the "brooding" publisher of the *Toronto Star*, "Bee and Pierre did not have a lot to say to each other. Both were rather professorial and Trudeau did not hide the fact that he did not care what Honderich had to say." Keith Davey has a similar recollection of one of Trudeau's first meetings with the *Globe and Mail* editorial board. "It was fascinating," Davey says. "Trudeau sat quietly as one editorial writer put a long preamble to a question. Trudeau turned to the paper's editor, Richard Doyle, and asked, 'You don't let that person write editorials do you?' Everyone was stunned and the rest of the conversation was like walking around on eggs."[10]

For sheer entertainment, nothing compared with a December 1976 Japanese lunch at the Prince Hotel in Toronto. Dining with Trudeau were the city's press and TV moguls: from the *Globe,* Clark Davey and Norman Webster, then respectively editor and Queen's Park columnist; Douglas MacFarlane, the editorial director of the *Toronto Sun;* the *Toronto Star*'s editorial-page editor, David Crane, and his television columnist Dennis Braithwaite; political editor Fraser Kelly of CFTO; and radio personalities Bob Hesketh of CFRB and Charles Templeton of CKEY. When, between sake and sushi, Trudeau commented matter-of-factly on the poor press he was receiving, Templeton suggested he use the media for his own political purposes. "Why do you think you're here for lunch?" Trudeau caustically replied, a comment to which Dennis Braithwaite took great exception. With some choice expletives, he told the prime minister what he could do "with his goddamn sake." Later Braithwaite admitted, "Trudeau's cynicism and the sake both hit me at once. I swore, I yelled, I told the PM he was responsible for splitting the country, him and his bilingualism. It was disgraceful."[11]

Many of the problems between Trudeau and the media can be traced to his Catholic upbringing and introverted nature. He had come to Ottawa in 1965 with few contacts or friends outside of Gérard Pelletier and Jean Marchand and courted no new network of Ottawa insiders. Trudeau was never the kind of leader to sit at his desk with a Rolodex in one hand and the telephone in the other, making calls to keep in touch with his army of supporters. "He didn't have the personal skills ... to make people feel at ease," says Tom Axworthy. "He was a Catholic intellectual, a rather private thinking man. He could inspire people by his depth of vision [and] could attract people like a magnet, but he couldn't make them feel part of a team."[12] On occasion, Trudeau could be insensitive. John Turner's resignation as finance minister in 1975 might have been avoided had Trudeau not been so indifferent to his feelings, and despite his great political success, members of the Liberal Party did not consider Trudeau one of their own. The members of the media, then, never had a chance.

All his life Trudeau had been an outsider. He was born in Montreal in 1919 into the bilingual household of Charlie and Grace Trudeau, a family "that was prototypical of the new French-Canadian bourgeoisie" trying to make it in an Anglo-dominated world. His education at the Jesuit Collège Jean-de-Brébeuf had disciplined his mind and given him a sense of "French Canadian moral superiority" that he carried with him for many years. His father, an ambitious and flamboyant businessman, died in 1935 when Trudeau was still a teenager. But thanks to Charlie, money was never an issue; the Trudeaus were wealthy. Not only did Pierre Trudeau pursue economic and political studies at the world's best universities and travel extensively, but he was in his thirties before he held a full-time job. Still, as Christina McCall has pointed out, in those early years and after, Trudeau's "pursuits were rarely idle. He was strongly motivated in everything he did, apparently driven on by an intense need to prove himself superior and to find a role that would satisfy the messianic streak in his nature."[13]

Trudeau always put forth the maximum effort, utilizing his considerable talents and all the resources available to him in everything he did. He might have refused to engage in public debate with the members of the media, but as a practical politician he understood the value of communication. And Trudeau, says his long-time friend and political associate Marc Lalonde, "was a damn good communicator."

Like President John F. Kennedy, with whom he has so often been compared, Pierre Trudeau had a special charisma. As noted by Stephen Clarkson and Christina McCall in their biography of Trudeau, he possessed the right number of "Weberian" attributes: "an element of foreignness, some obvious imperfections of feature and character, elevated social station, a sexual mystique, a facility for dramatic self-presentation, an unusual style of living, and above all, an extraordinary calling or vocation and along with it, the fighting stance of the crusader preaching social change."[14]

Television, with its focus on personality, style, and showmanship, was the ideal medium for transmitting the charisma of Kennedy and Trudeau. Indeed, Trudeau was the first prime minister to manipulate the power of television to his own advantage; he was "the premier Canadian performer in the age of telepolitics," as Jeffrey Simpson put it. But whereas JFK was fascinated with TV's "inner mechanics," analyzing news broadcasts endlessly and befriending the most important television executives and reporters in

Washington, Trudeau had little time for watching television or for chumming around with the CBC's star journalists. As an academic, he was more interested in the communication theory advanced by his friend Marshall McLuhan. In a decade-long correspondence, the 1960s media guru offered strategic advice and identified Trudeau's domination of the small screen. "Your own image is a corporate mask, inclusive, requiring no private nuance whatever," McLuhan wrote near the end of the 1968 federal election campaign. "This is your 'cool' TV power. Iconic, sculptural. A mask 'puts on' an audience. At a masquerade we are not private persons."[15]

Kennedy and Trudeau did share one other common characteristic: both men were magnificent and natural actors, aware of TV's powerful intimacy. Though he was not always at ease in front of a camera, from the moment he entered the political arena Trudeau understood that television put him in a room with one person, not twenty million. And despite the numerous problems he encountered during his prime ministership, including the rise and fall of his personal popularity, he never lost the ability to connect with his TV viewers. Whatever the occasion, "he knew how to appear charming or firm, how to be witty or sincere, [and] how to seem humble or shy."[16]

Trudeau took his television appearances very seriously. He prepared extensively for lengthy interviews, like a lawyer priming for a difficult legal case. His press assistants at the PMO, including communications expert Gabor Apor, who was instrumental in shaping Trudeau's TV image in the early 1980s, paid attention to such things as make-up and camera angles, and Trudeau readily followed their professional advice. Not surprisingly, most television journalists remember him as a tough interview. "He had these laser eyes that went right through you," says Peter Mansbridge of the CBC. "Even if you felt prepared about a topic you would feel like an absolute asshole for asking whatever it was you asked. No one tripped him up." Luc Lavoie, formerly with TVA in Quebec, adds that "he could be very intimidating, but not rude. He was the best I have ever seen. In my studio, he would make me feel so small."

Trudeau left a legacy of dramatic and electrifying television moments. As justice minister in 1968, he brilliantly duelled with Quebec premier Daniel Johnson at the televised hearings of the federal-provincial conference, a performance that solidified his election as the man to succeed Lester Pearson as Liberal leader. In an interview with Patrick Watson a few days prior to the leadership convention in April of the same year, he came across as "a man of great substance, depth [and] compelling honesty." It was time for "new guys with new ideas," Trudeau declared. The Liberal delegates seized upon these words and anointed him their new king. During the election campaign that followed, noted Jeffrey Simpson, Trudeau "and the kinetic reaction he generated across Canada, created scenes of action and excitement that television craved." On June 24, the day before the vote, people across Canada were awed by the televised image of Trudeau bravely remaining in his seat during the Saint-Jean-Baptiste Day celebrations in Montreal, defying the separatist protesters. It was an "image of courage" that affirmed everything "apologists had said about Trudeau as a leader for today and tomorrow."[17]

Nothing, however, quite compared with the confrontation between Trudeau and CBC reporter Tim Ralfe at the outset of the FLQ Crisis of October 1970. No friend of Trudeau's, Ralfe (who later left the CBC to work for the Conservatives) had been assigned to elicit a comment from the prime minister. On the steps of the Parliament Buildings, he caught Trudeau as he left his car.

"Sir, what is it with all these men with guns around here?" asked Ralfe, noting the soldiers guarding the Hill.

"Haven't you noticed?" Trudeau sarcastically shot back.

"Yes, I've noticed them. I've wondered why you people decided to have them," said Ralfe.

"What's your worry?" the prime minister asked.

"I'm not worried but you seem to be," Ralfe retorted.

"If you're not worried, I'm not worried."

"I'm worried about living in a town that's full of people with guns running around."

"Why? Have they done anything to you? Have they pushed you around or anything?"

This verbal joust continued until Ralfe asked Trudeau how far he'd go in dealing with the terrorists.

"Just watch me!" replied Trudeau. "Well, there are a lot of bleeding hearts around who just don't like to see people with helmets and guns. All I can say is, go on and bleed, but it is more important to keep law and order in the society than to be worried about weak-kneed people."[18]

CBC executives were upset with Ralfe's attitude. Knowlton Nash recalled: "Peter Trueman, then running 'The National,' was furious at what he felt was Ralfe's defiance of 'every journalistic standard I had ever heard of' in his harangue of the Prime Minister."[19] Before it was aired, the interview was severely edited. But in any event, the entire exchange was reported and debated by the press and has since been included in every documentary on the FLQ Crisis. It was a brilliant moment in Canadian television history and, as Nash says, provided "a rare look at Trudeau's inner thinking."

Beyond the appeal of such powerful images, Trudeau was attracted to TV because it allowed him an opportunity to speak directly to the people, one on one, free of media interpretation. He and his officials never hesitated to ask the networks for air time; in fact, he made personal appeals to

Canadians on a regular basis. Whether he spoke about the FLQ, wage and price controls, budget cuts, the air traffic controllers' strike, or the constitution, Trudeau was usually a star performer. His dress was always impeccable and his language cool and crisp. "Laws are made and changed in this country by elected representatives," he declared in October 1970, "not by assassins and kidnappers." On this occasion his passionate appeal for support was approved by more than 85 percent of Canadians, including the majority of journalists. (Critics like Richard Gwyn were much tougher on Trudeau when he unveiled his wage and price control package five years later. Gwyn portrayed Trudeau's TV performance as "stiff and awkward." He flubbed his lines half a dozen times with a text that "limped between clichés" about the "need to cool the fires of inflation." It was "the image of a leader trying to convince himself.")[20]

Whatever problems Trudeau encountered during the next fourteen years, and there were many, none of his political opponents were able to match his charismatic presence or domination of television. As he and those around him realized that his future success hinged on controlling that image, the contest with the media over access to information and setting the political agenda became even more strained. Suddenly backroom operatives and political consultants were feeding reporters what they wanted to see in print and on TV. Not at all happy with this turn of events, the Ottawa press corps could only complain about the manipulation. But they found that neither Pierre Trudeau nor the public was listening.

Just as politicians had to adapt to the realities of television, so too did Canada's print journalists. For one thing, it was during the 1970s that newspapers reluctantly relinquished to television their hold on advertising revenues as well as their position as the chief conveyors of the news. In the face of rising salaries and escalating ink and newsprint costs, publishers could no longer count on exclusive rights to mass-media advertising dollars. For newspaper owners, who for many years had related their paper's existence to its bottom-line performance, this contest with television had serious ramifications: a reduction in press competition and a dramatic increase in the concentration of ownership.

In 1982 there were 117 dailies published in ninety-seven Canadian cities. Of these, 88 papers were in the hands of twelve publishing groups, with two syndicates, Thomson and Southam, controlling 50. In only six cities was there any real competition (St. John's, Quebec City, Montreal, Toronto, Calgary, and Edmonton). In August 1980 the controversial decisions made by owners Thomson and Southam to close down the *Ottawa Journal* and the *Winnipeg Tribune,* respectively, underlined how much economic expediency had taken over the newspaper business.[21]

Television appealed to advertisers for the simple reason that more and more Canadians were watching it as part of their daily routine. (The 1981 Royal Commission on Newspapers, chaired by Tom Kent, learned that "98 percent of households had at least one [television] set, and the average Canadian was viewing about 191 minutes of television every day.")[22] Moreover, whatever political information most people were exposed to, it was often via television and not their local newspapers. Various studies have indicated that anywhere from 40 to 70 percent of Canadians depend on television as their main source of news. (The same studies have also shown that television – "which conveys images more adeptly than it does ideas, and impressions more easily than facts" – has not done a very good job of informing the public about critical issues. Individuals who said they relied on television "scored poorly on both factual and conceptual information.")[23] Such statistics had a tremendous impact on politics and, more significantly, on how it was covered.

During the Trudeau era, election campaigns became events managed in a way that would attract the maximum amount of television exposure. Everything was geared towards the production of a ninety-second clip for the nightly newscast. Media consultants became mandatory members of the campaign team. No one summed up the situation better than Conservative leadership candidate Brian Mulroney in 1983: "Every night I want to be on [television] news. It's fine to shake the delegates' hands but you can't win them in five minutes. You've got to reinforce it." (Politicians also had to be more careful. When TV cameras were finally allowed to record proceedings in the House of Commons in October 1977, the daily Question Period took on greater significance. But Canadians were not impressed with what they saw: images of their elected representatives exhibiting appalling behaviour. Polls showed that the public's perception of politicians, a perception largely derived from television, was declining rapidly.)[24]

What did all of this mean for print reporters? Television had already encouraged members of the Ottawa gallery to be more confrontational; now it pushed them to dwell on the image of the leader. Pierre Trudeau, with his keen intellect and sometimes outrageously arrogant behaviour, was the perfect subject for their investigations. He was stereotyped as "the swinger of 1968, the philosopher king of 1972, the embattled campaigner of 1974, and the unpopular vacillating leader of 1978."[25]

Journalists took themselves very seriously during the 1970s, even if Trudeau did not. The Watergate scandal in the United States in 1973–74 glorified the image of reporters everywhere, legitimizing journalism as an attractive profession for the increasing number of baby boomers entering university and the job market. It also made journalists more suspicious and critical of the politicians they were writing about. The gallery's membership list swelled, and more press and TV reporters were covering events in Ottawa than ever before. In 1968, when Trudeau came to power, the gallery had nearly 140 members; by 1982, near the end of his reign, the membership stood at 240 (a large part of the increase was due to the expansion of television news).

But the gallery had lost its hard-nosed whisky-drinking image of the 1950s. In a 1979 article, journalist Marjorie Nichols offered this assessment: "These days Parliament Hill guards are never called to scrape an errant scribe off the doorstep at 4 in the morning; the gallery is mostly made-up of serious-minded young men and women who limit themselves to one martini and change into their pyjamas before 'The National' ... The gallery lacks the excitement of yesteryear. Desk drawers are as likely to contain a bottle of Clearasil as a bottle of Scotch."[26]

In fact, the average Ottawa journalist was a "thirty-something" WASP male who had spent two or three years in university and was underpaid at a salary of about $32,000 a year.[27] The turnover rate was very high. Of the 140 reporters who greeted Trudeau in 1968, only 30 remained to wish him farewell when he first resigned in 1979. From a politician's point of view this was unacceptable. As Marc Lalonde asks, "How were journalists to acquire the in-depth knowledge necessary for covering national issues when the gallery was like a revolving door?"

While television had relegated print reporters to the back of the bus on the campaign trail, it also heightened the public's awareness of the media in general. Newspaper writers and commentators still "defined the issues and helped set the attitudes and myths of [Ottawa], spelled out who was good, who [was] bad, what the key issues and areas were, and thus profoundly affected the attitudes of those men who commanded the national mass audience. Television, rather than making [journalists] weaker, had amplified their power."[28]

Most importantly, they believed this to be so. As the self-proclaimed representatives of the public, the members of the Ottawa media expected to have, indeed they believed they had the right to, access to Pierre Trudeau, the members of his cabinet, and the government bureaucracy. Other prime ministers had generally, although sometimes begrudgingly, granted this privilege. Trudeau did not.

The only question Robert Stanfield, then the new Conservative leader, recalls he had in the spring of 1968 was "How badly was Trudeau going to beat us?" In the aftermath of the bitter ousting of John Diefenbaker the year before, the Tories were in an organizational mess when Trudeau called an election soon after he won the Liberal leadership that April.

Despite Trudeau's age – forty-eight – many Canadians, including most members of the media, were swept away by his youthful, fun-loving style, his dress and demeanour, and his wit. He was clever, sharp, and sexy. He was Canada's Kennedy, a man with a vision for the future. After the many tedious years of John Diefenbaker and Lester Pearson, politicians of another older generation, Trudeau seemed "too good to be true, let alone be prime minister," observed Peter Desbarats in a March 1968 *Saturday Night* profile. "He glitters and sparkles and purrs like a new car in a dealer's showroom."

In December 1967, as justice minister, he established his reputation as a reformer with a revised divorce bill and several key amendments to the Criminal Code, liberalizing laws relating to abortion and homosexuality; it didn't matter that these reforms had been planned by Justice officials long before Trudeau's arrival. "The state has no place in the bedrooms of the nation," he told reporters. Stephen Clarkson and Christina McCall observed: "That this idea was borrowed from an editorial written by Martin O'Malley that week for *The Globe and Mail* went unnoticed. Delivered by a minister of the Crown wearing a leather coat and sporting a Caesar haircut, it had an electrifying effect on the public imagination."[29]

At the press conference in February 1968, when he announced his candidacy for Lester Pearson's job, the media were already enthralled. Not many of their members knew him very well, although before he came to Ottawa he was the academic expert in Montreal they could count on for a good quote. Other Liberal leadership candidates had held brief meetings with the press to announce their future plans, but not Trudeau. The hour-long question-and-answer session that CBC Radio carried live was extensively reported on in the *Globe* the next day. Leaning back in a black leather chair in the packed theatre, a relaxed Pierre Trudeau responded to journalists' questions with outspoken candour. To a question on why he chose to run, he declared: "If I try to assess what happened in the past two months, perhaps, I have a suspicion you people (the press) had a lot to do with it. If anybody's to blame I suppose it's you collectively. If there's anybody to thank, it's you collectively. To be quite frank, if I try to analyze it well, I think in the subconscious mind of the press I think it started out like a huge practical joke on the Liberal party. It seemed to me, reading the press in the early stages a couple of months ago, it seemed to me as though many of you were saying you know, 'we dare the Liberal party choose a guy like Trudeau.'"[30]

After his victory at the Ottawa Civic Centre on April 4, there was no stopping him or curbing the unrealistically high expectations of the journalists watching him. In their columns and TV reports they created the campaign phenomenon of 1968 known as "Trudeaumania" – a Beatles-like public adulation. True, Trudeau played the game devised by his strategists, led by Bill Lee. He waded into the crowds at shopping plazas, kissed any female in sight, and shook hands in the Kennedy style. He did back flips at the hotel swimming pool to entertain the press corps. The TV and photo images of this new political messiah were powerful indeed.

But in fact his speeches were rather dull, full of vague declarations about his hopes for a "Just Society" and "participatory democracy." "We are not promising things for everybody and we are not seeing great visions," he proclaimed. "We are trying to make the people of the country understand that if they are to be governed well they will have to participate in the governing; that there are no magic solutions ... We will have to invent new things and will have to find new markets and fight for them."[31]

Had Robert Stanfield or NDP leader Tommy Douglas made similar statements, journalists would have challenged them; Trudeau – arrogant and impatient – got away with it. He did not make any attempt to soften his public persona for the benefit of the public or the press. Over the many years that journalists ran after Trudeau, he remained the same man; it was only their perception of him that changed so dramatically.

Near the end of the campaign, some editorial writers and columnists were beginning to see the candidate more clearly. They wondered about his intransigent position on Quebec's special status and his sketchy and undefined policies. Still, most newspapers, except a few Tory holdouts like the *Toronto Telegram* and *Ottawa Journal*, were willing to give Trudeau a chance to prove himself. Their opinion really didn't matter. Most Canadians were paying more attention to the powerful images they saw on their television sets, and neither Robert Stanfield nor Tommy Douglas, politicians of an older generation, could compete with "Pierre de la Plaza," as journalists dubbed him. On June 25 Canadians gave Trudeau the majority he wanted.

The honeymoon was over quickly. At his first press conference held in late August, Trudeau displayed a cool disdain for journalists' questions about his government's affairs.[32] He hadn't approved of the way Ottawa reporters had infiltrated the Pearson cabinet, even though he himself had passed on justice department secrets to such journalists as Peter Newman. But the leak of confidential government information had turned into a flood, and Trudeau determined to turn off the tap.

Newman, one of the first journalists to interview Trudeau following the Liberal leadership convention, found him quite different than before. "As I set up my tape recorder, I said, 'Hey I'm really glad you won the leadership. Now you'll be able leak news to me from *all* the ministries.' 'Listen,' Trudeau shot back, his face suddenly hard as a death mask, 'the first cabinet leak you get, I'll have the RCMP tap your phone.'" Newman had only been making a "tension-relieving joke"; Trudeau's response showed how the acquisition of power had affected him.[33]

There was little room for the press in the rational model of government established by Trudeau and his elitist "Supergroup" (Marc Lalonde, Ivan Head, Jim Davey, Gordon Robertson, and Michael Pitfield) during his first term. They wanted control of the lines of communication to be in their hands, not in those of journalists. As Christina McCall observed, members of the press now lamented for the chummier Pearson years, when phone calls to ministers were returned and contacts in the civil service were willing to talk openly.[34]

In clamping down on cabinet leaks, Trudeau merely reaffirmed the inviolability of cabinet secrecy, a tradition that harked back to Macdonald, Laurier, Borden, and King. But he also bruised the collective ego of the gallery – a gallery that believed it had had some major part in getting him elected prime minister – by so easily dismissing its role. "The disturbing thing," wrote Dennis Braithwaite in the *Toronto Telegram*, "is [that] the PM should have this anti-press bias; for even if its manners are deplorable ... even if it is occasionally venal or ill-informed, the press remains the only acceptable agent of public information in a democratic society."[35]

Pierre Trudeau begged to differ. Leaks, no matter how small or insignificant, upset him. It was as if the press were undermining his authority as prime minister. In June 1970, when the report of the Le Dain Royal Commission on the Non-medical Use of Drugs was leaked to reporters, Trudeau called out the RCMP to investigate. A few months later, in the midst of the FLQ Crisis, Bill Wilson, the highly respected Ottawa bureau chief of the *Montreal Star*, found himself in hot water. During Trudeau's first years in office, Wilson had had a good relationship with the prime minister – "friendly and confrontational" is the way he remembers it. He had written favourably of the government's official languages policy and in general had supported Trudeau's egalitarian views. Though he was less impressed with the prime minister's economic platform, he was trusted by many members of the cabinet.

Soon after the kidnapping of British trade minister James Cross on October 5, 1970, Wilson wrote that a "source" had informed him that the full cabinet had discussed the possibility of censoring the Montreal media, particularly several private Montreal radio stations that had carried inflammatory and often inaccurate news reports about the crisis. But his informant had slightly misled him; it had been only a cabinet committee that had discussed "controlling" – not censoring – the city's media (a moot point, since censorship was permitted and later carried out under the War Measures Act, passed on October 16). An angry Trudeau denied the story and started calling in ministers known to be friends of Wilson's.

The prime minister never discovered which minister on the committee had talked to Wilson (to this day, Wilson will not reveal his source). Once

Wilson learned of Trudeau's investigations, he checked back with his informant and wrote another story correcting the details. Immediately afterward, Wilson met with Trudeau. "We had an interesting encounter," recalls Wilson. "Neither of us were angry and there were no raised voices. But he told me that he found it intolerable that anything discussed at a cabinet committee would appear in a newspaper immediately afterwards. And he disputed that control as they had discussed it was tantamount to censorship. He told me that if I ever found out again what had been discussed in cabinet, I would be wise not to let him know because he intended to do everything he could to cut me off from every ministerial source that I had. On that friendly note we parted."

Of course, Trudeau could not follow through with his threat, but he did make one change in Wilson's work schedule that persists to this day. Wilson had dined regularly with his cabinet friends at the Grill in the Chateau Laurier Hotel. After this episode no minister or bureaucrat wanted to be seen with him in public. From then on he was forced to deal with his sources on the telephone – only a small inconvenience, since he found that they now talked even more freely.

More aggravating than the information leak, from Trudeau's point of view, was the media's enduring fascination with and probing of his private life. In January 1969 he attended the Commonwealth Conference in London and by all accounts performed reasonably well in his debut trip outside the country as prime minister.* But it was Trudeau's dinner (and breakfast) with a lovely German blonde woman named Eva Rittinghausen that attracted most of the headlines. The free-wheeling British popular press were the first to track down Miss Rittinghausen, who gave them lots to write about, and Canadian reporters followed their tracks to her door.

One of the first reporters to speak with her was Val Sears of the *Toronto Star*. "It was a remarkable interview," he remembers. "I had never before met an international courtesan. I asked her what attracted Trudeau to her when he has so many women. She said, 'I think it is because I am, how do

---

* Peter Newman, who was covering the trip for the *Toronto Star*, somehow managed to walk through the security and into the meeting room where the Commonwealth prime ministers were gathering. Wearing a three-piece suit, Newman was mistaken for Trudeau. He happily recalls the episode as follows: "Harold Wilson [prime minister of England] came up to me saying we must vote against Cyprus. 'Oh by all means,' I said. I was getting away with it when Trudeau saw me and asked what the hell I was doing. I just shrugged. He had me out of there in two seconds. Mike Pearson would have thought this was funny, but Trudeau called the police."

you say, très sportif.'" Sears's lengthy interview appeared the next day in the *Star*, and other Canadian newspaper stories quickly followed. At a press conference held soon after, as Sears recalls, Trudeau, "went through the roof," admonishing the reporters' "crummy" behaviour. "I really don't see the role that the press has to play in my private affairs," he told them. "I don't think it's any of your damn business, frankly, what a person thinks about me and how we behave together." This outburst astonished journalists.[36]

At first glance, it does seem that Trudeau's privacy, in London and after, was invaded more than that of any earlier prime minister. But never before had a "swinger" occupied the country's highest office. Here was a wealthy bachelor who dated scores of beautiful women, including Barbra Streisand, who jetted all over the world, and who danced at New York's finest discos. He taunted reporters with suggestive comments about his night life and was then surprised when stories about his escapades made the English-language papers (most French reporters and their newspapers displayed only a mild interest in Trudeau's peccadilloes). On this point, like many others, as journalist Geoffrey Stevens says, Trudeau was "a fascinating study in contradiction. He was a man who claimed he treasured his privacy and was offended when it was intruded upon, but he was a man who flaunted it in public."

Trudeau was not a victim of the press. (In contrast to the U.S. press's treatment of President Richard Nixon and his family in the same period, for example, Trudeau seems to have escaped very lightly.) In fact, the members of the Ottawa gallery – many of whom believed that they, on behalf of the public, had a legitimate right to know what the prime minister was doing and with whom – were quite unintrusive when it came to Trudeau's private life. They did not follow him during his vacations or snoop on him and his guests while he was at home or at his country residence at Harrington Lake. At the same time, there was no denying that he was wonderful copy and that some stories were too good to pass up. Moreover, despite the media's self-righteous cry about their "right to know," they no doubt found it far easier to write about Trudeau's personality and the women he dated than about the economic index and the rate of inflation – and such entertaining tidbits no doubt sold more papers.

Trudeau's marriage in March 1971 added a new angle to the press's coverage of the prime minister's private life. His bride, Margaret Sinclair, was a flower child of the sixties and at twenty-two years old young enough to be his daughter (Margaret's mother, Kathleen, was in fact only forty-nine, two years younger than the groom). There had never been anyone quite like Margaret Trudeau at 24 Sussex.

While Marshall McLuhan proclaimed the prime minister's marriage to be a great media event, from the beginning Trudeau made it clear to journalists that his wife was off-limits. (The Trudeaus had three sons: Justin, born Christmas day, 1971; Sacha, Christmas day, 1973; and Micha, October 1975.) During their first overseas trip together, to Russia in May 1971, Trudeau's press secretary, Peter Roberts, informed the corps of reporters on board "that they were on no account" to speak with Margaret, a request that was generally adhered to then and for the next few years. She made her splashing debut on the political stage during the election campaign of 1974. The so-called Margaret factor was regarded by the media as having contributed to Trudeau's impressive victory. In her speeches, she portrayed her husband as "a loving human being"; she reinvigorated the perhaps fading image of the charismatic man Canadians had first elected in 1968; and she gave journalists something fresh to write about.[37]

As Margaret later related in the first of her two sensational books, *Beyond Reason* (1979), her marriage to Trudeau started to unravel soon after that campaign ended. She was admitted to a Montreal hospital for "severe emotional distress" and, much to Trudeau's displeasure, started talking to the media about her cloistered life at 24 Sussex. It was impossible for the members of the Ottawa gallery – the English-speaking ones at least – to turn a blind eye to the prime minister's marital problems or the often outrageous activities of his troubled wife. "A split appeared in the ground between us and it widened with each episode – episodes that every newspaper reporter who wrote about us was by now on the alert for," Margaret recalled. "What *will* Mrs. Trudeau come out with next? Everyone it seemed to me, was watching me, longing to find a good juicy story for the front page."[38]

Indeed, Margaret gave the press plenty to write about: "She burst into song at a formal dinner in Venezuela, appeared sans underwear in a see-through T-shirt in Cuba, [and] yelled 'Fuck you!' in front of a group of Japanese dignitaries in Tokyo who witnessed one of her increasingly heated disagreements with her husband."[39] On the return flight from Venezuela in early 1976, she decided to fraternize with the journalists at the back of the plane. They were already in a state of revelry, as she later recalled: "'Will you sing to us?' asked one of the reporters in a friendly manner. I hesitated. Then I thought it would seem standoffish to refuse so in a wavering voice I obliged. Meanwhile another man had handed me a bottle of good Cuban rum, and though I don't drink, I took a swig to play my part. That was my error. The papers next day were full of stories about my carousing with newsmen and swigging back booze straight from the bottle, and transcripts (they had, it turned out, switched a tape on) of my song circulated around Ottawa for weeks. I felt shattered, totally betrayed."[40] Later her famous and (by her account) highly overblown weekend with the Rolling Stones in Toronto in 1977 and her subsequent separation from Trudeau set off a media frenzy unlike anything Ottawa had ever seen.

"Topic A," as Dalton Camp dubbed the Trudeaus' marriage problems, became the chief subject of debate in the gallery, overshadowing political and economic stories. The mood was especially tense at the first press conference held following the Rolling Stones' private concert at the El Mocambo in Toronto. Brian Nelson of Standard Broadcast News, the first reporter to be recognized, boldly asked *the* question. "Mr. Prime Minister," he began in a strained voice, "your wife's travels over the last week have been given a great deal of public attention ... Do you feel that your privacy or that of your wife has been violated, and perhaps more important, when does the wife of the prime minister of Canada suddenly cross the line from private to public person?" Trudeau and his aides had expected questions about Margaret's antics, and in the ensuing discussion he remained composed. "I think that if she goes to a rock concert that is very celebrated she has to expect to be noticed and written about. I have no complaint on that," he said. "But I still believe that my wife's private life is her affair and mine. If it becomes public, it's fair reporting. If it is private I don't think it should be dealt with by innuendo."[41]

At the time, Patrick Gossage was infuriated with the media's gossipy coverage of the marriage break-up. "Is the state of the PM's marriage really the most important issue in the country today?" he asked after another press conference had been devoted to Margaret's activities. But on reflection thirteen years later, he does concede that many members of the gallery were "good about Margaret. There was much they did not print. Many were reluctantly assigned to the 'Margaret beat' and felt demeaned by it." On one occasion, Margaret showed up at the National Press Club for drinks with, among others, her friend Claude Henault of the *Montreal Gazette*. When Trudeau came to fetch her, she told the bartender to "give the man a soda pop – that's about his speed."[42] This incident went unreported, as did stories about Margaret smoking marijuana (which she confirmed in *Beyond Reason*) in front of the Mounties at 24 Sussex Drive. According to Gossage, she revealed to Henault many other private and crude tales about her marriage, but he opted not to write about them.

By her actions and public confessions (for example, her infamous 1979 *Playgirl* interview and her book *Beyond Reason*), Margaret was her own worst enemy. The media, however, collectively failed by too often portraying her as the "prime minister's wife" rather than the immature twenty-seven-year-old mother of three she was. As is now clear, she was incapable of coping with the responsibilities of the position thrust upon her. Time and again, the media lost perspective. Beyond this, the saga of "Maggie and Pierre" established a precedent in Ottawa, forever changing the way Canadian journalists covered the private lives of prime ministers. As Joe

Clark, John Turner, Brian Mulroney, and their families would learn, anything and everything was now fair game.

In the immediate aftermath of the murder of Quebec labour minister Pierre Laporte in mid-October 1970, editorial writers who had questioned the imposition of the War Measures Act could not praise Pierre Trudeau enough. "Canadians can be thankful for the resolute leadership the prime minister is providing at this sad and difficult hour," declared the *Montreal Gazette* on October 19. "In the finest sense, the prime ministership of this country found itself in capable and sensitive hands at a moment of crisis," the *Montreal Star* added the following day. Columnists like Charles Lynch offered much of the same. "The sides of Mr. Trudeau that have been most in evidence in recent days," he wrote in the *Ottawa Citizen* on October 21, "are coolness, steadfastness and courage – he has met the professional terrorists eyeball to eyeball and stared them down." A majority of Canadians agreed, keeping Trudeau high in the opinion polls.

But by the time he called an election two years later, other issues had intervened. The Liberals' plan to fight inflation was not working, and the prime minister did not seem to care about the resulting rise in unemployment. The cabinet was divided on the question of foreign capital investment, and Trudeau failed to deliver a constitutional solution at Victoria in June 1971. What's more, he told strikers on Parliament Hill to "mangez de la merde" ("eat shit") and muttered "fuck off" (or "fuddle duddle," as he later claimed) in the House of Commons. In the view of political scientist James Eayrs, Trudeau was a "dilettante in power" who had failed to provide consistent leadership. Journalist Walter Stewart, in his diatribe *Shrug* (1971), painted a devastating picture of a "heartless, bloodless, [and] cold administration."[43]

During the 1972 campaign, Trudeau maintained the editorial support of such traditional Liberal newspapers as the *Montreal Star*, the *Ottawa Citizen*, and the *Winnipeg Free Press*, but lost the endorsement of the *Toronto Star*. After fifty years of fighting for the Grits, the *Star*, unhappy with the government's economic record, favoured the Conservatives for the first time. When the Liberals managed only a slim two-seat minority victory on October 30 (the Liberals won 109 seats, the Conservatives 107, the NDP 31, and the Social Credit 15), editors condemned Trudeau for hanging on to power, although it was his constitutional right to do so.[44]

In general, the reporters who covered the 1972 campaign came down hard on Trudeau as well. The glitz and glamour of 1968 had vanished. They rightly criticized the Liberals' inane slogan "The Land Is Strong" as well as Trudeau's reasoned academic approach. "We're really not fighting any other party," he declared. "The other parties can fight us if they want, but we're going to be talking to Canadians."

What further aggravated reporters travelling with Trudeau was his inaccessibility, a point of contention that would resurface to an even greater degree during the next three elections he contested and, in fact, in every Canadian campaign thereafter.* As Peter Desbarats recalled a decade later, in 1972 "journalists covering Pierre Trudeau still believed that they had a traditional right of reasonable access to a campaigning prime minister."[45] But the Liberal election team (led by MP Robert Andras, with help from Ivan Head and Jim Davey of the PMO), though it might have had its internal problems, did a good job of efficiently moving reporters from one locale to another and keeping them away from Trudeau.

"Mr. Trudeau rides at the front of the plane; his staff occupies a separate cabin behind; the more numerical press are aft," noted the *Globe and Mail*'s George Bain. "To see the Prime Minister it is necessary only for any reporter to nip quickly out the exit under the tail of the aircraft and run around to the front to watch him descending the ramp." When he did meet with reporters, it was on his terms. He preferred holding small, private, informal chats. This was a practice, lamented Bain, "about which many journalists have uneasy feelings because it introduces a grace-and-favour element into what ought to be a working relationship." Unable to get close to Trudeau, Charles Lynch, Hugh Winsor, and other members of the press corps resorted to criticizing the Liberals' "carefully orchestrated campaign" as if an efficient organization were one of the seven deadly sins.[46] Yet run a poor campaign full of gaffes, and critical media commentary is sure to follow.

The point these journalists missed was summed up by *Le Soleil* editor Marcel Pepin at a 1980 conference: "Politics is first and above all the art of winning. Contrary to what many people think, including newsmen, it is not the art of communicating with or through the press."[47] Cater to the press,

---

* Lack of access to Trudeau was nothing new by this point. As Christina McCall noted in a *Maclean's* article on Trudeau's trip to Russia in May 1971: "Since he took office, Trudeau has attempted rigorously to curb press activities, but his means of achieving news control on this Russian journey were ingenious in the extreme. He, or more particularly his aides in collaboration with the Russian press office, managed to turn the forty-person press corps into two busloads of croaking tourists who caught glimpses of the official party only on occasion … The press was housed in different quarters from the official party, transported in different airplanes as the group junketted around the country, and kept away from official talks and social functions." (Quoted in Stewart, *Shrug*, 210)

charm them, be their friend, and get them to write what you want, as Franklin Roosevelt and John Kennedy did, and they are forever grateful. But show indifference to their profession, don't be their best pal, don't feed them stories when it does not benefit you as a politician, like Lyndon Johnson, Richard Nixon, and Pierre Trudeau and you are charged with a heinous crime: news management.

Neither Trudeau nor his immediate prime ministerial predecessors were ever guilty of practising the kind of news management that, for example, was alleged to have been commonplace in the United States during the 1960s and 1970s – that is, they did not deliberately attempt to mislead or lie to the press. Even such a cynic as Walter Stewart conceded this. Trudeau was accused, however, of not treating all journalists the same when it came to granting interviews, of limiting access to himself, and of releasing reports and documents to suit his own agenda rather than to accommodate reporters with looming deadlines.[48]

It was the little things that really annoyed reporters. For instance, in August 1978 Trudeau unveiled some key economic proposals through what George Radwanski noted was a "strip-tease" series of late-evening announcements, so that any kind of analysis was impossible. In 1982, at budget time, the Liberals locked the journalists up with the proposed budget but in a small room that lacked a sufficient number of electrical outlets for their computer jacks. Of these crimes, Trudeau was guilty as charged, but so was every prime minister since John A. Macdonald. The game was to maintain power and thereby run the country. This meant that controlling the public agenda was crucial. Trudeau, like those before him, viewed this as a prime ministerial privilege that need not be shared with the unelected members of the media.

The return of Keith Davey and the arrival of Jim Coutts following the Liberals' near defeat in 1972 brought further charges of news manipulation. Despite being blamed for failing to deliver a majority to Lester Pearson, Senator Davey remained a popular Ontario Liberal organizer. Trudeau had never been comfortable with the partisan political style that had made Davey a legend (at least among Liberals), but he was astute enough to realize that his loss in the 1972 election was due in large part to his neglect of the party apparatus during the previous four years. Thanks to the deal he had made with the NDP, he was still in office, but that partnership had a limited life. After some protracted negotiations, Davey answered Trudeau's call in the spring of 1973 to become, along with Jean Marchand, co-chairman of the campaign committee for the next election. One of the first things Davey did was convince Trudeau to accept Jim Coutts as his chief election assistant – the person who would travel with him, liaise with the party, and deal with the media.[49]

In the books and articles written by journalists about the Trudeau era, Jim Coutts, the baby-faced lawyer with a Harvard MBA, has been consistently portrayed as the villain of the piece, a modern-day Machiavelli who was as ruthless and partisan as any ward boss operating out of Tammany Hall in New York City at the turn of the century. Coutts and Davey have gone down in the annals of Canadian politics as a dynamic duo – the greatest manipulators of all time.[50]

Coutts laughs off this depiction. "I don't think about it," he says, but adds, "In the story there have to be characters and a plot and we were part of the game." He had, in fact, from his earliest days been a bit of a political animal. Born in the small town of Nanton, Alberta, in 1938, he ran the federal election campaign of a local candidate when he was only fifteen years old. At the University of Alberta as an arts and law student, he was "the leading Liberal on campus" and faced off against another student, named Joe Clark, in the university's mock parliament. Coutts came to Ottawa in 1963 to work in Pearson's office but left for Harvard to further his education three years later. Around the time of Trudeaumania, he went into private business as a management consultant, but retained his contacts with the Liberal Party and just about everyone else in Ottawa whom he had so adeptly cultivated during his time there.[51] He dates the beginning of his nefarious reputation from the 1974 election campaign. In May of that year Trudeau had called an election after the NDP refused to support Finance Minister John Turner's budget.

Keith Davey, as he has conceded numerous times, was no political wizard. There was no plot in 1974 or later in 1979 and 1980, just a lot of common sense and hard work. (At a conference on the media and politics, Davey had this to say about the 1980 election that saw Trudeau's triumphant return after his defeat in 1979: "Ladies and gentlemen, if there was a plot, I wasn't part of it and if there had been a plot I think I would have been part of it. None of us are as clever as the plot theorists would suggest.") Davey had been working hard for over a year putting together an efficient team. He had recruited Martin Goldfarb to be his chief pollster and Dorothy Petrie, soon to be his wife, to manage the Ontario campaign. With Liberal lawyer Jerry Grafstein, he set up his own advertising agency, Red Leaf Communications, a consortium staffed by the best admen he could find, to sell the Liberals' platform. More importantly, he reminded Trudeau that politicking was still about people; he would first have to attract supporters and then keep them loyal. Though there were problems – a meeting Davey arranged for Trudeau with the editors of the *Toronto Star* backfired, for example – Davey recalls that Trudeau was "absolutely the best person to work with."[52]

The chief issues in the campaign were the perception that the Liberals were unable to deal with inflation and Trudeau's unpopular image as an insensitive leader. The reselling of Pierre Trudeau was made easier by the decision of the Conservatives to advocate wage and price controls as their solution to inflation. It was, as former Tory leader Robert Stanfield now says, "a stupid issue for us to get into because we ended up having to defend it [when Trudeau, once elected, instituted the controls himself] rather than being able to attack the government." Media commentary pointed to the vagueness of the policy as presented by Stanfield, while Trudeau ridiculed the proposal with the most memorable line of the campaign: "Zap! You're frozen!"

Stanfield had never really felt comfortable in front of a TV camera; nor could he trade barbs with the media in a heated scrum the way Trudeau could. On a personal level, newspaper editors and their reporters might have liked Stanfield more than Trudeau (he was certainly more accessible), but in an age of image politics, he could not compete with the Liberal master.[53] And then there was the infamous football fumble photo.

In mid-campaign at a refuelling stop in North Bay, Ontario, Stanfield had playfully tossed a football around with some of the reporters. CP photographer Doug Ball snapped a series of pictures of the game, most of them capturing Stanfield catching or throwing the football, but the photo that ended up on the front page of nearly every newspaper in Canada showed the Conservative leader clumsily fumbling the ball. Though this picture (as well as one showing him dressed as an uncomfortable cowboy) was by no means the only factor in the election loss sustained by the Conservatives, it did suggest that Stanfield was an old fogey and a bit of a bumbler.[54]*

Pierre Trudeau, on the other hand, at Keith Davey's behest, had adopted a more relaxed but "concerned, hard-working, and businesslike" persona. Accompanied by his young and beautiful wife, he provided the media with many dramatic images – whether he was flipping successfully on a trampoline, rescuing a helpless bird from a swimming pool, or boarding a train for an old-fashioned whistle-stop tour across Quebec and the Maritimes,

---

*Stanfield was amazed when the picture ran. "I was simply astounded that it became a prominent issue," he says. "To make a fuss of a sixty-year-old man taking part in tossing a football and dropping it is nonsense. I was stupified that this would be considered significant." He also remembered that about a year later he was playing softball with members of the gallery. "I went along just in fun … I used to catch when I was a kid, so I caught and John Laschinger pitched. I nearly broke a finger because John throws a pretty heavy ball. But what amused me was the number of press photographers, and others, hovering around taking pictures, trying to be another Doug Ball. And the number of pictures that got in the papers of me dropping a ball, or showing some tension when one of Laschinger's balls was coming in. How silly can grown men be?" (Reader's Digest Foundation of Canada, *Politics and the Media* [1981], 120–21)

reporters travelling with him were never at a loss for either photos or colourful copy.[55]

At first, journalists, many of whom had decided not to let their personal feelings about Trudeau interfere with their work, enjoyed the stunts and the prime minister's friendly style. But about halfway into the two-month campaign, they began to feel manipulated – and for good reason. Trudeau was still highly inaccessible. During his four-day train trip through eastern Canada, for example, he held only one twenty-minute press conference in a small and crowded parlour car and answered six questions (one of which was, "How do you like riding on a campaign train?"). He avoided radio call-in shows and consented to few television interviews. He unveiled a series of complex economic and social policies, but before the media could digest one proposal, there was another one to consider. The critical analytical commentaries that would be published a few days later were eclipsed by the latest announcement.[56] Journalists were up in arms. "Seldom has any Canadian political leader so fully evaded critical examination of his election proposals in the media and relied so much on the stage-managed announcement, the organized meeting, and the few words here and there at campaign stops," declared the *Toronto Star* in an editorial of June 25. "The boys on the bus are being used," cried columnist Richard Gwyn.

What exactly were Davey and his team guilty of? Academics and journalists have since accused the Liberals of devising one of the finest strategies for managing the media ever implemented. What they really did, however, was maintain control of the agenda. The Liberals gave "the press what it wanted, but in such a way as to get its message to the public with the greatest frequency and the least distortion possible."[57] Remembers Jim Coutts, "We decided that publishing a party platform in booklet form with 180 points is worth maybe fifteen minutes of attention from the media. It made more sense to bring it out in timely fashion and put it forward in such a way as to get the maximum amount of attention. The key was to do it on your time frame, not the media's. Halfway through the campaign we became diabolical for inventing this."

Keeping Trudeau away from media scrutiny made sense. Spared this ordeal, he did not lose his temper as he had so often done in 1972; nor did his negative feelings about the press become an issue. In response to the manipulation charges, Keith Davey has maintained that "while the reporters had their job to do, we also had ours. Of course, we timed our campaign to maximize its political impact. That is what political campaigns are all about!"[58]

More to the point, their strategy worked beautifully. Trudeau may not have received the endorsement of very many editors or reporters, but in the end he projected a very favourable image on both the front page and the television screen. For example, between May 4 and election day, July 8, Trudeau was on the front page of the *Globe* twenty-one times compared to nine times for Stanfield. Of the nineteen news items about the Liberal campaign carried on the *Globe*'s front page, only four were negative.[59] The truth was that journalists were the victims of their own system, which perpetuated extensive coverage of the leaders and encouraged a herd mentality – a common mind-set that ensured the same stories would be written and commented on in the same way.[60] From Davey's perspective, this made feeding the media the stories he wanted covered all the easier. The desired effect was achieved. On July 8, 1974, owing in large part to the Liberals' control of the campaign, Trudeau regained his majority government.

Back in power Trudeau continued to do things his own way, unconcerned about the negative publicity his actions generated. At the urging of the RCMP, he spent more than $80,000 on an armoured, silver-grey Cadillac complete with bullet-proof glass; he appointed his good friend Michael Pitfield to the powerful position of clerk of the Privy Council; and he arranged for a $200,000 swimming pool to be installed at the prime minister's residence. In January 1975 he told Canadians that the new year was going to be tough economically.[61] Eight months later, in a great reversal, he made a televised announcement that his government was imposing wage and price controls – the very action he had ridiculed the Conservatives for proposing fourteen months earlier. Even if they generally supported the initiative, political commentators derived great satisfaction in pointing out this significant change in Liberal policy.

Jim Coutts was now at the helm of the Prime Minister's Office. He had accepted Trudeau's invitation in August 1975 (urged by Davey) to serve as his new principal secretary. Coutts remoulded the PMO, making it more efficient and centralized. Yet, because he was much more politically partisan than any of his predecessors, he soon became unpopular with the Liberal caucus, the bureaucracy, and the media. Among the changes he and Davey brought about was the return of Richard O'Hagan, Lester Pearson's talented press secretary, from his hiatus at the Canadian embassy in Washington to take charge of the public relations for the Anti-Inflation Board. It was supposed to be a temporary move, but by early 1976 O'Hagan agreed to a permanent position as Trudeau's communications adviser at an annual salary of $40,000.[62]

O'Hagan's mandate was to devise some workable plan to improve Trudeau's deteriorating media relations. It was a tough assignment. The prime minister's popularity in the public opinion polls was dropping and journalists were leading the attack. "Day after day," wrote Christina McCall, "the editorial writers, columnists, and news commentators were bitterly and tellingly critical, the news reports on radio and television were doom-laden, the headlines in the newspapers unfavourable."[63]

By March 1976 even the French press in Quebec, which had stood by Trudeau through thick and thin, had turned against him. His refusal to contribute federal funds towards the $900-million Montreal Olympics deficit, his threats to patriate the constitution with or without the support of the provinces, his poor handling of the economy, his view that the Quebec media were largely separatist, and his insulting *joual* characterization of Quebec premier Robert Bourassa as a would-be populist leader "who, I hear, eats only hot dogs," all cost him dearly in such widely read papers as *La Presse.*[64]

For O'Hagan, one of the first orders of business was dealing with the parliamentary hallway scrums that had turned into hostile shoving matches. "We had to obviate the scrums," he says. "They brought out the worst in Trudeau and were a mutual provocation. We had to do something about it. The risk was that he would withdraw and become less effective in his public communication. We needed to institute some means to recover the public initiative." What he and the PMO press office – manned by Jean Charpentier and his assistants, Patrick Gossage and Ralph Coleman – came up with were weekly press conferences. It was the same ploy O'Hagan had tried with Mike Pearson back in 1965.

Not surprisingly, the members of the gallery considered O'Hagan's request that they limit their contact with Trudeau to these weekly conferences nothing less than a threat to the freedom of the press. But after the prime minister refused to answer their queries, except on Thursday afternoons, they had no choice but to accept the new situation. On the other hand, from the PMO's perspective, these conferences initially served two purposes. First, they gave the media access to Trudeau on conditions he could live with, making his inaccessibility a non-issue; and second, the conferences provided a showcase for Liberal policy, becoming media news events that were highlighted on the CBC "National News" and commented on in the next morning's *Globe and Mail*. Best of all, it didn't matter what Trudeau had to say, the reporters had to cover the conferences regardless.[65]

In time Trudeau tired of the weekly inquisitions, especially when the majority of questions began to focus around his marriage troubles. He skipped the conferences frequently. They did nothing to improve his relations with the press; instead, the personal resentment on both sides increased. Trudeau could be very cutting, and reporters who rose with a question never knew if they were going to get "a thoughtful response or an ego-crushing one-liner." His patience was extremely limited, and he regularly snapped "non-answers" at reporters or lectured them about how irresponsible they were.[66]

Consider this exchange between Trudeau and one reporter from a press conference held in November, 1978:

"What are some of the yardsticks that you personally use about your own performance as a prime minister as you assess yourself from month to month to decide how much longer you ought to continue in that office?" the reporter asked.

"Well, if you tell me the yardsticks you are using, I will tell you whether I share them. What yardsticks are you using?" Trudeau responded.

"Sir, you are the prime minister."

"You are asking if I share your yardsticks in assessing my future."

"No your yardsticks."

"I cannot answer until I know what your yardsticks are."[67]

Such confrontations obviously left most reporters feeling frustrated and angry.

The conferences had first been convened, starting in December 1976, at the theatre in the National Press Building and had been chaired by the gallery executive itself. But in November 1978, in an attempt to exercise greater control over the prime minister's meetings with journalists, O'Hagan moved the weekly gatherings down Wellington Street to the Canada Conference Centre. Now the conferences were chaired by Trudeau's press secretary Jean Charpentier, who decided which reporters could ask questions.

O'Hagan was also unhappy with the "wooden, remote and professorial" image of Trudeau "sitting behind the desk in the [Press Building's] Theatre, with a flag behind him and glass of Perrier Water (with a slice of lemon) at his right hand." At the Conference Centre he could stand in his "thumbs-in-the-belt gunslinger" pose. For O'Hagan, the image was perfect, but for journalists like Geoffrey Stevens of the *Globe*, the image served little purpose. In their view, Trudeau's press conferences had outlived their usefulness.[68]

In the two years leading up to the election of May 1979, O'Hagan tried every ploy he could think of to boost Trudeau's public image and improve his popularity with the media. The prime minister, he now admits, was "not always enthusiastic." O'Hagan was instrumental in convincing Trudeau to agree to journalist George Radwanski's request for several in-depth interviews; these led to a positive, though not uncritical, 1978 biography. "He has governed intelligently in a difficult time," Radwanski concluded, "and his record thus far makes him not a failed prime minister but an unfulfilled one."[69]

Luncheon meetings were arranged for Trudeau with Toronto press and television executives, but, O'Hagan says, they were usually unproductive. Trudeau was terrible at small talk and did not enjoy "good old boy" Anglo-Saxon humour. To show a side of the prime minister rarely seen by the public – the father and family man – O'Hagan encouraged Trudeau to take his sons on a train trip through western Canada, and he set up a CTV interview at Trudeau's home with his boys present.[70] These and other attempts at promotion usually fell flat. Trudeau's occasional outbursts did not help either. At a gathering of 800 Ontario Liberals in Toronto in late November 1978, he referred to the media in his speech as his "enemies," setting off a wave of columns about his Richard Nixon–like tendencies.

The mood in the gallery as the 1979 election loomed was not promising for Trudeau, nor did he seem to care. With his marriage falling apart, his government losing one minister after another, the federal deficit out of control, charges of corruption and scandal in every corner of Ottawa, Trudeau needed all the help he could get.[71] Rather than court the press, however, he alienated many journalists, ensuring that their personal feelings towards him would affect their judgment in the coming campaign. This was, Radwanski pointed out, "a course that is foolishly self-damaging for a practicing politician ... In the best of all possible worlds, the media coverage should not be affected by how graciously or roughly the prime minister treats journalists, but it does not work that way in real life. Whether it be due to an insufficient level of professionalism or to an inescapable human nature, the tone of media coverage Trudeau has received over the past decade has closely mirrored the ups and downs of his relationship with the working press."[72]

Inevitably, these negative feelings were passed on to the voters, who did not need much convincing that Trudeau's time was up. Indeed, when it came to Pierre Trudeau's media relations and public image in 1979, only one factor worked in the prime minister's favour, and that was that Joe Clark's were worse.

CHAPTER FIFTEEN

Judgmental Journalism

*The normal journalistic reaction is not to praise but to crit-
icize. There is a tacit understanding among journalists that
to write favourably about events or people is, if not per-
verse, at least gutless and certain to harm one's career.
Criticism, charges and accusations produce the most jolts
on television news and the biggest headlines in the papers.*

Clive Cocking, *Following the Leaders*, 1980

The rules of the politics-media game were altered for good during the
late seventies and early eighties. Influenced by American investigative
reporting techniques and hardened by a decade of dealing with Pierre
Trudeau, the younger generation of journalists in the press gallery were
forced to distance themselves more than they wished from the politicians
they covered.[1] No longer were private conversations between politicians and
journalists off the record; no longer were prime ministers and reporters
drinking buddies. Because it was Trudeau who, by his neglect of the gallery,
had defined this new relationship, only he survived these years in style and
unscathed. The same could not be said of the three other prime ministers of
this era: Joe Clark, John Turner, and Brian Mulroney.

It seemed like a great idea at the time, or so Douglas Roche, the Edmonton
MP and Tory foreign affairs critic thought. With the approach of an election
the Conservatives were destined to win, a quick trip around the world was
exactly what was required to establish Joe Clark's credentials as a masterful
statesman. Thus the plans were made in late December 1978 for the infamous twelve-day, 35,000-kilometre journey to Japan, India, Israel, and
Jordan that in all likelihood cost Clark his majority government on May 22,
1979.

Owing to the Conservatives' high standing in the polls, media interest
in Clark's tour of Asia, set to begin in the first week of January, was high,
too high in the view of Bill Neville, the Tory leader's chief of staff. "I didn't
think we were going to get the kind of media entourage we got," he recalls.

"I wasn't out there selling trips and I wasn't looking for twenty journalists to go with us. When I saw who was coming, I was worried right off the bat." In fact, fourteen journalists – eight from television – boarded the plane. And the six print reporters were an influential group: Jeffrey Simpson, then the *Globe*'s chief parliamentary bureau writer; Don Sellar of Southam; Doug Small of Canadian Press; Bob Lewis of *Maclean's;* Steve Handelman of the *Toronto Star;* and representing the *Vancouver Sun,* the witty and acerbic Allan Fotheringham, then the dean of Canadian pundits.[2] If they were look-ing to cut the prime minister-in-waiting down to size, here was the perfect opportunity.

Neville and other Tory officials scheduled the trip much too tightly. With no government jet at the disposal of the leader of the opposition, flights were arranged on various commercial airlines, including a gruelling fourteen-hour jaunt from Japan to India that depended on a one-hour plane change in Bangkok to Egypt Air (dubbed "Terror Air" by nervous journal-ists). It was an impossible connection. The Clark group, with the cranky and tired journalists in tow, barely made it, and their legendary luggage did not catch up with them until the next day.

By the end of the first week, the media were showing no mercy to Clark. Shut out of the Conservative leader's private meetings with prime ministers and kings, reporters had "only one thing to concentrate on – a search for the next Clark gaffe," wrote Fotheringham. Every blunder, every awkward gesture, every convoluted statement Clark made was played up in reports filed back to Canada. Asked to comment in Japan about the situation in Cambodia, he told the journalists that he "wouldn't want to be wrongly nuanced"; in India he inquired of a peasant, "What is the totality of your land?" and asked the age of a farmer's chickens; in Israel he pointed out that "Jerusalem is a very holy city."[3]

Headline writers and columnists in Canada had a field day – "Translation Hampers Clark in Japan"; "Globe-Trotting Clark Caught with-out His Pants; and "Around the World in 80 Gaffes." "From the press cover-age of his round-the-world trip," noted the *Globe*'s Geoffrey Stevens, "one gleans the impression that if Joe Clark were to form a government, it wouldn't be able to cross the street without the assistance of a seeing-eye dog, a troop of Boy Scouts and a first-aid brigade from St. John Ambulance."[4] Embarrassed Tories everywhere ran to hide.

Was the coverage fair to Clark? In their 1986 analysis of the Canadian media, Mary Anne Comber and Robert S. Mayne regarded the stories on Clark's 1979 tour "as one of the most destructive episodes of political reporting undertaken by Canadian journalists."[5] They pointed in particular to the articles on the "lost" luggage that was never actually lost, but delayed, as glaring examples of frivolous and unfair journalism. This sentiment is echoed by Bill Neville. When the luggage did not turn up in New Delhi, Conservative strategists and Canadian embassy officials tried to help. "It was the ultimate injustice," says Neville, still bitter a decade later. "We bust our ass delivering shaving supplies and other things to this media group who were with us for which they turn around and savage us."

Faced later with these charges, Allan Fotheringham, the leader of the pack, declared his innocence. "I didn't kill Joe Clark," he said in a 1985 interview, "Joe Clark committed suicide." Fotheringham maintained that he was telling it like it was. "Watching [Clark] at close hand," he wrote, "I saw a man who not only had no knowledge of history, art, culture, theatre or religion, but who had no *interest* in those areas ... What I saw was a one-dimensional man, uneasy and uninterested in the world outside the cosy political structure."[6] But that was not the point. Fotheringham took the easy way out, writing stories and columns of little substance instead of focusing on the Conservatives' foreign policy (his last piece on January 19 was a diary: "9:00 a.m. – Press party must rush to airport for 11 a.m. departure via Royal Jordanian airlines to New York and two optimistic changes later, Ottawa"). It was one thing to ridicule Clark's style, but was it fair to blame him for lost luggage, tight airline connections, and a smelly plane?[7] Did this make him unfit to be the next prime minister?

The most objective journalist on the trip was Jeffrey Simpson of the *Globe.* Not that he didn't play up the gaffes, but at least he put them in their proper context. The story he filed from New Delhi, for example, focused more on Canadian-Indian relations than on the "sour mood" among his media colleagues bemoaning their missing luggage. (Remarkably, as Richard Doyle relates in his memoirs, several *Globe* editors back in Toronto thought that "Sober Simpson" was not paying enough attention to the *real* story – Clark's blunders.)[8] Simpson, though, does believe that the trip was politically significant. "The tour said something about Clark's unpreparedness to be the prime minister," he now says. "That was the important part of the tour. The travel plans and awkwardness were not the issue. He did not have a grasp of the issues that he should have."

More than anything else, the image of Joe Clark as unprepared for the prime minister's job hurt his political career and nearly killed his quest for power. He was the Rodney Dangerfield of Canadian politics: no one gave him any respect. The irreverent "Joe Who?" headline that ran in bold print across the *Toronto Star* the day after he won the Conservative leadership on February 22, 1976, had been difficult, if not impossible, to shake. He was the Tories' second choice, a fact of political life he often joked about.

For many members of the parliamentary press gallery it was difficult to take the new, thirty-six-year-old Conservative leader seriously. As Dalton

Camp put it, Clark "was of their own age and too much one of them: they shared with Clark a common history, a life's experience as brief and unremarkable as their own." More significantly, Clark was forced to deal with the Trudeau myth, which defined the qualities the media and public expected of a prime minister. But Clark could not match Trudeau's sexy style, nor did he try. Lacking charisma, the Tory leader was, wrote Camp, a "hard man to find in a crowd." He looked "uncomfortable with his own body," observed Jeffrey Simpson. "He carried himself awkwardly, his arms pendulating in unnaturally long swings ... Clark had long, bony fingers, and his most instinctive mannerism – thrusting his left hand forward with fingers outstretched but slightly crooked – make the hand look like a chicken's foot scratching aimlessly at the air."[9] In short, he was an ordinary guy; in comparison to Trudeau, however, he looked like the wimp that journalists ridiculed.

Clark should have had an easier time of it. He had spent most of his life immersed in journalism and politics. His grandfather, Charles Clark, had established the weekly *High River Times* in the small town forty-eight kilometres south of Calgary where Joe was born in 1939. Not a great athlete, Clark found politics a good hobby. He worked as a reporter on the University of Alberta paper the *Gateway* and spent summers working for the *Edmonton Journal.* He dreamed of becoming the editor of a "truly Canadian national paper."[10]

Clark graduated in 1961 with a degree in history. He tried law school at Dalhousie but found it boring. He tried it again at the University of British Columbia, with the same results. But in Vancouver he spent much of his time working for Davie Fulton, then the provincial Conservative leader. He underwent his real initiation into the rough world of politics from 1962 to 1965, as the national president of the Progressive Conservative Students' Federation. Clark witnessed first-hand the deep divisions within the party caused by John Diefenbaker's leadership problems.

In 1967, when he was just twenty-seven, he took his first stab at politics, running in a provincial election in Alberta and losing by only 462 votes to the Social Credit candidate. He worked for a brief time alongside his close friend Lowell Murray in Robert Stanfield's office in Ottawa, but he was much too ambitious to remain in the background. In 1972 he won a federal seat in Alberta and quickly earned a reputation as a highly partisan and aggressive MP. Four years later he played both sides of the Conservative Party against the middle to capture the leadership.[11]

Politically, Clark was in a reasonable position in the spring of 1976. He had hired the well-connected Bill Neville, a successful lobbyist and a former journalist, as his chief of staff. A workaholic who smoked too much, Neville had earned his stripes during the sixties working for Liberal ministers Judy

LaMarsh, Paul Hellyer, and Edgar Benson. He switched party allegiances in 1968 after losing faith in Trudeau's policies. To show the Tories he meant business, he ran against John Turner in the 1974 general election, "one of the great kamikaze acts of all time," as he later called it. He lost by more than 10,000 votes. "That proved my loyalty, even if it did nothing for my intelligence," he said.[12]

In Clark's office, Neville was on top of everything. He was instrumental in shaping Clark's economic policies and preparing him for some tough media scrutiny. "From the beginning," he remembers, "the media reaction to Clark winning was the great 'Joe Who' line. That it was a fluke that this guy won." Neville's job was, he says, to put "some flesh" on Clark and "show the country what he stood for." In this task, he admits he failed. But he also blames Ottawa journalists for not being able to sell Clark's "community of communities" vision of small-town Canada. "Joe Clark is one of the most belief-driven politicians I know," Neville says. "But we were never able to convey his different view of the country because it wasn't given due consideration by many members of the media. Pierre Trudeau could have been for a 'community of communities' and it would have been a philosophy. 'Soft' guys, as Joe was perceived to be, are not allowed the luxury of conciliatory ideas." Yet even Neville admits that "community of communities" was never properly defined; it never conveyed more than Clark's desire to establish a better relationship with the provinces than had existed under Trudeau.[13]

Clark also had to work harder than Trudeau at managing the media. Whereas in press conferences the Liberal prime minister was clearly in control, Clark was nervous. Not that he didn't have a feel for the media; he knew, for instance, how to make the six o'clock news during an election campaign and one of his first press secretaries was Donald Doyle, a francophone and former parliamentary correspondent with *Le Soleil*. Clark genuinely wanted to establish an open relationship with the press. Equally he recognized that the critical bias in the media was usually against the political leader ahead in the polls, and in 1976 that was Clark.[14]

Instead of enunciating his policies and capturing the public's and the media's attention, Clark squandered away his first months as Conservative leader. According to Jeffrey Simpson, Clark travelled to Europe on an official trip that was anything but successful and "gave a series of bland speeches and interviews that left many voters wondering what all the fuss was about when Clark won the leadership convention."[15] Nevertheless, in October 1976 he was ahead of Trudeau in the polls, the first time the prime minister had trailed an opponent since 1968. This upward trend came to a halt a month later following the election of René Lévesque and the Parti Québécois. Canadians now looked to Trudeau, not Clark, to keep the country together.

Things got worse for the Tories before they got better. In 1977 the party lost five Quebec by-elections to the Liberals and a seat in Prince Edward Island it had held since 1957. This marked the start of the Conservative caucus's growing uneasiness with Clark, made evident by renegade MP Jack Horner's defection to the Liberals. Clark's media relations were less than amicable as well. After the by-election losses of May 24, Clark and his wife, Maureen McTeer, took a trip through British Columbia. Craig Oliver of CTV, travelling with the group, filed a critical report of Clark's "faltering" career. For that he received a tongue-lashing from McTeer that further aggravated an already tense situation.[16]

Clark's position improved slightly over the next twelve months as Canadians grew dissatisfied with the Liberals' economic management. Now watched over by both Neville and his old friend Lowell Murray, who was appointed Tory campaign chairman for the anticipated 1978 election, Clark started to look more like a potential prime minister. He adapted easily to the television cameras in the Commons, performing better than most of his colleagues and journalists had expected.[17]

The Liberals were on the ropes. They had lost ten of fifteen by-elections held in October 1978, and despite their best efforts to remould Trudeau, his public image remained arrogant and distant. An internal Conservative Party memo circulated in the summer of 1978 made this observation: "In short, the electorate perceived that the economy and the nation were in worse shape than ever before and that they were holding the Liberal government – and Trudeau, as the persona of that government – directly responsible."[18]

In light of all this, it is hard to comprehend the poor planning of Clark's round-the-world trip in January 1979, but easy to see why the ramifications were so disastrous. Allan Gregg's polls had told Murray and his team well in advance that Canadians still had "more questions" about Joe Clark's untested leadership abilities than they had about Trudeau.[19] Stories of incompetence overseas and lost luggage merely confirmed what many members of the public already believed about Clark: that he was weak intellectually and no match for Trudeau on the world stage. Worse, the trip seriously damaged Clark's shaky image with the media, whose members were gearing up for the coming electoral battle.

In the weeks after Clark returned from the Middle East, the gaffes continued. He announced that a Conservative government would stimulate the struggling Canadian economy by increasing the country's then $12-billion deficit "temporarily," a length of time publicly defined differently by Clark and his senior finance critic, Sinclair Stevens. Journalists were delighted to point out the conflicting interpretations. In early February, when asked about his party's response should Quebeckers choose sovereignty-association, Clark again clashed with a prominent member of his caucus, this time

David Crombie, a former mayor of Toronto. Crombie had stated that the Tories would negotiate for an independent Quebec if the need arose; Clark countered with the declaration that he basically would do nothing. Six weeks before Pierre Trudeau set the election date for May 22, 1979, the editors of the *Montreal Gazette* wondered about who was in charge of the Conservative Party and asked the poignant question: "Why should Canadians vote for whoever it is?"

In another era, the loss of editorial support would have been devastating for a government attempting to hold on to power. In 1979, however, the fact that nearly every Canadian newspaper, including the *Toronto Star* (which for the first time in its history supported the NDP), deserted the Liberals caused only a ripple, for even more than the preceding three federal election campaigns, the campaign of 1979 was truly a television event. "The party leaders," observes media expert Fred Fletcher, "crisscrossed the country speaking not so much to local audiences as to the television crews they brought with them." The campaign climaxed a week before the vote with a televised TV debate, "Encounter '79'" – "the ultimate media event."[20]

By now, print journalists had adapted to the new realities of their profession. Image, confrontation, and style were what counted, not editorial analyses of party policy. The election was treated as a horse race by both newspaper and TV reporters, who daily bombarded the public with a multitude of polling statistics but little explanation of sample sizes or a proper interpretation of the results.[21]

The media's power was heightened further in the spring of 1979 by the fact that both Trudeau and Clark were in difficult political positions. Cynicism about and critical judgments of the two leaders were more common than usual: the gallery's expectations of Joe Clark were so low that if he did not fall flat on his face, he was doing well; and journalists were determined not to allow Trudeau and his two strategists, Davey and Coutts, to manipulate them as in 1974. Seasoned reporters were assigned to both leaders with orders to write not only about policies but about tactics as well. In the words of one Ottawa TV producer, they saw themselves "as a kind of truth squad."[22]

Although the Liberals were portrayed as worn out and their leader as arrogant, Clark, owing to his wimpish image, could not capitalize on this decline in the government's popularity. The question which faced Canadians, as Val Sears explained in a *Toronto Star* article on April 14, was whether they "hated Pierre Trudeau enough to swallow Joe Clark." Believing it was their election to lose, Tory strategists Neville and Murray isolated Clark from the media horde travelling with him. After the fiasco of the world tour, who could blame them for adopting this no-access policy?

When Clark did appear, the reception accorded him was usually cold and critical. In early April he delivered a speech to the Quebec Chamber of Commerce in both English and French in an attempt to make some inroads in a province that had eluded the Tories since 1958. But according to the report of the meeting filed by Montreal columnist William Johnson, Clark "blew it" with a vague, statistic-laden speech about how he was going to save the economy.[23]

The Tories were determined not to be put on the defensive as they had been in 1974 over Robert Stanfield's commitment to wage and price controls. Yet in the end that was what happened. During the first month of the campaign, Clark made many expensive promises that returned to haunt him – none more damaging than a declaration that he would move the Canadian embassy in Israel from Tel Aviv to Jerusalem. Whatever honourable principles lay behind this controversial proposal, the media and public viewed it as a blatant attempt to buy Jewish votes in a few Toronto ridings. When asked by journalists about the cost of such other policies as the deduction of mortgage interest and property taxes, Clark replied vaguely that he did not have a "magic accountant" and "could not answer the question with 'specificity.'" Adding up the Conservatives' promises, the Liberals labelled Clark the "seven billion dollar man."[24]

Journalists also went after the Tory leader for snubbing the party's aging veteran John Diefenbaker, for giving speeches that lacked passion and emotion, and for his initial refusal to participate in a televised debate with Trudeau and NDP leader Ed Broadbent. Since the NDP had no realistic chance of forming the next government, Clark saw no reason to face off against Broadbent, but his reluctance only made him look like a coward. Neville and Murray had had enough. With about a month left in the campaign, the media's access was even more severely limited. There was to be no "football fumble" for Joe Clark.

At the same time, in small cities and towns across the country, Clark's weak image and negative media coverage actually started to work in his favour. "People are surprised when they see that I can connect a sentence and walk four steps without tripping," he explained after a speech in Regina. "And even more surprised, when they find I have some sense of economic policy and some sense of what makes the country work." It wasn't "Clarkamania," noted Charles Lynch after a visit by Clark to Timmins, Ontario, but the Conservative leader was "catching on." What's more, no matter how nasty the media were with Clark, he never fought back, accepting the critical commentary as part of his job.[25]

This was in sharp contrast to Pierre Trudeau in May 1979. In his gunslinger pose, thumbs in his belt loops, Trudeau had agreed to his handlers' plans for a more open campaign. Yet his bitterness over his marriage break-up and his too many years in power made him touchy and arrogant right from the start. In Quebec he declared that farmers were always complaining and told hecklers protesting unemployment in British Columbia to "get off their ass." While his confrontational style captured the headlines and the lead story on the TV news, the overall negative media assessment of Trudeau did not change. "If Clark was portrayed as weak, indecisive, and inexperienced," Fletcher noted, "Trudeau was presented as arrogant, bored, cynical and weary." Jim Coutts, who accompanied the prime minister throughout the campaign, did not help the Liberal cause or morale with his malicious Joe Clark jokes (Question: What do you do if Joe Clark throws a pin at you? Answer: Run, because he's got a grenade in his mouth). Journalists regarded him as devious, conniving, and a man not to be trusted.[26]

Any idea of maintaining a positive and open relationship with the media was soon forgotten. Remembered press assistant Patrick Gossage: "From a substantive, if not personal perspective we lost the press. We looked after them well; were the best. But given Trudeau's deeply held convictions about them and their role, and the actual content of the campaign, we couldn't hold them."[27] Coutts had invited Jeffrey Simpson, Mark Phillips of the CBC, and the *Toronto Star*'s Mary Janigan to dine with Trudeau aboard a flight from Ottawa to Winnipeg on April 23. Simpson opted not to attend, while Phillips and Janigan chose instead to have coffee with the prime minister. It was not made clear whether this was a private, off-the-record conversation or one that could be quoted. In any event, Trudeau probably did not care. In the interview, he speculated that should he lose his majority to the Conservatives by a few seats, he might be "inclined ... to put his policies to the test in the Commons."[28] While this was not an earth-shattering statement (Mackenzie King had done exactly this in 1925), its repercussions were considerable; it seems history and constitutional legalities have little place in campaign reporting. By the time the story was broadcast on the CBC and analyzed in the newspapers, Trudeau was accused, unjustly, of wanting to "cling to power." Here was a good example of the media's power to slant a story, thereby distorting the actual facts.

The campaign finale took place on Sunday evening, May 13, when the three leaders engaged in a televised debate watched by approximately 7.5 million Canadians. The only thing that mattered to the reporters covering the event was, not what was said, but who won the match. Though Clark held his own and Broadbent was competent, Trudeau excelled before the TV camera. Media assessments the next day declared the Liberal prime minister the victor. Trudeau was "sharp, perceptive, clear and precise," while Clark was "defensive, under pressure, nervous and short on specifics." "It was a debate," said novelist Mordecai Richler in a CTV interview, "between two men and a boy [Clark] with the most hollow laugh in the world."[29]

That Joe Clark narrowly managed to become the prime minister of Canada on May 22 was probably due more to the public's dissatisfaction with eleven years of Liberal rule than to anything else (the Conservatives won 136 seats, the Liberals 114, the NDP 26, and the Créditistes 6). The Liberal government had been guilty of mismanagement and of alienating members of its own party, the press, and the public. It would be difficult to argue with political scientist Stephen Clarkson's assessment that there was only one issue in this campaign – Pierre Trudeau.[30]

On the other side, the media's harsh treatment of Clark cost him a majority government. He could do nothing to counter the way the media portrayed him to Canadians – as a mild-mannered but ineffective bumbler. It would not be overstating the point to conclude that the Conservative leader, though guilty of numerous political errors, was an unwilling victim of judgmental journalism, in which strengths are overlooked and weaknesses played up.[31] And as the days ahead would show, Joe Clark's troubles with his media coverage were only beginning.

Charles Joseph Clark, at thirty-nine the youngest person ever to hold the office of prime minister, had an image problem – or rather, as pollster Allan Gregg put it, "no image at all." Despite his victory over Trudeau, Clark was regarded as a second-rate unknown. "It may not be an exaggeration to suggest," Gregg concluded in a report to the Conservative Party shortly after May 22, "that a national leader has rarely, if ever, assumed office with lower expectations concerning his ability to govern."[32]

Clark, however, brought to the prime ministership a refreshing attitude. He sincerely believed in an open and honest administration; he intended to be accessible to the media and to answer their never-ending questions. His regular Friday-morning press conferences were not always beneficial to him, but he refused to cancel them. Certainly, the gallery members appreciated the kindness and friendliness shown to them by Clark and his wife, Maureen McTeer; neither Pierre nor Margaret, for example, had ever served them coffee while they waited at Sussex Drive for an official dinner to end.

This, of course, did not stop journalists from being critical to the point of ruthlessness. The treatment Clark had received at the hands of the media during the 1979 campaign and earlier did not stop once he became prime minister. "No public man has ever been stalked as Clark has been," observed Dalton Camp. "Every waxed floor, curb, step, set of stairs or swinging doors on his route brings the suspense of myriad apprehensions ... Were he to drown in a bowl of soup tonight, all would mourn him but recall that he was never much of a swimmer."[33] Reporters jumped all over Clark's political gaffes and laughed behind his back. Within a few months, Clark was avoiding hallway scrums in the Langevin lobby.

Clark understood the mechanics of government and introduced several key reforms that the Liberals would later employ.[34] But he also wanted to keep the innumerable promises he had made during the campaign. Politically, this was not the wisest move. In fact, it was suicidal. At his very first press conference as prime minister, he foolishly announced his intention to move the Canadian embassy in Tel Aviv to Jerusalem. Unfortunately, he forgot to inform his external affairs minister, Flora MacDonald, about his plans. The Arab nations were upset, and journalists were soon writing stories tallying up the dollar and job total Canada stood to lose in foreign trade should Clark proceed. In response to the outcry, Clark appointed Robert Stanfield as a special Middle East envoy to study the issue further. Four months later, "Stanfield of Arabia," as he was dubbed by the press, urged the prime minister to cancel the planned relocation. Clark was forced to backtrack publicly, an act that seriously hurt his credibility.

At that same press conference, Clark also declared his intentions to go ahead with his promise to dismantle Petro-Canada, the government-owned oil company created by the Liberals. Polls indicated that only in Alberta was there real opposition to the crown corporation; in fact, most Canadians supported the government's foray into the oil business. Clark went ahead anyway, devising a restructuring plan that after much heated debate kept the control of Petro-Canada in the hands of the government. His administration looked "paradoxically stubborn and weak, and ultimately wrong."[35] Again media commentary was critical of this forced retreat.

It was the same story with Clark's constitutional policies. He declared that he was going to renew federalism his own way, gradually and peacefully. There was "no grand design for constitutional reform," he announced in the House – or was there? Two weeks earlier, Clark had quietly appointed Quebec senator Arthur Tremblay to produce a major constitutional report. Nothing upsets reporters more than politicians saying one thing in public and doing the opposite in private. When they found out about Tremblay's assignment in December, stories lambasted the prime minister for yet another flip-flop. And when he had to deal with the two most powerful Conservative premiers in the country, Bill Davis of Ontario and Peter Lougheed of Alberta, Clark looked like a junior minister fresh out of university.[36]

The final nail in the Tories' coffin was Finance Minister John Crosbie's controversial December 13 budget. Among other unpopular proposals, it included an eighteen-cents-per-gallon gasoline tax. Clark and Neville had miscalculated terribly. They did not believe that the Créditistes, who sharply disapproved of the fuel tax, would vote with the Liberals and the NDP to bring the government down. Nor did they believe that the Liberals, leaderless since November 21, when Trudeau had announced his intention to retire, wanted another election so soon. They were wrong. Joe Clark's world came crashing down on the evening of December 13 when his government's budget was defeated 139 to 133.

Pierre Trudeau had enjoyed a peaceful summer in 1979, travelling and canoeing. He had returned to Ottawa relaxed and sporting a grey beard. As opposition leader, he was nearly invisible, and journalists were busy writing his political obituary. "Pierre Trudeau will never again be prime minister," Richard Gwyn pontificated in the *Toronto Star* in mid-July. "He has no real future. He is an opposition leader on sufferance, occupying the post until some Liberal with better long-term prospects replaces him."[37]

Gwyn's predictions appeared accurate a few months later when Trudeau announced his retirement. Then every journalist and pundit in the land became an expert on Trudeau and his years in power. Much of the commentary was negative and confusing. After eleven years of dealing with Trudeau, editors were still not sure of who Trudeau really was; nor did they understand his true legacy. "He controlled the political system absolutely," said the *Globe*'s Geoffrey Stevens, "but he could not make it work." Editors at the *Ottawa Citizen* noted that "history will not be kind to Mr. Trudeau. Any enduring mark on either his party or the country remains strangely obscure." Douglas Fisher, no fan of Trudeau's, was more succinct: "[He had] deprived us of rising national confidence and feeling, and left us in constitutional and economic disarray." Such devoted Trudeau supporters as Tom Axworthy, Jim Coutts, and Keith Davey found these superficial media assessments galling.[38]

As soon as the Clark government fell, Coutts went to work to convince Trudeau to return for one last fight. Finally, after a week of negotiations, Trudeau stepped back into the arena. The challenge of battling his old nemesis Réne Lévesque in the coming Quebec referendum on sovereignty-association was too tempting to pass up. His announcement, on December 19, that he would return to politics was greeted with skepticism by the media, who were collectively saddened by Trudeau's last grasp for power. Perhaps the journalists were bothered by Trudeau's nonchalant statement that it was his "duty" to accept his party's draft even though he'd rather they chose a new leader. *Le Devoir* editor Michel Roy considered it a "bad decision," while the renegade *Toronto Sun* called it the "greatest flip-flop in Canadian political history."[39]

Nevertheless, this time around the real issue was not the return of Pierre Trudeau, but the seven-month, roller-coaster prime ministership of Joe Clark. The Conservatives tried to focus the campaign on the Liberals' decade of arrogant government, as they had in 1979, but the media kept the public's attention fixated on Clark's broken promises and political errors.[40] Because Clark wanted a second chance, he was forced to conduct a more open campaign than he would have liked, which meant he was even more at the mercy of the media than usual. Neither the journalists nor anyone else believed Clark when he declared he could negotiate a better deal with Quebec than Trudeau could. Beyond that, Clark's weak image on television and the old stories of his awkwardness proved more of a liability than he would have admitted. As a *Gazette* headline read: "Joe Clark's Wimp Image Is Hard to Shake Off."

To combat this problem, the Conservative leader adopted a more aggressive tone; he sounded more like Pierre Trudeau than Joe Clark. Here was a fundamental error in tactics that Bill Neville had long recognized: to attempt to out-Trudeau Trudeau was folly. Further, by attacking the Liberals, Clark's own decent personality was hidden from reporters and hence from the public.

Meanwhile, the Liberals adopted a strategy much different from that of a year earlier, when they had tried to make Trudeau more accessible. Now he was nowhere to be seen. Coutts and Davey decided that the less the media saw of him, the better. In the parlance of the campaign, they "low-bridged" him. Journalists travelling on the Liberal jet were outraged, dubbing the result the "peek a-boo campaign" and complaining about how undemocratic it was to keep the Liberal leader hidden. "It got to be a bigger thing in the minds of the members of the media than it was," recalls Jim Coutts. "We realized there was a great disenchantment with Clark. We were so high in the polls, in the 40 percent range. All we could do was lose the election once we started. So what advantage was there in putting forward a positive profile of Trudeau? That was not the issue; the issue was getting rid of Clark and the Tories. Why raise the profile of someone who was not the issue?"

The plan was to limit Trudeau's public appearances to about twenty minutes per day, giving reporters just enough for a short story or a sixty-second television or radio clip. Dalton Camp compared Trudeau to Richard Nixon, who as president had avoided the media. Finally, during the last week of January – more than six weeks since Trudeau's last official press conference – journalists travelling on the plane out of St. John's handed Patrick Gossage a petition demanding a meeting with Trudeau. As Gossage remembered: "I took it up to the front of the plane right away, and, with barely a word, gave it to the former PM. He put on his half glasses, studied it for a moment, looked at the names, and then wrote '*fiat medial conferenciam* – P.' This was probably as correct Latin as exists to permit a news conference to go ahead!"[41] Not surprisingly, Trudeau offered reporters little to write or comment about once the meeting took place.

The results on February 18, restoring the Liberal majority and gaving Trudeau his former job back, was a great victory for the party. But for the media, it meant things reverted to the norm in Ottawa: limited access, vague answers, and adversarial journalism. Had they given Joe Clark more of a chance, he might have made a real difference in their day-to-day work.

In his column of February 20, a few days after the election, Geoffrey Stevens recognized the tragic impact journalists had had on Clark's career. "The news media have never conveyed Mr. Clark's fundamental courtesy, consideration and decency," he observed, "mainly because it is easier to reinforce than to rebut the media-inspired image of the man as a walking disaster zone." Joe Clark would have to wait nearly a decade before the media and public gave him the respect he deserved. For the moment, however, the Liberals were back in control.

On May 20, 1980, the day Premier René Lévesque asked Quebeckers to give him a mandate to proceed with his plans for sovereignty-association, Geoffrey Stevens wrote that whatever the results of the referendum, the media had a special responsibility in the coming months to "exercise common sense." "We will have to look beyond the easy, instant sensation of the day, the conflict of a particular meeting, the outrage of a particular region, or government or leader," he added. "[Because] a press which reports the contestation and ignores the less dramatic more difficult-to-observe efforts at conciliation, will help destroy the process." This sage advice, offered by the then most influential political commentator in Ottawa, was all but ignored over the next eighteen months.

At first journalists were stunned and angered by Trudeau's return, believing it was only through the blatant manipulations of Coutts and Davey that the electorate had been tricked. As far as these wise pundits were concerned, the same arrogant Trudeau was back in power. He was as contemptuous of them as he had been for the previous decade. He stubbornly refused to speak at the gallery dinner in 1981. His press secretary, Patrick Gossage, tried to convince him to consent to weekly press conferences, but the most Trudeau would agree to was "news conferences on a regular basis." Reporters had no choice but to go after the prime minister in unwieldy scrums. (In one notable episode, Thomas Walkom of the *Globe and Mail* was mildly "roughed up" by Commons security guards after his aggressive attempt to question Trudeau about the government's cruise missile policy.) When Trudeau did grant journalists an audience, he was generally closed-mouthed, tight-lipped, and sarcastic.[42]

When it came to providing electrifying television images and sensational stories, however, few politicians could match Trudeau. More than at any time in the past, journalists of the 1980s thrived on confrontation, and the return of Pierre Trudeau fed the appetites of reporters desperate for lively copy. There was Trudeau versus Lévesque in a battle between two champion gladiators; Trudeau versus Claude Ryan, the intellectual Quebec Liberal leader and former editor of *Le Devoir* who wanted to fight the Parti Québécois in his own way; Trudeau versus Alberta and the West in a confrontation over his controversial National Energy Policy; and, the toughest down-in-the-dirt clash of them all, Trudeau versus the premiers in the feud over the constitution.

The saga of the patriation of the Canadian constitution was tailor-made for Ottawa's press gallery; it was a story filled with intrigue, back-stabbing, personal conflicts, and competing visions of the country's history and future. As an example, consider the 1982 book written by *Globe* reporters Robert Sheppard and Michael Valpy, appropriately entitled *The National Deal: The Fight for a Canadian Constitution.* It was an attempt to re-create television's thirty-second sound bites or short clips in printed form. Lacking in analysis and historical perspective, the book was largely a collection of anecdotal snapshots of the eighteen-month war between Trudeau and the provinces. "[Trudeau] scored divisions in the country that only future generations will be able to repair," the authors wrote. "He perhaps destroyed for years to come the Liberal Party as a representative national force; but he had warned his party colleagues at the outset that might likely be the case, that the battle would be bloody and the political costs high."[43]

For Sheppard, Valpy, and other reporters covering the constitutional story, the end of the world (or Canada, at least) was always around the corner. This penchant for doomsday journalism heightened the drama of each debate and meeting, and therefore raised the stature and significance of the messenger. Past constitutional negotiations were not relevant, nor was a century of history that suggested that Quebec independence was no more than the unrealistic dream of a small but vocal elite. Hence, the usually wise Geoffrey Stevens predicted on May 20 that "whatever happens in the referendum today, we have four years, possibly five, in which to save our country." Four months later, when yet another first ministers' conference fell apart without a deal being reached, *Maclean's* magazine writers Robert Lewis, Ian Anderson, and Roy MacGregor pessimistically noted that "the real loss in the impasse is that significant constitutional reform has been set back for years – if not for good."[44] Yet the best war stories have happy endings, and Trudeau and the premiers did not let the journalists down. The theme of Canada's demise would recur in the media for the next decade each time another solution to the constitutional quandary was proposed by the government. And each time, journalists in print and on television would carry on as if this proposal offered the last possible opportunity to avoid a national disaster.

Pierre Trudeau had always done things his own way, never more so than during his last four years in office. Re-elected in the spring of 1980, he was determined to resolve the Canadian constitutional dilemma that had eluded him and his predecessors for years. It was, as Clarkson and McCall have called it, his "magnificent obsession": "he was a re-empowered leader with a vision of his country that he had been ruminating on for decades and that he now intended to implement."[45] During the referendum campaign in Quebec, he had promised Quebeckers that a "Non" vote on sovereignty-association would mean a long-overdue redefinition of their place in Confederation. They gave him the mandate he asked for (the result of the referendum on May 20 was approximately 60–40 against proceeding with sovereignty-association), but when he could not sell his plans for a new division of powers, a charter of rights, and an amending formula to the premiers, he decided to take unilateral action.

While the national media, including editorialists from Quebec, had always respected Trudeau's intellect, his intransigent attitude on this issue was too much for many of them to stomach. How, they asked, could the federal government in good conscience patriate the constitution without the consent of the provinces? The prime minister was not listening. In early 1981 Trudeau initially refused to refer the matter to the Supreme Court. "Mr. Trudeau does not believe in the rule of law," declared the *Globe and Mail.* "He believes in the rule of men. One man. Himself." Once the court ruled in September that constitutional "convention" (though not law) dictated that the Liberal government have the consent of some, if not all, the provinces, commentators were even more critical of Trudeau's uncompromising approach. In an editorial echoing the view of many newspapers, the *Calgary Herald* decreed, "One thing is beyond question: if consensus cannot be achieved, Trudeau should abandon the initiative. National unity cannot stand anymore federal-provincial wrangling on this issue."[46]

Just when the country's future looked the bleakest, along came the best media story of them all. The first ministers' constitutional conference held in Ottawa from November 2 to 5, 1981, was perceived by journalists and the public as possibly the last chance to find a compromise. In the collective minds of the media, the meeting acquired a mythology all its own. The story reached its pinnacle on the evening of the third day, during the "Night of the Long Knives," when the anglophone premiers, once partners with Quebec premier René Lévesque in "The Gang of Eight," negotiated a deal behind his back.

Later commentators and analysts would blow out of proportion the significance of the the "kitchen accord," a deal struck between Justice Minister Jean Chrétien, Roy McMurtry, Ontario's attorney general, and Roy Romanow, Saskatchewan's attorney general, in a small kitchen in the Ottawa Conference Centre. As declared by a Canadian Press story carried across the country on November 6, "Canada's new constitution was conceived in a kitchen and born in a railway station after all-night gestation in two smoke-filled hotel rooms. The story of its birth is a pot-boiler political drama full of inevitable cliches – midnight telephone calls, and lawyers haggling over legal fine print as the sun came up." Actually, the Chrétien-McMurtry-Romanow meeting in the Convention Centre's kitchen took place late on Wednesday afternoon, November 4; nearly all the key players were asleep by 11 p.m. that evening; and the lawyers were tucked into their beds three hours later.[47]

When a final agreement was announced on November 5, the drama and excitement swept many journalists away in a sea of patriotism – Canada had been saved! But the deal was far from perfect, as editorials were quick to point out. Quebec had refused to sign; provinces were permitted to opt out of future constitutional changes affecting their powers; a "notwithstanding clause" gave politicians the opportunity to restrict the rights of citizens; and the rights of women and natives were not properly addressed.

The blame for these inadequacies, not surprisingly, lay with the man who had initiated the process. In caving in to the premiers' demands, he had produced "a typical Canadian document, complicated, untidy and not terribly inspiring," observed the *Winnipeg Free Press.* By his actions, he had "gutted the constitution of its purpose and efficacy," declared the *Toronto Star.* Other newspapers, like the *Globe, Montreal Gazette,* and *Ottawa Citizen,* were more optimistic, recognizing (as Trudeau was later forced to) that in politics the art of compromise is a prerequisite for success, even a limited one.[48] Though it was clear in November 1981 that Canada's constitutional difficulties were only beginning, Trudeau had achieved what other prime ministers had failed to do, and no amount of sniping from the media could erase that historic accomplishment.

Once the great task of patriating the constitution was completed, Trudeau turned his energies to more mundane matters like the economy, but never with quite the same enthusiasm. He was never able to solve the problem of inflation, though with hindsight one can see that Canada's economic performance in the early 1980s compares favourably with that of other Western countries. No matter, the $166-billion accumulated national debt that the Liberals passed on to the Mulroney government in 1984 was a difficult legacy to live down. Five and six years after Trudeau left office, the Conservatives, along with such prominent journalists as Jeffrey Simpson, were still blaming Trudeau's poor fiscal record for Canada's economic woes.[49] (In fact, while the Tories cut the operating deficit by about $10 billion during their first term, from 1984 to 1988, the accumulated national debt nearly doubled, reaching $320 billion.)

Trudeau's efforts in the area of world peace during his last year as prime minister equally did not draw rave reviews from the media. His interest in foreign affairs had never been strong – "sporadic" was how historians Jack Granatstein and Robert Bothwell characterized it in their 1990 book *Pirouette,* the first major study of Trudeau's foreign policy. No fan of the Lester Pearson approach to diplomacy (Trudeau had initially cut Canada's commitment to NATO in 1969 and disdained the country's role as a middle-power peacekeeper), he now employed Pearsonian strategy in attempting to reduce East-West nuclear tension. Moreover, his decision in the summer of 1983 to support the testing of American cruise missiles over Canadian soil diminished his stature as statesman of peace even before he began his tour of world capitals.[50] Journalists, who expected nothing but perfection from Canadian politicians, were happy to point out such inconsistencies.

The attitude of the press, as well as much of the public, to Trudeau's efforts to save the world was thus somewhat cynical. Trudeau launched the initiative with a major speech at the University of Guelph in late October 1983, but he did not announce his specific proposals until he returned from his first trip to Western Europe, and then did so at a $150-plate Liberal dinner in Montreal instead of in the House of Commons. This was, observed a *Winnipeg Free Press* editorial, "an insensitive way to develop public understanding." As his various proposals (including a five-power nuclear disarmament conference and a new emphasis on conventional-force reductions in Europe) were rejected one after the other by world leaders, reporters travelling with the prime minister were not impressed. "We joked to each other about the way Trudeau would come out of each meeting with each leader and solemnly pronounce himself 'very encouraged,'" Richard and Sandra Gwyn recalled. "The foreign reporters we encountered were mostly interested in the other Trudeau – Margaret had just filed for divorce."[51]

As unrealistic as it may have been, Trudeau's peace mission was eventually supported by the Canadian public. When he completed his work in early February 1984, several editors and columnists praised his attempts to renew the East-West dialogue; Charles Lynch even suggested Trudeau should be awarded the Nobel Peace Prize. But too many years had passed, too many battles fought, for most journalists to regard anything Trudeau did, no matter how honourable, with anything but skepticism, suspicion, and criticism.[52]

There was a similar response weeks later when Trudeau, following his famous walk in the snow on February 29, announced he was resigning as Liberal leader and prime minister. Called upon to assess the career of a man they never really understood, editorialists and reporters gushed about how Trudeau had saved the country by thwarting Quebec separatists and had transformed Canada by making it a truly bilingual nation, but in the innumerable articles and commentaries they also expressed a great deal of hostility and ambivalence. "The Country Will Be Better Off Without Him," a *Vancouver Sun* headline blared.

Like everyone else, however, journalists found Trudeau an irresistible subject. Had he only reciprocated the respect they begrudgingly accorded him, life in Ottawa would have been more tolerable for them. But that was never Trudeau's style or inclination. Unlike the other political leaders of the

1980s – Joe Clark, John Turner, and Brian Mulroney – Pierre Trudeau answered to no one but himself. Indeed, he got under the skin of the media like no other Canadian politician. When asked by reporters during one of his last press conferences if he had any regrets, he replied with a sly grin, "Well I won't have you guys to kick around anymore." No one but Trudeau could have made such a claim and meant it.

Today, nearly a decade after Pierre Trudeau's departure from public life, the media's obsession with the man continues. Word that at age seventy-one he had fathered a daughter with the considerably younger Deborah Coyne, constitutional adviser to Newfoundland premier Clyde Wells, set word processors going at full speed in September 1991. Trudeau's sexual prowess has long been a favourite topic of the media. A comment from Trudeau on just about anything can elicit pages of stories and commentaries in newspapers and endless discussions on television.* His virulent rejection of the Meech Lake Accord in May 1987 and his insulting references to Prime Minister Brian Mulroney as a "weakling" for capitulating to the provinces' demands particularly upset the Conservatives and renewed debate in the media about his own constitutional legacy.[53]

Yet no other former prime minister has ever commanded as much public attention. Most editors and journalists regarded Trudeau's criticism of and intervention in the 1992 constitutional referendum as one of the most significant factors in the victory of the "No" forces. Despite his arrogance and the hostile feelings he generated, journalists have judged his successors against the high standards of leadership he had set. "His absence haunts the stage," Michael Ignatieff wrote in 1987, "and we measure everyone who came after him by the length of his shadow."[54] Certainly this was the unhappy dilemma that confronted John Turner in the spring of 1984.

---

*A speech by Trudeau is a major media event. In October 1991 he delivered an address to 300 members of the Young Presidents Organization at a private meeting in Montreal. In his speech he alluded to the fact that under the proposed powers demanded by the Quebec government in its constitutional negotiations, it would be possible to "deport" anglophones if the need arose. Trudeau was obviously using an extreme example to illustrate, in no uncertain terms, the real dangers of Quebec nationalism. Attending the conference as an observer was Norman Webster, the editor of the *Montreal Gazette,* who had promised to respect the privacy of the gathering. Everything the former prime minister said was off the record. Yet Webster decided to print Trudeau's controversial remarks in his newspaper. This not only touched off a stormy debate in the media about the editor's ethics, but raised questions about Trudeau's "real" motives. Peter C. Newman, among others, suggested that it was time for Trudeau "to muzzle himself." (See *Globe and Mail,* October 6, 1991; George Galt, "Telling Tales," *Globe and Mail,* October 12, 1991; Letters to the Editor, *Globe and Mail,* October 16, 1991; Newman, "It's Time for Trudeau to Muzzle Himself," *Maclean's,* October 21, 1991, 86; George Bain, "Are Some Rules Made to Be Broken?" *Maclean's,* October 21, 1991, 97)

CHAPTER SIXTEEN

The Turner Follies of '84

*I have good friends in the media who have given me a good
dusting off. If it is professionally done, that's their job you
know ... But unprofessional work, I don't admire, anonymous source journalism, rumour mongering, I don't
admire, tattle-telling, I don't admire.*

John Turner, 1990

On May 10, 1984, two months into the Liberal leadership campaign,
John Turner was returning to Toronto by bus from nearby Trenton. He
had just finished delivering his standard noontime speech to a group of
potential delegates, a speech that stressed his love for Canada, family,
democracy, and God. Journalists who had travelled with him were not
impressed.[1]

Now on the bus, Turner – his suit jacket off – wandered to the back to
mingle with "the boys," as he liked to call the reporters. He ignored the fact
there were women among them. He joked with his old university friend Val
Sears of the *Toronto Star,* one of the few journalists aboard who had covered
Turner when he was a cabinet minister in the late sixties and early seventies.
Most of the other reporters had been in high school or university when
Turner was making headlines; now they were passing judgment on the fifty-
four-year-old man who wanted to be prime minister.

The bantering with Sears ended and the discussion turned to monetary
policy, interest rates, and the past. Why had Turner resigned as Pierre
Trudeau's finance minister in 1975, the reporters asked? Turner had never
talked publicly about this before, but he spoke of it now, believing his
remarks were off the record. In the old days, the back of the bus had been
sacred neutral territory where politicians could privately explain the secrets
of cabinet to trustworthy journalists.

Turner implied that Trudeau had failed to support his attempt to institute
voluntary wage and price controls, so he had had no choice but to quit.
"And you were not offered another portfolio?" they questioned. "Only the
Senate or the bench," he replied, his tone suggesting that Trudeau's offer
was a dreadful insult. The conversation ended and Turner returned to his

seat, happy that his relations with the younger journalists were starting to click and believing it was understood that his remarks about Trudeau were not for publication.[2] He was terribly mistaken.

None of the reporters had heard Turner say anything about his comments being off the record, and it might not have made a difference in any event. Stories like this could not be ignored. The leading Liberal leadership candidate had attacked the credibility of the man he wanted to replace. For Thomas Walkom, then a thirty-four-year-old reporter with the *Globe and Mail,* there was no question about it. The story had to be filed. Val Sears and Bill Casey of the CBC agreed. Reading the *Globe* the next day over breakfast, Turner was outraged. "In the bus, for God's sake," he said later. "And Tom Walkom of the *Globe and Mail* said he was going to file it, so Val [Sears] had to cover it for the *Star* and so did Bill Casey for the CBC. I don't blame Val or Casey. Those guys are all right. But that Walkom! This *Globe and Mail,* you know! I've never had a thing broken in a bus in my life."[3] Even more embarrassing for Turner was having to explain himself to an angry Pierre Trudeau, who remembered Turner's resignation very differently. Trudeau issued his own statement and Turner tried to clarify what he had been talking about, by then a common practice. (About this time, Jean Chrétien, also a leadership candidate, was asked in the House of Commons about another statement Turner had made. "Mr. Speaker," he said, "I will wait for the clarification." The House erupted in laughter.)[4] In reporting Turner's comments, the journalists were not betraying a confidence or being underhanded; it was just that in 1984 nothing was off the record. As Turner discovered that day in May, relationships and rules change.

John Turner missed the old days. He remembered the time, not so long ago, when Ottawa was a much smaller and friendlier "town," when everyone knew everyone else, when a mutual respect existed between members of the parliamentary gallery and the members of Parliament. He missed the evening sittings of the House, the confrontations between Jimmy Sinclair and Davie Fulton, the after-hours poker games. Most of all he missed the camaraderie.

They would meet for a late dinner, "ten or fifteen members of Parliament, with senior guys from the press gallery. It was part of the system," he recalls. "Nothing spilled out of these meetings and there was some rough talk from time to time and it got pretty personal." What counted were the virtues Turner had grown up with: loyalty, honour, respect for privacy, and fairness. "The good reporters could keep a confidence, building up their background, then breaking a story in their own time full of fact and interpretation, because they had the confidence of the men and women they were dealing with." Criticism was fine, as long as it was fair and accurate.[5]

In his younger days, he had had an easier time dealing with the media. Indeed, Turner had been a bit of a media celebrity, the man most likely to succeed. At the University of British Columbia, he was declared to be "the most popular student on campus." Liberal Donald Johnston, who had known Turner in the late fifties and was himself a Liberal leadership candidate in 1984, remembered "being aware that everyone assumed Turner one day would be prime minister. I sense he knew it too."[6]

Turner had not been born with a silver spoon in his mouth. His father, Leonard, a mysterious English adventurer and gunsmith, had died when he was only two years old. He had been raised by his hard-working mother, Phyllis Gregory, a brilliant economist who landed a job in Ottawa in an era when most women stayed at home. She was an exception, and she expected her two children, John and his sister, Brenda, to be exceptional as well. Turner was educated at the best private school in Ottawa, and later when his mother married Frank Ross, a wealthy Vancouver businessman, he attended the University of British Columbia. There "Chick" Turner, as he was known, was the golden boy of the campus – a jive-talking, speedy sprinter who wrote a popular sports column for the *Ubyssey,* "Chalk Talk, by Chick" ("This corner bills Doug Whittle's UBC mermen as odds-on-favourites to edge out the College of Puget Sound, Willamette and Lewis and Clark entries and to latch on to the first conference seaweed crown put on the velvet." Translation: Turner expected UBC's swimming team to win something). Turner enjoyed his foray into journalism and actually contemplated pursuing a career as a newsman.[7] But he turned to law instead, a safer, more conservative choice for a young man bent on success in post–Second World War Canada.

In 1949, at age twenty, Turner won a prestigious Rhodes scholarship. He studied jurisprudence at Oxford for two years and then spent a year improving his French at the University of Paris. He returned to Canada in 1953 to begin a successful law career in Montreal. Turner was on his way to the top. He first caught the attention of reporters when he danced with Princess Margaret at a ball hosted by his stepfather, then the lieutenant-governor of B.C. Gossip was rampant that the princess fancied this highly eligible Canadian bachelor, but nothing came of it. In 1963 Turner married Geills Kilgour, the daughter of a Winnipeg business executive, but he later remembered the "Margaret episode" as "a lotta fun – a real gas, you know what I mean?"[8]

He took the plunge into politics in the 1962 federal election and won impressively as a Liberal in a Montreal riding. He was exactly the kind of candidate party organizer Keith Davey wanted to attract. Not only did he have Kennedy-like looks, but he was articulate and progressive as well. As a backbencher, he was very popular, and in 1965 he was appointed to the cabinet as a minister without portfolio. Two years later he was given the position of registrar-general, and then he became the first minister of consumer and corporate affairs. In 1968 he believed he was ready for the leadership, but he had not counted on the rise of Pierre Trudeau.

Turner had never approved of Trudeau's confrontational style, the centralization of power in the Prime Minister's Office, the alienation of the West and of the business community, or the path Trudeau had chosen for the Liberal Party. On a personal level, the two men were very different. Whereas Trudeau was an introvert who guarded his private life, Turner genuinely liked people – he liked to touch them, in his words, "mano a mano, hand to hand." "Turner was a Rolodex politician with a filing-card network that was a legend," wrote journalist Ron Graham. "He boasted with some justification, that he knew more people on a first name basis in Canada than anyone else in the country."[9] Pierre Trudeau could not even remember the name of his biographer. Nevertheless, when duty called, Turner answered. He faithfully served Trudeau, first as justice minister, presiding over the passage of the War Measures Act during the FLQ Crisis of 1970, and then as finance minister for two years until he resigned in 1975.

He had been a popular politician in Ottawa and his relations with the press had always been good. In his early days, he had impressed journalists with his performance on the back benches. In 1965 Christopher Young of the *Ottawa Citizen* dubbed Turner "the most promising Liberal MP under the age of forty. He has ability, high educational qualifications [and] energy to burn." Assessments remained positive after Turner joined the Trudeau cabinet. He was praised for his work on the Official Languages Act in 1969, particularly for the way he negotiated with the premiers, "quietly and with reason," as the *Montreal Gazette* put it. As justice minister he was seen to be a leading reformer, and in Finance he was credited with saving Trudeau's minority government with a brilliant budget in 1973 that kept both the Conservatives and NDP on side. In the opinion of Geoffrey Stevens, the *Globe and Mail*'s Ottawa columnist, Turner was not only "attractive, forceful, intelligent and articulate," but he was equally "a politician with instinct, style and appeal all his own." Perhaps Brian Mulroney, then a Montreal lawyer and Conservative party organizer, summed up many people's feelings about Turner with these words: "Turner's so smooth, he's never made a mistake anybody can pin on him. He's the Liberal dream in motion."[10] In 1976 when Turner left Ottawa to build a successful corporate law practice in Toronto, the members of the gallery regarded this as a great loss to the government.

Turner, of course, was never really gone. He may not have had an office on Parliament Hill any longer, but journalists made sure his name was still prominent in their stories and columns. Often he inadvertently helped them out. Soon after the victory of the Parti Québécois in November 1976, Turner delivered a speech at a private gathering in Toronto in which he intimated that Trudeau was not doing enough to save the country. Much to Turner's dismay, a *Toronto Star* reporter in attendance wrote a story about his speech, playing up the rift between the former finance minister and the prime minister. Then he got caught with his name (along with that of one of his law partners, William Macdonald) on a series of private "newsletters" sent to his select corporate clients (for an annual fee of $15,000) that were critical of the Liberals' economic management. Again the media publicized Turner's discontent with the Trudeau administration, and this did not sit well with many members of the Liberal Party.[11]

At his regular table at Winston's in Toronto, he was the most famous public "private citizen" in the country. When he walked into a room, people stopped to stare. He never gave interviews, but everyone knew that he was the "Prince-in-Exile" waiting for the right moment to reclaim his throne. When Trudeau resigned for the first time in November 1979, journalists and politicians were very surprised that Turner said "Thanks, but no thanks." His wife was against the idea of returning to public life, his children were still relatively young, and his law practice was booming. He had been appointed a director on the most prestigious boards in the country, including Canadian Pacific, Massey-Ferguson, and Seagrams, and each carried a substantial annual stipend. Four years later, the situation had changed. His strategy team, led by the resourceful lobbyist Bill Lee and his mentor, John deB. Payne, a Montreal consultant and political guru, had been secretly meeting since September 1983 at the Royal York Hotel in Toronto, planning Turner's political rebirth.[12] And within time, Geills Turner gave her blessing.

On March 1, 1984, the day Trudeau announced his retirement for the second and last time, the media designated Turner, who had not yet declared his intentions, as the man to beat. Two weeks later at a crowded press conference at the Chateau Laurier, John Turner announced he was returning to public life. He believed he could bring fresh ideas to the political scene and made it clear that he was distancing himself from the Trudeau style of government. Turner argued that his eight and a half years on Bay Street had not pushed him to the right, as some critics charged, but his remarks about the need to cut the deficit sounded a lot like the economic policy of Brian Mulroney, the new Conservative leader.

He was rusty on some issues. Near the end of the conference, reporters asked for his opinion about the resolution recently passed in the House urging the Manitoba government to go ahead with its planned extension of French-language rights. He declared that he supported the spirit of the all-party resolution, but that in the end the issue would have to be solved by the province. In Turner's mind, he was making a distinction between the role of the federal government in protecting minority-language rights and the role of the Manitoba government in extending French-language services. Editors in Quebec and elsewhere, however, did not interpret his remarks in this way, and he was roundly criticized both for failing to comprehend the intricacies of the Manitoba language issue and for "rejecting the Trudeau government's long-standing commitment to use federal constitutional power, if necessary, to protect minority language rights."[13]

Journalists were equally surprised at how nervous he was, constantly wetting his lips and clearing his throat "machine-gun style." Still, most reporters were willing to give him the benefit of the doubt. After all, they (as well as many Liberals) had been hyping Turner for nearly nine years. Some of them were now treating him like a prophet who had been wandering in the desert and had finally found his way home. *Vancouver Sun* columnist Marjorie Nichols, however, observed that Turner would have to adapt quickly to the harsh new realities of media coverage in Ottawa – to the larger, less personal atmosphere driven by television – or he could find himself in serious trouble. She noted that when Turner was a cabinet minister, he had carried a stick of pancake make-up in his pocket, which he applied before stepping in front of a TV camera. This had never been reported back then, but would certainly be in 1984. As Nichols concluded, Turner had better learn quickly that "it's all on the record now."[14]

Turner's troubled relationship with journalists, which soon exploded in his face and hampered his leadership campaign, went beyond the fact that he was rusty or that he had not yet grasped all the new issues. Turner was a product of another era, championing traditional attitudes and values unlike the more cynical ones held by a new generation of reporters. He was a tough-talking, honourable man who sincerely believed he had a public duty to serve his country. His heroes were men of Canada's past, C.D. Howe, Lester Pearson, Jack Pickersgill, and John Diefenbaker. In private, his "gutsy, slangy" language was regularly laced with four-letter words, and he spoke about women as if he were still in a college locker room. He still believed he could go for late-night drinks with the "gentlemen of the press" or "the guys." When one female reporter became overly aggressive in questioning him, his response was, "Down girl!"[15]

To the journalists who had grown up with the myth that some day John Turner would return a mighty Liberal hero, he was a disappointment – more like a relic that belonged in a Grit museum than a leader for the 1980s. Turner, of course, understood that initially his relations with the media would be different as well as difficult. Television had already taken over politics in the early seventies and the gallery was starting to expand, making it impossible for politicians to be on good terms with every Ottawa journalist, as it had been when Turner first arrived in 1962. But even at the height of his power as finance minister, he was never scrutinized by journalists in the aggressive manner that Trudeau was. Now, as a potential prime minister in 1984, he was confronted with the same skepticism that had dogged Trudeau for more than a decade. And as much as he mentally prepared himself, he was not ready for reporters who thrust microphones in his face and "who dealt with each story as if it was their last."[16]

A month into the leadership campaign, Turner was stepping into an elevator in a Montreal hotel and suddenly found himself in a sea of microphones and cameras. What was his position on Quebec's controversial language law, Bill 101, reporters demanded to know. In French, he answered that he agreed "in principle," again trying to make the distinction between minority-language rights and services. When editorialists denounced his statement, he was once again forced to clarify his position on a sensitive subject. Then came his off-the-record/on-the-record discussion with Tom Walkom and other reporters at the back of the bus. By the time of the leadership convention in June, Turner did not know whom he could trust. "He discovered that reporters had no scruples about listening in on private conversations," Ron Graham observed. "He knew that every drink he took during a flight could be material for a 'campaign notebook' column, and he sat in terror through a meal in Saskatoon because it required him to pick up meatballs with a pair of chopsticks while the photographers waited for him to fumble."[17]

The majority of Liberals who met in Ottawa to elect a new leader on June 16 had not been swayed by the media's critical coverage of Turner, nor by his obvious rustiness. The consensus was that Turner, with all his faults, was more "saleable" to the country and a better opponent for Brian Mulroney than Jean Chrétien, the crowd favourite. As John Sawatsky noted, "The convention had to choose between sentiment and power and had chosen power."[18]

Even before he took over from Pierre Trudeau on June 30, Turner was caught in the eye of the media storm that would rage over the entire sixty-nine days of his unhappy term as Canada's seventeenth prime minister. From the start, he was indecisive and showed poor political judgment on a number of key issues. After having announced that he was a man with new ideas and a new image, that he was going to distance himself from Trudeau, he appointed a cabinet that was almost identical to the previous one. Of the twenty-nine ministers, twenty-four had served with Trudeau and eighteen were reappointed to the same portfolios, including Marc Lalonde in Finance, a man closely identified with Trudeau since 1968.[19] When he had decided to run for the Liberal leadership, Turner had refused to resign his lucrative corporate directorships, and it took him until June 30, the day he officially assumed power, to do so. Editors lambasted him for placing his own interests before those of Canadians.

Turner's gravest error, however, was his handling of Trudeau's infamous patronage appointments. Trudeau decided to leave office with one final orgy of pork-barrelling. During his last month in office, his cabinet approved 225 appointments for Liberals everywhere – judgeships, Senate seats, and ambassadorships. Included in Trudeau's list were approximately seventeen members of Parliament, among them veteran Liberal Bryce Mackasey, who was appointed ambassador to Portugal. Trudeau wanted to make all the appointments official prior to his departure, but the shifting of Liberal ministers into the Senate would have wiped out the slim Liberal majority in the House. Turner feared that without his majority Governor General Jeanne Sauvé might refuse his request for a dissolution and ask the Conservatives to form a government. He was following advice he had received from the Privy Council Office, which he either misinterpreted or did not understand, for such constitutional experts as Eugene Forsey ridiculed his logic. Against the counsel of just about everyone, Turner agreed to Trudeau's demand that he sign a letter stating that the balance of the appointments would be made after the House was prorogued.[20]

True to his word, on July 9, the day he called an election, Turner publicly announced the patronage appointments, with a few of his own added. The response was predictable. "It's something out of an Edward G. Robinson movie," Conservative leader Brian Mulroney declared with all the humility he could muster. "You know, the boys cuttin' up the cash. There's not a Grit left in town. They've all gone to Grit Heaven." Commentators and editors again criticized Turner for so blatantly reneging on his promise to introduce a new style and set of values into the government. Throughout the long hot summer campaign of 1984, he was forced to carry – in the words of *Vancouver Sun* columnist Jamie Lamb – the "smelly baggage" of the patronage appointments. When asked to defend his actions, all he could do was repeat what he told Mulroney during the final electrifying moments of the leaders' debate on July 25: "I had no option." It was a pathetic response.

Turner had ignored the advice of his chief strategist, Bill Lee, and Jean Chrétien, among others, who strongly recommended he delay calling an election until late November so that he could accustom himself to his new job, appear with the Pope and Queen during their planned visits to Canada that summer, and gain the confidence of the public. But Turner was impatient. He was far ahead in the polls and economic forecasts were dismal for the fall. Moreover, he believed, as Bill Lee did, that "a well-oiled Liberal machine awaited his decision to call a national election." In fact, the party was not ready. During the Trudeau era, all key decisions about organization had come out of the Prime Minister's Office, which Turner had just dismantled. Consequently, the Liberals' national party headquarters was unprepared for a national campaign (among the authors of the numerous books and articles on the 1984 election, only Liberal organizer Senator Keith Davey disputes this point, arguing that the party was well organized).[21]

Nevertheless, Turner called the election for September 4.

For two months, John Turner faced one disaster after another. "Seldom, if ever," wrote Jeffrey Simpson, "has a major party conducted a campaign of such sustained ineptitude." No one, including Turner, knew who exactly was in charge. Internal bickering hampered work at all levels of the party's organization, and Turner himself made some bad policy decisions that alienated the Liberals' traditional voters: minorities, women, senior citizens, youth, and francophones. His economic platform, which focused on reducing the federal deficit and cutting government costs, made him seem a larger-C Conservative than Brian Mulroney was. And his declaration that he would not negotiate a new constitutional deal with the Parti Québécois pushed undecided voters in Quebec into the open arms of the Tories.[22]

Most importantly, he failed to appear prime ministerial on television; there was no greater blunder for a 1980s politician than this. On July 13 Turner was in Edmonton to open the party's Western and Northern Council. In front of the audience and CTV's cameras, he kissed Liberal Party president Iona Campagnolo on the cheek and then patted her bum. She responded in kind by patting his bum. That night Turner was lucky; CTV decided not to run the clip. Bill Lee warned him to refrain from doing this again, but a few days later in Montreal he was caught on camera patting the bum of Lise St. Martin-Tremblay, a Quebec Liberal Party vice-president. This time CTV repeatedly ran the shot, along with the one of Campagnolo. Bum patting emerged as a major issue of the campaign, commented on in editorials, immortalized in cartoons, and made the butt of many jokes. Reporters renamed Turner's jet "Derri Air" and the Kitchener-Waterloo Status of Women's Group designed cardboard Turner "bum shields" for protection. This embarrassing issue could have been quickly diffused had Turner immediately apologized, but he did not because he failed to understand what all the fuss was about. "I'm a hugger, I'm a tactile politician," he told reporters. "I'm slapping people all over the place. People are reaching out to me. That's my style." This weak defence merely reinforced his image, as columnist Marjorie Nichols put it, as "an arrogant, out-of-touch refugee from another time, another place … From the moment that he chucked his hat into the leadership ring, it has been apparent that Turner is a man out of sync with the issues and rusty in his role on the public stage."[23]

Meanwhile, Brian Mulroney's Conservative campaign was rolling along under the generalship of Norman Atkins, an Ontario advertising executive and the mastermind of the Big Blue Machine that had kept Bill Davis in power in Ontario from 1971 to 1984. The major criticism levelled against Mulroney and his team by the media was that his operation was too "slick" and "smooth." This was the classic Canadian media paradox: Turner was ridiculed for running a sloppy, unorganized fiasco and for giving reporters milkshakes instead of beer, while Mulroney was condemned for devising a slick operation "lifted from the movie 'The Candidate' with Robert Redford," complete with a portable backdrop and podium and a schedule that ran with precision. Atkins, however, was delighted. "Anybody who accuses someone who is running a campaign of being slick is acknowledging the fact that they are doing it well," he says. "In the 1971 campaign in Ontario, we used to say, 'slick is beautiful.' We were getting slammed for it everyday, but we were getting credit for it beyond the media in the public's mind. The results in 1971 (and 1984) were tremendous."[24]

In an otherwise perfect display of political savvy, Mulroney slipped only once. He had ridiculed Turner's patronage appointments, promising that Canadians could expect much more – "true change, true attitudinal change" – from a Tory government. Yet a short time later, travelling by air back to Montreal from a tour of the North Shore of Quebec, Mulroney made some offhand remarks to reporters that he thought were off the record. Like Turner, he had cultivated good relations with journalists over his many years as a lawyer and political player. He genuinely enjoyed their company and thought he could trust them to place their friendship with him above their profession. He failed to understand that the rules of the game had changed once he had declared his desire to be prime minister.

On the plane, reporters reminded him that a year ago at the Conservative leadership convention he had promised the partisan crowd that a Tory government would appoint Liberals "only when there isn't a living, breathing Tory left without a job in this country." The journalists challenged him to explain the contradiction and he took their bait. "I was talking to Tories then and that's what they want to hear," he said. "Talking to the Canadian public during an election campaign is something else." Of Bryce Mackasey's appointment as ambassador to Portugal, he observed, "Let's face it, there's no whore like an old whore. If I'd been in Bryce's position I'd have been right in there with my nose in the public trough like the rest of them."[25]

One of the reporters listening, Neil Macdonald of the *Ottawa Citizen,* decided not to abide by any off-the-record rules. On the following Monday the *Citizen*'s front page declared that "Mulroney admits altering patronage stand for election." Editorialists, cartoonists and columnists savagely attacked Mulroney's hypocrisy. His words confirmed their belief that he was insincere and "slippery."* Privately, Mulroney felt that his trust had been

---

*Keith Davey watched the first television news clip of Mulroney's comments with John Turner in the prime minister's library at 24 Sussex Drive. Later, as he was leaving, Davey remarked, "John, the kind of language Mulroney was using tonight is offensive to a lot of people. Believe me, it will not play small-town Ontario." "You're fucking right!" Turner replied. (Davey, *The Rainmaker,* 336)

betrayed. At first he only planned to explain that his comments had not been meant for the public. Then, thinking better of it, he issued a very humble apology a few days later. Members of the media were skeptical because he had waited so long to deliver a statement, but the immediate political damage was repaired. Later, Mulroney would realize the real importance of his apology. "I apologized for what I said about patronage. I knew I had to do it," he said. "But I never really appreciated how important it was until Turner did not [apologize for bum-patting]."[26]

Both Mulroney and Turner were hoping to pick up points during the two televised debates near the end of July. Turner had the most to lose in an event the media covered as if it were a Kentucky horse race. He held his own the first night in the French debate, although most Quebec newspapers declared Mulroney, a native-born Quebecker, the winner. The next evening, in English, Turner was far from relaxed, but as the debate progressed, he had yet to make any serious errors. Bill Lee had advised him to project the image of a statesman and above all to refrain from commenting on the patronage issue lest Mulroney bring up Trudeau's long list of appointments. Keith Davey suggested he "kick [Mulroney] in the nuts" over comments the Tory leader had made about Bryce Mackasey.[27]

The patronage question arose in the first part of the debate, when Mulroney was pitted against NDP leader Ed Broadbent. That was it, Lee thought. Then, in one of the great Canadian political gaffes of all time, Turner came back to it when he was debating Mulroney in the final segment. Sensing he was losing and trying to regain the advantage, Turner attacked the Conservative leader over patronage.

"I have been saying the same thing to my party on all the issues that I say to the country," he said. "We have this patronage issue brought up earlier. Mr. Mulroney has not been dealing with the issue in the same way. He told his party last year that every available job would be made available to every living, breathing Conservative."

"I beg your pardon, sir," replied Mulroney, not believing what his Liberal opponent was saying.

"I would say, Mr. Mulroney," Turner continued, "that on the basis of what you've talked about – getting your nose in the public trough – that you wouldn't offer Canadians any newness in the style of government. The style that you've been preaching to your own party reminds me of the old Union Nationale, it reminds me of patronage at its best ... "

"Mr. Turner," an outraged but humble Mulroney began, "the only person who has ever appointed around here, for the last twenty-odd years, has been your party, and 99 percent of them have been Liberals. And you ought not be proud of that. Nor should you repeat something that I think you know to be inaccurate. You know full well that that was a figure of speech that was used and I don't deny it. In fact, I've gone so far – because I believe what you did is so bad I've gone so far, sir, as to apologize for even kidding about it. I've apologized to the Canadian people for kidding about it. The least you should do is apologize for having made these horrible appointments ... "

"I told you and I told the Canadian people, Mr. Mulroney, that I had no option," Turner weakly replied.

"You had an option sir," Mulroney yelled back, ignoring the moderator. "You could have said, 'I'm not going to do it. This is wrong for Canada and I'm not going to ask Canadians to pay the price.' You had an option, sir, to say no and you chose to say yes to the old attitudes and the old stories of the Liberal Party. That, sir, if I may say respectfully, that is not good enough for Canadians."

"I had no option," Turner repeated, looking as if he had just been beaten up in a schoolyard fight. "I was able – "

"That is an avowal of failure," Mulroney interrupted. "That is a confession of non-leadership and this country needs leadership. You had an option, sir. You could have done better."[28]

It was the most electrifying two minutes of Canadian television since Pierre Trudeau had been challenged by CBC reporter Tim Ralfe during the FLQ Crisis. More significantly, Turner had committed "The Big Mistake," and clips of this exchange were replayed many times during the remainder of the campaign. Commentators awarded Mulroney a knockout. He had appeared confident, humble, and respectful of Canadians, while Turner had looked frightened, weak, and unsure. In the days that followed, the Conservative leader got wonderful laughs from crowds everywhere with his imitation of Turner's "I had no option," while the Liberals dropped in the polls. Desperate, Turner, at the urging of his caucus, accepted Bill Lee's resignation (it is not clear whether Lee was fired or quit) and invited Keith Davey to take charge of the disastrous campaign. During the Liberal leadership race earlier in the year, Turner had vowed that he would not follow Trudeau's path; "no more rainmakers, no more backroom boys," he had declared. Now, months later, he was calling on the ultimate rainmaker, the man who had guided Trudeau's last three campaigns. Some members of the media were justifiably cynical about Davey's return.

Senator Davey, who later had a falling-out with Turner over Meech Lake and other issues, does not have good memories of Turner's term as Liberal leader. "The single [worst] mistake in my political career," he says, "was that I voted for Turner at the 1984 convention." Of his appointment as chairman during the 1984 election he says, "You have no idea how much it galled Turner to have me come into the last half of that campaign because I represented Trudeau." Near the end, Davey convinced a reluctant Pierre

Trudeau to speak at a rally held in a church basement in the east end of Montreal. It was a humiliating moment for Turner, who refused to sanction the event. Jeffrey Simpson put Trudeau's last-minute appearance into perspective as follows: "Requested in panic, given with reluctance, crafted in indifference, his was a loon's cry before the terrible storm."[29]

On September 4, 1984, the Liberal Party suffered the "worst electoral disaster" in its history. From a majority of 146 seats in the House, it was reduced to a rump of 40 and received only 28 percent of the vote. Quebec, a Liberal stronghold for most of the twentieth century, deserted the party en masse for the promises of Brian Mulroney. Somehow John Turner managed to win his own seat in Vancouver-Quadra. The media's post-election analysis placed the blame for the defeat on Turner's broad shoulders. But did he deserve it? The day before the vote, a disgruntled Keith Davey had dispatched a short letter to the editor of the *Globe and Mail,* accusing the newspaper of practising "yellow journalism" during the campaign: "The *Globe and Mail* has been fascinated with tacky process stories usually based on this or that leaked memo from this or that anonymous source. Some integrity reporting! Some national newspaper!" In reply, editor-in-chief Norman Webster dismissed the criticism, suggesting Davey was merely looking for a scapegoat for his impending loss. Which was it? How much were journalists to blame for John Turner's defeat? Or as two media experts have asked, rephrasing a question from the popular television show "Dallas," "Who shot J.T.?"[30]

Appearing on the CBC news show "The Journal" on September 6, Izzy Asper, the Liberals' western organizer, stated that "the journalists of Canada have got to do a little soul searching." Douglas Creighton, the publisher of the *Toronto Sun,* a paper which endorsed the Conservatives, wrote that Turner was the victim of "cheap shot journalism."[31]

The 1984 campaign, like the past five, was dominated by television. In the end, two images of the election remained in voters' minds: clips of Turner patting bums and the final exchange between Mulroney and Turner in the English-language debate. The media generally were obsessed with personality items and public opinion polls, to the detriment of the full airing of the policies at issue. A survey of major TV networks and newspapers across the country revealed that the competence and performance of the party leaders were the focus of "26 per cent of all network television campaign reports and daily newspaper front-page stories, as well as 31 per cent of newspaper editorials and columns in 1984." Moreover, the tone of this coverage was much more negative for Turner than Mulroney.[32]

As previously noted, most reporters treated the election like a horse race. The twelve nationally-funded media polls (two more than in 1980) told the public, weekly, who was winning the race, who was losing, and why.

Polls were the media's scorecard and the "lens through which almost everything else was interpreted." For the Liberals the news was devastating. "Poll after poll from all kinds of media outlets told of our plight in excruciating detail," Keith Davey remembers. "Every time we got up off the floor the next polls would knock us down."[33]

The image of Turner as a loser, deserved or not, was reinforced constantly throughout the election, especially following the TV debates. Three weeks before voting day, reporters were already writing their commentaries on why Turner lost.[34] As though subject to a domino effect, each gaffe and each negative poll result influenced the next. The following are only a few such examples.

The *Globe and Mail* ran several unkind photographs of Turner. On July 10, following his election announcement, he was pictured – a ridiculous grin on his face – saluting the press corps with a glass of water. A more controversial photo, on the *Globe*'s front page on August 25, showed Turner with the shadow of two forks (displayed on a banner behind him) coming out of his head. It made him look like the devil, a fool, or both.

CBC stories on "The National" repeatedly confirmed what Canadians already suspected: "Turner's handlers are worried that he can't perform under pressure" (July 11); "Turner is still learning on the job" (July 26); "Turner fumbled on equal pay for equal work and had to be prompted [at the debate on women's issues]" (August 13); "The P.M. needs every shot in the arm he can get nowadays" (August 19); "[Turner] is trying to save his campaign" (August 23).[35]

On August 9 CBC reported that a waiter had spilled coffee on Turner's pants and his wife, Geills, had to clean the stain while Turner waited in the washroom. This was followed the next day with a *Globe* front-page article headlined "Spill on PM's Pants a Job for PM's Wife." As Mary Anne Comber and Robert Mayne argued in their 1986 book, *The Newsmongers,* "the story managed to link Turner's promotion of women's issues with the incident by telling us that his wife 'dutifully went to wash away the offending spots.'"[36]

On August 31 the CBC reported that Turner had attended a local fair in southern Ontario, but had *not* won a prize!

In the *Maclean's* issue published the week of the election, Carol Goar's cover story included the tidbit – "a cruel twist," she called it – that when Turner became prime minister he had sold his stock market portfolio in accordance with conflict-of-interest guidelines for more than $80 million. She pointed out that had he not re-entered politics, his stocks would have been worth another $10 million owing to the boom in the market. The story left the impression, totally undeserved, that Turner was a poor business manager.[37]

That some journalists were out to crucify John Turner – or that one gaffe reinforced another – is difficult to dispute. "With Turner, we always went after him as a group," admitted Bob Hepburn of the *Toronto Star* after the fact. "We smelled blood, and we attacked. With Mulroney, we attacked at the end, but at the end people had already made up their minds."[38] Turner was indeed the object of sarcastic and cruel humour, and journalists, as they had done with Joe Clark, made ridiculing his personal idiosyncrasies – his throat-clearing, his two-fisted handshakes – a popular national pastime.

Turner himself did not hold the media responsible for his loss. "I think the country wanted some change, the Liberals had been in for a long time," he conceded six years later, prior to his retirement as leader. "When I decided to run for the leadership, I felt we were not going to win the '84 election ... but I do not blame the media [although] the *Globe and Mail* picture [on August 25] was pretty contrived journalism and I thought some of the over-attention on bum patting maybe we could do without. I didn't worry about it."

Nevertheless, Turner made many mistakes that contributed to his own defeat and allowed the media to abuse him. Most notably, he mishandled the patronage issue and was thus forced to account for sixteen years of often-unpopular Liberal rule. Equally, he failed to adapt to a 1980s-style, TV-driven election campaign and as a consequence appeared to voters just as the media and Mulroney portrayed him, as yesterday's man. In answering "Who Shot J.T.?," journalists Alan Frizzell and Anthony Westell concluded that "the best answer is that the [Liberal] party shot itself, with some help from journalists, who were extremely interested in its problems with patronage, organization and campaign difficulties."[39]

From a political strategist's point of view, Turner's gravest error was that he allowed the media to gain control of his agenda, something that Pierre Trudeau never did. Instead of leading the way and discussing the issues he wanted, Turner was too often forced to react to the media's polls, stories, and negative reports. In the public's mind, it was the sign of a weak, unconfident, and insecure leader.

Brian Mulroney, on the other hand, had a superb organization behind him. Every detail was carefully planned and executed, and he maintained control of his agenda throughout the campaign. This was no better illustrated than by the fact that he refused the media's demands to reveal the price tag of his numerous election promises until he was ready, which wasn't until the last week of August. All the journalists could do was criticize him for being too slick. Their relations with the new prime minister had yet to be fully worked out.

Chapter Seventeen

Media Junkie

*The drawbacks are that in the 1980s and 1990s we are
living with the kind of scrutiny and criticism that you read
of and see every day, and that can unintentionally or otherwise, wound people and hurt children, offend families, and
hurt friends. Innocent people can get caught up in these
attacks. Some people feel that there is a culprit behind
every transaction and there is malevolence in every
statement.*

Brian Mulroney, 1988

It remains a mystery why Prime Minister Brian Mulroney would have agreed to an interview with three reporters from the *Globe and Mail* in the midst of the most critical negotiations he had ever undertaken and why he would then talk so candidly. But on Monday, June 11, 1990, he did exactly that and lived to regret it. It was not the first or last time Mulroney behaved so impulsively; in this instance, however, the consequences were so serious that the whole country paid the price.

Late in the evening of Saturday, June 9, 1990, it looked as if Mulroney had done the impossible: after a week of hectic constitutional discussions in Ottawa, the first ministers had apparently agreed that the Meech Lake Accord of 1987 could be ratified. Quebec would again be a member of the constitutional family, as Mulroney liked to put it. Newfoundland premier Clyde Wells, a disciple of Pierre Trudeau's, had not been happy with Meech's decentralizing principles, but he had agreed to put the constitutional agreement before his Legislative Assembly before the June 23 deadline. Manitoba premier Gary Filmon thought he would be able to convene the mandatory public hearings and ratify the accord in time.

Mulroney had gone to bed at about 4 a.m., but he only slept for a few hours. Soon after he woke, he started phoning a variety of people who had supported Meech, including his former UN ambassador, Stephen Lewis, and the Quebec Liberal and commentator Eric Kierans. Later in the day, he called William Thorsell, the editor-in-chief of the *Globe*. Listening to Mulroney rave about the accord, Thorsell asked if the prime minister would be interested in speaking to three of the *Globe*'s Ottawa journalists. No doubt Thorsell also thought this would be a great copy to mark the newspaper's new format, to be introduced that Tuesday morning. Inexplicably, Mulroney agreed to Thorsell's request.

On Monday, at precisely 11 a.m, the *Globe*'s Jeffrey Simpson, Graham Fraser, and Susan Delacourt arrived at 24 Sussex Drive. Because work the previous week had been so demanding, the three journalists were exhausted. "We considered it an achievement just to get a taxi," Fraser recalls. The prime minister, too, was tired, and this, Fraser believes, may explain the tone of his remarks that day. The *Globe* team was ushered to the back lawn by press secretary Gilbert Lavoie for some small talk and photos, and then led into Mulroney's study, where small microphones were already set up so that the Prime Minister's Office would have its own tape of the interview. Lavoie sat by himself in the corner of the room.

The discussion with the journalists was straightforward. Mulroney talked of the high and low points of the past week and provided some historical context for the Meech negotiations. Relaxed and at ease with his company, he referred to the Fathers of Confederation in Charlottetown as "the boys" who "spent a long time in places other than the library." In defending the closed-door constitutional sessions, he offered his own version of Canadian history: "One of the greatest problems [John A. Macdonald] had [in London] was being stuck in this traffic jam on his way in from another weekend in the country; how depressed he was that the boys they had drank everything they had, and they were stuck in this bloody traffic jam getting back to the hotel. This is the way it was done. This is the way Confederation came about. There was no public debate."

Continuing, he explained why he had opted to call a first ministers' conference for the first week of June. "And so I decided, after consultations with my colleagues, mostly with Senator (Lowell) Murray and Paul Tellier, Norman Spector, people like this, that ... I remember when I told them, I called them right here, I asked them to come and see me, and I told them when this thing was going to take place. I told them a month ago, when we were going to start meeting. It's like an election campaign, you've got to work backwards. You've got to pick your dates and you work backward from it. And that ... and I said that's the day I'm going to roll all the dice. It's the only way to handle it." "And this was a month ago?" asked Graham Fraser. "About a month ago," said the prime minister. "Roll of the dice, this was a conscious, obvious decision," said Jeffrey Simpson. Mulroney asserted: "You had to roll all the ... the only way that this could be done was to roll all the dice."[1]

Back at the *Globe* office on Sparks Street, Fraser, Delacourt, and Simpson debated the significance of the "roll all the dice" phrase as a lead for their story. Mulroney had also revealed that he was planning to accept Clyde Wells's invitation to speak to the Newfoundland assembly about Meech Lake's merits, and Fraser argued that this was a more newsworthy detail. He wrote his article accordingly. Delacourt, however, disagreed and wrote her own version of the interview in which she emphasized the roll-all-the-dice strategy. Both stories were sent to Toronto, where *Globe* editors selected Delacourt's piece (with Fraser's name on it also) for the front page.[2]

In the next morning's *Globe*, under the headline "Marathon Talks Were All Part of Plan, PM Says," there appeared the statement "that's the day we're going to roll all the dice." Predictably, these few words caused a major upheaval across the country, an indication that even in the age of "telepolitics," print journalism still had some real power. In the minds of just about everyone, but especially Clyde Wells, poker talk of this sort confirmed yet again what many people had thought of Brian Mulroney for more than a decade: that he was a partisan, manipulative deal-maker who was willing to play "Russian roulette with Canada," as Christopher Young of Southam News put it in his *Ottawa Citizen* column on June 14. Serious damage to the fragile constitutional agreement had been done.

Wells, who had not been happy with either the process or the latest revision of the accord, had his out – despite an early morning telephone call from Mulroney assuring him that the federal government had no "secret plan to turn the Meech Lake impasse into an 11th-hour crisis." A week later, however, when Mulroney and his constitutional minister Senator Lowell Murray attempted a last-ditch effort to extend the June 23 deadline for Manitoba, whose legislature was mired in a procedural muddle, Wells refused to hold a vote in the Newfoundland assembly. "That is the final manipulation," declared the premier. "We are not prepared to be manipulated any longer."[3] Meech died and with it Brian Mulroney's dream, for the moment at least, that he would be the prime minister to lead Quebec back into the Canadian family.

Prime Minister Mulroney later insisted that the impression created by the *Globe* was false, but on June 20 the newspaper published a partial transcript of the interview verifying that he had said substantially what Fraser and Delacourt had written a week earlier. As an experienced prime minister who had been burned more than once by the media in the past six years, Mulroney should have been more careful. Certainly by this time he had gained a keen insight into the inner workings of modern Canadian political journalism. He understood that the boys in the gallery (many of whom by the late 1980s were women) were not his buddies, that nothing was ever off the record, and that when he spoke to three reporters in the quiet surroundings of his prime ministerial study, he may as well have been speaking to the entire country. But as long as anyone could remember, Brian Mulroney had been a "schmoozer," a hard-working "stiff" who had once enjoyed fine Scotch, beautiful women, and a night out with the guys. Those who know him well regard him as a charming man with a good sense of humour – hardly the slick and devious operator so many journalists have portrayed. This pleasant side of his personality, as well as his overwhelming desire for affection and notoriety, however, also proved to be a political liability when it came to dealing with the tough, cynical, and all too moralistic Canadian media of the 1980s.

Thanks to journalist John Sawatsky and his 1991 book *Mulroney: The Politics of Ambition,* we know a great deal about Brian Mulroney's past. Certainly no other Canadian leader, while in office, has ever had such an extensive study done of his life. Sawatsky claimed that he and his assistants conducted 600 interviews and dug up each and every indiscretion made by Mulroney since birth. Since Sawatsky did not include footnotes, sources, or lists of the people interviewed, we have to take him at his word. Typically, in its coverage of the book, the media played up stories about Mulroney's drinking habits and sexual escapades.

Nevertheless, there is much in the book about Mulroney's personality that rings true – the ambitious nature, sizable ego, intellectual weaknesses, and the ability to bounce back from a setback. Born on March 20, 1939, in Baie-Comeau, Quebec, into an Irish working-class family, young Brian had big plans, though he would never forget where he came from. In early profiles about him, his North Shore roots were a natural hinge for journalists. "Charm and hardwork have taken Brian Mulroney from his humble background to the Tory leadership," wrote Robert Mackenzie in a *Toronto Star* feature on June 12, 1983, after Mulroney's victory at the Conservative leadership convention that month.

Mulroney did not have an easy time in university, but he apparently had a good time. He received a B.A. from St. Francis Xavier University in Antigonish, Nova Scotia, then failed a year of law at Dalhousie before transferring to Laval University's law program, where he eventually was awarded a law degree. More importantly, his education in Quebec and Nova Scotia provided him with the network of friends, associates, and political hacks that would play such a significant role in his ascent to power. Loyalty and friendship were the two virtues that mattered most to Mulroney, then and later. In a September 1986 series in the *Globe and Mail* about the Conservative government, called "The Troubled Mandate," reporter Jeff Sallot caustically observed that "everyone in town knows that the real centres of power shift easily and can be charted only with reference to yearbooks and alumni lists from St. Francis Xavier and the law school at Laval

University, Prime Minister Brian Mulroney's alma maters." Included among those who counted were PMO strategists and Tory politicians of later years: Bernard Roy, Lowell Murray, Fred and Gerald Doucet, Sam Wakim, Michael Meighen, Patrick MacAdam, and Lucien Bouchard. Mulroney's experience at Laval equally ingrained in him a Quebec-centred view of Canadian politics and history that he would carry with him to the prime ministership.[4]

Following graduation in 1964, he went to work for a Montreal law firm, eventually making a name for himself as a top labour lawyer, not to mention as a key Quebec Tory fund raiser and organizer. As he worked his way up the corporate law ladder – settling a labour dispute at *La Presse* and securing an appointment on the 1974 Cliche Commission (which investigated unrest in the Quebec construction industry) – he earned a reputation as a shrewd negotiator. Nevertheless, Mulroney continued to dabble in politics. It satisfied his craving for attention. When someone asked about a particular issue he was more than willing to offer his opinion, laced with the appropriate colourful adjectives. In 1976, when he was only thirty-six, Mulroney sought the Conservative leadership for the first time. He believed his numerous contacts in the media would be helpful. He was wrong.

Since his days at university, Mulroney had been fascinated with the media and the supposed glamorous life of journalists. He devoured newspapers and was addicted to news.[5] Media junkie, news freak, mediaphile, and media groupie are a few of the ways writers and associates describe this affliction. Perhaps more significantly, he enjoyed seeing his name in print and cared what was said about him on TV. From the time Mulroney was featured in a 1961 *Maclean's* interview with Peter Newman and Peter Gzowski about young politicians of the future, he started cultivating contacts. (Interestingly, the contact with Newman has remained close. Newman has been guaranteed access to Mulroney and members of his cabinet to write the definitive story of "The Mulroney Years.")

Within time, Mulroney became a popular source for journalists covering the Quebec political scene. He was also very adept at planting and manipulating stories. According to Sawatsky, during Mulroney's stint as a member of the Cliche Commission, "he leaked stories shamelessly and would often call up a particular reporter just before deadline with a few extra nuggets to give him an edge on the competition ... He loved to take a reporter confidentially aside for a little tete-a-tete, soliciting his views on what the commission should do next, then offering some inside information. He often gave a journalist a preview of upcoming events and got him to sit on the news until he gave the signal ... He had mastered the art of making deals with the media, and the reporters liked him for it."[6] Among those journalists he befriended were Bill Fox of the *Toronto Star*, who covered the Cliche

Commission hearings and would later become Mulroney's first press secretary, and L. Ian Macdonald of the *Montreal Gazette,* his biographer and speech writer.

Initially when Mulroney decided to run in 1976, journalists were very positive in their profiles and coverage of his speeches. One reporter from the *Edmonton Journal* gushed about his "Paul Newman eyes," his Robert Redford "wavey hair" and his deep voice, "the resonance of a Lorne Greene school of broadcasting grad."[7] Mulroney ate it up, as if the opinion of a young reporter from Edmonton or Montreal made a difference in the whole scheme of things. But like John Diefenbaker, Mulroney worried incessantly about everything written about him, significant or not.

By entering the Conservative leadership race in 1976, Mulroney stepped over the invisible line that separated the "background source" (the feeder of rumour and gossip) and the subject of the story (the one gossiped about). In failing to see that his relationship with journalists had been altered, he paid a heavy price. In his memoirs, Senator Keith Davey included sage "advice to aspiring politicians." His first rule was that "no matter how close your relationship with any member of the working press, that person will put his craft ahead of your friendship."[8] Mulroney did not understand this in 1976, nor when he returned seven years later; he mistakenly expected his media friends to be loyal.

In his attempt to capture the Tory crown, Mulroney, the newcomer with no real public political experience, put on a flashy campaign. Unlike his opponents, he leased his own private jet and was perceived to be the "Cadillac" candidate in the pocket of such tycoons as Paul Desmarais. Nothing bothers the Ottawa press gallery more, or makes them more suspicious, than a showy capitalist with an abundance of funds (delegates of other candidates folded over Mulroney stickers so that they would read MONEY). The word "slick" came to be the journalists' adjective of choice when describing Mulroney.

Mulroney himself was not used to reporters trailing after him, watching for any slip they could write about. When he finally lost to Joe Clark, he was miserable. But it got worse in the next few days. At 3:15 a.m., the night the convention ended, Richard Cleroux of the *Globe* discovered one of Mulroney's Quebec workers, Paul Gauthier, paying off delegates $150 each for their hotel expenses. Gauthier was angry that the number of envelopes he handed out (400) was more than the number of votes Mulroney had received on the final ballot (369). Though this kind of payment was not unusual, Cleroux made the most of it in a scathing story that appeared in the *Globe* the following day: "Money was one of the big reasons why Brian Mulroney, the front-runner of the campaign for so long ... lost this campaign that he had dreamed about ... The Mulroney campaign was a media myth, plastered together with dollar bills, free lunches, paid organizers, lots of hoopla and little content. The real Brian Mulroney is somebody other than what the Conservatives saw." While Cleroux's story was substantially correct, it had a moralizing tone. Mulroney was livid. He tore into the *Globe* reporter in a telephone call full of yelling and swearing. Mostly though, Mulroney was personally hurt, believing that Cleroux had betrayed his trust and friendship.[9]

In the years that followed, Mulroney was very bitter about his loss. He started drinking heavily and, among friends, was not discreet about his negative opinion of Joe Clark. But he managed to keep his true feelings from the members of the media – until he spoke with Stephen Kimber, a freelance journalist from Ottawa who was preparing a profile of Mulroney for *Financial Post Magazine*. By this time Mulroney was president of the Iron Ore Company of Canada and Kimber was mainly interested in his success in the business world; all Mulroney was interested in, however, was talking about politics and the coming federal election. He met Kimber in Ottawa at the Chateau Laurier Hotel, where he was attending a meeting, and invited the writer to join him for a two-hour car trip back to Montreal.

His critical comments about Clark and the Tory organization were published two months later: "After Joe, Who? Brian Mulroney, perhaps. He's bitter as hell, but he does say he's only 39." The article may as well have been entitled "Brian Mulroney: Sore Loser." Kimber had written: "Talking with Brian Mulroney about the 1976 leadership convention is like scraping sandpaper over an exposed nerve. With even the gentlest encouragement, the hurt tumbles out into the open." When they had sat down for dinner at Mulroney's house in Montreal, Mulroney had told Kimber that "if Joe Clark wins the next election, I'll eat this plate. I mean, let's look at it. Can you see any way that he can win? Any way at all?" Later Mulroney deeply regretted this public catharsis and implied that Kimber had "broken a confidence."[10]

After this episode, Mulroney quietly bided his time, watching from the sidelines as Clark won power in 1979 and then lost it within nine months. Mulroney's role in undermining Clark's leadership over the next three years has been widely speculated about and has provided fodder for journalists ever since. Sawatsky's research indicates that while Mulroney was supporting Clark in public, he and his associates were harassing the embattled Conservative leader behind the scenes. It is alleged, for instance, that in the summer of 1981 Mulroney planted stories in *Le Devoir* through his contact on the paper, Pierre O'Neill, to the effect that the Conservative Party was deep in debt "because major donors had lost confidence in Clark." (In his biography of Mulroney, Ian Macdonald blamed some of Mulroney's supporters for these dirty tricks.)[11] It got so bad that in December 1982 Mulroney (with Clark at his side) held a press conference at Montreal's

Ritz-Carlton Hotel to declare his support for Clark as leader. The reporters were skeptical about his sincerity.

A month later, at the party's convention in Winnipeg, Clark received 66.9 percent of the delegates' support and opted to call a leadership convention. Most journalists singled out Mulroney as the chief culprit in Clark's political demise. If Mulroney had indeed been trying to undermine Clark, he had done a lousy job; after all, 66.9 percent support is nothing to slough off. Yet Clark believed that anything less than a vote of 70 percent would have continued to split the caucus. Perhaps he was right.

"He [Mulroney] is definitely a phony human being," says Ottawa columnist Don McGillivray, who claims he went through a "conversion process." McGillivray once lived in the same neighbourhood as Mulroney, in fashionable Westmount in Montreal. "The thing that shocked me," he says, "was when he had a joint press conference with Joe Clark and told the public that he was with Joe. But after, we found out it was all a put-up job. His friends had advised him to get out of the 'traffic.' It was a lie; all the while he was working to unseat Clark when he was saying he was not doing it."

Mulroney declared himself a candidate for the Tory leadership on March 21, 1983, and was forced to confront his image as a slick and shallow politician. While he ran a campaign that was low-key compared to his 1976 outing, he was still overly sensitive to media criticism. On more than one occasion, he phoned the CBC to berate both Knowlton Nash and Peter Mansbridge for what he regarded as an unfavourable or mistaken story on "The National." He was jealous too when *Maclean's* put Tory leadership candidate John Crosbie, not him, on the cover of its magazine three weeks before the convention. "Those myopic, incestuous bastards!" Mulroney said about the journalists in Ottawa. "They're skeptical because they don't know me. Believe me their time will come!"[12]

But the press corps were a tough group to win over. Mulroney's image, declared journalist Ron Graham in his 1986 book *One-Eyed Kings*, "was the first to come through the door; it dominated the room while he was talking; and it was the last thing to leave the memory." In his story about Mulroney's subsequent 1983 leadership victory, the *Globe and Mail*'s John Gray wrote: "Mr. Mulroney is a curious mixture, an unpredictable combination of sweet talk and harsh talk, a consummate charmer whose words can become cruel in a moment. And almost everything about him seems deliberate and calculated."[13]

As journalists watched Mulroney work his way up to the office of prime minister in September 1984, their opinions about him were mixed. Most reporters respected his landslide victory and hailed it as the beginning of a new era in Canadian politics. In Quebec, particularly, where the

Conservatives won fifty-eight out of seventy-five seats in 1984, editorialists were very positive about Mulroney's prospects. And journalists who had travelled on Mulroney's campaign plane through Quebec also judged him favourably.

But there were others who criticized his lack of specific policies and questioned his integrity.[14] In their view, the real Brian Mulroney was not the family man with the stunning wife and three beautiful children, who spoke about infusing "our federalism with a spirit of fraternity and creativity," but the partisan politician who had cuttingly called Liberal Bryce Mackasey a whore for accepting a patronage appointment as ambassador to Portugal. As he took office in the fall of 1984, Mulroney was obviously going to have to deal with these negative perceptions.

As veteran Southam columnist Charles Lynch recalls, Prime Minister Brian Mulroney must have caught a glimmer of his new reality during one of his first media scrums, when "the boys were jostling him." "Hey wait a minute," said Mulroney, "we are all friends here." Almost in unison "a large groan came from the group," says Lynch. Every prime minister since Pearson learned that it was difficult, if not impossible, to be chummy with members of the press gallery. Relationships with journalists must change with the acquisition of power. "You go from being a source and only dealing with the media when you want to," Bill Fox, Mulroney's former press secretary says, "to someone who has to deal with them on a daily basis." Mulroney did not find this transition easy (an error in judgment he later recognized in an interview published in the *Globe and Mail* on June 11, 1992. "I made a mistake. I thought it was possible to maintain this kind of relationship," he said about his past friendships with journalists).

At first the prime minister, who had himself charged the Liberals with secrecy, adopted the same approach, on the council of his advisers. Afraid that the new Tory administration would slip up, Mulroney, assisted by Bill Fox, attempted to centralize all government communication through the PMO. Leaks were to be halted, media sources were to be silenced. But the arrangement was unworkable and led to the implementation of draconian guidelines that unhappy civil servants were to follow in their dealings with the media. By the end of November 1984, Mulroney was forced to revise his plans, though off-the-record discussions between journalists and bureaucrats were still theoretically forbidden.

Ottawa journalists lambasted Mulroney and his "cronies" for trying such a misguided manoeuvre. They also didn't appreciate press secretary Bill Fox's gruff manner. Fox had known Mulroney since the mid-1970s, when he had covered Montreal for Southam News. In 1983 he was the Washington bureau chief for the *Toronto Star.* With his burly, down-to-earth style he was a natural choice for Mulroney's first press secretary.[15] For Fox, however, the transition from journalist to press secretary was difficult. "Journalists who leave journalism," he says, "are likened to people with a religious vocation who leave the monastery. You really are deemed to have 'sold out.' I had very close friends tell me after the fact that they couldn't deal with the notion that I would do something like that."

During his five years with Mulroney (he was made the PMO communications director in 1985), Fox was very efficient when it came to details. Though he takes exception to the term "spin doctor" as a description of his job, he does admit that there was a master plan for dealing with the media. He left nothing to chance. "The reason you plan," he explains, "is so that nothing distracts from or distorts the message you are trying to put out. If the prime minister is standing on a podium and a flag drops on his head, you will be hard pressed to find anybody there who knows what he said."

Fox rubbed many reporters the wrong way, and he discovered that his own skin was thinner than that of most politicians – "I had a lot of bums question my competence, people I would not have hired on a bet." Fox especially took exception to negative stories about his boss, once going so far as to threaten to "rip" *Toronto Star* reporter Joe O'Donnell's "fucking lungs out" for a story about renovations to the prime minister's residence.[16]

All of this contributed to a growing distrust of Mulroney and his strategists. Reporters did not respect or fear Mulroney as they had Trudeau. In the spring of 1986 allegations were made in the *Globe and Mail* that Industry Minister Sinclair Stevens had committed a serious breach of the government's conflict-of-interest guidelines (he was eventually forced to resign from the cabinet). Away on a trip in the Far East when the news first broke, Mulroney was reluctant to meet with the reporters travelling with him. Finally, after a certain amount of harassment levelled at his press secretary Michel Gratton, the prime minister held a brief press conference, declaring that within time Stevens would be totally vindicated (something which, in fact, did not come to pass).

After reading his prepared statement, he refused to answer any questions. "Then suddenly," as Gratton recalled, "through the din, he distinctly heard the blunt question yelled by Derik Hodgson of the *Toronto Sun:* 'Are you afraid to go back and face it?' He stopped momentarily, turned abruptly to me, and barked, 'Who said that?' I'd never seen such an expression on his face ... He was clearly enraged. You can accuse Brian Mulroney of a lot of things, but not of being a coward."[17]

A few years later on another overseas trip, this time to attend the Francophonie summit in Senegal, journalists wanted Mulroney to answer questions about a budget leak, but he refused. They persisted, yelling after Mulroney while he was touring a Senagalese village. "Have some class, for

God's sake," the prime minister told them. "We will when you do, sir," Patrick Doyle of the *Toronto Sun* replied.[18]

Some reporters tended to regard anything Mulroney did with a mixture of suspicion and cynicism, usually believing that he had a devious ulterior motive. For instance, in a 1990 article on Mulroney's success at keeping his caucus united, *Saturday Night's* Ottawa editor, Charlotte Gray, portrayed the prime minister as an unprincipled man who did almost anything, used every manipulative trick in the book, to win over his MPs. (This included apparently flattering their wives – "It removes the danger of an unbelieving spouse mouthing off at breakfast about the funding cuts to women's groups," Gray wrote, as if she had the evidence to back up such a charge).[19]

It seemed that journalists conjured up controversy when there was none and deliberately distorted Mulroney's words. In an interview in August 1989, Greg Weston of the *Ottawa Citizen* did not listen to what the prime minister actually said about lowering the goods and services tax from the proposed 9 percent to 7 percent; instead he observed Mulroney's "body language" and from that deduced that a drop in the rate was in the works. He wrote his story accordingly. This created the typical media domino effect. Other reporters, editors, and columnists reacted to Weston's original article as if it were the gospel truth. The Canadian Press added in its version that "there was confusion on the weekend after statements by Prime Minister Brian Mulroney and Finance Minister Michael Wilson about whether the rate could be lowered." The only thing that was confusing was the media's interpretation of Mulroney's statements in the *Citizen's* story. Veteran press watcher George Bain regarded the whole episode as "wilful ignorance, and an indecent lusting after page 1, where it is known that conflict and confusion play better than concord."[20]

Feelings towards Mulroney were so hostile among many members of the media that there were loud complaints when, in a September 1985 (and 1986) interview with the Global TV team of Doug Small, Peter C. Newman, and Peter Trueman, the prime minister was treated gently, decently, and with respect. Owing to mainly negative past perceptions about him, Mulroney was never accorded the traditional honeymoon treatment, when journalists go easy on their prey. From the beginning "there was always this notion of the sleaze factor about him," said Anthony Westell, the director of the school of journalism at Carleton University. "I don't know if it is right or not. Is he more untrustworthy than any other prime minister? I don't think so."[21]

Clearly, a large part of the problem was Mulroney himself and his habit for lapsing into overblown rhetoric. No politician could have lived up to the kinds of grandiose election promises Mulroney made about altering the structure of the Canadian political system. In the television debate with Liberal John Turner, Mulroney took the moral high ground on the patronage issue, but once his government was in office, Tories replaced Grits on most major government boards. As Conservative leader, before his election, he referred to the universality of such social programs as family allowances and old age pensions as a "sacred trust," but in his government's first major budget, in May 1985, he supported his finance minister's plans to partially de-index pensions. When challenged by little old ladies shaking their fists in his face, Mulroney backed down. The media portrayed him as vascillating and weak at the knees. He spoke about reducing the deficit and then was forced to explain why he spent $13,000 so Michael Wilson and two advisers could fly to Florida at taxpayers' expense for a brief meeting with him. He accepted a $7,000 salary cut and then spent more than $100,000 redecorating his official residences.[22] Members of the Ottawa gallery live for such inconsistencies, since it allows them to publicly spank the prime minister – which they did, and regularly.

Had they been ignored, many of these incidents would have been forgotten. The public has a short memory; the prime minister did not. "From the very outset, and for the duration of my sojourn in the Prime Minister's press office," wrote Michel Gratton, who worked in the PMO during the Conservatives' first term, "the media held a disproportionate importance and fascination for Brian Mulroney. What hurt most is that the media knew it. After the ego-bruising they suffered at the hands of Pierre Trudeau, who regarded them all as some sort of lower life form, they were served up a media junkie on a silver platter." "So, what are the boys saying?" (as Gratton's controversial best-selling memoirs were titled) became the cry from the prime minister that Gratton dreaded most. "Just once," he reflects, "I should have responded, 'it doesn't matter Sweet Fanny Adams what the boys are saying. Get on with the job.'"[23]

Gratton paints an unflattering portrait of Mulroney as a shallow politician who cared too much about tomorrow's headline and not enough about where he was taking the country. Not surprisingly, the publication of the book, in the fall of 1987, stirred up a lot of resentment at the PMO, where, says Bill Fox, Gratton was considered a "lout." Fox, who had hired Gratton as his assistant in June 1984, dismisses much of the book. "First, Michel was a press secretary, so whatever conversations he had with the prime minister are obviously going to be about the press! Secondly, Michel's view of the world isn't everyone's ... just because Michel never figured out there was a plan, one shouldn't leap to the conclusion that there wasn't one ... A lot went on that Michel did not understand. The whole fiscal side, for example. Michel, not unlike a lot of journalists, understands 'poached eggs' about the economy."

Fox maintains that Mulroney has a "tougher skin" than Gratton and other journalists have suggested. "The prime minister regularly reads that he is a vacuous, unctuous, intellectual pygmy whose wife only knows how to shop, whose kids are rented, and whose dog belongs to somebody else. How many people in society would put up with that? Not very many."

Occasionally, Mulroney lost his temper, particularly when journalists went after his wife, Mila, and their children. While he accepted that the public had a right to know "relevant" aspects of his private life – and even ridiculed rumours in 1991 that he had started drinking again after the failure of the Meech Lake Accord and that his marriage was on the rocks – he drew a line. In September 1991, *Frank Magazine,* the satirical Ottawa journal, carried a mock ad that urged young Conservatives to enter a contest to "deflower" Mulroney's seventeen-year-old daughter, Caroline. Later, when a CBC interviewer asked Mulroney for his reaction to this, he responded like any angry father: "When a trash magazine puts that on the cover of a magazine – an incitement to gang-rape my daughter – I wanted to take a gun and go down there and do serious damage to these people." Though the anger was real, his reference to taking a gun was an obvious exaggeration. Several newspapers, though, followed this up with interviews with anti-gun lobbyists and spokespeople from the National Action Committee for the Status of Women, who lectured the prime minister on the use of violence. Better still, in a CP story, Julie McGregor Mason, the mother of Glen McGregor, *Frank's* assistant editor, claimed that Mulroney owed her son an apology!

Owing to the demands of television, the growing complexities of government, and an unhealthy dose of professional cynicism, too many Ottawa reporters have resorted to petty and frivolous journalism. Joe Clark and John Turner were victims of this, as was Brian Mulroney. When the prime minister travelled, he was accompanied by a great deal of technical equipment and the people who operated it. The PMO requires film and recordings of speeches no less than the journalists who cover a trip. Bill Fox recalls a brilliant idea he had in 1986: "One day I asked the chief of staff about Hercules transport planes. Could we save money shipping all this electronic stuff? It was estimated that $100,000 could be saved on trips if the transport planes were used." But when reporters got hold of these facts, they pictured a vain Mulroney wasting taxpayers' dollars on "home movies." Gratton called the media's treatment of this story "one of the worst distortions of reality that I saw during three years with Mulroney."[24]

Indeed, in the larger scheme of things, does it matter that the prime minister of Canada used the government jet, that he stayed at an expensive hotel in Paris, or that the Mulroneys had a nanny on the government payroll? "The intense search for significance in what politicians ate for lunch ... the altogether too common assumption that only political considerations drive decisions, the reduction of complex matters to 15-second clips followed by instant analyses from those who do not know that they should know better – these are signs," the *Globe and Mail*'s Jeffrey Simpson wisely observed, "of a press badly in need of a wider perspective and an extensive bout of soul-searching."[25]

Sometimes it has been difficult to distinguish real investigative journalism from the variety found in *People Magazine*. In April 1987 *Globe and Mail* reporters Stevie Cameron and Graham Fraser got their hands on Conservative Party cancelled cheques that showed that the PC party fund had paid for $308,000 worth of renovations at the prime minister's residences at 24 Sussex Drive and Harrington Lake.

The first part of the story, published on April 16, noted that the arrangement was a private deal worked out between Brian Mulroney and David Angus, the chairman of the fund, and that Mulroney had already paid back "a substantial amount" of the loan (declared by the PMO the next day to be more than half the total). Well into the article, Cameron and Fraser wrote that "according to an official at Elections Canada, use of the PC Canada Fund in this way is not against the law." But the hook was in the third column: "On November 30, 1984, Mr. Mulroney told reporters he would personally pay for any renovations to 24 Sussex Drive above the $97,500 that the Government spent on the house after he was elected September 4, 1984." The implication: the *Globe* had apparently caught Mulroney lying – again. On the other hand, if Mulroney had already paid back $158,000 and the remaining $150,000 constituted a loan between the leader and the party, why the fuss?

The cheque in question had been discovered among the papers of Giovanni Mockwinkel, an Ottawa interior designer who had worked for the Mulroneys but had fled the country (to Italy) owing about $400,000. From these documents came the titillating details about Brian and Mila's "huge" closets. It was revealed, among other things, that the prime minister's bedroom closet had enough room for thirty suits and eighty-four pairs of shoes, fifty of which were Gucci loafers. For Mila Mulroney there was a special storage closet – which was always kept locked – with "nine meters of hanging space for blouses and suits, 3½ meters of hang storage for evening dresses and storage for 100 pairs of shoes." About a year later, Cameron's industrious digging turned up the fact that PC funds apparently had been used to purchase an expensive piece of jewelry for Mrs. Mulroney as well. Cameron's main source for this story was a Miss Danielle Letarte, who three years earlier had spent seven weeks working as Mockwinkel's temporary bookkeeper.[26]

These stories damaged the Mulroneys' public image, portraying them rather unfairly as a vain couple consumed by their wealth and status. All of the articles lacked perspective and context. Was the prime minister of Canada supposed to show up for an official engagement in an off-the-rack seersucker suit from K-Mart and wearing Hush Puppies? Interestingly, Quebec journalists did not pay a great deal of attention to these stories. "No one in Quebec has ever written much about shoes and nice clothes," says *La Presse* columnist Lysiane Gagnon. "It was considered normal. What was wrong with Mila Mulroney shopping at Holt Renfrew?" she asks. Gagnon believes that this fascination with Mulroney's personal habits reflected a Puritanical streak among members of the English media. It was also one of the reasons why Mulroney was always more at ease with French reporters; they respected his privacy.

Most amazing of all was the reaction of Stevie Cameron when she learned that Mulroney and PMO officials were angry with her. As Michel Gratton related, "Stevie confided in me that she had felt harassed and taken aback by the personal attacks launched against her after that, and was genuinely surprised at the wrath she had unleashed in Mulroney."[27] If not anger, what did she expect Mulroney's reaction to be? He and his wife had been accused of pilfering party funds to feed their materialistic lifestyle; he was entitled to be angry.

Further complicating life for Mulroney was the access to information legislation passed in July 1983. Reporters could now produce sensational stories about hotel room and other travel expenses. As he explained in a *Winnipeg Free Press* interview in September 1988, "Ours was the first government to begin a term and complete a term under access to information. As prime minister I did not contemplate, because no one had done it before me, the reality of some persons off the street writing to a government department and asking for someone's expense account and that expense account being dropped on somebody's desk and published in a newspaper without any perspective." (In fact, of 10,234 information requests made in 1989–90, for example, only 8.4 percent originated with the media; business accounted for more than 50 percent.) No doubt Mulroney was thinking of a Southam News report of June 1986 that documented his trip to Paris that supposedly cost Canadians $520,024.17, including a bill for $28,525 ($3,400 a night) for a hotel suite. There was no mention of the fact that this was one of the hotels on the list of three provided by the French government for security reasons. Moreover, a month later the CBC reported that officials in Paris had, in fact, paid Mulroney's hotel bill.[28] By then, however, no one was paying attention.

In itself the freedom of information legislation was important. The prime minister and the cabinet members should have to be accountable to the public for their various trips and expenses. But the manipulation of this information by some journalists – the process of selecting, distorting, and publicizing it – has created an untrusting relationship between the media and the government. Government paranoia has been the result.

In the summer of 1992 the government was locked in a clash with its own information commissioner, John Grace, as well as Southam News, the Canadian Press, and the *Globe and Mail,* over its refusal to release constitutional polls done in 1991. For Grace, who requested a ruling on the government's decision in the Federal Court, this was a serious problem. "The paradox, if not the contradiction here," he wrote in his 1991–92 annual report, "is that the denial came against the background of the government's own much stated intention and unprecedented efforts to bring the constitutional renewal exercise out from behind closed doors into the stark light of public consideration ... Is it not unfair to ask: can the public mood of cynicism [about the government and constitutional process] come as a surprise to anyone?"[29]

Fair enough. Yet because Mulroney and his strategists were burned so often in the past, who could blame them for believing that the publication of poll results could have been manipulated so as to damage the tenuous constitutional negotiations then under way? (The polls, which showed the public's negative views on further constitutional discussions, were finally released in November 1992, with a flurry of front-page stories about how the government had ignored them. In his judgment of this case, Mr. Justice Marshall Rothstein of the Federal Court ruled against the government's argument that the polls should remain confidential, and ordered the government to pay the legal costs of the applicants.)[30]

After about a year and half of dealing with scandals (most of them concerning conflicts of interest involving half a dozen members of his cabinet) and watching his public image deteriorate drastically, Brian Mulroney started to fight back. There was no doubt that the prime minister received bad press in both English and French newspapers, but in defending himself, he sounded a little too much like the overly sensitive John Diefenbaker. He blamed the parliamentary press gallery for his low standing in the polls and referred to it as "a cottage industry ... that deals with facile and mostly pejorative references to what any given prime minister is doing." He told reporters they were failing the country by ignoring his government's "tremendous record," and started seeking out reporters from other parts of the country. This strategy created a backlash. Though obviously not monolithic, the media tend to regroup when attacked. At the end of January 1986, from one end of the country to the other, editorialists were criticizing Mulroney for whining about press coverage. As *London Free Press* columnist Gary May put it, "Mulroney's problem does not lie with the admittedly flawed press gallery, but within his own government." French commentators in Quebec, many of whom had been optimistic about the Conservative victory in 1984, were just as critical. (It needs to be pointed out, however, that Quebec journalists did not then or after criticize Mulroney personally; nor were they disturbed by his bombastic style.)[31]

Any attempt to build up his credibility was seriously damaged when the Sinclair Stevens conflict-of-interest case was broken by the *Globe and Mail* in April. Added to this were charges of real and imagined favouritism shown towards Quebec (for example, the awarding of the CF-18 contract to Canadair of Montreal instead of Bristol Aerospace in Winnipeg, which had submitted a lower and technically superior bid); overblown stories about the prime minister's trip to Paris; accusations (with the help of records obtained through access to information legislation) that Bill Fox padded his expense account on an official trip to Nassau in 1985; and, finally, allegations that Michel Gratton had harassed two female reporters. Journalistic overviews of the first two years of the Conservative administration published in the fall of 1986 singled out Mulroney as the "untrustworthy leader of an unmitigated public relations disaster." By the end of the year, veteran Ottawa reporter Arch MacKenzie described the relations between Mulroney's press office and the gallery as "trench warfare."[32]

In the new year, matters remained the same. On Saturday, January 17, 1987, the *Montreal Gazette* ran a front-page story claiming that André Bissonnette, the minister of state for transport, was mixed up in a complicated land flip – known as the Oerlikon affair because the land in question was to be the home of a defence plant operated by the Swiss manufacturing company Oerlikon Aerospace Ltd. The next day a forlorn-looking Mulroney announced at a gathering at the National Press Theatre that Bissonnette had been asked to resign from the cabinet pending an investigation, but he noted that this decision had nothing whatsoever to do with the *Gazette*'s damaging article. It was the prime minister's last formal conference with the national media for more than three years. After this Mulroney adopted the habit of stopping on the stairs on his way out of the Commons; looking down at reporters, he would answer only those questions he wished to hear.

The Oerlikon affair was symbolic of the problems besetting the Conservative administration during the latter part of its first term. As Mulroney set out to transform the country with a free trade agreement with the United States and a new constitutional arrangement with Quebec, he was forced to defend himself and his ministers against charges of "patronage, favouritism and cronyism." In some instances, the negative coverage was deserved. But Mulroney and his various advisers believed, and rightly in many cases, that the media played up any story that had a whiff of dirt, whether all the facts were known or not.

Typical was the exaggerated coverage given to allegations made by disgruntled Quebec Conservative Suzanne Blais-Grenier in August 1988 that there existed in Quebec a vast system of kickbacks and payoffs for federal government contracts. Though Blais-Grenier produced no evidence for the RCMP, the headlines were damaging to the government's, and especially Mulroney's, image.[33] Earlier, in a speech to the Canadian Daily Newspapers Association in April, Mulroney complained that the media were ignoring his "good" patronage appointments and concentrating solely on the more partisan ones. "If the cousin of the brother of the wife of the (Conservative riding) association president in Sudbury is appointed to the Unemployment Insurance Commission, it gets an eight column headline. Yet if you appoint the first Acadian in history to the Supreme Court of Canada, it's not mentioned," he told the journalists.

And it was true. No matter what Mulroney said or did, television portrayed him as journalists wrote about him – as a one-dimensional character, a man who was too partisan, political, and slick for his own good. ("Brian Mulroney and TV are perfect allies: he's so slick in front of the cameras that you can almost see the sheen on his utterances," observed the *Globe*'s Matthew Fraser in a September 2, 1985, article.) The result was that any real achievements – like tackling the deficit and placating Quebec – were overshadowed by the overly critical media assessment Mulroney received during his first four years in office. "He wanted, above all, to be liked by the Canadian people," wrote Jeffrey Simpson on the eve of the 1988 election, "instead, he has been widely vilified."

Just as Pierre Trudeau's personality had irritated or enraged Ottawa journalists, Mulroney's personality, as perceived by the media, got in the way of objective reporting. Too often reporters saw only Mulroney's petty, blustery side. When André Bissonnette was cleared of fraud, conspiracy, and breach-of-trust charges in February 1988, Mulroney lectured reporters for twenty minutes for the way they had treated his minister: "You seem to be the only people who don't understand how tough and unfair it has been … for an ordinary Canadian citizen to see himself lynched, drawn and quartered on the front page of a newspaper with no evidence." This was too much for reporters to swallow. Recalling this episode several months later, Terence Wills of the *Montreal Gazette* wrote: "So Mulroney fired Bissonnette based on information not in the media, then 13 months later blamed the media for Bissonnette's woes."[34] Such sniping set the tone for the election campaign that shortly followed.

CHAPTER EIGHTEEN

The Comeback Kid's Last Ride

To think of [John A.] Macdonald and [Brian] Mulroney in the same breath is a leap of logic that will baffle and even anger most Canadians. Yet the two men (who also hold in common the fact that no other Conservative prime minister has ever won two electoral majorities in a row) believed with equal ferocity in the country they governed – and both moved its prospects significantly forward.

Peter C. Newman, *Maclean's,* September, 1992

Not since 1911 has there been as divisive and dramatic an election as there was in 1988. The Mulroney government's proposed free trade agreement with the United States "dominated debate and aroused political passions to a degree seldom seen in Canada."[1] On the hustings, the three political parties continued to battle with the media for control of their images.

Since Liberal leader John Turner was trailing in the opinion polls, he was forced to be the most accessible to press and TV reporters travelling with him. Consequently, during the first part of the campaign, in October, he set himself up as a target for media criticism and was perceived to have made the most mistakes. There has long been a tendency for journalists to go easy on the NDP and its leader (since the chance that the party might actually win a federal election has been so slight), and the same pattern developed during this campaign; John Turner's vigorous criticisms of the trade deal drew much more commentary than those of Ed Broadbent.

With the Conservatives slightly more popular than the two other main parties, Brian Mulroney was in a position of power in dealing with the media. His strategists maintained tight control over his agenda, and access to him was limited. The Conservative campaign team, led by Norman Atkins, the mastermind of the 1984 victory, adopted the classic low-bridging technique that had worked so well for the Liberals and Pierre Trudeau in the 1980 election.

As usual, reporters complained about the lack of access to the prime minister and the Tories' blatant manipulation of information; they were also cynical about the use of the most advanced technology – direct mailings, mechanically signed letters, and voter tracking. Mulroney's campaign was "tightly wrapped," observed *Maclean's;* Jeffrey Simpson wrote of the prime minister's "politics of the cocoon"; Val Sears of the *Toronto Star* commented on Mulroney's "buttery campaign" that "slid smoothly to the next photo opportunity"; and *Ottawa Citizen* reporter Robert Mason Lee wrote an entire book – *100 Monkeys: The Triumph of Popular Wisdom in Canadian Politics* – on how the Tory team slyly attempted to hoodwink the voters. But who ultimately lost the election? Who made the most gaffes? And who was distracted and forced to defend himself against media-generated stories? John Turner, not Brian Mulroney.

The Conservative leader played the game as it had to be played in the 1980s. As Alan Frizzell and Anthony Westell explained in their analysis of the election, "[Mulroney's] national tour was carefully organized to move him across the country from planned picture opportunity to stage-managed rally, and the frustrated reporters hardly laid a glove upon him."[2] It was not by accident that reporters dubbed the Liberals', NDP's, and Conservatives' planes, respectively, "DespAir," "Air Apparent," and "No Comment Air."

The Tory strategy was deliberate – the only response possible to the sixty-second clip, a media format Luc Lavoie calls "ridiculous." "John Turner says to seniors that they are going to lose their pensions [under the trade agreement] and you have to counter that in a one-minute clip," says Lavoie, a former Quebec TV reporter who travelled with Mulroney during the campaign. "That's horseshit, man!" Since TV can be such a manipulative medium, Lavoie saw his role as being Mulroney's guardian; he was there to ensure that the prime minister was "on even ground." "We consciously decided that the PM would not be trapped by a scrum of media around him and the image we would be projecting would be our image," he adds. "We basically decided the election campaign was a show and it was our show. I call the shots, [the journalists] do not call the shots."

On the campaign plane, Mulroney sat at the front in the first-class section, his handlers in the middle, and the reporters at the back. No one crossed the imaginary lines without an invitation. Initially, the usual routine at every stop was to keep the journalists behind either white plastic chains or a cordon of RCMP officers. There was little opportunity for reporters to question the prime minister, let alone get close enough to him for a scrum. "He will speak to you if he has something to say," Mulroney's press secretary, Marc Lortie (who joined him in 1987), told members of the media. This was "a protocol suited more to royalty than to a party leader in a parliamentary system," remarked the *Globe*'s Jeffrey Simpson. Such tactics obviously created tension and uneasy feelings. But Mulroney successfully maintained control of his agenda, and by convincing enough Canadians that the free trade agreement would not cripple the country's economy or social programs, he won the election. Liberal leader John Turner was not as fortunate.

Since his devastating defeat in the 1984 election, Turner's media image was a sore point with the party faithful. He soldiered on, however, working with experts like Gabor Apor and Dr. Henry Comor, who taught him how to improve his public-speaking skills. With a background in the British theatre and television, Henry Comor had made a name for himself as a high-priced media consultant. He worked as an adviser to ABC News on its show "World News Tonight" and trained the CBC's Peter Mansbridge, among other media stars, in the use of the autocue technique. In 1987, when he joined the Liberal team, he taught Turner how to relax through a series of breathing exercises. "I was not John Turner's Svengali," he says. "I just helped him understand the media better ... We analyzed his TV performance and I pointed out how he could improve." And it worked. Within time, the hacking and lip wetting – subjects of ridicule in 1984 – vanished. By the fall of 1988 a polished Turner knew the issues and could handle himself in a scrum.

Still, it was not all smooth sailing. On January 17, 1988, during a taping of the CTV news show "Question Period," interviewer Pamela Wallin asked Turner if he had a real or potential drinking problem. For months rumours about Turner's appetite for Scotch had been circulating through the corridors of power in Ottawa. (Those close to him, like Peter Connolly, his principal secretary from 1987 to 1989, considered the drinking charge "absurd.") As he was having his make-up applied, Wallin had warned Turner that she was going to raise the issue. As she later explained it, "We were heading into an election year and this man wanted to be prime minister. Too many people – in his caucus, on the Hill, in the press corps – had witnessed it [Turner's drinking] too many times. Too many people were pointing the finger ... Yes, we do invade people's lives. But people who run for public office forfeit their right to complain about that. They sign a blank cheque when they embark on public life."[3]

Ray Heard, Turner's communications strategist in 1987, was also aware of the rumours in Ottawa about Turner's drinking. A few days before the CTV interview, he warned the Liberal leader that Wallin might question him about it, and urged Turner to challenge Wallin on camera to name her sources. Instead, Turner took a more diplomatic course. When questioned, he acknowledged that he enjoyed a "good party" but said he had never allowed it to interfere with his work. Whether or not Wallin's question was fair is another matter. While both Knowlton Nash and Peter Mansbridge of the CBC regard it as legitimate, they say they would not have asked it if they had not had a specific example to peg it on. As Mansbridge puts it, "Only about one percent of things happened the way the press club said it did." Turner himself accepts such intrusions as the heavy price one must pay for serving in public life. Yet he points out that "there is a difference between probing public policy and curiosity. It really does not advance the cause of the country to know how many Guccis Mr. Mulroney's got in his closet. That's crap!" In the end, although people sympathized with Turner, this episode reinforced his image as a weak and troubled leader.

More serious were Turner's problems with his own caucus, which had stubbornly refused to rally around him. He had survived a 1986 leadership review with an impressive 76.3 percent vote of confidence, but Liberal unity fell apart months later when Turner, following the advice of his Quebec lieutenant, Raymond Garneau, decided to support the Meech Lake constitutional accord. That crucial decision cost him the support of former cabinet minister Don Johnston as well as ten other Liberals, and brought Pierre Trudeau out of retirement to denounce the deal. During this period, Turner's office was usually in turmoil. The party had little money and the Liberals had difficulty attracting potential candidates for the next election. On top of this, in April 1988 the media gave a great deal of publicity to the unhappiness of Senator Pietro Rizutto and twenty-two Liberal MPs who challenged Turner's leadership. For that matter, every apparent disagreement of opinion or policy among members of the Liberal caucus, and every private Liberal meeting, was treated by journalists as another full-scale assault on Turner's leadership.

The other chief problem was Turner's position on the free trade agreement. He hedged as the negotiations were proceeding; then, in October 1987, he declared in a passionate outburst that if he was elected prime minister he "was going to tear the deal up." Much was made in the media about how Turner had abandoned the traditional free trade principles of Laurier and King. But as Turner tried to explain, he was not against free trade, only against the Mulroney-Reagan trade deal, which he felt left Canada too vulnerable on energy, culture, and social policies. He challenged the Conservatives to call an election and then ordered Liberal senators to block passage of the bill until Mulroney succumbed to his demands. Journalists jumped all over him for this anti-democratic action.

Once an election was called for November 21, John Turner transformed himself into Canada's saviour. He adopted the politics of fear. His anti–free trade speeches were so loaded with dire predictions for the future – particularly his charges that medicare was threatened and that Canada would become a "colony" of the U.S. – that Canadians did not know whom or what to believe. In fact, everyone entered the fight. The *Toronto Star* denounced the agreement as vehemently as the *Globe* supported it; organized labour fought big business; and authors Margaret Atwood, Pierre Berton, and Timothy Findley went toe to toe with Michael Bliss, Morley Callaghan, and Robert Fulford. Midway through the campaign, Canadians started to become nervous and the relatively high Conservative numbers in the polls began to decline.

This should have helped Turner, but it did not. His campaign had a terrible start. Even before the election was officially called, there was the publication of *Ottawa Citizen* reporter Greg Weston's muckraking book *Reign of Error: The Inside Story of John Turner's Troubled Leadership.* The book was a fine example of a hatchet job. Weston portrayed Turner as a callous, insecure, swearing lout with few redeeming qualities. Likewise, his wife, Geills, was painted as an overbearing spouse who treated Turner's staff as if they were her personal servants and who had little regard for money, which she spent lavishly.

Here was how Weston described a typical Turner afternoon: "Turner returns to his office after lunch before 2:00 p.m. in time for the daily House of Commons made-for-TV melee called Question Period at 2:15. The leader usually asks three questions one of his aides has written for him, expresses moral indignation about whatever issues his image consultants and caucus members will think will grab a spot on the newscasts that night, sits through the rest of the parliamentary sideshow and heads back to the office."[4] Weston saw Turner as a politician with no vision and no mind of his own – "a leader without conviction."

Reviews of *Reign of Error* were very critical. Weston noted that he started writing the book "from a standing start" in February 1988 and dashed it off in a few months. And it showed. There was little analysis, no footnotes, no sources, no index. According to Geoffrey Stevens, then managing editor of the *Globe and Mail,* "Weston … has delivered himself of a book that is so biased in its approach, so loaded in its language, so shallow in its analysis, and so slight and selective in its facts as to discredit itself from serious consideration."[5]

Weston relied too heavily on the testimony of lobbyist Bill Lee, Turner's disgruntled 1984 campaign manager, and other unhappy staffers in Turner's office. Worse, however, was his overwhelming use of anonymous sources. There is nothing wrong with quoting from anonymous sources – it is the kind of journalism that made Bob Woodward and Carl Bernstein of Watergate fame so successful – but Weston took this art to a new level. There is scarcely a page in his book in which he does not quote from "a former staffer," "a senior aide," "a close confidant," or "a volunteer on the 1984 campaign." Far too much of *Reign of Error* was a collage of gossip and hearsay. Weston reported what a friend of a friend of a friend told his wife about what Jean Chrétien had said about Turner. He reconstructed private conversations between Turner and Pierre Trudeau, between Turner and Chrétien, and between Turner and his wife. It is unlikely that his own newspaper, the *Ottawa Citizen,* would have published most of these quotes in the context in which he presented them.[6]

The book, lacking credibility, did minimal damage, but it did attract headlines and its serialization in the pro-Liberal *Toronto Star* did not help the party's cause. Turner, who refused to be interviewed by Weston, was particularly upset about the attacks on his wife. And he had contempt for the author's style. "I don't mind adversarial or investigative journalism," he said two years later, "but I think journalists ought to declare sources. Weston's book was anonymous source journalism at its worst. Period. And it is more fiction than fact, believe me."

The sad part for Turner was that he initially looked like the bumbler Weston had described. Three days into the election campaign, the media played up the confusion within Liberal ranks over the exact cost of the party's daycare policy. John Turner said $4 billion; principal secretary Peter Connolly estimated it could be "$8 billion, it could be 10 billion"; Quebec MP and Liberal finance critic Raymond Garneau said it was less than $4 billion. (A clarification a few days later settled on more than $10 billion for 400,000 daycare spots.)

After this, every gaffe or mispronunciation, no matter how minor, received critical coverage. In Toronto on October 12 at the Liberals' Confederation dinner, in front of 4,200 people, Turner, in pain from a pinched nerve in his back and without notes, delivered a passionate speech. When he accused Mulroney of selling out Canada's birthright, he got tongue-tied and said "birth rate." No one noticed except the cameras of CBC-TV. On "The National" that night, those three seconds of a forty-five-minute speech were the focus of the report. (CBC producer Mark Bulgutch weakly defended the clip by pointing out that in the shot they used, "Turner's body language showed passion. That is why we showed that part of the speech. We were not poking fun at him.")[7]

The situation deteriorated to the point that Peter Connolly lost his temper at a few unruly reporters in the bar at Toronto's Royal York Hotel after they had inquired rudely about some lost luggage. "For two weeks, Turner performed very, very well – and got awful, awful, awful coverage," Connolly told Graham Fraser. "TV was just brutal. But he continued to perform well. He did things, and you'd look at the television that night and say 'Jesus Christ, was I there?'" Connolly himself contributed to the campaign chaos by inadvertently suggesting to David Vienneau of the *Toronto Star* that Turner intended to make a major policy statement on abortion – something Liberal strategists were planning to have happen only in the leaders' debates and only if it was absolutely necessary. Despite Connolly's assertion that he had been misquoted, the damage had been done. Some Liberals were so upset with the way the campaign was being handled that they started talking about replacing their leader. Morale was so low that editorialists began writing that the "Liberals were a vanishing breed," columnist Bill Wilson wondered if the Liberals were "facing doom," and political cartoonists portrayed John Turner as an "endangered species."[8]

What happened next showed the awesome power of television to control an election agenda. On "The National" the evening of October 19, CBC anchor Peter Mansbridge, standing out of doors in a trenchcoat, announced that six days earlier Liberal strategists Michael Kirby, John Webster, Al Graham, and André Ouellet had met to talk about Turner's poor performance. At the conclusion of their discussion, Mansbridge continued, they had signed a memo. "They did not include their thoughts about leadership, but they did ask to see Turner in a face-to-face meeting." The story included references to a "frenzied series of cross-country phone calls" in response to low poll results and to the fact that a small group of key caucus members – Herb Gray, Lloyd Axworthy, Robert Kaplan, and Raymond Garneau – also wanted to meet with Turner but had been "blocked" by Peter Connolly. (In fact, Garneau had not been part of this group, and Connolly had agreed to schedule such a meeting for the following Friday, but Gray changed his mind.) "It's not clear yet what the five M.P.'s wanted to tell Turner, but it is known that asking Turner to step aside had been discussed by some of this group," Mansbridge added.[9]

The denials were heard immediately from everyone implicated. "It is an insulting and false piece of news," declared an angry Raymond Garneau. The four strategists issued a carefully worded news release denying the impression the CBC had given of their meeting. There was no plot, they maintained.[10] What really bothered all concerned was that the CBC had not contacted the principals involved, although Mansbridge had had a luncheon date with Kirby on October 14 that had been cancelled.

John Turner was terribly upset. On October 19, in Vancouver, he was told of the story a few minutes before he had to deliver a major speech. Afterwards he called it "the craziest thing I've heard in the last four years."[11] Two years later he was still bitter. "That Mansbridge story on the so-called revolt; there was no factual basis to it," he said. "It wasn't checked with me; it wasn't checked with the national director of the campaign, John Webster; it was checked with no one who would have known. That I consider total irresponsible journalism and it had its effect. They all denied it. It did not happen. That's pretty irresponsible stuff. We were told five minutes before a major fund-raising dinner in Vancouver before 1,800 people. I couldn't believe it. It was nonsense. I mean, what party would want to dump a leader in the middle of a campaign. It doesn't make any sense, for goodness sakes. It's so nuts. We just couldn't believe it. Can you believe anyone dumping the leader before the debates?"

Turner had a point. What had Mansbridge actually related? That Liberals met and talked. Indeed, when does a meeting stop being a meeting and become plans for a coup? Mansbridge and Elly Alboim, CBC Ottawa bureau chief, had worked diligently on the story for two or three weeks, piecing together all the leaks and rumours they could corroborate. It is highly likely, almost certain, that someone very high up in the Liberal Party spoke with Mansbridge, planting the seed from which the main story grew (though Alboim maintains that "there was no 'deep throat' on this story"). When they felt they had the correct facts, they decided to run the story, even though they knew it would have serious consequences and that it was unlikely Turner would resign in the middle of a campaign.

While Mansbridge did not report that an actual coup was under way, his words did leave that impression. Moreover, the use of the chief anchor and the decision (much to the horror of Mansbridge and Alboim) to put up a simulated memo (as if the CBC had such a document in its possession) contributed to a sense of the report's authenticity and importance. Mansbridge remains adamant about the gist of the story. "The only thing we did wrong ... was put up the memo behind me," he says. "[But] it was the right story. It was not what people were thinking, it was what people did. They had a meeting, they did not think about it ... TV has always been accused of covering the façade during the elections, here was a story of substance." In hindsight, Knowlton Nash wonders if Mansbridge should have been the one to deliver the report. "You have to think very carefully when the anchor does the story," says Nash. "The anchor doing the story suggests that this is *really* important – the Second Coming practically."

In the days following the news report, the CBC was criticized, not just by politicians, but by many print journalists. The late Marjorie Nichols regarded the broadcast as a "wild and wooly" story for which the CBC "has much to be ashamed about." Bill Johnson of the *Montreal Gazette* analyzed the story word for word and concluded that "this was television at its most allusive, most impressionistic, least precise, and most irresponsible."[12] The CBC's Don Newman, who also worked on the story, dismisses such attacks as "penis envy." "If that story appeared first in the *Globe* and then on CBC, it would not have been a bad story," he maintains.

There is no question that John Turner's public image had been damaged – again. For the Liberal leader the main issue was the free trade agreement. But for the media and the public, it was Turner's credibility: why should they help Turner be the prime minister when his own party was trying to knife him in the back? Meanwhile, as a consequence of the CBC report, senior Liberals were forced to declare publicly their loyalty to their embattled leader.[13] Under all this pressure, Turner did not fold; instead he prepared himself even more diligently for the TV debates.

This time John Turner was ready. He had learned from his terrible performance in 1984 never to "back down on camera, no matter how great the pressure." His team, including Henry Comor and André Morrow, a Montreal media consultant, had thoroughly rehearsed him. The French debate on October 24 came first. Mulroney stressed that he was a native son, Turner sounded polished, while Broadbent survived the ordeal. The next night was more interesting. The CBC's David Halton, who had the first question, curiously asked Mulroney about patronage. Watching in a Regina hotel room, critic Rick Salutin couldn't believe it. "It is an illuminating example of the power of the press to subvert public discussion," he wrote in his election journal, *Waiting for Democracy*. "The people of the country have made it clear that free trade is what matters to them, that they feel terribly uninformed about it, that they're waiting to hear about it – so Halton raises patronage."[14]

Beyond the cameras, other members of the media, relegated to spectator status, eagerly awaited "the clip." In 1984 it had been Mulroney's exchange with Turner over the Liberals' patronage appointments. In this debate it turned up in the third hour during a bout between Mulroney and Turner over free trade. The Liberal leader accused the prime minister of selling out the country. "You do not have a monopoly on patriotism," replied Mulroney. "I resent the fact of your implication that only you are a Canadian. I want to tell you that I come from a Canadian family and I love Canada and that's why I did it, to promote prosperity, and don't you impugn my motives!"

The two men bickered back and forth for a few more minutes until Turner declared: "We are just as Canadian as you are. Mr. Mulroney, but I will tell you this: you mentioned 120 years of history. We built a country east and west and north. We built it on an infrastructure that deliberately resisted the continental pressure of the United States. For 120 years, we have done it. With one signature of a pen, you've reversed that, thrown us into the north-south influence of the United States, and will reduce us, I am sure, to a colony of the United States, because when the economic levers go, the political independence is sure to follow."

"Mr. Turner," Mulroney fought back, "it is a document that is cancellable on six months' notice."

"Cancellable?" Turner said, as if he could not believe his ears. "You're talking about our relationship with the United States."

"A commercial document that's cancellable on six months' notice," repeated Mulroney.

The dramatic exchange continued for a few more seconds as each man tried to score a knockout.[15] When it was over, the press declared the Liberal leader the winner. It was Turner's "best hour," claimed Jeffrey Simpson the next day in his *Globe* column. The Canadian Press, in its main story on the debate, distributed an article that had little news but a lot of opinion: "Unlike 1984, Opposition Leader Turner did his homework, rehearsed his lines and dominated the stage, while Prime Minister Mulroney had to reach deep into his bag of tricks to keep the Liberal leader from stealing the show."

The media had treated John Turner miserably but were now suddenly in his corner again. In the days following the debates, Turner's poll numbers started to rise, but only temporarily. His vague economic plans about how he was going to pay for his $20 billion worth of promises and the public's concern about what might happen if he really tore up the trade deal ultimately cost him votes. Turner wanted Canadians to "just trust him," but that was not good enough because he had nothing to offer them in place of free trade. The pivotal moment for Turner may have come near the end of the campaign when Judge Emmett Hall, the eighty-nine-year-old former justice of the Supreme Court and framer of Canada's medicare system, announced that nothing in the free trade deal threatened the country's health care system. Turner had no reply.

On election day, the perception that Turner had been making wild statements about the deal's effect on the Canadian economy, management of energy resources, and health care system perhaps contributed to his defeat. Enough Canadians, especially in Quebec, where Mulroney was seen as the only leader who could deliver a new constitutional proposal, took the "leap of faith" urged by the prime minister to give him a victory. Brian Mulroney and the Conservatives won impressively on November 21 with 169 seats and 43 percent of the popular vote, while Turner and the Liberals improved to 83 seats (32 percent) and Broadbent and the NDP to 43 seats (20 percent).

The Tories had proven to be much more adept than the Liberals or NDP in employing modern campaign techniques, including ensuring that the media did not become a major factor. The party's realization that Mulroney did not need the media, or at least that he could control it, meant that things would be quite different during his second term as he faced his greatest political and personal challenge: Quebec and the constitution.

John Turner, on the other hand, had failed miserably in his media relations during the 1988 campaign, having had to defend himself or his associates from the moment the election was called. And so it had been since his return to political life in 1984. He announced his resignation as Liberal leader on May 3, 1989, to a chorus of media platitudes similar to those bestowed upon Arthur Meighen more than six decades earlier. Now that he was departing, journalists wrote about his dignity, his sense of duty, and his commitment to the country. Newspaper editorials marked him as the last honourable politician in the country.[16]

But some things remained the same. In March 1989 Turner had to deal with a *Toronto Sun* story, written by reporters Tim Naumetz and Robert Fife, alleging that he had demanded a $500,000 payoff in money and director- ships before he would retire. Turner called the story a "sleazy personal attack" and threatened to sue if no retraction was forthcoming. The matter was eventually settled out of court, and the *Sun* issued an apology.

It was not by accident that Brian Mulroney and the Conservatives captured sixty-three out of seventy-five Quebec seats in the 1988 election. Even though he was a child of anglophone parents, Mulroney had a Quebecker's view of Canadian history. And as a student of politics, he had long under- stood that no government could hold power in Canada very long without controlling a large bloc of Quebec votes. Thus, he did what he had to do. He made dangerous deals with Quebec politicians like Marcel Masse, Benoît Bouchard, and his close friend Lucien Bouchard (all of whom had voted "Oui" in the 1980 referendum on sovereignty-association), bringing into his caucus nationalists who believed him when he said that he would negotiate a new and fair constitutional arrangement with Quebec; he turned his back on the centralized federalism of Trudeau and accepted the reality of a decen- tralized, province-centred country; he went out of his way to appease Quebec with fat government contracts, earning the disdain of the West and setting in motion the cry for a Senate that was elected, effective, and equal; he yelled passionately about the trampling of French-language rights in English Canada but remained strangely silent in December 1988, when the Quebec Liberal government led by Robert Bourassa ignored a Supreme Court ruling and banned the use of English on outdoor commercial signs; and most dangerous of all, he came to the mistaken conclusion that he was indispensable to Canadian unity.

Mulroney has always been concerned about his place in Canadian histo- ry. Why else would he have secured journalist Peter C. Newman as his offi- cial biographer? In the prime minister's view, there was only one way for him to leave his mark and that was to achieve what Pierre Trudeau had not. If he could use his great negotiating skills to find a constitutional compro- mise that would allow Quebec to rejoin "the Canadian family" with dignity, then his life's political work would be truly fulfilled. This was easier said than done, and Mulroney became too desperate for a deal. Journalists could legitimately write about Pierre Trudeau's vision of Canada, but what was Brian Mulroney's, other than the appeasement of Robert Bourassa and the nationalist members of his cabinet?

The constitutional accord signed at Meech Lake in principle on April 30, 1987, and confirmed on June 3 in an all-night session at the Langevin Block in Ottawa seemed to have solved Mulroney's problems. Quebec's five demands had been met, including recognition of Quebec as a "distinct society" and the transfer of various federal powers to the provinces, and thus the way was now clear for Quebec to sign the Constitution of 1982. Two key issues remained. The first was the provision for unanimity – the accord had to be passed by the federal government and each of the ten provinces; the second was the three-year time limit placed on its ratification. Mulroney should not have been surprised when over the course of that three-year period, the players around the table changed for the worse. The elections of Frank McKenna in New Brunswick, Clyde Wells in Newfoundland, and Gary Filmon in Manitoba brought into the picture premiers who had not been at the 1987 meetings, and more significantly, who had serious reservations about the Meech Lake deal. Though it was not directly related to the accord, Robert Bourassa's decision to override the Supreme Court ruling on his French-only sign law confirmed to many in the "rest of Canada" exactly what the distinct society clause implied. In Manitoba, for example, Bourassa's actions gave Premier Gary Filmon, who faced opposition on Meech Lake from members of his own party as well as the Liberals and the NDP, ample excuse to halt proposed ratification of the accord in the provincial legislature.

As lunch after lunch and meeting after meeting during 1989 and 1990 failed to provide a solution to the constitutional impasse, the *Globe and Mail* predicted that "Meech Lake is likely to die." Most journalists portrayed Mulroney as weak and stubborn. In February 1990 he refused to support a Liberal-NDP resolution reaffirming Canada's commitment to bilingualism unless the resolution was tied to a reaffirmation of the Meech Lake Accord (which would have made the accord difficult for some Liberals and New Democrats to accept). He then turned around and told an audience in Kitchener that Canada "will rise or fall on the bilingual nature of its character. What is Canada without it? There's no country; it's like an adjunct of the United States." Such "hyperbole," as the *Globe* termed it, was proof that Mulroney had lost perspective.[17]

Near the end of March 1990, when matters seemed bleakest, a haggard prime minister appeared on television to announce that the end of Canada was near. Yet, as always with Mulroney, he left room for a glimmer of hope. Premier Frank McKenna had formulated a companion resolution that might reopen the discussion, and Mulroney seemed open to the New Brunswick leader's ideas. A few days later, in the face of tough opposition from key Quebec caucus members as well as the Quebec media, he backed down, distancing himself from the McKenna proposal and insisting that the accord had to be passed as is. "Once again," observed the *Ottawa Citizen,* "the prime minister leaves the impression (perhaps false) that he is working for Quebec rather than the entire country."[18]

All the while the June 23, 1990, deadline hung like a deadweight around Mulroney's neck. Then came a devastating blow. On May 22 his confidant and friend Lucien Bouchard, who had joined the government in 1988, suddenly resigned his cabinet seat. Away attending a conference in Norway, Bouchard, then the minister of the environment, had read a faxed copy of the report of the House of Commons Committee on Meech Lake that had been prepared by Jean Charest. In order to break the impasse, the committee had recommended twenty-three modifications to the accord (among them, a companion resolution "that would affirm the supremacy of the Charter of Rights and Freedoms while acknowledging Quebec's role as a distinct society). This was unacceptable to Bouchard, a staunch Quebec nationalist. An intellectual but passionate man, he quickly dispatched a telegram to the annual Parti Québécois meeting, which was marking the anniversary of the 1980 referendum with praise for René Lévesque and the "Oui" side. On his return to Ottawa, Bouchard refused to apologize for embarrassing the government with his telegram. He then submitted his resignation to the prime minister, ending a thirty-year friendship.

At last – a constitutional story the media could sink its teeth into. It contained all the ingredients of high drama – passion, betrayal, confusion. Print reporters tried to outdo their colleagues in television. In their minds, this was much more than the resignation of a cabinet minister. As Val Sears of the *Toronto Star* described it, "In the gathering dusk, Lucien Bouchard, a brown envelope in his hand, walked through the aura of television lights and up the steps of his friend Brian Mulroney's house. Once, in the 30 turbulent years they had been the closest of friends, Bouchard had said: 'Sometimes Brian needs a slap in the face.' Now he was about to give such a blow as would sting not only the Prime Minister of Canada, but would reverberate through Quebec and indeed send a shiver through the country's foundations."[19] And the press accused Mulroney of hyperbole!

In the days that followed, media reports had Mulroney "ashen faced," "feeling abandoned," and as upset as when "his father died." Clearly, in the collective opinion of journalists, Bouchard was the villain of this story for deserting his friend in his hour of need – "an emotional and theatrical gesture" was what Alain Dubuc, the chief editorial writer of *La Presse,* called it. Such sensational coverage not only exaggerated the significance of the Bouchard resignation, but pushed the Charest report, which might well have saved the day, to the back pages of the newspaper, off the television screen, and out of the government's agenda.[20] What was Bouchard doing in federal politics in the first place? And why did Mulroney think Bouchard would have accepted a watered-down version of the accord? These were the questions that needed to be answered, but they got lost in the emotional tempest.

Bouchard's resignation set in motion the final act of the Meech drama, staged when the prime minister and the premiers gathered at the Conference

Centre in Ottawa during the first week of June. As had been the case with Trudeau's efforts in the early 1980s, the media approached these discussions as if they were a constitutional poker game, a conflict of personality rather than policy. Because constitutional law makes for dull reading and boring TV, the personal angle was stressed. Who is holding all the cards? Who is bluffing? Hence you had the embattled Brian Mulroney; the desperate Robert Bourassa, who was forced to answer to the Quebec media for his every decision; the bitter Clyde Wells, clearly the rogue of the affair; and finally a distraught Sharon Carstairs, the Liberal leader of Manitoba, who prevented Gary Filmon (leader of a minority government) from committing himself to ratification.

Since the main discussions took place behind closed doors, journalists had no choice but to wait for the first ministers to break each night. The emerging participants would then face a barrage of TV cameras, dominated by the CBC, its new twenty-four-hour "Newsworld" station, and its star reporters, Don Newman and Wendy Mesley. It was in the interest of dramatic television that the June negotiations be made a great national soap opera, and the CBC did just that. They set the stage on May 23 with a three-hour program on Meech ("three hours of anxiety," according to Rick Salutin). "It's as if the fuse had been lit on a time bomb," Barbara Frum declared. Peter Mansbridge added: "There's a widespread feeling that this is a decisive time, that the days ahead could be the most important we've ever lived through as a nation. Canada has endured for 120 years but all of that is now on the line ... Can Canada work, or is Canada drifting apart?"[21]

Things really started to cook during the first week of June, and the CBC dominated the scrums as if the corporation owned them. Rick Salutin wrote: "[CBC] showed the premiers going into the [conference] room in the morning, to a martial air (*Dumdadum* – 'The talks go on,' said [Peter] Mansbridge), and when they emerged at night, subjecting an already morbid nation to those mediocrities twice a day. It was like a walk into The Club: CBC's Don Newman acting as head waiter, showing them to choice tables, while Wendy Mesley took their dinner orders."[22]

Other journalists had to scramble for the crumbs. Even CTV reporters used "CBC-framed" questions in their reports. In the follow-up on "The Journal" both Clyde Wells and Gary Filmon faced tough questions from Barbara Frum for sticking stubbornly to positions that she found unacceptable. So commanding was the power of the TV journalists outside the conference centre that the first ministers found themselves reacting to the positions of other premiers as "conveyed" to them by "hovering journalists." "Of course," observed media expert David Taras, "the politicians are often the ones who seek out journalists, who crave the intoxicating glow of publicity."[23]

Relegated to the back of the pack, print reporters attempted to outdo each other: after speaking to aides, they reconstructed meetings and conversations as if they had been at the table. To emphasize the accuracy of their work, they used quotation marks to suggest to readers that these were the exact words spoken by the participants. If such stories are done well, they can be significant journalistic achievements, but in this case, more often than not, the work was sloppy and the sources not confirmed. Moreover, the reporters never made it clear that a given story merely represented the facts as perceived by one of the players, as told to an assistant, as told to an aide, as told to the reporter.[24]

On June 11 Graham Fraser wrote in the *Globe* that Joe Ghiz, the premier of Prince Edward Island, had called Clyde Wells "a prick." "You were a prick when we were at Dalhousie Law School together; you're a prick now, and you'll always be a prick!" Ghiz had apparently said. Ghiz vehemently denied that the exchange had ever taken place; furthermore, Fraser had not confirmed the remark with the P.E.I. premier's office. In fact, Ghiz and Wells had not even attended law school together. While Fraser still stands by the story, he admits that the tone of the conversation may have been different than what he portrayed. "There is no question that re-creation is tricky," he says. "But the art of writing is to re-create a new reality that is not the old reality. What you try to do is to capture what the people there would feel would be a fair and insightful representation of what took place." Still, Fraser acknowledges, in certain situations (the case just cited isn't one of them), it is possible to get all the facts right but still have the story wrong. The nuances or the message conveyed might be ultimately incorrect.

On Saturday, June 9, it looked as if constitutional victory was at hand. Clyde Wells was not happy, but he had agreed to submit the new compromise to a vote in the Newfoundland assembly. Manitoba still had to conduct public hearings. Editorialists in Quebec praised the work of both Mulroney and Bourassa, while those in English Canada expressed relief but questioned the secretive and desperate process.[25] At the *Globe,* Jeffrey Simpson was relieved both for the country and for Brian Mulroney. "A defeat for Meech Lake would have been a defeat for Mr. Mulroney," he wrote in his June 11 column, "a defeat so shattering his political coalition and his political career would have been broken."

Then, disaster. On Monday Mulroney spoke with *Globe* reporters about "rolling all the dice," in particular angering Premier Clyde Wells, who eventually withdrew his decision to hold a vote on Meech in the Newfoundland legislature. Less than two weeks later, Meech died. Rather than blaming himself and his "image as a manipulator," Prime Minister Mulroney singled out Clyde Wells as the chief culprit.

The national media contributed to this distorted view of history by feeding into Mulroney's sense of desperation – making it seem as if the country was indeed hanging together by a thread – and then going after Premier Wells with the same vengeance as the prime minister and his henchman, Senator Lowell Murray. In her *Ottawa Citizen* column of June 26, Marjorie Nichols wrote that "constitutional reform, as we now know it, is finished. Senate reform is also dead, along with plans for further first ministers meetings to discuss the economy, the fishery, and the aspirations of the aboriginal people." Peter C. Newman blamed Pierre Trudeau and his puppet Clyde Wells for destroying the country. On the CBC, the Newfoundland premier was deemed the father of "deconfederation."

A few days later, on "The Journal," Barbara Frum consoled Mulroney: "You have had a lot of low moments as prime minister, but I expect this is somehow different. Am I right?" Mulroney's only possible response was, "That's right, Barbara." She then allowed him to publicly lambaste Wells. ("I think Clyde Wells gave you supper at his house. Is that right?") The week before, Frum had taken a much harsher tack with Wells, "stopping just short of calling him a liar," as one TV critic put it. Two years later, Frum, reflecting on those interviews, agreed that they were less than objective. "[Mulroney] had just suffered a mortal blow, and I thought 'What is achievable here? Would he speak directly? Would he open up?' You always hope and try. Unfortunately, it didn't work."[26]

The entire Meech Lake experience showed both politicians and journalists at their worst. Feeding off each other's anxieties and needs, both parties heightened the tension of the event through their use of overwrought rhetoric. In the fall of 1990, when the smoke from Meech Lake finally cleared, it was Brian Mulroney, not Clyde Wells, Gary Filmon, or the media, who took the brunt of the blame. His preoccupation with Quebec, together with the battle in the Senate to pass the goods and services tax legislation (Mulroney had to appoint eight extra senators to combat the Liberal majority) and the continuing recession, pushed his popularity to lows never seen before in the history of modern polling. Now Jeffrey Simpson could declare that "the public doesn't like or trust him, and they object to all of his government's policies." (It is interesting that in the contest of trust between politicians and the media, the latter were far ahead. A *Maclean's*/Decima poll conducted in November 1990 indicated that a majority of Canadians considered the media's coverage "somewhat accurate," believed that the media helped them to understand world events, and thought that the media were not responsible for the high degree of cynicism in Canada).[27]

This was a theme that Simpson and other journalists hammered away at during the next year. Even when Mulroney made his next constitutional move – appointing Keith Spicer to chair a commission that would study

Canadian attitudes to their country – members of the media, perhaps reflecting public opinion, had all but given up on his ability to save Canada from the impending crisis.[28] The failure of Meech Lake did not halt Quebec premier Robert Bourassa from pursuing his own agenda: a restructuring of Canadian federalism that would give Quebec almost as much power as it would have if it were a sovereign state. With or without Ottawa's cooperation, he intended to solve the constitutional question. This might mean holding a referendum in the fall of 1992 on whether or not Quebec should separate from Canada. Neither Mulroney nor members of the media believed he was bluffing. Never one to quit when faced with defeat, the prime minister slowly started to fight back. In February, English and French editorialists in Toronto and Quebec City were impressed with speeches by Mulroney that put a high price on Quebec separatism.

But the crisis atmosphere was kept alive. "Canadians have less than two years to decide if their country has a future," declared *Maclean's*. It was at least the sixth time in the past two years that the magazine had made such a black prediction. Each time the Quebec government made some pronouncement or issued a new report, the media reminded Canadians out in Moosejaw just how serious life was in Ottawa.

In mid-April 1991, when Mulroney moved Joe Clark out of External Affairs and appointed him the new constitutional minister, journalists praised the selection (ironic in itself, considering Clark's past relations with the media) but could not resist bringing up the long-term rivalry between the two men. This had been a constant theme during the last few years. Each time there had been the slightest hint of a rift between Clark and Mulroney on Canadian foreign policy, reporters had yelled, "Aha, they're at it again." In fact, only weeks earlier the two men had appeared to differ on the role of the Palestine Liberation Organization in Arab-Israeli peace talks. Stating that he and Mulroney were in agreement about the PLO, Clark said "There are some people who think the point of life is to find some differences between myself and the Prime Minister."[29]

Thus, over the next year while Clark battled his way through endless meetings and constitutional discussions, forging a reasonable proposal by the summer of 1992, he had to reassure journalists constantly that he and Mulroney were on the same team. "Do you believe some people close to the prime minister are trying to undermine you?" a reporter asked Clark after he had negotiated what seemed like a workable agreement with all the premiers except Bourassa. "Oh no, I don't believe that," said Clark, laughing. "I've passed beyond that state of paranoia a long time ago."[30] Some journalists even went so far as to suggest that Mulroney hoped that Clark's multilateral talks with the premiers would fail so that he could implement his own deal. The prime minister dismissed this notion as nonsense.

Throughout 1991 and 1992 Mulroney's usual brand of blustery rhetoric had needlessly confused the issue. He called the Beaudoin-Dobbie constitutional committee report "the most important and substantial report in 125 years" – and then was forced to distance himself from it to appease some of his disenchanted Quebec MPs. Similarly, after Clark and the premiers had come to an understanding on a Triple-E Senate, Mulroney again initially voiced his support for the deal, only to change his mind later when this proposal proved to be unacceptable to the Quebec government and several key members of his cabinet. Who could blame journalists this time for wondering exactly what was going on inside Mulroney's head?

Equally, a strong case could be made that, in general, the media, at every turn of the constitutional story, emphasized the negative. The silence of Quebec Tory ministers was interpreted as an indictment of the government's proposals, and the organizational problems experienced by the travelling Commons' constitutional committee received front-page coverage. In Quebec no compromise was good enough for such a "Notable" (to use Laurier LaPierre's marvellous term) as *Le Devoir* editor Lise Bissonnette, whose response to the Clark initiative of early July was a one-word editorial: "NON!" When a compromise was at last agreed to at the end of August, the media, perhaps reflecting the national mood, remained skeptical, doubting that the new constitutional proposal – the so-called Charlottetown Accord – could be sold to the country. And indeed the results of the constitutional referendum held at the end of October justified their apprehensions. Canadians rejected the agreement.

During the six-week referendum campaign, it seemed that journalists had learned a lesson from their Meech Lake experience. Gone for the most part were the hysterical cries that the country was about to fall apart. The media did what it was supposed to do: inform the public on the various constitutional options. As George Bain noted in his *Maclean's* column on November 2, "Both the print and electronic media made serious, honest efforts to make the Charlottetown accord understandable, both as to the necessary compromises that went into it, and the details of the thing itself. And they did a good job of it."

The innate journalistic tendency to dwell on the personal and the negative was also evident. It was easy to focus on the clash between Brian Mulroney and Bloc Québécois leader Lucien Bouchard ("Ex-friends Set to Rumble," declared the headline in the *Winnipeg Free Press*) or to magnify the emotional appeal of former prime minister Pierre Trudeau's denunciation of the accord. In Quebec both English and French journalists were captivated by bugged cellular telephone conversations ("L'affaire Wilhelmy") and leaked briefing notes that implied that Premier Robert Bourassa had "caved in" during the constitutional negotiations.

In covering these stories, the media unwittingly gave the "No" forces a distinct advantage, despite the fact that most editors supported the agreement. As several politicians later pointed out, the media treated the non-partisan, all-party "Yes" side as nothing more than the handiwork of Brian Mulroney and his Tory henchmen – or worse, as the work of the country's "elite," a term used a lot but never actually defined. Too often the focus of the TV cameras and headlines was on what the prime minister said or did and not on the other spokespersons, who represented a variety of interests and political factions. The "Yes" side's message was thus distorted.

Mulroney, too, could be blamed for the "Yes" defeat. Once again his penchant for overdone dramatics made matters worse. The picture of the prime minister, before a Quebec audience, tearing up a list of the constitutional gains that could be lost with a "No" vote was a riveting television image and a captivating news photo, but nothing more.

In the days following the referendum defeat of the Charlottetown agreement, stories in newspapers and reports on television generally concluded that Brian Mulroney's time in office was up. This time the rumours were true. On February 14, 1993, Mulroney announced that he was stepping down as Conservative leader and prime minister. He was no fool. For months the polls had indicated that his party would stand a better chance in the next election without him. Despite his insistence that his decision was based on family considerations and a desire to pass on the prime ministership and power to his successor (unlike every other Conservative leader in this century), he really had no other option.

Editors, media commentators, and most English-speaking Canadians for that matter were hardly sorry to see him go. "Good riddance" was how the *Globe and Mail* summed up the sentiment of cross-Canada English-language editorials. The consensus among sympathetic Quebec journalists, on the other hand, was more like "He did his best." The visceral dislike, even hatred, of Mulroney, so common across the country, was rarely apparent in Quebec. Even those French Canadians who objected to the Conservatives' economic policies appreciated Mulroney's effort, albeit a failed one, at national reconciliation.[31]

Mulroney's inability to sustain public support may be an inherent part of the Canadian political culture, as *Globe* editor William Thorsell suggested in his political obituary of the Tory leader.[32] Indeed, who was the last prime minister to leave office with a high public approval rating? You would probably have to go all the way back to Sir John A. Macdonald in 1891, and it was not his choice to die in office.

In fact, several factors hampered Mulroney's media relations. The harder he tried to get journalists to like him and understand his tough political decisions, the worse the criticism often became (though the *Globe* and the

Financial Post, among other newspapers, while not always favourable to Mulroney personally, usually supported his government's economic and constitutional policies). In general, he failed to manage the media or keep them from perpetuating his image as a political Darth Vadar. This was a serious liability for a politician in the 1990s who had to confront, as a routine part of his job, a cynical and often hostile press.

Throughout his nine years in office, Muloney spent far too much of his time responding to the media's agenda rather than following his own. Consequently, any economic or constitutional achievements – incomplete as they may have been – were lost in the negative coverage about his personal unpopularity.

When things got tough, Mulroney liked to invoke the image of Sir John A. Macdonald and the drama of the first Conservative prime minister's fight for national unity.[33] Whether Mulroney will be as fondly remembered as Sir John A. remains to be seen. Approval of either Meech or Charlottetown would have cemented Mulroney's place alongside Macdonald as a giant in the country's constitutional history. While he fell short of his goal, future historians may judge his efforts to bridge the gap between English and French Canadians more favourably than current pundits have.

The two prime ministers shared something else: Macdonald was castigated in the press at least to the same degree that Mulroney has been. Sir John A., however, had unquestioning support from Tory papers and the loyalty of journalists like Martin Griffin. If George Brown's Toronto *Globe* distorted Macdonald's words and intentions, the prime minister could always call upon a Conservative editor somewhere to counter the attack. But the days have long gone since a prime minister could manipulate the news and editorial pages the way Macdonald did. More than at any time in the past, journalists' own interpretations shape the reporting and, more significantly, the public's perception of government policies.

All this being said, despite the astounding technological advancements in communications, despite the impact of television, and despite the oligopolistic nature of the newspaper business in the 1990s, the fundamental relationship between the prime minister and the journalist has remained constant over the decades. Although today's younger reporters might not believe it, the search for the truth in Canadian politics and government has been going on for generations. And the weaknesses in journalism have also endured: the misinterpretations, the biased reporting, the quick judgments, the fascination with the trivial, the lack of historical perspective, and the inherent conflict between making news informative and making it entertaining.

In his memoirs, Tom Kent, Lester Pearson's former adviser, observed that "most politicians exaggerate ... the influence of the press on public opinion. They are themselves the most avid readers of newspapers, and nowadays watchers of TV news and public affairs programs. The consequence is a mutually-regarding relationship between the media and public personalities. The media feel important because they constantly see how much their subjects care, while the vanity of the subjects makes them take the media much more seriously than do other readers, listeners and viewers. The mirrors of this relationship magnify, within the small world of active politics, the importance of the press."[34]

There is a great deal of truth in what Kent wrote. Politicians play far too much to the television camera, while journalists have long overvalued their own influence. There is obviously a need for both sides to practise self-criticism and correct their inadequacies. Still, in recent years, the price of power has been great. Stories that focus on private lives and past mistakes have become routine in newspapers and television, while so-called authoritative judgments on politicians' personalities and motivations are delivered daily by journalists who have, in some cases, never actually met those they have written about. This is, as Prime Minister Mulroney said shortly before leaving office, "an absolutely extraordinary phenomenon." And he gave this example: "You turn on a television set and there is somebody describing you and your wife. And I say, 'Honey, who is this guy?' She says, 'I don't know.' This is the latest expert on Brian Mulroney."[35]

The most recent victim of such reporting and analysis has been Prime Minister Kim Campbell. She won the Conservative leadership *despite* the treatment she received from journalists. In less than six months, she went from being the darling of the media – the politician almost certain to succeed Brian Mulroney – to a candidate whose credentials, family background, and abilities were highly suspect.

In a classic case of applying a double-standard, many male journalists castigated Campbell's ambition and aggressive behaviour as if these traits were somehow unbecoming for a woman. On the other hand, her opponent Jean Charest's enthusiastic quest for the leadership was regarded as a natural progression in his political career. Even more damaging from Campbell's point of view, was the *Toronto Star*'s distortion of her wide-ranging interview with Peter C. Newman in *Vancouver* magazine, a misrepresentation that was compounded as other reporters and commentators also took her words out of context.[36]

The time has come to take a step back. Too often there is little distinction made between what the public has a right to know and what journalists say it should know. The chaos of the scrum must be controlled. Otherwise, fewer and fewer talented individuals will choose a career in politics. Canadians will then not get the leaders they want, but those deemed acceptable by the members of the media.

Notes

ABBREVIATIONS

AO	Archives of Ontario	MS	*Montreal Star*
CAR	*Canadian Annual Review*	NA	National Archives of Canada
CH	*Calgary Herald*	NLF	National Liberal Federation
CHR	*Canadian Historical Review*	NW	*News* (Toronto)
DHC	*Debates of the House of Commons*	OC	*Ottawa Citizen*
DR	*Dalhousie Review*	OFP	*Ottawa Free Press*
DT	*Daily Telegraph* (Toronto)	OJ	*Ottawa Journal*
FP	*Financial Post*	SN	*Saturday Night*
GL	*Globe* (Toronto)	TS	*Toronto Star*
GM	*Globe and Mail*	TT	*Toronto Telegram*
ME	*Mail and Empire* (Toronto)	VS	*Vancouver Sun*
MFP	*Manitoba Free Press*	WFP	*Winnipeg Free Press*
MG	*Montreal Gazette*	WT	*Winnipeg Tribune*
ML	*Mail* (Toronto)		

PREFACE:
THE BATTLE OF THE SCRUM

1. *GM*, Nov. 5, 1981.
2. Erik Nielsen, *The House Is Not a Home* (Toronto, 1989), 206-7.
3. *GM*, Jan. 25, 1992
4. NA, National Liberal Federation (NLF) Papers, vol. 724, "List of Newspapers Received in the Prime Minister's Office, 1963-64"; J.S. Willison, *Reminiscences: Political and Personal* (Toronto, 1919), 46.
5. David Hayes, *Power and Influence: The Globe and Mail and the News Revolution* (Toronto, 1992), 198.
6. Arthur Siegel, *Politics and the Media in Canada* (Toronto, 1983), 19-20.
7. *GM*, Apr. 28, 1992
8. Cited in *GM*, Nov. 14, 1989.
9. George Bain, "Parliamentary Press Gallery," *Saturday Night,* July 1985, 26.
10. Ramsay Cook, *The Politics of John W. Dafoe and the Free Press* (Toronto, 1963), 285.

PROLOGUE:
THE VIEW FROM THE GALLERY

1. P.B. Waite, *Canada 1874-1896: Arduous Destiny* (Toronto, 1971), 97-98.
2. P.B. Waite, *The Man from Halifax: Sir John Thompson, Prime Minister* (Toronto, 1985), 29; *OC*, Mar. 2, 1921; *SN*, Apr. 2, 1921.
3. Sandra Gwyn, *The Private Capital: Ambition and Love in the Age of Macdonald and Laurier* (Toronto, 1984), 401.
4. P.B. Waite, *Sir John A. Macdonald: His Life and World* (Toronto, 1975), 71; Gwyn, *Private Capital*, 400-1; NA, William Lyon Mackenzie King Papers, J4, vol. 157, "I Remember," transcript of speech delivered by John W. Dafoe on CKY Radio, Winnipeg, Oct. 19, 1937.
5. Cited in Gwyn, *Private Capital*, 412.
6. Paul Rutherford, *A Victorian Authority: The Daily Press in Late Nineteenth Century Canada* (Toronto, 1982), 82.
7. Hector Charlesworth, *Candid Chronicles* (Toronto,

1925), 125; Rutherford, *Victorian Authority,* 79.
8. Willison, *Reminiscences*, 121.
9. Rutherford, *Victorian Authority*, 88-110.
10. Brian P.N. Beaven, "Partisanship, Patronage and the Press in Ontario, 1880-1914: Myths and Realities," *CHR* 64, no. 3 (Sept. 1983): 341.
11. Ibid., 326; Rutherford, *Victorian Authority*, 216; NA, Sir John A. Macdonald Papers, vol. 334, Auditor General's Report, 1888-89.
12. Rutherford, *Victorian Authority*, 219.
13. Macdonald Papers, vol. 503, John Young to Macdonald, May 29, 1891.
14. Willison, *Reminiscences*, 128.
15. *DHC*, Mar. 7, 1878, 803-54.
16. Waite, *Arduous Destiny*, 94; Willison, *Reminiscences*, 188.
17. Halifax *Herald*, Mar. 14, 1878.

CHAPTER ONE:
A CONTROLLING INTEREST

1. Cited in P.B. Waite, "Sir John A. Macdonald: The Man," *DR* 47, no. 2 (Summer 1967): 148.
2. J.S. Willison, *Laurier and the Liberal Party* (Toronto, 1908), 19-26. On Macdonald's character, see also Waite, "Sir John A. Macdonald," 143-58; Donald Creighton, *John A. Macdonald: The Old Chieftain* (Toronto, 1965), 251; Jeffrey Simpson, *Spoils of Power: The Politics of Patronage* (Toronto, 1988), 66.
3. Simpson, *Spoils of Power*, 66; Macdonald Papers, vol. 573, Macdonald to Morrison, Dec. 30, 1868.
4. Macdonald Papers, vol. 573, Macdonald to Morrison, Jan. 7, 1870.
5. Donald Creighton, *John A. Macdonald: The Young Politician* (Toronto, 1965), 96-97.
6. Creighton, *Old Chieftain*, 73-78.
7. Ibid., 86-97.
8. Macdonald Papers, vol. 574, Macdonald to Morrison, Apr. 21, 1871.
9. Ibid., Apr. 21, 1871; Creighton, *Old Chieftain*, 103-4.
10. Creighton, *Old Chieftain*, 113.
11. Ibid., 123-28.
12. J.M.S. Careless, *Brown of the Globe: The Voice of Upper Canada*, vol. 1 (Toronto, 1959), 8.

13. Rutherford, *Victorian Authority*, 41-42.
14. *Nation* (Toronto), June 4, 1874, cited in Waite, *Arduous Destiny*, 21; Sir Richard Cartwright, *Reminiscences* (Toronto, 1912), 9-10.
15. Creighton, *Young Politician*, 159; Waite, "Sir John A. Macdonald," 144.
16. Careless, *Brown of the Globe*, vol. 1, 218-19.
17. AO, M.O. Hammond Papers, Box 2, "Unpublished History of the Globe," 165-66.
18. *GL*, Nov. 5, 1873; see also J.M.S. Careless, *Brown of the Globe: Statesman of Confederation*, vol. 2 (Toronto, 1963), 309-10.
19. Cited in Waite, *Arduous Destiny*, 22.
20. NA, Alexander Mackenzie Papers, M-198, Mackenzie to Brown, July 25, 1877.
21. E.B. Biggar, *Anecdotal Life of Sir John A. Macdonald* (Montreal, 1891), 163.
22. Creighton, *Old Chieftain*, 239; Mackenzie to Brown, Apr. 12, 1878, cited in Cynthia Smith and Jack MacLeod, eds., *An Anecdotal Life of Sir John A. Macdonald* (Toronto, 1989), 76-77.
23. *GL*, Apr. 16, 1878.
24. Macdonald Papers, vol. 350, H.M.K. Wilson to Macdonald, June 10, 1878; vol. 303, Robert Henry to Macdonald, Apr. 22, 1878; vol. 349, Boyd to Macdonald, Apr. 24, 1878; A.H. Mac to Macdonald, Apr. 29, 1878; Clementi to Macdonald, May 7, 1878; Smith and MacLeod, *An Anecdotal Life*, 77.
25. On Quebec: Macdonald Papers, vol. 204, Chapleau to Macdonald, Nov. 20, 1885; vol. 425, E. Tasse to Macdonald, Apr. 6, 1886; vol. 455, J. Tasse to Macdonald, Feb. 24, 1888; vol. 458, J. Tasse to Macdonald, May, 1888; vol. 205, Chapleau to Macdonald, 1887, cited in Norman Ward, "The Press and Patronage," in J.H. Aitchison, ed., *The Political Process in Canada* (Toronto, 1963), 7. On the West: Macdonald Papers, vol. 246, George McMicken to Macdonald, Dec. 27, 1877; vol. 361, C.R. Tuttle to Macdonald, Oct. 28, 1879; vol. 311, Charles Allen to Macdonald, Dec. 23, 1879; vol. 362, Allen to Macdonald, Nov. 14, 1879; vol. 364, Tuttle to Macdonald, Jan. 15, 1880; vol. 311, Allen to Macdonald, Mar. 16, 1880; vol. 328, W.B. Scarth to Macdonald, Jan. 14, 1888; vol. 467, Acton Burrows to Macdonald, Dec. 9, 1888.
26. J.M.S. Careless, *Toronto to 1918: An Illustrated History* (Toronto, 1984), 124.
27. Careless, *Brown of the Globe*, vol. 1, 176-77, 260, 301; Paul Rutherford, *The Making of the Canadian Media* (Toronto, 1978), 28; *DT* (Toronto), Apr. 12, 1870.
28. Macdonald Papers, vol. 247, Macpherson to Macdonald, Feb. 1867; vol. 514, Macdonald to White, June 5, 1868; vol. 515, Macdonald to Macpherson, Feb. 16, 1869; vol. 519, Macdonald to Belford, Oct. 16, 1871.
29. Ibid., vol. 191, Brydges to Macdonald, Mar. 11, 1869; Mar. 18, 1869; Mar. 22, 1869; vol. 522, Macdonald to Brydges, Dec. 16, 1872; Ron Poulton, *The Paper Tyrant: John Ross Robertson of the Toronto Telegram* (Toronto, 1971), 50-52.
30. *DT*, May 11, 1871; Poulton, *Paper Tyrant*, 55, 48.
31. Poulton, *Paper Tyrant*, 56; Macdonald Papers, vol. 519, Macdonald to John Carling, Nov. 24, 1871; vol. 119, Carling to Macdonald, Nov. 30, 1871; vol. 301, Carling to Macdonald, Dec. 18, 1871; vol. 520, Macdonald to Macpherson, Feb. 20, 1872.
32. Poulton, *Paper Tyrant*, 59; Macdonald Papers, vol. 520, Macdonald to Brydges, Feb. 16, 1872; AO, T.C. Patteson Papers, vol. 1, Macdonald to Patteson, Feb.

20, 1872; *DT*, May 6, 1872, cited in Poulton, *Paper Tyrant*, 60.

CHAPTER TWO: PARTY ORGANS

1. Macdonald Papers, vol. 520, Macdonald to Thomas Gibbs, Jan. 31, 1872.
2. AO, MS49, "Unpublished Reminiscences of Thomas Patteson," 5-6; Patteson Papers, vol. 1, "Minutes of Mail Printing and Publishing Company," Feb. 23, 1872.
3. Macdonald Papers, vol. 520, Macdonald to Macpherson, Feb. 20, 1872; Macdonald to Patteson, Feb. 27, 1872.
4. Patteson Papers, vol. 1, Patteson to Macdonald, Feb. 23, 1872; Macdonald Papers, vol. 301, "Toronto Mail Stock List."
5. O.D. Skelton, *Life and Letters of Sir Wilfrid Laurier* (Toronto, 1921), 371.
6. "Reminiscences of Thomas Patteson," 92.
7. Macdonald Papers, vol. 521, Macdonald to Patteson, Sept. 20, 1872.
8. "Reminiscences of Thomas Patteson," 19-20; *ML*, Apr. 4, 1873.
9. Patteson Papers, vol. 1, Patteson to Langevin, July 31, 1873.
10. "Reminiscences of Thomas Patteson," 6; Rutherford, *Victorian Authority*, 59.
11. Rutherford, *Victorian Authority*, 59-60.
12. NA, Martin Griffin Papers, vol. 1, Macdonald to Griffin, July 7, 1881; Oct. 31, 1881; Macdonald Papers, vol. 379, Griffin to Macdonald, Dec. 12, 1881; Rutherford, *Victorian Authority*, 60.
13. Waite, *Arduous Destiny*, 209-10.
14. Rutherford, *Victorian Authority*, 60.
15. *ML*, Sept. 19, 1882, Nov. 20, 1882; Griffin Papers, vol. 1, Griffin to Macdonald, Nov. 1, 1882.
16. Macdonald Papers, vol. 400, Griffin to Macdonald, Feb. 21, 1884.
17. Griffin Papers, vol. 1, Griffin to Macdonald, Feb. 7, 1884; Macdonald Papers, vol. 403, Griffin to Macdonald, May 1, 1884.
18. Paul Bilkey, *Persons, Papers and Things* (Toronto, 1940), 54; NA, Edward Farrer Papers, vol. 1; Willison, *Reminiscences*, 207-15; Macdonald Papers, vol. 432, T.M. Daly to Macdonald, Dec. 31, 1886. For a full account of Farrer's life, see Carmen Cumming, *Secret Craft: The Journalism of Edward Farrer* (Toronto, 1992).
19. Rutherford, *Victorian Authority*, 60. For a different interpretation of Farrer's motives, see Cumming, *Secret Craft*, 66-72. Cumming suggests that Farrer used the Catholic issue as a way to stir up trouble in order to achieve his real objective: the break-up of Confederation and the annexation of the country by the United States.
20. Macdonald Papers, vol. 526, Macdonald to Thomas Robertson, June 2, 1886; vol. 325, "A loyal Conservative" to Macdonald, Sept. 14, 1886; vol. 427, T.H. McGuire to Macdonald, June 16, 1886; vol. 526, Macdonald to McGuire, June 18, 1886.
21. Waite, *Arduous Destiny*, 190.
22. This was the *Globe*'s view, in any event. See *GL*, Dec. 29, 1886.
23. Macdonald Papers, vol. 432, G. Coughlin to Macdonald, Dec. 29, 1886; John McIntyre to Macdonald, Dec. 30, 1886; vol. 433, McGurie to Macdonald, Jan. 5, 1887; Joseph Pope, *Correspondence of Sir John A. Macdonald* (Toronto, 1921), 392.

24. Rutherford, *Victorian Authority*, 60; Macdonald Papers, vol. 527, Macdonald to McCarthy, Jan. 1887.
25. Waite, *Arduous Destiny*, 205; W.R. Graham, "Sir Richard Cartwright, Wilfrid Laurier and Liberal Trade Policy, 1887," *CHR* 33, no. 1 (Mar. 1952): 2-3.
26. Charlesworth, *Chronicles*, 126; Macdonald Papers, vol. 250, Macpherson to Macdonald, Sept. 28, 1887.
27. Macdonald Papers, vol. 324, "Prospectus of the Empire," July 1887.
28. Ibid., vol. 527, Macdonald to Creighton, Dec. 10, 1887; vol. 551, Creighton to Pope, Aug. 29, 1891; vol. 198, Campbell to Macdonald, Nov. 29, 1887.
29. Ibid., vol. 228, McCarthy to Macdonald, Sept. 3, 1887; Creighton, *Old Chieftain*, 482.
30. Charlesworth, *Chronicles*, 77; Floyd S. Chalmers, *A Gentleman of the Press* (Toronto, 1969), 39.
31. Macdonald Papers, vol. 528, Macdonald to Livingston, June 7, 1888.
32. Ibid., vol. 530, Macdonald to Creighton, Dec. 13, 1890; Waite, *Thompson*, 417.
33. Macdonald Papers, vol. 208, Creighton to Macdonald, July 21, 1890; Chalmers, *Gentleman of the Press*, 55.
34. Waite, *Arduous Destiny*, 210-13.
35. Ibid., 211-13.
36. Willison, *Reminiscences*, 170-71; AO, Edward Blake Papers, E.W. Thomson to Blake, Mar. 1889; Blake to Jaffray, Mar. 19, 1889; Jaffray to Blake, Mar. 20, 1889, cited in Waite, *Arduous Destiny*, 310, n. 42; Macdonald Papers, vol. 208, Creighton to Macdonald, Feb. 8, 1889; Oct. 1, 1889.
37. Waite, *Arduous Destiny*, 200-2.
38. Ibid., 223; Creighton, *Old Chieftain*, 548-51.
39. Cumming, *Secret Craft*, 147-62.
40. *OFP*, Jan. 29, 1891; Creighton, *Old Chieftain*, 551; R.C. Brown, *Canada's National Policy* (Wesport, Conn., 1978), 204-5.
41. Waite, *Arduous Destiny*, 222; *GL*, Feb. 19, 1891; Macdonald Papers, vol. 68, "Affadavit of Christopher St. George Clark," Jan. 30, 1891.
42. Brown, *National Policy*, 206-7 (in another version of this intrigue, Farrer's pamphlet was given to Macdonald by Col. George T. Denison with the assistance of Major Percy Sherwood of the Dominion Police; see Cumming, *Secret Craft*, 177-78); Macdonald Papers, vol. 68, "Affadavit of Christopher St. George Clark," Jan. 30, 1891.
43. Cartwright, *Reminiscences*, 310; Waite, *Arduous Destiny*, 223; Sir Charles Tupper, *Recollections of Sixty Years in Canada* (Toronto, 1914), 212.
44. *Empire* (Toronto), Feb. 7, 15, 1891.
45. *GL*, Feb. 19, 25, 26, 1891.
46. *Empire*, Feb. 18, 1891.
47. Willison, *Reminiscences*, 209.
48. *GL*, Feb. 19, 1891.
49. Macdonald Papers, vol. 68, Louis Kribs to Macdonald, Feb. 19, 1891.
50. Willison, *Laurier*, vol. 1, 168; Macdonald to Stephen, Mar. 31, 1891, cited in Pope, *Macdonald*, 485.
51. NA, Sir John Thompson Papers, vol. 266, Thompson to Kelly, Feb. 16, 1894.
52. Ibid., vol. 177, Douglas to Thompson, Feb. 22, 1893; vol. 260, Thompson to Douglas, Feb. 28, 1893.
53. Ibid., vol. 223, Smith to Thompson, Oct. 18, 1894.
54. Rutherford, *Victorian Authority*, 107; *World* (Toronto), Feb. 2, 1895.
55. NA, Sir Charles Tupper Papers, vol. 11, J. Stewart Tupper to Charles Tupper, Apr. 11, 1896; Bilkey, *Persons, Papers and Things*, 12.

CHAPTER THREE:
LAURIER AND THE *GLOBE*

1. H. Blair Neatby, *Laurier and a Liberal Quebec* (Toronto, 1973), 226; Gwyn, *Private Capital*, 243.
2. M.O. Hammond, "The Parliamentary Press Gallery," *Westminister* 10, no. 4 (Apr. 1907): 226; NA, Grattan O'Leary Papers, vol. 1, "The Gallery – 50 Years Ago" (undated article by Grattan O'Leary).
3. Gwyn, *Private Capital*, 414-15; NA, Sir Wilfrid Laurier Papers, vol. 25, Magurn to Laurier, "Memo. Re: Press," Nov. 1896; Willison, *Reminiscences*, 121-22.
4. Simpson, *Spoils of Power*, 115.
5. Gwyn, *Private Capital*, 425; Arthur Ford, *As the World Wags On* (Toronto, 1950), 69; *DHC*, May 29, 1906, 4031-34; June 6, 1906, 4707-11.
6. Ford, *As the World Wags On*, 69-70; *DHC*, June 6, 1906, 4711.
7. Bruce Hutchison, *Mr. Prime Minister* (Toronto, 1964), 115-16; Marcel Hamelin, ed., *The Political Ideas of the Prime Ministers of Canada* (Ottawa, 1969), 80.
8. Neatby, *Laurier and a Liberal Quebec*, 203; cited in Simpson, *Spoils of Power*, 115.
9. Willison, *Reminiscences*, 55-58.
10. Careless, *Brown of the Globe*, vol. 2, 368.
11. Richard T. Clippingdale, "J.S. Willison, Political Journalist" (Ph.D. thesis, University of Toronto, 1970), 21; Hammond, "History of the *Globe*," 214; Michael Bliss, *A Canadian Millionaire: The Life and Times of Sir Joseph Flavelle* (Toronto, 1978), 53-82; Laurier Papers, vol. 435, H.M. Mowat to Laurier, Nov. 29, 1906.
12. Clippingdale, "Willison," 39; *GL*, Apr. 16, 1888.
13. Willison, *Reminiscences*, 203.
14. Clippingdale, "Willison," 70; Willison, *Reminiscences*, 201.
15. Clippingdale, "Willison," 53-54, 74.
16. Cited in Paul Stevens, "Laurier and the Liberal Party in Ontario, 1887-1911" (Ph.D. thesis, University of Toronto, 1966), 288-89.
17. Laurier Papers, vol. 6, Willison to Laurier, Dec. 14, 1892.
18. *ME*, Oct. 9, 1895; Waite, *Arduous Destiny*, 259-60.
19. *GL*, Feb. 3, 1891; Mar. 21, 1892; Clippingdale, "Willison," 171, 185-86.
20. A.H.U. Colquhoun, *Press, Politics and People: The Life and Letters of Sir John Willison* (Toronto, 1935), 42 (Willison to Laurier, Mar. 5, 1895), 43-44 (Laurier to Willison, Mar. 7, 1895).
21. NA, Sir John Willison Papers, vol. 11, folder 86, Willison to Dafoe, Mar. 7, 1923.
22. Ibid., folder 169a, Laurier to Willison, July 17, 1895.
23. Clippingdale, "Willison," 205.
24. Ibid., 216-17; *GL*, Jan. 16, 1896.
25. Paul Cruncian, *Priests and Politicians: Manitoba Schools and the Election of 1896* (Toronto, 1974), 135-36, 190-95.
26. Willison Papers, vol. 24, folder 169a, Laurier to Willison, May 16, 1896; Colquhoun, *Letters of Willison*, 40-41; Clippingdale, "Willison," 226.
27. Laurier Papers, vol. 59, Tarte to Willison, Dec. 16, 1897; Willison to Tarte, Dec. 17, 1897; Clippingdale, "Willison," 385; NA, Sir Clifford Sifton Papers, vol. 55, Willison to Sifton, Apr. 1, 1898; Apr. 20, 1898; Willison Papers, vol. 24, folder 169a, Laurier to Willison, Apr. 21, 1898.

28. Clippingdale, "Willison," 403-5; Willison Papers, vol. 37, folder 286, Sifton to Willison, May 6, 1899; Sifton Papers, vol. 74, Willison to Sifton, May 7, 1899.

29. Clippingdale, "Willison," 410-13; *GL*, Jan. 9, 1900; Willison Papers, vol. 24, folder 169b, Laurier to Willison, Jan. 10, 1900.

30. Ross Harkness, *J.E. Atkinson of the Star* (Toronto, 1963), 21-24.

31. Colquhoun, *Letters of Willison*, 97-100 (Willison to Sifton, Jan. 29, 1901).

32. Bliss, *Flavelle*, 149.

33. Ibid., 170.

34. Ibid., 172, 182; Colquhoun, *Letters of Willison*, 150-51, 154; Willison Papers, vol. 24, folder 169d, Laurier to Willison, Feb. 5, 1908.

35. Charlesworth, *Candid Chronicles*, 210.

36. Cited in Hammond, "History of the *Globe*," 246-47.

37. R.C. Brown and Ramsay Cook, *Canada 1896-1921: A Nation Transformed* (Toronto, 1974), 77-78; Laurier Papers, vol. 36, Laurier to Preston, Mar. 23, 1905.

38. Brown and Cook, *Canada 1896-1921*, 168-69; *GL*, Mar. 23, 1909; Poulton, *Paper Tyrant*, 134-35.

39. *GL*, editorials of Aug. 1, 19, 24, 25, 1911; *CAR*, 1911, 230.

40. Brown and Cook, *Canada 1896-1921*, 180-85; Skelton, *Life and Letters of Sir Wilfrid Laurier*, 370-71.

CHAPTER FOUR:
UNDER LIBERAL MANAGEMENT

1. Neatby, *Laurier and a Liberal Quebec*, 100-2.

2. Rutherford, *Victorian Authority*, 51-52.

3. Ibid., 53; NA, Sir Robert Borden Papers, vol. 277, Macnab to Borden, July 23, 1932.

4. Neatby, *Laurier and a Liberal Quebec*, 106.

5. Willison, *Reminiscences*, 303-4.

6. Neatby, *Laurier and a Liberal Quebec*, 107.

7. Ibid., 106.

8. Ibid., 108; Lucien Pacaud, *Sir Wilfrid Laurier: Letters to My Father and Mother* (Toronto, 1935), 112-13.

9. Neatby, *Laurier and a Liberal Quebec*, 109, 110.

10. Waite, *Arduous Destiny*, 44.

11. Neatby, *Laurier and a Liberal Quebec*, 138-39.

12. Ralph Heintzman, "The Struggle for Life: The French Daily Press of Montreal and the Problems of Economic Growth in the Age of Laurier" (Ph.D. thesis, York University, 1977), 39; Laurier Papers, vol. 271, Langlois to Laurier, July 3, 1907.

13. Pacaud, *Letters to My Father*, 44, 56-57.

14. Ibid., 82.

15. Neatby, *Laurier and a Liberal Quebec*, 40.

16. Brown and Cook, *Canada 1896-1921*, 15.

17. Simpson, *Spoils of Power*, 115.

18. Rutherford, *Victorian Authority*, 68-71; Mackenzie Porter, "The Pulse of French Canada," *Maclean's*, Mar. 15, 1954, 18-19, 63-68.

19. Neatby, *Laurier and a Liberal Quebec*, 127-28.

20. Heintzman, "The Struggle for Life," 51-52.

21. Ibid, 52; Tupper Papers, vol. 18, Tupper to Henry Darby, Feb. 6, 1899.

22. Heintzman, "The Struggle for Life," 46-49.

23. Skelton, *Letters of Laurier*, vol. 2, 209-16; R.C. Brown, *Robert Laird Borden: A Biography*, vol. 1 (Toronto, 1975), 78-85; T.D. Regehr, "The Canadian Northern Railway: Agent of National Growth, 1896-1911" (Ph.D. thesis, University of Alberta, 1967), 134-42.

24. Skelton, *Letters of Laurier*, vol. 2, 204.

25. Brown and Cook, *Canada 1896-1921*, 150-52.

26. Ibid., 150-52.

27. Brown, *Borden*, vol. 1, 81; Skelton, *Letters of Laurier*, vol. 2, 211.

28. Skelton, *Letters of Laurier*, vol. 2, 211-12; Heintzman, "The Struggle for Life," 55-56.

29. Brown, *Borden*, vol. 1, 81.

30. Ibid., 83-84; Heintzman, "The Struggle for Life," 53; Borden Papers, vol. 327, Hunt to McLeod, Oct. 17, 1904; McLeod to Borden, Dec. 10, 1907; Hunt to McLeod, Oct. 18, 1904; R.B. Fleming, *The Railway King of Canada: Sir William Mackenzie, 1849-1923* (Vancouver, 1991), 107; Cyrille Felteau, *Histoire de La Presse*, vol. 1 (Montreal, 1984), 323-35.

31. Neatby, *Laurier and a Liberal Quebec*, 146-47.

32. Brown, *Borden*, vol. 1, 81-82; Regehr, "Canadian Northern Railway," 135-36; Joseph Schull, *Laurier: The First Canadian* (Toronto, 1965), 444.

33. Côté to Laurier, Nov. 19, 1904; Dandurand to Laurier, Nov. 19, 1904; Laurier to Graham, Jan. 12, 1905 – all cited in Heintzman, "The Struggle for Life," 54; Borden Papers, vol. 391, Russell to Laurier, Dec. 12, 1905; Fleming, *Mackenzie*, 108.

34. Borden to Laurier, Mar. 21, 1905, cited in Heintzman, "The Struggle for Life," 56, 57.

35. Borden Papers, vol. 391, Russell to Laurier, Dec. 12, 1905; *MG*, Oct. 25, 1907.

36. Brown, *Borden*, vol. 1, 82-83. In his memoirs, Borden continued to assert that he had done nothing wrong; see, Henry Borden, ed., *Robert L. Borden: His Memoirs* (Toronto, 1938), 132.

37. Pierre Berton, *The Promised Land: Settling the West 1896-1914* (Toronto, 1984), 8; Skelton, *Letters of Laurier*, vol. 2, 371.

38. Berton, *Promised Land*, 23-25.

39. D.J. Hall, *Clifford Sifton: The Young Napoleon*, vol. 1 (Vancouver, 1981), 289-90; Berton, *Promised Land*, 34; Ramsay Cook, *The Politics of John W. Dafoe and the Free Press* (Toronto, 1963), 16.

40. Hall, *Sifton*, vol. 1, 222.

41. *CAR*, 1911, 230.

42. D.J. Hall, *Clifford Sifton: A Lonely Eminence*, vol. 2 (Vancouver, 1985), 146.

43. Hall, *Sifton*, vol. 1, 212.

44. Ibid., 216, 223.

45. Berton, *Promised Land*, 34.

46. Hall, *Sifton*, vol. 2, 21.

47. Berton, *Promised Land*, 35.

48. Hall, *Sifton*, vol. 2, 226.

49. Frank H. Underhill, "J.W. Dafoe," *Canadian Forum* 13, no. 145 (Oct. 1932): 23-24.

50. Neatby, *Laurier and a Liberal Quebec*, 234.

51. Cook, *Dafoe*, 85.

CHAPTER FIVE:
POLITICS OF VIRTUE

1. *TS*, Apr. 7, 1910. I am assuming the writer of this article was Gerald Brown, as he is identified as the *Toronto Star's* man in the gallery during this period. See M.O. Hammond, "The Parliamentary Press Gallery," *Westminister* 10, no. 4 (Apr. 1907): 228.

2. Brown, *Borden*, vol. 1, 89, 104.

3. Ibid., 132.

4. John English, *The Decline of Politics: The Conservatives and the Party System 1901-20* (Toronto, 1977), 6; Brown, *Borden*, vol. 1, 85, 248, 266.

5. Borden, *Memoirs*, 289; Brown, *Borden*, vol. 1, 168.

6. Brown, *Borden*, vol. 1, 168, 169; *NW*, Nov. 7, 1910.

7. Borden Papers, vol. 260, Borden to Lord Beaverbrook, Feb. 12, 1926.

8. Ford, *World Wags On*, 43, 190; *OJ*, Dec. 10, 1954.

9. Willison Papers, vol. 15, folder 116, Ford to Willison, Sept. 3, 1915.
10. Ibid., vol. 4, folder 32, Borden to Willison, May 2, 1903.
11. Chalmers, *Gentleman of the Press*, 166-68.
12. Colquhoun, *Letters of Willison*, 237.
13. On Willison's views, see his column "Month to Month," *Canadian Magazine*, Aug. 1920, 340; English, *Politics of Decline*, 218; Sifton Papers, vol. 268, Willison to Sifton, Dec. 28, 1920; Willison Papers, vol. 37, folder 286, Sifton to Willison, Dec. 29, 1920.
14. Frank Cochrane to Willison, Jan. 30, 1915, cited in English, *Politics of Decline*, 28.
15. Borden Papers, vol. 327, Borden to London, Oct. 16, 1916; Borden to Perley, Oct. 17, 1916; Borden to Perley, Dec. 6, 1916; Borden, *Memoirs*, 611-12; Borden Diary, May 4, 1916, cited in Roger Graham, *Arthur Meighen*, vol. 2, 149-50.
16. Borden Papers, vol. 327, Graham to Borden, July 18, 1903; Graham to Borden, July 15, 1904; Graham to Borden, Aug. 19, 1904; Borden to Graham, Dec. 17, 1904; Brown, *Borden*, vol. 1, 84.
17. *Herald* (Montreal), Oct. 25, 1907.
18. *CAR*, 1908, 169; Borden Papers, vol. 334, "Memoir Notes," 81 (this was not included in the published version of his memoirs).
19. *CAR*, 1911, supplement, 24.
20. Brown and Cook, *Canada 1896-1921*, 171.
21. English, *Decline of Politics*, 50; Brown, *Borden*, vol. 1, 128-29.
22. English, *Decline of Politics*, 64; Laurier Papers, vol. 681, Murphey to Laurier, May 20, 1911.
23. Bilkey, *People*, 134; English, *Decline of Politics*, 77.
24. Engish, *Decline of Politics*, 64-65; Brown and Cook, *Canada 1896-1921*, 181.
25. NA, R.B. Bennett Papers, M-1114, "History of Editorial Committee."
26. Ford, *World Wags On*, 42.
27. Willison Papers, vol. 15, folder 116, Ford to Willison, Nov. 8, 11, 1915; Ford, *World Wags On*, 102.
28. Willison Papers, vol. 15, folder 116, Ford to Willison, Nov. 30, 1914; Ford, *World Wags On*, 139.
29. English, *Decline of Politics*, 70-72; Brown and Cook, *Canada 1896-1921*, 193, 194.
30. Brown and Cook, *Canada, 1896–1921*, 207; cited in Brown, *Borden*, vol. 1, 246.
31. Brown, *Borden*, vol. 1, 208, 240; Brown and Cook, *Canada 1896-1921*, 208.
32. O'Leary, "50 Years Ago."
33. Brown and Cook, *Canada 1896-1921*, 208; AO, MU-1543, Borden to Jennings, May 8, 1913.
34. Brown and Cook, *Canada 1896-1921*, 210.
35. Ford, *World Wags On*, 43; English, *Decline of Politics*, 29.

CHAPTER SIX: WARTIME HEADLINES

1. R.C. Brown, *Robert Laird Borden*, vol. 2 (Toronto, 1980), 21.
2. Borden Papers, *OC*, vol. 230, "Memo: Press and War," Oct. 30, 1914.
3. English, *Decline of Politics*, 92; Brown and Cook, *Canada 1896-1921*, 252.
4. Borden Papers, vol. 263, Chambers's Report on Censorship to Borden, July 16, 1915.
5. Borden Papers, *OC*, vol. 343, Chambers to Meighen, Dec. 19, 1916; John H. Thompson, *The Harvests of War: The Prairie West, 1914-1918* (Toronto, 1978), 34; Borden, *Memoirs*, 629-31.
6. Borden, *Memoirs*, 493; W.H. Kesterton, *A History of Journalism in Canada* (Toronto, 1967), 184.
7. Willison, *Laurier*, 439; English, *Decline of Politics*, 90.
8. Cook, *Dafoe*, 67, 53-63.
9. Borden to Laurier, Nov. 3, 1915, cited in Borden, *Memoirs*, 514.
10. Laurier to Borden, Nov. 13, 1915, cited in Borden, *Memoirs*, 518-19.
11. English, *Decline of Politics*, 96-100.
12. Ibid., 98-101; Brown and Cook, *Canada 1896-1921*, 216; Brown, *Borden*, vol. 2, 55-58.
13. Willison Papers, vol. 15, folder 116, Ford to Willison, Sept. 23, 1914.
14. English, *Decline of Politics*, 100 (John Ross Robertson of the *Toronto Telegram*, for example, was very angry with Borden for supporting Hughes; see Poulton, *Paper Tyrant*, 141-42); Brown, *Borden*, vol. 2, 57-59; Borden *Memoirs*, 571.
15. Ford, *World Wags On*, 90.
16. NA, John W. Dafoe Papers, vol. 1, Dafoe to Wrong, Dec. 12, 1916.
17. English, *Decline of Politics*, 101.
18. Beaven, "Partisanship," 336; Charles Bruce, *News and the Southams* (Toronto, 1968), 67-91.
19. Bruce, *Southams*, 94; Willison, vol. 115, folder 116, Ford to Willison, May 18, 1916; Hughes to Alderson, Mar. 7, 1916, cited in Col. G.W.L. Nicholson, *Canadian Expeditionary Force 1914-1919* (Ottawa, 1964), 158.
20. Bruce, *Southams*, 94; *DHC*, May 17, 1916, 4105.
21. *DHC*, May 17, 1916, 4104-16.
22. Bruce, *Southams*, 96.
23. Ibid., 101; *OC*, Feb. 1, 1917; cited in Bruce, *Southams*, 102.
24. Bruce, *Southams*, 103-4; Borden Papers, vol. 82, Borden to W. Southam, Feb. 10, 1917.
25. Kesterton, *History of Journalism*, 159.
26. Ford, *World Wags On*, 43-44.
27. Borden Papers, vol. 28, L.J. Tarte to Borden, Sept. 10, 1917.
28. Mason Wade, *The French Canadians* (Toronto, 1955), 735, 737-39.
29. English, *Decline of Politics*, 157.
30. Ibid., 141-57.
31. Borden Papers, vol. 79, Rogers to Borden, Aug. 15, 1917; vol. 78, Willison to Borden, June 12, 1917; Reid to Borden, "Memo, June, 1917."
32. *CAR*, 1917, 567.
33. Dafoe Papers, Sifton to Dafoe, Oct. 1917, cited in English, *Decline of Politics*, 159.
34. *MFP*, Dec. 11, 1917; Cook, *Dafoe*, 81-82.
35. *GL*, Dec. 14, 1917; Wade, *French Canadians*, 752.
36. English, *Decline of Politics*, 181, 193-94; *CAR*, 1917, 610; Wade, *French Canadians*, 752.
37. Wade, *French Canadians*, 752; *CAR*, 1917, 608-9.
38. Borden Papers, vol. 16, Borden to Foster, Doherty, and Reid, Nov. 13, 1917.
39. Ibid., vol. 101, Borden to McCurdy, Carvell, and Rowell, Jan. 28, 1918; F.L. Smith to Borden, Feb. 25, 1918.
40. Brown and Cook, *Canada 1896-1921*, 306; Borden, *Memoirs*, 787-89; Borden Papers, vol. 101, "Memo to English Press," May 3, 1918; various editors to Borden, May 3, 4, 5, 1918; English, *Decline of Politics*, 208.
41. English, *Decline of Politics*, 205.
42. Ibid., 212.
43. Borden Papers, vol. 96, Rowell to Borden, Sept. 5, 1918.

44. Ibid., vol. 245, Rowell to Borden, Nov. 7, 1918; Borden to Rowell, Nov. 20, 1918; Rowell to Borden, Feb. 6, 1919; Cook, *Dafoe*, 89-90.
45. *GL*, July 28, 1919; Willison Papers, vol. 29, folder 219, Meighen to Willison, June 20, 1919.

CHAPTER SEVEN:
THE UNDEPENDABLE PARTY PRESS

1. Peter Desbarats, *Guide to the Canadian News Media* (Toronto, 1990), 117; Rutherford, *Canadian Media*, 50-53; Beaven, "Partisanship," 348-51; NA, P.D. Ross Papers, vol. 1, "Ottawa Journal Balance Sheet," 1920; Rutherford, *Victorian Authority*, 98.
2. *CAR*, 1922, 342; 1926-27, 595; *TS*, Oct. 25, 1926.
3. Desbarats, *News Media*, 55.
4. Bruce, *Southams*, 183, 154, 181.
5. Dafoe Papers, vol. 3, Dafoe to Sifton, May 30, 1924.
6. Douglas Fetherling, *The Rise of the Canadian Newspaper* (Toronto, 1990), 112; Rutherford, *Canadian Media*, 38; Desbarats, *News Media*, 54.
7. *OJ*, "Responsibilities of the Press," June 10, 1922.
8. Graham, *Meighen*, vol. 1, 295-96.
9. Ibid., vol. 2, 139, 121; Brown and Cook, *Canada 1896-1921*, 334.
10. *Le Devoir*, July 9, 1920; Graham, *Meighen*, vol. 1, 299-300.
11. Eugene Forsey, *A Life on the Fringe* (Toronto, 1990), 100.
12. NA, J. Alex Hume Papers, vol. 1, "CBC interview transcript," Dec. 4, 1972; NA, William Lyon Mackenzie King Papers, J1, vol. 117, King to Larkin, Nov. 26, 1925.
13. I.N. Smith's postscript in Grattan O'Leary, *Recollections of People, Press and Politics* (Toronto, 1977), 195-202.
14. NA, Grattan O'Leary Papers, vol. 1, Alan Phillips, "The Last Angry Tory," *Maclean's*, undated article.
15. Ibid.; Dafoe Papers, vol. 3, Dexter to Dafoe, May 4, 1926.
16. O'Leary, *Recollections*, 38.
17. Graham, *Meighen*, vol. 2, 103; Willison Papers, vol. 39, folder 286, Willison to Sifton, June 28, 1921; vol. 31, folder 237, O'Leary to Willison, Nov. 1, 1921; Willison to O'Leary, Nov. 4, 1921.
18. Graham, Meighen, vol. 2, 103; O'Leary, *Recollections*, 44.
19. NA, Arthur Meighen Papers, vol. 43, undated speech, "Power of the Press."
20. Cook, *Dafoe*, 54, 135-37, 157-59; Meighen Papers, vol. 116, Meighen to Nichols, Jan. 15, 1924; Meighen to F.G. Taylor, May 3, 1926.
21. Meighen Papers, vol. 5, Meighen to Jennings, Nov. 22, 1920; Jennings to Meighen, Nov. 25, 1920; *GL*, Aug. 4, 1920; Nov. 22, 1920.
22. Graham, *Meighen*, vol. 2, 182-83.
23. See the Canadian Press dispatch in the *WT*, Apr. 18, 1923; *DHC*, Apr. 17, 1923, 1928-38; Meighen Papers, vol. 89, Ford to Meighen, Mar. 8, 1923; Meighen to Ford, Apr. 18, 1923; vol. 116, Meighen to E. Norman Smith, president of CP, May 29, 1926; vol. 176, Meighen to Howard Robinson, vice-president of CP, July 15, 1940; Meighen to Rupert Davies, July 17, 1940.
24. O'Leary, *Recollections*, 46.
25. Bennett Papers, M-1114, "History of Editorial Committee"; Meighen Papers, vol. 21, "Memo: Regarding Publicity and Propaganda in a General Election," 1921.
26. Cited in Graham, *Meighen*, vol. 2, 141, 143.

27. Cited in ibid., 150.
28. Bliss, *Flavelle*, 404, 405.
29. Ibid., 409-10; *MS*, Dec. 3, 1921.
30. Meighen Papers, vol. 40, Flavelle to J.A. Stewart, Dec. 5, 1921; Bliss, Flavelle, 409.
31. Bliss, Flavelle, 410; *CAR*, 1921, 490-91; Graham, *Meighen*, vol. 2, 163-64; Meighen Papers, vol. 40, Meighen to Calder, Dec. 15, 1921.
32. Meighen Papers, vol. 116, H.G. Richardson to Meighen, Apr. 12, 1922; Meighen to I.E. Bowell, May 9, 1922; Bowell to Meighen, May 9, 1922; Meighen to Hugh Clark, June 19, 1922; Bowell to Meighen, Mar. 29, 1923; E. Guss Porter to Meighen, June 21, 1923; Dawson to Meighen, July 20, 1923; Meighen to Sam Charters, Aug. 17, 1923; Hocken to Meighen, Oct. 29, 1923; Porter to Meighen, Nov. 1, 1923; Dawson to Meighen, Nov. 21, 1923; E.B. Eddy Company to *Intelligencer*, Dec. 28, 1923.
33. *CAR*, 1921, 499-500; see Douglas How, *A Very Private Person: The Story of Izaak Walton Killam* (Halifax, 1976).
34. Beaven, "Patronage," 338-39; O'Leary, *Recollections*, 21; Ross Papers, vol. 2, undated speech, 1930s file.
35. Graham, *Meighen*, vol. 2, 231-33.
36. Ross Papers, vol. 2, Meighen to Ross, June 9, 1923; Ross to Meighen, June 12, 1923; Meighen to Ross, July 2, 1923; Graham, *Meighen*, vol. 2, 237-38.
37. Graham, *Meighen*, vol. 2, 242; *MS*, July 12, 1923.
38. Graham, *Meighen*, vol. 2, 243.
39. Ibid., 256.
40. Ibid.
41. Ibid., 262-67.
42. Ibid., 277-83.
43. Ibid., 325, 338.
44. Forsey, *Fringe*, 102; *WT*, Dec. 3, 1925; Willison Papers, vol. 15, folder 116, Ford to Willison, Dec. 2, 1925; *OJ*, Dec. 11, 1927; Ross Papers, vol. 2, Ross to Meighen, Dec. 2; Meighen to Ross, Dec. 4, 1925; O'Leary, *Recollections*, 63.
45. Cited in Graham, *Meighen*, vol. 2, 204, 210.
46. Ross Papers, vol. 2, O'Leary to I.N. Smith, June 11, 1973; Graham, *Meighen*, vol. 2, 367.
47. Dafoe Papers, vol. 3, Dexter to Dafoe, May 4, 1926; *CAR*, 1926-27, 595.
48. Eugene Forsey, *The Royal Power of Dissolution of Parliament in the British Commonwealth* (Toronto, 1943); see also Graham, *Meighen*, vol. 2, 414-51, for a vindication of Lord Byng.
49. Cook, *Dafoe*, 162-65, 167; Dafoe Papers, vol. 3, Dafoe to Dexter, Sept. 17, 1926.
50. Meighen Papers, vol. 238, Meighen to O'Leary, July 11, 1952; University of Calgary, Bruce Hutchison Papers, 2.14, Meighen to Max Freedman, Dec. 30, 1952.
51. Graham, *Meighen*, vol. 2, 473.

CHAPTER EIGHT:
THE TRIALS OF MACKENZIE KING

1. *OJ*, July 31, 1987; H. Blair Neatby, *William Lyon Mackenzie King, 1932-1939: The Prism of Unity* (Toronto, 1976), 128-33.
2. See Joy E. Esberey, *Knight of the Holy Spirit: A Study of William Lyon Mackenzie King* (Toronto, 1980); John English and J.O. Stubbs, eds., *Mackenzie King: Widening the Debate* (Toronto, 1978).
3. R.M. Dawson, *William Lyon Mackenzie King: A Political Biography 1874-1923* (Toronto, 1958), 50-51; Pierre Berton, *The Great Depression 1929-1939* (Toronto, 1990), 60-61.

4. Charles Lynch, *You Can't Print That!* (Toronto, 1988), 128.
5. Ford, *World Wags On,* 176.
6. David Halberstam, *The Powers That Be* (New York, 1979), 8-9.
7. Ibid., 8, 12, 9.
8. Bruce Hutchison, *The Incredible Canadian* (Toronto, 1952), 218.
9. Bruce Hutchison, "Press Conference in Room 16," *Victoria Daily Times,* Mar. 19, 1937.
10. King Papers, J4, vol. 172, W. Turnbull to King, Dec. 30, 1938.
11. J.W. Pickersgill, *The Mackenzie King Record,* vol. 2 (Toronto, 1968), 640.
12. *OJ,* Apr. 16, 1939.
13. Esberey, *Holy Spirit,* 105.
14. Dafoe Papers, vol. 2, Stevenson to Dafoe, Jan. 23, 1920; Harkness, *Atkinson,* 122, 162.
15. Meighen Papers, vol. 99, Meighen to Jennings, June 12, 1923; *OJ,* Feb. 23, 1970.
16. King Papers, J1, vol. 193, King to Rev. A.J. Vining, July 9, 1926; vol. 188, King to M.W. Rossie, n.d., 1931; vol. 191, King to Harry Johnson, Sept. 15, 1932; Johnson to King, Sept. 22, 1932.
17. Meighen Papers, vol. 176, Nichols to Meighen, Sept. 6, 1940.
18. Bruce Hutchison, *The Far Side of the Street* (Toronto, 1976), 69; King Papers, J1, vol. 252, Hutchison to King, Dec. 22, 1938; vol. 289, King to Hutchison, Feb. 20, 1940; vol. 306, Hutchison to King, Jan. 29, 1941.
19. Queen's University Archives, Grant Dexter Papers, vol. 2, Dexter to Ferguson, Jan. 20, 1942; Hutchison, *Far Side,* 198-99.
20. Patrick Brennan, "A Responsible Civilized Relationship: Reporting the Nation's Business, 1935-1957" (Ph.D. thesis, York University, 1989), 105; James Gray, *Troublemaker!* (Toronto, 1983), 145.
21. Dexter Papers, vol. 1, "Dexter autobiography," n.d.; Dafoe Papers, vol. 5, Dexter to Dafoe, Oct. 25, 1930; Pickersgill, *King Record,* vol. 2, 294, 236 (see also Dafoe Papers, vol. 12, Dexter to Dafoe, Apr. 21, 1941; Dexter Papers, vol. 3, Dexter to Dafoe, Feb. 28, 1942).
22. Dexter Papers, vol. 2, Dexter to Ferguson, Feb. 14, 1940.
23. Dafoe Papers, vol. 5, Dexter to Dafoe, June 29, 1931; vol. 8, Dexter to Dafoe, Sept. 3, 1935.
24. Charles P. Stacey, *A Very Double Life: The Private World of Mackenzie King* (Toronto, 1976), 133.
25. Ibid., 163-64.
26. Blair Fraser, "The Secret Life of Mackenzie King, Spiritualist," *Maclean's,* Dec. 15, 1951, 7-9, 60-61; *OC,* Oct. 10, 1950; *TS,* Nov. 9, 1950.
27. Hume Papers, vol. 1, Hume to Neatby, Nov. 19, 1963; O'Leary, *Recollections,* 87.
28. Stacey, *Double Life,* 18-21.
29. Reginald Whitaker, *The Government Party* (Toronto, 1977), 5-6; King Papers, J1, vol. 66, King to St. Morris, Jan. 21, 1921.
30. King Papers, vol. 87, Southam to Haydon, May 2, 1923; M.E. Nichols, *The Story of the Canadian Press* (Toronto, 1948), 174.
31. King Papers, vol. 74, Haydon to King, Feb. 25, 1922; vol. 87, Haydon to King, May 26, 1923.
32. Michael Nolan, *Walter J. Blackburn: A Man for All Media* (Toronto, 1989), 22-23; Harkness, *Atkinson,* 204; King Papers, J1, vol. 75, King to A.R. Kennedy, Feb. 11, 1922; Kennedy to A.T. Low, May 6, 1922.
33. King Papers, vol. 74, King to Purdom, Sept. 27, 1922; King to Purdom, Oct. 2, 1922; Harkness, *Atkinson,* 204; Nolan, *Blackburn,* 23.
34. Harkness, *Atkinson,* 205.
35. Bruce, *Southams,* 178; Kesterton, *Canadian Journalism,* 100; Fetherling, *Canadian Newspaper,* 102.
36. King Papers, J1, vol. 59, King to Cromie, Nov. 12, 1921; King to Congdon, June 9, 1921; vol. 65, Odlum to King, Dec. 8, 1921; vol. 100, King to Graham, Oct. 20, 1924; vol. 113, Cromie to Robb, June 26, 1925; vol. 142, Cromie to King, July 11, 1927; vol. 151, King to Cromie, July 17, 1928; vol. 165, King to Odlum, Feb. 6, 1930.
37. J.L. Granatstein, *Mackenzie King: His Life and World* (Toronto, 1977), 91-92; H. Blair Neatby, *William Lyon Mackenzie King, 1924-1933: The Lonely Heights* (Toronto, 1963), 369.
38. King Papers, J1, vol. 187, Manson to King, Oct. 24, 1931; King to Manson, Nov. 6, 1931; vol. 191, Johnson to King, Oct. 5, 1932; King to Johnson, Oct. 6, 1932.
39. Frank Underhill, "J.W. Dafoe," *Canadian Forum,* Oct. 1932, 23.
40. Ramsay Cook, "J.W. Dafoe at the Imperial Conference, 1923," *CHR* 41, no. 1 (Mar. 1960): 160; Cook, *Dafoe,* 141, 128-30 (for Dafoe's views on foreign policy).
41. Cook, *Dafoe,* 159.
42. Dafoe Papers, vol. 8, Lambert to Dafoe, Feb. 2, 1935; Dafoe to Lambert, Feb. 13, 1935.
43. Hutchison, *Far Side,* 194; King Papers, J1, vol. 283, King to Atkinson, Mar. 17, 1940; Harkness, *Atkinson,* 162; Wilfrid Eggleston, "Leaves from a Press Man's Log," *Queen's Quarterly* 63 (Winter 1957): 550.
44. Brennan, "Reporting the Nation's Business," 10; Harkness, *Atkinson,* 122, 319.
45. Pierre Berton, "The Amazing Career of George McCullagh," *Maclean's,* Jan. 15, 1949, 42.
46. Neatby, *King, 1924-1933,* 205; Esberey, *Holy Spirit,* 101-2.
47. Neatby, *King, 1924-1933,* 206.
48. *GL,* Mar. 2, 1923; *DHC,* June 26, 1925, 4975; May 28, 1930, 2743; *Senate Debates,* May 29, 1930, 395; *GL,* May 30, 31, 1930.
49. King Papers, J1, vol. 163, J.W. Lawrason to King, Nov. 14, 1929.
50. Neatby, *King, 1924-1933,* 58-59; King Papers, J1, vol. 103, King to Larkin, Sept. 6, 1924.
51. *King Papers,* J1, vol. 103, Larkin to King, Sept. 29, 1924; vol. 119, Mackinnon to King, June 22, 1925.
52. NA, The Diary of William Lyon Mackenzie King, Oct. 10, 1925 (hereafter King Diary).
53. King Papers, J1, vol. 117, King to Larkin, Nov. 26, 1925.
54. Ibid., vol. 111, Jaffray to Aylesworth, Nov. 18, 1925.
55. Ibid., vol. 146, King to Mullock, Feb. 26, 1927; Meighen Papers, vol. 238, O'Leary to Meighen, Feb. 20, 1927.
56. King Papers, J1, King to Jaffray, Aug. 12, 1929.
57. King Papers, J1, vol. 175, Johnson to King, Feb. 24, 1930; Jaffray to King, May 3, 15, 1930; *GL,* May 2-6, 1930.
58. Neatby, *King, 1924-1933,* 318-40.
59. King Papers, J1, vol. 186, Johnson to King, Aug. 1, 1931.
60. Ibid., Johnson to King, Aug. 18, 20, 1932.

CHAPTER NINE: R.B. IN CHARGE

1. Berton, *Great Depression*, 73. Traditional assumptions about Bennett's stern character and structured life have been recently challenged in two interesting books: James Gray, *R.B. Bennett: The Calgary Years* (Toronto, 1991); and P.B. Waite, *The Loner: Three Sketches of the Personal Life and Ideas of R.B. Bennett, 1870-1947* (Toronto, 1992).
2. Berton, *Great Depression*, 74; author's interview with Bruce Hutchison, June 11, 1990.
3. Berton, *Great Depression*, 15; Ernest Watkins, *R.B. Bennett: A Biography* (Toronto, 1963), 92-93.
4. Watkins, *Bennett*, 167; Berton, *Great Depression*, 72.
5. Dafoe Papers, vol. 8, Dexter to Dafoe, Jan. 23, 1935.
6. Larry A. Glassford, "Retrenchment – R.B. Bennett Style: The Conservative Record before the New Deal," *American Review of Canadian Studies* 19, no. 2 (Summer 1989): 142, 153.
7. Neatby, *King, 1924-1933*, 231, 232; *WT*, Oct. 13, 1927.
8. Bennett Papers, M-920, "Memo: Re: weekly papers in B.C.," 1927; M-922, Bennett to Wright, Apr. 1928; M-923, Brown to Ryckman, Feb. 2, 1929.
9. Ibid., M-943, Turnbull to Bennett, Oct. 24, 1927.
10. Ibid., Campbell to Blacklock, June 20, 1928; Memo, Sept. 4, 1928; Bennett to Gordon, Oct. 2, 1928.
11. Ibid., Campbell to Gordon, Feb. 12, 1929; M-1307, Gordon to Bennett, Aug. 4, 1929; Sept. 4, 1931; Dec. 31, 1931.
12. Watkins, *Bennett*, 77-78; Kesterton, *Canadian Journalism*, 75.
13. Bennett Papers, M-1114, Sauvé to Bennett, Nov. 3, 1931.
14. Ibid., Webster to Bennett, July 5, 1932; Sauvé to Bennett, Sept. 28, 1933; Bender to Bennett, Sept. 18, 1933.
15. *WT*, Oct. 8, 1927; Ford, *World Wags On*, 145-46.
16. Cited in John Thompson, with Allan Seager, *Canada 1922-1939: Decades of Discord* (Toronto, 1985), 201.
17. Ford, *World Wags On*, 146.
18. Ibid., 144-45; Berton, *Great Depression*, 65.
19. Ford, *World Wags On*, 146.
20. Bennett Papers, M-1114, Lipsett to Bennett, Aug. 1930.
21. Ford, *World Wags On*, 146, 145.
22. Harkness, *Atkinson*, 259.
23. Dafoe Papers, vol. 5, Dexter to Dafoe, Aug. 18, 1930.
24. E.C. Buchanan, column, *Saturday Night*, Sept. 27, 1930, 1.
25. Dafoe Papers, vol. 5, Smith to Dafoe, Sept. 25, 1930; *OJ* editorial in *Moncton Transcript*, Sept. 18, 1930.
26. O'Leary, *Recollections*, 74; Dafoe Papers, vol. 5, Smith to Dafoe, Sept. 25, 1930; Stevenson to Dafoe, undated letter from Jan.-July 1931 file.
27. Cited in Chalmers, *Gentleman of the Press*, 281.
28. *WFP*, July 2, 1931.
29. Chalmers, *Gentleman of the Press*, 282.
30. Ibid., 282-83; Floyd Chalmers, *Both Sides of the Street* (Toronto, 1983), 86-87.
31. Chalmers, *Both Sides of the Street*, 87.
32. Ibid., 88.
33. Ibid., 89-90; Bennett Papers, M-1278, Smith to Bennett, Nov. 23, 1933; Bennett to Smith, Nov. 24, 1933; Smith to Bennett, Dec. 1, 1933.
34. *The Saskatchewan Liberal*, Nov. 30, 1933; Chalmers, *Both Sides of the Street*, 90.
35. Dafoe Papers, vol. 4, Dafoe to Condliffe, n.d., 1928; George V. Ferguson, *John W. Dafoe* (Toronto, 1948), 78.
36. Dafoe Papers, vol. 5, Dafoe to Dexter, Aug. 8, 1930.
37. Ibid., Aug. 8, 1930.
38. Ibid., Aug. 22, 1930.
39. Dexter Papers, vol. 1, John Sifton to Dexter, Jan. 26, 1931.
40. Bennett's comments to Geoffrey Dawson of the *Times* (London) are in Dafoe Papers, vol. 6, Dawson to Dafoe, July 7, 1932; Cook, *Dafoe*, 196.
41. Cook, *Dafoe*, 196; Dafoe Papers, vol. 6, Dafoe to Bennett, July 2, 1932; Dexter to Dafoe, July 12, 1932.
42. Dafoe Papers, vol. 6, Dexter to Dafoe, Oct. 16, 1932.
43. Ibid., Oct. 19, 1932.
44. O'Leary, *Recollections*, 75.
45. *DHC*, May 17, 1934, 3119-20.
46. Neatby, *King, 1932-1939*, 59-60, 80-81; Berton, *Great Depression*, 237-80.
47. Halberstam, *Powers*, 15.
48. E. Austin Weir, *The Struggle for National Broadcasting in Canada* (Toronto, 1965), 8-18; John A. Irving, *The Social Credit in Canada* (Toronto, 1959), 30-32.
49. Berton, *Great Depression*, 229; James Gray, *The Roar of the Twenties* (Toronto, 1982), 216.
50. Desbarats, *News Media*, 36; Siegel, *Politics*, 166-72.
51. Bennett Papers, M-1277, O'Leary to Bennett, Sept. 4, 1931; Bennett to O'Leary, Sept. 10, 1931; Weir, *Broadcasting*, 67-70.
52. Halberstam, *Powers*, 15.
53. *GL*, June 19, 1930; *OJ*, Aug. 9, 1935, King Papers, J1, vol. 160, H. Cartwright to King, Dec. 5, 1929; Victoria *Colonist*, Dec. 30, 1939.
54. King Papers, J4, vol. 204, "Memo: Radio," 1936; author's interview with J.W. Pickersgill, Feb. 1, 1990; Michael Nolan, *Foundations: Alan Plaunt and the Early Days of CBC Radio* (Toronto, 1986), 136.
55. O'Leary, *Recollections*, 39; King Diary, June 9, 1930; Neatby, *King, 1924-1933*, 335.
56. Herr to Bennett, Apr. 12, 1934, cited in J.R.H. Wilbur, *The Bennett New Deal: Fraud or Portent?* (Toronto, 1968), 69.
57. Dafoe Papers, vol. 8, Dexter to Dafoe, Jan. 4, 1935.
58. Berton, *Great Depression*, 282; Nolan, *Foundations*, 118.
59. Wilbur, *New Deal*, 80-81; Thompson, *Canada 1922-39*, 262.
60. Cited in Neatby, *King, 1932-1939*, 88.
61. King Diary, Jan. 9, 1935; Neatby, *King, 1932-1939*, 89; Dafoe Papers, vol. 8, Dafoe to Dexter, Jan. 10, 1935.
62. Cited in Thompson, *Canada 1922-39*, 272.
63. Berton, *Great Depression*, 342.
64. Whitaker, *Government Party*, 72-83.
65. King Papers, J4, vol. 204, "Mr. Sage Broadcasts," 1935.
66. Ibid.; Weir, *Broadcasting*, 201, 76.
67. King Papers, J4, vol. 204, Charlesworth to Howe, Nov. 20, 1935; Weir, *Broadcasting*, 201-2.
68. Cited in Weir, *Broadcasting*, 204.

CHAPTER TEN: MANAGING THE WAR

1. Berton, "McCullagh," 43.
2. R.E. Knowles, "Presidents and Publishers," *Saturday Night*, Nov. 14, 1936, 5.
3. Berton, "McCullagh," 42; Doyle, *Hurly-Burly*, 17; Maggie Siggins, *Bassett* (Toronto, 1979), 19.
4. Berton, "McCullagh," 43.
5. Ibid., 43; Siggins, *Bassett*, 21.
6. King Papers, J1, King to McCullagh, Nov. 13, 1936; McCullagh to King, Nov. 17, 1936; King Diary, Nov. 19, 1936; John T. Saywell, *'Just Call Me Mitch': The Life of Mitchell F. Hepburn* (Toronto, 1991), 281.

7. Whitaker, *Government Party*, 316.
8. Cited in Brian J. Young, "C. George McCullagh and the Leadership League," in Ramsay Cook, ed., *Politics of Discontent* (Toronto, 1967), 78-81; Whitaker, *Government Party*, 319; Siggins, *Bassett*, 36; Saywell, *Hepburn*, 529.
9. Saywell, *Hepburn*, 327; King Diary, Apr. 13, 1937; Whitaker, *Government Party*, 320-21; Doyle, *Hurly-Burly*, 22.
10. Neil McKenty, *Mitch Hepburn* (Toronto, 1967), 122.
11. King Papers, J4, vol. 204, Pickersgill to King, Dec. 4, 1939; T.J. Allard, *Straight Up: Private Broadcasting in Canada 1918-1958* (Ottawa, 1979), 169-71; King Papers, J1, vol. 246, Brockington to King, May 11, 1938; King to Brockington, June 14, 1938.
12. Doyle, *Hurly-Burly*, 27-28.
13. Siggins, *Bassett*, 39; King Papers, J1, vol. 255, King to Mulock, Sept. 21, 1938.
14. David Mackenzie, "The Bren Gun Scandal and the Maclean Publishing Company's Investigation of Canadian Defence Contracts 1938-1940," *Journal of Canadian Studies* 26, no. 3 (Fall 1991): 141-52.
15. *FP*, Aug. 26, 1939; Mackenzie, "Bren Gun," 151-52; *DHC*, Mar. 1, 1939, 1452.
16. Mackenzie, "Bren Gun," 153-54; *FP*, Oct. 7, 14, 1939.
17. *MG*, Jan. 26, 1940; J.L. Granatstein, *Canada's War: The Politics of the Mackenzie King Government 1939-49* (Toronto, 1975), 80; Doyle, *Hurly-Burly*, 29, 44; Meighen Papers, vol. 175, Knowles to Meighen, June 19, 1940.
18. *GM*, Oct. 9, 1941; Dafoe Papers, vol. 12, Dafoe to Crerar, May 5, 1941; *WFP*, May 10, 1941; Granatstein, *Canada's War*, 359.
19. Granatstein, *Canada's War*, 423.
20. King Papers, J1, vol. 270, Heeney to Lapointe, Oct. 4, 1939; see also King Papers, J4, vol. 155, "Memo on Public Information," Nov. 15, 1939.
21. Granatstein, *Canada's War*, 285; Hutchison, *Incredible Canadian*, 323.
22. King Papers, J1, vol. 302, Claxton to King, May 1941.
23. NA, Wilfrid Eggleston Papers, vol. 29, "Press Censorship in Canada in World War II," n.d.
24. King Papers, J1, vol. 283, Bertrand to King, Sept. 9, 1940; vol. 285, Charpentier to Pickersgill, Sept. 11, 1940; J4, vol. 321, Pickersgill to King, Sept. 11, 1940; Gille Purcell, "Wartime Censorship in Canada," *International Journal* 2 (Summer 1947): 257.
25. Meighen Papers, vol. 175, Knowles to Meighen, June 19, 1940.
26. Granatstein, *Canada's War*, 85; Pickersgill, *King Record*, vol. 2, 378.
27. Harkness, *Atkinson*, 335-36; *GM*, Apr. 16, 1942.
28. Neatby, *King, 1932-1939*, 174-75; *WFP*, Oct. 1, 1936; June 18, 1937; Dexter Papers, vol. 1, Dafoe to Dexter, Oct. 30, 1936.
29. John Dafoe, "Press, Politicians and People," *Canadian Historical Review* 27, no. 1 (Mar. 1936): 59.
30. Dafoe Papers, vol. 13, Dafoe to Stevenson, Feb. 12, 1942; Cook, *Dafoe*, 268-71.
31. Dexter Papers, vol. 2, Ferguson to Dexter, July 12, 1941.
32. *WFP*, Feb. 2, 1942; Cook, *Dafoe*, 269.
33. *WFP*, May 10, 1941; King Papers, J1, vol. 337, *WFP* clipping, Aug. 1943.
34. Dafoe Papers, vol. 13, Dafoe to Stevenson, Feb. 12, 1942.

CHAPTER ELEVEN: UNCLE LOUIS

1. *Hamilton Spectator*, Oct. 30, 1948.
2. Chalmers, *Both Sides*, 112; June Callwood, "The Truth about Parliament," *Maclean's*, Apr. 17, 1965, 41.
3. Brennan, "Reporting the Nation's Business," 195.
4. Peter Dempson, *Assignment Ottawa: Seventeen Years in the Press Gallery* (Toronto, 1968), 21.
5. Hume Papers, vol. 1, Hume to St. Laurent, Nov. 26, 1948; NA, Louis St. Laurent Papers, vol. 139, see file 40-1-H for correspondence with Hume; vol. 194, Hume to St. Laurent, June 4, 1956.
6. Author's interview with Tom Earle, Apr. 25, 1991.
7. Brennan, "Reporting the Nation's Business," 379 n. 60.
8. Dale C. Thomson, *Louis St. Laurent: Canadian* (Toronto, 1967), 350.
9. *CH*, May 27, 1950; Vancouver *Province*, May 25, 1950; Thomson, *St. Laurent*, 375.
10. Hutchison, *Far Side*, 219; J.W. Pickersgill, *My Years with Louis St. Laurent: A Political Memoir* (Toronto, 1975), 175; Ian Sclanders, "How the Prime Minister Became Uncle Louis," *Maclean's*, Jan. 1, 1955, 42.
11. Hutchison Papers, 2.1.6, Power to Hutchison, May 21, 1951.
12. Peter C. Newman, column, *Maclean's*, Oct. 22, 1960, 21.
13. Thomson, *St. Laurent*, 324-25; Pickersgill, *My Years*, 174-79; St. Laurent Papers, vol. 137, Pickersgill to St. Laurent, July 12, 1952; Pickersgill to Howe, July 21, 1952; Whitaker, *Government Party*, 187.
14. Dexter Papers, vol. 6, Hutchison to Dexter, Nov. 5, 1952.
15. Whitaker, *Government Party*, 186, 236.
16. Ibid., 238; St. Laurent Papers, vol. 171, Pickersgill to Kidd, Oct. 7, 1948; vol. 123, Claxton to Pickersgill, July 4, 1952; Claxton to Pickersgill, Oct. 29, 1952.
17. Ibid., vol. 123, Kidd to Pickersgill, Feb. 28, 1949.
18. Dexter Papers, vol. 5, Bloom to Dexter, Feb. 11, 1949.
19. Whitaker, *Government Party*, 237; Sclanders, "Uncle Louis," 41.
20. Whitaker, *Government Party*, 237.
21. Dalton Camp, *Gentlemen, Players and Politicians* (Toronto, 1970), 137-38.
22. *OJ*, Apr. 19, 1950; Whitaker, *Government Party*, 237-38.
23. Dempson, *Ottawa*, 60.
24. Whitaker, *Government Party*, 205.
25. Harkness, *Atkinson*, 340.
26. Cited in Siggins, *Bassett*, 60; Harkness, *Atkinson*, 355; *TT*, Nov. 26, 1948.
27. Dempson, *Ottawa*, 62.
28. Harkness, *Atkinson*, 365.
29. Ibid., 365.
30. Ibid., 366; Sydney Katz, "How Toronto's Evening Papers Slanted the Election News," *Maclean's*, Aug. 15, 1949, 54.
31. Siggins, *Bassett*, 72.
32. *OJ*, Aug. 1, 1953.
33. Robert Bothwell and William Kilbourn, *C.D. Howe: A Biography* (Toronto, 1979), 79; O'Leary, *Recollections*, 106.
34. Tom Kent, *A Public Purpose* (Montreal, 1988), 21.
35. Thomson, *St. Laurent*, 385; Dexter Papers, vol. 7, Dexter memo of May 23, 1954.
36. St. Laurent Papers, vol. 206, memo from Pierre Asselin, Mar. 9, 1954.
37. Bothwell and Kilbourn, *Howe*, 294-95.

38. Kent, *Public Purpose,* 25.
39. Bothwell and Kilbourn, *Howe,* 300.
40. *OJ,* Aug. 12, 1955.
41. *Maclean's,* July 7, 1956, cited in Peter C. Newman, *Renegade in Power: The Diefenbaker Years* (Toronto, 1963), 37-38.
42. June Callwood, "The Truth about Parliament," *Maclean's,* Apr. 17, 1965, 11.
43. Brennan, "Reporting the Nation's Business," 359-61; Kent, *Public Purpose,* 28; *WFP,* May 15, 1956; *OJ,* May 29, 1956.
44. Newman, *Renegade in Power,* 43, 44.
45. St. Laurent Papers, vol. 193, Pearson to St. Laurent, Jan. 9, 1957 (Heeney's report of Dec. 1956 attached).
46. Callwood, "Truth about Parliament," 50.
47. *CH,* Nov. 2, 1956; *St. John's Telegraph,* Nov. 7, 1956; *WFP,* Nov. 26, 1956; Thomson, *St. Laurent,* 470.
48. Paul Rutherford, *When Television Was Young: Prime Time Canada 1952-1967* (Toronto, 1990), 59; Blair Fraser, column, *Maclean's,* Mar. 31, 1956, 58.
49. Rutherford, *When Television Was Young,* 58-59; Frank Peers, *The Public Eye: Television and the Politics of Canadian Broadcasting 1952-1968* (Toronto, 1979), 119-21.
50. St. Laurent Papers, vol. 206, St. Laurent to Dunton, Oct. 23, 1956; Dunton to St. Laurent, Oct. 29, 1956; St. Laurent to Dunton, Oct. 29, 1956; Peers, *Public Eye,* 121-23.
51. NA, NLF Papers, vol. 626, Report of Mar. 27, 1950; Camp, *Gentlemen,* 209.
52. Halberstam, *Powers That Be,* 225-26; Michael Cockerell, *Live from Number 10: The Inside Story of Prime Ministers and Television* (London, 1988), 27-44.
53. Halberstam, *Powers That Be,* 246; *WFP,* May 3, 1957; Whitaker, *Government Party,* 250.
54. NLF Papers, vol. 637, "Confidential Memo: Radio – TV," Mar. 18, 1957; Newman, *Renegade,* 54; Rutherford, *When Television Was Young,* 69; NLF Papers, vol. 837, Kidd to Harwood, Feb. 22, 1956; memo by Gordon Atkinson, July 2, 1957; vol. 836, Kidd to Archibald, May 25, 1957; Kidd to MacTavish, May 15, 1957; Aug. 8, 1957; Whitaker, *Government Party,* 250-51.
55. Rutherford, *When Television Was Young,* 70; Camp, *Gentlemen,* 262. In his memoirs, Diefenbaker suggested that Camp's role in the 1957 campaign was minimal: "I have read that Dalton Camp played a major role in the 1957 victory. At the time, I knew nothing of him whatever; and he did not operate under an assumed name at that time." (In 1966 Camp, as national president of the Conservative Party, was behind the movement to oust Diefenbaker as leader.) (John G. Diefenbaker, *One Canada,* vol. 2 [Toronto, 1976], 29.)
56. John Meisel, *The Canadian General Election of 1957* (Toronto, 1962), 81, 162-64, 285-89; Rutherford, *When Television Was Young,* 170.
57. Lynch, *Print That,* 139-41.
58. Camp, *Gentlemen,* 295; cited in Newman, *Renegade,* 57-58.
59. Newman, *Renegade,* 55; Kent, *Public Purpose,* 35-36.
60. NA, C.D. Howe Papers, vol. 108, Howe to Mackenzie, Aug. 27, 1957; Whitaker, *Government Party,* 251.
61. Rutherford, *When Television Was Young,* 171; Camp, *Gentlemen,* 262.

CHAPTER TWELVE: DIEF VS. THE GALLERY

1. Dempson, *Ottawa,* 95; Newman, *Renegade,* 59.
2. Knowlton Nash, *Diefenbaker and Kennedy* (Toronto, 1990), 121-59, 215-16.
3. Peter Stursberg, *Diefenbaker: Leadership Gained 1956-62* (Toronto, 1975), 77-78.
4. Diefenbaker, *One Canada,* vol. 2, 108; John G. Diefenbaker, *One Canada,* vol. 3 (Toronto, 1977), 141, 182.
5. Garrett Wilson and Kevin Wilson, *Diefenbaker for the Defence* (Toronto, 1988), 216-17.
6. Newman, *Renegade,* 25.
7. John G. Diefenbaker, *One Canada,* vol. 1 (Toronto, 1975), 268; Meighen Papers, vol. 238, O'Leary to Meighen, Oct. 15, 1957; O'Leary to Meighen, June 23, 1958; Diefenbaker, *One Canada,* vol. 3, 156.
8. University of Saskatchewan, Diefenbaker Centre, John G. Diefenbaker Papers, vol. 188, speech of Oct. 26, 1966.
9. Newman, *Renegade,* 232.
10. Ibid., 163-64; NA, Progressive Conservative Party Papers, vol. 387, "Strategy Paper by Dalton Camp, 1962."
11. Diefenbaker Papers, vol. 512, Nelson to Grosart, July 29, 1957.
12. Stursberg, *Diefenbaker, 1956-62,* 157.
13. Newman, *Renegade,* 234.
14. Rutherford, *When Television Was Young,* 428.
15. Cited in Robert MacDonald, "His Face Spelled News," *Toronto Sun,* Mar. 14, 1980.
16. Thomas Van Dusen, *The Chief* (Toronto, 1968), 118-19.
17. Peers, *Public Eye,* 230; Siggins, *Bassett,* 130; Dempson, *Ottawa,* 118.
18. Doyle, *Hurly-Burly,* 112, 133; Diefenbaker Papers, vol. 514, Dalgleish to Diefenbaker, Dec. 16, 1957.
19. Donald M. Fleming, *So Very Near: The Political Memoirs of the Honourable Donald M. Fleming,* vol. 2: *The Summit Years* (Toronto, 1985), 430-35.
20. Dempson, *Ottawa,* 104.
21. Ibid., 112, 117.
22. *DHC,* June 16, 1958, 1156; cited in Newman, *Renegade,* 232-33.
23. Dempson, *Ottawa,* 99-100; Patrick Nicholson, *Vision and Indecision* (Toronto, 1968), 188.
24. *OC,* Sept. 28, 1958; Dempson, *Ottawa,* 108.
25. Diefenbaker Papers, PMO Series, vol. 123, Dean to Diefenbaker, June 27, 1957; vol. 512, Waring to Diefenbaker, Aug. 5, 1957; *OC,* July 8, 1957; *GM,* July 11, 1957.
26. Nicholson, *Vision,* 64-72.
27. Newman, *Renegade,* 67; author's interview with Mitchell Sharp, May 8, 1990.
28. Nash, *Diefenbaker,* 73.
29. Stursberg, *Diefenbaker, 1956-62,* 104.
30. Diefenbaker, *One Canada,* vol. 2, 276; Nicholson, *Vision,* 105, 318.
31. Nash, *Diefenbaker,* 74-76.
32. Michael Bliss, "Shutting Down the Avro Myth," *Report on Business Magazine,* Feb. 1989, 32.
33. NA, Cabinet Conclusions, vol. 69, 1647, 57-59, Apr. 21, 1959; Margaret Conrad, *George Nowlan: Maritime Conservative in National Politics* (Toronto, 1986), 226.
34. Conrad, *Nowlan,* 226; Rutherford, *When Television Was Young,* 58; Newman, *Renegade,* 236.
35. Conrad, *Nowlan,* 227.
36. Diefenbaker Papers, vol. 514, Memo: *Toronto Star,* Nov. 24, 1959, 1.

37. Newman, *Renegade,* 295; Fleming, *So Very Near,* vol. 2, 337; *TS,* editorials of June 15, 17, 27, 1961; *WFP* editorials of June 15, 17, 27, 1961; J.L. Granatstein, *Canada 1957-1967: The Years of Uncertainty and Innovation* (Toronto, 1986), 77.
38. Fleming, *So Very Near,* vol. 2, 347; *TS,* June 27, 1961.
39. Fleming, *So Very Near,* vol. 2, 234-44; Granatstein, *Canada 1957-1967,* 83.
40. *OC,* Sept. 15, 1961; Newman, *Renegade,* 238; Donnelly's story is cited by Christopher Young in "What Happened at Accra," *OC,* Jan. 27, 1962.
41. Newman, *Renegade,* 239; Fleming, *So Very Near,* vol. 2, 393; *DHC,* Sept. 28, 1961, 9054-80.
42. *OC,* Jan. 27, 1962; Fleming, *So Very Near,* vol. 2, 390.
43. *OJ,* Nov. 4, 1961; *GM,* Jan. 15, 1962; Newman, *Renegade,* 244-45; Diefenbaker Papers, Speeches Series, vol. 78, speech of Jan. 13, 1962, 8.
44. *GM,* Aug. 12, 1960; J.M. Beck, *Pendulum of Power: Canada's Federal Elections* (Scarborough, 1968), 330; *TS,* Mar. 16, 1963 (op-ed article by Frank Underhill).
45. Newman, *Renegade,* 245.
46. Diefenbaker, *One Canada,* vol. 3, 6; Nash, *Diefenbaker,* 164; Newman, *Renegade,* 246.
47. PC Papers, vol. 387, "Strategy, 1962 Election."
48. Nash, *Diefenbaker,* 164-65.
49. Ibid., 165; Beck, *Pendulum,* 334, Stursberg, *Diefenbaker, 1956-62,* 251; Diefenbaker, *One Canada,* vol. 3, 123; *WFP,* May 4, 1962.
50. Dempson, *Ottawa,* 121-22.
51. *OC,* May 26, 28, 1962.
52. Stursberg, *Diefenbaker, 1956-62,* 266-67; *OC,* June 1, 1962.
53. Beck, *Pendulum,* 347.
54. Van Dusen, *The Chief,* 112, 116.
55. Peter Stursberg, *Leadership Lost: 1962-1966* (Toronto, 1976), 4; cited in Nash, *Diefenbaker,* 170.
56. Nash, *Diefenbaker,* 137-40.
57. Ibid., 145, 147; Granatstein, *Canada 1957-1967,* 122; Diefenbaker, *One Canada,* vol. 3, 3.
58. Nash, *Diefenbaker,* 143.
59. Newman, *Renegade,* 353; Pierre Sévigny, *This Game of Politics* (Toronto, 1965), 258.
60. *WFP,* Jan. 28, 1963; *GM,* Jan. 27, 1963; Nash, *Diefenbaker,* 235-36.
61. Nash, *Diefenbaker,* 249-53.
62. Doyle, *Hurly-Burly,* 174.
63. Sévigny, *Game,* 278.
64. Nicholson, *Vision,* 180-84; Stursberg, *Leadership Lost, 1962-1966,* 40-41.
65. Stursberg, *Leadership Lost, 1962-1966,* 63.
66. *GM,* Feb. 6, 1963; *Hamilton Spectator,* Feb. 7, 1963.
67. *GM,* Feb. 7, 8, 1963.
68. Diefenbaker, *One Canada,* vol. 3, 176.
69. Beck, *Pendulum,* 355-56.
70. Diefenbaker Papers, vol. 291, 1963 Election, Dalton Camp memo to constituency presidents, Feb. 13, 1963.
71. Ibid., cited in Newman, *Renegade,* 248.
72. Stursberg, *Leadership Lost, 1962-1966,* 44; Siggins, *Bassett,* 148.

CHAPTER THIRTEEN: ONE OF THE BOYS

1. Meighen Papers, vol. 238, O'Leary to Meighen, Mar. 15, 1952.
2. John English, *Shadow of Heaven: The Life of Lester Pearson,* vol. 1: *1897-1948* (Toronto, 1989), 255-56.
3. Lester B. Pearson, *Mike: The Memoirs of the Rt. Hon. L.B. Pearson,* ed. John A. Munro and Alex I. Inglis, vol. 3 (Toronto, 1975), 163-64.
4. Brennan, "Reporting the Nation's Business," 294.
5. Ibid., 34-35; Dexter Papers, vol. 1, Dexter to Ferguson, Oct. 19, 1937.
6. Dexter Papers, vol. 1, Dexter to Ferguson, Sept. 20, 1938.
7. Hutchison, *Far Side,* 249.
8. Hutchison Papers, 1.2.2, Hutchison to Dexter, Feb. 17, 1955.
9. Hutchison, *Far Side,* 243-44.
10. Ibid., 245-46.
11. Ibid., 246-47, 248.
12. Peter C. Newman, *The Distemper of Our Times* (Toronto, 1968), 212.
13. Hutchison Papers, 1.2.7, Hutchison to Dexter, July 20, 1961; see also Jan. 17, Feb. 8, Apr. 7, 1961.
14. Hutchison, *Far Side,* 213; Newman, *Distemper,* 64.
15. Kent, *Public Purpose,* 79-89; Hutchison Papers, 1.2.7, Hutchison to Dexter and Richard Malone, Sept. 29, 1961; Kent, *Public Purpose,* 111.
16. Hutchison Papers, 1.2.7., Hutchison to Dexter and Malone, Oct. 14, 1961.
17. Ibid.
18. Allan Fotheringham, column, *Toronto Sun,* Sept. 9, 1984; Christina McCall-Newman, *Grits: An Intimate Portrait of the Liberal Party* (Toronto, 1982), 5.
19. Keith Davey, *The Rainmaker: A Passion for Politics* (Toronto, 1986), 45; McCall-Newman, *Grits,* 41-42.
20. NA, Lester Pearson Papers, N2, vol. 105, file on Liberal Party colleges.
21. NLF Papers, vol. 712, O'Hagan to Davey, Apr. 24, 1962.
22. Pearson Papers, N3, vol. 256, O'Hagan to Pearson, Dec. 10, 1963; O'Hagan to Wilson, Dec. 10, 1963.
23. Dempson, *Ottawa,* 46.
24. NLF Papers, vol. 712, O'Hagan memo, 1961.
25. Pearson Papers, N2, vol. 28, O'Hagan to Davey, Sept. 5, 1961.
26. Ibid., vol. 28, Davey to Pearson, Nov. 13, 1962.
27. Davey, *Rainmaker,* 46.
28. Newman, *Distemper,* 69.
29. Peter C. Newman, column, *Maclean's,* Feb. 25, 1961, 54.
30. Cited in Peter Stursberg, *Lester Pearson and the Dream of Unity* (Toronto, 1978), 72-73.
31. Pearson Papers, N5, vol. 47, CBC interview, n.d.
32. Eric Koch, *Inside Seven Days* (Toronto, 1986), 22; Kent, *Public Purpose,* 334-35.
33. Kent, *Public Purpose,* 335.
34. Newman, *Distemper,* xii.
35. Ibid., 42.
36. Pearson, *Mike,* vol. 3, 109.
37. Judy LaMarsh, *Memoirs of a Bird in a Gilded Cage* (Toronto, 1968), 5; O'Leary, *Recollections,* 138; Kent, *Public Purpose,* 214.
38. Hutchison's comments on Pearson's mind are cited in Newman, *Distemper,* 82; *VS,* Dec. 16, 1967; Hutchison, *Far Side,* 250.
39. Cited in *WFP,* Dec. 28, 1972.
40. Kent, *Public Purpose,* 233; Newman, *Distemper,* 21; Walter Gordon, *A Political Memoir* (Toronto, 1977), 141-55.
41. Newman, *Distemper,* 22; Gordon, *Political Memoir,* 149; Kent, *Public Purpose,* 233-34.
42. Hutchison Papers, 2.1.2, Crerar to Hutchison, July 12, 1963.
43. *Time Magazine,* Nov. 13, 1964, 17.

44. Callwood, "Truth about Parliament," 44.
45. Dempson, *Ottawa*, 143; LaMarsh, *Memoirs*, 54.
46. *Ottawa Times Weekly*, Jan. 15, 1964.
47. Dempson, *Ottawa*, 144; *TT*, Feb. 18, 1966.
48. Rutherford, *When Television Was Young*, 409-14; *OC*, Dec. 23, 1965.
49. Pearson Papers, N4, vol. 228, LaPierre to Pearson, Feb. 19, 1965; Pearson to LaPierre, Mar. 9, 1965; Warner Troyer, *200 Days* (Toronto, 1980), 19-20.
50. Peers, *Public Eye*, 335; Rutherford, *When Television Was Young*, 414-15; Koch, *Seven Days*, 104-11.
51. Koch, *Seven Days*, 189-91; LaMarsh, *Memoirs*, 256; *GM*, May 28, 1966.
52. Koch, *Seven Days*, 116-18; *TS*, May 30, 1966; Rutherford, *When Television Was Young*, 404.
53. Rutherford, *When Television Was Young*, 403.
54. Elspeth Cameron, "Newman's Progress," *Saturday Night*, Sept. 1982, 13-17.
55. Ibid., 18; Cameron, *Newman's Progress*, 17.
56. Robert Fulford, *Best Seat in the House* (Toronto, 1988), 149-50; see also reviews of *Renegade* in *Saturday Night*, Nov. 1963, 38-39; *GM*, Nov. 9, 1963; *OJ*, Nov. 2, 1963.
57. Peter Newman, letter to editor, *MS*, Nov. 16, 1963.
58. Denis Smith, Introduction to Carleton Library edition, *Renegade in Power* (Toronto, 1971), xi.
59. *TT*, Nov. 5, 1963.
60. Van Dusen, *The Chief*, 114; Diefenbaker, *One Canada*, vol. 3, 209; Dave McIntosh, *Ottawa Unbuttoned* (Toronto, 1987), 32-33.
61. Diefenbaker Papers, vol. 171, "Peter Newman file," 105339-41; Steven Billinton, Diefenbaker Archives, to the author, Apr. 16, 1993.
62. Diefenbaker Papers, vol. 299, "Renegade in Power" file, Commentary, Nov. 1963, 14-17.
63. Pearson Papers, N4, vol. 109, Dornan to Pearson, Nov. 25, 1966.
64. Peter C. Newman, *Home Country: People, Places and Power Politics* (Toronto, 1973), 17.
65. Pearson Papers, N4, vol. 109, Dornan to Pearson, Nov. 25, 1966.
66. Ibid., Newman to Dornan, Nov. 24, 1966; Dornan to Newman, Nov. 25, 1966; Newman to Dornan, Dec. 7, 1966; *TS*, Dec. 24, 1966.
67. Pearson, *Mike*, vol. 3, 205.
68. Newman, *Distemper*, 285; Robert Bothwell, Ian Drummond, and John English, *Canada Since 1945: Power, Politics, and Provincialism* (Toronto, 1981), 293-94, 264-87, 389-406.
69. NLF, vol. 724, "List of Newspapers received by Prime Minister's Office," 1963, marked confidential; Callwood, "Truth about Parliament," 41.
70. Callwood, "Truth about Parliament," 41; Dempson, *Ottawa*, 149-50.
71. Callwood, "Truth about Parliament," 41-42.
72. *DHC*, May 21, 1964, 3428.
73. Pearson Papers, N4, vol. 232, Peacock to Pearson, Apr. 12, 1967; MacFarlane to Pearson, Apr. 10, 1967.
74. Pearson, *Mike*, vol. 3, 201-2.
75. Pearson Papers, N3, vol. 60, Tom Kent memo, Aug. 10, 1965.
76. Beck, *Pendulum*, 381.
77. Doyle, *Hurly-Burly*, 212-13; Beck, *Pendulum*, 381.
78. K.Z. Paltiel, *Political Party Financing in Canada* (Toronto, 1970), 90; Pearson Papers, N3, vol. 60, "Memo: Broadcasting and 1965 Campaign."
79. McCall-Newman, *Grits*, 48; Beck, *Pendulum*, 382-83.
80. PC Papers, vol. 398, "Election Campaign and Press Arrangements," 1965.
81. See Newman, *Distemper*, 378-79.
82. Ibid., 37. See also John English, *The Worldly Years: The Life of Lester Pearson*, vol. 2: *1949-1972* (Toronto, 1993).

CHAPTER FOURTEEN: THE "CRUMMY" PRESS

1. George Radwanski, *Trudeau* (Toronto, 1978), 121.
2. Ibid., 120.
3. Herbert F. Quinn, *The Union Nationale: A Study in Quebec Nationalism* (Toronto, 1963), 140.
4. Pierre Trudeau, *Federalism and the French Canadians* (Toronto, 1968), xxi; Radwanski, *Trudeau*, 227.
5. Siegel, *Politics and the Media*, 17; Radwanski, *Trudeau*, 119; Stephen Clarkson and Christina McCall, *Trudeau and Our Times: The Magnificent Obsession* (Toronto, 1990), 62-67.
6. Radwanski, *Trudeau*, 229.
7. Patrick Gossage, *Close to Charisma: My Years between the Press and Pierre Elliott Trudeau* (Toronto, 1986), 113, 215.
8. Cited in Radwanski, *Trudeau*, 228.
9. *Maclean's*, Mar. 12, 1984, 18.
10. Davey, *Rainmaker*, 248; McCall-Newman, *Grits*, 56-58.
11. *WFP*, Dec. 11, 1976.
12. Cited in Ron Graham, *One-Eyed Kings* (Toronto, 1986), 116.
13. Clarkson and McCall, *Trudeau and Our Times*, 25-51; McCall-Newman, *Grits*, 72.
14. Clarkson and McCall, *Trudeau and Our Times*, 111.
15. Jeffrey Simpson, *Discipline of Power: The Conservative Interlude and the Liberal Restoration* (Toronto, 1980), 292; see Halberstam, *Powers That Be*, 383-90; McLuhan to Trudeau, June 12, 1968, in M. Molinaro, C. McLuhan, and W. Toye, eds., *Letters of Marshall McLuhan* (Toronto, 1987), 354.
16. Rutherford, *When Television Was Young*, 431.
17. Ibid., 431-32; Clarkson and McCall, *Trudeau and Our Times*, 110; Richard Gwyn, *The Northern Magus* (Toronto, 1981), 68; Simpson, *Discipline of Power*, 285.
18. Gwyn, *Magus*, 120; Knowlton Nash, *Prime Time at Ten: Behind the Camera Battles of Canadian TV Journalism* (Toronto, 1987), 110.
19. Nash, *Prime Time*, 110.
20. Rutherford, *When Television Was Young*, 433-34; Richard Gwyn, column, *TS*, Oct. 14, 1975.
21. Siegel, *Politics and the Media*, 105, 110, 135.
22. Cited in Desbarats, *Canadian News Media*, 21.
23. *Maclean's*, Oct. 31, 1988, 24; *GM*, Apr. 2, 1988; June 28, 1988; Simpson, *Discipline of Power*, 286.
24. For Mulroney's comments and the impact of television on politics, see "Prime Time Politics," *GM*, Apr. 2, 1988.
25. Rick Butler and Jean-Guy Carrier, eds., *The Trudeau Decade* (Toronto, 1979), 386.
26. Marjorie Nichols, "Over the Hill," *Weekend Magazine*, Mar. 17, 1979, 16-18.
27. Desbarats, *Canadian News Media*, 88-91.
28. Halberstam, *Powers That Be*, 318.
29. Clarkson and McCall, *Trudeau and Our Times*, 107.
30. *GM*, Feb. 17, 1968.
31. Radwanski, *Trudeau*, 108.
32. *TT*, Sept. 3, 1968.
33. Peter C. Newman, *Drawn and Quartered: The Trudeau Years* (Toronto, 1984), 7.
34. Christina Newman, column, *Saturday Night*, Sept. 1968, 8-9.

35. *TT*, Sept. 5, 1968.
36. *GM*, Mar. 14, 1975; Butler and Carrier, *Trudeau Decade*, 89-92.
37. McCall-Newman, *Grits*, 157; Clarkson and McCall, *Trudeau and Our Times*, 133; Stephen Clarkson, "Pierre Trudeau and the Liberal Party," in Howard Penniman, ed., *Canada at the Polls: The General Election of 1974* (Washington, D.C., 1975), 85; *Le Devoir*, June 4, 1974.
38. Clarkson and McCall, *Trudeau and Our Times*, 125; Margaret Trudeau, *Beyond Reason* (New York, 1979), 193-95.
39. Margaret Trudeau, *Beyond Reason*, 201-4; Clarkson and McCall, *Trudeau and Our Times*, 135.
40. Margaret Trudeau, *Beyond Reason*, 206.
41. *VS*, Mar. 15, 1977; *OJ*, Mar. 12, 1977.
42. Gossage, *Charisma*, 69-70; McCall-Newman, *Grits*, 170; author's interviews with Geoffrey Stevens, May 30, 1990; Charles Lynch, May 8, 1990; Anthony Westell, Apr. 30, 1990.
43. James Earys, "Dilettante in Power: The First Three Years of Pierre Elliott Trudeau," *Saturday Night*, Apr. 1971, cited in Butler and Carrier, *Trudeau Decade*, 209-19; Walter Stewart, *Shrug: Trudeau in Power* (Toronto, 1971), 228-29; Radwanski, *Trudeau*, 257.
44. *OC*, Oct. 31, 1972; *OJ* and *VS*, Nov. 3, 1972.
45. *Financial Post*, Sept. 29, 1984.
46. *GM*, Oct. 6, 14, 1972; *OC*, Oct. 28, 1972.
47. *Reader's Digest, Politics and the Media* (Toronto, 1981), 195.
48. Stewart, *Shrug*, 209-10.
49. McCall-Newman, *Grits*, 148-53.
50. Ibid., 140-46; Simpson, *Discipline of Power*, 256-57; Gwyn, *Magus*, 168-72.
51. Simpson, *Discipline of Power*, 259; McCall-Newman, *Grits*, 142-45.
52. Davey, *Rainmaker*, 165-75.
53. Richard Gwyn, "The Boys on the Bus Are Being Used," *TS*, June 18, 1974.
54. Fred Fletcher, "The Mass Media in the 1974 Canadian General Election," in Penniman, *Election of 1974*, 272-73; John Burns, "Dogging the Campaign Trail to Check on the Press," *GM*, June 21, 1974.
55. Fletcher, "Mass Media," 273.
56. Burns, "Press," *GM*, June 21, 1974; Clive Cocking, *Following the Leaders* (Toronto, 1980), 23.
57. Cocking, *Following the Leaders*, 23; Simpson, *Discipline of Power*, 254; Clarkson, "Trudeau," 84; Fletcher, "Mass Media," 254, 284-85.
58. Davey, *Rainmaker*, 184.
59. Clarkson, "Trudeau and the Liberal Party," 84-85.
60. Fletcher, "Mass Media," 285-88.
61. McCall-Newman, *Grits*, 162.
62. Ibid., 162-68; Gwyn, *Magus*, 170-71; Simpson, *Discipline of Power*, 259-60.
63. McCall-Newman, *Grits*, 171.
64. *TS*, Mar. 26, 1976.
65. Geoffrey Stevens, column, *GM*, Dec. 28, 1976.
66. Don Braid, "Trudeau versus the Media," *MS*, Dec. 3, 1977; Gossage, *Charisma*, 116.
67. *MG*, Nov. 25, 1978.
68. Geoffrey Stevens, column, *GM*, Nov. 15, 1978.
69. Radwanski, *Trudeau*, xi, 355.
70. McCall-Newman, *Grits*, 56-57, 341.
71. Stephen Clarkson, "The Defeat of the Government, the Decline of the Liberal Party, and the (Temporary) Fall of Pierre Trudeau," in Howard Penniman, ed., *Canada at the Polls 1979 and 1980: A Study of General Elections* (Washington, D.C., 1981), 153-56.
72. George Radwanski, column, *Financial Post*, Nov. 27, 1978.

**CHAPTER FIFTEEN:
JUDGMENTAL JOURNALISM**

1. George Bain, "Parliamentary Press Gallery," *Saturday Night*, July 1985, 28.
2. Allan Fotheringham, *Look Ma No Hands* (Toronto, 1984), 62.
3. Ibid., 69; Simpson, *Discipline of Power*, 83.
4. For headlines, see *GM*, Jan. 9, 1979; *OJ*, Jan. 11, 1979; *La Presse*, Jan. 20, 1979; *GM*, Jan. 16, 1979.
5. Mary Anne Comber and Robert Mayne, *The Newsmongers: How the Media Distort the Political News* (Toronto, 1986), 50.
6. Lloyd Tataryn, *The Pundits: Power, Politics and the Press* (Toronto, 1985), 149; Fotheringham, *Look Ma*, 71-72.
7. Allan Fotheringham, column, *WFP*, Jan. 19, 1979; Cocking, *Leaders*, 221; Stewart McLeod, column, *St. John's Evening-Telegram*, Jan. 16, 1979.
8. *GM*, Jan. 12, 1979; Doyle, *Hurly-Burly*, 330.
9. Dalton Camp, *Points of Departure* (Ottawa, 1979), 14, 172; Simpson, *Discipline of Power*, 76-77.
10. David Humphreys, *Joe Clark: A Portrait* (Toronto, 1978), 38.
11. Ibid., 53; Kenneth Whyte, "Back in the Saddle," *Saturday Night*, Feb. 1992, 52; John Sawatsky, *Mulroney: The Politics of Ambition* (Toronto, 1991), 243.
12. Simpson, *Discipline of Power*, 100-1; *GM*, Mar. 10, 1979.
13. Simpson, *Discipline of Power*, 74.
14. Michael Nolan, *Joe Clark: The Emerging Leader* (Toronto, 1978), 97.
15. Simpson, *Discipline of Power*, 79.
16. Humphreys, *Clark*, 252.
17. John C. Courtney, "Campaign Strategy and Electoral Victory: The Progressive-Conservatives and the 1979 Election," in Penniman, ed., *Canada at the Polls 1979 and 1980*, 131.
18. Ibid., 133-35.
19. Allan Gregg to Lowell Murray, June 12, 1978, cited in Courtney, "1979 Election," 136.
20. Fredrick J. Fletcher, "Playing the Game: The Mass Media and the 1979 Campaign," in Penniman, *Canada at the Polls 1979 and 1980*, 280-81, 286.
21. Ibid., 297, 319.
22. Ibid., 292.
23. *GM*, Apr. 4, 1979.
24. Simpson, *Discipline of Power*, 84.
25. *MG*, Apr. 21, 1979; *TS*, May 4, 1979.
26. Fletcher, "Playing the Game," 287, 310; Clarkson, "The Defeat of the Government," 182, 179.
27. Gossage, *Charisma*, 171.
28. Clarkson, "Trudeau," 182; Cocking, *Leaders*, 134-41.
29. Fletcher, "Playing the Game," 310; cited in Cocking, *Leaders*, 250.
30. Clarkson, "Trudeau," 183.
31. Fletcher, "Playing the Game," 318, 321.
32. Cited in Simpson, *Discipline of Power*, 86-89.
33. Camp, *Departure*, 170.
34. Sawatsky, *Mulroney*, 377.
35. John Sawatsky, *The Insiders: Government, Business and the Lobbyists* (Toronto, 1987), 120; Simpson, *Discipline of Power*, 159-65.
36. Troyer, *200 Days*, 134, 149.
37. Cited in Clarkson and McCall, *Trudeau and Our Times*, 148, 421 n. 6.

38. Ibid., 152, 422 n. 11; cited in Gwyn, *Magus*, 341-42; Clarkson and McCall, *Trudeau and Our Times*, 152.
39. Of the twenty major Canadian dailies, thirteen were negative and six were more critical than positive. Only the *Toronto Star* was positive. See *Windsor Star*, Dec. 20, 1979.
40. Simpson, *Discipline of Power*, 328.
41. Gossage, *Charisma*, 192.
42. Clarkson and McCall, *Trudeau and Our Times*, 188; Gossage, *Charisma*, 221; *VS*, Dec. 1, 1982; *Toronto Sun*, Dec. 3, 1982; *TS*, Mar. 28, 1983.
43. Robert Sheppard and Michael Valpy, *The National Deal: The Fight for a Canadian Constitution* (Toronto, 1982) – see chapter 8.
44. *Maclean's*, Sept. 22, 1980, 21.
45. Clarkson and McCall, *Trudeau and Our Times*, 183-87.
46. *GM*, Feb. 4, 1981; cited in *TS*, Sept. 30, 1981.
47. Jean Chrétien, *Straight from the Heart* (Toronto, 1985), 184; Clarkson and McCall, *Trudeau and Our Times*, 381-84; Sheppard and Valpy, *National Deal*, 288-302.
48. *WFP, TS, GM, OC, MG*, Nov. 6, 1981; Clarkson and McCall, *Trudeau and Our Times*, 383-84.
49. Ian Stewart, "Global Transformation and Economic Policy," in Pierre Trudeau and Thomas Axworthy, eds., *Towards a Just Society: Governing Canada 1968-1984* (Toronto, 1989), 107-25; *GM*, Apr. 24, 1989; Apr. 25, 1989; Mar. 18, 1992; Simpson, column, *GM*, May 2, 1989.
50. J.L. Granatstein and Robert Bothwell, *Pirouette: Pierre Trudeau and Canadian Foreign Policy* (Toronto, 1990), 376-80; Richard Gwyn and Sandra Gwyn, "The Politics of Peace," *Saturday Night*, May 1984, 19-32.
51. Gwyn and Gwyn, "Politics of Peace," 19, 25.
52. Ibid., 28; *OC*, Feb. 9, 1984; see editorials of *VS, OC, WFP, GM*, Feb. 10, 1984.
53. *La Presse, TS*, May 27, 1987; *GM*, May 30, 1987; *Maclean's*, June 8, 1987, 10-11; Sept. 7, 1987, 14-19; *GM*, Mar. 6, 1990; *OC*, Mar. 11, 1990; *GM*, Mar. 20, 1990.
54. Michael Ignatieff, "The Longest Shadow," *Saturday Night,* Oct., 1987, 26; Clarkson and McCall, *Trudeau and Our Times*, 6.

CHAPTER SIXTEEN:
THE TURNER FOLLIES OF '84

1. Graham, *One-Eyed Kings*, 198-99.
2. Ibid., 201; author's interview with Thomas Walkom, June 1992.
3. Cited in Jack Cahill, *John Turner: The Long Run* (Toronto, 1984), 215.
4. Chrétien, *Straight from the Heart* (Toronto, 1985), 202.
5. Author's interview with John Turner, June 6, 1990.
6. Donald Johnston, *Up the Hill* (Montreal, 1986), 22.
7. Cahill, *Turner*, 52-53.
8. McCall-Newman, *Grits*, 244.
9. Graham, *One-Eyed Kings*, 190-91.
10. Young cited in Cahill, *Turner*, 104; Cahill, *Turner,* 133, 60-67; Mulroney cited in McCall-Newman, *Grits*, 249.
11. McCall-Newman, *Grits,* 316-17; Cahill, *Turner*, 192.
12. Sawatsky, *Insiders*, 193.
13. Jeffrey Simpson, "The Vincible Liberals," in A. Frizzell and A. Westell, eds., *The Canadian General Election of 1984* (Ottawa, 1985), 20.
14. Sawatsky, *Insiders*, 199; *VS*, Mar. 17, 1984; see also *GM, OC, CH*, Mar. 17, 1984.

15. Sawatsky, *Insiders*, 191; McCall-Newman, *Grits*, 243; Graham, *One-Eyed Kings*, 188.
16. Cahill, *Turner*, 214.
17. Graham, *One-Eyed Kings*, 194.
18. Sawatsky, *Insiders*, 215.
19. Stephen Clarkson, "The Dauphin and the Doomed: John Turner and the Liberal Party's Debacle," in Howard Penniman, ed., *Canada at the Polls 1984* (Washington, D.C., 1988), 104-5.
20. Simpson, *Spoils of Power*, 352-53.
21. Sawatsky, *Insiders*, 229-31, 226-31; Davey, *Rainmaker*, 328.
22. Simpson, "Vincible Liberals," 15-16; Clarkson, "John Turner," 107-14.
23. Sawatsky, *Insiders*, 239-40; Greg Weston, *Reign of Error: The Inside Story of John Turner's Troubled Leadership* (Toronto, 1988), 81-83; Comber and Payne, *Newsmongers*, 46; *VS*, July 24, 1984.
24. Richard Gwyn, "Disorder Raises Doubts," *WFP*, Aug. 8, 1984; author's interview with Senator Norman Atkins, May 10, 1990.
25. Sawatsky, *Mulroney*, 533.
26. Ibid., 534; Michel Gratton, *So What Are the Boys Saying?* (Toronto, 1987), 40-46.
27. Sawatsky, *Insiders*, 243.
28. Cited in Sawatsky, *Mulroney*, 538-40.
29. Jeffrey Simpson, column, *GM*, Sept. 3, 1984.
30. Ibid.; Frizzell and Westell, *General Election of 1984,* 55.
31. Cited in Fredrick J. Fletcher, "The Media and the 1984 Landslide," in Penniman, *Canada at the Polls 1984*, 183.
32. Fletcher, "Media and the 1984 Landslide," 172-76; Comber and Payne, *Newsmongers*, 101-3.
33. Davey, *Rainmaker*, 353.
34. Charles Lynch, *Race for the Rose: Election 1984* (Toronto, 1984), 149.
35. Comber and Payne, *Newsmongers*, 118-19.
36. Ibid., 106.
37. Carol Goar, "Down to the Day of Decision," *Maclean's*, Sept. 3, 1984, 14.
38. Hepburn cited in Frizzell and Westell, *General Election of 1984*, 55-56.
39. Frizzell and Westell, *General Election of 1984*, 71.

CHAPTER SEVENTEEN:
MEDIA JUNKIE

1. *GM*, June 20, 1990.
2. Author's interview with Graham Fraser, Apr. 25, 1991; Dec. 23, 1992; see also Hayes, *Power and Influence*, 280-92.
3. *GM*, June 13, 1990; Wells cited in *Maclean's*, July 2, 1990, 23.
4. Sawatsky, *Mulroney*, 51-56.
5. Ibid., 200.
6. Ibid., 255-56.
7. Cited in ibid., 280.
8. Davey, *Rainmaker,* 254.
9. *GM*, Feb. 24, 1976; Sawatsky, *Mulroney*, 319-20.
10. *FP Magazine*, June 20, 1978, 18-20, 54-56; Sawatsky, *Mulroney,* 351-56.
11. Sawatsky, *Mulroney,* 391; L. Ian Macdonald, *Mulroney: The Making of the Prime Minister* (Toronto, 1984), 131.
12. Macdonald, *Mulroney*, 194; Sawatsky, *Mulroney*, 474-75; Mulroney cited in Graham, *One-Eyed Kings*, 140.
13. Graham, *One-Eyed Kings,* 139; Gray's article is cited in Doyle, *Hurly-Burly*, 479.

14. For differing views on journalists' opinions of Mulroney in 1984, see Fletcher, "Media and the 1984 Landslide," 168; *Maclean's*, Sept. 17, 1984, 10-11; Richard Gwyn, column, *WFP*, Sept. 5, 1984; George Perlin, "Opportunity Regained: The Tory Victory in 1984," in Penniman, *Canada at the Polls 1984*, 93-95; Claire Hoy, *Friends in High Places* (Toronto, 1987), 320-21.
15. Macdonald, *Mulroney*, 229.
16. *OC*, Nov. 15, 1986.
17. Gratton, *So What Are the Boys Saying?*, 214-15.
18. Charlotte Gray, "Massaging the Beast," *Saturday Night*, Jan./Feb. 1990, 12.
19. Charlotte Gray, "Caucus Charisma," *Saturday Night*, July/Aug. 1990, 15-18.
20. *OC*, Aug. 17, 26, 1989; George Bain, column, *Maclean's*, Sept. 25, 1989, 52; Gray, "Massaging the Beast," 12-13; see also George Bain, column, *Maclean's*, Aug. 22, 1988, 44.
21. Cited in *MG*, Oct. 1, 1988.
22. Graham, *One-Eyed Kings*, 328.
23. Gratton, *So What Are the Boys Saying?*, 3, 235.
24. Ibid., 226.
25. Jeffrey Simpson, "Everybody Wants to Be a Critic," *GM*, May 2, 1988.
26. *GM*, Apr. 16, 1987; Mar. 12, 1988.
27. Michel Gratton, *Still the Boss: A Candid Look at Brian Mulroney* (Toronto, 1990), 57.
28. Gratton, *So What Are the Boys Saying?*, 225-26.
29. *Annual Report of the Information Commissioner, 1991-1992* (Ottawa, 1992), 6.
30. *GM*, Nov. 19, 20, 1992.
31. Gratton, *So What Are the Boys Saying?*, 188-89; *TS*, Jan. 27, 1986; Stewart MacLeod, column, *Charlottetown Guardian*, Nov. 13, 1985; Jan. 23, 1985. On the Quebec press, see MacLeod, column, *Charlottetown Guardian*, Jan. 30, 1986.
32. *WFP*, Aug. 30, 1986; *OC*, Nov. 15, 1986.
33. Jeffrey Simpson, column, *GM*, Aug. 24, 1988; Stevie Cameron, column, *GM*, Aug. 25, 1988; James Stewart, column, *WFP*, Aug. 29, 1988.
34. *MG*, Oct. 1, 1988.

CHAPTER EIGHTEEN:
THE COMEBACK KID'S LAST RIDE

1. A. Frizzell, J.H. Pammett, and A. Westell, *The Canadian General Election of 1988* (Ottawa, 1989), 131.
2. Alan Frizzell and Anthony Westell, "The Media and the Campaign," in Frizzell et al., *Election of 1988*, 76.
3. Linda Frum, ed., *The Newsmakers* (Toronto, 1990), 15-16.
4. Weston, *Reign of Error*, 135.
5. *GM*, Sept. 17, 1988.
6. See, for example, Weston, *Reign of Error*, 48, 55, 57, 85, 106, 197.
7. Cited in *Maclean's*, Oct. 31, 1988, 24-25.
8. *GM*, Oct. 22, 1988; Fraser, *Playing for Keeps*, 232, 241; *WFP*, Oct. 14, 18, 1988.
9. Fraser, *Playing for Keeps*, 253; Mansbridge cited in Frizzell et al., *Election of 1988*, 81-82.
10. Gerald Caplan, Michael Kirby, and Hugh Segal, *Election* (Toronto, 1989), 138-44.
11. Cited in Fraser, *Playing for Keeps*, 255.
12. *OC*, *MG*, Oct. 22, 1988.
13. Caplan et al., *Election*, 142.
14. Norman Snider, "The Fixer," *Saturday Night*, Nov. 1988, 35-41; Rick Salutin, *Waiting for Democracy* (Toronto, 1989), 146.

15. Cited in Fraser, *Playing for Keeps*, 290-91.
16. Jeffrey Simpson, column, *GM*, May 5, 1989; Christopher Young, column, *OC*, Feb. 8, 1990.
17. *GM*, Feb. 9, 13, 1990.
18. *OC*, Mar. 29, 1990; *GM*, Mar. 24, 1990.
19. *TS*, May 23, 1990.
20. David Taras, "How Television Transformed the Meech Lake Negotiations," in David E. Smith, Peter Mackinnon, and John C. Courtney, eds., *After Meech Lake* (Saskatoon, 1981), 175.
21. Rick Salutin, "Brian and the Boys," *Saturday Night*, Nov. 1990, 16.
22. Ibid., 85.
23. John Meisel, "Mirror? Searchlight? Interloper?: The Media and Meech," in Smith et al., *After Meech Lake*, 156; *OC*, June 12, 1990; Salutin, "Brian and the Boys," 85; Taras, "How Television Transformed," 178.
24. *OC*, June 9, 1990 (article by Greg Weston).
25. *GM*, *Le Devoir*, *La Presse*, June 11, 1990; *OC*, June 12, 1990.
26. Salutin, "Brian and the Boys," 87; cited in *GM*, Feb. 1, 1992.
27. *GM*, Oct. 29, 1990; *Maclean's*, Jan. 7, 1991, 24, 32-33. The results were similar in 1993; when asked whether journalists or politicians have the most honesty and integrity 10 percent of the respondents chose journalists, while only 2 percent chose politicians (*Maclean's*, Jan. 4, 1993, 43).
28. Jeffrey Simpson, column, *GM*, Dec. 6, 1990; Jan. 31, 1991; *GM*, Nov. 22, 1990; *Maclean's*, Nov. 19, 1990, 17; Jan. 7, 1991, 12-15.
29. Cited in *GM*, Mar. 12, 1991.
30. Ibid., July 18, 1992.
31. Lysiane Gagnon, column, *GM*, Feb. 27, 1993; "Good Riddance or Mission Accomplished," *GM*, Feb. 26, 1993; Pauline Couture, column, *GM*, Mar. 4, 1993.
32. William Thorsell, column, *GM*, Feb. 27, 1993.
33. Ibid., Aug. 12, 1991.
34. Kent, *A Public Purpose*, 17.
35. Mulroney interview in *Maclean's*, Mar. 8, 1993, 39.
36. Lysiane Gagnon, column, *GM*, June 5, 1993; George Bain, column, *Maclean's*, June 21, 1993, 56; Christina McCall, "This PM Is Looking Like One of the Boys," *GM*, June 25, 1993.

Bibliography

PRIMARY SOURCES

MANUSCRIPT COLLECTIONS

**Archives of Ontario,
Toronto**

Leslie Frost Papers
M.O. Hammond Papers
Thomas Patteson Papers

**National Archives of
Canada, Ottawa**

The Prime Ministers
J.J. Abbott Papers
R.B. Bennett Papers
Robert Borden Papers
Mackenzie Bowell Papers
William Lyon Mackenzie
   King Papers
Wilfrid Laurier Papers
John A. Macdonald Papers
Alexander Mackenzie Papers
Arthur Meighen Papers
Lester Pearson Papers
Louis St. Laurent Papers
John Thompson Papers
Charles Tupper Papers

The Politicians
Edward Blake Papers
Henri Bourassa Papers
John Bracken Papers
George Brown Papers
C.D. Howe Papers
A.E. Kemp Papers
R.J. Manion Papers
J.W. Pickersgill Papers
Clifford Sifton Papers
Robert Stanfield Papers
Israel Tarte Papers
National Liberal Federation
   of Canada Papers
Progressive Conservative
   Party of Canada Papers

The Journalists
Charles Belford Papers
John W. Dafoe Papers
Norman DePoe Papers
Wilfrid Eggleston Papers
Edward Farrer Papers
Martin Griffin Papers
J. Alex Hume Papers
Stewart Lyon Papers
James Moylan Papers
M. Grattan O'Leary Papers
Ernest Pacaud Papers
P.D. Ross Papers
E. Norman Smith Papers
John Stevenson Papers
John Willison Papers

**Queen's University
Archives, Kingston**

Grant Dexter Papers

**University of Calgary
Special Collections**

Bruce Hutchison Papers

**University of
Saskatchewan, Saskatoon,
The Rt. Honourable John
G. Diefenbaker Centre**

John G. Diefenbaker Papers

INTERVIEWS

Note: All interviews were
conducted by the author
between 1990 and 1993.

Norman Atkins
Thomas Axworthy
George Bain
Henry Comor
Peter Connolly
Jim Coutts

Pauline Couture
Clark Davey
Keith Davey
Peter Desbarats
Richard Doyle
Philipe Dubuisson
Tom Earle
Douglas Fisher
Bill Fox
Graham Fraser
Lysiane Gagnon
Patrick Gossage
Gowan Guest
Roy Heard
Beland Honderich
Bruce Hutchison
Arthur Irwin
Marc Lalonde
Gilbert Lavoie
Luc Lavoie
Romeo LeBlanc
Charles Lynch
L. Ian Macdonald
Peter Mansbridge
Don McGillivray
Knowlton Nash
Jim Nelson
Don Newman
Bill Neville
Peter C. Newman
Richard O'Hagan
Jock Osler
Don Peacock
Jack Pickersgill
Doug Richardson
Val Sears
Mitchell Sharp
Jeffrey Simpson
Robert Stanfield
Geoffrey Stevens
Walter Stewart
John Turner
Thomas Walkom
Anthony Westell
W.A. Wilson
Christopher Young

SELECTED PUBLISHED SOURCES

Berton, Pierre. *The Promised Land: Settling the West 1896–1914.* Toronto: McClelland & Stewart, 1984.

_____. *The Great Depression: 1929–1939.* Toronto: McClelland & Stewart, 1990.

Bilkey, Paul. *Persons, Paper and Things.* Toronto: Ryerson Press, 1940.

Borden, Henry, ed. *Robert L. Borden: His Memoirs.* 2 vols. Toronto: Macmillan, 1938.

_____. *Letters to Limbo.* Toronto: University of Toronto Press, 1971.

Brown, R.C. *Robert Laird Borden: A Biography.* 2 vols. Toronto: Macmillan, 1975, 1980.

Brown, R.C., and Ramsay Cook. *Canada 1896–1921: A Nation Transformed.* Toronto: McClelland & Stewart, 1974.

Bruce, Charles. *News and the Southams.* Toronto: Macmillan, 1968.

Cahill, Jack. *John Turner: The Long Run.* Toronto: McClelland & Stewart, 1984.

Camp, Dalton. *Gentlemen, Players and Politicians.* Toronto: McClelland & Stewart, 1970.

Careless, J.M.S. *Brown of the Globe: The Voice of Upper Canada.* Vol. 1. Toronto: Macmillan, 1959.

_____. *Brown of the Globe: Statesman of Confederation.* Vol. 2. Toronto: Macmillan, 1963.

Chalmers, Floyd S. *A Gentleman of the Press.* Toronto: Doubleday, 1969.

_____. *Both Sides of the Street.* Toronto: Macmillan, 1983.

Charlesworth, Hector. *Candid Chronicles.* Toronto: Macmillan, 1925.

_____. *More Candid Chronicles.* Toronto: Macmillan, 1928.

Clarkson, Stephen, and Christina McCall. *Trudeau and Our Times: The Magnificent Obsession.* Vol. 1. Toronto: McClelland & Stewart, 1990.

Cocking, Clive. *Following the Leaders.* Toronto: Doubleday, 1980.

Colquhoun, A.U.H. *Press, Politics and People: The Life and Letters of Sir John Willison.* Toronto: Macmillan, 1935.

Comber, Mary Anne, and Robert Mayne. *The Newsmongers: How the Media Distort the Political News.* Toronto: McClelland & Stewart, 1986.

Cook, Ramsay. *The Politics of John W. Dafoe and the Free Press.* Toronto: University of Toronto Press, 1963.

Creighton, Donald. *John A. Macdonald: The Young Politician.* Vol. 1. Toronto: Macmillan, 1965.

Creighton, Donald. *John A. Macdonald: The Old Chieftain.* Vol. 2. Toronto: Macmillan, 1965.

Cumming, Carman. *Secret Craft: The Journalism of Edward Farrer.* Toronto: University of Toronto Press, 1992.

Dafoe, J.W. *Laurier: A Study in Canadian Politics.* 1922. Reprint. Toronto: McClelland & Stewart, 1963.

Davey, Keith. *The Rainmaker: A Passion for Politics.* Toronto: Stoddart, 1986.

Dawson, R.M. *William Lyon Mackenzie King: A Political Biography 1874–1923.* Toronto: University of Toronto Press, 1958.

Dempson, Peter. *Assignment Ottawa: Seventeen Years in the Press Gallery.* Toronto: General Publishing, 1968.

Desbarats, Peter. *Guide to Canadian News Media.* Toronto: Harcourt Brace Jovanovich, 1990.

Diefenbaker, John G. *One Canada: The Crusading Years 1895–1956.* Vol.1. Toronto: Macmillan, 1975.

_____. *One Canada: The Years of Achievement 1956–1962.* Vol. 2. Toronto: Macmillan, 1976.

_____. *One Canada: The Tumultuous Years 1962–1967.* Vol. 3. Toronto: Macmillan, 1977.

Doyle, Richard. *Hurly-Burly: My Time at the Globe and Mail.* Toronto: Macmillan, 1990.

English, John. *The Decline of Politics: The Conservatives and the Party System 1901–1920.* Toronto: University of Toronto Press, 1977.

_____. *Shadow of Heaven: The Life of Lester Pearson.* Vol. 1. Toronto: Lester & Orpen Dennys, 1989.

Esberey, Joy E. *Knight of the Holy Spirit: A Study of William Lyon Mackenzie King.* Toronto: University of Toronto Press, 1980.

Ford, Arthur. *As the World Wags On.* Toronto: Ryerson Press, 1950.

Fraser, Graham. *Playing for Keeps: The Making of the Prime Minister, 1988.* Toronto: McClelland & Stewart, 1989.

Fraser, John, and Graham Fraser, eds. *Blair Fraser Reports.* Toronto: Macmillan, 1969.

Frizzell, A., and A. Westell, eds. *The Canadian General Election of 1984.* Ottawa: Carleton University Press, 1985.

Frizzell, A., J.H. Pammett, and A. Westell, eds. *The Canadian General Election of 1988.* Ottawa: Carleton University Press, 1989.

Gordon, Walter. *A Political Memoir.* Toronto: McClelland & Stewart, 1977.

Gossage, Patrick. *Close to Charisma: My Years between the Press and Pierre Elliott Trudeau.* Toronto: McClelland & Stewart, 1986.

Graham, Roger. *Arthur Meighen.* 3 vols. Toronto: Clarke Irwin, 1960, 1963, 1965.

Graham, Ron. *One Eyed Kings.* Toronto: Collins, 1986.

Granatstein, J.L. *Canada's War: The Politics of the Mackenzie King Government 1939–1949.* Toronto: Oxford University Press, 1975.

_____. *The Ottawa Men.* Toronto: Oxford University Press, 1982.

Gratton, Michel. *"So What Are the Boys Saying?" An Inside Look at Brian Mulroney in Power.* Toronto: McGraw-Hill Ryerson, 1987.

_____. *Still the Boss: A Candid Look at Brian Mulroney*. Scarborough: Prentice-Hall, 1990.

Gwyn, Richard. *The Northern Magus*. Toronto: McClelland & Stewart, 1980.

Gwyn, Sandra. *The Private Capital*. Toronto: McClelland & Stewart, 1984.

Halberstam, David. *The Powers That Be*. New York: Alfred A. Knopf, 1979.

Hall, D.J. *Clifford Sifton: The Young Napoleon*. Vol. 1. Vancouver: University of British Columbia Press, 1981.

_____. *Clifford Sifton: A Lonely Eminence*. Vol. 2. Vancouver: University of British Columbia Press, 1985.

Harkness, Ross. *J.E. Atkinson of the Star*. Toronto: University of Toronto Press, 1963.

Hayes, David. *Power and Influence: The Globe and Mail and the News Revolution*. Toronto: Key Porter, 1992.

Hutchison, Bruce. *The Far Side of the Street*. Toronto: Macmillan, 1976.

Irving, John. *The Social Credit Movement in Alberta*. Toronto: University of Toronto Press, 1955.

Kesterton, W.H. *A History of Journalism in Canada*. Toronto: McClelland & Stewart, 1967.

Kent, Tom. *A Public Purpose*. Montreal: McGill-Queen's University Press, 1988.

La Marsh, Judy. *Memoirs of a Bird in a Gilded Cage*. Toronto: McClelland & Stewart, 1968.

Lynch, Charles. *You Can't Print That!* Edmonton: Hurtig Publishers, 1983.

MacDonald, L. Ian. *Mulroney: The Making of the Prime Minister*. Toronto: McClelland & Stewart, 1984.

McCall-Newman, Christina. *Grits: An Intimate Portrait of the Liberal Party*. Toronto: Macmillan, 1982.

Nash, Knowlton. *Prime Time at Ten*. Toronto: McClelland & Stewart, 1987.

_____. *Diefenbaker and Kennedy*. Toronto: McClelland & Stewart, 1990.

Neatby, H. Blair. *William Lyon Mackenzie King 1924–1932: The Lonely Heights*. Toronto: University of Toronto Press, 1963.

_____. *Laurier and a Liberal Quebec*. Toronto: McClelland & Stewart, 1973.

_____. *William Lyon Mackenzie King 1932–1939: The Prism of Unity*. Toronto: University of Toronto Press, 1976.

Newman, Peter C. *Renegade in Power: The Diefenbaker Years*. Toronto: McClelland & Stewart, 1963.

_____. *The Distemper of Our Times*. Toronto: McClelland & Stewart, 1968.

Nichols, M.E. *The Story of the Canadian Press*. Toronto: Ryerson Press, 1948.

Nolan, Brian. *King's War*. Toronto: Random House, 1988.

O'Leary, Grattan. *Recollections of People, Press and Politics*. Toronto: Macmillan, 1977.

Pearson, Lester B. *Mike: The Memoirs of the Rt. Hon. L. B. Pearson*. 3 vols. Toronto: University of Toronto Press, 1972, 1973, 1975.

Peers, Frank. *The Public Eye: Television and the Politics of Canadian Broadcasting 1952–1968*. Toronto: University of Toronto Press, 1979.

Pickersgill, J.W. *My Years with Louis St. Laurent: A Political Memoir*. Toronto: University of Toronto Press, 1975.

Radwanski, George. *Trudeau*. Toronto: Macmillan, 1978.

Rutherford, Paul. *A Victorian Authority: The Daily Press in Late Nineteenth Century Canada*. Toronto: University of Toronto Press, 1982.

_____. *When Television was Young: Prime Time Canada 1952–1967*. Toronto: University of Toronto Press, 1990.

Sawatsky, John. *The Insiders: Government, Business and the Lobbyists*. Toronto: McClelland & Stewart, 1987.

_____. *Mulroney: The Politics of Ambition*. Toronto: Macfarland, Walter and Ross, 1991.

Siegel, Arthur. *Politics and the Media in Canada*. Toronto: McGraw-Hill Ryerson, 1983.

Siggins, Maggie. *Bassett*. Toronto: James Lorimer & Co., 1979.

Simpson, Jeffrey. *Discipline of Power*. Toronto: Personal Library Publishers, 1980.

_____. *Spoils of Power: The Politics of Patronage*. Toronto: Collins, 1988.

Smith, I. Norman. *The Journal Men*. Toronto: McClelland & Stewart, 1974.

Stacey, C.P. *A Very Double Life: The Private World of Mackenzie King*. Toronto: Macmillan of Canada, 1976.

Stewart, Walter. *Shrug: Trudeau in Power*. Toronto: New Press, 1971.

Tataryn, Lloyd. *The Pundits: Power, Politics and the Press*. Toronto: Deneau, 1985.

Trudeau, Pierre, and Tom Axworthy. *Towards a Just Society: Governing Canada 1968–1984*. Toronto: Viking, 1989.

Waite, P.B. *Canada 1874–1896: Arduous Destiny*. Toronto: McClelland & Stewart, 1971.

_____. *Sir John A. Macdonald: His Life and World*. Toronto: McGraw-Hill, 1975.

_____. *The Man from Halifax: Sir John Thompson, Prime Minister*. Toronto: University of Toronto Press, 1985.

Watkins, Ernest. *R.B. Bennett: A Biography*. Toronto: Kingswood House, 1963.

Whitaker, Reginald. *The Government Party*. Toronto: University of Toronto Press, 1977.

Willison, J.S. *Reminiscences: Political and Personal*. Toronto: McClelland & Stewart, 1919.

INDEX